TAKEOVERS AND MERGERS LAW
IN IRELAND

UNITED KINGDOM
Sweet & Maxwell
London

AUSTRALIA
LBC Information Services
Sydney

CANADA and the USA
Carswell
Toronto

NEW ZEALAND
Brooker's
Auckland

SINGAPORE and MALAYSIA
Thomson Information (S.E. Asia)
Singapore

TAKEOVERS AND MERGERS LAW IN IRELAND

BLAINAID CLARKE

*B.C.L., M.B.S. (Banking and Finance),
Barrister-at-Law, Statutory
Lecturer in Law, U.C.D.*

DUBLIN
ROUND HALL SWEET & MAXWELL
1999

Published in 1999 by
Round Hall Sweet & Maxwell
Brehon House
4 Upper Ormond Quay
Dublin 7

Typeset by Carrigboy Typesetting Services, County Cork
Printed by ColourBooks Ltd, Dublin.

ISBN 1–899738–98–3

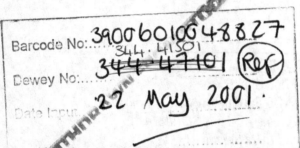

To Alan
and to my parents

FOREWORD

The past 30 years have witnessed an ever increasing volume of takeover and merger activity within Ireland of both private and public companies by national and international companies. In this period, and particularly the latter half thereof, a sophisticated network of regulation of both domestic and European origin has been put in place to monitor such activity and to provide in many instances welcome protection for those directly or indirectly affected by such transactions (e.g. employees' rights on the transfer of undertakings). This book not alone expertly addresses the detail of such regulation but it reviews it within the contractual framework of mergers and acquistions.

The title *Takeovers and Mergers Law in Ireland* greatly understates the ambit of transactions encompassed by the book. The author demonstrates the knowledge of her subject matter in considering the various economic and financial theories attributable to takeover activity.

In July 1997 the Irish Takeover Panel, established by statute, commenced the regulation and monitoring of takeovers of Irish companies whose shares are listing on the Irish Stock Exchange. Blanaid Clarke deals extensively and comprehensively with the new statutory framework and Rules which, in many ways, mirror the London City Code. The new statutory framework, while giving extensive power to the Panel in order to regulate takeovers, also provides for the right to apply to the High Court for judicial review of a ruling or direction by the Panel or where it avails of its disciplinary powers. As yet, the High Court has not been required to exercise this jurisdiction. However, it is likely to be called upon more extensively in the granting of relief than the English courts have been since their decision in the Datafin case in 1987 held that decisions of the London Takeover Panel were subject to judicial review, albeit in a restricted manner.

Blanaid Clarke is to be congratulated for her detailed analysis of the Irish Takeover Panel Act 1997 and the Panel Rules, which is I believe the first comprehensive commentary on the Irish Takeover Code. She also details the current status of the Draft of the 13th Company Law Directive regulating takeover bids. First proposed in 1989, the 13th Directive is ten years later the subject of much debate and amendment.

This book is, however, highly instructive for all those engaged as advisers (or regulators) in takeovers whether large or small, public or private. It addresses the relevant principles to be considered under competition law, both Irish and European and the many different forms in which a takeover can be effected. Consideration is given to different forms of acquisitions from the common offer for the shares of the company in return for shares or cash or Court-approved schemes of arrangement to mergers pursuant to the European Communities (Mergers and Divisions of Companies) Regulations 1987 which to date have been little availed of in this country. The reader's attention is directed to the importance of a proper consideration of employees' rights under the European Communities (Safeguarding of Employees' Rights on Transfer of Undertakings) Regulations 1980.

The chapter on "Introduction of Pre-Contractual Negotiations" is I believe of considerable relevance to all advisers and emphasises the importance of and ultimate enforceability of a Confidentiality Agreement, in particular where negotiations do not come to fruition. The reader is further alerted to the legal difficulties (often created by time pressures for completion) attendant to provisions which are tantamount to an agreement to negotiate or to agree in the future. In this review, she highlights the difficulties in attempting to force agreements "to use reasonable endeavours" or to buy or sell at a fair and reasonable price or in a manner to be agreed between the parties. She also expresses her own opinion as to how judicial opinion in Ireland and elsewhere is likely to develop in the future in this complicated area.

Blanaid Clarke rightly refers to the legal responsibilities of advisers whether accountants, stockbrokers or solicitors (or others). She summarises such duties, distinguishing between UK and Irish judicial developments. Her treatment of the existence and effectiveness of "Chinese walls" within firms highlights the necessity for general awareness when and where relevant. Her reference to the recent House of Lords decision in *Prince Jefri Bolkiah v. KPMG* where the Court upheld the principle that a fiduciary (whether a solicitor or other adviser) cannot act at the same time both for and against the same client is instructive and relevant for all those concerned.

Lastly, Blanaid Clarke is to be complimented for the manner in which she so successfully interweaves in her subject matter the many Irish Court decisions, in particular those of recent origin. Such decisions firmly underlie the many legal propositions which she recites and, where appropriate, give authority to her book. Students and practitioners alike from many disciplines will find this work most instructive and of practical benefit.

DANIEL O'KEEFFE
Chairman, Irish Takeover Panel
September 10, 1999

PREFACE

My objective in writing this book was to attempt to address equally the needs of two categories of reader, the practitioner and the student. In relation to the former, my intention was to produce a text which would be a useful guide for corporate finance practitioners, lawyers, accountants, stockbrokers, fund managers, compliance officers, company secretaries, company directors and shareholders. Because of the substantial growth in takeover activity, practitioners both legal and non-legal, are being called on increasingly to consider the legal aspects of takeover transactions. From my own experience working as a corporate finance practitioner, I realised the importance of an awareness of the law at all stages of the takeover process. Despite this, no Irish text exists to meet the needs of the practitioner in this respect. In writing this book, I have also sought to meet the needs of the student reader by setting out the rules and regulations which are relevant to students of mergers and takeovers law or corporate finance law and, more generally, to students of company law, securities regulation and investor protection regulation. In my capacity as a lecturer in Corporate Finance Law on the LL.M Commercial Law programme in University College Dublin, I lecture postgraduate students on the subject of mergers and takeovers law. Again, the need for an Irish text focusing on this area of the law is apparent.

Over the past few years, a number of significant changes have occurred in the Irish market for mergers and takeovers. For example, in 1997, the Irish Takeover Panel Act, 1997 was passed and a statutory system was established to regulate takeovers of relevant companies. The rules introduced pursuant to this Act provide a statutory framework for the conduct of takeovers of Irish listed companies. Previously, the acquisition of such companies was supervised by the London Panel on Takeovers and Mergers, a self-regulatory body. These changes provided a further impetus to produce an up to date Irish text on mergers and takeovers law.

The subject of mergers and takeovers law requires an examination of aspects of a broad range of laws including company law, securities regulation, corporate governance, the law of tort, employment law, the law of contract and financial services regulation. There are of course many excellent texts on these general areas. For example, Patrick Ussher's *Company Law in Ireland* (Sweet & Maxwell) although published in 1986 continues to be one of the definitive texts in general company law.

Similarly, Robert Clark's *Contract Law in Ireland* (Round Hall Sweet & Maxwell, 1998) and Tom Courtney's *The Law of Private Companies* (Butterworths, 1994) contain many invaluable sections on issues relevant to mergers and takeovers law. However, none of these texts are intended to offer a comprehensive treatment of the law applicable to mergers and takeovers.

Part 1 of the text introduces the reader to the area of mergers and takeovers. At this stage, I have sought to describe the myriad of conflicting theories which attempt to establish a rationale for takeovers. An understanding of these theories will provide a framework for the analysis of the regulations that follow. In addition to the general legal principles which regulate takeovers, a number of specific rules and regulations merit particular consideration and are the subject of Part 2 of the text. For example, a thorough examination is undertaken of the Irish Takeover Panel Act, 1997 which effected a domestic system of regulation of the takeovers of Irish listed companies. The text also analyses the latest version of the proposed 13th Directive on company law concerning takeovers which, if implemented, will have a significant impact on both domestic and cross-border takeovers. Stock Exchange regulations, competition law and financial services law also merit special attention as they seek to offer particular protection to shareholders, consumers and clients in the context of a takeover. Part 3 of the text considers the most expensive takeovers – takeovers of public companies and, in particular, public listed companies. Such takeovers may involve either the acquisition of the undertakings or the acquisition of the shares of the companies. The procedures involved in both forms of acquisitions and the legal considerations are evaluated in detail. The parties involved in takeovers and their particular roles and legal responsibilities are also examined. Finally, the restrictions on dealing and the disclosure requirements which are relevant to parties during the course of a takeover are considered. Part 4 of the text considers the acquisition of private companies. An analysis is undertaken of the legal principles applicable from the entry into pre-contractual negotiations through the due diligence exercise, the drafting of the relevant documentation and up until the completion agenda. Part 5 examines the rationale for management buy-outs and the special rules which apply to these acquisitions. The final Part of the text examines the possibility of management taking action to pre-empt any possible takeover bid or to frustrate an existing takeover bid. The various theories which have been advanced in favour of and against allowing management take action are considered. Having considered the advisability of regulating conduct, the actual regulation itself is considered. This involves both general rules such as section 205 of the Companies Act, 1963 and Rule 21 of the Irish Takeover Panel Act 1997 (Takeover) Rules, 1997 which apply to all such tactics and specific rules which apply to particular actions such as the prohibition on giving financial assistance for the purchase of own shares.

Although this text attempts to set out the legal principles applicable to mergers and takeovers, it is not intended to constitute an exhaustive treatise on every aspect of the takeover or merger process. In particular, no attempt is made to deal with the accounting implications of mergers and takeovers and the relevant taxation issues are merely sign-posted generally for the reader. These are the subjects of separate books in themselves and are outside the scope of this text.

Any opinions stated and interpretations suggested constitute personal opinions and interpretations and are not intended to represent the views or practices of any other person or body. In addition, I would add that this book is intended as a guide for practitioners and students and is not intended to replace the need for professional advice on individual transactions. As a result, no liability is accepted for any shortcomings in the text.

Various people read and provided comments on drafts of individual chapters or parts of chapters. Because of the wide range of legal areas covered, such co-operation and help was invaluable. Colleagues in University College Dublin to whom I am indebted include John Breslin, Philip Bourke, Dermot Cahill, Robert Clark, Tony Kerr, Andrew Lyall, Barbara Maguire, Paul McDermott, Mary Catherine Lucey, Jonathan Newman and Paul Ward. Less captive but equally approachable commentators were Leo Conway, Ann Corrigan, Tom Courtney, Alan Doolin, Noel Gaughran, Hugh Lynn, David Milman and Sean O'Flaherty. In addition, I would like to thank the various guest lecturers who have contributed to my Corporate Finance Law course over the years and in doing so have given me the benefit of their invaluable insight and experience on various aspects of mergers and takeovers law. I am particularly grateful to Maurice Curran, Rebecca Maguire and Brian O'Connor in this regard. I would also like to thank Paul O'Connor, Dean of the Faculty of Law for his encouragement, Tony Eckloff and Ann Cooney in the Law Library in UCD for their help sourcing material; and Suzanne Egan for checking a vast number of references at severe cost to her social plans. Finally, I would like to thank the staff at Round Hall Sweet & Maxwell especially Therese Carrick who agreed to produce the text and Joanna McAdam, Selga Medenieks and Amy Hayes who worked on the various drafts.

Finally, I would like to thank Mr. Dan O'Keeffe, Senior Counsel, who agreed to write the forword to this book. In addition to providing such a kind foreword, he generously gave me the benefit of his own expertise and experience in making comments on a number of the issues raised.

I have attempted to deal with the law as it stood in June 1999 although limited references to certain later developments have proved possible.

BLANAID CLARKE
August 1999

TABLE OF CONTENTS

PART 1 – INTRODUCTION

PART 4 – ACQUISITION OF PRIVATE COMPANIES

TABLE OF CASES

IRELAND

U.K.

EUROPE

Decisions of the European Commission

Cases of the European Court of Justice

OTHER JURISDICTIONS

Australia

Canada

TABLE OF EUROPEAN LEGISLATION

TABLE OF LEGISLATION

Table of Legislation

Civil Liability Act 1961
s.34(1) 10–57
Companies Acts 1963–1990 7–92,
12–35, 12–36, 16–17,
16–23, 20–37
Companies Act 1963 .... 5–10n
First Schedule, Table A,
Part 1, Arts 2, 4 & 5 ... 8–08n,
20–08n
s.2(1) 14–05
s.8(1) 8–05
s.10 20–63
(1) 8–04
(3) 8–04
s.13(2) 20–21n
s.15 8–04
(1) 20–23
s.20 20–24
s.25 19–32
s.31 19–34
s.32(1) 20–07
(2) 20–07
s.33 1–12
(1) 14–03
(a) 15–06
s.39(1) 10–58
s.44(1) 14–05n
(3) 5–61
s.45 .... 5–61n
(1) 5–61n
(2) 5–61n
(3) 5–61n
s.49 .... 5–61n, 14–05
(1) 14–05
(3) 14–05n
s.50 .... 5–61n, 14–05n
s.51(1) 14–06n
s.60 ... 11–22n, 11–42, 11–43, 14–14,
14–17, 18–04, 18–35
(1) 11–43, 14–12
(2) 11–45, 14–14, 14–14n
(3) 14–15n
(5) 14–15n
(6) 14–14n
(8) 14–16
(10) 14–16n
(11) 14–14n, 14–16n
(12) 11–45, 14–13
(13) 11–45, 11–45n, 14–13,
14–13n
(a) 11–45n, 14–13n
(b) 11–45n, 14–13n
(c) 11–45n, 14–13

(14) 11–46, 14–17n
(15) 11–46n
(15A) 11–45, 14–14n
(15B) 11–45n, 14–13n
s.61 .... 5–61n, 14–06n
(1) 14–06, 14–06n
(2) 1–12n, 14–07
s.62 .... 8–18n, 11–40
(1) 8–18
(2) 8–20
s.65 20–63
s.72 20–24
s.79 15–05
s.81 15–05
s.83 15–05
s.99 15–34
(1) 15–19
s.100(1) 15–19
s.101 15–19
s.102 15–19
s.103(1)(b) 15–20n
s.103(2) 15–20n
s.125 15–18
s.136(1) 20–15
(2)(b) 20–15
(3) 20–15n
(5) 20–15n
(6) 20–15n
s.141(1) 8–38n, 14–14n
(2) 14–14n
s.143(4)(f) 15–11n
(g) 15–11n
s.148 18–21
s.155 6–43
s.180 13–30
s.182 3–22
(1) 20–34
(7) 20–36
s.186 .... 8–29, 11–55, 11–55n,
18–32, 20–38, 20–40
s.187 .... 8–29, 11–55, 11–55n,
18–32, 20–40
(1) 20–38
(2) 8–29n, 20–38
s.188 .... 11–55n, 18–32, 20–40
(1) 20–39
(2) 20–39
(3) 20–39
s.189(3) 8–29n, 11–55n,
18–32n, 20–40
(4) 20–41
s.194 18–15
(1) 18–15

xl

TABLE OF STATUTORY INSTRUMENTS

IRISH STATUTORY INSTRUMENTS

1

UK STATUTORY INSTRUMENTS

TABLE OF TAKEOVER RULES

PART 1

INTRODUCTION

CHAPTER 1

INTRODUCTION TO MERGERS AND TAKEOVERS

Introduction

1–01 Takeovers are an increasingly important aspect of corporate life. In 1998, an estimated 179 takeovers or mergers were completed by Irish companies, amounting to a total value of more than £5.7 billion in consideration.[1] These figures, however, include the Irish Life/Irish Permanent merger which was announced in December 1998 and which offered a consideration of £2.8 billion. This is the single biggest acquisition between two Irish companies. The active state of the market has been attributed to a move towards consolidation in the market, and to some extent the reduction in the rate of capital gains tax on business disposals from 40 per cent to 20 per cent.[2] A recent survey of the chief executives of Irish companies indicates a confidence that acquisitions are the best way of achieving substantial growth quickly.[3] From an investment perspective, the prospect of acquiring a company and increasing its turnover and profits is extremely attractive and potentially highly lucrative. Such an increase might result from operating synergies or alternatively through more efficient management. Less meritorious perhaps is the prospect of acquiring a company and making a profit through the divestiture of its assets. From a management perspective, acquisitions as a form of expansion often prove a popular option to the high costs and risks associated with organic growth. Particularly in this era of international cross-border business, the opportunity to acquire active operations in other countries is highly valuable. As post acquisition experiences appear to have proved favourable with Irish companies, it is likely that over the next few years acquisitions will continue to increase in number and size.

---

[1] Chapman Flood 1998 Acquisition Survey (Dublin, 1999).
[2] Taxes Consolidation Act 1997, s.78.
[3] *op. cit.*, n.1.

A. Definitions

I. TAKEOVER

1–02 The term "takeover" refers to a situation where one party, the "bidder", or "offeror" acquires control of another company, "the target" or "offeree". In the case of the takeover of a private company, the terms "purchaser" and "vendor" tend to be used. A "takeover" is defined by Weinberg and Blank as:

> "a transaction or series of transactions whereby a person (individual, group of individuals or company) acquires control over the assets of a company, either directly by becoming the owner of those assets or indirectly by obtaining control of the management of the company".[4]

Section 1(1) of the Irish Takeover Panel Act 1997[5] defines a "takeover" more broadly as:

> "(a) any agreement or transaction (including a merger) whereby or in consequence of which control of a relevant company is or may be acquired; or
>
> (b) any invitation, offer or proposal made, or intended or required to be made, with a view to concluding or bringing about such an agreement or transaction."

The term "control" in turn is defined in the same subsection of the Act as:

> "the holding, whether directly or indirectly, of securities of the company that confer, in aggregate, not less than 30 per cent (or such other percentage as may be prescribed) of the voting rights in that company".

II. MERGER

1–03 The term "merger" refers to a situation where two companies, generally of similar size, join together.[6] It is effected either by shareholders exchanging their shares or alternatively by the formation of a new holding company to which the shares or the assets and liabilities of the original two companies are transferred. In the latter situation, the shareholding in this new company will be spread between the shareholders of the original two companies. Where the companies are public listed companies, the new company will apply to the Stock Exchange

---

[4] Weinberg and Blank, *Takeovers and Mergers* (Sweet & Maxwell, London, 1989) Part 1, Chap. 1.
[5] See below para. 3–18; this Act generally applies to public limited companies rather than private companies.
[6] It should be noted, however, that the term "merger" is often used loosely to indicate any combination of two companies.

for a listing for all of its issued shares immediately upon the offer becoming unconditional.

1–04 Mergers or takeovers are often classified as horizontal, vertical or conglomerate. An horizontal takeover involves the acquisition of a company in the same line of business. For example, the acquisition of a printing company by another printing company. A vertical takeover, involves the acquisition of a target company by another company which is at a different stage in the "raw material to ultimate consumer flow", *e.g.* the acquisition of a printing company by a paper manufacturing company. Large industrial companies appreciate this form of takeover as it gives them greater control over the production process by allowing them to expand back towards the output of raw materials and forward towards the sale to the ultimate customer. A conglomerate takeover involves the acquisition of a company in a totally unrelated line of business. These have not proved to be very popular however, and in 1998, 99 per cent of all acquisitions by Irish companies were in core business areas.[7]

III. TENDER OFFER

A "tender offer" is defined in Rule 2.1 of Part A of the Irish Takeover Panel Act 1997 (Takeover) Rules, 1997 as:

> "an invitation made by a person by public advertisement to holders of a class of securities of a relevant company to tender securities of that company, up to a stated number, for purchase by that person, on terms stipulated in the advertisement."

Tender offers are mechanisms designed to allow an acquisition of shares in a company be made at a faster rate than would otherwise be allowed by the Irish Takeover Panel Act 1997 (Substantial Acquisition) Rules, 1997. This is permitted since the opportunity to sell is open to all shareholders.

IV. SUBSTANTIAL ACQUISITION OF SHARES

1–06 Finally, a substantial acquisition of shares is defined in Rule 3 of the Irish Takeover Panel Act 1997 (Substantial Acquisition) Rules, 1997 as an acquisition or a series of acquisitions by a person of voting securities of a relevant company or of rights over voting securities of that company where:

> "(i) any voting securities so acquired by that person and the voting securities the subject of any rights so acquired by that person confer in the aggregate 10% or more of the voting rights in the company; and

---

[7] Chapman Flood 1998 Acquisition Survey.

(ii) any voting securities so acquired by that person and the voting securities the subject of any rights so acquired by that person, when aggregated with any voting securities already held by that person and any voting securities over which that person already holds rights, confer 15% or more, but less than 30%, of the voting rights in the company; and

(iii) in the case of a series of acquisitions of securities, all of such acquisitions are made within a period of 7 days."

These rules are intended to slow down the rate at which stakes may be built up in companies in order to allow small shareholders to participate in any premium which may be payable in connection with the establishment or consolidation of a large holding. The Rules also serve to provide management with sufficient time to consider the acquisition and to take whatever steps, if any, are necessary to safeguard the interests of the shareholders.

B. Methods of Acquiring Control

1–07   A takeover may involve the acquisition of the business or undertaking[8] of a target by the transfer of the entire undertaking or merely the transfer of certain assets to the offeror. Where the offeror pays the target in cash and the entire undertaking is acquired, the target will be left as a cash-rich shell company. Where the offeror pays for the target with its own shares, and the entire undertaking is acquired, the target will end up as an investment company holding a block of shares in the offeror. An offeror may also effect a merger, by acquiring the assets and liabilities of the target in exchange for the issue of its shares to the target's shareholders. This may be effected under section 201 of the Companies Act 1963.

1–08   Alternatively, instead of actually acquiring the undertaking from its current corporate owner, a takeover may involve acquiring control of the target by the acquisition of its shares from its shareholders. If all the shares are acquired, the target will become a wholly-owned subsidiary of the offeror. Where the offeror wishes to acquire control of the company in this way, an offer is made to its shareholders. An "offer" is defined in section 1(1) of the Irish Takeover Panel Act 1997 as:

> "an offer (by whatever name called), made to the holders of securities in a relevant company, to acquire some or all of those securities by the payment

---

[8] An undertaking is generally taken to mean any entity involved in commercial activity.

of cash or other valuable consideration or in exchange for other securities or by means of both such a payment and such an exchange."

If a takeover offer is supported by the target's management, the effect will generally be the same as a merger, with the two companies being brought under the unified control of representatives from both sets of management. If the offer is not supported by management, the offer is made directly to the shareholders of the target. This is commonly known as a "hostile takeover".

1–09 There are both benefits and drawbacks to these two methods of acquiring control. Where an undertaking is acquired, desirable assets can be appropriated leaving behind the unwanted assets and also the company's liabilities. The offeror can thus be sure that no hidden liabilities are being acquired. The disadvantage, however, is that the assets acquired will have to be identified very precisely in order to ensure the transfer of separate title to each individual asset. This will give rise to much administrative and legal paperwork. By contrast, where all the shares of the target are acquired, the offeror cannot leave behind undesirable liabilities. The offeror is also responsible for latent liabilities which may arise at some stage in the future. Difficulties may also arise if the target's assets are subsequently used to finance the purchase of the shares. On the positive side, however, the transfer procedure is a lot less complex. Tax considerations may play an important role in the form of acquisition used. Firstly, stamp duty must be paid (generally by the purchaser or offeror) in respect of certain instruments and certain transactions. Duty is imposed on the consideration paid or the market value if that is higher. The rate of duty which applies to conveyances on sale of non-residential property exceeding £60,000 in value is £6 per £100 or part of £100. For stocks and marketable securities the rate of stamp duty is 1% per £100 or part thereof. For shares transferred electronically under the Crest System, the rate is also 1%.[8a] Certain reconstructions and amalgamations of companies involving the transfer of shares in one company to another attract no stamp duty.[8b] A second consideration relevant to the purchaser is the acquisition of tax losses where the shares of the company are acquired. For example, a trading loss may be set off against future profits. Section 396(1) of the Taxes Consolidation Act, 1997 allows a company to make a claim to carry forward a loss in its trade for set off for the purposes of corporation tax against any trading income from the same trade in succeeding accounting periods. Section 400 of the Taxes Consolidation Act, 1997 allows for the transfer of

---

[8a] Finance Act, 1996 s.103. See para. 5–04 below. See generally, O'Connor and Cahill, *The Law of Stamp Duties*, (The Institute of Taxation in Ireland, 1998).
[8b] Finance Act 1965, section 31.

trading losses from one company to another provided that 75% of the shareholders of the successor company were shareholders in the original company in the period, one year before and two years after the reconstruction. Section 401 of the Taxes Consolidation Act, 1997 deals with company reconstructions leading to changes of ownership. Section 401(2) provides that if (a) within any three year period there is both a change in ownership of a company and a major change in the nature and conduct of a trade carried on by the company or (b) at any time after the scale of the activities in a trade carried on by a company has become small or negligible and before any considerable revival of the trade, there is a change in the ownership of the company, no relief will be allowed for trading losses forward from any accounting period ending before the change of ownership against subsequent income.[8c] It should also be noted that a new Schedule 18A was inserted into the Taxes Consolidation Act, 1997 by section 57 of the Finance Act 1999 in order to impose restrictions on the ability of corporate groups to utilise capital losses in companies bought into the group with unused capital losses. While the target company will be able to use its capital losses against future capital gains in the normal manner, such "pre-entry losses" are not transferrable to other members of the group.

For the target company and its shareholders, tax plays a fundamental role in determining the appropriate method of disposing of their interests. Firstly, where the shareholders are selling their shares or assets to the offeror, each individual shareholder will be liable to pay capital Gains Tax ("CGT") at a rate of 20% on chargeable gains made on the disposal of the shares or the assets. An exception exists where the shares derive the greater part of their value from development land. In this case a 40% CGT rate is applicable. The first £1,000 of chargeable gains is exempt. Where the company is selling its undertaking, any capital gain (apart from development land gains) is treated as part of the company's total profits subject to corporation tax, albeit a formula is applied so that the capital gains element of those profits is taxed at the CGT rate (currently 20%). Development land gains are taxed at the CGT rate of 40%.

C. Form of Consideration

1–10 Where the offeror is a public company, the acquisition may be financed by cash payment, by issuing shares or debentures or by a combination of both. Cash is generally the most attractive option from the target's point of view. Where the offeror offers cash in exchange for

---

[8c] See generally, Brennan & Moore, *Corporation Tax* (Institute of Taxation in Ireland, 1998). Chapter 4 – Losses.

shares in the target, a premium on the market price is always included. One disadvantage of a purely cash consideration is that it denies the target's shareholders the opportunity to maintain a holding in the company and to participate in its future development. From the offeror's perspective, if sufficient cash is not available, it will have to borrow to finance a cash offer. A decision to alter a company's capital structure in this way will involve a number of considerations addressed in Chapters 8 and 11.[9] For example, although debt may be cheaper than equity, the offeror's gearing may already be perceived as high and it may have to pay a premium.

1–11 If the offeror offers consideration in the form of shares, a number of potential problems may arise. First the offeror's earnings per share ratio "EPS" may decrease after the acquisition. This ratio is measured as being equal to the profit after tax (and after preference dividends) divided by the number of ordinary shares outstanding. It is a measure of what the company is actually earning on behalf of its shareholders. This is a vital ratio as shareholders are always concerned about the earnings which will eventually be available to pay their dividends, or which will be used as retained earnings to expand their company. Although in theory, the additional earnings acquired in the acquisition should make up for the increased number of shareholders, for various reasons this may not be so. A second concern for the offeror is to ensure compliance with the pre-emption rights of existing shareholders.[10] Where consideration takes the form of debentures, some element of convertibility is often included in order to make the offer attractive to shareholders who wish to participate in the company's future.

Tax considerations play an important role in this context. Section 55(1) of the Stamp Act, 1891 provides that where all or part of the consideration for a conveyance on sale consists of stocks or marketable securities, the conveyance is to be charged with ad valorem stamp duty in respect of the value of the stocks or securities. However, where all or part of the consideration consists of non-marketable securities, section 55(2) provides that the duty is assessed on the amount due on the day of the conveyance for principal and interest on the securities. It should be noted that a conveyance of shares in one company in exchange for shares in another company is assessed as two separate conveyances on sale of the respective lots of shares.[10a] It should also be noted that reconstructions of companies effected by share for share swaps or share for undertaking swaps may qualify for relief from stamp duty/capital

---

[9] See below paras 8–07–8–11 and 11–38–11–40.
[10] See below paras 8–12–8–16.
[10a] *J. & P. Coats Ltd. v. IRC* (1897) 1 QB 778, O'Connor & Cahill, *op. cit.*, n.8a Chap. 20.

duty pursuant to section 31 of the Finance Act 1965 and section 72 of the Finance Act, 1973.[10b]

A transfer of other property in exchange for shares is liable to ad valorem stamp duty in respect of the conveyance of the property.[10c] As noted in para. 1–09 above, individuals are generally subject to CGT on any chargeable gains. However, a share for share exchange in a takeover situation where the offeror obtains control does not give rise to a disposal for CGT purposes.[10d] Where an individual transfers a business together with the assets of the business to a company in exchange for shares in that company, section 600 of the Taxes Consolidation Act, 1997 provides that the chargeable gain arising is deferred until the shares are disposed of by the person. This relief involves reducing the market value of the shares received in exchange for the transfer of the business to the company by the amount of the capital gain on the tranfer. The tax is, therefore, collected if the shares are subsequently sold as the base cost applicable has been decreased and therefore the corresponding CGT liability is increased. Thus the rate of CGT paid will be the rate prevailing at the date the shares are sold, not the date of the transfer to the company.[10e]

1–12   Where the offeror is a private company, the choice as to the form of the consideration is more limited. A private company is defined in section 33 of the Companies Act 1963 as a company which, by its articles "restricts the right to transfer its shares", which "limits the number of its members to fifty" and which "prohibits any invitation to the public to subscribe for any shares or debentures of the company". It is unlikely, therefore, that a private company can offer consideration in the form of shares as this would increase the number of its shareholders above the maximum limit. Also, the offer would fall within the prohibition of an offer of shares to the "public", unless the offer could be deemed as being "a domestic concern of the persons making and receiving it".[11] Private companies are thus restricted to offering consideration in the form of cash. Obviously, this may place a severe restriction on the quality and size of companies and businesses which such companies may acquire.

D. Valuation of the Target

1–13   The valuation of the target is one of the most important decisions the offeror will make. It will ultimately determine whether an acquisition

---

[10b] O'Connor & Cahill, *op. cit.* n.8a, Chap. 32.
[10c] Finance Act, 1993, s.104.
[10d] Taxes Consolidation Act, 1997 ss. 584–587.
[10e] See also "Capital Gains – the Transfer of Business Reliefs" (1997) *Irish Tax Review* 581.
[11] Companies Act 1963, s.61(2). See below paras 14–06–14–11.

is successful or not. The valuation process depends on a number of factors, such as future turnover and costs, which are difficult to predict. Another difficulty is that the offeror will not generally have access to detailed financial information in respect of the target. This is true particularly in the case of a hostile takeover. Even where the target's board are working with the offeror and willing to make the relevant information available, insider dealing restrictions may prevent its dissemination.[12]

1–14 A number of separate techniques may be used to value companies, the most common of which include: the net asset value, the dividend valuation, the discounted cash flow value and the earnings value. Alternatively, a combination of a number of techniques may be used.

Before examining each of these techniques, it should be borne in mind, that if the company is private, the shares will not be as marketable as those of a public company, particularly a listed company. This will be especially true where the company's own regulations are restrictive, *e.g.* pre-emption rights may apply to transfers. In addition, shareholders agreements may exist which regulate the transfer of shares and determine a share pricing mechanism. As a result, the value of a private company is generally discounted. A discount of 10 per cent would seem to be typical.

I. NET ASSET VALUE

1–15 The net asset value of the company is the value of all the assets, when all the liabilities have been met. Since it is assumed that this figure will be available for division amongst ordinary shareholders upon a liquidation, it is possible to calculate the net asset value attributable to each share. This figure is determined by the formula:

$$= \frac{\text{net assets (i.e. assets} - \text{liabilities)}}{\text{total number of shares}}$$

A major difficulty arises in determining what value should be attributed to assets. One possible solution is to value assets at their book values. Assets are normally recorded in the balance sheet at cost and a charge is included in the profit and loss account annually to account for depreciation.[13] A depreciation charge is designed to factor in the age and relative obsolescence of the assets. This historical book value is not usually

---

[12] See below paras 13–03–13–86.
[13] Statement of Standard Accounting Practice No. 12 defines depreciation as "the measure of the wearing out, consumption or other loss of value of a fixed asset whether arising from use, effluxion of time or obsolescence through technology and market changes".

an accurate reflection of the assets' current value. Often, for example the market value of land exceeds the figure reflected in the company's balance sheet. In addition, other items such as old machinery with a negligible book value may retain some resale value. A second possibility is to value assets on the basis of their liquidation value. Unfortunately, unless the company or business being acquired is no longer a going concern or is being sold by a receiver, this method tends to undervalue the company. A further method of valuing the assets is by calculating their depreciated replacement cost. This method involves calculating the present cost of replacing assets in their present state. The cost of replacing the assets is thus reduced by a charge to account for their depreciation.

1–16 In addition to the difficulty of determining a suitable method of valuing the assets, this method of valuing a company is subject to certain other difficulties. First, in agreeing to a valuation, the offeror will have to ensure that no contingent liabilities or charges on assets exist. Secondly, as Professor Krishna points out "asset valuation runs counter to the fundamental concept of a going concern business, namely, that an ongoing enterprise is something more than an aggregation of its assets. A shareholder in a corporation buys an aliquot share of a business, not just its assets. In other words, the value of a share is not simply its pro rata interest in the assets of the corporation but is a proportionate claim to a going concern".[14] In order to factor this consideration into the equation, a figure will have to be calculated on top of the pure asset value to account for "goodwill". Goodwill represents the difference between the net asset value of the company and the value the purchaser is willing to pay. Again, determining a mutually acceptable figure to account for goodwill will involve a large element of speculation.

II. DIVIDEND VALUATION

1–17 The dividend valuation model values the company shares in terms of dividends and growth in capital value. The dividend yield per share is calculated as:

$$= \frac{\text{current dividend}}{\text{the investors cost of capital} - \text{company's growth rate}}$$

While this method may be suitable to value shares for individual shareholders, for a potential corporate acquirer it does not take into account the value of any expected synergies.

---

[14] Krishna, "Determining the Value of Company Shares" 8 *The Company Lawyer* No. 2, 66.

III. DISCOUNTED CASH FLOW

1–18 A company may also be valued in terms of the discounted cash flow it is capable of generating. The term "cash flow" is not synonymous with the term "profit". Instead it constitutes revenues directly attributable to the business less costs directly attributable to the business. It therefore involves making an adjustment to the "profit after tax" figure to account for non-cash items. The resultant figure represents the actual value for cash generated from activities.[15]

1–19 There are a number of steps to be followed in obtaining this valuation. First, cash flows must be estimated for a number of years ahead. This involves predicting a growth rate for cash flows and, using the current year's cash flow as a base, calculating cash flows for the future. Since it is not possible to estimate cash flow for an infinite term, a terminal value must be placed on the business at the end of the predictable period. The terminal value is calculated as follows:

$$= \frac{\text{cash flow for the last year}}{\text{required rate of return}^{16} - \text{growth rate estimated for the company}}$$

The second step is to take into account the time value of money, *e.g.* £100 obtained in December 1997 will be worth more than £100 obtained in December 1998, and more still than £100 in 1999. An amount of money must be paid to an investor to reward the investor for doing without the money for 12 months. The discount rate used will depend on the rate of return required by the investor. If we assume that an investor in Government Bonds for a 12–month period could earn 8 per cent virtually risk free, one would have to be paid a premium on top of the 8 per cent in order to account for the additional risk involved and to induce the investor to wait for the year. A yield of 10 per cent for example might be required. This 10 per cent figure is known as the "discount rate" or the "after tax cost of capital". By discounting future cash flows, we can obtain the present value of the cash flows. Discounted cash flow tables are available to show the discount factors for cash receivables at certain stated future times and at certain stated rates of discount. Alternatively, the calculations may be done manually.[17] Calculations

---

[15] The anticipated inflows and outflows arising from fixed asset disposals and purchases should be taken into account in estimating cash flow.

[16] The required rate of return will be at least the return available on government bonds.

[17] *e.g.* if our required rate of return is 10 per cent, we can calculate what £100 in one year's time will be worth today. It is equal to – 100 *(i.e. amount)* x 100/110 *(i.e. 100 + required rate)* = £90.9 Thus, £90.9 now and £100 in one year's time are equivalent. Likewise, we can calculate what £100 in two years' time will be worth today. It is equal to 100 *(i.e. amount)* x (100/110)(100/110) = £82.6. See Brockington, *Financial Management* (DP Publications Ltd. 1987) Chapter 9.

show that £100 in one years time at a discount factor of 10 per cent will be worth £90.90 today. The third and final step in the valuation process is to add up all the discounted cash flows expected over a period. This gives us the company's present value. Again, this method of valuation depends on a number of uncertainties and variables which may lead to the under valuation or over valuation of the target. Although sensitivity analysis may be used to factor in the risk and uncertainties involved in any of these estimates, this is still a risky valuation technique.

IV. EARNINGS VALUE

1–20   A valuation based on earnings value is commonly used. The first step is to calculate the company's predicted future earnings after tax. This figure must be a maintainable figure. There must be no aberrations for revaluation of assets, changing accounting standards or sales of property. Often an average or weighted average of the past earnings will used. Alternatively, prospective earnings may be used. There is a body of opinion which suggests that in calculating this maintainable earnings figure, expected synergies and cost savings should not be factored in. The purpose of this is to ensure that the target is not given the benefit of future actions by the acquirer.[18] On the other hand, clearly this figure is relevant in determining what the offeror can afford to pay. Although all of the savings should not be transferred to the target, some may have to be.

1–21   The second step in the valuation process involves applying a multiple to this figure in order to determine the company's value. The multiple is normally the price earnings or "PE" ratio. This ratio is measured as:

$$= \frac{\text{market price of the ordinary shares}}{\text{Earnings per share (EPS)}}$$

The PE ratio is a measure of the relative expense of the share. A PE ratio of 10 for example, tells us that the share can be purchased for 10 times its annual earnings. This ratio is probably the most important measure of value used by investors in the market place and thus a significant figure for companies. If the company's shares have a low ratio, it may be viewed as undervalued and become a potential takeover target. If it is too high, however, the shares may be viewed as over-valued. In evaluating the

---

[18] Byrne, "Target Valuation and Structuring the Acquisition" Commercial Law Centre, Conference on Corporate Acquisitions and Disposals, March 26, 1996.

possibility of a takeover, the effect on the offeror's EPS is important. The EPS will decrease anytime the PE ratio paid for a company is greater than the PE ratio of the offeror. The greater the PE of the offeror in comparison to that of the target, the lower the EPS of the offeror in comparison to the target's EPS and the greater the increase in the EPS of the offeror after the acquisition. The PE also reflects the rate of return investors require before they purchase stock or alternatively the return required by bidders before they purchase the target. The PE multiple is the inverse of the required rate of return, *e.g.* a multiple of 10 suggests a required rate of return of 10% and likewise a multiple of five suggests a required rate of return of 20%. Where the target is a private company or an unlisted public company, this method may still be used by estimating a PE ratio as appropriate for the target. This will generally be a multiple based on the PE of a comparable firm (size, stage, prospects, gearing) in the same industry. The main problem with using market value to determine the multiple is that the market price reflects a derived demand; it can be influenced by irrational motives and rumours. If the market is at an abnormal high for example, a company may be overvalued.

V. CAPITAL ASSET PRICING MODEL

1–22 A further mechanism used to value companies is the capital asset pricing model (CAPM). As noted in Chapter 2, below, this mechanism would allow the offeror to calculate the expected rate of return of securities. It is not uncommon for this method of valuation to be used in conjunction with the discounted cash flow model.[19]

VI. CONCLUSION

1–23 Whilst many Irish companies seeking to value a target would appear to use all the aforementioned methods of valuation, the most popular single method is the discounted cash flow method. The price earnings method would appear to be the next most popular technique.[20] At the end of the day, however, a valuation of a company prior to its acquisition will be a complex and difficult task, often involving a large element of subjective assessment and instinct.

---

[19] The CAPM can be used to estimate the required rate of return which can then be used to discount the cash flows to take into account the time value of money.
[20] Chapman Flood 1998 Acquisition Survey.

CHAPTER 2

RATIONALE FOR MERGERS AND ACQUISITIONS

2–01 In order to understand more fully the rules and regulations applying to takeovers, it is necessary to consider why takeovers and mergers occur. This Chapter examines the various theories put forward to explain the causes of mergers and acquisitions.[1] These theories may be analysed in terms of one of two assumptions. Underlying each assumption is the fact that target shareholders receive a premium on market price from the successful offeror for their securities. The first assumption is that the market correctly prices corporate securities. This leads to the conclusion either that the offeror places a higher value on the securities or alternatively, that the premiums on takeovers amount to over-payment. The second assumption is that the market has incorrectly priced the securities and the price paid by the offeror reflects the true value of the securities.

---

[1] See generally H. Manne "Mergers and the Market for Corporate Control" 73 (1965) J. Pol. Econ. 110; Kraakman "Taking Discounts Seriously: The Implications of "Discounted" Share Prices as an Acquisition Motive" 88 Col. Law Rev. 891 (1988); M. Jensen & R. Ruback "The Market for Corporate Control: the Scientific Evidence" J of Financial Econ. (1983) pp. 5–50; Black "Bidder Overpayment in Takeovers" 41 Stan. Law Rev. 597; Coffee "Regulating the Market for Corporate Control: A Critical Assessment of the Tender Offer's Role in Corporate Governance" 84 Col. Law Rev. 1145–1296; Easterbrook & Fischel "The Proper Role of a Target's Management in Responding to a Tender Offer" 94 Harv. Law Rev. 116 (1981); Easterbrook & Fischel "Corporate Control Transactions" 91 Yale. L.J. 698 (1982; Easterbrook & Fischel "Auctions and Sunk Costs in Tender Offers" 35 Stanford Law Rev. 1; Bebchuk "The Case for Facilitating Competing Tender Offers" 95 Harv. Law Rev. 1029 (1982); Lipton, "Takeover Bids in the Target's Boardroom" 35 Bus. Law. 101 (1979); Lipton, "Takeover Bids in the Target's Boardroom: An Update After One Year" 36 Bus.Law. 1017 (1980); (1979 Lowenstein "Pruning Deadwood in Hostile Takeovers: A Proposal for Legislation" 83 Col. Law Rev. 49 (1983); S. Deakin and G.Slinger "Hostile Takeovers, Corporate Law and the Theory of the Firm" (1997) 24 J. Law & Soc. 124.

A. Assumption One – The Market Accurately Prices Securities
(Traditional Hypothesis)

2–02 The assumption that the market accurately prices securities is popular. Three economic theories are relevant here, portfolio theory, capital markets theory and the efficient market hypothesis. An important implication of these theories is that securities are correctly priced to reflect their intrinsic value. If this is correct, the premium on market price paid to shareholders upon the completion of a successful takeover can only be explained in one of two ways. Either, the offeror places a higher value on securities because the company is worth more to it or alternatively, the offeror over-pays for the target.

I. SECURITIES MARKETS THEORY

(1) Portfolio Theory

2–03 Portfolio theory deals with the selection by investors of share portfolios based on their assessment of expected return and acceptable risk.[1a] The idea is that in constructing their portfolios, investors will seek to maximise their returns for the level of risk they are prepared to accept. Risk may be classified either as systematic risk or non-systematic risk. The first category of risk, systematic risk, reflects the company's sensitivity to fluctuations and changes in the general market.[2] Systematic risk results from the tendency of share prices to "move together" with the general market. For example, as a result of the economic downturn in Asia, the share prices of all the companies listed on the Irish Stock Exchange decreased substantially in September 1998. The recession affected all shares listed in the market not just shares in a particular industry or a particular company. Similarly, a change in Irish interest rates will affect the prices of all shares listed on the Irish Stock Exchange. Systematic risk is thus inherent in all investments. However, some securities and portfolios are particularly sensitive to changes in the market, while others are more independent and stable. In other words, some shares appear to bear a higher degree of systematic risk than others. The Greek letter beta "B" is the measure given to a stock's systematic risk based on past record. A company's beta is calculated by measuring the covariance between the return on its common stock and the market index. The second category of risk affecting corporate secu-

---

[1a] See generally, Sharpe, *Portfolio: Theory and Capital Markets* (McGraw-Hill, New York, 1970).
[2] For this reason, it is also referred to as "market risk".

rities is non-systematic risk. This form of risk results from variations peculiar to a particular company or industry. For example, a labour strike or a new product failure in a particular company will generally only affect the price of that company's shares. Similarly, a particular industry may be affected by the entry of a new competitor or by new legislation *e.g.* a law prohibiting tobacco advertising will affect the share prices of all tobacco companies.

2–04   Instead of investing all his money in one company or even in one industry, an investor may choose to diversify his share portfolios. By investing in a range of companies and perhaps a range of industries, the investor avoids "putting all his eggs in the same basket". In this way, diversification allows investors to ensure that their portfolios are insulated against non-systematic risk. If one company fares badly, the investor will, to some extent, be insulated by his other investments. Clearly, however, only non-systematic risk will be eliminated by diversification. Systematic risk such as the risk of a downfall in the general level of share prices will affect all shares and a diversified portfolio will fare no better than a non-diversified one.

2–05   Diversification leads to the construction of portfolios which have the highest expected return for the lowest possible risk. These portfolios are termed "efficient portfolios" or "Markowitz efficient portfolios" after Professor Harry Markowitz, the developer of portfolio theory. In constructing this efficient portfolio, a number of assumptions are made.[3] First, it is assumed that investors' decisions are affected only by two considerations risk and return. Secondly, it is assumed that investors are risk adverse, *i.e.* they prefer shares that offer less risk to shares that offer high risk for the same expected return. Finally, it is assumed that investors seek the highest possible return for a given level of risk.

(2) Capital Market Theory

2–06   Capital market theory deals with the effect of investors' decisions on security prices. It is assumed that the logical investor will avoid non-systematic risk by diversification and the only relevant form of risk will be systematic risk. This, therefore, is the only form of risk an investor must be compensated for holding. Capital markets theory suggests that if investors constructed efficient portfolios as indicated by portfolio theory, shares with identical levels of systematic risk would trade at prices that imply an identical estimated rate of return. The reason for this is that if two shares offered similar risks for different returns, the

---

[3] Fabozzi and Modigliani, *Capital Markets* (Prentice-Hall International Inc., 1996), Chap. 8: Risk and Return Theories I.

share offering the higher return would pose better value for the investor. The investor would thus buy these shares and sell any shares already held offering the lower return. The investor might also borrow to buy these higher return shares. The result of this would be that the supply of high return shares would decrease as the demand increased and consequently the share price would rise. Conversely, the share price of the share offering the lower return would decrease as supply exceeded demand. By this process, which is termed "arbitrage", the prices of the two shares would eventually be identical.

2–07   An important implication of this theory is that by estimating a shares' beta or systematic risk, it should be possible to estimate the required rate of return for that investment. This is known as the Capital Assets Pricing Model (CAPM).[4] One major drawback to the CAPM is that it makes a number of important assumptions which may not always be correct. For example, it assumes that risk free assets such as government bonds are available to investors in unlimited supply for inclusion in their portfolios. It assumes that investors may borrow and lend at this risk free rate and that there are no transactional or information costs. It also assumes that all investors have identical expectations concerning assets' risk and return.

(3) The Efficient Market Hypothesis

2–08   The CAPM relies upon the ability of arbitrageurs to recognise when share prices are out of line and to make a profit by driving them back to an equilibrium value which is consistent with available information. The efficient market hypothesis suggests that the capital market is efficient in the sense that share prices fully reflect all available information.[5] Share prices thus, represent unbiased estimates of the intrinsic value of the shares. Efficient markets have been described in terms of "a fair game" where share prices fully reflect the information available.[6] It has also been suggested that the efficient market hypothesis may be divided into three categories: the "weak form", the "semi-strong form" and the "strong form". Weak form efficiency means that historical share prices are fully reflected in share prices. Certain empirical evidence

---

[4] The standard form CAPM was developed independently by Sharpe and Lintner. See Sharpe, "Capital Asset Prices: A Theory of Market Equilibrium Under Conditions of Risk" (1964) *Journal of Finance* 425–442 and Litner, "Security Prices, Risk and Maximum Gains from Diversification" (1965) *Journal of Finance* 587–615.

[5] Copeland and Weston, *Financial Theory and Corporate Policy*, (3rd ed., Addison-Wesley, Reading Mass., 1988) Chap. 9, Elton and Gruber, *Modern Portfolio Theory and Investment Analysis*, (4th ed., Wiley, New York, 1991) Chap. 15.

[6] Fama, "Efficient Capital Markets: A Review of Theory and Empirical Work, (1970) *Journal of Finance* 383.

suggests that price behaviour is largely random. For example, the "random walk" model describing the time-path of share prices predicts that in any future period the share price will be equal to the price of that security in the immediately preceding period plus some randomly chosen number. This means that the expected value of future price changes is independent of past price changes. Semi-strong form efficiency means that all publicly available information is reflected in share prices. Semi-strong form tests have been performed with respect to many different types of information such as earnings announcements, dividend announcements and stock splits. All tests have indicated that the market adjusts to new information rapidly with much of the impact taking place in advance of the announcements. This means that investors will not be able to earn abnormal rates of return utilising trade strategies based on publicly available information. Finally, strong form efficiency suggests that share prices fully reflect all information, including unpublished information. Tests, however, suggest that insiders can earn excess returns.[7] Empirical tests of the efficient market hypothesis, thus, suggest that the market is reasonably efficient or "semi-strong"[8] rather than perfectly efficient or "totally strong".[9]

II. EFFICIENCY THEORY

2–09 Efficiency theory attempts to explain why offerors would place a value on securities in excess of their market value. It suggests that as securities markets price securities precisely in accordance with their real value, the only opportunity for an offeror to profit by a takeover is where that offeror can re-deploy assets or manage the assets more efficiently. A premium is justified therefore because the target has a unique value to the offeror.

(1) Synergies

2–10 An offeror may determine that "synergies" exist such that the value of the combined companies is greater than the sum of the two individual companies. Synergies may enhance revenues, reduce costs, lead to lower taxes and a lower cost of capital. Revenue enhancing synergies result where the combined firms are capable of producing greater benefits than the two separate entities. An example of such a synergy is

---

[7] Jaffe, "Special Information and Insider Trading" (1974) 47 No. 3 *Journal of Business* 410–428.

[8] Fama, Fisher, Jensen and Roll, "The Adjustment of Stock Prices to New Information" (1969) 15 *International Economic Review* 15.

[9] Jaffe "The Effect of Regulation Changes on Insider Trading" (1974) *The Bell Journal of Economics and Management Science* 93.

product complementality. For example, the acquisition by a health food company of an exercise equipment manufacturer leads to a more balanced product mix. Another synergy under this heading is strategic advantage which gives the offeror an opportunity to take advantage of a competitive environment should the timing be appropriate. One commonly cited example of strategic advantage is Procter and Gamble's initial acquisition of the Charmin Paper Company. This acquisition allowed Procter and Gamble to exploit perceived opportunities in the form of developing interrelated paper products such as disposable nappies, paper towels and bathroom tissue. Examples of potential cost reducing synergies include, economies of scale or economies of production, marketing or finance. Such economies are typical of horizontal acquisitions. Vertical acquisitions may also lead to economies. For example, the acquisition of a printing company by a paper manufacturer provides the manufacturer with a ready market and the printing company with a ready source of paper. Tax synergies may also prove useful where, for example, one company through an acquisition acquires, the use of tax losses from net operating losses. A lower cost of capital may result from the acquisition of a company rich in cash. In addition, the costs of issuing securities will be subject to economies of scale.

(2) The Market for Corporate Control

2–11 A second form of efficiency involves the replacement of underperforming or inept management with experienced and efficient management. Where incumbent management are performing poorly, share prices will decrease below their highest potential value. A profit opportunity then exists for the offeror to purchase the undervalued shares, replace the poor management, operate the company more efficiently and reap the rewards. This is called the "market for corporate control" because it involves alternative management teams vying for the right to manage corporate assets. In terms of economic theory, the Coase theorem predicts that if one firm is making inefficient use of assets, that another firm which can obtain greater value from the same assets will bribe the less efficient firms' stockholders to let it do so.[9a]

2–12 This form of market control exercises a disciplinary effect on management. In his seminal article on the subject, Manne suggested that the control of corporations may constitute a valuable asset which exists independently of any interest in either economies of scale or

---

[9a] "The Nature of the Firm" (1937) NS. 4 *Economica* 386; "The Problem of Social Cost" (1960) 3 *Journal of Economics* 1.

monopoly power.[10] A fundamental premise underlying the market for corporate control is the existence of a high positive correlation between corporate managerial efficiency and the market price of shares for that company. Manne suggests that there are compelling reasons apart from empirical data for believing that this correlation exists. Insiders (those with the most knowledge about corporate affairs) are strongly motivated financially to perform a kind of arbitrage function for their company's stock. The effect of this reliable information is stronger than the ignorant information which, over a period of time, will be randomly distributed with an overall neutral effect:

> "Decisions made by those with a higher degree of certainty will to that extent not meet a concealing effect since they will not be made on a random basis. Over some period of time, it would seem that the average market price of a company's shares must be the correct one."[11]

The market price of the shares declines because the company is not being managed well enough to give shareholders as great a return as could be accomplished under other more efficient management.

2–13   This theory suggests that instead of attempting to change poor management, shareholders will sell their shares causing an overall drop in the value of the company's shares. Although shareholders should be able to reap substantial benefits from improving the performance of managers, this improvement is difficult to achieve. Easterbrook and Fischel point out that agency costs will typically go undetected by individual shareholders, most of whom are passive investors seeking liquid holdings with no interest in managing the company:

> "No one shareholder can collect all or even a little of the gains available from monitoring the firm's managers. The benefits would be dispersed among all stockholders according to their investments, not according to their monitoring effects"[12]

This is the "free rider" issue. The "Wall Street Rule" suggests that shareholders sell rather than attempt change. In addition, shareholders have no authority to compel the company to change its ways. For this reason, Manne noted:

> "Only the takeover scheme provides some assurance of competitive efficiency among corporate managers and thereby affords strong protection to the interests of vast numbers of small, non-controlling shareholders".[13]

---

[10] Manne, "Mergers and the Market for Corporate Control" (1965) 73 Journ. Pol. Econ. 110.
[11] *ibid*. at 112.
[12] Easterbrook and Fischell, "The Proper Role of a Target's Management in Responding to a Tender Offer" 94 Harv. L. Rev. 1161 at 1171.
[13] *op. cit.*, above, n.10 at 113.

Other forms of monitoring which seek to achieve the same objective are common law fiduciary duties, statutory restrictions and corporate governance codes.[14]

2–14   Coffee maintains that the market for corporate control is not as efficient as Manne suggests. Coffee states that internal monitoring should detect inefficiencies before outsiders and before the market discounts the shares by a sufficient amount. Easterbrook and Fischel would appear to accept this, their argument being that shareholders may perceive the problem but they have no incentive to act upon it. Coffee has also argued that the market for corporate control is only effective within a limited range. Most instances of managerial inefficiency or self dealing will not result in a significant enough discount in the company's share price to justify the substantial takeover premium that normally prevails. On the other end of the scale Coffee also points out that the level of risk required to accept a financially distressed company is high. Extremely badly managed companies may be perceived as carrying excessive risk and may thus become indigestible and survive. They are immune from attack precisely because of their pervasive inefficiency. As a result, Coffee states "companies where the level of inefficiency is either not extreme enough to justify the necessary premium or so extreme as to surpass the bidder's level of risk aversion" fall outside the range and will not be considered as targets.[15] This means that the market for corporate control is "sufficiently limited that it can serve only as a remedy of last resort for massive managerial failures and not as the principal enforcer of corporate accountability".[16] Another flaw in the corporate control argument is that it would appear to suggest that offerors will search constantly and evenly throughout the marketplace to find mismanaged targets. This does not explain why takeovers tend to be cyclical and concentrate on first one industry and then another. Nor does it explain why offerors seem to pursue companies with strong operating management or why the search undertaken by offerors for potential targets seems to be a restricted one that is strongly schewed by internal organisational considerations. Finally, Coffee points out that if the market for corporate control alone were adequate to monitor and replace corporate management, then much of existing corporate law, (such as the legal rules governing self dealing and fiduciary duties) should either wither away as obsolete or be viewed as simply non-mandatory provisions, which the parties to the corporation could

---

[14] See Clarke, "Corporate Responsibility in Light of the Separation of Ownership and Control" (1997) 19 *Dublin University Law Journal* at 50–76.
[15] Coffee, "Regulating the Market for Corporate Control" (1984) 84 Col. L.Rev 1145 at 1204.
[16] *ibid.*, at 1153.

modify as they wished. Easterbrook and Fischel, Coffee argues, are close to this position because they argue that the principal value of fiduciary duties is that the existence of such "off-the-rack" rules reduces the cost of transacting and of enforcing restrictions on the agents powers. In summary, while Coffee accepts that the market for corporate control has a disciplinary effect, he opines that the scope of that effect tends to be more limited than neo-classical theory has admitted.

III. EXPLOITATION THEORIES

2–15 While efficiency theory suggests that acquisitions create private gains for the participating parties and net social gains, other less prominent theories suggest that these gains are achieved at an unacceptable cost to third parties. It is argued that offerors can afford to pay a premium on the market price, not because they are creating wealth but, because they are transferring wealth to the target shareholders at a cost to third parties. Such costs may be imposed for example by exploiting monopoly power or by breaching implicit contracts between shareholders and creditors, employees or incumbent managers. It is argued that takeovers decrease welfare because they divert resources which would otherwise be used for capital investments or dividends and instead are used only to rearrange the ownership of existing corporate assets. Takeovers are castigated for their detrimental effect on employees who may loose their jobs or be dislocated. Takeovers are also criticised for leading to increased gearing.

2–16 In a related argument, Lipton argues that takeover offers decrease social welfare because they "adversely affect long-term planning and thereby jeopardise the economy".[17] The threat of takeovers may alter decision making within target companies and may distract management from the more important business of running the company. Potential targets may seek to reduce their vulnerability by divesting themselves of cash or other assets desired by the offeror. A related consequence is that targets stalk other targets to grow in size and deplete their cash to reduce the likelihood of their being taken over. Easterbrook and Fischel reject this arguing that if the market perceives that management has a successful long-term strategy, this will be reflected in a higher share price.[17a]

2–17 U.S. commentators suggest that target shareholders can be exploited by being trapped in a "prisoners dilemma" faced with a choice

---

[17] Lipton, "Takeover Bids in the Target's Boardroom" (1979) 35 Bus Law 101 at 105.
[17a] *op. cit.*, above, n.12, 1184.

between an unsatisfactory current price offered by the offeror and a potentially even lower price in the future. Because shareholders cannot communicate and co-ordinate in a two-tier bid their actions to resist the offer, they are vulnerable to "the second stage merger" at a worse price.[17b] As will be seen in Chapter 11, under current takeover rules, this cannot happen in Ireland as all shareholders will be entitled to sell their shares at the same price in the event of the offer proving to be successful.

IV. OVERPAYMENT THEORY

2–18   Overpayment theory suggests that the premium successful offerors pay on market price is unjustified and that there is no real opportunity for acquisitions gains at all. The overpayment hypothesis suggests that the shareholders of an offeror expect it to reinvest its cash flow poorly. Black has described this as "extending the free cash flow model to bidders, adding in rational investor expectations, and then exploring bidding dynamics in a world where many bidders are likely to overpay".[18] The result of this expectation is that the offeror's share price will not fall as a consequence of the overpayment because the expected loss was already built into the offeror's price. Black also notes that bad financial managers outbid good financial managers. A contributing factor to this is that good financial managers are not expected to overpay and if they do, their share price will go down. Although this explains why offerors are able to overpay, it does not in itself explain why they would want to overpay. Two possible explanations have been put forward to do this.

(1) Empire Building

2–19   It has been suggested that offerors overpay because they are engaged in "empire building". There are a number of reasons why managers might seek to increase the size of their companies. Their objectives may be to increase the size of their companies in order to leave a legacy, to increase performance related perquisites, to lessen the chances of being taken over, to increase the likelihood of promotion or to increase their standing in the business community. There is a common element in the writings of such economists as William Baumol, J.K. Galbraith, Oliver Williamson, Robin Harris and Harvey Leibenstein arguing that management seek to maximise growth even when it is contrary to the shareholders best interests.[18a] There is thus a tendency

---

[17b] Bebchuck, "Toward Undistorted Choice and Equal Treatment in Corporate Takeovers" 98 *Harv. L. Rev.* 1963; Brudney and Chirelstein, "Fair Shares in Corporate Mergers and Takeovers" 88 Harv. L. Rev. 277.

[18]   Black, "Bidder Overpayment in Takeovers" 41 Stan.Law Rev. 597 at 600.

[18a] Coffee, *op. cit.*, above, n.15, p. 1167.

for growth maximisation to be preferred by management over profit maximisation. Agency theory informs us that some divergence is inevitable, given the costs of monitoring management and the substantial opportunities for managerial discretion. It may be argued that growth maximising acquisitions are socially undesirable because they produce "bureaucratic layering" which in turn implies that corporate decision-making will become more sluggish. If this argument is accepted, the necessary implication is that takeovers do not lead to greater efficiency but rather to a net transfer of wealth from the offeror's shareholders to those of the targets. Small companies may be vulnerable to takeovers by larger inefficient companies.

The potential for empire building is not however without its limitations. There are for example product, capital and labour market constraints. In addition, there are corporate control market constraints. Easterbrook & Fischel, *e.g.* point out that a company headed by an empire builder would fare poorly in the product market and the capital market and its low share price would render it a takeover target.[18c]

(2) Error

2–20   A second explanation for over payment is error. The offeror's management may overestimate their own abilities to manage the target more efficiently. Alternatively, they may incorrectly value the target by placing too high a value on future sales, growth rates, discount rates etc. Alternatively, the error may be caused by "winner's curse".[19] This latter concept stems from an ignorance of the basic principles of bidding theory. Competition between offerors will drive the market price of a desired target up to a level where some level of overpayment becomes the norm. This theory envisages a successful offeror in an auction situation having to pay more than original intended in order to avoid a situation where it has nothing to show for all the investigation and negotiation costs. Winner's curse problems apply only to an asset whose value is common to all offerors. An offeror with a unique synergy faces winner curse only to the extent of that target's value to other offerors. Black suggests that winners curse theory dictates that offerors must offer substantially less than their estimate of the worth of an asset and be prepared to succeed in only a fraction of their bids. Black points out that "the potential for overpayment is substantially increased by the limited supply of targets at a modest premium to the

---

[18c] *op. cit.*, n.12 at p. 1185.

[19] Roll, "The Hubris Hypothesis of Corporate Takeovers" (1986) 59 J.Bus.197; Capen, Clapp & Campbell, "Competitive Bidding in High-Risk Situations" (1971) 23 J. Petroleum Tech. 641.

market".[20] One source of supply limits is target management resistance". Other reasons are substantial transaction costs, potential negative synergies and shareholder insistence on some premium.

Kraakman, however, has discounted this theory arguing that that the prosperous acquisitions market and a large empirical literature both suggest that most acquisitions do generate private gains, at least as measured by their impact on share prices. Target shareholders earn large returns in the form of premium and the offerors shareholders do not seem to suffer losses and may also register gains.[20a]

B. Assumption Two – The Market Does not Accurately Price Securities
(Discount Hypothesis)

2–21   If the market has not correctly priced the securities, then the offeror need not be paying in excess of the value of the shares. Instead, the payment may reflect the true value of securities discounted by the market. Kraakman describes this as a form of "recaptured discount".[21] The difficulty with this approach is that it would seem to run contrary to a wealth of evidence which suggests that the capital markets are "speculatively efficient". Easterbrook and Fischel deduce thus, that "it is unlikely that price and 'value' will diverge in large markets for shares."[22] This may not necessarily be true. Kraakman suggests two theories to explain why the share price may be inaccurate: the mis-investment hypothesis and the market hypothesis.

I. THE MIS-INVESTMENT HYPOTHESIS

2–22   The mis-investment hypothesis suggests that investors rationally expect managers of target firms to mis-invest the future returns on corporate assets and investors discount the value of these assets accordingly. The mis-investment hypothesis, Kraakman argues belongs to the "broader family of agency cost theories".[23] Managers are said to exercise discretionary control over "free cash flows" or cash flows exceeding the investment requirements of the firms existing projects. This theory suggests that target firms tend to waste the cash flow on excessive growth rather than return it to shareholders. The implication

[20] Black, *op. cit.*, above, n.18 at 629.
[20a] Kraakman, "Taking Discounts Seriously: The Implications of Discounted Share Prices as an Acquisition Motive" 1988 Colum. L. Rev. 891.
[21] Kraakman, "Discounted Share Prices as a Source of Acquisition Gains" in *Corporate Law & Economic Analysis*, (Bebchuk, ed., Cambridge University Press, 1990) Chap. 2, p. 29.
[22] *op. cit.*, above, n.12, p. 1165.
[23] Kraakman, *op. cit.*, above, n.21, 35.

of the mis-investment hypothesis is that share prices for well managed firms will always equal or exceed corporate asset values. Hostile take-overs thus, serve a useful purpose in forcing these firms to disgorge excess cash. The effect of individual takeovers is then to move share prices in the right direction.

II. THE MARKET HYPOTHESIS

2–23   The second theory suggested by Kraakman to explain why share prices may be inaccurate is the market hypothesis which asserts that the share prices themselves may be "noisy or skewed" resulting in the failure of market prices to reflect informed estimates of likely cash-flows generated by the target. Kraakman suggests that large scale noise trading may arise from misconceived strategies, erroneous valuation assumptions, fashions and fads, or simply pleasure in trading. This market theory is a popular one. Black also agrees that share prices reflect less the perceived value of the company than the noise or other factors with no bearing on intrinsic value.[23a]

2–24   Lowenstein has pointed out that the market is only efficient at what it seeks to do.[24] He argues that the day-to-day trading market is distinct from the market for corporate control. Its efficiency in terms of investor or institutional pricing is only loosely related to its efficiency in terms of a willing buyer looking at its intrinsic value. The intrinsic value to the buyer is based on book value or liquid value. The focus is thus on earning power. The trading market on the other hand represents a form of derived demand. Keyes summarised this as follows:

> "professional investment may be likened to those newspaper competitions in which the competitors have to pick out the six prettiest faces from a hundred photographs, the prize being awarded to the competitor whose choice most nearly corresponds to the average preferences of the competi-tors as a whole; so that each competitor has to pick, not those faces which he himself finds prettiest, but those which he thinks likeliest to catch the fancy of the other competitors, all of whom are looking at the problem from the same point of view. It is not a case of choosing those which, to the best of one's judgment, are really the prettiest, nor even those which average opinion genuinely thinks the prettiest. We have reached the third degree where we devote our intelligence to anticipating what average opinion expects the average opinion to be. And there are some, I believe, who practice the fourth, fifth and higher degrees."[25]

[23a] *op. cit.*, n.18.
[24] Lowenstein, "Pruning Deadwood in Hostile Takeovers: A Proposal for Legislation" (1983) 83 Col. L.Rev. 249 at 273.
[25] Keyes, *The General Theory of Employment, Interest and Money* (1936 ed.), 156.

2–25   Many investors admit to having no deep knowledge of the companies in which they invest. They principally invest on the basis of anticipated price movements. The value of the shares to them is thus intrinsically different to the value to a potential purchaser of the company. Another complicating factor is that investors entertain heterogeneous beliefs about the value of their shares. As a result, Stout explains that the market price for shares is likely to be higher than the average investor's estimate of its value.[26] The slope of the demand function should increase as it approaches the vertical axis. Because shareholders have different expectations of value and thus different reservation prices, market price is set by the most pessimistic of company's current shareholders. Under this hypothesis, the price of a single share can no longer be viewed as an accurate reflection of market value of each of the company's outstanding shares. There are also different perceptions and degrees of acceptability of risk, especially the financial risks associated with leverage. Lowenstein suggests that the stockmarket is dominated either by an extreme pessimism which results in arbitrarily low valuations or a preoccupation with short term trading profits. The latter exists because institutional investors focus on the prospect of short term price changes in securities.[26a]

2–26   The implication of this hypothesis remains a moot point. On the one hand, it may mean that hostile offerors exploit the prices and are in fact no more than asset strippers. Asset stripping occurs when it is cheaper to purchase control of the company than to purchase assets in the market for such assets. Offerors are able to earn a large return by purchasing the shares and then selling the assets. On the other hand, Coffee suggests that hostile offerors should be viewed positively as "the saviour" who pays back some premia to shareholders which they would otherwise have been unable to release. As Coffee warns "under-valued stocks can easily remain undervalued stocks".

III. PRIVATE INFORMATION THEORY

2–27   A third explanation for market undervaluation is that the offeror may in the course of negotiations have accessed information which was not available to the market but which when disseminated causes the market to re-evaluate the shares. This private information theory according to Kraakman "straddles the line between traditional and discount hypotheses".[27] This theory assumes that the market may be

---

[26] Stout, "Are Takeover Premiums Really Premiums? Market Price, Fair Value and Corporate Law" 99 *Yale Law Journal* 1235.

[26a] *op. cit.*, No. 24 at Pp. 268–309.

[27] Kraakman, *op. cit.*, above, n.21, 32.

uninformed about the real value of target assets. As noted above, tests suggest that the market is not strong form efficient. Insiders who privately learn key information can thus exploit true discrepancies between share prices and asset values. One flaw with this theory is that there is no reason to believe that hostile acquirers have access to inside information. This theory "demands the acquirers routinely discover dramatic good news relative to market expectations about targets". In addition, as Kraakman points out, evidence that unsuccessful bids fail to increase the share prices of target firms over the long run also suggests that hostile bids do not release key inside information.[27a]

C. Conclusion

2–28 From even this brief analysis it becomes clear, that it is not possible to adopt a monolithic approach to takeovers. Certain takeovers may be beneficial and certain detrimental depending on many factors, among them the relative skills of target and offeror control groups. Under a pluralistic interpretation, each theory may have a partial validity and may accurately describe motivations underlying some but not all takeovers. The implication of this finding for regulators is that a delicate balance needs to be struck between safeguarding the needs of target shareholders and other relevant parties and ensuring that unnecessary obstacles are not placed in the way of parties intending to make offers for target companies. This issue will be pursued in greater detail in Chapter 19.

[27a] *ibid.*, at p. 33.

PART 2

REGULATORY FRAMEWORK

CHAPTER 3

THE IRISH TAKEOVER PANEL

Introduction

3–01   Until July 1997, the London Panel on Takeovers and Mergers regulated offers for Irish companies if their shares were listed on the Irish Stock Exchange or dealt in on the Unlisted Securities Market.[1] This situation changed with the introduction of the Irish Takeover Panel Act 1997 which establishes an Irish Takeover Panel to regulate the conduct of takeovers of Irish companies. The implementation of the Act marked a further step in the development of an autonomous system of regulation in Ireland.[2] By 1995, stock exchanges, stock exchange member firms and investment business firms were all regulated by the Central Bank of Ireland,[3] roles previously performed by UK regulatory bodies. Following the separation of the London and Irish Stock Exchanges, there no longer seemed any logical reason for the London Panel to continue its regulatory role in the Republic of Ireland. The time was ripe thus for the establishment of a domestic supervisory authority.

3–02   The first issue to be determined was whether a self regulatory Panel could work in Ireland. The main attractions of a self regulating body such as the London Panel are its abilities to react instantly to new situations, to amend its rules at short notice and to adopt a flexible purposive interpretation of its rules. However, concerns about the legal difficulties which would arise from the exercise of its functions by a Panel which did not have adequate powers derived from legislation led to the decision to establish a statutory Panel in Ireland. In forming a Panel and introducing rules to regulate the conduct of takeovers in Ireland, much reliance was placed on the structure of the London Panel and the takeover rules used by the London Panel. Therefore, before the

---

[1]   The London panel supervised Irish companies whose securities were listed on the Unlisted Securities Market until it closed at the end of 1996.
[2]   See Clarke, "The Irish Takeover Panel Act 1997 – A Further Cutting of the UK Regulatory Ties" *Palmer's in Company*, Issue No. 1, 1998.
[3]   Under the Stock Exchange Act 1995 and the Investment Intermediaries Act 1995, respectively.

35

Irish Panel is examined, the first part of this Chapter will examine the operational structure of the London Panel.

A. The London Panel on Takeovers and Mergers

3–03 The London Panel on Takeovers and Mergers was set up in 1968 under the auspices of the Governor of the Bank of England in response to growing concern about unfair practices during the course of takeover bids. The Panel regulates the conduct of takeover bids for all listed and unlisted public companies resident in the UK, the Channel Islands and the Isle of Man. It also applies to offers for private companies so resident in certain limited circumstances, where for example their equity share capital has been listed on the Stock Exchange or dealt in on the Unlisted Securities Market at any time during the previous 10 years. In the year ended March 31, 1999 there were 235 published takeover or merger proposals of which 231 reached the stage where documents were sent to shareholders. In carrying out its functions, the London Panel strives to ensure fairness and equality of treatment of shareholders. It is not concerned with the commercial merits of takeovers or wider questions of public interest.

I. THE CITY CODE

3–04 The London Panel regulates conduct in the course of a takeover through the City Code on Takeovers and Mergers ("the City Code") and the Rules Governing Substantial Acquisitions of Shares. The City Code is a self regulatory code which operates to ensure fair and equal treatment of all shareholders in relation to takeovers and to provide an orderly framework within which takeovers can be conducted. The City Code is intended to represent the collective opinion of those professionally involved as to good and fair practice.

3–05 The City Code is based upon ten General Principles which are described by the London Panel as "good standards of commercial behaviour".[4] These General Principles are set out in Appendix 1. These General Principles ensure that all shareholders of the same class of the target company are treated equally and are provided with sufficient information in time to make an informed assessment of the offer. They also require directors of the target to act in good faith and not to frustrate an offer without the shareholders' authorisation. The General

---

[4] The City Code on Takeovers and Mergers – Introduction, A3.

Principles are expressed in broad terms and the spirit as well as the precise wording of the General Principles and the ensuing rules must be observed.[5] As a result, the London Panel may modify or relax the effect of the precise wording of the General Principles accordingly. These principles are supplemented by a series of 38 rules some of which are expansions of the General Principles and examples of their application and others of which are provisions governing specific aspects of takeover procedure. The rules are augmented by notes setting out interpretations and practices. The London Panel also administer the Rules Governing Substantial Acquisitions of Shares. The objective of these latter rules is to slow up the rate at which substantial holdings in shares may be built up. This will deter the occurrence of what became known as "dawn raids".

II. COMPOSITION OF THE LONDON PANEL

3–06 The London Panel's membership is drawn from major financial and business institutions, giving it a broad spread of expertise. The Governor of the Bank of England appoints the chairperson, two deputy chairpersons and three non-representative members, two of whom are industrialists. The Panel works on a day-to-day basis through its executive, headed by the Director General. The latter is normally a senior merchant banker on secondment. The executive's other staff are permanent employees or persons on secondment from accountancy firms, legal firms, stockbroking firms, clearing banks and also the Department of Trade and Industry and the Bank of England. This system enables the Panel to maintain a high calibre of personnel. The high turnover of staff provides the Panel with expertise, a constantly fresh approach, enthusiasm and an up to date view of the market. The Panel is self financing, generating its income primarily from a levy on transactions in UK securities and charges on offer documentation. In the year ended March 31, 1999, the London Panel in its Annual Report noted income from document fees of Stg £3,715,500 and income from the contract note levy of Stg £955,318.

III. LONDON PANEL PROCEDURE

3–07 A ruling on the application of the City Code will be given initially by the executive. Where there is a particularly unusual, important or difficult point at issue, the executive may refer the matter to the London Panel itself for a decision without giving a ruling. If a party, an adviser or in certain circumstances a shareholder wishes to contest a ruling of the executive, they may ask for the matter to be reviewed by the Panel.

---

[5] City Code, Introduction to the General Principles, B1.

3–08   The executive may institute disciplinary proceedings when it believes that there has been a breach of the City Code. The person suspected of committing the breach is invited to appear before the Panel. If a breach is found to have occurred, the Panel possesses a number of potentially potent sanctions. It may: reprimand the person privately or publicly; report the affair to another regulatory authority such as the Stock Exchange, the Department of Trade and Industry or the Financial Services Authority; or take any other action it deems appropriate. Such actions might involve halting a bid or organising the withdrawal of the UK securities markets' facilities from the wrongdoer. The Panel may also ask a party to remedy any wrongdoing *e.g.* in 1989, the Panel ruled that Guinness should pay approximately £75 million to former Distillers shareholders who received a lower than required consideration for their shares in breach of Rule 11 of the City Code.

3–09   An Appeal Committee exists to hear appeals in the following three cases: where the Panel intends to take disciplinary action as a result of a finding that the City Code has been breached; where it is alleged that the Panel has exceeded its jurisdiction; or where the Panel refuses to recognise a market maker or fund manager as an exempt market maker or fund manager. The Appeal Committee consists of two members of the London Panel who were not involved in the decision in issue and a chairperson who will usually have held high judicial office. In the year ended March 31, 1999, only three appeals were heard, none of which was successful.

IV. SELF-REGULATORY BASIS

3–10   The City Code does not have the force of law. It is not created by statute, or under an authority delegated by Parliament. This allows it to act quickly and flexibly. For example, it can react rapidly to new market developments by immediate amendment of the City Code. Rules can be fashioned to meet new contingencies. One disadvantage of this approach, however, is that rulings may be inconsistent. As a result of the London Panel concentrating on the spirit rather than the letter of the law, it is often difficult to give definitive legal advice.

Since its establishment, the London Panel has operated its non-statutory system with enormous success. Indeed, it has been the prototype for many other European supervisory systems. For this reason, the London Panel has been a vehement opponent of the draft European Directive on Takeovers, fearing that its self-regulatory system would be jeopardised.[6] The draft Directive will be examined in the next Chapter.

---

[6] House of Lords Select Committee on the European Communities (1996 H.L.Q. 214).

V. ENFORCEMENT

3–11   The operation of the City Code is, however, recognised and supported by the Financial Services Act 1986 which provides the regulatory framework for the protection of investors and the conduct of the financial markets in the UK. Authorised bodies under the 1986 Act such as Financial Services Authority and the relevant self regulatory bodies impose rules providing that authorised firms should not act for clients who are unprepared to comply with the City Code (the "cold shouldering rule"). Furthermore, the Financial Services Authority requires authorised persons to co-operate with the Panel in providing relevant information, documentation and assistance. In addition, where the Panel reports a breach of the City Code by a practitioner to the appropriate authority which authorises that person under the Act, the practitioner may be disciplined or have restrictions placed on his or her business.

VI. JUDICIAL REVIEW

3–12   In *R v. Panel on Takeovers and Mergers; ex parte Datafin plc*,[7] the Court of Appeal held that decisions of the London Panel are subject to judicial review. Although it is not a body created by the legislature, the Panel was acknowledged to operate as an integral part of a system which performs public law duties. The Court held that having regard to the wide-ranging nature and importance of the matters covered by the Code and to the serious public consequences of non-compliance with the Code, the Panel was performing a public law function when prescribing and administering the Code. As a consequence, it was deemed subject to public law remedies including judicial review. The Court then went on to consider the manner in which the court's jurisdiction should be exercised given the nature of the Panel's activities in the financial markets and the need for speed and certainty in its decisions.

3–13   The grounds upon which an application for judicial review could be based were seen by the court to be limited. Such a finding is consistent with the Panel's character as the controlling body for the self-regulation of takeovers and mergers. It was noted that "the Panel combines the functions of legislator, court interpreting the Panel's legislation, consultant, and court investigating and imposing penalties in respect of alleged breaches of the Code".[8] Against this background, it is clear it would be difficult to prove any wrongdoing on the Panel's part. Firstly, Donaldson M.R. stated that there could be "little scope for

---

[7]   [1987] 1 All E.R. 564.
[8]   *ibid.*, at 579.

complaint that the Panel has promulgated rules which are ultra vires, provided only that they do not clearly violate the principle proclaimed by the Panel of being based on the concept of doing equity between one shareholder and another".[9] The Court stated that the Panel was unlikely to violate this, its guiding principle. Secondly, Donaldson M.R. stated that it would be difficult to argue that the Panel had erred in interpreting its own rules and he suggested that the Panel was to be given "considerable latitude" both "because, as legislator, it could properly alter them at any time and because of the form which the rules take, i.e. laying down principles to be applied in spirit as much as in letter in specific situations".[10] A court might intervene, his lordship believed only where the interpretation "were so far removed from the natural and ordinary meaning of the words of the rules that an ordinary user of the market could reasonably be misled".[11] Even in this case, it was suggested the court might decide that it would be more appropriate to declare the true meaning of the rule, leaving it to the Panel to promulgate a new rule accurately expressing its intentions than to quash the Panel's original decision. Similarly, his Lordship stated that the Panel's discretionary power to grant dispensations from the operation of the rules was fettered only by the obligation to seek equity between shareholders. As a result, the Panel could only be challenged "in wholly exceptional circumstances" and there again, he indicated the appropriate relief would be likely to be declaratory rather than remedial. Finally, the Panel's disciplinary function was said to be open to challenge only if a lack of bona fides could be proven and even then the appropriate remedy would again be a declaration. His Lordship noted that "it is not for a court exercising a judicial review jurisdiction to substitute itself for the fact-finding tribunal, and error of law in the form of a finding of fact for which there was *no* evidence or in the form of a misconstruction of the Panel's own rules would normally be a matter to be dealt with by a declaratory judgement."[12] Indeed the only circumstances in which the learned judge could anticipate the use of the remedies of *certiorari* and *mandamus* was in the unlikely event of the Panel acting in breach of the rules of natural justice. Thus, Donaldson M.R. stated that the role of a court in an appropriate case is:

> "to review the decision of the Panel and to consider whether there has been 'illegality' *i.e.* whether the Panel has misdirected itself in law, 'irrationality', *i.e.* whether the Panel's decision is so outrageous in its defiance of logic or accepted moral standards that no sensible person who had applied his mind

---

[9]   *ibid.*, at 579.
[10] *ibid.*, at 579.
[11] *ibid.*, at 579.
[12] *ibid.*, at 579.

to the question to be decided could have arrived at it, or 'procedural impropriety', *i.e.* a departure by the Panel from any procedural rules governing its conduct or a failure to observe the basic rules of natural justice . . ."[13]

3–14 In the *Datafin* case, the jurisdiction of the court was also said to be limited in terms of the time factor involved. Donaldson M.R. stated that in light of "the special nature of the Panel, its functions, the market in which it is operating, the time scales which are inherent in that market and the need to safeguard the position of third parties, who may be numbered in thousands, all of whom are entitled to continue to trade on an assumption of the validity of the Panel's rules and decisions, unless and until they are quashed by a court, the relationship between the Panel and the court has to be historic rather than contemporaneous."[14] Thus his Lordship went on to explain that he would expect "the contemporary decisions to take their course, considering the complaint and intervening, if at all, later and in respect by declaratory orders which would enable the Panel not to repeat any error and would relieve the individuals of the disciplinary consequences of any erroneous findings of breach of the rules".[15] This decision ensures that judicial review cannot be used as a delay tactic in takeover battles. In addition, since an applicant for judicial review must obtain leave before applying, the court is in a position to refuse unmeritorious applications which are made merely as a tactical ploy.

3–15 In *R v. Panel on Takeovers and Mergers, ex.parte Guinness*, Lord Donaldson elaborated further on the grounds for granting relief holding that:

> "Illegality would certainly apply if the Panel acted in breach of the general law, but it is more difficult to apply in the context of an alleged misinterpretation of its own rules by a body which under the scheme is both legislator and interpreter. Irrationality, at least in the sense of failing to take account of relevant factors or taking into account irrelevant factors, is a difficult concept in the context of a body which is itself charged with the duty of making a judgement on what is and what is not relevant, although clearly a theoretical scenario could be constructed in which the Panel acted on the basis of considerations which on any view must have been irrelevant or ignored something which on any view must have been relevant. And similar problems arise with procedural impropriety in the narrow sense of failing to follow accepted procedures, given the nature of the Panel and of its functions and the lack of any statutory or other guidance as to its procedures which are intended to be of its own devising. Similarly, in the broad sense of breach of the rules of natural justice, what is or is not fair may depend on underlying value

---

[13] *ibid.* at 580.
[14] *ibid.* at 579.
[15] *ibid.* pp. 579–580.

judgements by the Panel as to the time scale which is appropriate for decision, the consequences of delay and matters of that kind".[16]

In this case, the Court of Appeal also held that where a right of appeal from the decision-making body existed but was not exercised, the court would only grant relief by way of judicial review in exceptional circumstances.

B. The Irish Takeover Panel

3–16   The Irish Takeover Panel Act 1997 ("the Act") establishes the Irish Takeover Panel ("the Panel") as the body responsible for the monitoring and supervision of takeovers and other relevant transactions in relation to securities in relevant companies in Ireland. The Panel commenced operations in Ireland with effect from July 1, 1997.[17]

I. TAKEOVERS AND OTHER RELEVANT TRANSACTIONS

3–17   Section 7 imposes a duty on the Panel to monitor and supervise "takeovers" and "other relevant transactions" in order to ensure compliance with the provisions of the Act and the Panel's rules.

A "takeover" is defined in section 1(1) as:

"(a) any agreement or transaction (including a merger) whereby or in consequence of which control of a relevant company is or may be acquired; or

(b) any invitation, offer or proposal made, or intended or required to be made, with a view to concluding or bringing about such an agreement or transaction."

The term "control" means, in relation to a relevant company:

"the holding, whether directly or indirectly, of securities of the company that confer, in aggregate, not less than 30 per cent (or such other percentage as may be prescribed) of the voting rights in the company".[18]

This figure is in keeping with the City Code definition of control. Although this figure may be amended by prescription of the Minister for Enterprise and Employment ("the Minister"), the draft regulations must be laid before each House of the Oireachtas and may not be made until a resolution approving the draft has been passed by each House.[19]

---

[16] [1989] 1 All E.R. 509 at 512.
[17] Irish Takeover Panel Act 1997 (Commencement) Order 1997 (S.I. No. 158 of 1997) and Irish Takeover Panel Act 1997 (Commencement) (No. 2) Order 1997 (S.I. No. 255 of 1997).
[18] s.1(1).
[19] s.22(3).

The term "security" is defined in section 1(1) of the Act in relation to a company as:

> "(a) any interest in the capital of the company and includes any interest in the nature of a share, stock, debenture or bond, by whatever name called, and irrespective of the rights, if any attaching thereto, of or issued by the company,
>
> (b) an interest in a security falling within paragraph (a) of this definition".

The definition of the term "voting right" is also important. It is defined in section 1(1) of the Act in relation to a company as:

> "a right exercisable for the time being to cast, or to control the casting of, a vote at general meetings of members of the company, not being such a right that is exercisable only in special circumstances".

As noted above, the Panel's jurisdiction also extends to monitoring and supervising "other relevant transactions". The term "other relevant transactions" is defined in section 1(1) of the Act as:

> "(a) any offer, agreement or transaction in relation to the acquisition of securities conferring voting rights in a relevant company (including a substantial acquisition of securities) which the Panel specifies, in rules under section 8, to be a relevant transaction for the purposes of this Act,
>
> (b) any agreement, transaction, proposal or action entered into, made or taken in contemplation of ,or which is consequent upon or incidental to, a takeover or an offer, agreement or transaction referred to in paragraph (a) of this definition."

Transactions which are deemed relevant by the Panel in the Rules include, for example, the substantial acquisitions securities[20] and reverse takeovers.[21]

II. RELEVANT COMPANIES

3–18 In determining whether the Act applies, it is the nature of the target company to whom the offer is made ("the offeree") or the potential offeree which is important. Where the offeree is a "relevant company" as defined by section 2, the Act will apply. Three categories of company are deemed "relevant" for the purposes of the 1997 Act. The first category of company is a public limited company or other corporate body incorporated in the State whose securities are currently being traded on a market regulated by a recognised Stock Exchange.[22] The Irish Takeover

---

[20] R.3.1(a).
[21] R.3.1(c).
[22] s.2(a).

Panel Act 1997 (Prescribed Stock Exchange) Regulations 1997[23] prescribe the Irish Stock Exchange as a stock exchange for the purposes of the Act. Thus, all the companies whose securities are traded on the Irish Stock Exchange are relevant companies. The second category of company is a public limited company or other corporate body incorporated in the State whose securities, though not currently traded, were so traded in the five years prior to the takeover.[24] The City Code applies to offers for a wider category of private companies including companies whose equity share capital has been listed on the London Stock Exchange at any time during the previous ten years. The third category of company deemed relevant is any public limited company prescribed by the Minister "in order to secure more fully the protection of shareholders".[25] The Minister is required to consult with the Panel before making such a prescription. Any regulations proposed by the Minister under this section must be laid in draft form before each House of the Oireachtas and may not be made until a resolution approving the draft has been passed by each House.[26] To date, no other companies have been so prescribed by the Minister. However, it is possible that Regulations may be introduced in the near future pursuant to section 22(1) of the 1997 Act prescribing for the purposes of section 2(c) of the definition of "relevant company" public limited companies whose securities are for the time being traded on the London Stock Exchange, the New York Stock Exchange, NASDAQ and EASDAQ. Similarly, public limited companies whose securities are not traded on the aforementioned markets at present but were traded on such a market at any time within a period of five years prior to the date on which the proposed takeover or other relevant transaction was made may be included.

Companies expressly excluded from this definition are undertakings for collective investment in transferable securities[27] or investment companies within the meaning of Part XIII of the Companies Act 1990.[28] These companies are excluded as the manner and purpose for which the shareholding of such companies are brought together denote investors with a common purpose.[29] As of June 30, 1999, 79 companies were deemed relevant for the purposes of the Act.

---

[23] S.I. No. 256 of 1997.
[24] s.2(b).
[25] s.2(c).
[26] s.22(3).
[27] Within the meaning of the European Communities (Undertakings for Collective Investment in Transferable Securities) Regulations, 1989 (S.I. No. 78 of 1989).
[28] s.2(i) & (ii).
[29] See 470 *Dáil Debates*, Col. 1603, (Second Stage) the Minister of State at the Department of Enterprise and Employment, Mr. Rabbitte.

III. PARTIES TO THE TAKEOVER

3–19　The Act allows for the imposition of obligations and responsibilities on "parties to a takeover or other relevant transaction". These parties are defined in section 1(1) to include:

(a)　the offeror;

(b)　any person acting in concert with the offeror;

(c)　the directors of the offeror if the offeror is a company;

(d)　the offeree;

(e)　the holders of the securities to whom the offer is made;

(f)　the directors of the offeree;

(g)　any person acting as an adviser to any of the foregoing persons in relation to the takeover or other relevant transaction;

(h)　any person who, following a request made of him or her to do so by the offeror pursuant to rules under section 8, confirms that the offeror has access to sufficient resources as will enable the offer, if it is fully accepted, to be implemented;

(i)　such other persons as are specified in rules under section 8 for the purposes of this definition or whom the Panel deems in the circumstances of a particular takeover or other relevant transaction to be parties to that takeover or transaction.

This is thus an extremely broad ranging definition and the power of the Panel referred to in the last subparagraph of the definition allows the Panel to regulate all necessary persons.

3–20　In this context, it is worth noting that the definitions of the terms "offeror" and "offeree" provided in the Bill were amended to allow the Panel regulate for a broad range of scenarios including actions taken prior to the stage where an offer is actually made. Thus, the term "offeror" is defined in section 1(1) as:

> "a person who makes, or intends or is required to make, an offer or does any act in contemplation of making an offer".

Similarly, the term "offeree" is defined as:

> "a relevant company (a) any securities of which are the subject of an offer that has been made or is intended or required to be made, or (b) in respect of which, or in connection with which, a person does any act in contemplation of making an offer to holders of securities in that company".

Section 1(3) of the Act states that persons will be deemed to be "acting in concert":

"if, pursuant to an agreement or understanding (whether formal or informal) between them, they actively co-operate in the acquisition by any one or more of them of securities in the relevant company concerned or in doing, or in the procuring of the doing, of any act that results in an increase in the proportion of such securities held by any one or more of them".

The role of relevant parties and their rights and obligations will be examined in greater detail in Chapter 10.

IV. MEMBERSHIP AND BOARD OF THE IRISH PANEL

3–21 The Irish Takeover Panel was registered under the Companies Acts 1963 to 1990 as a company limited by guarantee. As with the London Panel, membership is drawn from the financial, business and legal communities. The members comprise the following five bodies, or in certain cases, their corporate or personal nominee: the Law Society of Ireland, the Irish Association of Investment Managers, the Irish Bankers Federation, the Irish Stock Exchange and the Consultative Committee of Accountancy Bodies – Ireland.[30] Each member represents different interests, provides different perspectives and contributes different expertise. The collective fund of knowledge represented by such a Board is of crucial importance to the Panel, particularly in these early years. Section 6(5)(a) of the Act allows the Minister to introduce regulations adding other members to this list or deleting other members from the list. Where a member is removed from the list, their nominee director will also cease to hold office.

3–22 The Panel is currently comprised of seven directors. Each of the five bodies referred to above is entitled to appoint a director to the board of the Panel. In addition, the Governor of the Central Bank is responsible for nominating and appointing the chairperson and deputy chairperson to the board. Section 6(1)(e) allows the Governor of the Central Bank and each of the five bodies named above to nominate and appoint alternate directors. This is a useful provision which will allow a director to step down, *e.g.* where he or she is unavailable or has a conflict of interest in relation to a case under consideration. Three of the members have chosen to appoint alternates to date. In addition, section 6(d) allows the directors to co-opt three further directors. It seems that such an appointment was viewed as necessary in circumstances where "the expertise available to the panel may be wanting in some respects". It was also envisaged that the term of office of such directors might relate to the individual takeovers, but is not so limited.[31] Again, this provision may also be

---

[30] s.6(1)(b).
[31] See 470 *Dáil Debates*, Col. 1604 (Second Stage), Rabbitte.

useful where conflicts of interest arise in particular cases. To date, however, this has not proved necessary. Once appointed, the directors are expected to carry out their functions in an independent fashion. The members of the Panel are expressly prohibited from instructing directors regarding the carrying out of their duties under the Act.[32] In addition, in order to ensure that the Panel's directors remain totally independent of the members who nominated them, section 182 of the Companies Act 1963 which allows for the removal of directors by ordinary resolution, does not apply to the Panel.[33]

3–23 The day-to-day work of the Panel is carried out by the Executive through the office of the Director General. The Executive deals with the general administration of the Panel and the Rules. Section 6(2)of the Act allows the Panel, where it deems it appropriate, to delegate its functions to any of its officers, employees or authorised persons. The executive may thus deal with any queries and submissions which do not require the Board's attention. It consults with parties and provides guidance before and during takeovers and other relevant transactions. The Executive is also responsible for monitoring dealings in the securities of relevant companies to ensure compliance with the General Principles and Rules. The Board of the Panel itself will be responsible for making formal rulings and giving directions on the interpretation and enforcement of the General Principles and Rules. The directors are entitled to meet for the despatch of business, adjourn and otherwise regulate their meetings as they deem fit. Questions arising at meetings of the Board will be decided by a majority of votes, with the chairperson having a second or casting vote.[33a] The quorum necessary for the transaction of the business of the Board of the Panel is three.[33b]

3–24 The Panel produced its first annual report in Autumn 1998 in accordance with its obligations under section 19 of the Act. This section imposes an obligation on the Panel to submit annual reports to the Minister which must then be laid before the Dáil and Seanad. The form of the report may be prescribed by the Minister after consultation with the Panel. However, in doing so, the Minister must ensure that his or her powers are not being exercised in such a manner as to require the disclosure of information which could "materially injure" or "unfairly prejudice" the legitimate interests of any person.[34]

---

[32] s.6(3).
[33] s.6(4).
[33a] Article 47, Articles of Association of the Irish Takeover Panel.
[33b] Article 48, Articles of Association of the Irish Takeover Panel.
[34] s.19(2).

V. CHARGES

3–25 The Panel, like its UK counterpart, is intended to be self financing. Thus, section 16(1) of the Act empowers the Panel to impose charges for the purpose of defraying its expenses. These charges may be imposed:

(a) on relevant companies;

(b) on a person (not being a relevant company) in respect of an offer made by that person

(c) on any person in respect of dealings in the securities of relevant companies

(d) on any person furnishing documentation to the Panel in accordance with rules under section 8, in connection with a takeover or relevant transaction

(e) on any person furnishing documentation to the Panel in relation to any proceedings of the Panel concerning a takeover or other relevant transaction.

Obviously, the Irish Panel does not deal with the same quantity of cases as the London Panel and thus income generated from documentation fees is greatly reduced. Also, as the turnover of securities in the Irish Stock Exchange is considerably lower, income from this source too is lower.

3–26 The rates of the charges must be approved in advance by the Minister. Where the Minister considers it appropriate, this approval should not be given until he or she has consulted with any persons deemed interested in the matter.[35] Section 16(3) allowed for the recovery of expenses incurred by members or their agents before the formation of the Panel, once ratified subsequently by the Panel. Such ratification was duly given. Currently, annual fees for relevant companies are based on market capitalisation. Companies falling into the following bands of market capitalisation pay the following annual fees; under Euro 12 million pays Euro 1,250; Euro 12–31 million pays Euro 2,500; Euro 31–62 million pays Euro 3,750, Euro 62–125 million pays Euro 5,000, Euro 125–625 million pays Euro 6,250; Euro 625–1250 million pays Euro 12,500, and more than Euro 1,250 million pays Euro 18,750. An offeror which is not a relevant company is liable to a charge when it makes an offer for securities of a relevant company. The amount of the charge will be equal to the annual charge for a relevant company, corresponding to the capitalisation of the offeree company by reference to the highest value of the relevant offer. Where such an offer is partly financed by the

---

[35] s.16(2).

issue of securities, the Panel will determine its value for the purposes of establishing the charge.[35a]

In addition, every offeror is liable to pay a document charge based on the value of the offer. Offers valued under Euro 5 million will give rise to a charge of Euro 2,500, offers valued between Euro 5–15 million will give rise to a charge of Euro 2,500, offers valued between Euro 15–35 million will give rise to a charge of Euro 17,500, offers valued between Euro 35–65 million will give rise to a charge of Euro 35,000, offers valued between Euro 65–125 million will give rise to a charge of Euro 50,000 and offers valued over Euro 125 million will give rise to a charge of Euro 62,500. In the case of a merger effected by a bidding company making offers for two existing companies, the document charge is based on the value of the lower of the two offers, unless only one of the offerees is a relevant company, in which case it will be based on the value of the offer for that company.[35b] A document charge of Euro 2,500 is also imposed in connection with a "whitewash"[35c] and a charge of up to Euro 900 is imposed in respect of documents furnished to the Panel in relation to hearings conducted under section 11 of the Act.[35d]

Finally, a charge of Euro 1.25 is levied on each contract note in respect of dealings in quoted securities of relevant companies where the consideration (net of transaction costs) on the individual contract is more than Euro 12,500). This latter charge will be collected by the parties' brokers and remitted to the Panel.[35e] Section 16(4) is a particularly useful provision which allows the Panel recover outstanding charges as a simple contract debt in any court of competent jurisdiction.

VI. OBJECTS OF THE PANEL

3–27 The two principal objects of the Panel which are set out in section 5(1) of the Act are:

"(a) to monitor and supervise takeovers and other relevant transactions so as to ensure that the provisions of this Act and any rules thereunder are complied with as respects each such transaction;

(b) to make rules under section 8 for the purposes mentioned in that section in relation to takeovers and other relevant transactions."

These objects must be stated in the Panel's memorandum and articles of association. The Panel may also include in its memorandum of

---

[35a] Notes on the Irish Takeover Panel Act 1997 (Takeover) Rules, 1997 p. C1–C2.
[35b] Notes on the Irish Takeover Panel Act 1997 (Takeover) Rules, 1997 p. C2.
[35c] Notes on the Irish Takeover Panel Act 1997 (Takeover) Rules, 1997 p. C3.
[35d] Notes on the Irish Takeover Panel Act 1997 (Takeover) Rules, 1997 p. C3.
[35e] Notes on the Irish Takeover Panel Act 1997 (Takeover) Rules, 1997 p. C2.

association such other objects and powers as are reasonably necessary or incidental to the due attainment of the principal objects.[36] The Panel is empowered to do anything which appears to it to be "requisite, advantageous or incidental to, or which appears to it to facilitate, either directly or indirectly, the performance by it of its functions".[36a] The actual memorandum of association of the panel lists 19 objects and powers as subsidiary and ancillary to the two principal objects. They include, *e.g.* the power to enter into arrangements and co-operate and share information with governmental and non-governmental authorities, bodies and persons with specific reference to stock exchanges and those responsible for supervising takeovers and other relevant transactions.

VII. GENERAL PRINCIPLES

3–28 The City Code is based upon ten General Principles which are applied in accordance with their spirit in order to achieve the underlying purpose of the Code. The Schedule to the Act contains twelve General Principles ("the General Principles") which serve to ensure that all shareholders are dealt with fairly and treated equally. The Minister is entitled under the Act, to make regulations adding or deleting anything to or from the Schedule,[37] but such regulations must be approved by both Houses of the Oireachtas.

PRINCIPLES APPLICABLE TO THE CONDUCT OF TAKEOVERS, ETC.

1. *All shareholders of the same class of the offeree shall be treated similarly by an offeror.*
2. *Where information is tendered by the offeror or offeree of their respective advisers to shareholders of the offeree in the course of any offer it shall be made available equally to all of the shareholders who may accept the offer.*
3. *No offer shall be made and no announcement of a proposed offer shall be made save after careful and responsible consideration of the matter by the offeror and any advisers of the offeror and only if the offeror and any advisers of the offeror are satisfied that the offeror will be able to implement the offer if it is accepted.*
4. *Shareholders to whom an offer is made shall be entitled to receive such information and advice as will enable them to make an informed decision on the offer. For that purpose the information and advice should be accurate and adequate and be furnished to the shareholders in a timely fashion.*

---

[36] s.5(2).
[36a] s.5(2).
[37] s.7(3).

5. *It is the duty of all parties to a takeover or other relevant transaction to prevent the creation of a false market in any of the securities of the offeror or offeree and to refrain from any statement or conduct which could mislead shareholders or the market.*

6. *It is the duty of the directors of an offeree when an offer is made or when they have reason to believe that the making of an offer is imminent to refrain from doing anything as respects the conduct of the affairs of the offeree which might frustrate that offer or deprive shareholders of the opportunity of considering the merits of the offer, except upon the authority of those shareholders given in general meeting.*

7. *Directors of the offeree shall give careful consideration before they enter into any commitment with an offeror (or any other person) which would restrict their freedom to advise shareholders of the offeree in the future.*

8. *The directors of the offeree and (if it is a company) of the offeror owe a duty to the offeree and the offeror respectively and to the respective shareholders of those companies to act in disregard to personal interest when giving advice and furnishing information in relation to the offer; in discharging that duty the said directors shall be bound to consider the interests of the shareholders as a whole.*

9. *Rights of control must be exercised in good faith and the oppression of a minority is not acceptable in any circumstances.*

10. *Where an acquisition of securities is contemplated as a result of which a person may incur an obligation to make an offer, he or she must, before making the acquisition, ensure that he or she can and will continue to be able to implement such an offer.*

11. *An offeree ought not to be disrupted in the conduct of its affairs beyond a reasonable time by an offer for its securities.*

12. *A substantial acquisition of securities (whether such acquisition is to be effected by one transaction or a series of transactions) shall take place only at an acceptable speed and shall be subject to adequate and timely disclosure.*

3–29   Ten of the principles stated reflect the ten City Code principles with some small but potentially significant differences. For example, the second of the Irish General Principles refers to information tendered to shareholders "in the course of any offer". The City Code principles also includes information tendered "when an offer is in contemplation". In addition, whilst the City Code principles require directors to act in the best interests of shareholders together with those of employees and creditors, the Irish General Principles are silent as to the interests of employees or creditors. Two new principles are included in the Irish principles which though reflected in the London Panel's rules are not contained in the City Code principles. The first is principle 11 which seeks to avoid causing excessive disruption to a target. This principle is reflected in Rule 35 of the City Code which restricts subsequent offers or purchases of offeree company securities by the same bidder. The purpose of this is to prevent management being distracted for too long from the running of their business. It is submitted that such a fundamental point is correctly inserted as an underlying principle. The other new principle in the Irish General Principles is principle 12. This principle is reflected in the London Panel's Rules governing substantial acquisition of shares.

VIII. RULES

3–30   Section 8 of the Act provides the Panel with both general and specific rule making powers. The Panel fulfilled its duty under section 8 by the introduction of the Irish Takeover Panel Act 1997 (Takeover) Rules 1997 ("the Rules") and the Irish Takeover Panel Act 1997 (Substantial Acquisition) Rules 1997 ("the SARs"). Both sets of rules came into operation on July 1st 1997. These rules will be examined in greater detail in the course of the Chapters 11, 12 and 13.

The Panel is empowered generally to make rules for the purpose of:

(a)   specifying offers, agreements or transactions in relation to the acquisition of securities conferring voting rights in a relevant company to be considered relevant for the purposes of the Act;

(b)   ensuring that takeovers and other relevant transactions comply with the General Principles and other provisions of the Act;

(c)   otherwise providing, where it deems it desirable to do so in the interests of the shareholders, for the manner in which relevant transactions and activities relating to them are to be conducted or carried out and otherwise for the governance of such transactions and activities;

(d)   specifying circumstances in which a person shall be presumed to be acting in concert with another person as respects a takeover or other relevant transaction.

The Act also requires the Panel to make rules in three specific areas. These latter rules must be approved by the Minister in advance.[38]

(1) Substantial Acquisition Rules

3–31   Section 8(2) requires the Panel to make rules specifying the conditions under which an acquisition by a person of securities conferring voting rights in a relevant company is to be regarded as a substantial

---

[38] s.8(5).

acquisition of securities. These conditions should be specified by reference to:

(a) the proportion which the amount of securities conferring voting rights acquired or, to be acquired, bears to the total amount of such securities held in the company;

(b) the extent to which the acquisition of such securities increases or will increase any existing holdings of such securities in the company; and

(c) in the case of a series of acquisitions of such securities, the periods of time that elapses between each such acquisition being effected.

The purpose of such rules is to slow down the rate at which stakes may be built up in companies in order to allow small shareholders participate in any premium which may be payable in connection with the establishment or consolidation of a large holding. These rules also serve to provide management with sufficient time to consider the acquisition and to take whatever steps, if any, are necessary to safeguard the interests of the shareholders.

3–32 In introducing the SARs, the Panel fulfilled its obligation under section 8(2). Rule 3 of the SARs states as follows:

> "an acquisition or a series of acquisitions by a person of voting securities of a relevant company or of rights over voting securities of that company shall be regarded, for the purposes of the Act, as a substantial acquisition of securities if:
> (i) any voting securities so acquired by that person and the voting securities the subject of any rights so acquired by that person confer in the aggregate 10% or more of the voting rights in the company; and
> (ii) any voting securities so acquired by that person and the voting securities the subject of any rights so acquired by that person, when aggregated with any voting securities already held by that person and any voting securities over which that person already holds rights, confer 15 per cent or more, but less than 30%, of the voting rights in the company; and
> (iii) in the case of a series of acquisitions of securities, all of such acquisitions are made within a period of 7 days."

(2) Mandatory Offer Rules

3–33 Section 8(3)(a) obliges the Panel to make rules requiring the making of a mandatory offer in certain specified circumstances. Offers must be made where a person, or persons acting in concert, acquire control of a relevant company (other than by reason of a redemption or purchase by the company of its own securities). Such offers must also be made where a person, or persons acting in concert, controlling a relevant company acquire a specified amount of additional securities in that company within a specified period. Section 8(3)(b) gives the Panel discretion as to whether to make rules requiring a mandatory offer where the two circumstances specified above are triggered as a result of the redemption or purchase by the relevant company of its own securities.

3–34 The Panel has fulfilled its obligation under section 8(3)(a) by introducing Rule 9 of the Rules. Rule 9.1 states that where a person acquires (whether by a series of transactions over a period of time or otherwise) securities in a company which of themselves, or when aggregated with securities already held, carry 30 per cent or more of the voting rights, that person will be obliged to extend the offer to the holders of each class of equity share capital in the company and to the holders of each class of voting non-equity share capital in the company of which such person holds shares. This rule mirrors Rule 9 of the City Code. The 1991 Annual Report of the London Panel explained the rational for the rule as follows:

> "the philosophy underlying this Rule is that, if effective control of a company is obtained by the acquisition of shares, the principle of equality of treatment for shareholders requires that all shareholders should have the opportunity to obtain the price per share paid for that control (it will usually be a premium price) and that they should have the opportunity to get out of the company if they do not like what has happened".

Such an offer is also required where a person holding 30–50 per cent of the voting rights acquires further securities carrying 1 per cent of such rights in any 12 month period. In the UK any acquisition whether less than 1% or not triggers this second requirement and a similar amendment is being considered at present by the Irish Panel. Rule 37 of the Takeover Rules provides for the making of mandatory offers in circumstances where the acquisition of control results from the redemption or purchase by a company of its own securities.

(3) Competition Legislation Rules

3–35 Section 8(4) requires the Panel to make rules specifying the requirements to be complied with by a party to the takeover or other relevant transaction, being requirements the specification of which the Panel considers necessary or expedient for the purpose of any case in which the provisions of the Mergers, Takeovers and Monopolies (Control) Act 1978 fall to be applied. The Panel fulfilled its obligation in this respect with the introduction of Rule 12 of the Rules. Rule 12(a) requires every offer to which the Mergers, Takeovers and Monopolies (Control) Act 1978 applies to be made subject to a condition that will be satisfied if the Minister decides not to prohibit the merger or takeover. In addition, Rule 12(b) requires every offer to which the European Merger Regulation might be relevant, to contain a term whereby the offer will lapse if, before the first closing date or the date when an offer becomes or is declared unconditional as to acceptances, the European Commission initiates proceedings under the Merger Regulation or refers the matter back to a competent authority of a Member State.

(4) Procedures

3–36 Although the Panel is authorised to make the rules, a draft of the rules proposed to be made under section 8(2) and 8(4) must be submitted to the Minister in advance. If the draft is not approved by the Minister, the Panel must submit a further draft for approval and must keep resubmitting until approval is obtained. There is no such requirement to submit the rules made under section 8(3) on mandatory offers to the Minister. During the course of the debate on the Bill, the Minister of State at the Department of Enterprise and Employment had to assure senators who were concerned at the power vested in the Minister that the Minister would not use the powers of the Act to intrude into the affairs of the Panel and its method of doing business.[39]

(5) Waivers & Derogations

3–37 Section 8(7) of the Act allows the Panel to grant derogations from, or waive, any of these rules in relation to a particular matter in exceptional circumstances if, having considered the General Principles, it deems it appropriate to do so. This power is essential as it allows the Panel to remain flexible. Given the many different situations which could arise in the marketplace, no piece of legislation or list of rules could anticipate all eventualities. No supervisory authority could thus be expected to operate effectively without such a power. In its first year of operation, its annual report noted that the Panel granted two waivers and thirteen derogations from the requirements of the Rules.

IX. ENFORCEMENT

3–38 One of the main reasons why the Panel was set up as a statutory body was that statutory enforcement provisions were deemed to be necessary. In a small market such as Ireland's, the threat of public censure or the removal of Irish authorisation or an Irish listing might not have the same deterrent effect as in the UK market especially for a large foreign multinational company.

---

[39] 149 *Seanad Debates*, Col. 1709.

(1) Rulings & Directions

3–39 Section 9 was described in the Seanad as "one of the central pillars of the activities of the Panel".[40] Section 9(1) of the Act gives the Panel statutory authority to make rulings as to whether any activity or proposed activity as respects a takeover or other relevant transaction, complies with the General Principles and the Rules. The Panel may make such a ruling of its own volition or on the application of any interested person. It is important to note that the term "interested person" is used here as opposed to any "party to the takeover". This allows other parties such as, for example, an individual shareholder of the offeror, the Director of Consumer Affairs, a competitor or a potential offeror to complain.

3–40 In order to ensure compliance with the General Principles and the Rules as respects the manner in which a takeover or other relevant transaction is conducted, section 9(2) empowers the Panel to give a direction to any party to the takeover or other relevant transaction to do or to refrain from doing anything which the Panel specifies in its direction. Section 9(3) provides a non-exhaustive list of directions which may be issued to the parties. Included are directions: to acquire, issue, allot or dispose of securities or to refrain from doing so; to refrain from exercising voting or other rights attached to securities; to make an offer on specified terms; to announce that the offer has lapsed or to renew an offer; to disclose any information or; to obtain or to communicate advice to shareholders. The Panel has discretion as to whether a ruling or a direction should be published or not and as to the form of any such publication.[41]

The Panel may amend, revoke or suspend any ruling or direction except:

(a) where the Court has made an enforcement order in relation to the direction or ruling under section 12;

(b) where the Court has made an order on foot of an application for leave to apply for judicial review; or

(c) where the Court has made an order on foot of an application for such judicial review.[41a]

Furthermore, section 9(5) allows the Panel by notice in writing served on the party or stock exchange, to require any party to a takeover or relevant transaction or the stock exchange to furnish any information it may reasonably require for the performance of its functions and which is specified in the notice.

---

[40]   149 *Seanad Debates*, Col. 1690, Rabbitte.
[41]   s.9(1)(b) and s.9(2)(b).
[41a] s.9(4).

(2) Enquiries

3–41   The Panel is entitled under section 10 to enquire into the conduct of any person where it has reasonable grounds for believing that a contravention of the Rules or General Principles has occurred or may occur. The Panel may initiate such an enquiry on its own initiative, at the request of a party to the takeover or other relevant transaction or at the request of a recognised stock exchange. Unlike section 9(1) thus, the Panel cannot act on the application of "any interested party". Clearly however, where an interested party makes a sufficient case to the Panel to justify an enquiry, the Panel could decide to act on its own volition.

Following an enquiry into the conduct of any person, where the Panel deems it proper, it may advise, admonish or censure such a person.[42] Notice of the giving or administering of any such advice, admonition or censure and of the terms thereof may, at the discretion of the Panel, be published. A person who has been advised, admonished or censured under this section may appeal the matter to the High Court. The court may confirm the Panel's decision or it may annul it directing the Panel either to conduct a fresh enquiry into the matter or to publish a notice of the court's decision.[43]

(3) Hearings

3–42   In the exercise of its powers under sections 9 and 10, the Panel may conduct a hearing under section 11. The Panel may decide to hold the whole or part of the hearing in public or in private. It may decide to hold it in private, if it considers this to be more appropriate having regard to the interests of any party concerned or of any company, a transaction or proposed transaction affecting the securities of which is the subject of the hearing.[44] The Panel have suggested that any party which considers that its interests justify a private hearing should submit a written request stating the reasons why it is considered appropriate that the hearing should be held in private. Any such request will be considered by the Panel before the relevant hearing.[45] Prior to such a hearing, the parties concerned will be given an opportunity to set out their arguments briefly in writing. The Executive may also submit its views on the matter under consideration to the Board and the parties.[46]

3–43   For the purposes of such a hearing, the Panel shall have the same powers, rights and privileges as are vested in the High Court or a

---

[42]   s.10(2).
[43]   s.10(4).
[44]   s.11(2).
[45]   Takeover Rules, Introduction, TI7.
[46]   Takeover Rules, Introduction, TI7.

High Court judge in relation to compelling attendance, examination on oath, and compelling the production of documents.[46a] A witness before the Panel is also entitled to the same privileges and immunities as witnesses before the High Court.[46b] These are important powers not enjoyed by the self regulating London Panel. At the hearing, arguments may be presented by the parties themselves or their advisers, including legal advisers. The parties may call witnesses and question any witnesses called. The Board of the Panel may question or invite statements from any of those present and may call additional witnesses. Parties and their advisers are entitled to be present throughout the hearing and to see papers submitted to the Board in connection with the hearing. The parties involved in the hearing are absent however during the Board's consideration of the matter.[47]

3–44 Section 11(5) prohibits a person:

(a) disobeying a valid summons to attend without just cause or excuse;

(b) when called as a witness, refusing to take an oath, to make an affirmation, to produce documentation under their control or to answer any question to which the Panel may legally require an answer;

(c) wilfully giving material evidence which is false and known to be false or not believed to be true; or

(d) by act or omission, obstructing or hindering the Panel in the conduct of the hearing.

If a person does or fails to do anything referred to in section 11(5)(a),(b) or (d), the Panel may seek a High Court order requiring compliance.[47a] In addition, the Panel may itself prosecute such an offence and the maximum fine upon summary conviction is £1500 or 12 months in prison.[48]

(4) Court Orders

3–45 Finally, if the Irish Panel believes that a ruling or direction is unlikely to be complied with or has not been complied with, it may apply to the High Court in a summary manner under section 12(1) for an enforcement order. This may include an order requiring a party to do, or not to do, something, an order annulling any transaction carried out otherwise than in accordance with the said ruling or direction; an order

---

[46a] s.10(3).
[46b] s.10(4).
[47] Takeover Rules, Introduction, TI7.
[47a] s.11(6).
[48] s.25(1), (2).

providing for any consequential relief or an order providing restitutionary relief. The Panel may also make an application under section 12(2) for an order annulling any transaction carried out by a party in connection with a ruling or direction, where the ruling or direction has subsequently been amended or revoked because it was given on the basis of false or misleading information provided by that party. The Court may make or refuse to make any such order.

3–46   An application for an order under this section should be made by motion, and the Court when considering the motion may make such interim or interlocutory order as it deems appropriate.[49] The application by the Panel may not be made earlier than seven days from the date on which the ruling or direction was given. The purpose of this is to allow the other party to consider their position and to decide whether they wish to seek judicial review of the ruling or direction. If they do apply for judicial review or for leave to seek judicial review, an order under section 12 cannot be made while their application is pending.[50]

X. JUDICIAL REVIEW

3–47   Section 13(1) of the Act expressly confers the right to apply for judicial review of a rule, a derogation or waiver of such a rule, or a ruling or direction of the Panel under Order 84 of the Rules of the Superior Courts.[51] Indeed, this is stated to be the sole method of questioning the validity of the foregoing. However, section 13(2) provides that a rule may only be challenged in a situation where the Panel has made a ruling or given a direction based on that particular rule in relation to a takeover or other relevant transaction to which the applicant is party. Section 13 was stated to be designed to provide "a balanced approach to ensure that parties can protect their interests while at the same time ensuring that takeover activity is not unduly impeded".[52]

3–48   Section 13(3)(a) provides that the application for leave to apply for judicial review must generally be made in the case of a rule, within seven days of the date when the related ruling or direction is made, and in the case of a derogation, waiver, ruling or direction, within seven days from the date the derogation, waiver, ruling or direction is granted, made or given. This period may only be extended in circumstances where the delay was not caused by the default or neglect of the applicant or any person acting for them and where an extension would

---

[49] s.12(3).
[50] s.12(5).
[51] S.I. No. 15 of 1986.
[52] 149 *Seanad Debates*, Col. 1692, Rabbitte.

not cause injustice to any other party concerned in the matter. In considering whether injustice would be done, the Court must consider (a) the length of time which has elapsed since the completion of any takeover or other relevant transaction to which the rule, derogation, waiver, ruling or direction the subject to the application relates or any substantial step in the effecting of such a takeover or other relevant transaction and (b) the nature of the relief that could ultimately be granted to the applicant.[53] The uniquely strict time limit set out in the Act demonstrates the commitment of the legislature to a swift settlement of any disputes. It is entirely consistent with the acceptance of the Court in *Datafin* of "the special needs of the financial markets for speed on the part of decision-makers".[54] In that case, the Court suggested that the Panel and those affected should treat its decisions as valid and binding, unless and until they are set aside. The Court advised the Panel that it should ignore applications for leave to apply since to do otherwise would enable such applications to be used as "a mere ploy" in takeover battles. The strict time limit imposed in the Act avoids the need for the parties to ignore any applications, as the application will generally be settled within a short period.

The application for leave to apply for judicial review should be made by motion on notice to the Panel and, unless they are seeking the application themselves, to the offeror and offeree.[55] Before hearing an application, the Court may direct that notice of the application also be served on other specified persons.[56] Such persons might include for example the shareholders or the offeror's financiers.

3–49 Section 13(3)(b) provides further that leave to apply for judicial review is not to be granted unless the Court is satisfied that there are substantial grounds for contending that the rule, derogation, waiver, ruling or direction is invalid or ought to be quashed. Section 13(6) provides that the decision of the Court on the application for leave to apply or on the judicial review itself is final and leave to appeal to the Supreme Court will only be granted where the court certifies that its decision involves a point of law of "exceptional public importance" and that it is desirable in the public interest that an appeal should be taken. Clearly, however, this will not prevent an appeal being taken on the issue of the constitutionality of any law.[57] In *Datafin*, Donaldson M.R. suggested that the court should grant certiorari and mandamus

---

[53] s.13(5).
[54] *R. v. Panel on Takeovers and Mergers; ex parte Datafin plc* [1987] 1 All E.R. 564 at 578.
[55] s.13(3)(b).
[56] s.13(4).
[57] s.13(7).

only where there had been a breach of natural justice and that in all other cases contemporary decisions of the Panel should take their course and the relationship of the court and Panel should be "historic rather than contemporaneous".[58] Clearly, there is an acceptance in the Act that the remedy of judicial review should not be lightly available, and that there should be a minimum degree of delay to the transaction. It remains to be seen, however, whether an Irish Court in its choice of orders will limit itself to a declaration with prospective effect.

3–50 While an application for leave to apply for judicial review or for such judicial review is pending or during the seven day period within which such an application may be made, the Panel may apply to the court for an order providing for appropriate interim or interlocutory relief.[59] This allows the Panel to approach the court at an early stage where the circumstances of the case demand immediate action.

3–51 Section 14(1) provides that appeals or applications provided for in the Act should be heard by one judge and, if possible, by the same judge. This will enable the chosen judge to become familiar with the operation of the Panel and its Rules. It was also hoped that it would "assist the process of ensuring speedy decisions from the court".[60] Section 14(2) provides that the proceedings may be held wholly or partly in private if the court, in the interests of justice, considers that the interests of any party concerned or of any company, a transaction or proposed transaction affecting the securities of which is the subject of the appeal or application, so require.

XI. EFFECT OF THE ACT

3–52 As noted above, the Panel may apply to the Court under section 12 for an order to have its rulings and directions enforced which may involve an order annulling any transaction carried out otherwise than in accordance with the said ruling or direction or annulling a transaction carried out in accordance which a ruling or direction made or given on the basis of false information. Apart from the powers of the Court under section 12, section 15 states that it will not be possible to annul or rescind transactions which are carried out: (a) otherwise than in accordance with the General Principles, a rule under section 8, a ruling or a direction under section 9 or (b) in accordance with a rule, ruling or directions which is

---

[58] *op. cit.* at 579.
[59] s.13(8).
[60] 470 *Dáil Debates*, Col. 1608, Rabbitte.

subsequently declared invalid or quashed on an application for judicial review. This section was included in order to ensure that takeovers which have been completed cannot be unwound, except upon application by the Panel itself under section 12. To allow otherwise, particularly in circumstances where property had changed hands, facilities had been reorganised and management redeployed, would lead to a situation described by the Minister in the Dáil as "invidious".[61] Indeed, the Minister suggested that before the Panel sought an order from the Court annulling any transaction under section 12, it would need to be of the view that "the circumstances justified the unscrambling of the takeover and the fair treatment of all the shareholders involved".[62]

XII. SECRECY

3–53 Section 17(1) makes it an offence to disclose information obtained by virtue of the performance by the Panel of any of its statutory functions where that information is not otherwise in the public domain. This obligation is imposed on all persons including specifically a member or director of the Panel, an adviser to the Panel or a Panel employee or former employee. Also included, of course, would be parties to whom the Panel had conveyed confidential information. There are a number of exceptions to this obligation. The first is referred to in section 17(1) where information may be disclosed in "accordance with law". This would include a situation where in order to comply with the principles of constitutional justice, particularly the *audi alteram partem* rule, the Panel has to notify persons of the charges made against them and the evidence supporting those charges. The Panel must disclose this information despite the fact that the evidence was obtained from persons in the course of the performance by the Panel of its functions under the Act and is unpublished. The other exceptions to this obligation of secrecy are set out in section 17(2). Section 17(2)(a) allows for the disclosure of information where this is necessary to allow the Panel publish the basis of a ruling or direction or censure or the grounds on which it has advised, admonished or censured a person under section 10. Section 17(2)(b) allows for the disclosure of information to certain specified persons. Such persons include the Minister, the Garda Síochána, the Director of Public Prosecutions, a statutory inspector, a Stock Exchange, the Central Bank, any other foreign supervisor of takeovers or any other person prescribed by the Minister.

---

[61] 470 *Dáil Debates*, Col. 1608, Rabbitte.
[62] 149 *Seanad Debates*, Col. 1693, Rabbitte.

Section 18 provides for the protection under this legislation of confidential information which would not normally be disclosable in legal proceedings on the grounds of legal professional privilege.

XIII. LIABILITY OF THE PANEL

3–54 In introducing a statutory supervisory authority in place of a private body, one obvious concern was that persons would be encouraged to seek remedies against the Panel and private parties. Section 20 of the Act sets out to avoid just such an outcome. Section 20(1) protects the Panel itself, its directors, members, officers and employees from liability in damages in respect of actions or omissions in the performance of their statutory functions, unless committed in bad faith. Section 20(2)(a) provides specifically that immunity will lie in an action for damages in respect of any ruling, direction, report, statement or notice made, given, prepared, published or served unless the ruling, direction or other matter was made, given, prepared, published or served in bad faith. Section 20(3) notes that the appointment of a director of the Panel will not render the appointer liable for acts or omissions of the director in the performance of his or her functions. This subsection also notes that the fact of appointment may not be held to have created a duty owed by the appointer to any person to supervise or superintend the director. The inclusion of this provision may to some extent be merely cautionary. In practice, the courts appear reluctant to accept that regulators owe investors a duty of care in negligence. The case of *Yuen Kun-yeu and Others v. AG of Hong Kong*[63] and *Davis and Another v. Radcliffe and Others*[64] are prime examples of this. In the latter case, the Privy Council stated that "it is now clear that foreseeability of loss or damage provides of itself no sufficient criterion of liability".[65] It is also necessary to establish proximity, *i.e.* "an expression which refers to such a relation between the parties as renders it just and reasonable that liability in negligence may be imposed on the defendant for loss or damage suffered by the plaintiff by reason of the act or omission of the defendant of which complaint is made".[66] This general principle was accepted by the Irish courts in *Ward v. McMaster*[67] and *McMahon v. Ireland & Others*.[68] However, an exemption from liability like this is common in modern legislation providing authorities or bodies with financial regulatory control. Section 53 of the Stock Exchange Act 1995 similarly exempts the Central Bank from liability for damages.

---

[63] [1987] 3 W.L.R. 776. See also *Three Rivers District Council and Others v. Governor and Company of the Bank of England (No. 3)*, *The Times*, December 10, 1998; [1996] 3 All ER 558.
[64] [1990] 1 W.L.R. 821.
[65] *ibid.* at 826.
[66] *ibid.*
[67] [1988] I.R. 337.
[68] [1988] I.L.R.M. 610.

3–55   Section 20(4) allows the Panel to indemnify the members, directors, officers or employees in respect of acts or omissions in the performance of their duties. Section 20(5) provides that these persons may also be indemnified in respect of certain liabilities on their parts determined in proceedings before a foreign court or tribunal to pay damages or costs by reason of acts or omissions in the carrying out of their duties. This latter subsection was included in order to ensure that, in line with the practice of the London Panel, the Panel could take out insurance policies in respect of its officers against possible legal actions against them for defamation in other jurisdictions. However, section 200 of the Companies Act 1963 was seen as an obstacle prohibiting it from taking out insurance. Under section 200, any policy to indemnify an officer against any liability which by virtue of any rule of law would otherwise attach to him or her in respect of any negligence, default, breach of duty or breach of trust of which he or she may be guilty in relation to the company is deemed void except in specified restricted circumstances. During the parliamentary debates, the Minister of State explained that it was necessary not to disapply section 200 in respect of the Panel, but rather to amend section 200 in order to ensure that the indemnity will apply in a case arising in another jurisdiction. It does not prevent a company which believes it has been the subject of negligence from initiating legal action. It merely means that the directors of the Panel would be indemnified.[69]

XIV. TRANSITION FROM A SELF-REGULATORY FRAMEWORK TO A STATUTORY FRAMEWORK

3–56   The transition from a self-regulatory framework to a statutory framework naturally brings its own difficulties. The two main advantages of the former framework are flexibility and speed. The London Panel is renowned for its ability to make decisions quickly and to react instantly to new situations. The City Code may be amended very quickly and is subject to a flexible purposive interpretation. Although the Act establishes the Panel as a statutory body, it attempts to imbue it with as much flexibility as possible. The powers of the Panel to draft and to apply rules is evidence of this. In addition, it is clear from the foregoing that the Act has also sought to avoid many of the limitations which are inherent in the self regulatory system such as restricted sanctions, lack of formal powers to conduct hearings and perhaps to some degree a loss of certainty.

---

[69]   475 *Dáil Debates*, Col. 1646.

CHAPTER 4

THE DRAFT 13TH COMPANY LAW DIRECTIVE

A. Background

4–01   The Commission first put forward a proposal for a 13th Directive on Company Law concerning takeover bids in 1989.[1] This Directive was scheduled to be adopted by Member States by January 1992 and implemented by January 1993. It laid down minimum requirements for the conduct of takeovers of listed public companies in the European Union. A system of regulation was envisaged with rules having the force of law. The stated objective of this proposed Directive was to create a level playing field by ensuring that differences in national regulation of public takeovers did not encourage offerors to concentrate their acquisition searches in certain Member States with little or no regulation. A second objective of the proposed Directive was to encourage private investors to place their capital in the most efficient and most profitable companies. The proposed Directive sought to impose detailed and standardised rules governing: the timetable for offers, transparency during the offer period, obligations on the offeree and offeror during the offer period, the content of the offer and defence documents, the publication of the offer document, the mandatory bid, frustrating actions and the independent supervision of the entire takeover process. The proposal received general support from the Economic and Social Affairs Committee[2] and the European Parliament[3] and was in fact amended in 1990 to take into account the comments of these bodies.[4]

4–02   However, the proposal failed to achieve the necessary degree of support from Member States. For example, Germany was not happy with the concept of a mandatory general bid for an offeree in circumstances where a certain minimum shareholding had been reached by the offeror. The United Kingdom argued against a move from its current self regulatory scheme.[5] The view was expressed that such a

---

[1]   [1989] O.J. No. C 64/8.
[2]   [1989] O.J. No. C298/56.
[3]   [1990] O.J. No. C38/41.
[4]   [1990] O.J. No. C240/7.
[5]   para. 3–10.

move would lead to a loss of flexibility and increased legalism and court involvement. The proposal was put forward by the European Commission at the Edinburgh European Council in 1992 as one of a number of proposals to be reviewed in accordance with the principle of subsidiarity. Following detailed consultation with Member States, a majority of Member States agreed that some form of regulation was required and most of those agreed that a framework directive would be the most appropriate instrument. Such a framework directive would establish general principles to regulate takeovers but would not involve detailed provisions for the harmonisation of implementing arrangements.

4–03　As a result, the Commission introduced a further amended proposal in 1996[6] and yet a further proposal in 1997 ("the 1997 Proposal").[7] The text of these documents is contained in Appendix 2. The 1997 Proposal was criticised for its lack of clarity and for not bringing about any sufficient method of harmonisation.[8] Furthermore, it was argued that it did not satisfy the subsidiarity criteria as it was not certain that it would provide a sufficient minimum level of protection for shareholders which would be equivalent throughout the Community.[9] In the UK in particular, it has met with vociferous opposition where many felt that it would not bring sufficient advantages to outweigh its potentially serious disadvantages. One of the primary fears in the UK was that the statutory basis would lead to more judicial interference and the possibility of tactical litigation. On the other hand, it was opined that there was every reason to expect that the adoption of the 1997 Proposal would lead to harmonised takeover regulation which might be "an important contribution to the internal market and reduce barriers to takeovers".[10] In Ireland, as a statutory system already operates, there is probably less to fear in respect of the encouragement of tactical litigation from a Directive. However, the 1997 Proposal contained a number of ambiguities and anomalies which made it inappropriate from the Irish perspective. Key amongst these were the inability to derogate from the provisions of the Directive, the availability of an alternative mechanism to a mandatory bid and the exposure of the supervisory authorities to liability.

4–04　In June, 1999, following substantial discussions at Council working group level, a further proposal for a directive was submitted by

---

[6]　[1996] O.J. No. C162/5.
[7]　[1997] O.J. No. C378/10.
[8]　Dine, "The Proposal for a Thirteenth Directive on Takeovers" 12 Co.Law 83; Digest, Takeover Directive Amended after Political Pressure" 19 Co. Law 14
[9]　House of Lords Select Committee on the European Communities, Session 1995–1996, 13th Report (HL Paper 100) p. 14, Dine "Subsidiaririty, Datafin and the DTI" 17 Co.Law 248.
[10]　Adenas, "European Takeover Legislation and the City Code" 17 Co.Law 150.

the Presidency to the Internal Market Council. After the Internal Market Council of June 21, 1999, an amended proposal was published ("the 1999 Proposal"). The text of this latest proposal is contained in Appendix 3 and is discussed below. Despite the existence of different views on many of the issues, political agreement was reached on all but one aspect of the 1999 Proposal. Spain maintained its general political reservation linked to the definition of supervisory authorities. As a result of this ongoing dispute over recognition of the independent Gibraltar authorities by the Spanish, the 1999 Proposal was not voted upon at the Internal Market Council in June. Although Gibraltar is unlikely to establish its own domestic authority to supervise takeovers, the wording of the references to the supervisory authorities in the Proposal must be satisfactorily agreed by all Member States. At the Council meeting, the Council agreed that the UK and Spain should attempt to reach a compromise at the level of the Committee of Member States' Permanent Representatives (COREPER) and, at the time of writing, negotiations were still ongoing.

B. Objectives

4–05 The stated aims of the 1999 Proposal are to ensure an adequate level of protection for shareholders throughout the European Union and to provide for minimum guidelines on the conduct and transparency of takeover bids. In the Recitals to the 1999 Proposal, the Commission emphasises that "only action at Community level can ensure an adequate level of protection for shareholders throughout the Union and provide for minimum guidelines for the conduct of takeover bids". It is stressed that "Member States acting independently are not able to establish the same level of protection especially in the case of cross-border takeovers or purchases of control". The 1999 Proposal establishes six general principles and a number of general requirements which Member States are required to implement through more detailed rules according to "their national systems and their cultural contexts".

C. Framework Directive

4–06 Article 3(2) of the 1999 Proposal constitutes a significant improvement on the 1997 Proposal. It provides that whilst Member

---

[11] Directorate General XV "21 June 1999, Internal Market Council Close to Agreement on Proposal Takeovers Directive" (Europa, European Commission Website, 21 June 1999)

States are obliged to ensure that rules are in force to satisfy the minimum requirements of the Directive, Member States are free to introduce additional conditions and more stringent provisions to regulate bids. This means that where provisions of the 1999 Proposal do not adequately protect shareholders, Member States may implement national legislation to do so. The effect of this would be to allow the Irish Takeover Panel ("the Irish Panel") to maintain those parts of The Irish Takeover Panel Act, 1997 (Takeover) Rules 1997 ("the Irish Rules") which are not directly required by the Directive. The implementation period for the Directive was agreed by the Council as four years from the date of its adoption.[11a]

A further advantage of the 1999 Proposal is that Article 4(4) allows Member States to provide in their rules that their supervisory authorities may "in particular types of cases" and "on the basis of a reasoned decision, in specific appropriate cases grant derogations from these rules". This provision will allow the supervisory authorities to make both general and specific derogations. The existence of such a power is acknowledged in the Recitals to be essential in order for takeover regulation to be flexible and capable of dealing with new circumstances as they arise. A similar power to derogate is contained in section 8(7) of the Irish Takeover Panel Act, 1997 ("the Act"). Article 4(4) of the 1999 Proposal provides one limitation to this power. Member States must ensure that the general principles referred to in Article 3(1) are respected. Similarly, section 8(7) requires the Panel in making any derogations to take into consideration the scheduled principles in the Act.

A specific derogation may be granted pursuant to Article 4(4) on the basis of "a reasoned decision". One possible interpretation of this phrase is that it requires a written decision. Such an interpretation would place a huge administrative burden on the London Panel on Takeovers and Mergers ("the London Panel"). In practice, as a result of the large number of bids regulated, the London Panel grants many hundreds of derogations each year and it would be impractical to communicate them all in writing. To resolve this issue, the Commission proposed including a declaration in the Council Minutes to the effect that the words "on the basis of a reasoned decision" do not impose on the supervisory authorities an obligation to issue a written decision when granting derogations of minor importance.

[11a] *ibid.*

D. Scope of the 1999 Proposal

4–07 Article 2 sets out the scope of the proposed Directive. The Directive applies to:

> "takeover bids for the securities of a company governed by the law of a Member State where such securities are admitted to trading on a regulated market within the meaning of Article 1(13) of Directive 93/22/EEC in one or more Member States".

I. TAKEOVER BIDS

4–08 A "takeover bid" is defined as:

> "a public offer (other than by the offeree company itself) made to the holders of the securities of a company to acquire all or part of such securities. A bid may be either mandatory or voluntary, and must follow or have as its objective the acquisition of control."

The term "securities" is defined in turn in Article 2(e) as "transferable securities carrying voting rights in a company". The definition of a "takeover bid" in the 1999 Proposal is far superior to the definition in the 1997 Proposal which made no reference to the passing of control.[12] In order to fall within the ambit of the 1999 Proposal, either a bid must follow the obtainment of control or the bid must have as its objective the obtainment of control. The latter scenario would apply in the case of a voluntary offer and the former would apply where a party triggered the requirement to make a mandatory offer in accordance with Article 5. Article 5(3) notes that the percentage of voting rights which confers control for the purposes of a mandatory bid and the manner of its calculation will be determined by the rules of the Member State where the offeree company has its registered office. As noted in chapter 3 above, the term "control" is defined in section 1(1) of the Act as a holding of securities of a company conferring not less than 30 per cent of the voting rights in that company.[13] The term "securities" is defined in section 1(1) of the Act as:

> "(a) any interest in the capital of the company and includes any interest in the nature of a share, stock, debenture or bond, by whatever name called, and irrespective of the rights, if any attaching thereto, of or issued by the company,
> (b) an interest in a security falling within paragraph (a) of this definition."

In the event of the implementation of the 1999 Proposal, it is likely that these definitions would continue to apply.

---

[12] Article 2 of the 1997 Proposal referred to "an offer made to the holders of the securities of a company to acquire all or part of such securities by payment in cash and/or in exchange for other securities".

[13] See para. 3–17 above.

4–09 It is important to note that the definition of takeover bid in Article 2(a) expressly excludes offers by a company to buy its own shares. From the shareholders' perspective such an offer is obviously unlike any offer made by a third party.

It should also be noted that companies whose shares were listed on a recognised stock exchange within the previous five years which currently fall within the scope of the Act would not fall within the ambit of the 1999 Proposal. However, as noted above, as additional obligations may be imposed by supervisory authorities in Member States, such companies could continue to be supervised by the Irish Panel under the Act. This would be important in ensuring that a company intending to privatise and wishing to avoid the scrutiny of the Irish Panel could not do so by simply delisting prior to a change of control.

II. RELEVANT SECURITIES

4–10 The 1999 Proposal only applies to takeover bids for the securities of a company admitted to trading on a regulated market within the meaning of Article 1(13) of Directive 93/22/EEC (the Investment Services Directive). Article 1(13) of that Directive defines a regulated market as a market which:

– appears on the list provided for in Article 16 drawn up by the Member State which is the home Member State as defined in Article 1(6)(c);
– functions regularly;
– is characterised by the fact that regulations issued or approved by the competent authorities define the conditions for the operation of the market, the conditions for access to the market and, where Directive 79/279/EEC[14] is applicable, the conditions governing admission to listing imposed in that Directive and, where that Directive is not applicable, the conditions that must be satisfied by a financial instrument before it can effectively be dealt in on the market;
– requires compliance with all the reporting and transparency requirements laid down pursuant to Articles 20 and 21.

Public limited companies whose securities are not listed on a recognised stock exchange in any of the Member States will not thus fall within the ambit of the Directive.

---

[14] The Admissions Directive

III. UCITS AND INVESTMENT COMPANIES

4–11   Article 1(2) expressly excludes from the scope of the 1999 Proposal:

"takeover bids for securities issued by companies the object of which is the collective investment of capital provided by the public, and which operate on the principle of risk spreading, and the units of which are, at the holders' request, repurchased or redeemed, directly or indirectly, out of the assets of those companies. Action taken by such companies to ensure that the stock exchange value of their units does not significantly vary from their net asset value shall be regarded as equivalent to such repurchase or redemption".

This is consistent with the definition of "collective investment undertakings" in Article 3(a) of the Prospectus Directive (Directive 89/298/EEC).[15] This paragraph serves thus to exclude from the scope of the proposed Directive UCITS and other open-ended variable capital investment companies. The shareholders of these categories of company are deemed to be adequately protected by existing regulation.

4–12   At present, section 2 of the Act excludes both UCITS and investment companies within the meaning of Part XIII of the Companies Act 1990 ("the 1990 Act"). Originally, Part XIII of the 1990 Act only applied to open-ended investment companies. Section 253(2) provides that such a company[16] is limited by shares and set up with the sole object of "the collective investment of its funds in property with the aim of spreading investment risk and giving members of the company the benefit of the results of the management of its funds". In addition, the articles or memorandum of such a company must provide:

"(i) that the actual value of the paid up share capital of the company shall be at all times equal to the value of the assets of any kind of the company after the deduction of its liabilities, and
(ii) that the shares of the company shall, at the request of any of the holders thereof, be purchased by the company directly or indirectly out of the company's assets."

Section 253 of the 1990 Act was amended by section 80 of the Investment Intermediaries Act 1995 in order to apply Part XIII of the 1990 Act to closed-ended companies whose articles or memorandum do not provide that their shares are repurchasable at the request of any holders. As a result, both open-ended and closed-ended investment companies fall outside the scope of the Act.[16a] As Article 1(2) excludes

---

[15] [1989] O.J. No. L124/8.
[16] Such a company not being a company to which the European Communities (Undertakings for Collective Investment in Transferable Securities) Regulations, 1989 (S.I. No. 78 of 1989) apply.
[16a.] Although section 253 is due to be amended as a result of the forthcoming

only the latter and closed-ended companies would be subject to the Directive if implemented, the Act would need to be amended in this respect following implementation of the 1999 Proposal.

E. Definitions

4–13   Article 2 contains definitions of certain key terms. The term "offeree company" is defined in Article 2(b) as:

> "a company whose securities are the subject of a bid".

A company is deemed to be an offeree company therefore only when a bid has been made. The definition is rather limited in that it does not include, for example, a company in negotiations with a potential offeror with a view to making an offer for its securities. As noted in chapter 3,[17] such a company would however be deemed an "offeree" under the Act.

The term "offeror" is defined in Article 2(c) as:

> "any natural person or legal entity in public or private law making a bid".

Again, unlike the Act, no reference is made in the definition to a person who intends to make a bid or is required to make a bid.

Whereas the 1997 Proposal did not refer to or define the term "persons acting in concert", the term is defined in Article 2(d) of the 1999 Proposal as:

> "persons or legal entities who co-operate with the offeror or the offeree company on the basis of an agreement, either express or tacit, either oral or written, and aimed respectively at obtaining control of the offeree company or frustrating the successful outcome of the bid."

Section 1(3) of the Act refers similarly to "an agreement or understanding (whether formal or informal)" between persons. However, it also refers as respects a takeover or other relevant transaction to active co-operation in the acquisition by any one or more of the persons, or in the doing, or in the procuring of the doing, of any act leading to an increase in the proportion of securities held by any one or more of the persons. An acquisition by a person in co-operation with a person already in control *i.e.* a consolidation of control would in certain circumstances thus be included. It would not appear however to be included in the 1999 Proposal unless the acquisition served to frustrate a bid made by a third party. In addition, Article 2(d) of the 1999 Proposal provides that persons

---

Companies (Amendment) No. 2 Act 1999, the amendment is unlikely to affect the Act in this regard.
[17] para. 3–20.

controlled by another person with in the meaning of Article 8 of Directive 88/627/EEC ("the Transparency Directive") are deemed concert parties. Article 8(1) provides that a "controlled undertaking" means:

> "any undertaking in which a natural person or legal entity:
> (a) has a majority of the shareholders' or members' voting rights: or
> (b) has the right to appoint or remove a majority of the members of the administrative, management or supervisory body and is at the same time a shareholder in, or member of, the undertaking in question; or
> (c) is a shareholder or member and alone controls a majority of the shareholders' or members' voting rights pursuant to an agreement entered into with other shareholders or members of the undertaking."

For the purposes of Article 8(1), a parent undertaking's rights as regards voting, appointment and removal will include the rights of any other controlled undertaking and those of any person or entity acting in his own name but on behalf of the parent undertaking or of any other controlled undertaking.[18]

4–14 The term "parties to the bid" is defined in Article 2(f) of the 1999 Proposal as:

> "the offeror, the members of the offeror's administrative or management board, if the offeror is a company, the offeree company, holders of securities of the offeree company and the members of the administrative or management board of the offeree company, or persons acting in concert with such parties".

This definition marks a significant improvement on the definition in the 1997 Proposal in that the latter did not include either the offeree company or concert parties. One notable omission however, is the advisers of the parties in relation to the takeover. It is particularly important in the Act that such persons be deemed parties in order to ensure that they may be the subject of rulings and directions.

F. General Principles

4–15 Article 3(1) sets out six general principles ("the General Principles") which generally reflect the General Principles in the Act and in the City Code on Takeovers and Mergers ("the City Code") operated by the London Panel. The General Principles are very broad in nature and seek to ensure fair and equal treatment of all shareholders in relation to takeovers. Member States are required to ensure

---

[18] Directive 88/627/EEC, Article 8(2).

that any rules or arrangements introduced pursuant to the Directive respect these principles. The General Principles are:

> "(a) all holders of securities of an offeree company of the same class are to be given equivalent treatment; in particular, if a person acquires control of a company, the other holders of securities are to be protected;
>
> (b) holders of securities of an offeree company are to have sufficient time and information to enable them to reach a properly informed decision on the bid;
>
> (c) the board of an offeree company is to act in all the interests of the company as a whole; and must not deny the holders of securities the opportunity to decide on the merits of the offer;
>
> (d) false markets must not be created in the securities of the offeree company, of the offeror company, or of any other company concerned by the bid in such a way that the rise or fall in the prices of the securities becomes artificial and the normal functioning of the market is disrupted;
>
> (e) an offeror shall announce a bid only after ensuring that it can fulfill any cash consideration if so offered and after having taken all reasonable measures to secure the implementation of any other type of consideration;
>
> (f) offeree companies must not be hindered in the conduct of their affairs for longer than is reasonable by a bid for their securities."

A number of points merit particular consideration. Principle (a) in the 1999 Proposal provides for the equal treatment of all shareholders. This mirrors General Principle 1 of the Act. As an amendment to the 1997 Proposal, the 1999 Proposal also emphasises that where control of a company is acquired, the minority shareholders must be protected.

4–16   In the 1997 Proposal, Principle (c) imposed a duty on the board of the offeree company "to act in all the interests of the company, including employment". The Company and Commercial Law Committee of the Law Society of Ireland noted that this principle could cause difficulties in situations where there are conflicts between the interests of the shareholders and the interests of the employees. Such a conflict would arise for example where a generous offer had been made to shareholders but in circumstances where the bidder made clear its intention to dismiss a large portion of the workforce following the acquisition. Modern corporate theory would appear to suggest that the claims of the shareholders should be paramount.[19] The 1999 Proposal is more appropriate to current corporate governance in that it omits the reference to employees referring instead to the interests of the company

---

[19]   See, for example, Parkinson, *Corporate Power and Responsibility*, (Clarendon Press, Oxford, 1993) Chaps 9 and 10; Engel, "An Approach to Corporate Social Responsibility (1979) 32 Stan L. Rev. 1; Easterbrook and Fischel "The Corporate Contract" (1989) 89 Colum. L.Rev. 1416; Clarke, "Corporate Responsibility in Light of The Separation of Ownership and Control" (1997) Vol. 19 *Dublin University Law Journal* 50.

"as a whole". In addition, it contains a further provision to the effect that the offeree board should not deny shareholders an opportunity to "decide on the merits of the offer". This limits the ability of the board to frustrate the offer and will be considered in greater detail in paragraphs 4–47—4–49 below.

4–17   A new principle introduced in the 1999 Proposal is Principle (e) which mirrors General Principle 3 of the Act which requires the offeror to ensure that it will be able to "implement the offer if it is accepted". Whilst the Irish Panel have interpreted this as obliging the offeror to ensure finance is in place to satisfy the consideration for the acquisition rather than the medium or long term working capital needs of the enlarged offeror following the acquisition, Principle (e) avoids any ambiguity by referring expressly to the consideration provided.

G. Supervisory Authority

4–18   According to Article 1(1) of the 1999 Proposal, the co-ordination measures prescribed by the Directive will apply to "the laws regulations, administrative provisions, codes of practice or other arrangements of the Member States, including arrangements established by organisations officially authorised to regulate the markets". The reference to "codes of practice" and "arrangements" was included in order to allow the UK to retain its self-regulatory code. For this reason too, Article 4.1 specifically states that the supervisory authorities may be either "public authorities or associations" or "private bodies recognised by national law or by public authorities expressly empowered for that purpose by national law". Whereas Article 4.1 of the 1997 Proposal required Member States to designate a supervisory authority to supervise "the entire course of the bid", Article 4(1) of the 1999 Proposal merely refers to supervising the bid. In the case of the London Panel, this is more appropriate as the latter may not be responsible for all aspects of enforcement of the City Code. Under the Financial Services Act 1986, the Financial Services Authority may take action against a person authorised under that Act for breach of the Code at the request of the London Panel. Clause 114 of the Financial Services and Markets Bill suggests this endorsement is likely to continue.

I. JURISDICTION AND APPLICABLE LAW

4–19   Article 4(2)(a) provides for the most typical scenario in the regulation of takeovers. It provides that where an offeree company has its registered office in a Member State and its securities are admitted to trading on a regulated market in that same Member State, the relevant authority for supervising the bid will be the authority of that Member State. For example, in the case of a takeover bid for a company incorporated in Ireland whose securities are listed on the Irish Stock Exchange, the Irish supervisory authority (the Irish Panel) will be responsible for supervising the bid.

Article 4(2)(b) deals with the situation where the securities of the offeree company are not admitted to trading on a regulated market in the Member State in which the company has its registered office. In such cases, the authority competent for supervising the bid will be that of the Member State on whose regulated market the securities of the company are admitted to trading or, where the securities are admitted to trading on markets in more than one Member State, the Member State on whose regulated market the securities were first admitted. If the securities were admitted to trading on regulated markets simultaneously, Article 4(2)(c) provides that the offeree company may determine the competent authority.

4–20   Having determined which authority should be the competent supervisory authority, Article 4.2(e) proceeds to determine which law or rules should be applied by that supervisory authority in cases referred to under Article 4(2)(b) and 4(2)(c). There are two possible options in this regard – the law of the Member State in which the offeree company has its registered office ("the Home Member State") or the law of the Member State of the competent authority ("the Host Member State").

It is submitted that it would seem more correct to apply the law of the Home Member State on the basis that as an integral part of a company law directive this would be more suitable. However, a contrary argument would suggest applying the law of the Host Member State as the law of the market on the basis that the Directive is in essence a financial services law directive. Article 4.2(e) currently divides issues into two categories. It provides that the applicable rules and the competent authority will be those the Host Member State in respect of:

> "matters relating to the consideration offered in the case of a bid and particularly the price, and matters relating to the procedure of the bid, in particular the information on the offeror's decision to make an offer, the contents of the offer document and the disclosure of the offer".

The law of the Home Member State is stated to apply and the competent authority will be the authority in the Home Member State in respect of:

> "matters relating to the information of employees of the offeree company and in matters relating to company law, in particular the percentage of

voting rights which confers control and any derogation from the obligation to launch a bid, as well as the conditions under which the board of the offeree company may undertake any action which might result in the frustration of the offer".

4–21   One difficulty with Article 4.2(e) as it currently stands is that it is not sufficiently clear what issues constitute matters relating to "the procedure of the bid" and what issues constitute "matters relating to company law". For example, although it is assumed that key issues such as timetable and conditions might be deemed procedural, this is clearly a moot point. This lack of clarity will cause uncertainty which will in turn lead to delays, conflicts and possibly legal challenge. As a result, this may jeopardise what has been recognised as "the special needs of the financial markets for speed on the part of decision-makers"[20] It may even encourage tactical litigation. In a hostile takeover bid situation, one of the parties may argue that a particular issue, for example a minimum acceptance condition, has been incorrectly classified and, as a result, that the wrong law has been applied. This would cause enormous delays to the takeover timetable. In addition, in certain cases, a determination that a particular law applies might even be central to a company's decision as to whether to make a bid or not. A final problem with this lack of clarity is that it will cause significant problems for legislators attempting to transpose this Article into national law. For all these reasons, it is imperative that sufficient guidance be given in the Directive.

In an attempt to resolve this problem, it is proposed to assign the contact committee a role in the development of some form of guidelines for supervisory authorities. The following declaration is thus proposed for inclusion in the Council Minutes:

> "The Commission and the Council agree that it should be a priority for the Contact Committee provided for in Article 10a to develop guidelines to facilitate agreement on the respective roles of supervisory authorities in Article 4(2)(e) cases."

As a further means of ensuring the best possible protection for shareholders, Article 10c provides that the Council and the Parliament, acting on a proposal from the Commission, are obliged to examine and, if necessary, revise Article 4(2) in the light of the experience acquired in applying the Article. Such an examination is required three years after the deadline for introduction of the Directive into national law. Whilst this ensures that the matter will at least be re-visited, it is submitted that many problems could be pre-empted by attempting to identify the grey areas and controversial issues at an earlier stage.

---

[20]   *R v. Panel on Takeovers and Mergers; ex parte Datafin plc* [1987] Q.B. 815.

4–22   A further problem with Article 4(2)(e) is that it does not contain any guidance as to how conflicts between the rules of Member States and/or the decisions of supervisory authorities are to be resolved. The authorities of the Home and Host Member States may not be able to reach a mutually satisfactory conclusion on the categorisation of an issue. Even where they do, the parties may not agree to this categorisation. Since the decisions of the supervisory authorities are not stated to be binding, it would be open to one of the parties to claim that this paragraph had not been incorrectly interpreted. The only method of solving this dispute would be to refer the matter to the European Court of Justice. The ensuing delays might make such an action attractive as a frustrating tactic in a hostile takeover.

Whilst it might be argued that Article 4(2)(e) will apply only to a small number of cases each year, because of the unpredictability of market development in the next few years and the accepted competition amongst the smaller stock exchanges, this provision may increase in importance in future years. It would seem preferable, at the outset, to develop a suitable system which can be guaranteed to lead to a uniform, fair and predictable method of regulation of transactions of this type.

II. CONFIDENTIALITY

4–23   Article 4.3 requires Member States to ensure that individuals employed or formerly employed by the supervisory authorities be bound by professional secrecy. As a result, confidential information may only be disclosed "by virtue of provisions laid down by law". Section 17 of the Act sets out the obligations of professional secrecy and prohibits the disclosure of information obtained by parties directly or indirectly involved in the operation of the Irish Panel.[21]

III. CO-OPERATION

4–24   In cross-border transactions the ability of supervisory authorities to co-operate with each other and with authorities supervising capital markets such as stock exchanges[22] is crucial. Article 4(3a) requires such authorities to "co-operate and supply each other with information", where necessary for the application of rules drawn up in accordance with the Directive and especially cases covered by Article 4(2)(b), (c) and (e).

---

[21]   para. 3.53
[22]   Reference is made in Article 4(3.a) to authorities supervising capital markets in accordance with Directive 88/627/EEC (the Transparency Directive), Directive 89/592/EEC (the Insider Dealing Directive) and Directive 93/22/EEC (the Investment Services Directive.

Subject to this requirement to co-operate, the information is covered by the obligation of secrecy to which employees and ex-employees of the supervisory authorities receiving the information are subject. A new provision in Article 4(3a) of the 1999 Proposal states rather unclearly that this cooperation should include "the ability to serve the legal documents necessary to enforce measures taken by the competent authorities in connection with the bid". It should also include "other such assistance as may be reasonably requested by the supervisory authorities concerned for the purposes of investigating any actual or alleged breaches of the rules made or introduced to implement this Directive." The first part of this provision deals with the service of legal documents out of juris-diction. As such, the powers of a supervisory authority to serve or otherwise enforce decisions of competent authorities in other juris-dictions may be restricted. For this reason, a declaration is to be included in the Council Minutes confirming the interpretation of the Irish delegation that compliance will be on the basis of what is reasonably possible for supervisory authorities to deliver in this area of cooperation.

IV. POWERS

4–25   Article 4(4) provides that the supervisory authority is to have "all the powers necessary for the exercise of their functions, which shall include the duty to ensure that the parties to a bid comply with the rules made pursuant to this Directive".

As noted above, express discretion is given to Member States to allow their supervisory authorities to grant derogations from the rules provided that the General Principles are respected. This flexibility will allow, for example, Italy to retain its partial offer rule referred to in paragraph 4–34 below.

V. COURT INVOLVEMENT

4–26   Because of the framework nature of the Directive, it is possible to allow Member States discretion as to the judicial remedies available, subject, of course, to Community law. Article 4(5) notes that the 1999 Proposal:

> "does not affect the power of Member States to designate the judicial or other authorities responsible for dealing with disputes and for deciding on irregularities committed during the bid procedure".

It also provides that the Directive does not affect "the power of Member States to regulate whether and under which circumstances parties to the bid are entitled to bring administrative or judicial proceedings". This paragraph is clearly inserted to meet the concerns of

UK critics that the existence of a European Directive on takeovers would necessarily involve the Panel in increased litigation.[23] Whether Article 4(5) is successful in meeting this objective is debatable.

4–27   The latest version of Article 4.5 contains the following two sentences:

> "In particular this Directive does not affect the power which courts may have in a Member State to decline to hear legal proceedings and to decide whether or not such proceedings affect the outcome of the bid. This Directive shall not affect the powers of the Member States to determine the legal position concerning the liability of supervisory authorities or concerning litigation between the parties to a bid".

Again, the purpose of this provision is to ensure that a self regulatory system can continue to operate and that the Directive will not give rise to an increase in litigation. A declaration is to be included in the Council Minutes to the effect that it the U.K. regards the wording in Article 4(5) as a fundamental pre-requisite of its support for the Directive as a whole. Of particular concern would be the possibility that parties could claim that additional rights were created on foot of the Directive – rights which could be enforceable against other parties or against the supervisory authorities. The existence of such rights could delay the takeover process and could expose the supervisory authorities to litigation.

4–28   In an attempt to allay concerns, the Recitals have been amended to include the following provision:

> "Whereas, in accordance with general principles of Community law, and in particular the right to a fair hearing, decisions of a supervisory authority will in appropriate circumstances be susceptible to review by an independent court or tribunal; whereas, however, this Directive leaves it to Member States to determine whether rights are to be made available which may be asserted in administrative or judicial proceedings, whether in proceedings against a supervisory authority or proceedings between parties to a bid."

This seeks to emphasise that decisions of a supervisory authority are not being rendered immune to review. Even in the UK, decisions of the London Panel are currently subject to judicial review.[24] However, Member States are authorised to ensure that this system of review operates only in appropriate circumstances and that the Directive does

---

[23] Article 4(5) of the Directive proposed in 1996 was particularly objectionable to the UK in that it stated that an injured party must enjoy "adequate remedies, whether through an appeals procedure operated by the supervisory authority or through the right to take proceedings before the court to claim compensation."

[24] paras 3–12—3–15.

not lead to the creation of additional rights enforceable in administrative or judicial proceedings.

H. Protection of Minority Shareholders

4–29 Article 5 of the 1999 Proposal deals with the protection of minority shareholders after an acquisition of control. In the majority of Member States, a general offer for all the remaining shares is currently required following an acquisition by a person of control of a company. This mandatory bid provision is not however universal. In Germany and the Netherlands, for example, no such provision exists. These countries do however operate alternative means of protecting minority shareholders in these circumstances. This has proved to be one of the most difficult aspects of takeover regulation to harmonise.

I. TRIGGERING THE MANDATORY BID

4–30 Article 5(1) provides that where a person makes an acquisition of securities which, when aggregated with any existing holdings, give that person a specified percentage of voting rights in that company, conferring on him the control of the company, rules must be in place requiring him to make a bid in order to protect the minority shareholders of the company. As noted above, there is no set definition of "control" and Article 5(3) provides that Member States may determine the percentage of voting rights which confers control and its method of calculation.[25] Failure to set even a minimum threshold has been a cause for concern of a number of bodies including the English and Irish Law Societies and the London Panel. The English Law Society noted that if control was left open to a variety of different interpretations, then it would clearly be open to give less protection to minorities in some jurisdictions than others depending on where the level of control is fixed.[26]

4–31 Although the requirement provided for in Article 5(1) to make a general offer only applies where an acquisition of securities has taken place and securities are defined in Article 2 as "transferable securities carrying voting rights in a company", this is only a minimum requirement. Member States can avail of the discretion provided for in Article

---

[25] An earlier proposal requiring Member States, when calculating control, to adopt the methodology contained in Directive 88/627/EEC (the Transparency Directive) was fortunately rejected.

[26] *op. cit.*, n.9 at pp. 61–62.

3(2)(b) to introduce more stringent provisions. In order to make this clear, the Recitals state that Member States may extend the mandatory offer to the acquisition of securities which only carry voting rights in specified circumstances or which do not carry voting rights.

4–32   One significant flaw of the 1997 Proposal is that it made no provision for the obtaining of control by concert parties. It was suggested that the protection devised for shareholders could be circumvented if the offeror was able to acquire control by means of parties acting in concert with the offeror acquiring shares in the company.[27] Article 5(1) of the 1999 Proposal includes acquisitions by persons acting in concert with a person and existing holdings of such persons. This is in keeping with Rule 9 of the Irish Rules.

Where a person acquires control of a company as a result of a general offer to all shareholders, it would be nonsensical to subject that person to the mandatory bid provision of Article 5. Shareholders would already have been given an opportunity to accept the offer. Such a situation would clearly be excluded from the mandatory bid provision. In addition, Article 5 will not be applied to require offers from those controlling holdings at the time the Directive enters into force.[28]

II. ADDRESSEES OF THE OFFER

4–33   Article 5(1) of the 1999 Proposal provides that the bid must be addressed to "all holders of securities for all their holdings". By contrast, the 1997 Proposal merely required a "bid" which was defined as including both general offers and partial offers. Indeed, Article 10 of the 1997 Proposal stated that the offers had to be launched to all shareholders "for all or for a substantial part of their holding". Member States did not thus need to require the offeror to launch a bid for 100 per cent of the shares as is currently the case under the Irish Rules. The 1997 Proposal emphasised that "the term "substantial" should not be interpreted as meaning less than 70 per cent of the securities, except where duly justified authorization has been given by the supervisory authority." This, it is submitted, did not go far enough. The Department of Trade & Industry in the UK warned that this provision could lead to the creation of a smaller minority shareholding without offering the minority shareholders any additional protection.[29]

---

[27] *op. cit.*, n.9 at p. 37, and Commentary of the Company and Commercial Law Committee of the Law Society of Ireland on the proposal.
[28] Recital 6.
[29] *op. cit.*, n.9 at p. 87

4–34   It was agreed that only a bid to all shareholders would adequately protect shareholders. However, the possibility exists that exceptions may be required. For example although Italy operates a full mandatory bid situation, in certain specific circumstances it allows for the making of a voluntary public offer to acquire 60 per cent or more of the securities of a company without requiring the successful offeror to then make a mandatory offer. The objective of this partial offer rule is to render it easier to acquire control of an Italian listed company. This provision is based loosely on Rule 36 of the City Code. Such an offer would not be inconsistent with the General Principles as it would only be allowed where the offer has been approved by the majority of all shareholders with voting rights, excluding from the calculation securities held by the offeror and concert parties and by any shareholder who alone or in concert holds more than 10 per cent of the voting rights. Because this condition would be deemed to offer sufficient protection to shareholders, such an offer would probably be allowed pursuant to Article 4(4) permitting derogations. In order to clarify the compatibility of this Partial Offer Rule, the Commission proposed including the following declaration in the Council Minutes:

> "The Council and the Commission agree that national law may provide that when a natural person or a legal entity makes a voluntary public offer to acquire the securities of a given company conferring the control, this offer may be limited to the acquisition of at least 60% of the voting rights on condition that the offer has been approved by the majority of all shareholders with voting rights, excluding from the calculation securities that are held by the offeror and persons acting in concert with the offeror and by any shareholders, who alone or in concert holds more than 10% of the voting rights. The above-mentioned approval is independent from the decision by each individual shareholder whether or not to accept the offer."

It is interesting to note that whereas Rule 36 of the Irish Rules and the City Code allows for the making of partial offers in exceptional cases, subject to shareholder approval, large shareholders holding more than 10 per cent of the voting rights are not automatically excluded.[30] Such shareholders would only be excluded if they were otherwise deemed to be concert parties.

III. THE AMOUNT OF THE CONSIDERATION

4–35   The price which had to be paid to shareholders under the 1997 Proposal was "a price which ensures equal treatment for shareholders". This was an improvement on the wording of Article 10 in the 1996

---

[30]   paras 11.26–11.36.

proposal which referred to a price which "meets the objective of protecting their interests". The 1999 Proposal requires that "an equitable price" must be paid. The Commission have explained that as the definitions of such price are too divergent in the different Member States it is not possible to be more specific.[30a] Rule 9 of the Irish Rules and City Code provides that the price offered must not be less than the highest price paid by the offeror or any concert parties for shares in the offeree of that class during the period beginning 12 months prior to the commencement of the offer period and ending on the expiry of the offer period.[31] The purpose of this requirement is to allow minority shareholders to participate in the premium paid by the bidder in acquiring control. It is likely that if the Directive was implemented into Irish law, this price would be deemed "an equitable price" for the purposes of the Directive.

IV. THE FORM OF THE CONSIDERATION

4–36 At present both the Irish Rules and the City Code require the consideration for a mandatory offer to be in cash or at least accompanied by a cash alternative offer.[32] A contrary view was expressed during the consultation process for the 1999 Proposal that each Member State should be given discretion to determine the form of consideration to be offered. A number of member states would appear to support this view on the basis that a mandatory cash consideration makes a takeover more expensive.

One of the difficulties with allowing a securities exchange offer as opposed to a cash offer is that the offeror may offer any form of unmarketable securities as consideration. In order to avoid this, Article 5(1) requires a cash consideration or a cash alternative when the consideration offered by the offeror "does not consist of liquid securities admitted to trading on a regulated market in the sense of Article 1(1)". Although, in theory this allows dissenting shareholder to sell their new offeror securities for cash in the market, this may not always prove possible. For example, institutional shareholders or other large shareholders may only be able to dispose of their shares on the market at a discount. These shareholders may thus be locked into what they perceive to be an unattractive investment.

[30a] Directorate General XV "Takeovers Directive — Questions and Answers" (Europa, European Commission Website, June 18, 1999).
[31] paras 11.71–11.72.
[32] paras 11.71–11.72.

V. EQUIVALENT MEANS OF PROTECTION

4–37 The 1997 Proposal did not treat the mandatory bid as the only means of protecting minority shareholders where control had been acquired. It allowed for "other appropriate and at least equivalent means in order to protect the minority shareholders". The provision for other "equivalent means" was designed to accommodate Member States such as Germany and the Netherlands which did not support the idea of a mandatory bid. It is submitted that the full mandatory bid is the only effective way of protecting minority shareholders.[33] It provides them with an opportunity to exit the company without being discriminated against in terms of the price offered for their shares. As the Irish Law Society have noted "it is difficult to imagine any exit mechanism for minority shareholders as satisfactory as that afforded by the mandatory bid at an appropriate price". The term "equivalent means" thus becomes incomprehensible in this context.

A majority of Member States, including Germany, have subsequently agreed upon the introduction of a mandatory bid rule. As a result, the 1999 Proposal requires all Member States to introduce mandatory bid provisions. In order to allow Member States to implement the necessary changes, Article 5(2) provides that Member States which provide for other appropriate and at least equivalent means may continue to apply such means for one year following the date for compliance[34] by Member States with the Directive. In order to avail of this extended period, the equivalent means must be specific to the transfer of control and must include specific financial compensations for the minority shareholders.

VI. ADDITIONAL MEASURES

4–38 As noted above, Article 3(2) allows Member States to have additional conditions and more stringent provisions than required by the Directive. This endows Member States therefore with a large degree of flexibility. In addition, reference is made in the text of the Directive to a number of specific additional measures pertinent to Article 5.

Firstly, Article 5(2.a) provides that Member States may provide for further instruments aiming at the protection of security holders "as far as these instruments do not hinder the normal course of the bid" referred to in Article 5(1). This ensures that the one year transition period allowed by Article 5(2) is not viewed as establishing a deadline for the abolition of such measures.

---

[33] *op. cit.*, n.9 at pp. 22–24 & 38.
[34] As set out in Article 11(1).

Secondly, the Recitals cite two examples of "further instruments" which may be established for the protection of the interests of security holders. The first is "the obligation to make a partial bid where the offeror does not acquire control of the company". Clearly such a provision would not be incompatible with Article 5. The second example cited in the Recitals is "the obligation to make a bid simultaneously with the acquisition of the control of the company." At present the Spanish regulatory system includes a requirement to launch a bid simultaneously with the acquisition of control. The effect of the Recital is to clarify the compatiblity of the Spanish system with Article 5.

I. Amendment to the Transparency Directive

4–39   Council Directive 88/627/EEC[35] ("the Transparency Directive") sets out the information to be published when a major holding in a listed company is acquired. This Directive is analysed in greater depth in chapter 13[36] Article 1(1) of the Transparency Directive currently provides as follows:

> "Member States shall make subject to this Directive natural persons and legal entities in public or private law who acquire or dispose of, directly or through intermediaries, holdings meeting the criteria laid down in Article 4(1) which involve changes in the holdings of voting rights in companies incorporated under their law the shares of which are officially listed on a stock exchange or exchanges situated or operating within one or more Member States."

Article 5a of the 1999 Proposal provides for the amendment of Article 1(1) of the Transparency Directive by referring not to shares "officially listed in a stock exchange" but to shares "admitted to trading on one or several regulated markets within the meaning of Article 1(13) of Directive 93/22/EEC" ("the Investment Services Directive"). This reference to a regulated market as defined in the Investment Services Directive is consistent with Article 1(1) of the 1999 Proposal setting out the ambit of that Directive. The effect of this amendment is to extend the Transparency Directive to regulated markets, ensuring that both the 1999 Proposal and the Transparency Directive refer to similar securities.

---

[35] [1988] O.J. No. L348/62.
[36] paras 13.97–13.100.

J. Information

4–40   Article 6 imposes an obligation on Member States to ensure that companies comply with certain informational requirements.

I. THE DECISION TO MAKE A BID

4–41   Article 6.1 requires that the decision to make an offer be made public without delay. It also provides that the supervisory body must be informed of the bid. Indeed Member States are expressly permitted to require that the supervisory authority be informed before the decision is made public. According to the Recitals, the requirement to publish this information without delay will reduce the scope for insider dealing. At present the Irish Rules also regulate the conduct of the parties in negotiations prior to the making of a decision to make a bid.[37] As soon as the offer has been made public, Article 6(1) requires the board of the offeree to inform representatives of its employees, or where there are no representatives, the employees themselves of this fact. This is in keeping with a recommendation of the EU Economic and Social Committee.[38] As a result of concerns about insider dealing, it would not be possible to inform employees before the bid is made public.

II. PUBLICATION OF THE OFFER DOCUMENT

4–42   Article 6(2) provides that Member States must ensure that rules are in place requiring that a properly detailed offer document should be made available to the supervisory authority prior to publication. Rules should also require that upon publication, the document should be sent to the shareholders of the offeree company in sufficient time to allow them to make a properly informed decision. The offer document should also be communicated by the board of the offeree company to their employees' representatives. Again, where there are no representatives, the document should be communicated to the employees themselves. In most cases, this requirement would appear to be superfluous in that when an offer document has been published, the employees will have direct access to the information contained therein. (It may, however, be useful where the company's securities are traded on a stock exchange in a different Member State and the information is not as readily available.) It will not be important that this information was

---

[37]   Rule 2.2(c). See paras 12.02–12.05.
[38]   C295/1 7/10/1996.

not passed to them directly by the directors as required by the 1999 Proposal but was obtained by the employees or their representatives acquiring copies of the offer document.

The second paragraph of Article 6(2) provides for the mutual recognition of offer documents in Member States on whose markets the securities of the offeree company are admitted to trading without it being necessary to obtain the approval of the supervisory authorities of those Member States and without their being able to require additional information to be included in the offer document. The only exceptions to this rule are firstly, market specific information concerning the formalities to be complied with in accepting the bid and receiving consideration and secondly, tax arrangements applicable to the consideration. In order to avail of this mutual recognition provision, the offer document must be subject to the prior approval by the competent supervisory authority. Similar provisions for mutual recognition exist in Directive 80/390/EEC (the Listing Particulars Directive)[39] and Directive 89/298/EEC (the Prospectus Directive).[40] At present, neither the Irish Rules nor the City Code provides for prior approval of offer documents. This is unlikely to change, however, as the first paragraph of Article 6(2) provides merely for communication of the document not for its' approval. There is, therefore, no obligation to introduce a system of prior approval.

III. CONTENTS OF THE OFFER DOCUMENT

4–43 Article 6(3) sets out the minimum informational requirements to be included in the offer document. This document should include:

    (a) the terms of the bid;
    (b) the identity of the offeror and where the offeror is a company, the type, name and registered office of that company;
    (c) the securities or class, or classes of securities for which the bid is made;
    (d) the consideration offered for each security or class of securities and, in the case of mandatory bids, the basis of the valuation used in determining it, with particulars of the way in which that consideration is to be given;
    (e) the maximum and minimum percentages or quantities of securities which the offeror undertakes to acquire;
    (f) details of any existing holdings of the offeror, and of persons acting in concert with him, in the offeree company;
    (g) all conditions to which the offer is subject;
    (h) the offeror's intentions with regard to the future business and undertakings of the offeree company, its employees and its management, including any material change in the conditions of employment;

---

[39] [1980] O.J. No. L100/1.
[40] [1989] O.J. No. L124/8.

    (i) the period for acceptance of the bid;

    (j) where the consideration offered by the offeror includes securities of any kind, information about those securities;

    (k) information on the financing for the bid;

    (l) the identity of persons and entities acting in concert with the offeror or with the offeree company, in the case of companies together with their type, name and registered office, and their relationship with the offeror and where possible with the offeree company."

These provisions are compatible with Rule 24 of the Irish Rules and the City Code which sets out the minimum informational requirements of the offer document.[41]

4–44 In relation to paragraph (h) above, it is important to note that the 1997 Proposal required disclosure of "any change in the conditions of employment" irrespective of its importance. For example, an increase in the time available for lunch by five minutes would constitute a change in the conditions of employment and would thus have required disclosure in the offer document. This latter problem has been resolved by the inclusion of the word "material" in the 1999 Proposal. This is in keeping with the Irish Rules and the City Code which require only that "major changes" must be notified.[42] A remaining problem with paragraph (h) identified by the Company and Commercial Law Committee of the Law Society of Ireland is that it would be difficult, if not impossible in the case of a hostile bid, for the offeror to give any indication of any changes in the conditions of employment in the offeree company as it would be unlikely to be aware of pre-existing conditions.

K. Period for Acceptance of the Bid

4–45 Article 6a(1) provides that that the period for acceptance of the offer may not be less than two weeks[43] or more than ten weeks from the date of publication of the offer document. Member States are expressly authorised to extend this ten weeks period subject to the condition that the offeror must give at least two weeks prior notice of its intention to close the bid. Such flexibility is essential. It would allow for an extension of the period, where, for example, regulatory approval had not been obtained. In addition Article 6a(2) authorises Member

---

[41] paras 12.29–12.44.
[42] Rule 24(1)(b).
[43] Under the 1997 proposal, the minimum period was four weeks. Such a time period would not have suited all the Member States. France, for example, operates a system of simplified bids lasting 10 days.

States to provide for rules modifying this period in "specific appropriate cases". Under the Irish Rules, the offer must be open for at least 21 days after the posting of the offer document[44] and should lapse unless it has become or been declared unconditional as to acceptances on the 60th day after the date the offer document was posted or unless the Panel agrees otherwise.[45] In addition, offers may be left open for a longer period after they have gone wholly unconditional, or in the event a competing offer has been made or finally, where there are delays for regulatory reasons relating to the Mergers, Takeovers and Monopolies (Control) Act, 1978 or the European Commission.[46]

Article 6a(2) also provides that Member States may authorise the supervisory authority to grant a derogation from the offer period specified "in order to allow the offeree company to organise a general meeting to consider the bid". As the notice required for the calling of a shareholders' meeting varies in different Member States, it is essential to have a provision such as this in a framework directive. It ensures, for example, that sufficient time is available to allow the board of the offeree company to call a general meeting of shareholders to consider the adoption of defensive measures.

L. Disclosure

4–46   Article 7(1) provides that Member States must also issue rules providing for the disclosure of bids in order to avoid the creation of a false market.

Article 7(2) provides that Member States must ensure that rules are in force providing for the disclosure of all information or documents required in such a manner as to ensure that they are both readily and promptly available to the holders of securities "at least in those Member States where the securities of the offeree company are admitted to trading on a regulated market". The last proviso weakens the protection offered by the Article 7 obligation but is perhaps administratively justifiable. The information and documentation must also be made available to the representatives of the employees of the offeree company or, where there are no such representatives, to the employees themselves. This provision enforces the informational requirements of Article 6.

---

44   Rule 31.1.
45   Rule 31.6(a)(I).
46   Rule 31. See generally paras 12.56–12.60.

M. Obligations of the Board of the Offeree Company

4–47   Article 8(1)(a) of the 1999 Proposal prohibits the board of the offeree company from engaging in frustrating actions. This is one of the cornerstones of the Directive and the objective of this Article is "to limit the powers of the board of directors of the offeree company to engage in operations of an exceptional nature without unduly hindering the offeree company to carry out its normal course of business."[47]

I. THE PROHIBITION

4–48   The prohibition commences at the latest after receiving the information referred to in Article 6(1) first sentence concerning the bid and applies until the result of the bid is made public or until the bid lapses if it is unsuccessful. The first sentence of Article 6(1) refers to the publication of the decision to make a bid. During this period, the board of the offeree company are required to "abstain from completing any action other than seeking alternative bids which may result in the frustration of the offer." In particular, the board is prohibited from "the issuing of shares which may result in a lasting impediment to the offeror to obtain control over the offeree company". The existence of a prohibition on defensive measures is central to the protection of shareholders. Particularly, in a hostile takeover, the interests of the directors of the offeree company may conflict with the interests of the shareholders of the offeree company. In such a case, it is essential that the directors do not deny shareholders the opportunity to consider any offer which may be made.[48]

It is not the intention of Article 8(1)(a) to prevent the board of the offeree company mounting a robust defence to the bid by trying to persuade shareholders to reject the offer. Neither does it seek to prevent the board from seeking a white knight and promoting an auction. In both cases, the actions of the directors are acceptable in that the shareholders are not deprived of the opportunity to make an informed assessment and ultimately to accept the offer.

Rule 21 of the Irish Rules and the City Code contains a prohibition on frustrating actions by the offeree company board.[49] In both cases, however, the prohibition commences at the commencement of the offer period or "at any earlier time at which the offeree board has reason to believe that an offer in respect of the offeree may be imminent". This is

---

[47]   Recital 14.
[48]   See Chapters 19 and 20.
[49]   para. 19.60 *et seq.*

clearly preferable to a prohibition which commences at the time the decision to make a bid is made public. The latter gives the board of the offeree company greater latitude to act to ensure that an imminent bid is not put before shareholders.

II. EXCEPTIONS TO THE PROHIBITION

4–49   The only circumstances envisaged by Article 8(1)(a) in which the board of the offeree company is permitted to take frustrating action is where it has obtained "the prior authorisation of the general meeting of the shareholders given for this purpose, during the period of acceptance of the bid." This paragraph is similar to Rule 21 of the Irish Rules and the City Code. The effect of this provision is that shareholders who do not wish to accept the offer may authorise their directors to take defensive action to prevent the offer being implemented. Because this authorisation may only be given during the period of acceptance of the bid, the shareholders will have received the information contained in the offer document and will thus be in a position to assess the offer on its merits. It is important thus to note that this authorisation may not be given at a time when the existence of a bid or the terms of the bid is unknown to the shareholders.

Article 8.2 of the 1999 Proposal contains a further exemption. This provision was viewed as a compromise solution between the position of Member States which indicated a preference for allowing defensive measures against hostile takeovers and that of Member States such as Ireland, and the UK which prohibit defensive measures. It states as follows:

> "Member States may allow the board of the offeree company to increase the share capital during the period of acceptance of the bid on the condition that prior authorisation has been received from the general meeting of shareholders not earlier than 18 months before the beginning of the period of acceptance of the bid, with full recognition of the right of preemption of all shareholders as provided for in Article 29(1) of the Directive 77/91/EEC."

The main difficulty with this paragraph is that it anticipates seeking the consent of the shareholders to a specific frustrating action at a time when they obviously would be unaware of the terms of the offer and probably even the existence of a possible offer by the offeror. Although Article 8(3) is permissive and Member States would not thus need to provide an exemption of this sort in their domestic regulation, it is submitted that the operation of such a provision in any of the Member States undermines the objective of the Directive of providing equivalent safeguards for the protection of shareholders throughout the European Union.

III. THE OFFEREE CIRCULAR

4–50 A further obligation is imposed by Article 8(1)(b) which requires the board of the offeree company to draw up and publish a document informing shareholders of its "opinion on the bid" together with its reasons for forming this view. Such a document must also include the board's views on "the effects of implementation on all the interests of the company, including employment". Similar obligations are already imposed by the Irish Rules and City Code.[50]

N. Conduct of the Bid

4–51 Article 9 provides that rules should be in place to govern the conduct of bids. As a minimum, rules should be introduced in respect of: the lapse of the bid; the revision of bid; competing bids, the disclosure of the results of a bid; and the irrevocability of the bid and the conditions permitted. All these matters are currently regulated by the Irish Rules.

O. Contact Committee

4–52 Article 20 of the Admissions Directive (Directive 79/279)[51] provided for the establishment of a contact committee to facilitate the harmonised interpretation of that Directive. This committee is already in operation. Article 20(3) of the Admissions Directive provides that the Committee should be composed of persons appointed by the Member States and of representatives of the Commission. Article 10a of the 1999 Proposal authorises this same Committee to perform certain functions with respect to the 1999 Proposal. The Committee is required to facilitate the harmonised application of the Directive. This function is to be performed through regular meetings dealing in particular with practical problems arising in connection with its application. In the Recitals, it is noted that the task of assisting Member States and supervisory authorities in the implementation of the Directive will be particularly important in areas such as cross-border takeover bids and the mutual recognition of offer documents.

A second function of the contact committee is to advise the Commission, if necessary, on additions or amendments to the Directive.

---

[50] See generally Chapter 12.
[51] [1980] O.J. No. L100/1.

In order to avoid confusion, Article 10a(2) expressly provides that this Committee will not appraise the merits of decisions taken by any of the supervisory authorities in individual cases. This would not, of course, prevent the Committee discussing individual cases with a view to identifying issues which merit inclusion in the Directive or provisions requiring amendment in the Directive.

P. Sanctions

4–53   Article 10b obliges each Member State to determine the sanctions to be applied for infringement of the measures taken pursuant to the Directive. These sanctions may thus involve civil or criminal penalties as the Member States deem appropriate. However, it is expressly provided that the sanctions must be "sufficient to promote compliance with those measures".

Conclusion

4–54   Despite the progess made in recent years towards the harmonisation of company law and financial services law in different Member States, clearly differences exist. As a result of the disparate systems of takeover regulation in Member States, the drafting of a directive seeking to harmonise certain safeguards throughout the Community will necessitate compromises by all Member States. The transposition of any such directive will necessarily involve substantial changes to domestic regulation. Yet, it is stated in the Recitals that only action at Community level can ensure adequate protection for shareholders throughout the Community.

In a number of key areas, the 1999 Proposal is an improvement on its predecessor. By allowing Member States to grant derogations from the rules made pursuant to the Directive and by allowing Member States to introduce additional provisions, the 1999 Proposal introduces greater flexibility. Such flexibility is essential for the effective supervision of takeovers. The 1999 Proposal empowers Member States to determine the legal position concerning the liability of supervisory authorities or concerning litigation between the parties to a bid. Such a provision should reduce the incidence of tactical litigation. Following a transition period, the 1999 Proposal provides that mandatory bids will be required following the acquisition of control. This will ensure that the rights of minority shareholders are safeguarded. Despite these improvements, the 1999 Proposals is not without its flaws. In its 1998–1999 Annual Report, the London Panel state that "the text agreed in the Council reflects the lowest common denominator of what is capable of agreement between the Member States". The lack of a harmonised approach in a number of the key areas such as the provision of cash consideration for mandatory offers and the prohibition of any form of frustrating action casts doubt on the achievement of the very purpose of the Directive. In other areas such as the determination of jurisdiction and law in Article 4(2)(e), a lack of clarity may give rise to problems of transposition and implementation.

Agreement on the final version of a Directive on Company Law concerning takeover bids has not yet been reached. The political reservation made by Spain linked to the definition of a supervisory authority in Gibraltar is currently the subject of negotiation. Any wording suggested will have to be approved of by all Member States. In addition, as the 1999 Proposal is subject to co-determination procedures, the approval of both the Council and the European Parliament is required. Further amendments could be suggested at either stage. Indeed, it is submitted that in a number of areas highlighted above, further consideration might be advisable and might lead to an overall improvement in the level of protection afforded to shareholders.

CHAPTER 5

STOCK EXCHANGE REGULATIONS

Introduction

5–01 Stock exchanges facilitate companies in the raising of capital through the listing of corporate securities. In addition to providing the market, stock exchanges regulate the admission of securities to listing on the market and the maintenance of that listing. Consequently, companies whose securities are listed on a stock exchange must comply with the listing rules established by that exchange. These rules will impose obligations on companies during the takeover process in two main ways. Firstly, where either the offeror or the offeree is a listed company, certain continuing obligations apply which may have an impact on the procedure to be followed. The continuing obligations of the Irish Stock Exchange are examined in Part B of this Chapter. Secondly, where the offeror is a listed company, as part of the consideration for the acquisition it may issue new securities and apply to have these securities listed. Part C of this Chapter examines the rules which apply when an issuer seeks to list securities on the Irish Stock Exchange.

At the outset however, Part A of the chapter contains a brief review of the markets operated by the Irish Stock Exchange, a prescribed stock exchange for the purposes of section 2(a) of the Irish Takeover Panel Act, 1997 ("the Act").[1] Part A also considers the markets operated by the London Stock Exchange and NASDAQ and EASDAQ as the possibility exists that public limited companies whose securities are traded on these markets may, in the future, be deemed "relevant companies" under section 2(c) of the Act.

---

[1] The Irish Takeover Panel Act, 1997 (Prescribed Stock Exchange) Regulations, 1997 (S.I. No. 256 of 1997).

A. Stock Exchanges

I . THE IRISH STOCK EXCHANGE

(1) Background

5–02   The Stock Exchange in Dublin was established by "An Act for the Better Regulation of Stockbrokers" referred to as the Stockbrokers (Ireland) Act 1799, 39 Geo.III, c40 (Ir.).[1a] At this time, apart from government debentures ("gilts"), there were only three stocks traded on the Dublin Stock Exchange: Bank of Ireland, the Grand Canal and the Royal Canal. In 1822, the Stock Exchange published its first code of "Laws, Rules, and Regulations" to govern the admission of members to the Exchange. In 1918, the Stockbrokers (Ireland) Act, was passed allowing the Dublin Stock Exchange, with the approval of the Lord Lieutenant,[2] to regulate the fixing of commission for dealings by licensed stockbrokers in gilts. A second Irish stock exchange was established in Cork in 1886, adopting certain of the regulations of the Dublin and London Stock Exchanges. In 1971, the Dublin Stock Exchange merged with the Cork Stock Exchange to form the newly titled "Irish Stock Exchange". Two years later, in 1973, the Irish Stock Exchange and the London Stock Exchange merged to form "the International Stock Exchange of the United Kingdom and the Republic of Ireland Limited". As part of this Exchange, the Irish unit was supervised under the rules of the International Stock Exchange which had force of law in the UK under the Financial Services Act 1986. The listing rules used by the International Stock Exchange of the United Kingdom and the Republic of Ireland Limited to regulate the admission of securities to a listing and the maintenance of that listing were considered to be amongst the most stringent in the world, and this proved an enormous help to the marketing of Irish securities abroad. At this time, member firms of the Irish unit of the Exchange were regulated by the Securities and Futures Authority, a UK based, self regulatory organisation authorised under the Financial Services Act 1986.

5–03   The regulation of the securities market in Ireland changed dramatically in 1995 with the introduction of the Stock Exchange Act 1995. This Act led to the provision of a domestic regulatory and supervisory authority for stock exchanges and member firms. The Central Bank was authorised as the regulatory authority for the Irish Stock Exchange, any other stock exchange which subsequently establishes

---

[1a] For an excellent account of the history of the Irish Stock Exchange, see Thomas, *The Stock Exchanges of Ireland* (Francis Cairns (Publications) Ltd., 1986).

[2] After 1922, the Minister for Finance fulfilled the role of the Lord Lieutenant.

itself in Ireland and the member firms of these exchanges. The main instigator of this change was the Investment Services Directive[3] which was intended to open the way for investment firms authorised in their home Member States to have access to financial markets throughout the Community. It was believed that although the Directive did not strictly require the establishment of an Irish supervisory institution, nor prevent two supervisors from two different Member States supervising a transnational institution, in practice, the legal complexities involved would have made this inoperable. Ironically thus, although the objective of the Investment Services Directive was to secure a harmonised European market, one of the most important consequences of its implementation in Ireland was its facilitation of the separation of the London and Dublin Exchanges. The two Exchanges became separate with effect from the December 8th, 1995.

(2) The Official List

5–04 The Irish Stock Exchange ("ISE") operates three markets: the main market (the Official List), the Developing Companies Markets and the Explorations Companies Market.[4] The Official List is the largest and longest established of these three markets. The Official List provides listing facilities for corporate securities, gilts, local authority bonds and investment funds. At the end of June 1999, there were 74 companies whose securities were listed on the Official List. The total market capitalisation was £58,345 million. No market makers exist to trade in Irish equities and the market is therefore order driven rather than price driven. The CREST equity settlement system[5] is used to allows shares to be held and traded in an electronic form. This system operates by responding to electronic messages from stockbrokers to transfer securities between accounts. Although, the articles of association of companies previously required the transfer of shares to be evidenced by a stock transfer form and the issuance of paper share certificates, the Companies Act 1990 (Uncertified Securities) Regulations, 1996 provide for electronic transfer.[5a]

5–05 In order to have its securities listed on this market, a company must meet stringent entry criteria. Subsequently, it must adhere to rules

---

[3] Council Directive 93/22/EEC O.J L141/27. See Chap. 7, paras 7–53–7–57.
[4] Two other markets, the Smaller Companies Market and the Unlisted Securities Market, both closed at the end of 1996.
[5] CREST is a paperless share settlement system which was introduced by CREST Co. in 1996.
[5a] S.I. No. 68 of 1996. In addition ss. 101–110 of the Finance Act 1996 were introduced to ensure that stamp duty is still levied in respect of transfers of shares under the best system despite the fact that no transfer instrument exists. A change of 1% is currently imposed on the transfer of electronic shares.

and guidelines monitored by the ISE in order to ensure that investors are adequately protected. These rules are referred to as the "Listing Rules". In order to ensure that international investors maintained their trust and confidence in the strict level of supervision of the Irish market following its separation from the London Stock Exchange, the ISE made a commitment to maintain the existing standards. Thus, the Listing Rules which apply to companies seeking a listing on the ISE remain essentially the same as those applied by the London Stock Exchange. The London Stock Exchange Listing Rules are contained in a folder which is referred to as the "Yellow Book". The ISE, however, has developed a series of explanatory notes for companies seeking admission to, or listed on the Official List of the ISE. These notes, which are contained in the "green pages", are to be read in conjunction with the London Stock Exchange Listing Rules. Parts B and C of this Chapter consider the effect of these Listing Rules on the takeover process.

5–06   The Listing Rules do not, however, have statutory force in Ireland except insofar as they mirror the requirements of the Admissions Directive,[6] the Listing Particulars Directive[7] and the Interim Reports Directive.[8] The purpose of the Admissions Directive is to co-ordinate the conditions for the admission of securities to official listing on stock exchanges operating in Member States in order to provide equivalent protection for investors at Community level. Such co-ordination is expected to facilitate the admission of securities from other Member States on national stock exchanges and the listing of securities on a number of different European stock exchanges. The Listing Particulars Directive seeks to eliminate the differences in Member States rules governing the contents and scrutiny of listing particulars and their publication. The existence of these differences made it more difficult for undertakings to list in several Member States and also hindered the acquisition by investors residing in one Member State of securities listed on a stock exchange in another Member State. The Interim Reports Directive seeks to co-ordinate the requirements for appropriate regular information throughout the entire period of listing in order to make investor protection more equivalent throughout the Community. The overall objective of these three Directives is to ensure greater inter-penetration of national securities markets. The three Directives were implemented into Irish law by the European Communities (Stock

---

6 Council Directive 79/279/EEC. ([1979] O.J. L66/21).
7 Council Directive No. 80/390/EEC ([1980] O.J. L100/1) as subsequently amended by Council Directive 87/345/EEC ([1987] O.J. L185/81), Council Directive 90/211/EEC ([1990] O.J. L122/24) and Council Directive 94/18/EC. [1994] O.J. L135/1.
8 Council Directive No. 82/121/EEC. ([1982] O.J. L48/26).

Exchange) Regulations 1984.[9] These 1984 Regulations designated "the Irish Stock Exchange" as the competent authority for authorising the admission of companies to listing and for supervising the listed companies. The Irish Stock Exchange was defined then as "the Committee of the Irish Unit of the International Stock Exchange of the United Kingdom and the Republic of Ireland Ltd.". Following the separation of the exchanges, the European Communities (Stock Exchange) (Amendment) Regulations 1995[10] amended this definition and "the Irish Stock Exchange Ltd." is now the competent authority for the purposes of the aforementioned Directives.

(3) The Developing Companies Market and the Explorations Securities Market

5–07 The Developing Companies Market ("the DCM") was launched on January 31, 1997 to meet the needs of young and growing public limited companies. It was hoped that this market would attract small and medium sized high growth companies in electronics, telecommunications, media etc. Limited tax incentives are available to companies quoted on the DCM. In addition, admission to the DCM is substantially less expensive than to the Official List. It is expected that a flotation on the DCM could cost approximately £80,000. A flotation on the Official List by contrast can cost up to £1 million. At the end of June 1999, six companies were listed on this market and the total market capitalisation was £164 million.

5–08 The DCM has its own specific rules ("the DCM Rules") governing the admission and ongoing requirements of companies joining the market. A sponsor must be appointed which must satisfy itself that the applicant has satisfied the admission requirements. The sponsor's functions are to guide and advise the applicant as to the relevant Stock Exchange requirements and to conduct the admission process with the Stock Exchange on the applicant's behalf. An applicant must prepare a DCM admission document in accordance with Chapter 3 of the DCM Rules. This document must include all information within their knowledge necessary to allow investors make an informed assessment of the applicant's assets, liabilities, financial position, profits and losses,

---

[9] S.I. No. 282 of 1984 European Communities (Stock Exchange) Regulations, 1984. Council Directive 87/345/EEC was implemented by S.I. No. 18 of 1991, European Communities (Stock Exchange) (Amendment) Regulations, 1991. Council Directive 90/211/EEC was implemented by S.I. No. 202 of 1992, European Communities (Transferable Securities and Stock Exchange) Regulations, 1992. Council Directive 94/18/EEC was implemented by S.I. No. 234 of 1994, European Communities (Stock Exchange) (Amendment) Regulations, 1994.

[10] S.I. No. 311 of 1995.

prospects and rights attaching to the securities.[11] Details about the persons responsible for the document, the applicant, its capital, its activities, its management and any recent developments and prospects must be included together with a statement of responsibility from the directors and any proposed directors. The admission document must be submitted to and approved by the ISE.[12]

5-09 In the case of further issues of shares by an issuer whose shares are already quoted, an admission document is necessary only where those shares are to be offered to the public.[13] An admission document will not be required for issues of shares by a company whose shares are already quoted where the number or the estimated market value or the nominal value or, in the absence of a nominal value, the accounting par value of the shares offered amounts to less than 10 per cent of the number or of the corresponding value of shares of the same class already quoted provided the applicant confirms that investors possess up to date information about the applicant equivalent to that required under Section III of the Prospectus Regulations.[14]

5-10 As with any public offer, the applicant must publish a prospectus in accordance with the Prospectus Regulations. The DCM Rules are less restrictive than the Official Listing Rules thus making it easier for smaller companies to list on this market. Thus, while an applicant for admission to the DCM must normally have a minimum one-year trading record, the ISE has discretion to admit companies with a shorter record. At least 10 per cent of the company's shares (which must be valid and freely transferable) should be in public hands at the time of entry to the DCM compared to 25 per cent for the Official List. However, in order to ensure a reasonably wide share ownership when the securities are listed, most DCM companies will aim to have 20–30 per cent of their shares in public hands.

5-11 The continuing obligations for quoted companies are set out in Chapter 4 of the DCM Rules. A general obligation exists to notify the Companies Announcements Office of the ISE ("the CAO") immediately of any major new developments in its sphere of activities which are not publicly known and which are price sensitive. Other matters which must be notified are board changes, certain interests of directors and

---

[11] para. 3.5, DCM Rules.
[12] This is in contrast to the equivalent UK market, the Alternative Investment Market, where responsibility for the admission document lies with the nominated adviser or sponsor. See paras 5–17–5–18.
[13] para. 2.4, DCM Rules.
[14] European Communities (Transferable Securities and Stock Exchange) Regulations, 1992, S.I. No. 202 of 1992 and the relevant provisions of the Companies Act 1963.

connected persons, major interests in shares, certain capital changes and stated financial information. The disclosure requirements for major transactions in companies quoted on the DCM are less onerous than those for companies listed on the Official List. For example, where a company on the Official List contemplates an acquisitions of a target which represents a substantial acquisition of more than 25 per cent of the bidder under a number of headings (profits, net assets etc.), the listed company must prepare a very detailed circular to shareholders and must also seek shareholder approval at an Extraordinary General Meeting giving 21 days notice.[15] A substantial transaction for a DCM quoted company is a transaction where any percentage ratio is above 10 per cent but each is less than 100 per cent.[16] In such cases, the Rules require merely the notification of the CAO. This will allow DCM companies to complete major transactions more quickly. Only in the case of a reverse takeover must a circular be prepared for shareholders and their approval sought.[17] A reverse takeover is defined as an acquisition by a quoted company of a business, unquoted company or assets where any percentage ratio is 100 per cent or more or which would result in a fundamental change in the business or in a change in board or voting control of a quoted company.[18]

At the end of June 1999, there were 11 companies listed on the Explorations Securities Market with a total market capitalisation of £213 million. All are oil and mineral exploration companies. The admission requirements are less onerous than a full listing and a minimum trading record of one year is required. Relatively undemanding disclosure requirements apply to these companies.

II. THE LONDON STOCK EXCHANGE

5–11A The London Stock Exchange is one of the oldest and most established stock exchanges in the world.[19] The first joint stock company was established in London in 1553 in order to obtain funding from the public to finance trips to the Orient. As far back as 1697, legislation existed to prohibit any malpractice by brokers. In 1760, 150 stockbrokers formed a club at Jonathan's Coffee House in the City of London. This club was renamed the Stock Exchange in 1773. Two hundred years later in 1973, the new trading floor opened for business and 20 provincial exchanges and the Irish Stock Exchange amalgamated to form the International Stock Exchange of the United Kingdom and the Republic of Ireland Limited. As noted above, the Irish unit of this Exchange separated in December

---

[15] See Chap. 5–38.
[16] para. 4.43.
[17] para. 4.47.
[18] para. 4.43.
[19] For a detailed discussion of the history of the UK Stock Exchanges see: Morgan, *The Stock Exchange, its History and Functions* and Scott, *Joint-Stock Companies to 1720* Vol. 1.

1995. In 1998, the London Stock Exchange and the Deutsche Börse unveilled plans for an alliance intended to create a pan-European share trading platform. Six other continental exchanges agreed to become involved in this venture. In July 1999, the London Stock Exchange announced its intention to discontinue its mutual status and convert itself into a shareholder-owned company. This was stated to be a response to competition from new electronic communications networks ["ECNs"].

5–12 Like, the ISE, the London Stock Exchange regulates both capital raising and market trading. The London Stock Exchange has the third largest domestic equity market in the world after New York and Tokyo. It operates two markets: the main market (the Official List) and the Alternative Investment Market. By June 1990, 2,031 UK companies were listed on the Official List with a total equity value of £1,638 billion and 323 UK companies were listed on the Alternative Investment Market with a total equity value of £6.17 billion. The London Stock Exchange also has 502 international companies listed with a total equity value of £3,147 billion making London the world's leading exchange for overseas listings. During 1998, the London Stock Exchange recorded its largest UK and international equity turnover – £1,037 billion and £2,183 billion, respectively.

(1) The Official List

5–13 For FTSE 100 securities, trading on the London Stock Exchange has been conducted through SETS since October 1997. SETS is the acronym for "the Stock Exchange Electronic Trading Service" a screen based order-driven trading facility. Non-FTSE 100 UK companies are traded on SEAQ (the Stock Exchange Automated Quotations System) which provides a database of market makers' bid and offer prices. Market makers are obliged to display to the market their bid and offer prices for all their registered stocks and the maximum size transaction to which these prices relate. SEAQ International is a comparable quotations system for international companies. Finally, smaller companies with fewer than two market makers use the SEATS PLUS (Stock Exchange Alternative Trading Service) which is a combination of competing market makers quotes and/or firm orders. There is thus an order board through which orders to buy and sell shares can be displayed and matched, and a facility for competing quotations allowing one or more market makers to display prices in a company's shares.

5–14 The Admissions Directive, the Listing Particulars Directive and the Interim Reports Directive were implemented by Part IV of the Financial Services Act 1986 and Regulations made thereunder. The London Stock Exchange which is a "Recognised Investment Exchange" under the 1986 Act is answerable to the Financial Services Authority[20] and is responsible for ensuring that the market operates in an orderly fashion and for providing proper protection for investors. Under the 1986 Act, the London Stock Exchange is the competent authority in the UK for authorising the admission of companies to listing and for supervising the listed companies. Although this role was examined as part of the UK Government's review of financial regulation, the Government have now confirmed that the London Stock Exchange will continue in this role.[21] The admission requirements and the continuing obligations of listing are determined by Part IV of the 1986 Act and the London Stock Exchange Listing Rules.

5–15 At the time of the separation of the London and Dublin Stock Exchanges, the Irish Stock Exchange negotiated special arrangements for Irish Listed companies which were also listed in London. These companies were allowed primary listing status on both Exchanges, and are regulated by both Exchanges to Listing Rules standards in parallel. Companies listing on the Dublin Stock Exchange since the separation, while not benefiting from duel primary listing status, will often obtain a secondary listing on the London Stock Exchange.

(2) The Alternative Investment Market

5–16 The Alternative Investment Market ("AIM") commenced operations on June 19th, 1995 and represented the first new equity market created by the London Stock Exchange for 15 years. It's objective is to provide a new source of finance for smaller higher risk growing companies. At present there are 331 companies listed including 21 overseas companies. The total market capitalisation is £6,734 million. More than £2.38 billion was raised by companies on the market at admission or by further share issues up to June 1999. Tax breaks are available to investors due to the status of AIM companies as "unquoted". Many companies perceive the AIM as a gateway to a full listing and to date 54 AIM companies have progressed to the official list.

5–17 An applicant seeking a quotation must be a public limited company whose securities are freely tradable. In order to allow young companies to participate in this market, neither a trading record nor a profit forecast will be required. Minimum liquidity requirements are also being waived. Unlike the Official List, there is no minimum requirement for any percentage of share capital to be publicly available,

---

[20] The successor body to the Securities Investments Board.
[21] London Stock Exchange Annual Report 1998.

although it is expected by the London Stock Exchange that most firms will have around 25 per cent of its equity available to the public. An applicant for an AIM quotation must appoint a nominated adviser and a broker. The broker's responsibility relates solely to trading AIM company's shares using the SEATS PLUS trading facility. The broker will seek to match bargains in the company's shares if there is no market maker. In order to quash the fears of institutional investors about possible lack of regulation, the onus of compliance is placed on the nominated adviser. Nominated advisers are responsible for determining the suitability of the applicant for the market and for guiding and advising it on compliance with the AIM Rules. Unlike a sponsor for a listed company, the adviser will work with the DCM company throughout its quoted life. The London Stock Exchange has approved a list of 60 nominated advisers from a variety of backgrounds including stockbroking, accounting and banking.

5–18 An admission document must be produced. This document should include details of the applicant, its directors, substantial shareholdings and certain financial information. As a prospectus is necessary for the initial quotation and subsequent capital raisings, the requirements of the Prospectus Directive[22] must also be satisfied. A prospectus will not be vetted by the Stock Exchange in the same way as a company seeking a full market listing. Instead, the company's adviser reviews the prospectus. The adviser owes a duty to the Stock Exchange to ensure that due diligence has been carried out. In this way, an adviser's reputation will depend upon the accuracy of information contained in the prospectus. The Stock Exchange will then conduct annual performance reviews of the advisers. Poor performance may result in fines or removal from the register.

5–19 AIM companies are required to meet less onerous disclosure requirements. Price sensitive information must be disclosed, including transactions with related parties, as well as interim figures and audited accounts. Substantial transactions have to be published but only reverse takeovers have to be approved by shareholders. In May 1997, the London Stock Exchange announced a change of rules requiring companies to disclose the name of anyone who has received fees or shares worth £10,000 or more in the 12 month period prior to the company joining the market. Details of shadow directors should also be disclosed. In addition, the companies and their nominated advisers are required to review the actual financial performance of the company compared with

---

[22] Council Directive 89/298/EEC implemented in the UK by The Public Offers of Securities Regulations, 1995, S.I. No. 1537 of 1995.

public profit projections made in their admission documents. They must notify the market immediately if there has been a material change in the company's trading performance.

The exchange fee is £2,500 for the first year. The costs of joining are considerably lower than a full listing, with some nominated advisors offering to bring new companies to the market for £50,000. The real cost saving however is the reduced expenditure incurred in managing the quotation and meeting AIM's requirements.

III. NASDAQ

5–20   The US market is attractive to Irish companies because of its vast size and because of the competitive cost of capital. The NASDAQ Stock Market, Inc is a subsidiary of the National Association of Securities Dealers (NASD), a self-regulatory organisation registered with the U.S. Securities Exchange Commission ("the SEC"). In 1998, when NASD and the American Stock Exchange (AMEX) merged, the NASDAQ–AMEX Market Group Inc. was formed as a subsidiary of the NASD. NASDAQ and AMEX continue to operate, however, as separate markets. In July 1999, NASDAQ also announced plans for demutualisation and to explore a public offering in the exchange. The NASDAQ[23] market is an "over the counter" market which means that there is no physical location or exchange facility. Instead, securities are traded back and forth by NASD securities firms through various NASDAQ computer terminals. These persons engage in matching buyers and sellers. Vendor terminals located all around the world carry detailed quote and last-sale information to traders, fund managers and brokers who then place orders with the NASD securities firms in the U.S. who execute the orders on their behalf. The NASDAQ market is thus primarily an electronic price quotation system.

5–21   All companies quoted on NASDAQ must have at least two market makers competing for investors' orders. Market makers are obliged to report each completed trade in a NASDAQ security to the NASD within 90 seconds. Information on the size and price of trades is then immediately relayed to all NASDAQ screens and vendor terminals world-wide. Market makers are allowed to sponsor stocks as well as trade them. These firms have specialised in producing reliable research on small companies, helping investors separate the high quality investments from the others and generally promoting interest in the sector. NASDAQ's use of sophisticated technology offers unique market access and liquidity to Irish companies.

---

[23]   The title "NASDAQ" stems from the fact that the market originated from the NASD Automated Quotation System, an electronic system which collected and disseminated quotations from competing dealers.

5–22 Although the NASDAQ exchange only opened in 1971, it is second only to the New York Stock Exchange in the U.S. and its trading in volume terms often surpasses the other Exchange. In addition, NASDAQ has more foreign companies listed. NASDAQ has become the U.S. trading exchange for the shares of entrepreneurial start up companies especially those focusing on growth sectors such as electronics and biotechnology. Technology companies account for 16 per cent of all the stocks listed on NASDAQ and 41 per cent of the market's total capitalisation. The NASDAQ market has two tiers for listing: the NASDAQ National Market for larger well established companies and the NASDAQ SmallCap Market for smaller emerging companies. As of the end of June 1999, there were 3,817 companies listed on the NASDAQ National Market® and 1,027 companies listed on the NASDAQ SmallCap Market. U.S. examples are Microsoft and Intel. Currently, over 25 per cent of the companies listed on NASDAQ are non-US.[24] Examples of such companies are Toyota, Cadbury Schweppes and Ericsson. Irish companies perceive this to be a market where they can raise money cheaper, and at an earlier stage in their development than would be possible in Ireland. Irish companies currently listed include Elan, Institute of Clinical Pharmacology, CBT and Ryan Air.

5–23 Listing on NASDAQ involves appointing a U.S. broker. This broker prepares a prospectus to comply with SEC Regulations and with the Irish prospectus rules. A company listing shares on a U.S. stockmarket must first register with the SEC. This involves filling in a Form 20–F registration statement and having the SEC complete its review. For companies offering securities for sale, the SEC requires a Form F–1 initially, followed by a Form 20–F. Following the initial registration process, companies must continue to file a Form 20–F with the SEC every year. Companies must meet specific financial and qualitative criteria to be listed and remain on the NASDAQ National Market® and the NASDAQ SmallCap Market. To be listed on the NASDAQ National Market, a company must: have a minimum level of net tangible assets, a minimum number of shares outstanding, a minimum number of Market Makers; outside members of the board of directors; independent accountants; and meet other similar criteria. To be listed on the SmallCap Market, companies are required to meet less stringent entry requirements. In August 1997, the SEC approved changes to the listing requirements of both tiers setting out a $1 minimum bid price, quantitative requirements, peer review requirements for auditors and requiring compliance with corporate governance rules.

---

[24] "NASDAQ: An Alternative Listing Route for Irish Business" *Finance* Vol. 10 No. 3.
[25] EASDAQ website — www.easdaq.

IV. EASDAQ

5–24 EASDAQ was launched at the end of September 1996 as a pan European market for growing companies. It mirrored itself on the NASDAQ market and maintains a cross link with NASDAQ allowing companies traded on NASDAQ to be crosstraded on EASDAQ. EASDAQ is based in Brussels and is incorporated as a societe anonyme under Belgian law. The main objective of EASDAQ thus is "to provide a well-regulated, pan-European stock market which is liquid, efficient and fair, where fast-growing companies with international aspirations can raise capital from investors."[25] It was intended to build upon the passport provided by the Investment Services Directive to E.U. securities firms to offer cross border securities services. There are currently 49 companies listed, the only Irish one being ESAT Telecom. The first 19 companies raised 508 million ECU on admission and had a market capitalisation at admission of almost 3 billion ECU.

5–25 EASDAQ members, of which there are approximately 250, are authorised intermediaries or authorised credit institutions under the terms of the Second Banking Directive.[26] Members can act as brokers, market makers and sponsors. Brokers trade in the shares of EASDAQ companies on behalf of private and institutional clients. Market makers commit capital to buying and selling shares in certain companies. Market makers enter firm quotes on the EASDAQ quotation management system for those securities and these quotes are displayed on-screen to be viewed by all the brokers. At least two EASDAQ registered market makers must be appointed for each security.[27] This is a continuing obligation of listing. Trading will be done over the phone and transactions are then reported to EASDAQ via a trade confirmation system called TRAX within three minutes. Reported trades will be published over the EASDAQ quotation network and to information vendors immediately.

The new EASDAQ rule book was approved by the Belgian Minister of Finance in September 1998. Sponsors are responsible for ensuring that companies adhere to the rules by preparing the companies for flotation and ensuring they meet the continuing obligations set out therein. Companies seeking a listing are expected to have total assets of at least ECU 3.5 million and capital and reserves of at least ECU 2 million. A listing prospectus must be prepared in English setting out certain financial and organisation details about the company and the securities to be listed. The securities being issued must be freely transferable and EASDAQ must be satisfied that there is likely to be an adequate spread of shareholders immediately after admission. Whilst the guideline minimum is

[26] Directive 89/646 [1989] O.J. L386/1.
[27] Art. 7.

100 shareholders after admission, this requirement is dependant upon the particular characteristics of the company. In order to ensure liquidity, a sufficient proportion of the total share capital should be available to the public. Normally a figure of 20% would be adequate. EASDAQ also conducts a qualitative review of the company, its business and its management in order to ensure that accurate, comprehensive and timely information will be available to investors. Companies coming to the public market for the first time are prohibited from disposing of any shares for a period of at least six month from the date of admission to trading on EASDAQ. An exception is made where the shares are disposed of through a public offering. To an extent, EASDAQ has been overshadowed by EURO.NM, a pan-European grouping of regulated markets. The members of EURO.NM include the Paris Stock Exchange (Le Nouveau Marché), Deutsche Börse, Amsterdam Exchanges, the Brussels Stock Exchange and the Italian Stock Exchange.

V. THE NEW YORK STOCK EXCHANGE

5–25A   The New York Stock Exchange ("NYSE") evolved from a two-sentence agreement entered into by 24 Wall Street brokers to trade in the five securities existing at that time to become the largest equities market in the world with a market capitalisation of almost $12 trillion. In July 1999, the NYSE announced its intention to de-mutualise and to offer its shares to the public. At the end of July 1999, 3,100 companies are listed on this Exchange including 382 non-US companies. Trading volume averages $36.2 billion in a single day. For Irish companies, the NYSE presents an opportunity to raise capital in the US by accessing a very large shareholder constituency. The marketability of the company's shares are significantly increased. This in turn enhances the visibility of the company and its products or services and facilitates acquisitions in the United States through the use of domestically listed securities. Five Irish companies have securities listed on the NYSE, Allied Irish Bank, Elan, Jefferson Smurfit, Telecom Eireann and Bank of Ireland.

The NYSE may be described as an "agency auction market". This means that trading takes place by means of open bids and offers by Exchange members acting as agents for institutional investors or for individual investors. Like any other auction situation, buy and sell orders are matched and prices are determined according to the supply and demand of shares. An electronic order routing system called "SuperDOT" is used by member firms to transmit orders directly to the trading post where the security is traded and to report on the execution of the order after the order has been completed in the market.

Non-US companies have the choice of qualifying for listing under the NYSE domestic listing criteria or the alternate listing standards for non-

US companies. The principal criteria of the latter focus on worldwide distribution of shares and are relevant where there is a broad liquid market for the company's shares in its home country. Often, a NYSE member firm will be appointed as a corporate sponsor. The minimum listing requirements are: 5,000 round-lot holders[27a] world wide; 2.5 million public shares worldwide with a market value of $100 million and; aggregate net tangible assets for the last three years of $100 million with a minimum of $25 million for any one of the three years. Domestic listing criteria require a minimum distribution of shares with the US. The minimum listing requirements in this case are: 2,000 round-lot holders in the US;[27b] 1.1 million public shares in the US with a market value of $40 million; net tangible assets of $40 million and; most recent pre-tax income of $2.5 million with each of the preceding two years income of $2 million.[27c] In addition, domestic listing criteria includes certain corporate governance criteria in respect of a minimum number of outside directors, audit committee composition, voting rights and related party transactions.

B. Continuing Obligations of Listed Companies

5–26 Companies listed on the Official List of the ISE are required both by the Admissions Directive[28] and by the ISEs own Listing Rules to comply with certain ongoing obligations. Many of these obligations will have serious implications for the takeover process itself. Failure to comply with these Rules may lead to public or private censure or more seriously to the suspension or ultimate cancellation of the listing.

I. THE ADMISSIONS DIRECTIVE

5–27 A listed company is required to observe certain obligations once its securities have been admitted to listing. Schedule C to the Admissions Directive sets out the obligations of companies whose shares are admitted to official listing on a stock exchange. These obligations require the company: to list newly issued shares of the same class as those already officially listed; to ensure equal protection for all share-

---

[27a] Holders of at least 100 shares.

[27b] As alternatives, a figure of 2,200 US shareholders together with an average monthly trading volume for the most recent six months of 100,000 shares or a figure of 500 US shareholders together with an average monthly trading volume for the most recent 12 months of one million shares are acceptable.

[27c] As alternative quantitative standards, an aggregate pre-tax income for the three years of $6.5 million and a minimum pre-tax income in the most recent year of $4.5 million or an aggregate adjusted net income for the three years of $25 million.

[28] Council Directive 79/279/EEC.

holders who are in the same position; to communicate a draft of any amendment to its instrument of incorporation or its statutes; to publish its annual accounts and report; to inform the public of any major new developments which may lead to substantial share price movements; and to ensure that equivalent information is made available to the market at each of the stock exchanges on which its shares are listed. Schedule D sets out similar obligations in respect of issuers whose debt securities are listed. Article 4(2) provides that the issuers of securities admitted to official listing must fulfil these obligations. In addition, Article 17 deals with the method of publishing the information required to be made available to the public in accordance with the requirements of Schedule C and D. The requisite information must either be published in one or more newspapers distributed throughout the Member State, distributed widely therein or alternatively be made available in writing at certain specified places. On a more general level, Article 13(1) imposes a duty on the issuer to provide the competent authorities with all the information which the latter consider appropriate in order to protect investors or ensure the smooth operation of the market.

5–28   Under Article 5 (2), Member States may also impose "more stringent" or "additional obligations" on issuers once these obligations are applied generally for all issuers or for individual classes of issuer and have been published before the issuer applies for a listing. Similarly, Regulation 3(2) of the European Communities (Stock Exchange) Regulations 1984[29] which implements the Admissions Directive, allows for additional or alternative conditions or obligations, provided they apply generally, are published in advance and "are not otherwise inconsistent with, or imposed in a manner inconsistent with, any provision of the Directives".

II. THE IRISH STOCK EXCHANGE LISTING RULES

5–29   The continuing obligations imposed by the ISE on listed companies are in many places more detailed than those set out in the Admissions Directive. The rules in respect of continuing obligations are set out in Chapters 9–16 of the Listing Rules. Additional and alternative requirements are set out in Chapters 17, 18, 21 to 24 and 26 dealing with overseas companies, property companies, investment entities, public sector issuers, issuers of specialist securities and miscellaneous securities and venture capital trusts.

---

[29] S.I. No. 282 of 1984.

(1) General Obligations

5–30   Chapter 9 of the Listing Rules sets out the general obligations of listed companies. Paragraphs 9.1 to 9.10 impose general obligations of disclosure on companies. The purpose of these obligations is to ensure that companies disclose any information in respect of substantial new developments in its sphere of activity which are not public knowledge and which may lead to substantial movements in the price of its listed securities. Of particular interest are paragraphs 9.11 to 9.14 which require that acquisitions or disposals of major interests in shares must be disclosed to the Exchange. Finally, the Listing Rules restrict a company dealing in securities when a director would be prohibited from doing so under the Model Code.[30] These obligations are examined in Chapter 13.[30a]

5–31   Companies must also notify the Exchange of certain information relating to its capital, *e.g.* any changes in the rights attaching to the various classes of securities must be disclosed.[31]

Paragraph 9.16 provides that a company having listed shares must ensure equality of treatment for all holders of such shares who are in the same position. For this reason pre-emption rights apply, unless shareholders otherwise permit. These rights are discussed further at paragraphs 5–58–5–60 below.

5–32   Communication with shareholders is strictly regulated by paragraphs 9.24 to 9.31 of the Listing Rules in order to ensure that shareholders receive adequately and timely information. The final paragraphs of Chapter 9 set out further miscellaneous obligations for companies. For example, in order to monitor the liquidity of the market, the issuer must inform the Stock Exchange immediately if the proportion of listed equity shares in public ownership falls below 25 per cent of the total issued share capital.[32] An acquisition which gives the offeror more than 75 per cent of the company could cause difficulties in this regard and could lead to the removal of the company's listing facility.

(2) Further Obligations

5–33   Chapters 12 to 16 of the Listing Rules set out further obligations of listed companies. Chapter 12 sets out the continuing obligations relating to matters of a financial nature. For example, the CAO must be notified immediately after board approval of a preliminary statement of annual

---

[30]   Listing Rules, para. 9.38.
[30a]   See below paras 13–55–13–68.
[31]   Listing Rules, para. 9.10(c).
[32]   Listing Rules, para. 9.37.

results or a decision to pay dividends.[33] Listed companies are required to issue an annual report and accounts and a half-yearly report containing certain specified information.[34]

5–34   Chapter 13 of the Listing Rules lists certain documents which do not require the prior approval of the ISE before they may be issued. Included in Chapter 13 are memoranda and articles of association, trust deeds, employees' share schemes and proxy forms. Chapter 14 sets out the general requirements applicable to all circulars sent by a company to holders of listed securities. Circulars not generally requiring prior ISE approval under Chapter 14 include circulars in respect of the allotment by the directors of shares, the disapplication of pre-emption rights, an increase in authorised share capital, a reduction in capital and a capitalisation issue. Documents or circulars not complying with the relevant requirements of Chapters 13 and 14 must be discussed with the Exchange and possibly submitted to them in draft form for approval.

5–35   Chapter 15 of the Listing Rules sets out the rules which apply to a company intending to purchase its own listed securities. These requirements related primarily to the notification of proposed and actual purchases. These rules are considered further in Chapter 20 of this text.[34a]

5–36   Finally, Chapter 16 of the Listing Rules imposes obligations relating to directors of listed companies. This Chapter deals with directors personal responsibility for listing particulars, directors services contracts and the notification of their interests in company securities. A Model Code is included for transactions in securities by directors, certain employees and connected persons. These rules are detailed in Chapter 13 of this text.[34b]

(3) Major Transactions

(a) Classifications

5–37   Chapters 10 and 11 of the Listing Rules set out the requirements relating to major transactions by listed companies.[35] Chapter 10 describes the manner in which transactions are classified. Essentially, a transaction is classified by assessing its size relative to the size of the listed company proposing to make the transaction. The size of the transaction is determined by examining the following ratios:

---

[33] Listing Rules, para. 12.40.
[34] paras 12.41 and 12.46.
[34a] See below, paras 20–72–20–77.
[34b] See below, paras 13–55–13–68.

(a) assets — the gross assets acquired or disposed off divided by the gross assets of the listed company;

(b) profits — the profits[36] attributable to the assets acquired or disposed of divided by the profits of the listed company;

(c) turnover — the turnover attributable to the assets acquired or disposed of divided by the turnover of the listed company;

(d) consideration to market capitalisation — the consideration[37] divided by the aggregate market value of all the ordinary shares of the listed company;

(e) gross capital — the gross capital of the company or business being acquired divided by the gross capital of the listed company.[38]

In addition, since January 1999, industry specific tests may be submitted, where relevant, by the issuer to support the above standard calculations.[39] Where any of the above calculations produces an anomolous result or where the calculations are inappropriate to the sphere of activity of the listed company, the ISE reserves the right to disregard the calculation and substitute other relevant indicators of size, including industry-specific tests.[39a]

A comparison of size is then made by reference to a number of percentage ratios which are set out in Chapter 10 of the Listing Rules for this purpose. An examination of these percentage ratios allows a transaction to be classified and thus determines the extent of announcement, circularisation and approval necessary.

(b) A Class 1 Transaction

5–38   A "*Class 1*" transaction is a transaction where any aforementioned percentage rating is 25 per cent or more.[40] Such a transaction requires an announcement to the CAO as soon as the terms are agreed. Paragraph 10.37 of the Listing Rules requires the notification to include:

---

[35]   para 9.45 of the Listing Rules provides that companies without listed equity securities need not comply with chaps 10 and 11 which set out requirements in respect of acquisitions and disposals by listed companies. Para. 9.46 of the Rules provides that companies which have only debt securities listed are required to comply with a lesser number of obligations.

[36]   Profits means profits after deducting all charges except taxation and extraordinary items (Listing Rules, para. 10.13)

[37]   See Listing Rules, para. 10.14.

[38]   This ratio is only applied in the case of an acquisition.

[39]   Listing Rules, para. 10.5A.

[39a] Listing Rules, para. 10.6.

[40]   Listing Rules, para. 10.4.C. Until January 1999, such a transaction used to be known as a "super class 1 transaction".

(a) particulars of the transaction;

(b) a description of the business carried on by, or using, the net assets the subject of the transaction;

(c) the consideration, and how it is being satisfied;

(d) the value of the net assets the subject of the transaction;

(e) the profits attributable to the net assets the subject of the transaction;

(f) the effect of the transaction on the listed company including any benefits which are likely to accrue to the company as a result of the transaction;

(g) details of any service contracts of proposed directors of the listed company;

(h) in the case of a disposal, the application of the sale proceeds; and

(i) in the case of a disposal, if securities are to form part of the consideration received, a statement whether such securities are to be sold or retained.

If, subsequent to this notification, any significant change occurs affecting any matter notified or any significant new matter arises, the Exchange must be advised without delay.[41] A supplementary notification must then be sent to the CAO.

5–39 In addition, an explanatory circular must be sent to shareholders who must give their prior approval in general meeting. Any agreement affecting the transaction must be conditional upon obtaining this approval.[42] The circular which must be submitted to the Exchange for approval prior to its publication, must contain certain information set out in paragraph 10.38 of the Listing Rules and the appendix to Chapter 10 which includes: the information given in the notification; details of the effect of the transaction on the earnings or assets and liabilities of the group; a directors' responsibility statement; an expert's consent statement; directors interests in shares and transactions; material contracts; litigation; group prospects; and certain specified financial information such as a statement of indebtedness and working capital. Where a Class 1 circular relates to a takeover offer which is not recommended by the Board of the offeree at the time of publication of the circular, it will be more difficult for the offeror to obtain the necessary information. The offeror may publish its own working capital and indebtedness statements and the statements on the combined basis must be given later in a circular published within

---

[41] Listing Rules, paras 10.32–10.34.
[42] Listing Rules, para. 10.37.

28 days after the offer is declared wholly unconditional. Other information required by the appendix to Chapter 10 should be disclosed in the circular on the basis of information published by the offeree and of which the listed company is aware and is free to disclose. If the takeover offer becomes unconditional, any change or supplement to the disclosed information which is material should be disclosed in a circular published within 28 days after the offer is declared wholly unconditional.[43]

(c) Class 2 Transaction

5–40   A "Class 2" transaction is a transaction where any percentage ratio is 5 per cent or more, but each is less than 25 per cent.[43a] While such a transaction must be notified to the CAO, a circular does not have to be sent to shareholders for their approval. The notification to the CAO must contain the same information as that required for a Class 1 notification.[44]

(d) Class 3 Transaction

5–41   Finally, a "Class 3" transaction is a transaction where all percentage ratios are less than 5 per cent.[44a] An announcement to the CAO is necessary in the case of an acquisition all or part of the consideration of which is satisfied by the issue of securities for which a listing is sought.[45] The notification in such a case must include:

(a) the amount of the securities being issued.

(b) particulars of the transaction, and

(c) either the value of the consideration, and how this is being satisfied, or the value of the net assets acquired, whichever is the greater.

In the case of other Class 3 transactions, if the company releases any details to the public, they must also be notified to the CAO. In this case, the notification must include:

(a) particulars of the transaction,

(b) either the value of the consideration, and how this is being satisfied, or the value of the net assets acquired or disposed of and

(c) in the case of a disposal, the effect on the company of the disposal.[46]

---

[43] Listing Rules, para. 10.45.
[43a] Listing Rules, para. 10.4.b.
[44] Listing Rules, paras 10.31–10.34.
[44a] Listing Rules, para. 10.4.a.
[45] Listing Rules, para. 10.29.
[46] Listing Rules, para. 10.30.

(e) Reverse Takeover

5–42 A reverse takeover is defined as "an acquisition by a listed company of a business, an unlisted company or assets where any percentage ratio is 100 per cent or more or which would result in a fundamental change in the business or in a change in board or voting control of the listed company".[47] Upon the announcement of a reverse takeover which has been agreed or is in contemplation, the Exchange will suspend listing of the company's securities. The company must prepare a Class 1 circular for shareholders. It must also obtain the prior approval of shareholders to the transaction. If, as is likely, the company wishes to remain listed following the completion of the acquisition, it must also prepare listing particulars as if it were a new applicant. One exception, however, is that audited accounts need only be in respect of one year rather than three. Upon publication of the circular and listing particulars, the listing will be restored.[48]

In certain circumstances, para. 10.21 of the Listing Rules provides that a reverse takeover will be treated as a Class 1 transaction. This will occur where the following four conditions are fulfilled:

(a)   the subject of the acquisition is of a similar size to that of the offeror;

(b)   the subject of the acquisition is in a similar line of business to that of the offeror;

(c)   the undertaking the subject of the acquisition complied with the conditions of listing set out in chapter 3 of the Listing Rules; and

(d)   there will be no change of board or voting control.

(f) Transactions with Related Parties

5–43 Chapter 11 of the Listing Rules concentrates on transactions involving directors. It provides that where any transaction is proposed between a listed company (or any of its subsidiary undertakings) and a related party, a circular and the prior approval of the company in general meeting will generally be required. A "transaction with a related party" is defined as:

> "(i) a transaction (other than a transaction of a revenue nature in the ordinary course of business) between a company, or any of its subsidiary undertakings, and a related party; or
>
> (ii) any arrangements pursuant to which a company, or any of its subsidiary undertakings, and a related party each invests in, or provides finance to, another, undertaking or asset."[49]

---

[47]   Listing Rules, para. 10.4(d).
[48]   Listing Rules, para. 10.39.
[49]   Listing Rules, para. 11.1(a).

The definition of "related party" includes a substantial shareholder and

"any person who is (or was within the 12 months preceding the date of the transaction) a director or shadow director of the company or any other company which is (and, if he has ceased to be such, was while he was a director or shadow director of such other company) its subsidiary undertaking or parent undertaking or a fellow subsidiary undertaking of its parent undertaking."

The definition also includes any associate of such person.[50]

5–44 A "substantial shareholder" is defined in paragraph 11.1(c) of the Listing Rules as:

"any person (excluding a bare trustee) who is, or was within the 12 months preceding the date of the transaction, entitled to exercise or to control the exercise of 10 per cent or more of the votes able to be cast on all or substantially all matters at general meetings of the company (or any other company which is a subsidiary undertaking or parent undertaking or is a fellow subsidiary undertaking of its parent undertaking)."

Paragraph 11.1(d) of the Listing Rules provides that an "associate" of a director or substantial shareholder who is an individual would include:

 (i) the individual's spouse or child ('the individual's family')

 (ii) the acting trustees of any trust of which the individual or any of the individual's family is a beneficiary or discretionary object[51]

(iii) any company in whose equity shares the individual or any member or members (taken together) of the individual's family or the individual and any such member or members (taken together) are directly or indirectly interested (or have a conditional or contingent entitlement to become interested) so that they are (or would on the fulfilment of the condition or the occurrence of the contingency be) able to exercise or control the exercise of at least 30 per cent of the votes or to appoint or remove directors holding a majority of the voting rights at board meetings.[52]

5–45 Where the substantial shareholder is a company, paragraph 11.1(e) of the Listing Rules provides that the term "associate" means:

---

[50] Listing Rules, para. 11.1(b).
[51] Other than an occupational pension scheme or an employee's share scheme which does not confer benefits on persons all or most of whom are related parties.
[52] Listing Rules, para. 11.2 provides that for the purposes of determining whether a company is an associate of a director under this sub-paragraph, it should be noted that where more than one of the directors of the listed company, its parent undertaking or any of its subsidiaries is interested in the equity shares of a company, the interests of those directors and their associates are aggregated.

(i) any other company which is its subsidiary or parent or fellow subsidiary of the parent;

(ii) any company whose directors are accustomed to act in accordance with the substantial shareholder's directions or instructions; and

(iii) any company in the capital of which the substantial shareholder, and any other company under (i) or (ii) taken together, is (or would on the fulfilment of a condition or the occurrence of a contingency be) able to exercise or control the exercise of at least 30 per cent of the votes or to appoint or remove directors holding a majority of the voting rights at board meetings.

5–45A　Where a company proposes to enter into a transaction with a related party, the company must make an appropriate announcement, circularise its shareholders, obtain the prior approval of its shareholders and ensure that the related party abstains from voting.[53] The company must make any announcement required by Chapter 10 depending on the classification of the transaction. The announcement must contain the details required to be included in a Class 1 or 2 transaction notification,[54] the name of the related party concerned and details of the nature and extent of the interest of the related party in the transaction. The circular to shareholders must contain even further information.[55] It must include:

(a) the name and address of the company, documents on display, major interests in shares, material contracts, details of the consideration and significant changes;

(b) where the related party is a director, or an associate of a director, of the company the directors' interests in shares, the directors' interests in transactions and the directors' service contracts;

(c) full particulars of the transaction, including the name of the related parties concerned and the nature and extent of their interests in the transaction;

(d) in the case of an acquisition or disposal of an asset, an independent valuation;

(e) a statement by the directors (other than the directors involved) that the transaction is fair and reasonable so far as the shareholders are concerned and that the directors have been so advised by an independent adviser acceptable to the Exchange;

---

[53] Listing Rules, para. 11.4.
[54] Listing Rules, para. 10.31.
[55] Listing Rules, para. 11.10.

(f) where applicable, a statement that the related party will abstain and has taken all reasonable steps to ensure that its associates will abstain from voting at the meeting;

(g) if the transaction also falls within the Class 1 classification, the information required to be included in a Class 1 circular;

(h) details of any other transactions entered into by the company (or any of its subsidiaries) with the same related party and (any of its associates) which have not been approved by shareholders, if required by paragraph 11.9; and

(i) where an expert statement is included in any circular not constituting listing particulars, a statement of consent to its inclusion.

Shareholder approval must be obtained either prior to the transaction being entered into, or if it is expressed to be conditional upon such approval, prior to the completion of the transaction. The related party must not vote on the resolution for this approval.[55a]

(4) Exceptions to the Usual Requirements

5–46 The requirements will not however apply in certain circumstances set out in paragraph 11.7 and 11.8. They will not thus apply to a company where it or any of its subsidiaries proposes to enter into a transaction with a related party if:

"(a) it does not have any equity securities listed;

(b) it is an overseas company with a secondary listing on the Exchange;

(c) the transaction is an issue of new securities either:

   (i) for cash by the company (or any of its subsidiary undertakings) pursuant to an opportunity which (so far as it is practicable) is made to all holders of the company's securities (or to all holders of a relevant class of its securities) on the same terms; or

   (ii) made pursuant to the exercise of conversion or subscription rights attaching to a listed class of securities or previously approved by the company's shareholders in general meeting;

(d) the transaction:

   (i) involves the receipt of any asset (including cash or securities of the company or any of its subsidiary undertakings) by a director of the company, its parent undertaking or any of its subsidiary undertakings; or

   (ii) is a grant of an option or other right to a director of the company, its parent undertaking, or any of its subsidiary undertakings to acquire (whether or not for consideration) any asset (including cash or new or existing securities of the company or any of its subsidiary undertakings);

[55a] Listing Rules, paras 11.4(c) and 11.4(d).

in accordance with the terms of either an employees' share scheme or a long-term incentive plan;

(e) the transaction is a grant of credit (including the lending of money or the guaranteeing of a loan) to the related party or, on an unsecured basis, by the related party:

   (i) upon normal commercial terms in the ordinary course of business; or

   (ii) in an amount and on terms no more favourable than those offered to employees of the group generally;

(f) the transaction is the grant of an indemnity to a director of the company (or any of its subsidiary undertakings) to the extent not prohibited by section 200 of the Companies Act 1963,[56] or the maintenance of a contract of insurance to the extent contemplated by that section (whether for a director of the company or a director of any of its subsidiary undertakings;

(g) the transaction is an underwriting by the related party of all or part of an issue of securities by the company (or any of its subsidiary under-takings) and the consideration to be paid by the company (or any of its subsidiary undertakings) in respect of such underwriting is no more than the usual commercial underwriting consideration and is the same as that to be paid to the other underwriters (if any);

(h) the terms and circumstances of the investment or provision of finance by the company, or any of its subsidiary undertakings are, in the opinion of an independent adviser acceptable to the Exchange, no less favourable than those applicable to the investment or provision of finance by the related party; or

   (i) the transaction is one where each of the percentage ratios referred to in paragraph 10.5 is equal to or less than 0.25%."

5–47 Paragraph 11.8 of the Listing Rules provides that the usual requirements set out in paragraph 11.4 do not apply in the case of a transaction with the related party where each of the percentage ratios referred to in paragraph 10.5 of the Listing Rules is less than 5 per cent, but one or more exceeds 0.25 per cent. Instead however, prior to completing the transaction, the company must provide the Exchange with written details of the proposed transaction and written confirmation from an independent adviser, acceptable to the Exchange, that the terms of the proposed transaction are fair and reasonable so far as the shareholders of the company are concerned. The company must also furnish the Exchange with a written undertaking to include details of the transaction in the company's next published annual accounts. These details should include, where relevant, the identity of the related party, the value of the consideration for the transaction and all other relevant circumstances.

---

[56] As amended by section 3 of the Companies (Amendment) Act 1983.

C. Listing of Securities

5–48   If the offeror is a listed company, it may decide to finance the bid by issuing new securities and offering them to the public to raise cash for the acquisition. Alternatively, the offeror may issue new shares and offer them as consideration in exchange for shares in the offeree. Often a combination of shares and cash will be offered as consideration. In order to make these securities more marketable, the issuer will wish to apply to have them listed. Even if the issuer were not to make this decision voluntarily, a requirement exists to have the new securities listed. Paragraph I of Schedule C of the Admissions Directive states that in the case of a new public issue of shares of the same class as those already officially listed, the company shall be required, where the new shares are not automatically admitted, to apply for their admission to the same listing, either not more than a year after their issue or when they become freely transferable. Paragraph 9.33 of the Listing Rules implements this obligation in a more stringent manner by providing:

> "When further securities are allotted of the same class as securities already listed, application for listing such further securities must be made not more than one month after allotment."

I. BRINGING SECURITIES TO A LISTING

5–49   Chapter 4 of the Listing Rules describes the different methods by which securities may be brought to listing. Applicants with equity shares already listed generally bring securities to listing by one of the following methods: an offer for sale; a placing; a rights issue; an open offer; an acquisition or merger issue or a vendor consideration placing.

(1) An Offer for Sale

5–50   An offer for sale involves selling the shares to the public. The company normally agrees to allot the shares to an issuing house or broker who in turn makes an offer to the public to sell the shares. The issuing house is rewarded by selling at a somewhat higher price or by charging an underwriting commission. The shares would normally be sub-underwritten. An offer for sale is defined in the Listing Rules as:

> "an invitation to the public by, or on behalf of, a third party to purchase securities of the issuer already in issue or allotted. This may be in the form of an invitation to tender at or above a stated minimum price".[57]

---

[57] Listing Rules, para. 4.4.

The main advantage for the issuer is that the intermediary bears the entire risk and most of the administrative burdens.

5–51 By contrast, an offer for subscription involves the company offering the shares directly to the public. These shares will be under-written by a merchant bank or other intermediary. The company thus bears all the costs of the issue. This method is very uncommon in Ireland, and in the UK is only associated with very large and well known companies. An offer for subscription is defined in the Listing Rules as: "an invitation to the public by, or on behalf of an issuer to subscribe for securities of the issuer not yet in issue or allotted". This offer may also be in the form of an invitation to tender at or above a stated minimum price.[58]

(2) A Placing

5–52 A placing involves the sponsoring broker arranging to sell the majority of shares that the company is selling to institutions and private investors under firm commitments. Occasionally, the broker may simply arrange for investors to take the shares directly from the company itself. A "Private Placing" means selling shares without seeking a Stock Exchange quotation. The shares are sold to long term investors. A placing is defined in the Listing Rules as:

> "a marketing of securities already in issue but not listed or not yet in issue, to specified persons or clients of the sponsor or any securities house assis-ting in the placing, which does not involve an offer to the public or to existing holders of the issuer's securities generally".[59]

Where the securities are shares of a class already listed, the shares will normally be sold at a discount to the market unless there is strong institutional demand. However, the placing price may not be at a discount of more than 10 per cent to the middle market price of those securities at the time of the placing. An exception may be allowed, however, where the Exchange is satisfied that the issuer is in severe financial difficulties or there are other exceptional circumstances. The ISE will thus expect to receive a pricing statement completed by the issuer's sponsor before considering the application.[60]

(3) A Rights Issue

5–53 A rights issue involves an offer to existing holders of a com-pany's securities to subscribe for or purchase new securities in a fixed

---

[58] Listing Rules, para. 4.5.
[59] Listing Rules, para. 4.7.
[60] Listing Rules, paras 4.8–4.9.

proportion to their existing holdings. The objective of this is to raise capital while avoiding the dilution of existing holdings. Although, it might appear that pre-emption rights oblige a company to issue shares in this way, as will be seen in paragraphs 5–58–5–60 of this text, pre-emption rights may be disapplied. While, in theory, this method of raising capital is available to public and private companies, the practicalities are such that it will normally only be used by companies with a broad shareholder base, usually acquired as a result of a Stock Exchange quotation. The price of the issue will normally be at a discount to the market (typically around 13–15 per cent). A rights issue is defined in the Listing Rules as:

> "an offer to existing holders of securities to subscribe or purchase further securities in proportion to their holdings made by means of the issue of a renounceable letter (or other negotiable document) which may be traded (as 'nil paid' rights) for a period before payment for the securities is due".[61]

In a placing of rights arising from the issue of shares before the official start of dealings, paragraph 4.17 of the Listing Rules requires that a number of conditions must be satisfied. Firstly, the placing must relate to at least 25% of the maximum number of securities offered. However, a lesser amount may be allowed if the Exchange is satisfied that a requirement of at least 25% would be detrimental to the success of the issue. Secondly, the placees must have committed to take up whatever number of shares is placed with them. Thirdly, the price paid by the placees must not exceed the price at which the securities the subject of the rights issue are offered by more than one half of the calculated premium over the offer price. The premium is the difference between the offer price and the theoretical ex-rights price. Finally, the securities the subject of the rights issue must be of the same class as securities already listed. Paragraph 4.21 of the Listing Rules requires the offer to remain open for at least 21 days. In addition, the circular to shareholders must contain a table of market values for the securities of the same class as those offered for the first dealing day in each of the preceding six months, for the last dealing day before the announcement of the rights issue and the latest practicable date prior to the despatch of the circular.

If existing holders of securities do not take up their rights to subscribe in a rights issue, paragraph 4.19 of the Listing Rules provides that the securities must be offered for subscription or purchase on terms that any premium obtained over the subscription or purchase price net of expenses will be held on trust for such holders. There is a minimum provision however, and if the proceeds are £3 or less, they may be retained for the benefit of the company. The securities not taken up may be allotted or sold to underwriters if a premium has not been

---

[61] Listing Rules, para. 4.16.

obtained upon the expiry of the subscription period. Excess applications are only permitted upon the receipt of the Exchange's prior written permission.

An open offer is an invitation to existing holders of securities to subscribe or purchase securities in proportion to their holdings, which is not made by means of a renounceable letter (or other negotiable document).[62]

(4) An Acquisition or Merger Issue

5–54   An acquisition or merger issue (or vendor consideration issue) is "an issue of securities in consideration of an acquisition of assets, or an issue of securities on an acquisition of, or merger with, another company as consideration for the securities of that other company."[63] In this kind of issue, no marketing of any securities proposed to be issued as consideration for a takeover offer may be carried out during an offer period, as defined in the Takeover Rules.[63a]

(5) A Vendor Placing

5–55   A "Vendor Placing" is an arrangement whereby, on the acquisition of a target company by a quoted company, instead of the offeror issuing shares in consideration to the vendor, the offerors shares will be placed with institutional investors. The vendor then gets the cash proceeds. A vendor consideration placing is defined in the Listing Rules as: "a marketing, by or on behalf of vendors, of securities that have been allotted to them as consideration for an acquisition".[64] In such a placing, all vendors must have an equal opportunity of participating in the placing.[64a] Where the securities to be placed are equity securities of a class already listed, the placing price must not be at a discount of more than 10 per cent to the middle market price of those securities at the time of the placing, unless the Exchange allows otherwise and a pricing statement must be submitted.[65] Where the securities are equity securities of a class not already listed:[66] the securities in issue must be sufficiently widely held; no shares may be placed with connected clients of the sponsor or of any securities house or other intermediary assisting with the offer;[67] the results of the marketing must be notified

---

[62] Listing Rules, para. 4.22.
[63] Listing Rules, para. 4.27.
[63a] Listing Rules, para. 4.28.
[64] Listing Rules, para. 4.29.
[64a] Listing Rules, para. 4.30(a).
[65] Listing Rules, para. 4.30(b).
[66] Listing Rules, para. 4.30(c).
[67] Unless placed with a market maker or fund manager for the purpose of its business.

to the CAO before dealings commence; if following the placing, the sponsor or broker assisting with the offer becomes interested in 3 per cent or more of any class of equity shares being marketed, the interest must be notified to the CAO before dealings commence; and a shareholder statement should be completed by the sponsor and submitted to the Exchange before the consideration of the listing application.

5–56 The Irish Association of Investment Managers have suggested that a vendor placing should be made with "a clawback" if it involves more than 5 per cent of the issued share capital or if is issued at a discount of more than 5 per cent. The reason for this is that a vendor placing would otherwise avoids pre-emption rights because the shares are issued for a non cash consideration. A "placing with a clawback" is an option to an underwritten rights issue. The shares are placed initially with the investors, on terms that if any of the shareholders wish to take up their proportional entitlement, such shares will be "clawed back" from the placees. Such a placing does require the placees to be flexible as to the amount of shares they receive.

(6) Other

5–57 Other less common methods of bringing securities to listing are: a capitalisation issue, an offer for subscription; an issue for cash, a conversion of securities of one class into securities of another class, an exercise of options or warrants to subscribe securities; or any such other method as the Exchange accepts either generally or in any particular case.

II. PRE-EMPTION RIGHTS

5–58 The Listing Rules previously insisted as a requirement of listing that a company offer its shares on a pre-emptive basis unless the shareholders in general meeting decided otherwise. This meant that each specific allotment had to be put to shareholders for their approval. It subsequently became clear that this position was too restrictive and hindered companies' freedom to raise capital as quickly and as cheaply as possible. In addition, a rights issue rather than a cash placing did not lead to improved liquidity as the shareholder base was not expanded. The Listing Rules were thus modified.

5–59 Paragraph 9.18 of the Listing Rules provides that a company proposing to issue equity securities for cash must first offer those securities to existing equity shareholders and to holders of other equity securities of the company who are entitled to be offered them in proportion to their existing holdings. Only to the extent that the securities are not taken up by such persons under the offer may they then be issued for cash to others.[68]

5–60 In a rights issue or open offer, pre-emption rights need not apply in respect of securities representing fractional entitlement, or securities where the directors of the company consider it necessary or expedient to exclude securities from the offer on account of either legal problems or the requirements of a regulatory body.[69] In addition, the Exchange allows a disapplication of pre-emption rights to the extent that shareholders give their authorisation under section 24 of the Companies (Amendment) Act 1983, to the general disapplication of the statutory pre-emption rights set out in section 23 of the Companies (Amendment) Act 1983.[70] Circulars issued in connection with a resolution proposing to grant directors authority to allot relevant securities must include a statement of the maximum amount of relevant securities which the disapplication will cover. In the case of a general disapplication in respect of equity securities, the circular should also include the percentage which the amount generally disapplied represents of the total ordinary share capital in issue as at a date not more than one month prior to the date of the circular.[71]

III. PROSPECTUS REQUIREMENTS

5–61 In general, where shares are offered to the public[72] for which a listing is being sought, the rules governing prospectuses and listing particulars apply. Section 44(3) of the Companies Act 1963 renders it unlawful to issue any form of application for securities unless the form is issued with a prospectus. A prospectus is defined as:

> "any prospectus, notice, circular, advertisement or other invitation, offering to the public for subscription or purchase any shares or debentures of a company."[73]

All prospectuses must comply with the Companies Act 1963 and the Prospectus Directive.[74] The contents of the prospectus are strictly specified in order to ensure that investors have sufficient information to

---

[68] Listing Rules, para. 9.18.
[69] Listing Rules, para. 9.19.
[70] Listing Rules, para. 9.20.
[71] Listing Rules, para. 14.8.
[72] Section 61 of the Companies Act 1963 defines an offer of securities to the "public" as "including a reference to offering them to any section of the public, whether selected as members or debenture holders of the company concerned or as clients of the person issuing the prospectus or in any other manner". See paras 14–06–14–11.
[73] Companies Act 1963, s.2.
[74] Council Directive 89/298/EEC as implemented by the European Communities (Transferable Securities and Stock Exchange) Regulations, 1992 (S.I. No. 202 of 1992).

allow them make an informed decision.[75] Civil and criminal liability is imposed for misstatements in the prospectus.[76] Because of the overlap between the regulations governing prospectuses and listing particulars, where securities are offered to the public for which a listing is to be sought, the contents of the prospectus, the procedures for submission of the prospectus to and approval by the ISE and for the publication of the prospectus are generally deemed to be the same as those applicable to listing particulars.[77]

IV. LISTING PARTICULARS

(1) Conditions for Listing

5–62 Where securities are to be to be admitted to official listing, Schedules A and B of the Admissions Directive set out the conditions relating to the companies and the conditions relating to the securities for which the admission to official listing is sought. Article 3 of the Admissions Directive imposes an obligation on Member States to ensure that securities will not be admitted to official listing on any stock exchange situated or operating within their territory unless issuers are subject to the conditions sets out in the Directive. Article 5(1) of the Admissions Directive also allows Member States to impose "more stringent conditions" or "additional conditions" on the admission of securities "provided that these more stringent and additional conditions apply generally for all issuers or for individual classes of issuer" and provided that "they have been published before application for admission of such securities is made".[78] Additional conditions for listing have been introduced by the Irish Stock Exchange in Chapter 3 of the Listing Rules. The issuer must be duly incorporated or otherwise validly established according to the relevant laws of its place of incorporation or establishment.[78a] It must furnish audited accounts for at least three years although accounts for a lesser period may be accepted if the Stock Exchange feels that this is desirable in the interests of the company or investors and the investors have sufficient information to make an informed decision.[78b]

---

[75] Section 45(1) of the Companies Act 1963 requires the prospectus to meet the informational requirements set out in the Third Schedule. Sections II and II set out the contents and arrangements for the scrutiny and distribution of the prospectus for transferable securities.

[76] Companies Act 1963, ss. 49 & 50.

[77] Section 45 of the Companies Act 1963, Art. 7 of the Prospectus Directive and paragraph 5.1(d) of the Listing Rules.

[78] This is mirrored in r. 3 of S.I. No. 282 of 1984.

[78a] Listing Rules, para. 3.2.

[78b] Listing Rules, para. 3.3. Exceptions may also be made in respect of an issue of guaranteed debt securities where the guarantor has three year accounts or in respect

The issuer must be carrying on an independent business which is revenue earning and has been so for the period of the accounts and there should be continuity of management throughout the period of the accounts.[78c] Directors must have appropriate expertise and experience and be free from conflicts of interest or have made arrangements to avoid detriment to the company's interests.[78d] A working capital statement must be included in the listing particulars demonstrating that sufficient capital is available to meet present requirements.[78e] Finally, the issuer must be able to show that there is a decision making function independent of controlling shareholders.[78f] The rules relating to securities require that the securities be valid and freely transferable.[78g] Except where securities of the same class are already listed, the expected aggregate market value of all securities to be listed must be at least £700,000 for shares and £200,000 for debt securities. Securities of lower value may be admitted however, if the Exchange is satisfied that there will be sufficient liquidity.[78h] Where an application for listing of a class of shares has been made, a sufficient number of shares of that class must be distributed to the public no later than the time of admission. This generally means that at least 25% shares should be in public hands.[78i] If no securities of that class are already listed, an application for listing must relate to the whole class of securities, issued or proposed to be issued. If securities of that class are already listed, the application must relate to all further securities of that class.[78j] Where the issuer already has shares of the same class listed, the obligations are less onerous.

---

of debt securities generally where the obligations created by the securities are fully secured.

[78c] Listing Rules, para. 3.6. Para. 3.6A provides for the admission of a company which fails to meet this requirement, if the Exchange is satisfied that such admission is desirable in the interests of the company and investors and that investors have sufficient information to arrive at an informed decision concerning both the company and the securities.

[78d] Listing Rules, paras. 3.8 & 3.9.

[78e] Listing Rules, para. 3.10. Para. 3.11 exempts issuers from the requirement to prepare such a statement where the issuer's business is entirely or substantially that of banking, insurance or the provision of similar financial services. In such cases, the Exchange would need to be satisfied that a working capital statement would not provide significant information to investors and that the issuer's solvency and capital adequacy requirements are suitable regulated.

[78f] Listing Rules, para. 3.12.

[78g] Listing Rules, paras. 3.14 and 3.15.

[78h] Listing Rules, paras. 3.16 and 3.17.

[78i] Listing Rules, paras. 3.18–3.21.

[78j] Listing Rules, para. 3.22.

(2) Requirements Relating to Listing Particulars

5–63 In addition to complying with the conditions for listing, the issuer must generally compile and publish an informational document termed "the listing particulars" in accordance with the Listing Particulars Directive and Chapters 5 and Appendix 1 to Chapter 5 of the Listing Rules. The requirement to comply with Chapter 5 and appendix 1 is however subject to the following:

(a) references in Chapter 6 to the issuer's group will not generally include the offeree company and its subsidiaries unless it has become a member of the issuer's group by the time the listing particulars are published;

(b) the information regarding major interests in shares and directors' interests in shares must be given in relation to the issuer's share capital both as existing and as enlarged by the shares for which listing is sought; and

(c) If the offer is recommended by the offeree board at the time of publication of the offer document, the issuer must publish working capital and indebtedness statements on the basis that the acquisition has taken place. If the offer is not recommended, at the time of publication of the offer document, the issuer must publish its own working capital and indebtedness statements and then subsequently publish the statements on the combined basis in a circular or supplementary listing particulars published within 28 days after the offer is declared wholly unconditional. In the latter case, the listing particulars must state that the statements on the combined basis will be available as soon as possible.[79]

(3) Contents of Listing Particulars

5–64 Chapter 6 sets out the contents of the listing particulars. The listing particulars provide shareholders with very detailed information concerning: the persons for listing particulars, the auditors and other advisers; the shares for which application is being made; the issuer and its capital; the group's activities; the issuer's assets and liabilities, financial position and profit and losses; the management; and the recent development and prospects of the group.

(4) Supplementary Listing Particulars

5–65 Apart from being necessary as a result of the original terms of an offer consisting of securities for which a listing will be sought, listing particulars may also be necessary as a result of a revision of the terms

---

[79] Listing Rules, para. 10.47.

during the course of an offer. Where listing particulars have already been published and the offer is revised, supplementary listing particulars may also be required.[80] Where a securities exchange offer has been revised to include a new class of debenture for which listing is to be obtained, it will not be necessary to repeat the information contained in the original listing particulars, only any additional information appropriate to the issue of the securities.[81]

(5) Publication and Circulation

5–66   Listing particulars or supplementary listing particulars must be published and circulated as set out in Chapter 8 of the Listing Rules. Paragraph 8.1 of the Listing Rules prohibits the publication of listing particulars until they have been formally approved by the Stock Exchange. Listing particulars must be available for a period of at least 14 days commencing on the earliest of (a) the day the listing particulars or notice of them is published in the national press (b) the day after listing particulars are dispatched to shareholders and (c) the day on which admission to listing is expected to become effective.[81a] In addition, a formal notice must be inserted in a national paper no later than the next business day following publication of the listing particulars, unless the securities are of a class already listed. In the case of offers to the public for sale or subscription, the issuer may elect to insert either full listing particulars or a mini-prospectus or an offer notice, in a national paper.[81b] Listing Particulars must generally be published at least two business days prior to the expected date of the consideration of the application for admission to listing.[81c] Paragraphs 8.14–8.19 of the Listing Rules provide for the circulation of listing particulars. Where listing particulars are produced in respect of securities issued in consideration of a takeover or merger, the offeree's shareholders must be circularised by the issuer with either a copy of listing particulars, summary particulars or issue note with the offer document.[81d] Where supplementary listing particulars have been produced in respect of securities issued in consideration for a takeover or merger, the supplementary listing particulars must be published and circulated to the offeree's shareholders unless the Exchange agrees otherwise.[81e] The Listing Rules allow for the incorporation of listing particulars, supplementary listing particulars or issue note in the relevant circular or offer document only if they are set out in a separate specially

---

[80]   Listing Rules, para. 10.46.
[81]   Listing Rules, para. 10.50.
[81a] Listing Rules, para. 8.5
[81b] Listing Rules, para. 8.7
[81c] Listing Rules, para. 8.8
[81d] Listing Rules, para. 8.15.
[81e] Listing Rules, para. 8.16

designated section.[81f] On a reverse takeover, the issuers shareholders must receive listing particulars with the Class I circular.[81g] In other circumstances where holders of securities must be circularised, the listing particulars need not be sent out unless those shareholders are being offered an opportunity to subscribe for, or acquire, the securities concerned. If the listing particulars are not sent out with the circular, the circular should state that they are available on request from the issuer.[81h] Where the listing particulars are revised or supplementary listing particulars are published, they must normally be published and circulated to shareholders at the time of dispatch of the revised offer document.[82]

(6) Exemptions

5–67   In certain circumstances, the issuer may be exempt from the obligation to publish listing particulars. Article 6 of the Listing Particulars Directive allows Member States to permit the competent authorities to provide for complete or partial exemption from the obligation to publish listing particulars in certain situations. Article 6.1 allows exemptions where the securities for which admission to listing is sought are:

(a) securities which have been the subject of a public issue;

(b) securities issued in connection with a takeover offer; or

(c) securities issued in connection with a merger involving the acquisition of another company or the formation of a new company, the division of a company, the transfer of all or part of an undertaking's assets and liabilities or as consideration for the transfer of assets other than cash.

This exemption applies only where, not more than 12 months before the admission of the securities to official listing, a document containing information equivalent to that of the listing particulars has been published in the same Member State. Paragraph 5.23A(a) of the Listing Rules contains the same exemption.

In such a case where an exemption is given, an exempt listing document must be published, setting out details of any material changes which have occurred since the publication of the relevant document, a statement that an application has been made for the listing of the securities specifying the number and class of the securities in question, a directors' responsibility statement and the relevant document.[82a]

Further exemptions are set out in Articles 6.2–6–5 of the Listing Particulars Directive and paragraphs 5.23A(b) & (c) and 5.27. Listing

---

[81f] Listing Rules, para. 8.17.
[81g] Listing Rules, para. 8.18.
[81h] Listing Rules, para. 8.19.
[82]   Listing Rules, para. 10.48.
[82a] Listing Rules, para. 5.24.

particulars are not generally required for example, for issues of shares by an issuer whose shares are already listed where the issue would increase the shares of a class already listed by less than 10%.

V. ENFORCEMENT

5–68   The Stock Exchange Listing Rules expressly require issuers to comply with all Listing Rules applicable to them. Paragraphs 1.8–1.10 of the Listing Rules provide for the imposition of sanctions. If the Exchange considers that an issuer has contravened the Listing Rules, it will refer the issue to the Quotations Committee unless the issuer or director concerned agrees to a private censure by the Exchange and the Exchange considers this an appropriate sanction. If the matter is referred to the Quotations Committee and the Committee finds that the Listing Rules have been contravened by the issuer, the issuer may be censured and the censure may be published. As a more serious alternative, the Committee may decide to suspend or cancel the listing of the issuer's securities. If the Committee determines that any contravention is due to a failure of any of the issuer's directors to discharge their responsibilities under the listing rules, the director may be censured and the censure may be published. Where the director wilfully or persistently fails to discharge his responsibilities following such a censure, the Committee may recommend the removal of the director from his or her office, and they may suspend or cancel the issuer's listing if the director remains in office.

5–69   The threat of a suspension or cancellation is obviously more potent than that of censure. According to the Listing Rules a suspension will be effected where the "smooth operation of the market is, or may be, temporarily jeopardised or where protection of investors so requires".[83] A cancellation may take place where the Exchange is satisfied that "special circumstances exist which preclude normal regular dealings in the securities".[84] The consequences of a suspension or a cancellation are far reaching and these sanctions will only be imposed in extreme circumstances. One difficulty is that the effect of either a suspension or a cancellation is to penalise not only the issuer who has contravened the rules but also the shareholders whose shares suddenly become less marketable. In certain circumstances, this may amount to a double penalty: shareholders loose when the issuer contravenes the listing rules by not disclosing information to them and they loose when the share listing is suspended or cancelled.

---

[83]   Listing Rules, para. 1.19.
[84]   Listing Rules, para. 1.22.

CHAPTER 6

COMPETITION LAW

6–01   Part A of this chapter examines European Community competition law and policy. This is relevant to Irish companies in three regards. First, where Irish companies merge with or acquire or are acquired by companies incorporated in other Member States, European Community law applies. Secondly, mergers between Irish companies may affect trade between Member States and are subject in this way to European Community law. Thirdly, some domestic regulation contains similar concepts and similar wording to that in European Community law and the Irish Courts and regulatory authorities in resolving issues arising under domestic regulation have referred to, and in some cases followed, the approaches adopted by the European Commission, the European Court of First Instance and the European Court of Justice. Part B of this chapter examines domestic competition law in so far as it regulates mergers and takeovers. Finally, Part C of this chapter involves a brief analysis of UK domestic legislation. As UK companies remain the most likely foreign candidates as acquisition targets and as offerors, such a study is justified.

A. European Competition Law

I. ARTICLE 81 OF THE TREATY OF ROME (PREVIOUSLY ARTICLE 85)*

6–02   Article 81 of the Treaty of Rome deals with anti-competitive agreements which may appreciably affect trade between Member States. It states:

> "1.   The following shall be prohibited as incompatible with the common market; all agreements between undertakings, decisions by associations of undertakings and concerted practices which may affect trade between Member States and which have as their object or effect the prevention, restriction or distortion of competition within the common market, and in particular those which:

---

* NOTE   This chapter refers to Article 81 and 82 of the Treaty of Rome. As a result of the Ratification of the Treaty of Amsterdam, Articles 85 and 86 were renumbered Article 81 and Article 82, respectively. As the case law considered refers to the old numbering, references have been changed in this text for ease of reference.

(a) directly or indirectly fix purchase or selling prices or any other trading conditions;

(b) limit or control production, markets, technical development, or investment;

(c) share markets or sources of supply;

(d) apply dissimilar conditions to equivalent transactions with other trading parties, thereby placing them at a competitive disadvantage;

(e) make the conclusion of contracts subject to acceptance by the other parties of supplementary obligations which, by their nature or according to commercial usage, have no connection with the subject of such contracts."

Article 81(2) provides that "[a]ny agreements or decisions prohibited pursuant to this Article shall be automatically void".

In a *Memorandum on the Concentration of Enterprises in the Common Market* in 1966, the Commission stated that Article [81] was not applicable to agreements "whose purpose is the acquisition of total or partial ownership of enterprises or the reorganisation of the ownership of enterprises."[1] The suggestion was that structural changes would be dealt with under Article [82].[2] Subsequent European Court of Justice caselaw has however suggested that Article [81] may indeed be relevant to structural changes in the market.

(1) Agreements Producing Structural Changes

6–03   The most important case on the application of Article 81 to mergers and takeovers is *British American Tobacco Co Ltd. and R.J. Reynolds Industries Inc. v. Commission*.[3] In 1981, Philip Morris Inc. a New York cigarette manufacturer, purchased 50 per cent of the shares in Rothmans Tobacco (Holdings) Ltd. from a South African company Rembrandt Group Ltd.. Rothmans Tobacco (Holdings) Ltd. held a controlling interest in Rothmans International plc, another major cigarette manufacturer. Rembrandt Group Ltd. agreed with Philip Morris Inc. that the activities of Rothmans International plc should be managed on a joint basis. Following complaints by competitors, the Commission challenged this arrangement under both Articles [81] and [82]. Following discussions with the Commission, the parties proposed new arrangements under which Philip Morris Inc. gave up its shareholding in Rothmans Tobacco (Holdings) Ltd. in exchange for a direct shareholding in Rothmans International plc. That holding accounted for 30.8 per cent of the total shares in Rothmans International plc but represented only 24.9 per cent of the voting rights in the company. Rembrandt Group Ltd. thus retained

---

[1] EEC Competition Series Study No. 3 at para. 58.
[2] Article [82] prohibits the abuse of a dominant position. See below paras 6–10–6–16.
[3] Cases 142 and 156/84 [1987] E.C.R. 4487; [1988] 4 C.M.L.R. 24.

full control. The new agreement, which was approved of by the Commission, contained a number of terms restricting future disposals of shareholdings by each side. The agreement gave each side a right of first refusal should the other wish to dispose of its shareholding and if the other side chose not to exercise this right and a third party purchaser was found, the entire shareholding had either to be disposed of for cash to a single purchaser or to ten or more independent purchasers. Furthermore, the agreement stipulated that if Rembrandt Group Ltd. disposed of its shares to a single purchaser, this purchaser would be required to make a comparable offer for the shareholding of Philip Morris Inc. In the event of any such disposal, an adjustment of voting rights would be required. Philip Morris Inc. gave undertakings to the Commission not to be represented on the board of Rothmans International plc and that information of a sensitive competitive nature would not pass between the two companies. Two competitors of Philip Morris and Rothmans, British-American Tobacco (BAT) and R.J. Reynolds, appealed the Commission's decision to the European Court of Justice. In a landmark judgment, the Court upheld the Commission's assessment of the revised agreements but made it clear that Article [81] may apply to the acquisition of, at least, a minority shareholding in a competitor.

6–04   The Court identified the main issue as "whether and in what circumstances the acquisition of a minority shareholding in a competing company may constitute an infringement of Articles [81 and 82] of the Treaty."[4] (It might be argued thus that the case only holds that Article [81] applies to the acquisition of minority shareholdings.) The Court continued:

> "Since the acquisition of shares in Rothmans International was the subject matter of agreements entered into by companies which have remained independent after the entry into force of the agreements, the issue must be examined first of all from the point of view of Article [81]."[5]

A second potential limitation stemming from this statement is that Article 81 may only apply to companies which have remained independent after the entry into force of the agreements. None of the aforementioned factors were referred to by the Court in its broad statement of principle as follows:

> "Although the acquisition by one company of an equity interest in a competitor does not in itself constitute conduct restricting competition, such an acquisition may nevertheless serve as an instrument for influencing the commercial conduct of the companies in question so as to restrict or distort competition on the market on which they carry on business. That will be

---

[4]   *ibid.*, para. 30.
[5]   *ibid.*, para. 31.

true in particular where, by the acquisition of a shareholding or through subsidiary clauses in the agreement, the investing company obtains legal or *de facto* control of the commercial conduct of the other company or whether the agreement provides for commercial co-operation between the companies or creates a structure likely to be used for such co-operation. That may also be the case where the agreement gives the investing company the possibility of reinforcing its position at a later stage and taking effective control of the other company. Account must be taken not only of the immediate effects of the agreement but also of its potential effects and of the possibility that the agreement may be part of a long-term plan. Finally, every agreement must be assessed in its economic context and in particular in the light of the situation on the relevant market."[6]

One possible limitation which is, however, alluded to in the above general statement is that the use of Article [81] is limited to mergers involving competing companies. While this clearly includes horizontal mergers, it might not include vertical ones. A great deal of controversy has attended on the interpretation of this judgment and the limitations applicable to it.[7]

6–05   Subsequently, the Commission has intervened in several merger-type cases including the Irish Distillers case.[8] However, since 1989, no action has been taken by the Commission under Article [81] and it has confined its investigations of mergers to the Merger Control Regulation.[9] However, Korah has pointed out that:

"In Ireland, with only a weak merger control law but provisions modelled on Articles [81 and 82], the uncertainties of the judgment are highly relevant and may have to be worked out through the High Court".[10]

(2) Acquisition of Minority Holdings

6–06   There has, however, been caselaw on the application of Article [81] to transactions which do not involve the acquisition of control. In *BAT and Reynolds*, the complainants argued that a sale of a minority stake by an alleged dominant vendor to a competitor constituted a breach of Article [81]. This case confirmed beyond doubt that Article 81 (and Article 82) may apply to share acquisitions which do not give the acquirer either sole or joint control of the company in which the shares

---

[6] *ibid.*, paras. 37–40.
[7] Downes and Ellison, *The Legal Control of Mergers in the European Communities* (Blackstone Press Ltd. 1991) Chap. 1, para. 1.1.3.4. Van Bael and Bellis, *Competition Law of the European Community* (CCH Europe, 3rd ed., 1994), Chap. 6.
[8] 1988 21 Bulletin of EC 7–7/34.
[9] Council Regulation 4064/89 (as amended by Regulation 1310/97). See paras 6.19–6.39.
[10] Korah, "EC Precedents in Controlling Mergers before implementation of the Mergers Regulation" in *Second Annual Seminar on Mergers & Competition Law*, p. 9, (Competition Press Dublin, 1997). Irish competition law will be examined below in paras 6–60 *et seq.*

are purchased. By contrast, in *Warner-Lambert/Gillette*,[11] it was the purchase of a minority stake by a dominant purchaser which constituted the breach. In that case, Gillette, a company with a dominant position in the wet shaving products market, acquired a 22 per cent non-voting equity holding in Eemland, a major competitor. Gillette was also Eemland's largest creditor. Eemland owned Wilkinson Sword in Europe and in the U.S. while Gillette had already purchased outright the Wilkinson Sword business in the rest of the world The acquisition of the interest in Eemland gave Gillette a number of important pre-emption and conversion rights in Eemland. The Commission admitted that the acquisition of the non-voting equity interest did not in itself infringe Article [81]. However, the trade mark separation agreement between Eemland and Gillette not to sell products under the Wilkinson Sword trade mark in each other's territories was viewed as liable to result in co-ordination between the two companies in breach of Article [81]. The purchase by Gillette of products from Eemland for sale outside the E.C. was also held to result in co-ordination between Eemland and Gillette in violation of Article [81]. The Commission also found that there was an abuse of a dominant position contrary to Article [82] because, despite the fact that the acquisition gave Gillette no board representation and no voting rights, the Commission determined that it would allow Gillette by other means exercise some influence over Eemland's commercial conduct. The Commission stressed that special responsibility was placed on a dominant company not to allow its conduct to impair genuine undistorted competition. The Commission thus ordered Gillette to dispose of its equity interest in Eemland. Van Bael and Bellis have stated that this case suggests that the effects of the acquisition of a minority stake by a dominant company may be viewed more strictly under Article [82] than Article [81].[12]

(3) Exemptions

6–07   Article 81(3) allows the Commission to exempt certain agreements from the prohibition contained in Article 81(1) where their net effect for consumers is positive. It provides as follows:

> "The provisions of paragraph 1 may, however, be declared inapplicable in the case of;
> – any agreement or category of agreements between undertakings;
> – any decision or category of decisions by associations of undertakings;
> – any concerted practice or category of concerted practices;
> which contributes to improving the production or distribution of goods or to promoting technical or economic progress, while allowing consumers a fair share of the resulting benefit, and which does not:

---

[11] [1993] O.J. L116/21.
[12] *op.cit.*, n.7 at 370.

(a) impose on the undertakings concerned restrictions which are not indispensable to the attainment of these objectives;

(b) afford such undertakings the possibility of eliminating competition in respect of a substantial part of the products in question."

In order to obtain an exemption the four criteria referred to above must be satisfied. The agreement must: improve the production or distribution of goods or promote technical or economic progress; allow consumers a fair share of the benefit; contain only restrictions which are indispensable to the attainment of the agreement's objective; and not lead to the elimination of competition in respect of a substantial part of the goods in question. Having met these criteria, either an individual exemption or a block exemption may be sought. The latter is used to exclude certain generic agreements from the scope of Article 81 obviating the need for a separate notification to the Commission each time an agreement of this type occurs. Block exemptions have been granted by the Commission in the past for a number of areas including research and development, technology transfer and exclusive distribution agreements. The main advantage of notifying an agreement and seeking an exemption is that it provides the companies with an immunity from fines in the event that the agreement is ultimately found to be unlawful.

6–08   The Article 81(3) exemption mechanism is not really appropriate for a merger or acquisition. Only a small number of individual exemptions are granted each year and comfort letters may be sent instead to the parties. These letters express merely the opinion of the Commission. Although a comfort letter is not binding, the European Court of Justice in *Guerlain*[13] noted that a national court may take the views expressed by the Commission in such a letter into account. In addition, completing the notification form involves a lot of time and effort and a delay may be expected before the Commission responds to the notification. The exemption once received may be absolute or it may be subject to conditions and obligations. Furthermore, exemptions are only granted for a limited time subject to renewal and clearly this would not be appropriate in the case of a merger or acquisition agreement.

(4) Enforcement

6–09   There is no requirement to notify the Commission in advance of likely infringements. This means that the Commission may only become aware of certain anti-competitive agreements at a late stage. Although Article 81(2) provides that all agreements which violate

---

[13] *Procureur de la Republique and Others v. Bruno Giry and Guerlain* Case 253/78 E.C.R. 2327; [1981] 2 C.M.L.R. 99.

Article 81(1) are null and void, it is expensive and administratively difficult to unwind a completed takeover or merger. Pre-notification of such an agreement would obviously be more efficient.

II. ARTICLE [82] OF THE TREATY OF ROME (PREVIOUSLY ARTICLE [86])

6–10 Article 82 prohibits the abuse of a dominant position within or in a substantial part of the European Community. It states:

> "Any abuse by one or more undertakings of a dominant position within the common market or in a substantial part of it shall be prohibited as incompatible with the common market in so far as it may affect trade between Member States. Such abuse may, in particular, consist in:
> (a) directly or indirectly imposing unfair purchase or selling prices or unfair trading conditions;
> (b) limiting production, markets or technical development to the prejudice of consumers;
> (c) applying dissimilar conditions to equivalent transactions with other trading parties, thereby placing them at a competitive disadvantage;
> (d) making the conclusion of contracts subject to acceptance by other parties of supplementary obligations which, by their nature or according to commercial usage, have no connection with the subject of such contracts."

(1) Relevant Market

6–11 In order to determine whether a firm enjoys a dominant position in the market, it is necessary firstly to define that market. This may be done in terms of the product or service provided and in terms of the geographic area. In determining the relevant product market, both the product or service provided by the firm and any substitutable or interchangeable products or services on both the supply and the demand side are considered. Substitutability is determined on the basis of the products' characteristics, their prices and their intended use.[14] The relevant geographic market is defined as "the area in which the undertakings concerned are involved in the supply and demand of products or services, in which the conditions of competition are sufficiently homogeneous and which can be distinguished from neighbouring areas because the conditions of competition are appreciably different in those areas."[15] In order to assess whether an undertaking has a dominant position, the relevant market is assessed in terms of the combination of product and geographic markets. The relevant market is currently defined in a Commission Notice mainly by reference to substitutes on the demand side. Demand substitution is stated to

---

[14] Commission Notice on the Definition of Relevant Markets [1997] C372, para. 7.
[15] *ibid.*, para. 8.

constitute the most immediate and effective disciplinary force on the suppliers of a given product, especially in relation to their pricing decisions. While this Notice is not a binding instrument, it does serve as a useful indicator of Commission policy.

(2) Dominant Position

6–12   An assessment of a firm's dominance involves more than a consideration of its market share, although this may be an important determinant. In *United Brands Company and United Brands Continental BV v. Commission*,[16] the European Court of Justice defined a "dominant position" as:

> "a position of economic strength enjoyed by an undertaking which enables it to prevent effective competition being maintained on the relevant market by giving it the power to behave to an appreciable extent independently of its competitors, customers and ultimately of consumers."

The concept thus indicates an ability to foreclose and keep other firms out of the market.[17] Such a position would usually arise when a firm or group of firms accounts for the large share of the supply in any given market, provided that other factors analysed in the assessment point in the same direction.[18] These other factors would include an appraisal of entry barriers and the capacity of reaction of customers.

(3) Abuse

6–13   The final constituent of Article 82 is the existence of an abuse. The existence of a dominant position without any abuse is not prohibited. The term "abuse" is translated in many of the other language versions as "abusive exploitation". Such an abuse includes both conduct that exploits the lack of competition and conduct that substantially reduces competition.[19]

(4) Mergers

6–14   Article [82] has been applied by the Commission to mergers which would result in a dominant undertaking increasing its market share in a manner which amounts to an abuse of its position. In *Europemballage Corporation and Continental Can Co. Inc. v. Commission*[20] in 1973, the European Court of Justice upheld the Commission's position that Article [82] prohibits a merger which would strengthen a dominant position. The

---

16 Case 27/76 [1978] E.C.R. 207; [1978] 1 C.M.L.R. 429 para. 65.
17 Korah, *EC Competition Law and Practice* (Hart Publishing, 6th ed., 1997), 78.
18 Commission Notice on the Definition of Relevant Markets, *op. cit.* above, n.14.
19 Korah *op. cit.*, above n.17, 95–121.
20 Case 6/72 [1973] E.C.R. 215; [1973] C.M.L.R. 199.

case involved a multinational corporation, Continental Can, a manufacturer of metal containers and other forms of packaging. It operated on
an international scale through locally based subsidiaries, one of which
was in Germany. A holding company (Europemballage) was established
and using funds supplied by Continental Can it acquired Thomassen &
Drijver Verblifa ("TDV"), the principal Benelux manufacturer of metal
containers for meat and fish. Defining the relevant product markets as
limited to tin cans for meat products, tin cans for fish products and metal
lids, the Commission found Continental Can's German subsidiary's
market share in Germany to range between 70 per cent, 80–90 per cent
and 50–55 per cent of those product markets respectively. TDV was found
to hold market shares of approximately 100 per cent in the Netherlands
and Belgium. The Commission concluded that the elimination of this
strong Dutch competitor in the relevant geographic market of North
Western Germany and the Benelux countries constituted an abuse
prohibited under Article [82] because it consolidated Continental Can's
already dominant position in that market. Continental Can challenged the
Commission's Decision on a number of grounds. It argued, *inter alia*, the
Article [82] did not apply to mergers because it was concerned with
conduct on the market which was directly prejudicial to consumers and
not with structural changes. It further argued that merger control was
deliberately omitted from the scope of the competition rules in Articles
[81] and [82]. The European Court of Justice reversed the Commission's
decision on the grounds that the Commission had inadequately defined
the relevant product market.[21] However, the Court confirmed that Article
[82] applied to mergers and stated:

> "abuse may therefore occur if an undertaking in a dominant position
> strengthens such position in such a way that the degree of dominance
> reached substantially fetters competition, i.e. that only undertakings remain
> in the market whose behaviour depends on the dominant one."[21a]

At this time, it was assumed that dominance required very high market
shares. Now, however, a dominant position is presumed at 50 per cent
and possibly even lower.[22] As a result, this case has a wider application
now than was perhaps understood or intended at the time.

6–15 The *10th Commission Report on Competition Policy* states that the
strengthening of a dominant position could amount to an abuse:

---

[21] The court stated that the Commission had not overcome the burden of proving that
the relevant market was the very narrow market it had defined and not a more
general market for light metal containers for all sorts of products.

[21a] *op. cit.*, above, n.20 at para. 26.

[22] *AKZO Chemie BV v. Commission* Case 62/86 [1991] E.C.R. I–3359 [1993] 5 C.M.L.R. 215.

"if any distortion of the resulting market structure interferes with the maintenance of remaining competition (which already has been weakened by the very existence of the dominant position), or its development. Such an effect depends, in particular, on the change in the relevant market strength of the participants after the merger, *i.e.* the position of the new unit in relation to remaining competitors."

One obvious limitation to the use of Article 82 to control mergers and acquisitions is that it does not include within its scope the creation of dominance, merely the control of an undertaking which is already dominant. Prior to adoption of the Merger Control Regulation, the Commission initiated numerous investigations of mergers applying the *Continental Can* doctrine but issued formal decisions only in the *Tetra-Pak I (BTG Licence)*[23] and *Metaleurop*[24] cases. In the latter case, the Commission decided that since neither of the companies which merged had a dominant position prior to the merger, the *Continental Can* doctrine did not apply.

(5) No Exemptions

6–16 There is no equivalent to Article 81(3) in Article 82. There is no provision for exempting abuses of a dominant position irrespective of any ensuing improvements in production or distribution of goods or benefits to consumers. Licences are not available where an undertaking has abused its dominant position.

III. ENFORCEMENT OF ARTICLES 81 AND 82

6–17 As well as legal arguments about the use of Articles 81 and 82, there are procedural difficulties. As noted above, Articles 81 and 82 do not provide for the prior control of mergers. Regulation 17/62[24a] which sets out the procedural rules relevant to Articles [81] and [82] provides for a long and detailed investigative process allowing the Commission to make requests for information, carry out inspections and sectoral enquiries. The parties and any other parties demonstrating a sufficient interest in the agreement must then be given an opportunity to present their views to the Commission before a final decision is made. This slow decision making process is not suitable for assessing a takeover where rapid decisions are essential.

6–18 Although complainants may themselves bring breaches of Articles 81 and 82 to the attention of the European Commission, the

---

[23] [1990] O.J. L272/27.
[24] [1988] O.J. L179/41.
[24a] [1959–62] O.J. (Special Edition 87).

policy has been to take cases with a "Community dimension" and to encourage national competition authorities to deal with conduct which takes place within one particular Member State.[25] Competition rules have direct effect in the Member States and complainants should be able to enforce their rights in national courts. They may even be entitled to damages in the national courts. This process is not however without its problems. For example, only the Commission is entitled to grant individual exemptions under Article 82[26] and an investigation initiated by a national competition authority may be interrupted thus by one of the parties seeking an exemption.

IV. COUNCIL REGULATION 4064/89 (AS AMENDED BY REGU-LATION 1310/97)

6–19   The Merger Regulation was introduced following warnings by the then Competition Policy Commissioner, Peter Sutherland, that if the Regulation was not adopted, Articles [81] and [82] would be applied to all transactions leading to changes in corporate ownership.[26a] In the recitals to the Regulation, it is noted that while Articles [81 and 82] are applicable according to European Court of Justice caselaw to certain concentrations, the Articles are not sufficient to cover all operations which may prove to be incompatible with the system of undistorted competition envisaged in the Treaty. The objective of the Regulation thus is to create a new legal instrument to permit effective monitoring of all concentrations from the point of view of their effect on the structure of competition in the Community. It is also intended that this instrument should be the only instrument applicable to such concentrations.[27]

The Regulation requires the pre-notification to the Commission of concentrations having a "community dimension". Such concentrations will then be assessed by the Merger Task Force of DG IV which has responsibility for the area of competition.

(1) Concentration

6–20   The Regulation only applies where there has been a "concentration". Article 3(1) defines two categories of concentration.

Article 3(1)(a) provides that a concentration exists where "two or more previously independent undertakings merge". Such a merger

---

[25] The Commission's Draft Notice on Co-operation between National Competition Authorities and the Commission in handling cases falling within the scope of Articles 85 and 86, [1996] O.J. C262/9. See also *Automec SrL v. Commission* [1992] E.C.R. II–2223.

[26] Reg. 17, *op. cit.*, n.24a. Art. 9.

[26a] [1989] O.J. L395/1.

[27] Recitals 6 & 7.

may arise either where two or more undertakings amalgamate into a new undertaking and cease to exist independently or alternatively where one undertaking is absorbed by another, the latter retaining its legal identity while the former ceases to exist as a legal entity. The Commission Notice on the concept of a concentration clarifies that a merger may also occur where, in the absence of a legal merger, the combining of the activities of previously independent undertakings results in the creation of a single economic unit[28] Such a merger may arise in particular where two or more undertakings, while retaining their individual personalities, establish contractually a common economic management. Where this leads to a *de facto* amalgamation of the undertakings concerned into a genuine economic unit, the operation is considered to be a merger.

The Notice explains that a prerequisite for the determination of a common economic unit is the existence of a permanent, single economic management. Other relevant factors may include internal profit and loss compensation as between the various undertakings within the group and their joint liability externally. In addition, it is noted that the de facto amalgamation may be reinforced by cross-shareholdings between the undertakings forming the economic unit.

6–21 Article 3(1)(b) provides that a second category of concentration arises from an acquisition of control. It states that a concentration will be deemed to arise where:

"– one or more persons already controlling at least one undertaking, or
– one or more undertakings
acquire, whether by purchase of securities or assets, by contract or by any other means, direct or indirect control of the whole or parts of one or more other undertakings."

Provision is thus made for an acquisition of control by one undertaking acting alone or by two or more undertakings acting jointly. Control may also be acquired by a person in circumstances where that person already controls (whether jointly or solely) at least one other undertaking or, alternatively, by a combination of persons (which controls another undertaking) and/or undertakings. Under this second category of concentration, the definition of "control"[28a] becomes relevant.

6–22 Article 3(3) provides that for the purposes of the Regulation:

---

[28] Commission Notice on the concept of concentration under Council Regulation 4064/89/EEC on the control of concentrations between undertakings (98/CC 66/02), para. 7.
[28a] *ibid.*, para. 8.

"control shall be constituted by rights, contracts or any other means which, either separately or jointly and having regard to the considerations of fact or law involved, confer the possibility of exercising decisive influence on an undertaking, in particular by:
(a) ownership or the right to use all or part of the assets of an undertaking;
(b) rights or contracts which confer decisive influence on the composition, voting or decisions of the organs of an undertaking."

Unlike the definition of control in the Irish Takeover Panel Act 1997, this assessment of control is clearly based on qualitative rather than quantitative criteria. The Commission Notice[28b] indicates that the Commission will take account of issues of law and fact in determining whether an operation gives rise to an acquisition of control. It provides:

"The acquisition of property rights and shareholders' agreements are important, but are not the only elements involved: purely economic relationships may also play a decisive role. Therefore in exceptional circumstances, a situation of economic dependence may lead to control on a *de facto* basis where, for example, very important long term supply agreements or credits provided by suppliers or customers, coupled with structural links, confer decisive influence".

Nevertheless as Article 3.4 of the Merger Regulation notes, control is normally acquired by persons or undertakings which are the holders of rights or are entitled to rights conferring control or have the power to exercise the rights deriving therefrom.

6–23   The acquisition of control may be in the form of sole or joint control. Sole control is normally acquired on a legal basis where an undertaking acquires a majority of the voting rights of a company. The Commission Notice emphasises that it is not in itself significant that the acquired shareholding is 50 per cent of the share capital plus one share[29] or that it is 100 per cent of the share capital.[30] In the absence of other elements, an acquisition which does not include a majority of the voting rights does not normally confer control even if it involves the acquisition of a majority of the share capital.[30a] Sole control may also be acquired in the case of a qualified minority. This can be established on a legal and/or *de facto* basis. On a legal basis it can occur where specific rights are attached to the minority shareholding enabling the minority shareholder to determine the strategic commercial behaviour of the target company. On a *de facto* basis, a minority shareholder may have sole control in a situation where the shareholder is highly likely to

---

[28b] *ibid.*, para. 9.
[29] Case IV/M.296 – *Credit Lyonnais/BFG Bank of 11 January 1993.*
[30] Case IV/M.299 – *Sara Lee/BP Food Division of 8 February 1993.*
[30a] *op. cit.*, n.14, para. 13.

achieve a majority at the shareholders' meeting because the remaining shares are widely held.[31] Joint control may also be established on a legal or *de facto* basis. There is joint control if the shareholders (the parent companies) must reach agreement on major decisions concerning the controlled undertaking (the joint ventures). Article 3(2) of the Merger Regulation provides that a joint-venture performing on a lasting basis all the functions of an autonomous economic entity should also be considered to be a concentration.

(2) Exemptions

6–24   Article 3(5) of the Merger Regulation contains three exceptions from the definition of a concentration. The first refers to financial institutions and insurance companies which, in the ordinary course of their business, acquire securities in another enterprise with a view to reselling them. A concentration shall be deemed not to arise in such cases provided the firms observe certain restrictions as to the exercise of their voting rights and the envisaged sales take place within one year of the date of the acquisition. The second exception refers to the acquisition of control by an office holder according to the law of a Member State relating to liquidation, insolvency, cessation of payments composition or analogous proceedings. The third exception refers to financial holding companies as defined in the Fourth Council Directive[31a] on the annual accounts of certain types of companies. Once such companies observe certain restrictions as to the exercise of their voting rights, such enterprises may acquire control without falling within the scope of the Regulation.

(3) Community Dimension

6–25   For the Merger Regulation to apply, the merger or takeover must have a "community dimension". Article 1(2) of the Merger Regulation provides that

> "For the purposes of this Regulation, a concentration has a Community dimension where:
> (a) the aggregate world-wide turnover[32] of all the undertakings concerned is more than ECU 5,000 million, and
> (b) the aggregate Community-wide turnover of each of at least two of the undertakings concerned is more than ECU 250 million,

---

[31] *Arjoumari-Prioux/Wiggins Teape Appleton* IV/M.025 Merger Control Reporter B.23 para. 4.
[31a] Directive 78/660 (EEC [1978] O.J. L222/11) as amended by Directive 84/569/EEC ([1984] O.J. L314/28.)
[32] Article 5 of the Regulation explains how the turnover figure should be calculated.

unless each of the undertakings concerned achieves more than two-thirds of
its aggregate Community-wide turnover within one and the same Member
State."

Article 1(3) as amended[34] extends the criteria, providing that:

"For the purposes of this Regulation, a concentration that does not meet the
thresholds laid down in paragraph 2 has a Community dimension where:
(a) the combined aggregate world-wide turnover of all the undertakings is
    more than ECU 2,500 million;
(b) in each of at least three Member States, the combined aggregate turnover
    of all the undertakings concerned is more than ECU 100 million;
(c) in each of at least three Member States included for the purpose of point
    [b], the aggregate turnover of each of at least two of the undertakings
    concerned is more than ECU 25 million; and
(d) the aggregate Community-wide turnover of each of at least two of the
    undertakings concerned is more than ECU 100 million;
unless each of the undertakings concerned achieves more than two-thirds of
its aggregate Community-wide turnover within one and the same Member
State."

It was hoped that by extending the scope of the Regulation to concentrations with a significant impact in several Member States, a "one-
stop system" would apply. This amendment was made to obviate the
multiple notifications which were occurring where concentrations with
a significant impact in several Member States fell below the original
thresholds. This was leading to legal uncertainty, increased effort and
costs and the possibility of conflicting assessments.

The thresholds are so high that the majority of Irish companies
would not qualify. One of the few mergers with an Irish dimension
which was notified was the 1996 strategic alliance between Telecom
Éireann, Telia AB of Sweden and PTT Telecom BV of Holland.

(4) Criteria for Assessment

6–26   Article 2 of the Merger Regulation contains an appraisal mechanism for determining whether concentrations with a Community
dimension are compatible with the preservation and development of
effective competition in the common market. Article 2(1) requires the
Commission to consider:

"(a) the need to preserve and develop effective competition within the
     Common Market in view of, among other things, the structure of all the
     markets concerned and the actual or potential competition from under-
     takings located either within or without the Community;
 (b) the market position of the undertakings concerned and their economic
     and financial power, the opportunities available to suppliers and users,
     their access to supplies or markets, any legal or other barriers to entry,
     supply and demand trends for the relevant goods and services, the

interests of the intermediate and ultimate consumers, and the development of technical and economic progress provided that it is to consumers' advantage and does not form an obstacle to competition."

6–27   Article 2(2) provides that:

"a concentration which does not create or strengthen a dominant position as a result of which effective competition would be significantly impeded in the common market or in a substantial part of it shall be declared compatible with the common market."

On the other hand, Article 2(3) of the Merger Regulation provides that a concentration which does create or strengthen a dominant position as a result of which effective competition would be significantly impeded in the common market or a substantial part of it would be declared incompatible with the common market. Article 2(4)[34] of the Merger Regulation sets out the appraisal criteria for a joint-venture which co-ordinates the competitive behaviour of undertakings that remain independent.

As Craig and De Burca have pointed out, many of the issues which are encountered in a consideration of abuses under Article [82] are relevant to Article 2.[35] For example, in determining whether a concentration is compatible, it will be necessary to define the relevant market in geographical and product terms. It will also be necessary to determine whether there is a dominant position which has been created or strengthened by the concentration.

(5) Procedures

6–28   Article 4(1) of the Merger Regulation provides that concentrations with a Community dimension must be notified to the Commission within one week of the conclusion of the agreement, or the announcement of the public bid, or the acquisition of a controlling interest, whichever occurs first. Where the concentration consists of a merger or an acquisition of joint control, Article 4(2) provides that notification should be made by the parties to the transaction. In all other cases, notification should be effected by the person or undertaking acquiring control of the undertaking.[36]

6–29   Where a notification is deemed to fall within the ambit of the Merger Regulation, the Commission must publish the fact of notification, the names of the parties, the nature of the concentration and the economic sectors involved. To reassure companies concerned about the

---

[33]   Reg. 1310/97 ([1997] O.J. L180/1), Art. 1(1).
[34]   Reg. 1310/97, Art. 1(2).
[35]   Craig and De Burca, *EU Law, Text, Cases and Materials* (2nd ed., Oxford University Press, 1998) at 989.
[36]   Merger Regulation Art. 5(2).

confidentiality of information disclosed in this manner, Article 4(3) of the Merger Regulation emphasises that the Commission will take into account the legitimate interest of undertakings in the protection of their business secrets.

6–30 Article 7(1) of the Merger Regulation[36a] prohibits a concentration from taking effect either before its notification or until it has been declared compatible with the common market pursuant to a decision under Article 6(1)(b) or Article 8(2) or on the basis of a presumption according to Article 10(6). Article 7(3) provides that this obligation shall not, however, impede the implementation of a public bid which has been notified, provided that the offeror does not exercise the voting rights attached to the securities in question or does so only to maintain the full value of those investments and on the basis of a derogation granted by the Commission. Derogations may be granted by the Commission, on request, from the obligations imposed in paragraphs (1) or (3). In deciding whether to grant a derogation, the Commission must consider *inter alia* (i) the effects of the suspension on one or more undertakings concerned by the concentration or on a third party and (ii) the threat to competition posed by the concentration. The Commission may grant a derogation subject to certain conditions or obligations. A derogation may be applied for and granted at any time even before notification or after the transaction.[37]

6–31 Once the concentration has been notified, the Commission through the Merger Task Force can begin its investigation. There are, in effect, two stages to the investigation. At the first stage, the Commission will make one of the three possible decisions set out in Article 6(1).[38] It may decide that the concentration does not fall within the scope of the Regulation, in which case it will publish a decision to that effect. Alternatively, the Commission may find that the concentration does fall within the scope of the regulation, but does not cause serious doubts as to its compatibility with the common market. In this case, the Commission will declare that it is so compatible.[39] Finally, the Commission may find that the concentration falls within the scope of the Regulation and raises "serious doubts as to its compatibility with the common market". In this latter case, the Commission will initiate proceedings. Decisions under Article 6(1) must normally be made within one month of the date of notification.[40]

[36a] As amended by Reg. 1310/97, Art. 1(b).
[37] Art. 7(4) as amended by Reg. 1310/97, Art. 1(b).
[38] As amended Reg. 1310/97, Art. 1(5).
[39] This decision should also cover restrictions directly related and necessary to the implementation of the concentration.
[40] Art. 10(1). See Reg. 447/98, Arts 6–10.

6–32 At the second stage, the Commission will proceed with the investigation of concentrations which raise serious doubts as to their compatibility with the common market. Article 8(2) to (4) sets out the Commission's options at this stage. Firstly, the Commission may find that the concentration fulfils the criterion laid down in Article 2(2) above[41] and thus it will declare the concentration compatible with the common market. In order to ensure compatibility, modifications may need to be made by the undertakings to the original plans notified to the Commission.[42] Secondly, where the Commission finds that the concentration fulfils the criterion defined in Article 2(3),[43] it must declare that the concentration is incompatible with the common market.[44] Where a concentration has already been implemented, the Commission may demand that the merger be reversed.[45] Again, there are time limits imposed for the making of these decisions, the basic rule being that the decision must be made within four months.[46] Failure to comply with these limits will lead to the concentration being deemed compatible with the common market under Article 10(6).

6–33 A right to be heard is provided to a broad range of persons by Article 18 before decisions are made pursuant to Article 7(4) on derogations, Article 8(2) second paragraph, Articles 8(3)–(5), Article 14 and Article 15. In other cases, the Commission must consult the Advisory Committee on Concentrations which consists of one or two representatives from the Member States under the chairpersonship of the Commission.[47]

(6) Sanctions for Non-Compliance

6–34 The Commission is given wide investigative powers to determine if there have been breaches of the Merger Regulation and also strong enforcement powers. Article 11 of the Merger Regulation enables the Commission to obtain all the necessary information from the governments and competent authorities of the Member States, from the persons acquiring control and from undertakings and associations of undertakings. Article 12 of the Merger Regulation allows the Commission to request the competent authorities in Member States to undertake an investigation. Finally, Article 13 of the Merger Regulation gives the Commission power

---

[41] Or, in cases of joint ventures referred to in Article 2(4), the criteria laid down in Article 82(3) of the Treaty.
[42] Article 8(2) as amended.
[43] Or, in cases of joint ventures referred to in Article 2(4), does not fulfil the criteria laid down in Article 82(3) of the Treaty.
[44] Art. 8(3) as amended.
[45] Art. 8(4).
[46] Art. 10(2)(3) and (4). See also Reg. 447/98, Arts 9 and 10.
[47] Art. 19.

to conduct an on-site investigation into undertakings and associations of undertakings.

6–35 The validity of any transaction carried out before notification or before it has been declared compatible is dependent on (i) a decision of the Commission declaring that the concentration is compatible or that it is incompatible with the common market, or (ii) a presumption to the effect that the concentration is compatible with the common market which takes effect if the Commission fails to decide in a timely manner.[48] In effect thus, transactions are provisionally ineffective. An exception is made, however, in respect of transactions in securities admitted to trading on a regulated and supervised market which operates regularly and is accessible directly or indirectly to the public.[49] The Irish Stock Exchange or any other stock exchanged authorised under the Investment Services Directive would constitute such a market. Such transactions will not be rendered invalid unless the buyer and seller knew or ought to have known that the transaction was prohibited.

6–36 Article 14 of the Merger Regulation empowers the Commission to impose fines of between ECU 1,000 and ECU 50,000 for a variety of offences under the Merger Regulation. These include situations where persons or undertakings omit to notify a concentration, supply incorrect or misleading information in a notification, supply incorrect information or untimely information when requested for information, produce incomplete documentation when required to produce documentation or refuse to submit to an investigation under Article 13. In addition, Article 15 allows the Commission to impose periodic penalty payments of up to ECU 25,000 for each day of the delay in order to compel relevant persons or undertakings to supply complete and correct information in response to a request or to submit to an investigation.

(7) Member State Control

6–37 One of the main advantages of the Merger Regulation is that it provides a "one stop shop" procedure. Article 21(1) provides that the Commission has "sole competence" to take decisions provided for in the Regulation, subject to review by the Court of Justice. Article 21(2) emphasises thus that no Member State may apply its national competition legislation to any concentration which has a Community dimension. There are, however, a number of exceptions to this rule, where in the circumstances it is deemed appropriate that the individual Member State maintain an element of control.

---

[48] Art. 7(5) para. 1 as amended.
[49] Art. 7(5) para. 2 as amended.

Article 21(3) provides that, notwithstanding Article 21(1) and (2), Member States:

> "may take appropriate measures to protect legitimate interests other than those taken into consideration by this Regulation and compatible with the general principles and other provisions of Community law".

The term "legitimate interests" is stated to include "public security, plurality of the media and prudential rules". Any other public interest alleged must be communicated to the Commission by the Member State concerned and "shall be recognised by the Commission after an assessment of its compatibility with the general principles and other provisions of Community law". The Commission must inform the Member State concerned of its decision within one month of the communication.

6–38   Article 9(2) of the Merger Regulation allows the Commission to refer a notified concentration to the competent authorities of a particular Member State if, within three weeks of receiving a copy of the notification, a Member State informs the Commission that:

> "a concentration threatens to create or to strengthen a dominant position, as a result of which effective competition would be significantly impeded on a market, within that Member State, which presents all the characteristics of a distinct market be it in a substantial part of the Common Market or not".

The Commission must consider whether, having regard to (i) the market for the product or services in question and (ii) the geographic market,[50] such a distinct market exists. The Commission must also consider whether such a threat exists. Where it answers these two questions in the affirmative, Article 9(3) provides that the Commission may either deal with the case itself in order to maintain or restore effective competition on the relevant market or it may refer the matter to the competent authorities of the Member State concerned with a view to the application of that State's domestic competition law. If the Commission believes that a distinct market does not exist or that the threat is not real, it must inform the Member State of its decision. Strict time limits are set out for the making of this decision[51] and an appeal lies to the European Court of Justice against a decision not to refer.[52] Because of the large Irish dimension, it would have been within the jurisdiction thus of the Minister for Enterprise and Employment to have asked for a referral in respect of the acquisition by Tesco of Associated British Foods in 1998. The Minister, however, chose in the circumstances not to avail of this provision.

---

[50]   Art. 9(7).
[51]   Art. 9(4) & (5).
[52]   Art. 9(9).

6–39 Article 22(3) provides that a Member State may ask the Commission to investigate whether a concentration without a Community dimension creates or strengthens a dominant position leading to a significant impediment to competition within the territory of that Member State. If the concentration affects trade between Member States, the Commission may then take action. This provision was designed to provide a mechanism for the control of mergers where none existed at national level.[53]

In addition to the above, a number of articles require co-operation between the Commission and Member States. Article 19, for example, requires the Commission to act in close and constant liaison with the competent authorities of the Member States from which it obtains comments and information.

V. CONCLUSION

6–40 Whilst there still remains the theoretical possibility of the European Commission applying Articles 81 and 82 to certain types of mergers and acquisitions which do not fall under the Merger Regulation, it has made it clear that it has little interest in applying the two Articles to mergers and acquisitions. The main advantage of the Merger Regulation over Articles 81 and 82 are the time limits sets out in the former. In addition, because the Regulation was specifically designed with mergers and takeovers in mind, its provisions are more appropriate.

B. Domestic Competition Law

6–41 Two principal pieces of domestic competition legislation are relevant to mergers and acquisitions in Ireland: namely, the Mergers, Takeovers and Monopolies (Control) Act 1978 and the Competition Act 1991.

I. THE MERGERS, TAKEOVERS AND MONOPOLIES (CONTROL) ACT 1978

6–42 The Mergers, Takeovers and Monopolies (Control) Act 1978[54] ("the 1978 Act") governs merger control in Ireland. Under this Act, the Minister for Enterprise Trade and Employment ("the Minister") is responsible for assessing any merger or takeover involving firms above a certain size threshold. Such mergers or takeovers must be reported to

---

[53] Para. 29 of the recitals to the Regulation.
[54] As amended by the Competition Act 1991 and the Competition (Amendment) Act 1996.

the Minister and failure to notify will result in the transaction being deemed void. This sanction alone, apart from the criminal penalties which may be imposed, tends to ensure compliance with the provisions of this Act.

(1) The Existence of a Merger or Takeover

6–43   There are two situations in which a merger or takeover will be deemed to exist for the purposes of the 1978 Act.
Section 1(3)(a) provides that:

> "a merger or takeover shall be taken to exist when two or more enterprises, at least one of which carries on business in the State, come under common control."

Clearly, all three conditions must be met for a transaction to be deemed a merger or takeover under this subsection. The first condition is that there must be an agreement between "enterprises". An "enterprise" is defined in section 1(1) as:

> "(i) a person or partnership engaged for profit in the supply or distribution of goods or the provision of services, including –
>
>   (a) a society, including a credit union, registered under the Industrial and Provident Societies Acts 1893 to 1971,
>
>   (b) a society registered under the Friendly Societies Acts 1896 to 1977, and
>
>   (c) a society established under the Building Societies Act, 1976, or
>
> (ii) a holding company within the meaning of section 155 of the Companies Act 1963;"

6–44   The second condition is that at least one of the enterprises concerned in the merger or takeover must carry on business in Ireland. Thus for example, the Act will apply if either a French company acquires an Irish company or an Irish company acquires a French company. Furthermore, the Department of Enterprise, Trade and Employment has taken the view that the Act applies when the control of an Irish enterprise may pass as a result of a proposed acquisition of its foreign holding company, even if there is no transfer of shares or assets under Irish law.[55] The third condition is that the enterprises must be brought under "common control". Section 1(3)(b) provides that enterprises will be deemed to be under common control:

> "if the decision as to how or by whom each shall be managed can be made either by the same person, or by the same group of persons acting in concert".

---

[55] Competition and Mergers Review Group, *Proposals for Discussion in Relation to Mergers* (July 1998), p. 8.

6–45 Section 1(3)(c) provides further:

"Without prejudice to paragraph (b), where an enterprise (in this paragraph referred to as "the first enterprise"), whether by means of acquisition or otherwise, obtains the right in another enterprise (in this paragraph referred to as "the second enterprise") which is a body corporate:
(i) to appoint or remove a majority of the board or committee of management of the second enterprise; or
(ii) to shares of the second enterprise which carry voting rights, except where the voting rights in the second enterprise which are controlled by the first enterprise –
 (I) are not after the acquisition more than 25 per cent of the total of such voting rights,[56] or
 (II) are before the acquisition more than one half of the total of such voting rights
the said enterprises shall be deemed to have been brought under common control."

For the purposes of section 1(3)(c), section 1(c)(d)(i) provides that the term "voting rights" does not include voting rights which arise only in specified circumstances. Section 1(c)(d)(ii) provides in turn that voting rights shall be deemed to be controlled by an enterprise when it can determine how the votes concerned shall be cast.

6–46 Section 1(3)(e)[56a] provides that the second situation in which a merger or takeover shall be deemed to exist is where

"the assets, including goodwill, (or a substantial part of the assets) of an enterprise are acquired by another enterprise, the acquisition shall be deemed to constitute a merger or Takeover for the purposes of this Act, if upon the acquisition a result of the acquisition is to place the second-mentioned enterprise in a position to replace (or substantially to replace) the first-mentioned enterprise in the business in which that enterprise was engaged immediately before the acquisition and the value of those assets or the value of the turnover generated therefrom, exceeds the thresholds referred to in section 2(1)(a)."

It is interesting to compare this definition with the definition of a transfer of an undertaking developed by the courts for the purposes of the Transfer of Undertakings Directive.[57] The decisive criterion for establishing whether there is a transfer for the purposes of the Directive is whether the business in question retains its identity. The acquisition of goodwill whilst an important indicator of a transfer is not absolutely necessary.

[56] The 1978 Act initially provided that if 30 per cent of the voting rights in a company were acquired by a purchaser, the Minister had to be notified. This percentage would have been consistent with the percentage specified in the definition of control in the Irish Takeover Panel Act 1997. It was amended by the Competition Act 1991, s.15(2).
[56a] As amended by the Competition Act 1991, s.15(3).
[57] Council Directive 77/187/EEC, see Chap. 9 below.

6–47   There are a number of exceptional cases provided for in the 1978 Act. Section 1(3)(f) provides that where enterprises come under common control either because the acquirer is a receiver or liquidator or an underwriter or jobber, a takeover or merger for the purposes of the Act will be deemed not to have occurred. Similarly, section 1(3)(g) provides that a merger or takeover shall not be taken to exist where two or more wholly owned subsidiaries of the same body corporate are involved. Finally, section 2(3) provides that the Act will not apply to enterprises coming under common control solely as a result of a testamentary disposition or an intestacy.

(2) Thresholds

6–48   In order to come within the scope of the 1978 Act, the transaction must exceed certain size thresholds. Section 2(1) provides that the Act will apply if in the most recent financial year:

> "(I) the value of the gross assets of each of two or more of the enterprises to be involved in the proposal is not less than £10 million or
>
> (II) the turnover[58] of each of those two or more enterprises is not less than £20 million".

When introducing the Competition (Amendment) Bill 1994, the then Minister stated that the Department in practice applied this as a requirement that both sides of a merger would be above the *de minimis* level.[59]

6–49   Although the 1978 Act does not specify what enterprises are to be considered in the calculation of thresholds, it would appear the assets and turnover of affiliates need not be taken into account.[60] Section 2(4) allows the Minister to alter these limits from time to time by Order and this was done in 1985 and 1993 to bring the thresholds to their current levels.[61] In addition, section 2(5) provides that where the exigencies of the common good so warrant, the Minister may make an Order providing that the 1978 Act applies to any proposed merger or takeover of a particular class specified in the Order. Under the Mergers Takeovers and Monopolies (Control) Act (Newspapers) Order 1979,[62] the thresholds have been disapplied to newspaper companies. This

---

[58] Section 2(1)(b) provides that for the purposes of this subsection, "turnover" does not include any payment in respect of value-added tax on sales or in respect of excise duty.

[59] 444 *Dáil Debates* Col. 977.

[60] Competition and Mergers Review Group, Proposals for Discussion in Relation to Mergers (July 1998).

[61] S.I. No. 230 of 1985 and S.I. No. 135 of 1993.

[62] S.I. No. 17 of 1979.

Order reflects the political fears of the negative effects of concentrated ownership in the media. Similarly, in the UK, special rules have been applied to newspaper companies.[62a]

6–50 The Competition and Mergers Review Group, in its discussion document published in July 1998, has suggested retaining the system of mandatory notification where the defined financial thresholds are exceeded. However, the Group recommended retaining the thresholds for notification based on turnover criterion but abolishing the gross assets criterion. Whereas the turnover criterion was agreed to be relatively clear and simple to apply and easily verifiable, it considered that the gross assets criterion was too unrefined to be considered useful. Secondly, it recommended that thresholds be set in respect of each of the parties to a proposed transaction and that the threshold be fixed in respect of the level of activity within the State. Under the current system, the activities within the State of one of the parties to the proposed transaction might be minimal and yet the proposal might be notifiable in Ireland. In addition, in most situations where a large firm exceeding the thresholds acquires a small firm, no competition concerns arise. A majority of the Group also recommended that the thresholds be increased to £30 million. A further recommendation was that the methods of calculating turnover provided for in the Merger Regulation should be followed. Finally, it was recommended that the Minister should retain the power to disapply the thresholds.

(3) Notification

6–51 Section 1(2) of the 1978 Act provides that a merger or takeover shall be deemed to be proposed "when an offer capable of acceptance is made". Section 5[63] then provides that each of the enterprises involved has one month to notify the Minister in writing of the proposal. The notification should include full details of the proposal and be accompanied by the prescribed fee.[63a] Upon receipt of the notification, the Minister may decide that further information is necessary and may, within one month of the date of receipt of the notification, or of the last of such notifications, as the case may be, address a written request to any one or more of the enterprises concerned.[63b]

6–52 It is a criminal offence for a person in control of an enterprise to fail to notify the Minister within the specified period or to fail to

---

[62a] See para. 6–109.
[63] As amended by the Competition Act 1991, s.16.
[63a] s.5(1A) as inserted by the Competition Act 1996, s.10.
[63b] s.5(2).

comply with the Minister's request for further information.[64] In the case of non-compliance by a corporate body, any officer who knowingly and wilfully authorises or permits the contravention will be liable. In the case of a partnership, each partner who knowingly and wilfully authorises or permits the contravention will be liable. Finally, in the case of any other form of enterprise, any individual in control of that enterprise who knowingly and wilfully authorises or permits the contravention will be liable.[64a] In addition to a fine of £1,000 on summary conviction and £200,000 upon conviction on indictment, for continued contravention a daily fine may be imposed not exceeding £100 on summary conviction or £20,000 upon conviction on indictment.

The Competition and Mergers Review Group has stated that in view of the severity of these sanctions and the possible resulting failure to transfer title to shares or assets, some mechanism should be made available for remedying the failure to notify. Its suggestion was that retrospective notifications should be acceptable subject to the imposition of a fine and the imposition of conditions in respect of the retrospective approval.[65]

(4) Assessment

6–53   Upon receipt of the notification, section 7[65a] allows the Minister two possible courses of action. Under section 7(a), the Minister may, no later than three months after the notification, notify the parties concerned that he or she has decided not to make an order prohibiting the proposed merger or takeover. Alternatively, under section 7(b), the Minister may within 30 days of notification refer the notification to the Competition Authority for investigation. In the *Guinness/United Beverages* case, the Minister erroneously referred the matter to the Competition Authority after this time limit had expired. The Competition Authority stated that it no longer had jurisdiction to consider the matter. In such a case, the Minister would not under the Act have been authorised to made an order refusing consent. If she had not given her consent under section 7(a), at the expiry of the three month waiting period, the parties could have proceeded by default. As it happened, the agreement was notified to the Competition Authority under the Competition Act 1991 and the matter was dealt with by the Competition Authority under that Act.

Although the 1978 Act does not refer to the criteria relevant for the referral decision, the Minister's Annual Reports in the past have referred to issues such as competition, danger to continuity of supplies,

---

[64]   s.5(3)(a).
[64a] s.5(3)(c).
[65]   *op. cit.*, n.55 at p. 38.
[65a] As amended by the Competition Act 1991, s.17(2).

employment, consumers interests and generic ones such as "the scheduled criteria."[65b] A reference to competition is the most usual.

6–54 Where a proposed merger or takeover has been referred to the Competition Authority, it should investigate the proposal and report back to the Minister within the specified time limit which should not be less than 30 days.[66] In this report, the Competition Authority should state its opinion as to whether or not the proposed merger or takeover concerned "would be likely to prevent or restrict competition or restrain trade in any goods or services and would be likely to operate against the common good".[67] It is also required to give its views on the likely effect of the proposed merger or takeover on the common good in respect of certain scheduled criteria set out in section 8(2)(b) which are:

- (i)   continuity of supplies or services;
- (ii)   level of employment;
- (iii)   regional development
- (iv)   rationalisation of operations in the interests of greater efficiency;
- (v)   research and development;
- (vi)   increased production;
- (vii)   access to markets;
- (viii)   shareholders and partners;
- (ix)   employees;
- (x)   consumers.

Within two months of the report being made, the Minister is required to publish it.[68] However, confidential information will not be disclosed. The purpose of this requirement is "to ensure that assessments of significant merger proposals are carried out in a transparent way".[69]

To date, there has been just one report by the Competition Authority which related to the increase by Independent Newspapers plc of its shareholding in the Tribune Group from 29.99 per cent to a possible 53.09 per cent in 1992.[70] The Competition Authority recommended not to allow this as it could allow Independent Newspapers plc to "exercise

---

[65b] s.17(6) of the Competition Act 1991 repealed the schedule to the 1978 Act. The criteria in section 8(2)(b) of the 1978 Act are now the relevant criteria.

[66] s.8(1) as amended by the Competition Act 1991, s.17(3).

[67] s.8(2) as amended by the Competition Act 1991, s.17(4).

[68] Competition Act 1991 s.17(5).

[69] 407 *Dáil Debates* Col. 1497.

[70] Pl.8795.

an adverse and distorting effect on competition in the market." It submitted that such an acquisition could allow it to act in "both a predatory and an exclusionary manner."

6–55 The majority of the Competition and Mergers Review Group recommended that notifiable transactions should be notified to the Competition Authority rather than to the Minister. It was argued that this would avoid the possible duplication which arises where the Department conducts a preliminary investigation and the Competition Authority may then be required to conduct an in-depth investigation. When the matter is reported back to the Minister, an examination of the reasoning of the Competition Authority is then required before the Minister arrives at a final decision. The Group recommended a two-tier system be introduced allowing for a fast track procedure for mergers which give rise to few competition concerns and a second in-depth investigation phase for those which do.[71] It recommended that the Competition Authority should apply pure economic criteria, such as those heretofore applied. Since it was deemed appropriate that certain "common good" factors be taken into account, the Group favoured the view that the final decision should lie with the Minister. In making this decision, the Minister should then consider *inter alia* the interests of efficiency and consumer benefit envisaged by section 4(2) of the 1978 Act. Finally on this point, the Group recommended that the Minister be entitled to take account of industrial policy, employment, regional development and environmental policy.[71a]

(5) The Ministerial Decision

6–56 Having considered the Competition Authority's report, the Minister may, under section 9(1)(a), make an order prohibiting a proposed merger or takeover either absolutely or except on specified conditions. The Minister may take this decision if he or she thinks that "the exigencies of the common good so warrant". These exigencies shall include, but are not limited to, the criteria in section 8.[71b] In addition, the Minister should consult with any other Government Minister concerned, *e.g.* the Minister for Employment.

6–57 Any order under section 9 must be laid before each House of the Oireachtas and either House may pass a resolution annulling the order within 21 days. In addition, any enterprise referred to in the order may appeal, under section 12, to the High Court on a point of law within

---

[71] *op. cit.*, n.55 at pp. 34–39.
[71a] *op. cit.*, n.55 at pp. 39–42.
[71b] As amended by the Competition Act 1991, s.18.

one month of the coming into effect of the order. Where the terms of the order are not being complied with, the Minister or any other person, may seek an injunction under section 13 to enforce compliance. In addition, criminal penalties may be imposed under section 13(2) on persons who contravene a provision of an order. Fines may be imposed up to a maximum of £500 on summary conviction and for continued contravention, a daily fine not exceeding £100. For conviction on indictment a maximum fine may be imposed of £5,000 and for continued contravention, a daily fine not exceeding £500.

(6) Enforceability

6–58   In addition to, and independent of, the criminal penalties for non-compliance with the notification requirements or contravention of a prohibitory order, the 1978 Act contains one provision which makes it essential for firms to comply with the Mergers Act and to notify the Minister. Section 3(1) states that in order for title to shares or assets to pass in a merger or takeover regulated by the Act either:

(a)   the Minister must have stated in writing pursuant to section 7(a) that he or she has decided not to make an order prohibiting the proposed merger or takeover; or

(b)   the Minister must have stated in writing that he or she has made a conditional order in relation to the proposed merger or takeover; or

(c)   three months must have lapsed from the date of notification without the Minister's having made a prohibition order under section 9 in relation to the proposed merger or takeover.

An offeror is extremely unlikely to deliberately fail to notify the transaction and risk the transaction being deemed void and the acquisition being unravelled. Indeed, compliance with the 1978 Act is generally a condition of any offer falling within the scope of the Act.

II. THE COMPETITION ACT 1991

6–59   The Competition Act 1991, as amended by the Competition (Amendment) Act 1996, prohibits agreements which prevent, restrict or distort competition or which constitute an abuse of dominant positions in trade in the State. The long title to the Competition Act 1991 ("the 1991 Act") states that the prohibition is analogous to Articles [81] and [82] of the Treaty of Rome. The 1991 Act also establishes the Competition Authority as the relevant body to perform the functions assigned to it by the Act.[71]

---

[71]   s.10.

(1) The Competition Authority

6–60 The Competition Authority is responsible for monitoring the application of the 1991 Act. It is an independent body and the schedule to the 1991 Act provides that it shall consist of a chairperson and not less than two and not more than four other members, each of whom is appointed by the Minister. Section 11(1) allows the Competition Authority, on its own initiative, to carry out a study of "any practice or method of competition affecting the supply and distribution of goods or the provision of services". In addition, section 14(1) allows the Minister, where he or she is of the opinion that there is an abuse of a dominant position, to request the Competition Authority to investigate the abuse. The Competition Authority must then hold an investigation and report to the Minister whether a dominant position exists, and if it does, whether it is being abused. The Competition Authority is given wide powers to summon witnesses, to examine on oath, to require witnesses to produce relevant documentation and to authorise officers to perform such of its functions as it deems proper. Failure to co-operate with the Competition Authority in this respect is an offence punishable by a fine not exceeding £1,000 and/or imprisonment for a period not exceeding six months.[72]

(2) Prohibitions

6–61 Section 4(1) of the 1991 Act prohibits:

> "all agreements between undertakings, decisions by associations of undertakings and concerted practices which have as their object or effect the prevention, restriction, or distortion of competition in trade in any goods or services in the State or in any part of the State".

Such agreements are expressly stated to be void. The prohibition expressly applies to agreements between undertakings. Section 3(1) defines "an undertaking" as:

> "a person being an individual, a body corporate or an unincorporated body of persons engaged for gain in the production, supply or distribution of goods or the provision of services".

The term "gain" in this context has been held to mean "for charge or payment" not necessarily for profit.[73] Section 4(1) is modelled on Article 81 of the Treaty of Rome. The non-exhaustive list of anti-competitive agreements set out in section 4(1) refers to agreements which:

---

[72] Schedule to the 1991 Act.
[73] Competition Authority, *PRS/IMRO* June 30, 1992 and *Deane v. VHI* [1992] 2 I.R. 319.

164

"(a) directly or indirectly fix purchase or selling prices or any other trading conditions;
(b) limit or control production, markets, technical development or investment;
(c) share markets or sources of supply;
(d) apply dissimilar conditions to equivalent transactions with other trading parties thereby placing them at a competitive disadvantage;
(e) make the conclusion of contracts subject to acceptance by the other parties of supplementary obligations which by their nature or according to commercial usage have no connection with the subject of such contracts."

6–62 In its first decision *Nallen/O'Toole (Belmullet)*, the Competition Authority emphasised that the 1991 Act did not incorporate a *de minimis* provision. This case involved an agreement for the sale of a business which contained certain restraints on the vendor from competing with the business after the sale. The Competition Authority noted that:

> "there is no provision in the Competition Act which would exclude small undertakings from the provisions of the Act . . . given the size and distribution of population in Ireland, it is possible that a number of relatively small undertakings could, by acting together, prevent, restrict or distort competition in a part of the State. The exclusion of small undertakings from the provision of the Act could deny consumers in Parts of the State the protection against Anti-competitive activities which the Act provides".[74]

6–63 The second prohibition in the 1991 Act is contained in section 5(1) which prohibits:

> "any abuse by one or more undertakings of a dominant position in trade for any goods or services in the State or in a substantial part of the State".

The examples given of such abuses in section 5(2) are:

"(a) directly or indirectly imposing unfair purchase or selling prices or other unfair trading conditions;
(b) limiting production, markets or technical development to the prejudice of consumers;
(c) applying dissimilar conditions to equivalent transactions with other trading parties, thereby placing them at a competitive disadvantage;
(d) making the conclusion of contracts subject to the acceptance by other parties of supplementary obligations which by their nature or according to commercial usage have no connection with the subject of such contracts."

This section is analogous to Article 82 of the Treaty of Rome.

---

[74] Competition Authority Decision No. 1, April 2, 1992, para. 21.

(3) Certificates and Licenses

6–64   Section 4(2) of the 1991 Act allows the Competition Authority to grant an individual or category licence for the purposes of any agreement, decision or concerted practice or categories of the aforementioned which in its opinion:

> "having regard to all relevant market conditions, contributes to improving the production or distribution of goods or provision of services or to promoting technical or economic progress, while allowing consumers a fair share of the resulting benefit and which does not –
>
> (i) impose on the undertakings concerned terms which are not indispensable to the attainment of those objectives;
>
> (ii) afford undertakings the possibility of eliminating competition in respect of a substantial part of the products or services in question."

According to section 4(3)(a), such a licence permits "the doing of acts which would otherwise be prohibited and void under subsection (1)." No equivalent permission may be obtained in the case of a breach of section 5 of the 1991 Act.

6–65   In addition to issuing a licence, the Competition Authority may issue a certificate under section 4(4)(a)[75] of the 1991 Act to the effect that, in its opinion, on the basis of the facts in its possession, (i) an agreement, decision or concerted practice or (ii) a category of agreements, decisions or concerted practices does not offend against section 4(1).

6–66   Before granting a licence or issuing a certificate, the Competition Authority may decide to invite any relevant Government Minister to make any observations on the matter.[75a] In addition, it may accept observations or submissions from persons claiming to be interested if it deems this proper.[76] The Competition Act 1991 (Notices of Licences and Certificates) Regulations 1993[77] provides that where a licence or a certificate under section 4 of the 1991 Act covers a category of agreements, decisions or concerted practices, publication of the notice in An Iris Oifigúil will be deemed sufficient notice to every person to whom the licence or certificate relates. Section 9 of the 1991 Act provides that any undertaking, or association of undertakings, concerned or any other person aggrieved by a licence or a certificate may appeal to the High Court within 28 days of publication. By contrast, no appeal is provided for against the refusal of the Competition Authority to grant a licence or certificate.

---

[75] As amended by the Competition Act 1991, s.5.
[75a] s.4(5).
[76] s.7(5).
[77] S.I. No. 293 of 1993 Art. 2(2).

6–67 It is important to note that a certificate is not binding on a court. However, there is a distinct advantage to be gained by a party who obtains an individual certificate or falls within the terms of a category certificate. Although, section 6(5)(a) provides that where action is taken under section 6 by an aggrieved person which results in the court finding that an agreement infringes the prohibition in section 4(1), any certificate in force will cease to be effective from that date, section 6(6), provides the incentive. It provides that where a certificate has been issued, pursuant to section 4(4) and has not been revoked, a claimant will not be entitled to damages for a contravention of the prohibition in section 4(1) for loss suffered in consequence of that agreement in respect of the period during which the certificate is or has been in force.

(4) Notification

6–68 Unlike the 1978 Act, there is no general requirement to notify the Competition Authority of an agreement. Only where the parties are seeking an individual licence or certificate must they notify the agreement.[78] Until such a notification has been received,[79] the Competition Authority will not be in a position to grant a licence or a certificate. Unlike the 1978 Act, this Act seems to envisage a merger agreement being in existence prior to notification.

(5) Offences

6–69 Sections 2(2)(b) and (7)(a) of the Competition (Amendment) Act 1996 ("the 1996 Act") make it a criminal offence for an undertaking to breach section 4 or section 5 of the 1991 Act respectively. Section 3(5) of the 1996 Act authorises the Competition Authority to investigate any contravention of section 2(2) or 2(7) and to bring summary proceedings under section 3(6) of the 1996 Act.

6–70 However, a number of specific defences may be raised by the undertaking charged. In proceedings for an offence under section 2(2) of the 1996 Act, section 2(2)(c) provides that the following defences are available:

"(i) the defendant did not know, nor, in all the circumstances of the case, could the defendant be reasonably expected to have known, that the effect of the agreement, decision or concerted practice concerned would be the prevention, restriction or distortion of competition in trade alleged in the proceedings, or

---

[78] s.7(1).
[79] s.7(4) provides that a notification must be accompanied by a fee.

    (ii) at all material a licence or certificate was in force in respect of the agreement, decision or concerted practice concerned and, in the case of a licence –

      (I) the terms and conditions of the licence were at all material times being complied with by the defendant, or

      (II) subject to subsection (3) of this section, in case any terms or conditions of the licence were not being so complied with –

        (A) those terms or conditions are terms or conditions that had been amended, or inserted in the licence, under section 8 of the Principal Act,

        (B) the defendant was complying with the terms and conditions of the licence immediately before the making of such amendments or insertions, and

        (C) the defendant began to take, within 14 days after the date of publication, in accordance with the said section 8, of notice of the amendment or insertion of terms or conditions aforesaid, all reasonable steps for the purposes of complying with those terms or conditions and was proceeding with due expedition on the date on which the offence is alleged to have been committed with the completion of any step remaining for those purposes, or

   (iii) subject to subsections (3) and (4) of this section, in the case of an agreement, decision or concerted practice in respect of which a licence or certificate has been granted and such a licence has been revoked or suspended or, as the case may be, such a certificate has been revoked, the defendant began to take, within 14 days after –

      (I) in the case of the revocation of a licence or certificate, the date of publication, in accordance with section 8 of the Principal Act, of notice of such revocation, or

      (II) in the case of the suspension of the licence, the date of the order of the High Court or, as may be appropriate, the Supreme Court providing for such suspension,

all reasonable steps for the purposes of ensuring that any arrangements that had been made and which were necessary for the implementation of the agreement or decision or, as the case may be, which constituted the concerted practice were discontinued and was proceeding with due expedition on the date on which the offence is alleged to have been committed with the completion of any step remaining for those purposes."

Section 2(3) of the 1996 Act denies a defendant a right to claim the defences set out in sections 2(2)(c)(ii)(II) or 2(2)(c)(iii) if the date of the alleged offence is more than two months after the publication of the notice or order. Section 2(4) denies a defendant the right to claim the defence set out in section 2(2)(c)(iii) if the doing of the act or the making of any omission formed the basis for the revocation of the licence or certificate.

6–71 Section 2(7)(b) of the 1996 Act sets out the defences to a breach of section 5(1) of the 1991 Act. It shall be a good defence to prove that:

"(i) the defendant did not know, nor, in all the circumstances of the case, could the defendant be reasonably expected to have known, that the act or acts concerned done by the defendant would constitute the abuse of a dominant position in trade for goods or services alleged in the proceedings, or

(ii) the said act was done in compliance with the provisions of an order under section 14 of the said Act ('the first-mentioned order'), or

(iii) subject to subsection (8) of this section, in case any of those provisions were not being complied with –

　(I) those provisions are provisions that had been amended, or inserted in the first-mentioned order, by another order under the said section 14 ('the second-mentioned order'),

　(II) the defendant was complying with the provisions of the first-mentioned order immediately before the commencement of the second-mentioned order, and

　(III) the defendant began to take, within 14 days after the commencement of the second-mentioned order, all reasonable steps for the purposes of complying with the provisions so amended or inserted and was proceeding with due expedition on the date on which the offence is alleged to have been committed with the completion of any step remaining for those purposes, or

(iv) subject to subsection (8) of this section, in case an order under section 14 of the said Act prohibited the continuance of the act concerned except on conditions specified in that order and that order has been revoked by another order under the said section 14 ('the second-mentioned order'), the defendant began to take, within 14 days after the commencement of the second-mentioned order, all reasonable steps for the purposes of discontinuing the act concerned and was proceeding with due expedition on the date on which the offence is alleged to have been committed with the completion of any step remaining for those purposes."

Section 2(7)(c) provides a defence where it is alleged that there has been non-compliance with the provisions of an order under section 14 of the 1991 Act which had been amended or inserted by a second order. In such a case, it shall be a good defence to prove that the defendant had been complying with the first order immediately before the commencement of the second order and that within 14 days after the commencement of the second order, the defendant began to take all reasonable steps to ensure compliance and was proceeding with the completion of any remaining steps with due expedition on the date the offence allegedly occurred. Section 2(8) denies a defendant the defences set out in sections 2(7)(b)(iii) or (iv) or 2(7)(c) if the date of the alleged offence is more than two months after the order concerned.

6–72 Section 3 of the 1996 Act provides penalties for undertakings found guilty of the offences created in section 2 of the 1996 Act. The undertakings found guilty on summary conviction will be subject to a maximum fine of £1,500 and if found guilty on indictment to a maximum fine of £3 million or 10 per cent of the turnover of the undertaking in the previous financial year. In the case of an individual, a prison sentence not exceeding six months on summary conviction or two years on conviction on indictment may be imposed. A fine may also be imposed on an individual. On summary conviction, a fine not exceeding £1,500 may be imposed. On conviction on indictment, a fine not exceeding the greater of £3 million or 10% of the turnover of the individual in the previous financial year may be imposed. An undertaking which continues to contravene the Act may be liable to a fine of £1,500 per day.

(6) Rights of Action

6–73   Any person who is aggrieved in consequence of any agreement, decision, concerted practice or abuse prohibited under sections 4 or 5 may, under section 6(1) of the 1991 Act,[80] bring an action against:

> "(a) any undertaking which is or has at any material time been a party to such an agreement, decision or concerted practice or has been guilty of such an abuse;
> (b) any director, manager or other officer of such an undertaking, or a person who purported to act in any such capacity, who authorised or consented to, as the case may be, the entry by the undertaking into, or the implementation by it of, the agreement or decision, the engaging by it in the concerted practice or the doing by it of the act which constituted the abuse."

The action seeking relief is usually brought in the High Court by way of an injunction, declaration or damages, including exemplary damages.[80a] Section 6(4)(a) of the 1991 Act provides that both the Minister and the Competition Authority have a right of action in respect of an abuse under sections 4 and 5. This allows the Competition Authority to act in situations where the injured party does not have the financial resources to do so or wishes to avoid any adverse publicity. There is a rebuttable presumption that each director, manager and similar officer of the undertaking and any person who purported to act in any such capacity at the material time, consented to the acts of the undertaking.[81]

(7) Application of the Competition Act 1991 to Mergers — The *Woodchester* Case

6–74   In *Woodchester Bank Ltd/UDT Bank Ltd*,[82] the Competition Authority held that it had authority to review a merger under the 1991

---

[80] As amended by the Competition Act 1996, s.7.
[80a] s.6(2) and (3).
[81] s.6(4)(a).
[82] Competition Authority Decision No. 6, August 4, 1992.

Act notwithstanding that the merger had been notified to and approved by the Minister under the 1978 Act. In other words, it initiated a system of dual notification for mergers in Ireland.

The *Woodchester* case concerned an agreement between Hill Samuel Bank Ltd. and Woodchester Bank for the sale of UDT Bank to Woodchester. The agreement contained a number of non-compete clauses. The notifying parties made a submission to the Competition Authority to the effect that the acquisition was not reviewable under the 1991 Act. Firstly, they contended that it could not have been the legislature's intention that an agreement which had been notified and approved under the 1978 Act and the Central Bank legislation should also be reviewable under the 1991 Act. Secondly, they argued that serious uncertainty would be introduced into commercial transactions if such transactions were reviewable. Thirdly, they argued that because, pursuant to the Merger Regulation, acquisitions which result in concentrations are not reviewable under Article [81], then by analogy, section 4 should not provide the basis for such review in Ireland.

6–75   The Competition Authority addressed each of these arguments in turn. It stated that "a merger or takeover may, on occasion, prevent, restrict or distort competition"[83] but conceded that there was some merit in the argument that it could not have been the legislature's intention that notified mergers approved by the Minister, could be reviewable under the rules of competition as set out in the 1991 Act. However, it stated that a number of factors militated against such a finding. First, it emphasised that section 4(1) specifically refers to "all agreements" and provides for no exceptions. Secondly, it pointed out that mergers frequently include a number of ancillary clauses which may themselves involve some restriction on competition:

> "If notifiable mergers are not reviewable under the Competition Act then a number of practices which would be prohibited in other circumstances under Section 4(1) would escape the prohibition if they were part of a Merger agreement. The Authority does not believe that this was the legislature's intention."[83a]

A further complication arises on this point by virtue of the fact that mergers involving firms below a certain size are not subject to review under the 1978 Act. If the parties argument were accepted it could mean that mergers above the thresholds set in the 1978 Act were outside the 1991 Act while those below the threshold were subject to it. This in turn could mean that, where a merger below the threshold

---

[83]   *ibid.*, at para. 49.
[83a] *ibid.*, at para. 50.

prevented, restricted or distorted competition, aggrieved parties would have a right of relief under section 6 of the 1991 Act but that no such relief would exist in the case of a merger which had been notified to, and approved by, the Minister under the 1978 Act. It opined that this would appear highly inconsistent as the latter case would appear likely to give rise to more serious restrictions of competition than the former.[83b] Thirdly, the Competition Authority noted that:

> "the Minister must take account of the effects on competition of any notified merger before approving it. While this is so, the Minister might approve a merger which had adverse effects on competition because he believed that it was in the common good. While section 4(2) of the Competition Act allows the Authority to grant a licence to an anti-competitive agreement exempting it from the prohibition contained in section 4(1), strict criteria must be satisfied before such a licence can be granted. Section 4(2) does not allow a licence to be granted to an agreement on the grounds that it is in the interests of the common good. Thus, if the parties' argument was accepted, and section 4(1) was not to apply in the case of mergers notifiable under the Mergers Act, this would create a further inconsistency in the treatment of large and small mergers. The Authority believes that such an inconsistency was not intended."[84]

6–76 Although it accepted the parties' second argument that if mergers are reviewable under sections 4 and 5 of the 1991 Act, this could create considerable uncertainty for business, it went on to say that:

> "It is frequently the case that the enactment of new legislation results in uncertainty for business. Such uncertainty tends only to be eliminated over time as a result of court decisions which clarify the meaning of legislation. It has been claimed in some quarters that the entire Competition Act has created considerable uncertainty for business as people do not know exactly what sort of activities are prohibited by the legislation. The Authority cannot accept the view that it was not the legislature's intention that mergers would be subject to the Rules of Competition simply because this would create uncertainty."[85]

6–77 Finally, the Competition Authority referred to the parties' third argument that, by analogy with E.C. law, the acquisition does not come within the scope of section 4(1). The parties sought to rely on the decision of the European Court of Justice in *British American Tobacco Co Ltd.* and *R.J. Reynolds Industries Inc. v. Commission*[86] to the effect that the acquisition by one company of an equity interest in a competitor might

---

[83b] *ibid.*, at para. 51.
[84] para. 51.
[85] para. 53.
[86] Joined cases 142–156/84, [1987] E.C.R. 4487, [1988] 4 C.M.L.R. 24.

fall within Article [81(1)] where the acquirer obtained legal or *de facto* control of the commercial conduct of the other company. The parties argued that this only applies to an acquisition of a minority share-holding in the company and that the court's decision implies that where an undertaking acquires 100 per cent of the shares in another undertaking, Article [81] of the Treaty of Rome and hence section 4(1) of the Competition Act do not apply. The Competition Authority did not accept this argument and denied that the decision could be construed in this manner. It referred to Commission decisions such as *PPG/Mecaniver*[87] which, it stated, demonstrate that the sale of a business which gave rise to any restriction on competition would come within the scope of Article [81(1)]. By analogy therefore, the Competition Authority stated that such an agreement would offend against section 4 of the Competition Act.

6–78 The Competition Authority recognised that if mergers were subject to section 4 of the 1991 Act that this would create considerable uncertainty for business and also that the prospect of having to notify a merger to two separate bodies (the Competition Authority and the Minister) could impose a significant burden on the parties to a pro-posed merger. However, it stated that it had to operate on the basis of its interpretation of the Act. Even if it considered that mergers are not subject to the Act this would not prevent a challenge by an aggrieved person in the courts in respect of section 4 or section 5. In this instance, the parties had notified the acquisition to the Competition Authority and requested a certificate from it. In the Competition Authority's view for the reason stated, such arrangements do not enjoy any automatic exemption from the provisions of section 4(1). Given the particular market circumstances, however, the Competition Authority decided to issue a certificate under section 4(4).

6–79 There are many difficulties with a dual notification system. First, it is perceived to be cumbersome and costly for the parties involved in the merger or takeover. Secondly, the Minister may take a different view to the Competition Authority of the same transaction. This outcome is rendered more likely by the fact that the 1991 Act lists criteria which address purely competition issues, whilst other issues, such as employ-ment and "the common good", can be considered under the 1978 Act. Thus, the application of two systems causes uncertainty.

---

[87] Case No. 85/78/EEC, [1985] O.J. L35/54. [1985] 3 C.L.M.R. 359.

(8) Proposed Removal of Mergers and Takeovers from the Scope of the Act

6–80   Section 2 of the Competition (Amendment) Bill 1994 provided for the removal of mergers and takeovers from the scope of section 4 of the 1991 Act. Dissatisfaction had been expressed with the *Woodchester* decision in the Dáil.[88] A new section 19A was proposed to be added to the 1978 Act as follows:

> "(1) In this section 'merger or takeover' has the meaning assigned to it by section 1 of the Act of 1978.
> (2) (a) Subject to subsection (3), section 4 shall not apply to a merger or takeover.
> (b) This section shall have effect whether or not the merger or takeover is one to which the Act of 1978 applies by virtue of section 2 of that Act.
> (3) Subsection 2 shall not be construed as prejudicing the application of section 4 to anything done by any enterprise, the subject of the merger or takeover, not being the transfer of shares or assets or the doing of the other thing or things that constitute the merger or takeover.

The effect of this section thus would have been to remove merger and takeover agreements themselves.

6–81   Many arguments have been put forward to support this approach. First, the provisions of section 4(2) of the 1991 Act allowing the Competition Authority to grant licenses are inappropriate for the purpose of mergers. A license may only be granted for a specific period, whereas mergers and takeovers would require once off permanent approval. Secondly, there is no time limit provided for decisions under the 1991 Act. As speed tends to be of the essence in these type of transactions, this may create substantial difficulties for the parties. Thirdly, if sections 4 and 5 of the 1991 Act apply to mergers, a third party at any stage may initiate court proceedings in relation to a particular transaction. This could give rise to tactical litigation which would hinder the smooth operation of these transactions. Finally, in an acquisition of a listed public limited company by way of a general offer to shareholders, there will not merely be one agreement but rather a large number of individual agreements with shareholders many of whom are individuals who would not qualify as "undertakings" under the 1991 Act. In such a case, it seems clear that the application of the 1991 Act to the agreement *per se* is manifestly inappropriate.

6–82   Before the 1994 Bill could be enacted, the Government changed and the new Minister for Enterprise, Trade and Employment established

---

[88]   444 *Dáil Debates* Col. 1014, Ruairi Quinn.

the Competition and Mergers Review Group to consider this issue among others. The Group stated that the arguments in favour of streamlining the system so as to avoid the current double jeopardy were persuasive.[88a] The majority of the Group recommended that section 4 of the 1991 Act should no longer apply to mergers *per se* nor to any directly related restrictions which are notified as an integral part of the merger. It also recommended that section 5 of the 1991 Act should no longer be applicable to a proposed merger but that this should not affect the possibility of relying on section 5 in relation to actions of the merged entity. It accepted that by rendering section 4 and 5 of the 1991 Act inapplicable to mergers, there would be a risk that such acquisitions which might constitute abuses of section 5 but which would fall below the thresholds of the 1978 Act would avoid any regulatory scrutiny. The Group opined, however, that this situation would not arise very frequently. In addition and more importantly, it stated that even if mergers were not subject to the 1991 Act, the actions of the merged entity could always be subject to the application of section 5 of the 1991 Act by the Competition Authority or by way of private action where the actions of the group formed by the merger subsequently amounted to an abuse of its (dominant) position.

(9) Criteria for Assessment of Mergers under the Competition Act 1991

6–83 In the *Woodchester* case, the Competition Authority stated that while a merger frequently results in a reduction in the number of competitors in a market, it does not necessarily follow that this restricts competition. It stated that if section 4(1) were in fact to be interpreted in this way, it would amount to a *per se* prohibition of mergers which it did not believe was the legislature's intention. It is thus necessary to understand the criteria used by the Competition Authority to assess a merger or takeover under the 1991 Act in order to determine whether any breaches of that Act have occurred.

6–84 In the *Woodchester* case, the Competition Authority stated:

"before a merger can be found to offend against section 4(1) of the Competition Act, it must be shown that it would, or would be likely to, result in an actual diminution of competition in the market concerned. A reduction in the number of competitors or the fact that a merger will result in the merged entity having a larger share of the market than that previously held by either of the merged undertakings individually are not, of themselves, sufficient to establish that such a diminution of competition has occurred or would be likely to occur."[88b]

[88a] *op. cit.*, n.55 at pp. 42–45.
[88b] *op. cit.*, n.82 at para. 78.

Similarly, in *Scully Tyrell & Co./Edberg Ltd.* the Competition Authority stated:

> "In general, the Authority believes that a merger, per se, between competitors would not prevent, restrict or distort competition and thereby offend against section 4(1) unless the market is, or will as a result of the merger become, highly concentrated."[89]

6–85 In order to determine whether a merger results in an actual "diminution of competition" or "concentration", the Competition Authority has indicated that the economic circumstances prevailing in the market in question have to be taken into account.[90] It will consider whether the merger resulted in, or would be likely to result in, a lessening of competition in the relevant market such as would:

– allow the merged undertaking or all of the remaining firms in the market to raise their prices;

– reduce the ease with which new competitors could enter the market.[91]

It will also consider whether effective competition exists from overseas suppliers.[92]

6–86 Two tests for assessing market concentrations were set out in *Scully Tyrell & Co./Edberg Ltd.*[93] The first is the "four firm concentration ratio":

> "The four firm concentration ratio (the aggregate market share of the four largest firms) is a standard measure of market concentration used in economics. The Authority believes that it would generally be accepted that a market where the four firm concentration ratio fell below 40 per cent was effectively competitive."[94]

The other measure of market concentration is the Herfindahl Hirschman Index ("HHI"):

> "The HHI is the sum of the squares of the shares of all firms in a market. The HHI is used by the US Department of Justice to evaluate mergers and its guidelines classify markets into three categories.[95] Where the post-merger HHI is below 1000, the market is regarded as unconcentrated and mergers in such markets are considered unlikely to have adverse effects on

---

[89] Competition Authority Decision No. 12, January 29, 1993 at para. 65.
[90] *Nallen/O'Toole* op. cit., n.74.
[91] Woodchester, above, n.82, paras 77 and 78.
[92] *Scully Tyrell & Co./Edberg Ltd.* above, n.89, para. 65.
[93] *op. cit.*, n.89.
[94] *ibid.*, para. 54.
[95] U.S. Department of Justice Guidelines, issued June 14, 1984.

competition. Where the post merger HHI lies between 1000 and 1800, the market is regarded as moderately concentrated. Mergers which increase the HHI by more than 100 points in such markets are considered to potentially raise significant competitive concerns depending on other factors. When the HHI exceeds 1800, the market is regarded as highly concentrated, although even in this case, a merger raising the HHI by less than 50 points is considered unlikely to have adverse competitive consequences."[96]

However, the Competition Authority has recognised that in a small economy such as Irelands, market concentration ratios in many sectors may be high relative to those which exist in much larger economies.[96a]

6–87   In *Irish Distillery Group plc/Cooley Distillery plc*,[97] the Competition Authority for the first time determined that a merger agreement offended against section 4 of the 1991 Act. The merger agreement between Irish Distillers Group ("IDG") and Cooley Distillery ("Cooley) fell below the thresholds provided for in the 1978 Act and was not thus notified under that Act.[98] IDG was found to account for virtually 100 per cent of the Irish whiskey market which was defined as the "relevant market" with Cooley being the only other Irish producer. The Competition Authority found that the merger would have an impact on competition because of the significant impediments to entry into the Irish whiskey market and because of the fact that the merger would lead to the elimination of Cooley, a potential, although currently minor, competitor from the market. IDG argued that Cooley's financial difficulties meant that it was unlikely to remain in business and thus it should not be regarded as a potential competitor. This is known in the U.S. as the "failing firm defense". The Competition Authority rejected this argument, however, and opined that it was possible that an overseas drinks producer would acquire Cooley and real competition would develop. In *Barlo Group plc/Kingspan Group plc*[99] the failing firm defense was used more successfully. This case involved a potential acquisition by a subsidiary of Barlo Group plc of the assets of Kingspan Veha Ltd. The Competition Authority stated that the presence of other radiator manufacturers within Ireland and in other E.U. countries would ensure that the acquisition would not have the effect of preventing, restricting or distorting competition within the State. In addition, it referred to the "failing firm defence" noting that the target was in serious financial difficulties and that there was little

---

[96]   para. 55.
[96a] Competition Authority Decision No. 489 – Certificate in respect of agreements involving a merger and/or side of business, explanatory note para. 14.
[97]   Competition Authority Decision No. 285, February 25, 1994.
[98]   The Competition Authority denied that this fact raised a presumption that the proposed merger was not anti-competitive.
[99]   Competition Authority Decision No. 302, March, 15, 1994.

prospect of the plant continuing in operation unless the acquisition proceeded. Its point was not that it was concerned by the potential job losses *per se*, but that if the plant were to close, the degree of market concentration would increase anyway.[100] A certificate was issued under section 4(4).

(10) Merger Category Certificate

6–88   As noted in the previous section, while the Competition Authority has stated that section 4(1) of the 1991 Act applies equally to agreements which constitute a merger or takeover, it emphasises that this is not the same as stating that a merger offends against section 4(1).[101] In many cases a merger or sale of a business will not have any adverse effect on competition and so will not contravene the prohibition on anti-competitive agreements contained in section 4(1). Because the Competition Authority felt able to define the circumstances in which an agreement for a merger or sale of a business will not prevent, restrict or distort competition, it issued a category certificate with the aim of assisting businesses to ascertain whether an agreement would be regarded by the Competition Authority as anti-competitive. In issuing this category certificate, the Competition Authority hoped to reduce the number of unnecessary notifications *i.e.* notification of agreements which are not clearly anti-competitive. The introduction to the certificate specifically states that the certificate does not affect the requirement to notify mergers under the 1978 Act.[101a]

6–89   The category certificate indicates that agreements falling within the scope of the certificate do not, in the opinion of the Competition Authority, offend against Article 4(1). This certificate is not, however, binding on a court. As noted previously, it does limit the party's liability to damages pursuant to section 6 for a contravention of the prohibition in section 4(1) in any proceedings under section 6 commenced after the issue of the certificate for loss suffered as a result of the agreement in respect of the period the certificate was in force.[102] It should be noted that mergers which do not comply with the terms of the category certificate are not automatically prohibited, but are deemed to require closer investigation.

---

[100] In a submission to the Competition Authority, the Minister for Enterprise and Employment indicated that although he was concerned to see the growth and strengthening of Irish companies which would permit them to compete successfully in Europe, his main concern was safeguarding the employment of those in the plant being acquired. He stated that the target had been in a loss making situation for a number of years and that if the takeover did not proceed there would be a serious danger that jobs would be in jeopardy.

[101] *Scully Tyrell & Co.* above, n.89.

[101a] *op. cit.*, n.96a at para. 40.

[102] Competition Act 1991, s.6(6).

(a) Scope of the Certificate

6–90 Article 1 sets out the scope of the certificate. It covers agreements between undertakings, decisions of associations of undertakings and concerted practices which (1) involve a sale of business, including a merger or takeover and (2) satisfy the provisions of the certificate. Article 1(b) provides that a "sale of the business" takes place when all, or a substantial part, of the assets, including goodwill, of an undertaking are acquired by another undertaking. Article 1(c) provides that a "merger" takes place when two or more undertakings at least one of which carries on business in the State, come "under common control". Undertakings are deemed to be under "common control" if the decisions as to how or by whom each shall be managed can be made either by the same person, or by the same group of persons acting in concert. Article 1(c) notes that where one undertaking obtains the right to appoint or remove a majority of another corporate undertaking's board or management committee, the two undertakings are deemed to have come under common control. Similarly, where one undertaking obtains the right to shares in another corporate undertaking which carry 25 per cent or more of the voting rights, the two undertakings are deemed to have come under common control. For the avoidance of doubt, Article 1(d) provides that common control is stated to exist "in any circumstances where one undertaking controls the commercial conduct of the other".

6–91 The certificate is relevant to all mergers and sales of business without limitation as to size or turnover.[103] However, the acquisition of some or all of the assets of an undertaking by a receiver, liquidator or examiner is not included. Nor does the certificate apply to an agreement between undertakings by which one makes a loan to the other with the result that it may obtain the right to appoint a receiver over the other's assets on default.[104]

6–92 The certificate will not allow agreements containing unreasonable restraint of trade clauses to be cleared. Article 4(a) provides that the certificate will not apply to a merger or business sale agreement which involves a post-sale restriction on the vendor competing with the purchaser unless:

(a) the agreement includes the sale of the goodwill of the business and

(b) the restriction on the vendor competing, soliciting customers, soliciting employees and/or doing any other things in competition with the purchaser does not:

---

[103] Art. 1(f).
[104] Art. 1(e).

- exceed two years from the date of completion of the sale;
- apply to any location outside the territory where the products concerned were manufactured, purchased or sold by the vendor at the time of the agreement; and
- apply to goods or services other than those manufactured, purchased or sold by the vendor at the time of the agreement.

However, Article 4(b) provides that the certificate will apply to a merger or sale of business agreement which involves a post-sale restriction on the vendor's competing with the purchaser, soliciting customers or employees for a maximum of five years from the date of completion where the business involves the use of technical know-how. Once this technical know-how is in the public domain, the restriction must cease to apply. The term "technical know-how" is defined in this Article as "a body of technical information that is secret, substantial and identified in an appropriate form". Knowledge concerning a particular line of business will not constitute technical know-how for this purpose. Similarly, Article 4(c) provides that the certificate will apply to agreements which include restrictions on the vendor using or disclosing confidential information regarding the business for an unlimited period of time. It will not apply, however, where the agreement includes a restriction on the vendor using or disclosing technical know-how for a period exceeding five years.

6–93   Often the vendor will remain involved in the business, either actively as a director or employee or alternatively as a shareholder. In such cases it is not unusual to incorporate non-competition clause or non-solicitation clauses in the agreements for the sale of a business or mergers. Once, the time periods are reasonable, such clauses are acceptable. Article 5 thus provides that the certificate will apply where a vendor who has remained engaged in the business following completion is prevented from competing with the business or soliciting clients or employees as long as he or she remains engaged in the business. Similarly, if the vendor has retained at least a 10 per cent shareholding in the business after completion of the sale agreement, the certificate will still apply where the vendor is prevented from competing with the business or soliciting clients or employees of the business for a period of up to two years from the date of any future sale of such shares.

(b) Horizontal Mergers

6–94   The Competition Authority believes that where post-merger concentration levels are relatively low, a merger or sale of a business would not have any adverse effect on competition in the market. In the

Scully Tyrrell[105] decision discussed above, the Competition Authority set out two of the most popular methods of measuring market concentration, the Herfindahl Hirschman Index ("HHI") and the four firm concentration ratio.[106] Article 2(a) and (b) of the Certificate set out these two tests. Article 2 (a) of the Certificate relies on the HHI. It states:

> "Where a merger or sale of business involves two or more undertakings which are competitors in one or more markets then, in the Authority's opinion, such an agreement does not contravene Section 4(1) of the Competition Act 1991, where, following the merger, the level of market concentration as measured by the Herfindahl Hirschman Index ("HHI") is:
> (1) below 1000; or
> (2) between 1000 and 1800 but has increased by less than 100 points as a result of the merger; or
> (3) above 1800 but has increased by less than 50 points as a result of the merger."

The HHI index is defined as the sum of the squares of the market shares of all firms in the relevant market. Article 2(b) adopts the four firm concentration ratio as an alternative to the HHI.

> "Alternatively, where a merger or sale of business involves two or more undertakings which are competitors in one or more markets then, in the Authority's opinion, such an agreement does not contravene Section 4(1) of the Competition Act 1991, where following the merger, the combined market share of the four largest firms in terms of market share does not exceed 40 per cent of the total relevant market."

The Competition Authority has stated that the HHI should be used whenever possible as it provides more accurate information on market structure and concentration.[106a]

6–95 By contrast with Article 2(a) and (b), Article 2(c) considers not the post merger market and concentration, but rather the creation or strengthening of a dominant position:

> "Where a merger or sale of business involves two or more undertakings which are competitors in one or more markets then, irrespective of the level of market concentration following the merger, in the Authority's opinion, such an agreement could contravene Section 4(1) of the Competition Act 1991, if it led to the creation or strengthening of a dominant position in a relevant market. For this reason where any one of the parties already has a market share of 35 per cent or more this category certificate does not apply."

---

[105] Above, n.89.
[106] paras 54 and 55.
[106a] *op. cit.*, n.96a, para. 13.

To benefit from a certificate, the parties in such a case would have to notify the merger and seek an individual certificate.

6–96   Where post-merger concentration levels exceed the thresholds set out above, the Competition Authority believes that other factors must also be taken into account. It considers, for example, that, even in highly concentrated markets, a merger will not have any adverse effect on competition in the absence of any barriers to entry or where there is a significant level of competition from imports.[106b] The explanatory note to the category certificate also sets out the views of the Competition Authority on issues such as barriers to entry, potential competition from imports and the actual level of competition in the relevant market. It states that:

> "Where there is evidence that competition in the relevant market is relatively weak, the Authority believes that a more detailed analysis of any proposed merger would be required in order to establish whether or not it might have an adverse effect on competition. Consequently this certificate would not apply to mergers in such circumstances."[106c]

6–97   Finally, the Competition Authority decision in *Scully Tyrrell* is further reflected in Article 2(d) of the category certificate which states:

> "Where a merger or sale of business involves two or more undertakings which are competitors in one or more markets then, irrespective of the level of market concentration following the merger, in the Authority's opinion, such an agreement does not contravene Section 4(1) of the Competition Act, 1991,unless it can be shown that there are barriers which would prevent other firms entering the market or that there is little prospect for purchasers of the products concerned to obtain supplies from outside the State."

(c) Vertical Mergers

6–98   In general, vertical mergers are unlikely to restrict competition. The companies acquired or joined are not competitors and thus there is no question of eliminating a competitor. However, where an agreement was designed to block access either to raw materials or to distribution outlets, competition in the marketplace could be affected.
Article 3 of the category certificate provides that:

> "where a merger or sale of business involves two or more undertakings which operate at different stages in the production or distribution process in respect of the same product, i.e. between a firm and its suppliers or a firm and its distributors or retailers, it does not, in the Authority's opinion,

---

[106b] *op. cit.*, n.96a, para. 17.
[106c] *op. cit.*, n.96a, para. 22.

contravene section 4(1) unless it can be shown that an agreement would result in foreclosure of a relevant market by denying other undertakings access to sources of supply or distribution outlets which are independent of the undertakings which are parties to the sale of business agreement."

(d) Guinness Ireland Group Limited/United Beverages Holdings Limited

6–99 In *Guinness Ireland Group Limited/United Beverages Holdings Limited*,[107] the Competition Authority were notified of an agreement involving a share purchase agreement whereby Guinness Ireland Group Limited ("GIG"), which already owned 30.76 per cent of the shares in United Beverages Holdings Limited ("UBH"), wished to acquire 100 per cent of the company. GIG also owned a 49.6 per cent shareholding in C&C Wholesale Ltd ("C&C"), UBH's major rival in the packaged beer and soft drinks distribution market and a competitor in the soft drinks production market. GIG contended that the agreement complied with the Competition Authority's draft category certificate on mergers, in so far as the merger was horizontal, no party had a market share of 35 per cent or more of the relevant market and barriers to entry into the industry were low. Also, it argued that the vertical element of the merger would not have an exclusionary effect on existing or potential competitors in the market for beer products.

6–100 The Competition Authority repeated its assertion that where post-merger concentration levels exceed the thresholds set out in the category certificate, other factors must also be taken into account and that where there is evidence that competition in the relevant market is relatively weak, a more detailed analysis of any proposed merger would be required in order to establish whether or not it might have an adverse effect on competition. Consequently the certificate would not apply to mergers in such circumstances.

6–101 Since, the agreement under consideration had both horizontal and vertical aspects, the Competition Authority considered the effects of the merger under six headings: the HHI; the four-firm concentration ratio; barriers to entry; potential competition from imports; the actual level of competition; and the vertical effects. The Competition Authority determined that GIG's shareholding in C&C was relevant to the assessment of the effect on competition of the transaction. It stated that while the market shares of C&C are not necessarily ascribed to GIG in the calculations of HHI and four-firm concentration ratio, the overall

---

[107] Competition Authority Decision No. 512, June 17, 1998.

effect of the cross-shareholding must be taken into account in the analysis. It considered that it was an anti-competitive situation for a company with GIG's strength in the brewing market to own 100 per cent of companies with 30.4 per cent of the wholesale market while simultaneously owning 49.6 per cent of a company with 12.58 per cent of the market, these being the only two nationwide wholesalers. Further, GIG would have full control of the largest and fourth-largest wholesalers, and a 49.6 per cent share of the third-largest, with a first option on the purchase of the remaining shares. There would be only one other wholesaler of comparable size left in the market.

6–102 On the basis of this analysis, the Competition Authority determined that GIG's increase in shareholding from 30.76 per cent to 100 per cent restricted or distorted competition by virtue of its 49.6 per cent shareholding in C&C. Consequently, in the Authority's opinion, the notified agreement contravened section 4(1) of the 1991 Act. GIG provided certain undertakings in relation to C&C in respect of the reduction of this shareholding to below 10 per cent and the waiving of its rights to appoint a director and of its pre-emption rights. The Competition Authority accepted that if those undertakings were to have immediate effect, they would make the transaction eligible for a certificate. In this case, however, the arrangements would clearly require time to complete. The Competition Authority thus decided to grant a licence under section 4(3) of the 1991 Act on condition that the aspect of the transaction which the Authority found offensive, namely GIG's influence over C&C, be removed as soon as possible and at any rate within a certain specified time frame.

III. CONCLUSION

6–103 The application of the 1991 Act to mergers is unfortunate. For the reasons outlined in paragraph 6–81, the provisions of the 1991 Act are not appropriate to mergers and takeover agreements. The Category certificate on mergers provides some degree of comfort and promotes greater certainty for businesses. However, as the *United Beverages* decision demonstrates, in many cases a more detailed analysis of a proposed merger or acquisition will be required and the certificate will simply not apply. These cases are likely to involve large companies with a proportionately high market share. The great majority of these companies will be listed companies and the importance of speed in such cases must not be underestimated.

C. The UK System

6–104   In the UK, the regulation of mergers is governed by the Fair Trading Act 1973 ("the 1973 Act") as amended by the Companies Act 1989 and the Deregulation and Contracting Out Act 1994.[108] The competition bodies with responsibility for overseeing mergers are the Department of Trade and Industry ("the DTI"), the Office of Fair Trading ("the OFT") and the Competition Commission previously known as the Monopolies and Mergers Commission ("the MMC").[109]

I. MERGER OR TAKEOVER

6–105   Section 64 of the 1973 Act provides that a merger occurs where two or more enterprises have "ceased to be distinct". Enterprises may cease to be distinct either because they are brought under common ownership or control or because there is an arrangement or transaction between the persons carrying on the enterprises so that one of them will cease to be carried on in order to prevent competition between them. Section 65 identifies three levels of control. Firstly, a company may acquire the ability materially to influence the policy of another company. The size of a shareholding alone will not determine whether the holder can materially influence the policy of the company concerned. For example in Peninsular and Oriental Steam Navigation Co. ("P&O")/European Ferries Group plc,[109a] a shareholding of 16.1 per cent of the voting rights of European Ferries was deemed by the MMC to be sufficient to allow P&O to materially influence its policy. The distribution of the shares was a key determinant in this case as the other shareholdings were particularly fragmented. Other relevant factors in making this decision would be board representation, restrictions on voting rights and the existence of agreements with the company which would enable the holder to influence policy. The OFT has stated that as a shareholding of 25 per cent or more generally enables the holder to block special resolutions, this proportion is likely to be seen as automatically conferring the ability materially to influence policy — even when all the remaining shares are held by one person.[110] However the OFT may examine any case where there is a shareholding of 15 per cent or more. Secondly, a company may acquire the ability to control the policy of another company. This is *de facto* control. Finally, a

---

[108]   See the Office of Fair Trading booklet called "*Mergers: A Guide to Procedures under the Fair Trading Act 1973*".

[109]   Pursuant to the Competition Act 1998.

[109a]   Cm 31 (1986).

[110]   *op. cit.*, n.108 at para. 2.6.

company may acquire a controlling interest in another company. This is "legal control". A controlling interest generally means a shareholding carrying more than 50 per cent of the voting rights of the company.

II. CRITERIA FOR A REFERRAL TO THE COMPETITION COMMISSION

6–106 For a merger to qualify for investigation in the UK under section 64 of the 1973 Act, at least one of the enterprises merging must be carried on in the UK or under the control of a body corporate incorporated in the UK. A merger thus between two foreign companies may still qualify for investigation, if either of the two companies controls any enterprise which is carried on in the UK or by is controlled by a UK company. In addition to fulfilling this criterion, to qualify for investigation, the merger must satisfy either the "share of supply" test or the "assets test". The former requires that the enterprises which cease to be distinct must supply or acquire goods or services of a similar kind and must together supply or acquire at least 25 per cent of all those goods or services supplied in the UK or a substantial part of it. Although there is no definition in the Act of "a substantial part", in *R v. Monopolies and Mergers Commission and another ex parte South Yorkshire Transport Ltd.*[110a] the House of Lords held that while there cannot be a fixed definition of the term, an area must be of such size, character and importance as to make it worth consideration for the purposes of merger control. The alternative "assets test" requires that the gross value of the world-wide assets being acquired must be more than STG £70 million. Merger references may be made either before a merger has taken place or within four months of the merger having taken place.[111]

III. VOLUNTARY NOTIFICATION

6–107 Unlike the position in Ireland under the 1978 Act, there is no statutory duty to notify a merger. There are no penalties or sanctions under the 1973 Act for taking part in a non-notified merger. Sections 75A–75F of the Fair Trading Act 1973[112] provide for a system of voluntary notification. The advantage of notification for a company is that the Secretary of State is obliged within 20 working days to decide whether to refer the merger to the Competition Commission. A maximum extension of 15 working days is allowed.[113] If no reference

---

110a [1993] 1 W.L.R.
111 Unless there was no announcement to the public of the merger and no announcement to the Secretary of State or Director General.
112 Inserted by the Companies Act 1989 and amended by the Fair Trading Act (Amendment) (Mergers Pre-notification) Regulations 1994 (S.I. No. 1934 of 1994).
113 s.75B(2).

takes place during this time, the merger is automatically cleared.[114] A prescribed Merger Notice form must be completed and submitted to the OFT by post or by hand together with an appropriate fee. This procedure may only be used to provide formal notification of a proposed merger which has been announced to the public. It is not available in the case of completed mergers or proposed mergers which have not been publicly announced.

6–108 As in Ireland, the regulation of newspaper companies is particularly strict. In the U.K., the provisions for the control of newspaper transfers are contained in sections 57–62 of the 1973 Act. They arise from the 1961–62 report of the Royal Commission on the press which concluded that action should be taken to regulate the increasing concentration of newspaper ownership which could threaten the freedom and variety of expression of opinion and perhaps even the unbiased presentation of news. As a result, the proprietors of newspapers circulating in the U.K. must obtain the prior consent of the Secretary of State for Trade and Industry to acquire a newspaper (or newspaper assets) where the average paid-for daily circulation of the newspapers involved is 500,000 copies or more. The newspapers whose circulation is to be counted for this purpose are those being acquired and those already owned by the purchaser.

IV. THE DIRECTOR GENERAL'S ADVICE

6–109 The function of the Director General who heads the OFT is to monitor business transactions which may result in the merger of two distinct enterprises. The Director General advises the Secretary of State as to whether such mergers should be referred to the Competition Commission. The primary issue is to determine the effect of the merger on competition. The OFT has stated that every assessment follows a similar basic pattern. Firstly, the markets in which the enterprises are engaged are identified. This assessment is similar to that carried out by the Competition Authority in Ireland under the 1991 Act. The two main factors to be considered in defining the market are product dimension and geographic dimension. In the former, the OFT will consider the substitutability of products. The geographic dimension may lead to a decision that the UK as a whole is relevant or a particular part of the UK is relevant. The limits are determined by evaluating how readily customers in any particular area will switch between local suppliers and those based elsewhere in the event of a change in the relative prices charged by the two groups. Having identified the market, the OFT will then proceed to analyse the structure of the markets affected by the

---

[114] s.75A(3).

merger in order to determine the likely effects of the merger on the nature and degree of competition in those markets. Factors which will influence the OFT are the extent and impact of barriers to market entry, the buying power of customers and the size and rates of growth of the markets. Having made these assessments, the OFT will then be in a position to recommend whether or not a referral should be made or to recommend the imposition of undertakings on the parties.

6–110 In certain circumstances, the Secretary of State may accept binding undertakings from a merged enterprise as an alternative to making a reference to the Competition Commission. The enterprise may give structural undertakings agreeing to divest itself of part of its business. Typically, this will involve an undertaking to dispose of assets or shares within a stated period. Alternatively, behavioural undertakings may be given where the enterprise gives a formal commitment in respect of its future conduct. Once they are in place, these undertakings will be monitored by the OFT in order to ensure compliance.

V. THE COMPETITION COMMISSION EVALUATION

6–111 The Competition Commission is an independent body which examines any merger referred to it in order to determine whether it is contrary to the public interest. The Competition Commission performs the functions of the Mergers & Monopolies Commission which was dissolved pursuant to section 45(3) of the Competition Act, 1998. This transfer of functions to the Competition Commission is said to reflect the close relationship between chapter II of the Competition Act, 1998 which prohibits the abuse of a dominant position and the 1973 Act.[115] Section 84 of the 1973 Act provides that the Competition Commission "shall take into account all matters which appear to them in the particular circumstances to be relevant". In particular, however, the Competition Commission is required to consider the desirability:

– of maintaining and promoting effective competition between persons supplying goods and services in the UK;

– of promoting the interests of consumers, purchasers and other users of goods and services in the UK in respect of the prices charged for them and in respect of their quality and the variety of goods and services supplied;

– of promoting, through competition, the reduction of costs and the development and use of new techniques and new products; and of facilitating the entry of new competitors into existing markets;

---

[115] Corry, 1998 Current Law Statutes, (Sweet & Maxwell) pp. 41–59.

– of maintaining and promoting the balanced distribution of industry and employment in the UK;

– of maintaining and promoting competitive activity in markets outside the UK and on the part of producers of goods, and of suppliers of goods and services, in the UK.

6–112 In making its assessment, the Competition Commission hears evidence from all the relevant parties. It then draws up and delivers a report to the Secretary of State. The Competition Commission must exclude from this report any confidential information about the private affairs of individuals, and information about the affairs of businesses where disclosure could detrimentally affect such businesses.

VI. ACTION FOLLOWING THE COMPETITION COMMISSION REPORT

6–113 Once the Competition Commission report is received, the Secretary of State will attempt to publish it within 20 days. This is described as an "administrative target" rather than a statutory requirement.[115a] If the Competition Commission decides that the merger should be allowed to proceed, the Secretary of State must accept this finding and take no further action. If however, the report is adverse and the Competition Commission concludes that the merger should not be allowed to proceed, the Secretary of State may block the merger or require the parties to the merger to satisfy certain conditions before allowing the merger to proceed. In order to do this, undertakings may be required or alternatively, if the case is not suitable for undertakings, the Secretary of State may make an order after consulting on its terms.[116] Competition Commission reports are usually laid before Parliament and subsequently published. The announcement of publication is made via the Stock Exchange's Regulatory News Service. The DTI also issues a press statement.

[115a] For guidance on DTI procedures and handling Merger references and reports see dti.gov.uk website.
[116] Section 73 of the 1973 Act.

CHAPTER 7

REGULATION OF FINANCIAL INSTITUTIONS

7–01 The acquisition of holdings in certain types of undertaking attracts additional regulation. The undertakings in question are undertakings whose businesses are perceived to be of central importance to the economy and whose investors or creditors are deemed to require particular protection. In this regard, special provisions have been introduced in the form of both primary and secondary legislation in order to regulate the acquisition of large shareholdings in credit institutions, investment firms and insurance companies.

A. Credit Institutions

7–02 The Central Bank licenses and supervises credit institutions operating within the State. The credit institutions which are supervised by the Central Bank currently comprise licensed banks, building societies, TSB Bank, ACC Bank plc, ICC Bank plc and ICC Investment Bank. Credit institutions authorised in other Member States may also establish branches in the State or provide services in the State on the basis of the Banking Directives.[1] These institutions do not need to obtain licences from the Central Bank and are not supervised by the Central Bank.

7–03 Traditionally, merchant banks provided institutional services, large commercial financing, investment advice and underwriting services and industrial banks offered leasing and hire purchase services, factoring and export finance, etc. Competition between these institutions, however, has led to the gradual erosion of the distinction between the business activities of the merchant banks and industrial banks.[2]

In addition, the building societies, and other credit institutions supervised by the Central Bank have developed and consolidated their role in banking business over the last ten years. The final form of credit institution to be considered in this Chapter is the credit union. Because of their unique "common bond", credit unions are subject to separate

---

[1] para. 7–19–7–20.
[2] Foy, *The Capital Markets* (Round Hall Sweet & Maxwell, 1998), p. 46.

and special attention and do not fall within the ambit of Central Bank regulation.

I. THE CENTRAL BANK ACTS 1942–97

7–04　The Central Bank ("the Bank") is the competent authority for the licensing and supervision of banking business in the State under the Central Bank Acts, 1942 to 1997[3] and the European Communities (Licensing and Supervision of Credit Institutions) Regulations, 1992.[3a] In order to conduct banking business[4] in Ireland, a licence is required.[5] A number of categories of institutions are, however, exempt from the requirement to hold a banking licence.[6] These include: central banks in other Member States, the ACC, the ICC, the Post Office Savings Bank, the TSB, building societies, credit unions and unit trusts. In addition, the Minister is authorised to amend this list where he or she believes it necessary in the interest of the orderly and proper regulation of the financial market.[7]

7–05　The Central Bank Act 1989 ("the 1989 Act") strengthened the powers of the Bank in relation to the licensing and supervision of banking business. One of its main objectives was to provide for the prior notification to and approval by the Bank and, in certain cases, the Minister for Finance ("the Minister") of proposals to acquire specific holdings in a licensed bank in the State and of proposals by licensed banks to acquire certain holdings in other corporate bodies.

(1) Acquiring Transactions

7–06　Chapter VI of Part II of the 1989 Act[8] deals with acquiring transactions in respect of credit institutions. Section 75(1)(a) of the 1989 Act defines an "acquiring transaction" as:

> "any acquisition by a person or more than one person acting in concert of shares or other interest in a holder of a licence but does not apply to an acquisition where
> (i) after the proposed acquisition, the proportion of shares would not exceed the "prescribed percentage" and

---

[3]　These include the Central Bank Act 1942, the Central Bank Act 1971, the Central Bank Act 1989 and the Central Bank Act 1997.

[3a]　S.I. No. 395 of 1992.

[4]　As defined by section 2 of the Central Bank Act 1971 as amended by section 29 of the Central Bank Act 1989 and section 70 of the Central Bank Act 1997.

[5]　Central Bank Act 1971, s.7(1) as amended by the European Communities (Deposit Guarantee schemes) Regulations 1995 (S.I. No. 168 of 1995) and section 70(a) of the Central Bank Act 1997.

[6]　Central Bank Act 1971, s.7(4) as amended by section 30 of the Central Bank Act 1989.

[7]　Central Bank Act, 1971, s.7(4)(b) as amended by s.30 of Central Bank Act 1989.

[8]　ss. 74–88.

(ii) if the holder of the licence concerned is a body incorporated in the State, the acquisition, together with any other interest already held or controlled by the acquirer, would not confer a right to appoint or remove some or all of the board of directors or committee of management of the holder of that licence."

It is important to note that an acquisition by a concert party will also be considered to be an acquisition for the purposes of this Part of the Act. A "prescribed percentage" is defined by section 74 of the 1989 Act as "10 per cent. of the total shares or of the total voting rights attaching to shares". This figure may however be varied by order of the Minister following consultation with the Bank subject to the prior approval of the Dáil and Seanad.[9]

7–07 Not all such acquisitions are included, however, and section 75(2) of the 1989 Act empowers the Bank to exempt any acquiring transaction or any class of acquiring transaction, subject to any conditions it sees fit, where:

(a) the acquiring transaction is being, or has been entered into, by a licence holder as part of a bona fide underwriting of a share issue, or

(b) the acquiring transaction is being entered into with the prior approval of the Bank in the interests of the proper and orderly regulation of banking or financial markets in the State, or

(c) the interest in shares is not being beneficially acquired by a licence holder or is being acquired only in the course of its normal business to secure the issue of a loan to be made by the licence holder to the undertaking concerned.

The first and the third category of transaction above are exempted because they do not involve an attempt to secure control or influence over another company. These transactions are merely transactions entered into in the course of a licence holder's ordinary banking business. The second category of exemption was added by section 55 of the Central Bank Act 1997 and it gives the Bank greater discretion to exempt inappropriate transactions from the scope of Chapter VI. Once the Bank determines that the transaction is in the interests of the proper and orderly regulation of the market, it may approve the transaction and exempt the transaction.

7–08 Originally, the definition of an "acquiring transaction" also included acquisitions by licence holders of shares or other interests in any other undertaking.[10] Section 4 of the Central Bank Act, 1997 removes this provision which severely restricted a credit institution's ability to

---

[9] Central Bank Act 1989, s.79.
[10] Central Bank Act 1989, s.75(1)(b).

make investments in other companies. The European Communities (Licensing and Supervision of Credit Institutions) Regulations 1992 which are discussed below deal with this issue now.

(2) Notification of Proposed Acquiring Transactions

7–09   Section 82(1) of the 1989 Act places an obligation on each of the undertakings involved in the proposed acquiring transaction, who have knowledge of the existence of the proposal, to notify the Bank in writing. Where the Bank needs further information to assess the transaction, it may request any further information from any of the undertakings within one month of receipt of the notification.[11] Criminal penalties may be applied to the person in control of an undertaking who fails to notify the Bank.[12] Upon summary conviction, a maximum fine of £1,000 and/or a maximum prison sentence of 12 months may be imposed. Upon conviction on indictment, the maximum fine is £50,000 and the maximum prison sentence is five years. The "person in control" of an incorporated or unincorporated body is defined as "any officer of the body concerned who knowingly and willingly authorises or permits the contravention".[13]

(3) Validity of Certain Acquiring Transactions

7–10   In order to ensure that the Bank's approval is sought, section 76(1) of the 1989 Act invalidates any acquiring transaction in a license holder unless approved by the Bank or unless the "relevant period" has elapsed without the Bank refusing its approval. A "relevant period" for these purposes is six months.[14] The effect of this invalidity is that title to any shares or other interests will not pass and any consequential purported exercise of powers will be void. However, a degree of flexibility is allowed and section 76(2) of the 1989 Act[15] allows a person who has inadvertently breached the rules to seek a High Court order validating the transaction. A person may apply to the High Court for an order declaring that, notwithstanding the failure of the person to notify the Bank:

– the acquiring transaction is and always has been valid; and
– title to any shares or other interest concerned did pass; and
– that all purported exercise of powers is and always has been valid.

In order to make such an order, the High Court must find either that the failure to notify the Bank of the proposed acquiring transaction was due to inadvertence on the part of the person or that it is otherwise in

---

[11]   *ibid.*, s.82(2).
[12]   *ibid.*, s.82(3)(b).
[13]   *ibid.*
[14]   *ibid.*, s.83.
[15]   As inserted by section 56 of the Central Bank Act 1997.

the interests of justice to make the order. In granting an order under section 76(2), the court is authorised to impose conditions.

7–11 This is a sensible provision given that an acquisition by a concert party could easily lead to a licence holder exceeding the prescribed percentage without its knowledge. A similar power exists for the Irish Takeover Panel to grant a waiver from the Rule 9[16] of the Irish Takeover Panel Act 1997, (Takeover) Rules, 1997 requirement to make a mandatory general offer, where the thresholds are exceeded as a result of an inadvertent mistake.

7–12 Where a purported acquiring transaction is rendered invalid under section 76 of the 1989 Act, the purported vendor of shares is entitled, under section 81, to recover damages from the purported purchaser. This provision will act as a further incentive to persons to comply with the requirements of the Act. It will be a defence, however, for the purported acquirer to prove that the purported vendor was notified by him before the purported transaction of the circumstances which gave rise to the possibility of such an invalidity. Breslin has pointed out a deficiency in the drafting of section 81 which restricts the right to damages to cases where shares have been sold and does not cover situations where some other interest is sold.[17]

(4) Ministerial Consent and Central Bank Approval

7–13 Section 77(1) of the 1989 Act provides that the Bank must seek the approval of the Minister before it makes a final decision on whether or not to approve an acquiring transaction which would result in 20 per cent or more of the total assets of licence holders in the State being concentrated in the control of the acquirer. Section 77(2) provides that the Minister cannot give consent unless:

(a) he or she is satisfied that the Bank's decision to approve or refuse approval would be in the interests of the orderly and proper regulation of banking, and

(b) where, the proposed acquisition exceeds the thresholds of the Mergers, Takeovers and Monopolies (Control) Act, 1978, he or she has consulted with the Minister for Industry and Commerce [now the Minister of Enterprise, Trade and Employment] and any other Minister concerned.

---

[16] Irish Takeover Panel Act 1997, Takeover Rules, 1997.
[17] *Banking Law in the Republic of Ireland* (Gill & Macmillan, 1998), p. 87.

Furthermore, the Minister must refuse consent where he or she believes that the exigencies of the common good so warrant. Where the Minister decides to consent to the acquisition, he or she may require the Bank to make the approval conditional on any conditions the Minister deems necessary for the orderly and proper regulation of banking.[18] In addition to imposing these conditions, section 80 of the 1989 Act allows the Bank to attach any conditions which it deems necessary for the orderly and proper regulation of banking. These conditions may be amended or revoked by the Bank subsequently. However, in the case of conditions imposed at the request of the Minister, the Minister's consent will be required to such amendment or revocation.

Where the Bank has sought the consent of the Minister under this section and the Minister has decided that consent should not be granted, the Bank is obliged under section 78(2) to refuse its approval. In all other cases, the Bank will refuse approval only if it is satisfied that the transaction would not be in the interest of the orderly and proper regulation of banking.

7–14   Section 84(1) of the 1989 Act allows the Bank, on its own initiative, or at the request of the Minister for the purposes of making an assessment under section 77, to carry out any inquiries necessary to allow for proper consideration of the proposed acquiring transaction. Heavy penalties may be imposed on persons who impede inquiries or who provide false or misleading information.[19] On summary conviction, a maximum £1,000 fine and/or a maximum prison sentence of 12 months may be imposed. On conviction on indictment, a maximum fine of £50,000 and/or a maximum prison sentence of five years may be imposed.

(5) Communication of the Bank's Approval or Refusal

7–15   The Bank is required by section 85 of the 1989 Act to communicate its decision on the proposed transaction to the undertakings concerned. The Bank may have decided to grant either absolute approval or conditional approval or it may have decided to refuse to approve the proposed transaction. In the case of a refusal to grant approval, the Bank must state its reasons in writing, subject to certain secrecy requirements imposed on the staff of the Bank.[20]

---

[18] s.77(3).
[19] s.84(3).
[20] s.16.

7–16   In the case of a refusal or a conditional approval, section 86(1) of the 1989 Act authorises the relevant undertaking to appeal on a point of law to the High Court within one month of being notified of the decision. The Minister is entitled, at his request, to be included as a party to the proceedings. Any costs incurred by the Minister may be awarded by the Court against other parties to the proceedings. Unusually, section 86(6) provides that an appeal against a decision of the High Court will not lie to the Supreme Court.

(6) Compliance

7–17   Section 87(1) of the 1989 Act sets out the penalties for any person contravening the approval or the conditions of approval to enter an acquiring transaction. The contravention in question may be either by act or by omission. Upon summary conviction, a maximum fine of £1,000 and/or a prison sentence not exceeding 12 months may be imposed. Upon conviction on indictment, a maximum fine of £50,000 and/or a maximum five-year prison sentence may be imposed. Section 87(2) provides for a continuing offence for a person convicted of an offence under the section for failure to comply with the conditions of approval. The penalty provided is a fine not exceeding £1,000 for a summary conviction or £5,000 on conviction on indictment.

(7) Sections 201 and 203 of the Companies Act 1963

7–18   Sections 201 and 203 of the Companies Act 1963 enable acquisitions and disposals to be effected by means of a court order.[21] Section 88(2) of the 1989 Act prohibits the making of any such order until the Bank has been notified and given its approval to the acquiring transaction or until the expiry of the default period. The purpose of this provision is to ensure that the Bank is aware of any such transactions and is given the opportunity to supervise their suitability.

II. THE EUROPEAN COMMUNITIES (LICENSING AND SUPERVISION OF CREDIT INSTITUTIONS) REGULATIONS 1992

7–19   The First Council Directive on the Co-ordination of Laws, Regulations and Administrative Provisions relating to the taking up and pursuit of the business of credit institutions ("the First Directive")[22] removed many of the obstacles to freedom of establishment of banks and other credit institutions. It set out common standards for the

---

[21]   Chaps 8 and 11.
[22]   Council Directive 77/780, O.J. L322/30.

granting of banking licenses and introduced the basic principles of co-operation between competent authorities in Member States. The Second Council Directive on the Co-ordination of Laws, Regulations and Administrative Provisions relating to the taking up and pursuit of the business of credit institutions ("the Second Directive")[23] sought to remove the barriers to a unified Community banking market which still existed after the implementation of the First Directive.[24] By removing these barriers, the Second Directive achieved the essential harmonisation necessary to allow for the granting of a single banking licence recognised throughout the Community. A necessary part of this harmonisation is the application of the principle of home Member State prudential supervision. This ensures that similar conditions are imposed on credit institutions in terms of authorisation and continued supervision.

7–20   The Second Directive applies to all credit institutions except those exempted from the First Directive.[25] The First Directive excluded the central banks of Member States, post office giro institutions and in Ireland, credit unions. The Second Directive was implemented in Irish law by the European Communities (Licensing and Supervision of Credit Institutions) Regulations 1992 ("the Regulations") which came into force on January 1st, 1993.[26] The Regulations currently apply to the licensed banks, building societies, Trustee Savings Bank, ACC and ICC.

(1) Suitability of Shareholders as a Condition of Authorisation

7–21   One of the common conditions imposed on credit institutions relates to the suitability of large shareholders. Regulation 7(1) of the Regulations provides that the Bank may not authorise a credit institution until it has been informed of the identities of the shareholders or members, whether direct or indirect, natural or legal persons, that have "qualifying holdings" and the amounts of those holdings.[27] Regulation 7(2) requires the Bank to be satisfied that every person holding a qualifying holding is "a fit and proper person whom it is reasonable to expect will exercise his shareholding and other rights in the applicant in the interests of the orderly and proper regulation of credit institutions in the State". This gives effect to Article 5 of the Second Directive which prohibits the competent authorities from granting

---

[23] Council Directive 89/646, O.J. L386/1.
[24] See Claotti, "The Completion of the Internal Financial Market: Current Position and Outlook" *EC Financial Market Regulation and Company Law*, Mads Andenas & S. Kenyon-Slade, (Sweet & Maxwell, London, 1993) Chap. 1.
[25] Art. 2(1) & (2).
[26] S.I. No. 395 of 1992.
[27] See also Art. 5.

authorisation to credit institutions if they are not satisfied as to "the suitability" of the members and shareholders. In making this assessment, the supervisory authorities are directed to consider the need to ensure "the sound and prudential management of a credit institution".

(2) Qualifying Holdings

7–22 The definition in Regulation 2 of a "qualifying holding" refers to:

(a) a holding by a person, either on his own or in concert with another person, of 10 per cent. or more of the shares[28] or of the voting rights attaching to shares in an undertaking, or

(b) a shareholding or interest held by a person in an undertaking which either confers a right to appoint or remove one or more members of the board of directors or of the committee of management of the undertaking, however described, or otherwise allows that person to exercise a significant influence over the direction or management of the undertaking.

This is consistent with the definition in the Second Directive which refers to a "direct or indirect holding in an undertaking which represents 10 per cent or more of the capital or of the voting rights or which makes it possible to exercise a significant influence over the management of the undertaking in which a holding subsists".[29]

7–23 Clearly, where the shares of a company are very widely held, a shareholding of considerably less than 10 per cent may constitute a qualifying holding under the second part of this definition. It should also be noted that this definition includes both direct and indirect holdings and holdings by concert parties. Regulation 5 allows for the determination of qualifying holdings in credit institutions. It states that the following shares or rights in the credit institution are treated as held by a person:

(a) shares or rights held by another person on that person's behalf;

(b) shares or rights held by an undertaking which is under the effective control[30] of that person whether the shares or rights are held by that undertaking itself or by any other undertaking which is a subsidiary of the first mentioned undertaking or which is under the effective control of that undertaking;

---

[28] Reg. 5 provides that the term "shares" includes for the purposes of the regulations any interest in shares which are to be notified under section 77 of the Companies Act 1990.

[29] Art. 1.

[30] Reg. 4 defines the term "control" as including "any power, whether arising from a contract or agreement or otherwise, whereby one party can direct the affairs of another and a parent undertaking shall be deemed to control its subsidiaries".

(c)   shares or rights held by an undertaking in which that person holds 20 per cent. or more of the shares or of the voting rights;

(d)   shares or rights held by a partnership in which that person is a partner or by an undertaking of which that person is a director, or

(e)   shares or rights held by any person with whom that person has an agreement or arrangement with respect to that acquisition, holding or disposal of shares or interests in that credit institution or under which they undertake to act together in exercising their voting power in relation to that credit institution.

(3) Notification of Proposed Acquisitions of Qualifying Holdings in Credit Institutions

7–24   In addition to evaluating qualifying shareholders at the time of authorisation, the Regulations allow for their continuing scrutiny. Regulation 14 regulates the acquisition of shareholdings in credit institutions. Regulation 14(1) notes that, without prejudice to the provisions of Chapter VI of Part II of the 1989 Act, Regulation 14 applies to all acquisitions by any person of shares or other interests in a credit institution which is authorised by the Bank.

7–25   Regulation 14(2) obliges any person who proposes to acquire, directly or indirectly, a qualifying holding in a credit institution to notify the Bank in advance and to "supply such details of the proposal as the Bank may specify". Similarly, disclosure is required under Regulation 14(3) in advance of:

(a)   a proposal by a person to increase the size of their qualifying holding such that the holding would reach or exceed 20 per cent, 33 per cent or 50 per cent of the shares or voting rights attaching to shares in the credit institution; or

(b)   a proposal to acquire any shares or interest in the credit institution which would result in the credit institution becoming a subsidiary of that person.[31]

7–26   Under Article 11(1), the competent authorities are to be given a maximum of three months from the date of notification to oppose the acquisition on the grounds that they are not satisfied as to the suitability of the person making the acquisition. The basis for making this assessment is the need to ensure sound and prudent management of the credit institution. Regulation 14(4) prohibits a person from acquiring a

---

[31]   Art. 11.1.

qualifying holding, or increasing the size of the qualifying holding[32] unless either (i) three months has passed since notification or (ii) the Bank has notified the person that it will not object to the proposed acquisition or increase. The Central Bank may fix a deadline for the implementation of the acquisition and may make any notification by it to the person concerned conditional on the acquisition or increase being made by this time.[33]

7–27 Regulation 14(5)[34] deals with acquisitions by: (a) a credit institution authorised in another Member State; (b) the parent undertaking of a credit institution authorised in another Member State; or (c) a person controlling a credit institution authorised in another Member State. If as a result of an acquisition by such a person, the target institution would (a) become the acquirer's subsidiary or (b) come under its control, Article 11(2) requires the assessment of the acquisition to be the subject of the prior consultation provided for in Article 7. Article 7 requires prior consultation between competent authorities of Member States. Regulation 14(5) is a little more specific. It requires such consultation where (a) the acquirer proposes to acquire 50 per cent or more of the shares or voting rights attaching to shares or (b) the acquirer proposes to acquire any interest in a credit institution which would make it a subsidiary. It is submitted that an acquisition of a 20 per cent shareholding might allow the credit institution to come under that person's control within the terms of the Directive without triggering the Regulations.

7–28 Regulation 14(6)[35] provides for the advance notification of disposals of qualifying holdings. Notification is also required in advance of a proposed reduction in a qualifying holding below the aforementioned thresholds or a disposal which would result in the institution ceasing to be a subsidiary. However, there is no requirement that the transaction be approved by the competent authorities. Regulation 14(7) obliges every person to whom Regulation 14(6) applies to notify the Bank of the resultant size of its holdings after the proposed disposal has been effected.

7–29 Regulation 14(8)[36] place the onus on credit institutions to notify competent authorities of notifiable acquisitions or disposals of holdings in their capital. The Bank must be notified as soon as the credit institutions become aware of such transactions. In addition, Regulation 14(9)[37]

---

[32] In circumstances described in Reg. 14(2) or (3).
[33] Reg. 14(4)(b).
[34] Art. 11(2).
[35] Art. 11(3).
[36] Art. 11(4).
[37] And the second para. of Art. 11(4).

provides that at least once a year, credit institutions must notify the Bank of the names of shareholders and members possessing qualifying holdings and the size of such holdings. Article 11(4) suggests that such information may be obtained by the institutions at annual general meetings of shareholders or as a result of compliance with the regulations applicable to listed companies.

(4) Directions

7–30   Where the Bank has reason to believe that a person who has a qualifying holding in a credit institution is exercising an influence on the direction of the affairs of a credit institution which is, or is likely to be, "detrimental to the sound and prudent management of that credit institution," Regulation 14(10)[38] requires the Bank to notify the relevant person and direct the person to take specified steps to bring such an influence to an end within a specified period. Before issuing such a direction however, Regulation 14(11) requires the Bank to notify the person of its intention to issue the direction and to allow them an opportunity to be heard. Where a direction has been issued, Regulation 14(12) provides a right of appeal to the High Court. In the event of non-compliance with a direction or non compliance within the specified time, Regulation 14(b) allows the Bank to:

(a)   issue a direction to a credit institution under section 28 of the 1989 Act;

(b)   apply to the Court in a summary manner;

  (i)   for an injunction prohibiting the person from issuing directions to directors, officers or staff of the institution and prohibiting the aforementioned persons from seeking directions or consulting with that person without the Bank's consent,

  (ii)   to suspend the exercise by the person of any interest in or voting rights attaching to the shares held by that person in the credit institution,

  (iii)   for a Court order requiring the person concerned to dispose of some or all of his shareholding, interests or rights in the credit institution within a period specified by the Bank, or

  (iv)   for any other order the Court considers appropriate.

While, similar measures are provided by Article 11(5) for persons who fail to disclose a relevant acquisition in advance, Regulation 14(15) provides that such a failure will constitute an offence. In keeping with, Article 11(5), Regulation 14(16) provides that an acquisition against the wishes of the Bank or an acquisition, where the person has not made the relevant notification, will be invalid and:

---

[38]   Art. 11(5).

(a) title to any shares or other interest concerned shall not pass, and

(b) any consequential purported exercise of powers shall be void.

(5) Acquisitions of Holdings in Other Companies

7–31 Regulation 15 implements the provisions of Article 12 into law in respect of acquisitions by credit institutions of holdings in other companies.[39] Regulation 15(1) prohibits an authorised credit institution from investing more than 15 per cent of its own funds in the acquisition of a qualifying holding in any one "relevant body corporate".[40] In addition, the total amount of all such qualifying holdings in all relevant body corporates should not exceed the equivalent of 60 per cent of the credit institution's own funds.[41] Article 12(6) provides that compliance with these limits must be ensured by means of supervision and monitoring on a consolidated basis in accordance with Directive 83/350/EEC.[41a] Regulation 15(7) excludes from the definition of "relevant corporate bodies", companies which are credit institutions, financial institutions or, unless the Bank otherwise directs, authorised insurance companies.[42] In calculating the qualifying holding for the purposes of this Regulation, Regulation 15(2) provides that the following shares held by a credit institution should be disregarded:

(a) shares held on a temporary basis during a financial rescue or re-organisation of the relevant company;

(b) shares held on behalf of another person;

(c) shares held on a temporary basis with a view to re-sale; and

(d) shares held as part of a bona fide underwriting of a share issue.[43]

7–32 Regulation 15(4) acknowledges that the percentage thresholds may be exceeded in exceptional circumstances. It provides that where the Bank believes that a credit institution has exceeded these limits, it may require the credit institution to:

(a) increase the amount of its own funds;

(b) dispose of specified shareholdings in a relevant company; or

(c) take any other measures specified to meet the limits.

---

[39] Immediate compliance upon the entry into force of the regulations is not necessary and Reg. 15(3) allows the Bank to specify a period for compliance, which date should not be later than January 1, 2003. See also Art. 12(7).

[40] See also Art. 12(1).

[41] See also Art. 12(2).

[41a] O.J. L193/18.

[42] Arts. 12(1), (2), & (3).

[43] Reg. 15(3) & Art. 12(4).

Compliance by the credit institution with this direction is mandatory. Regulation 15(5) allows the Bank to refrain from applying the limits set out in Regulation 15(1) if it provides that 100 per cent of the amounts by which a credit institution's qualifying holdings exceed those limits are covered by its own funds and that the latter will not be included in the calculation of the solvency ratios. If both limits are exceeded, the amount to be covered by its own funds must be the greater of the excess amounts.[44]

7–33   Regulation 15(6) allows the Bank to prescribe rules and standards for the application of this Regulation to credit institutions either generally or in particular. The Bank has stated that notwithstanding the provisions of Chapter VI of the 1989 Act, section 28 of the Building Societies Act 1989 and Regulation 15, credit institutions should not acquire, directly or indirectly more than 10 per cent of the shares or other interests in another company without its prior written approval. In addition, it has required credit institutions to notify it of its divestment of the whole or part of such holdings. It has also emphasised that it would not be receptive to a proposal from a credit institution to acquire a qualifying holding in a general insurance company.[45]

III.   THE TRUSTEE SAVINGS BANK ACT 1989 AND THE ACC BANK ACT 1992

7–34   The Trustee movement was founded in the early years of the 19th century in order to provide safe repositories for small savings. A banking service developed which became identified with the smaller depositor and the smaller borrower and which had a special local character.[46] The trustee savings banks were founded and run under trusteeships. The Trustee Savings Bank Act 1989 effected the repeal of the Trustee Savings Banks Acts 1863 to 1979. The Trustee Savings Bank Act 1989 extended the range of banking activities carried out by trustee savings banks. It also transferred the role of supervisor of trustee savings banks from the Minister for Finance ("the Minister") to the Central Bank.

7–35   In order to survive in more recent times, local units were compelled to amalgamate. Part VI of the Trustee Savings Bank Act 1989 regulates the amalgamation of trustee savings banks. Section 47 allows existing trustee savings banks to amalgamate upon (a) the passing by

---

[44]   Art. 12(8).
[45]   "Licensing and Supervision Requirements and Standards for Credit Institutions" (1995) *Central Bank of Ireland, Quarterly Bulletin* para. 12–2.
[46]   392 *Dáil Debates* Cols. 1269–1270.

each of a resolution authorising the amalgamation and (b) the approval of the Minister and the Central Bank to a submitted amalgamation scheme as provided for under section 48. Subsequent to the introduction of the Trustee Savings Bank Act 1989, the last two remaining trustee savings banks, the Dublin TSB and the Cork & Limerick TSB amalgamated.

7–36 Section 57 of the Trustee Savings Bank Act 1989 authorises the Minister to reorganise the Trustee Savings Banks into companies and to arrange for the transfer of all assets and liabilities to the new companies. In the Dáil, the Minister stated that the "legal advice available to us is that the Oireachtas has the power to dispose of the assets of the TSBs or to alter their status as it seems fit".[47] Thus, any order made by the Minister to effect this reorganisation must be passed by both Houses of the Oireachtas in order to become effective. Section 57(4)(g) provides that an order authorising the re-organisation must provide for:

> "the prohibition of the transfer or alienation by the Minister of shares in the company held by him otherwise than for the purpose of providing a person appointed or intended to be appointed to be a director of the company with the necessary qualification and the prohibition, in any event, of the transfer for the purpose aforesaid of any number of shares in the company that would reduce the number of shares in the company held by him to less than 51 per cent of the shares of the company".

When the Bill was being introduced to the Dáil, the Minister of the time, Mr. Reynolds, stated that there were no plans for the banks reorganisation at that stage. However, the Minister stated that a company structure might prove necessary in the future in order to allow the banks greater flexibility in trading and in raising capital and to open the way for more direct links with other financial organisations. "In an increasingly competitive environment, we must recognise the possibility that the Trustee Savings Banks may find it necessary to become associated with larger financial groupings and some level of joint venture or an even close[r] relationship may be necessary in due course".[48]

7–37 In February 1999, the Minister announced that subject to the necessary regulatory approvals the Government had agreed to the proposals from the boards of ACC Bank plc and TSB that the banks be allowed to merge and float on the stock market. It was announced that

---

[47] At Col. 1272.
[47a] Section 57 of the Trustee Savings Bank Act 1989.
[48] 392 *Dáil Debates* Cols. 1276–1277.

the merger and flotation would probably take place simultaneously because of the complex legal structure of TSB.

7-38   ACC Bank plc, which was previously known as the Agricultural Credit Corporation,[49] was established by the Agricultural Credit Act 1978. Originally the services which could be provided by the ACC were extremely limited *e.g.* it was prohibited from lending more than 25 per cent of its loan book outside the agricultural sector. The Agricultural Credit Act 1978 was amended by the Agricultural Credit Act, 1982, the Agricultural Credit 1988 and most recently by the ACC Bank Act, 1992. The ACC Bank Act 1992 extended the range of services the ACC could provide to include full banking services.[50] It also allowed the Minister to appoint the Central Bank as the competent supervisor of the ACC.

7-39   Although section 7(4) of the Central Bank Act 1971[50a] exempts the ACC from the requirement to hold a banking licence and thus excludes it from the supervisory control of the Central Bank, section 4 of the ACC Bank Act 1992 allows this situation to be altered. It provides that notwithstanding section 7, the Minister after consultation with the Central Bank may prescribe that all or any of the supervisory provisions of Part II of the Central Bank Act 1971 or Chapters I to VI of Part II of the Central Bank Act 1989 apply to the ACC with such modifications or adaptations as the Minister considers necessary. The provisions in relation to supervision of acquiring transactions may thus be extended to the ACC. The Minister choose to exercise this discretion and the ACC Bank Act 1992 (Section 4) Regulations 1992[51] applies these provisions to the ACC.

IV. THE ICC BANK ACT 1992

7-40   The Industrial Credit Corporation which is now termed ICC Bank plc[52] was set up by the Industrial Credit Act 1933. The primary function of the ICC at that stage was to provide venture capital to Irish industry. The permitted objects were restricted to the acquisition of securities in, or the advancement of money to, companies carrying on, or proposing to carry on, any trade or industry in the State.[53] The 1933

---

[49] The name was changed by section 2 of the ACC Bank Act 1992.
[50] s.5.
[50a] Inserted by s.30 of the Central Bank Act 1989.
[51] S.I. No. 373 of 1992.
[52] The name was changed by section 2 of the ICC Bank Act 1992.
[53] Paragraph 2(c) of the Schedule to the Industrial Credit Act 1933 as amended most recently by section 3 of the Industrial Credit (Amendment) Act 1971.

Act was amended a number of times since then[54] most recently by the ICC Bank Act 1992. At the time this latter Act was passed, the Government's intention to privatise the ICC was evident. In addition to changing the name of the institution to ICC Bank, a more commercial title, the ICC Bank Act, 1992 broadens the scope of activities which may be carried out permitting it to provide a full range of banking and associated financial services. The Government have subsequently announced their intention to sell the bank, and advisers have been appointed.

7–41 Section 7(4) of the Central Bank Act 1971[55] exempts the ICC from the requirement to be licensed by the Central Bank before carrying on banking business. Notwithstanding this exemption, however, section 3 of the 1992 Act allows the Minister, after consultation with the Central Bank, to introduce regulations allowing the Bank to exercise supervision over the ICC. This is similar to section 4 of the ACC Bank Act 1992. All or any of the supervisory provisions of Part II of the Central Bank Act 1971 or Chapters 1 to VI of Part II of the Central Bank Act 1989 may be applied to the ICC. The Minister has since introduced the ICC Bank Act 1992 (Section 3) Regulations 1993[56] stating that all of the supervisory provisions of Part II of the Central Bank Act, 1971 and Chapters 1 to VI of Part II of the Central Bank Act 1989 apply to the ICC as if the ICC were the holder of a banking licence. The provisions in relation to the supervision of acquiring transactions are, therefore, relevant.

V. THE BUILDING SOCIETIES ACT 1989

7–42 The Building Societies Act 1989 effects the repeal of all existing building societies Acts.[57] Prior to the drawing up of the Act, a working party comprising government members, the Central Bank and the Registrar of Building Societies, in consultation with the building societies, made recommendations on the shape of this new legislation. The stated objectives of the Act are:

> "Firstly, to allow societies to compete and develop in the context of the internal market by offering new services and broadening the scope of their business. Secondly, to establish a modern and effective supervisory regime for societies. Thirdly, to improve the statutory provisions governing the running of societies, their accounts and audit. Fourthly, to put societies on the same footing as banks in regard to savings protection. Fifthly, to encourage

---

[54] In 1958, 1959, 1971, 1974, 1977, 1979, 1990.
[55] As amended by section 30 of the Central Bank Act 1989.
[56] S.I. No. 24 of 1993.
[57] The Building Societies Act 1976, the Building Societies (Amendment) Act 1980, the Building Societies (Amendment) Act 1983 and the Building Societies (Amendment) Act 1986.

societies to broaden the extent of their involvement in housing and sixthly, to provide a satisfactory mechanism for conversion to public status".[58]

The Building Societies Act 1989 extends the scope of activities which may be carried out by building societies. It also transfers the regulatory and supervisory function to the Central Bank. Previously, the Registrar of Building Societies performed this role in respect of building societies. The Building Societies Act 1989 also sets out the conditions for the conversion of building societies from mutual to public limited company status.

(1) Investment in Corporate Bodies

7–43   Section 28(1) of the Building Societies Act 1989 allows building societies to (a) invest in corporate bodies and (b) to support corporate bodies.[59] Investing in corporate bodies may involve either acquiring and holding shares or corresponding membership rights in companies or alternatively, forming or taking part in the formation of companies. Supporting corporate bodies involves providing companies in which the building society invests with loans, grants of money, guarantees or the use of services or property. However, in order to exercise either of these powers both a special resolution of the building society adopting the power and the approval of the Bank will be necessary.[60]

7–44   Section 28(2) prohibits building societies from investing in companies whose objects enable them to (i) carry on activities which are outside the powers of the building society, or (ii) invest in other bodies corporate. These restrictions ensure that building societies do not attempt to avoid statutory or Bank restrictions on investment by means of their investment in other companies. In order to retain a degree of flexibility, the Bank, where it considers it expedient to do so, may allow the building society to invest in a company which carries on activities which are outside the powers of the building society.[61] The Bank may decide to impose terms and limitations on this investment. The Bank is also allowed to set a specific percentage of a company's share capital or corresponding membership rights which a building society must hold in order to exercise the powers available under this section.[62] Where a building society invests or proposes to invest in a company engaged in the business of accepting deposits or other repayable funds, section 28(4) allows the Bank to specify such limits or restrictions on the business of the

---

[58]   386 *Dáil Debates* Col. 1532, Flynn.
[59]   Support to approved housing bodies is also allowed under section 28(1)(b).
[60]   s.36.
[61]   s.28(2)(b).
[62]   s.28(3).

company as it considers appropriate in the interests of "the orderly and proper regulation of building societies".

(2) Amalgamation of Building Societies

7–45 Part X of the Building Societies Act 1989 provides for the amalgamation of societies and the transfer of engagements. This part marks a re-enactment of similar provisions in the Building Societies Act 1976. The terms of amalgamation and the memorandum and rules of the new society must be approved by the members of each society by special resolution. Section 98 of the Building Societies Act 1989 provides that the Bank must also approve the amalgamation. On the date specified by the Bank as the date incorporation takes effect, section 95(4) of the Building Societies Act 1989 provides that all the property, rights and liabilities of each of the amalgamating societies stands transferred to and vested in the society incorporated as the successor.

(3) Demutualisation of Building Societies

7–46 Part XI of the Building Societies Act 1989 allows for the conversion of building societies to public limited companies. In the Dáil, the Minister commented that:

> "as demutualisation would be a quite fundamental change in the nature of a society, it is important that the Law should lay down certain safeguards to ensure that the decision is taken after due consideration of all the implications by all those concerned."[63]

7–47 Section 101(2) of the Building Societies Act 1989 sets out the conditions which a building society must fulfil in order to convert. There must, for example, be a conversion resolution pursuant to section 71 and the resolution must be confirmed by the Central Bank under section 104. Section 102 sets out the protective provisions for the company once registered. It provides that for a period of five years after conversion, the successor company must not:

> "(a) offer to the public, or allot or agree to allot with a view to their being offered for sale to the public, any shares in or debentures of the company,
> (b) allot or agree to allot any shares in or debentures of the company, or
> (c) register a transfer of shares in or debentures of the company,
> if the effect of –
> (i) the offer, the allotment or the registration of the transfer would be that 15 per cent. or more of the shares in or debentures of the company would be held by, or by nominees for, any one person, or

---

[63] Col. 1548.

(ii) the offer, the allotment or the registration of the transfer of shares would be that 15 per cent. or more of the voting rights attaching to the company's shares would be held by, or by nominees for, any one person or their nominees acting in concert."

In order to ensure compliance with this restriction, section 102(3) provides that any allotment or registration of a transfer of shares or debentures in contravention of subsection (1) will be void and any voting rights held by, or by nominees for, any one person or persons or their nominees acting in concert in excess of a figure representing 15 per cent of the total voting rights shall not be exercisable by that person or persons or by their nominees. This provision effectively prevents any person or their concert parties gaining control of the successor company for a period of five years. The Minister explained that the purpose of this section is to prevent "speculators attempting to bring about a conversion with a view to a takeover".[64]

VI. THE CREDIT UNION ACT 1997

7–48   The first credit union was formed in Ireland in 1958 under the Industrial and Provident Societies Acts 1893 to 1913. The Credit Union Act 1966 provided a separate statutory base for credit unions dealing with the basics of credit union establishment, organisation, operations and supervision. The Registrar of Friendly Societies was given responsibility for authorising credit unions in Ireland. The 1966 Act outlined the conditions for the registration of credit unions and the qualifications for membership. It provided for the rules of a credit union to be approved by, and registered with, the Registrar and established the general provisions relating to member's shares and deposits. One limitation of this Act, however, was that it provided the Registrar with very limited power to exercise a meaningful role in supervising established credit unions. Part III of the Industrial and Provident Societies Act, 1978 was introduced to provide the Registrar of Friendly Societies with additional supervisory powers in respect of existing credit unions. The Registrar was empowered to inspect and investigate a credit union's affairs and where necessary, to direct a credit union to suspend the acceptance of shares, deposits, loans and payments in certain specified circumstances. A working party comprising representatives of the Department of Enterprise and Employment, the Registrar of Friendly Societies, the Credit Union Advisory Committee and the Irish League of Credit Unions concluded that a new consolidating Act was required and identified the parameters of this new legislation.[65] The

---

[64] 390 *Dáil Debates* Col. 507.
[65] 475 *Dáil Debates* Cols. 524–525.

Act which was subsequently introduced, the Credit Union Act 1997 repeals the previous legislation on credit unions.

7–49 The stated objectives of the Credit Union Act 1997 are to consolidate all existing credit union legislation, to provide an updated statutory framework for the development and regulation of the credit union movement and to enable credit unions to provide an extended range of services to their members.

7–50 Credit unions are unique creatures whose *raison d'être* would appear to vary between the commercial and the altruistic. The objects of a credit union must be:

(a) the promotion of thrift among its members by the accumulation of their savings;

(b) the creation of sources of credit for the mutual benefit of its members at a fair and reasonable rate of interest; and

(c) the use and control of members' savings for their mutual benefit.

The only other objects allowable are:

(a) the training and education of its members in the wise use of money;

(b) the education of its members in their economic, social and cultural well-being as member of the community;

(c) the improvement of the well-being and spirit of the member's community; and

(d) subject to section 48,[66] the provision to its members of such additional services as are for their mutual benefit.[67]

7–51 Section 184 of the Credit Union Act 1997 provides inter alia that neither the Central Bank Acts 1942–1997, nor the Building Societies Act 1989 apply to credit unions. Also, as noted above, credit unions are exempt from the provisions of the European Communities (Licensing and Supervision of Credit Institutions) Regulations 1992. This is largely because the protection afforded by the regulations is unnecessary. Even if there was an economic rational for it, the acquisition of a credit union would be virtually impossible. Admission to membership of a credit union is restricted to persons who share a common bond. These common bonds are: following a particular occupation; residing or being

---

[66] Section 48 deals with a credit union's powers to provide additional services.
[67] s.6(1).

employed in a particular locality; being employed by a particular employer or having retired from employment with a particular employer; being a member of a bona fide organisation; or any other common bond approved by the Registrar.[68] While members may transfer their shares, they may only do so to other members and subject to the limits on shareholdings set out in the Credit Union Act 1997.[69] Similarly, restrictions are placed on the manner in which credit unions may invest their funds. Section 43 of the Credit Union Act 1997 provides that surplus funds may only be invested:

(a) in securities in which trustees are for the time being authorised by law to invest;[70]

(b) in the shares of or deposits with or loans to a credit union;

(c) in the shares of a society registered under the Industrial and Provident Societies Act, 1893–1978; or

(d) in such other manner as may be prescribed by the Minister which the Minister considers beneficial to the credit union.

7–52 Part IX of the Credit Union Act 1997 deals with the amalgamation of credit unions. Section 128 of the Credit Union Act 1997 allows for the amalgamation of two or more credit unions and sets out the conditions for the formation of the successor credit union. The terms of the amalgamation must be approved by each credit union by a special resolution and the Registrar must confirm the amalgamation under section 131. Where the Registrar approves, a date must be specified for the taking effect of the registration of the successor, and on this date all the property, rights and liabilities of each of the credit unions amalgamating shall stand transferred to and vested in the successor.

---

[68] s.6(3).
[69] s.29.
[70] Regulation 3 of the Trustee (Authorised Investments) Order 1998 (S.I. No. 28 of 1998) varies the investments specified in section 1 of the Trustee Act 1893 (inserted by section 1 of the Trustee (Authorised Investments) Act 1958) by deleting the instruments specified in that section and inserting the investments specified in the First Schedule of the Order. Included in this list are securities issued by the State, securities (other than shares) of authorised credit institutions, units of shares in collective investment schemes and securities of issuers with a specified rating.

B. Investment Business Firms

I. THE INVESTMENT SERVICES DIRECTIVE

7–53 The Investment Services Directive[71] ("the ISD") is an integral part of the internal market programme seeking to remove the barriers to the single market in financial services.[72] The ISD relates to the securities component of the financial services market. The Second Banking Directive, discussed above, plays a similar role in the banking component of the market. The stated objective of the ISD [according to its recitals] is to:

> "secure the mutual recognition of authorisation and of prudential supervision systems, making possible the grant of a single authorisation valid throughout the community and the application of the principle of home Member State supervision."

In this way, the ISD hopes to facilitate access to investment activities and facilitate the exercising of these activities. The ISD defines a set of common rules to protect investors and to ensure the smooth operation of the markets in transferable securities. One of these rules focuses on the suitability of large shareholders. The objective of the ISD in this regard, is to ensure that the ownership structure of an investment firm does not hinder the sound and prudent management of that firm. This objective is relevant both to the authorisation of the investment firm and to its continued supervision.

7–54 Article 4 of the ISD provides that the competent authorities may not authorise an investment firm until they have been informed of the identities of the shareholders or members, whether direct or indirect, that have "qualifying holdings" and the amounts of those holdings. The competent authorities are prohibited from granting authorisation to investment firms if they are not satisfied as to the suitability of the members and shareholders. In making this assessment, the supervisory authorities should consider the need to ensure "the sound and prudential management of an investment firm". Article 1 of the ISD defines a "qualifying holding" as:

> "any direct or indirect holding in an investment firm" which
> (a) "represents 10 per cent or more of the capital or of the voting rights or"
> (b) "which makes it possible to exercise a significant influence over the management of the investment firm in which that holding subsists".

---

[71] Council Directive on Investment Services in the Securities Field Directive No. 93/22/EEC, O.J. L141/27.

[72] Lomnicka, "The Internal Financial Market and Investment Services" in *EC Financial Market Regulation and Company Law* (Andenas & Kenyon-Slade ed., Sweet & Maxwell, London, 1993), Chap. 4; Ashall, "The Investment Services Directive: What Was the Conflict All About?" *ibid.*, Chap. 5.

Clearly, where the shares of a company are very widely held, a share-holding of considerably less than 10 per cent may constitute a qualifying holding under the second part of this definition. It should also be noted that this definition includes both direct and indirect holdings.

7–55   Article 9 of the ISD allows for the continuing supervision of shareholders or members with such qualifying holdings. Article 9(1) obliges Member States to require any person who proposes to acquire, directly or indirectly, a qualifying holding in an investment firm to notify the competent authorities in advance, informing them of the size of the intended holding. Similar disclosure is required in advance of an increase in a qualifying holding which would lead to a holding reaching or exceeding 20 per cent, 33 per cent or 50 per cent. Finally, advance disclosure is also required where the acquisition would result in the investment firm becoming a subsidiary of the person. The competent authorities are given three months from the date of notification to oppose the acquisition on the grounds that they are not satisfied as to the suitability of the person making the acquisition. The basis for making this assessment is the need to ensure sound and prudent management of the investment firm. Where there is no opposition, the competent authorities may fix a deadline for the implementation of the acquisition. Article 9(2) refers to acquisitions by:

(a)   an investment firm authorised in another Member State;

(b)   the parent undertaking of an investment firm authorised in another Member State; or

(c)   a person controlling an investment firm authorised in another Member State.

If, as a result of such an acquisition, the target firm would become the acquirer's subsidiary or come under its control, the assessment of the acquisition must be the subject of the prior consultation provided for in Article 6. Article 6 requires prior consultation between competent authorities of Member States. Article 9(3) provides for the advance notification of disposals which result in the disposer's holding ceasing to be a qualifying holding, or which reduce his qualifying holding below the aforementioned thresholds or which result in the firm ceasing to be a subsidiary. Unlike Article 9(1), there is no requirement that such a transaction be approved by the competent authorities.

7–56   Article 9(4) of the ISD places the onus on investment firms to notify competent authorities of acquisitions or disposals of holdings in their capital which cause holdings to exceed or fall below the thresholds. The competent authorities must be notified as soon as the investment firms become aware of such transactions. In addition, the second paragraph of Article 9(4) provides that at least once a year, the investment firms must notify the competent authorities of the names of shareholders and members possessing qualifying holdings and the size of such holdings. It is suggested that such information may be obtained at annual general meetings of shareholders or as a result of compliance with the regulations applicable to listed companies.

7–57   Where the influence likely to be exercised by the acquirer may be prejudicial to the sound and prudent management of an investment firm, Article 9(5) of the ISD obliges Member States to require the competent authorities to take appropriate action to end that situation. The examples of such action cited include obtaining injunctions or sanctions against directors or managers or the suspension of voting rights attaching to the shares held by such persons. Similar measures are required for persons who fail to disclose a relevant acquisition in advance. An acquisition against the wishes of a competent authority will lead to the suspension of the corresponding voting rights, the nullity of the votes cast or for the possibility of their annulment.

In Ireland, the Stock Exchange Act 1995 and the Investment Intermediaries Act 1995 implement the Investment Services Directive into Irish law.

II. THE STOCK EXCHANGE ACT 1995

7–58   The Stock Exchange Act 1995 fulfils the obligations of the ISD in respect of stock exchanges and stock exchange member firms. The main purpose of the Stock Exchange Act 1995 is to establish the Bank as the regulatory authority for the Irish Stock Exchange, any other stock exchange which may, in the future, establish itself in Ireland, and the member firms of these exchanges. Section 8 of the Stock Exchange Act 1995 makes it an offence to establish or operate a stock exchange in the State without the approval of the Bank. Similarly, section 17(1) makes it an offence to claim to be or to hold oneself out as a member firm without actually being a member firm of an approved stock exchange. Part II of the Stock Exchange Act details the procedure by which a stock exchange may be approved by the Bank and the conditions and requirements which may be imposed upon an exchange. Part III imposes similar rules in relation to the authorisation of stock exchange member firms and the imposition of rules and requirements. Section 17(2) lists three methods whereby a firm may become an authorised member firm of an approved exchange. Until a firm is authorised in one of these ways it will not be able to operate as a member firm in the State. The first method of authorisation is by the Bank under section 18 of the Stock Exchange Act, 1995. The second method is authorisation by a competent authority in another Member State for the purposes of the ISD whose authorisation includes investment services. The final method of authorisation is by a European Communities credit institution under the Banking Directives whose authorisation includes investment services.

7–59   One of the preconditions for Bank approval in respect of both stock exchanges and stock exchange member firms is that the proposed stock exchange or member firm satisfy the Bank as to the suitability of each of its qualifying shareholders.[73] A "qualifying shareholder" is defined in section 3(1) as a person who has or controls "a qualifying holding". There is no definition of the term "suitability" in the Stock Exchange Act 1995 and unlike the ISD there is no reference to the criteria by which suitability should be assessed. By referring back to the ISD, however, we can assume that the Bank, in making this assessment, should consider the need to ensure "the sound and prudential management of an investment firm". In keeping with the ISD, the Stock Exchange Act 1995 provides for the consideration of the suitability of stock exchanges and member firms not only at the time of authorisation but also throughout the period of authorisation. In this respect, sections 39 to 49 of the Stock Exchange Act 1995 deal with acquiring transactions in and disposals of approved stock exchanges or authorised member firms.

(1) Definitions

7–60   An "acquiring transaction" is defined by section 39(2) of the Stock Exchange Act 1995[74] as:

> "any direct or indirect acquisition by a person or more than one person acting in concert of shares or other interest in an approved stock exchange or authorised member firm, provided that, after the proposed acquisition –
> (a) the proportion of voting rights or capital held by the person or persons making the acquiring transaction would reach or exceed a qualifying holding, or
> (b) the proportion of voting rights or capital held by the person or persons making the acquiring transaction would reach or exceed 20 per cent., 33 per cent. or 50 per cent., or
> (c) the approved stock exchange or authorised member firm would become a subsidiary of the acquirer."

---

[73] ss. 9(5)(e) & 18(5)(e).
[74] As amended by the Investor Compensation Act 1998, s.77.

A "disposal" is defined in section 39(3) as:

> "any direct or indirect disposal by a person or more than one person acting in concert of a qualifying holding or a disposal which would reduce such a qualifying holding so that the proportion of the voting rights or of the capital held by the person or persons would fall below 20 per cent., 33 per cent. or 50 per cent. or so that the approved stock exchange or authorised member firm would cease to be its subsidiary."

7–61　In order to qualify as an acquiring transaction under paragraph (a), an acquisition of a holding greater than or equal to a qualifying holding is required. A "qualifying holding" is defined in section 3(1) of the Act as either:

(a) "a direct or indirect holding of shares or other interest in a proposed stock exchange or an approved stock exchange or a proposed member firm or authorised member firm which represents 10 per cent. or more of the capital or of the voting rights" or

(b) "any direct or indirect holding of less than 10 per cent. which, in the opinion of the Bank, makes it possible to control or exercise a significant influence over the management of the proposed stock exchange or approved stock exchange or proposed member firm or authorised member firm in which a holding subsists."

The second part of the definition gives the Bank a wide discretion to include any acquisition, no matter how minor, within the scope of this Part of the Act, if it believes that the result of the acquisition would be to give the acquirer control of or significant influence over the management of the exchange or firm. It is submitted that until the Bank forms this opinion, a transaction will not be an acquiring transaction requiring disclosure under the Act. The definition of a "qualifying holding" in Article 1 of the ISD is different. It merely refers to a holding which makes it possible to exercise a significant influence over the management of the firm without requiring the supervisory authority to take this view. Thus under a strict reading of the Article, any holding which gives a person significant influence is included. The approach in the Directive would be likely to create greater difficulties for legal advisers to those acquiring or disposing of shares. A decision would have to be made as to whether an acquisition of a holding less than 10 per cent should be characterised as an "acquiring transaction" and thus notified. Since an acquisition of a qualifying holding would not generally be valid unless notified to the supervisory authorities and approved, this decision would be crucial. Section 3(1), however, would seem to suggest that unless the Bank deemed that the acquisition of a qualifying holding of less than 10 per cent came within the section, the legal advisers would not have to ensure notification. While, in practice, this may prove a more pragmatic approach, it would seem that the requirements of the Act in this respect are not as extensive as the requirements of the ISD. This in turn raises doubts as to whether the Act completely implements the Directive in this regard.

7–62   In order to qualify as an acquiring transaction under paragraph (b) of section 39(2), an acquisition must result in the acquirer reaching or exceeding the percentage threshold. This also is slightly different to the ISD which refers to a person *increasing* his qualifying holding to reach or exceed the percentage thresholds. It would seem thus, that the threshold requirement in the ISD is only triggered where the acquirer before the acquisition holds a qualifying holding. In effect however, the result is the same. If a person does not have a qualifying holding at the outset, they will be required to notify the competent authorities if they reach or exceed the thresholds because they will have acquired a qualifying holding under the ISD.

7–63   One final point worth noting is that the definitions of an "acquiring transaction" or "disposal" in the Act and the ISD are broadened by the inclusion of indirect acquisitions and disposals. Section 3(1) of the Act provides that the terms "indirect acquisition" and "indirect disposal" shall be construed in accordance with the ISD. Article 1 of the ISD, in turn, refers to Article 7 of Council Directive 88/627.[75] Council Directive 88/627/EEC regulates the information to be published when a major holding in a listed company is disposed of or acquired. It is examined in greater depth in Chapter 13.[75a] Article 7 of Council Directive 88/627 emphasises that is not only the voting rights held directly by a person which will be considered relevant for the purposes of the notification requirements of that Directive. Other interests which will be considered relevant are:

- voting rights held by other persons on their behalf;
- voting rights held by an undertaking controlled[76] by that person;
- voting rights held by a third party with whom that person has concluded a written agreement obliging them to exercise their voting rights in concert in order to adopt a common policy towards the management of the company in question;

---

[75] [1988] O.J. L348/62.
[75a] See below paras 13–97–13–100.
[76] Article 8 provides a definition for a "controlled undertaking". For the purposes of the Directive the terms means any undertaking in which a natural person or legal entity:
   (a) has a majority of the shareholders' or members' voting rights;
   (b) has the right to appoint or remove a majority of the members of the board and is a shareholder or member of the undertaking; or
   (c) is a shareholder or member and alone controls a majority of the shareholders' or members' voting rights pursuant to an agreement entered into with other shareholders or members.

– voting rights held by a third party under a written agreement concluded with that person or with an undertaking controlled by them providing for the temporary transfer for consideration of the voting rights in question;

– voting rights attaching to shares owned by that person which are lodged as security;[77]

– voting rights attaching to shares of which that person has the life interest;

– voting rights which that person or one of the aforementioned persons is entitled to acquire, on his own initiative alone, under a formal agreement;

– voting rights attaching to shares deposited with that person which that person can exercise at its discretion in the absence of specific instructions from the holder.

(2) Notification of Acquiring Transactions

7–64   Sections 40(1) and (2) of the Stock Exchange Act 1995 require any persons proposing to make a relevant acquisition or disposal to notify the Bank "as soon as may be" and to provide it with whatever information the Bank has specified. Furthermore, the obligation to notify the Bank is extended to the stock exchange or member firm whose holdings are the subject of the acquisition or disposal. Section 40(3) requires the stock exchange or member firm to notify the Bank on becoming aware of any proposals for acquiring transactions or disposals. If the Bank needs further information in order to consider an acquiring transaction, it may, within one month of the receipt of the notification, request such further information from any one or more of the undertakings concerned.[78]

(3) Approval or Refusal of the Acquiring Transaction

7–65   It is only in relation to the acquiring transaction that the Bank's approval is necessary. Disposals per se do not require the Bank's approval. In respect of the notification, section 40(5) of the Stock Exchange Act 1995 authorises the Bank to adopt one of three positions. The Bank may approve the acquiring transaction absolutely, it may approve it subject to the imposition of conditions or it may refuse to approve it. Under section 41, the Bank has three months from the date of notification[79] to approve or refuse consent for the acquiring transaction. In

---

[77] An exception to this is provided where the person holding the security controls the voting rights and declares his intention of exercising them.
[78] s.40(4).
[79] Or the date of request of further information under section 40(4).

making its decision, section 47(1) allows the Bank to make any inquiries and obtain any information it considers necessary. Approval must take the form of written notification to the stock exchange or member firm and the party proposing the acquisition. In default of a decision from the Bank within three months, the transaction may proceed.

7–66   Section 45(1) requires the Bank to refuse approval where:

(a)   it is not satisfied as to the suitability of the person proposing the acquiring transaction; or

(b)   it considers that the acquiring transaction is likely to be prejudicial to the sound and prudent management of the approved stock exchange or authorised member firm; or

(c)   it considers that the acquiring transaction is likely to be prejudicial to the proper regulation of the approved stock exchange or authorised member firm.

Furthermore, section 45(2) authorises the Bank to issue directions under section 29 to the directors and managers of the approved stock exchange or member firm where it refuses approval or where it has not been notified of the acquiring transaction as required under section 40. These directions may extend to requiring the stock exchange or member firm to suspend business for up to 12 months. No direct penalty is imposed, however, on the proposed purchaser for failure to notify. Section 46(1) allows an appeal to the High Court against a refusal of approval or against the imposition of conditions or requirements on any approval. Where the appeal is successful, the High Court remits the matter to the Bank directing it to make a decision in accordance with the determination of the High Court.

(4) Implementation of the Acquiring Transaction

7–67   Section 42 of the Stock Exchange Act 1995 allows the Bank to specify a period for the implementation of an acquiring transaction. Section 43(1) provides that approval of the acquiring transaction shall be subject to any conditions or requirements or both as the Bank may impose. The only limitation on this power is that these conditions and requirements must, in the Bank's opinion, be necessary for the orderly and proper regulation of approved stock exchanges and authorised member firms. Any conditions imposed may be amended or revoked at any time under section 43(2).

(5) Validity of Certain Acquiring Transactions

7–68   Section 44 of the Stock Exchange Act 1995 invalidates any acquiring transactions which are:

(a) unapproved;

(b) not entered into within 12 months of the receipt of approval in writing; or

(c) in the case of approval by default, not entered into within 12 months of the end of the three month period.

The effect of this invalidity is that title to any shares or other interest will not pass and any consequential purported exercise of powers relating to such shares or other interest will be invalid.

(6) Ongoing Obligations

7–69 In keeping with paragraph 2 of Article 9(4) of the ISD, section 48 of the Stock Exchange Act 1995 requires approved stock exchanges and authorised member firms to inform the Bank at least one a year of the names of direct shareholders and members possessing qualifying holdings and the size of such holdings. Furthermore, at least once a year approved stock exchanges and authorised member firms must make best efforts to ascertain the identity of all indirect shareholders and members possessing qualifying holdings and notify the Bank of the names of such persons. This section recognises the difficulty of obtaining information about indirect shareholders. In the ISD, it is suggested that such information may be obtained at annual general meetings of shareholders or as a result of compliance with the regulations applicable to listed companies. For example, both the Irish Stock Exchange Listing Rules and the Companies Act 1990 contain disclosure requirements for acquisitions of interests in companies.[80]

(7) Sections 201 and 203 of the Companies Act 1963

7–70 Sections 201 and 203 enable acquisitions and disposals to be effected by means of a court order. Section 49(2) of the Stock Exchange Act 1995 prohibits the making of any such order in respect of a proposed amalgamation which is an acquiring transaction until the Bank has been notified and given its approval to the acquiring transaction or until the expiry of the default period. This ensures that the Bank is aware of such transactions and is given the opportunity to supervise their suitability.

III. THE INVESTMENT INTERMEDIARIES ACT 1995

7–71 The Investment Intermediaries Act 1995 ("the 1995 Act") established a comprehensive system of regulation of investment services. An

---

[80] See below paras 13–87 *et seq.*

"authorised investment business firm" is defined in section 2(1) of the 1995 Act as:

> "an investment business firm which has been authorised by a supervisory authority under section 10 or 13 of this Act or which is deemed to be authorised under Part IV or part VII of this Act".

Initially, there were two supervisory authorities for the purposes of the 1995 Act – the Central Bank and the Minister for Enterprise and Employment. The latter was responsible for supervising persons who did not have discretionary control over client assets and who confined themselves to acting as deposit agents or brokers, or to transmitting orders for listed shares or bonds or prize funds, or who provided services in relation to units in collective investment schemes. The core of the Minister's responsibilities were investment product intermediaries. The Bank regulated all other investment business firms. Part VI of the Central Bank Act 1997 transferred sole responsibility to the Bank. The decision to remove these functions from the Minister was taken in the wake of the default of a number of these firms.[81]

7–72   Section 10 of the 1995 Act allows the Bank to grant or refuse authorisation to operate as an authorised investment business firm to firms which meet certain specified preconditions and certain ongoing obligations. Section 13 of the 1995 Act deems existing investment business firms to be authorised until authorisation is subsequently refused or granted. Restricted activity investment product intermediaries are deemed authorised under Part IV of the 1995 Act subject to the conditions imposed by section 26(2) of the 1995 Act. Finally, certified persons controlled by approved professional bodies under Part VII of the 1995 Act are deemed authorised subject to the conditions imposed by section 63 of the 1995 Act. Section 2(4) of the Investor Compensation Act 1998 notes that unless the Minister prescribes otherwise, restricted activity investment product intermediaries who are practising solicitors and who have not informed the Bank and the Investor Compensation Company Ltd. that they are such intermediaries are excluded from this definition unless the Minister prescribes otherwise.

7–73   The implementation in the 1995 Act of the provisions in the ISD in respect of acquiring transactions and significant shareholdings is almost identical to the implementation of these provisions in the Stock Exchange Act 1995. Thus, section 10(5)((e) of the 1995 Act makes it a precondition of authorisation that a proposed investment business firm satisfy the Bank as to the suitability of each of its qualifying shareholders.

---

[81]   495 *Dáil Debates* Col. 64.

Sections 38 to 48 of the 1995 Act regulate "acquiring transactions" in "authorised investment business firms".

(1) Definitions

7–74 An "acquiring transaction" is defined by section 38(2)[82] as:

> "any direct or indirect acquisition by a person or more than one person acting in concert of shares or other interest in an authorised investment business firm, provided that, after the proposed acquisition –
>
> (a) the proportion of voting rights or capital held by the person or persons making the acquiring transaction would reach or exceed a qualifying holding, or
>
> (b) the proportion of voting rights or capital held by the person or persons making the acquiring transaction would reach or exceed 20 per cent., 33 per cent. or 50 per cent., or
>
> (c) an authorised investment business firm would become a subsidiary of the acquirer."

A "disposal" is defined in section 38(3) as:

> "any direct or indirect disposal by a person or more than one person acting in concert of a qualifying holding or a disposal which would reduce such a qualifying holding so that the proportion of the voting rights or of the capital held by the person or persons would fall below 20 per cent., 33 per cent. or 50 per cent. or so that an authorised investment business firm would cease to be its subsidiary."

7–75 In order to qualify as an acquiring transaction under paragraph (a) of section 38(2), an acquisition of a holding equal to or greater than a qualifying holding is required. A "qualifying holding" is defined in section 2(1) of the 1995 Act as either:

> (a) "a direct or indirect holding of shares or other interest in a proposed investment business firm or an authorised investment business firm which represents 10 per cent. or more of the capital or of the voting rights" or
>
> (b) "any direct or indirect holding of less than 10 per cent. which, in the opinion of the supervisory authority, makes it possible to control or exercise a significant influence over the management of the proposed investment business firm or authorised investment business firm in which a holding subsists."

The second part of the definition gives the Bank a wide discretion to include any acquisition, no matter how minor, within the scope of this Part of the Act, if it believes that the result of this acquisition is to give the acquirer control of or significant influence over the management of

---

[82] As amended by the Investor Compensation Act 1998, s.63.

the investment business firm. It is submitted thus that until the Bank forms this opinion, a transaction will not be an acquiring transaction requiring disclosure under the 1995 Act. As noted in paragraph 7.54, the definition of a "qualifying holding" in Article 1 of the ISD is different. It merely refers to a holding which makes it possible to exercise a significant influence over the management of the firm without requiring the supervisory authority to take this view. Thus under a strict reading of Article 1, any holding which gives a person significant influence is included. The approach in the ISD would be likely to create greater difficulties for legal advisers to those acquiring or disposing of shares in investment intermediaries. A decision would have to be made as to whether an acquisition of a holding less than 10 per cent should be characterised as an "acquiring transaction" and thus notified. Since an acquisition of a qualifying holding would not generally be valid unless notified to the supervisory authorities and approved, this decision would be crucial. Section 2(1), however, would seem to suggest that unless the Bank deemed that the acquisition of a qualifying holding of less than 10 per cent came within the section, the legal advisers would not have to ensure notification. While, in practice, this may prove a more pragmatic approach, it would seem that the requirements of the 1995 Act in this respect are not as extensive as the requirements of the ISD.

7–76   In order to qualify as an acquiring transaction under paragraph (b) of section 38(2), an acquisition must result in the acquirer reaching or exceeding the percentage threshold. This also is slightly different to the ISD which refers to a person increasing his qualifying holding to reach or exceed the percentage thresholds. It would seem thus that the threshold requirement in the ISD is only triggered where the acquirer before the acquisition holds a qualifying holding. In effect however, the result is the same. If a person does not have a qualifying holding at the outset, they will be required to notify the competent authorities if they reach or exceed the thresholds because they will have acquired a qualifying holding under the ISD.

7–77   The ambit of the definitions of "acquiring transaction" and "disposal" in the 1995 Act is broadened considerable by the inclusion of indirect acquisitions and disposals. The ISD also includes indirect acquisitions. Section 2(1) of the 1995 Act provides that the terms "indirect acquisition" and "indirect disposal" shall be construed in accordance with the ISD. Article 1 of the Directive, in turn, refers to Article 7 of Council Directive 88/627.[83] Council Directive 88/627/EEC regulates the information to be published when a major holding in a

---

[83] [1988] O.J. L348/62.

listed company is disposed of or acquired. It is examined in greater depth in chapter 13.[83a] Article 7 of Council Directive 88/627 emphasises that is not only the voting rights held directly by a person which will be considered relevant for the purposes of the notification requirements of that Directive. The other interests which will be considered relevant are set out above in paragraph 7.63.

(2) Notification of Acquiring Transactions

7–78   Section 39(1) and (2) of the 1995 Act require any persons pro-posing to make a relevant acquisition or disposal to notify the Bank "as soon as may be" and to provide it with whatever information the Bank has specified. The obligation to notify the Bank is extended to the authorised investment business firm whose holdings are the subject of the acquisition or disposal. Section 39(3) requires the investment business firm to notify the Bank on becoming aware of any proposals for acquiring transactions or disposals. If the Bank needs further information in order to consider an acquiring transaction, it may, within one month of the receipt of the notification, request such further information from any one or more of the undertakings concerned.[84]

(3) Approval or Refusal of the Acquiring Transaction

7–79   It is only in relation to the acquiring transaction that the Bank's approval is necessary. Approval of a disposal is not necessary. Section 39(5) of the 1995 Act authorises the Bank to adopt one of three positions. It may approve the acquiring transaction absolutely, it may approve it subject to the imposition of conditions or it may refuse to approve it. Under section 40, the Bank has three months from the date of notifi-cation[85] to approve or refuse consent for the acquiring transaction. In making its decision, section 46(1) allows the Bank to make any inquiries and obtain any information it considers necessary. Approval must take the form of written notification to the investment business firm and the party proposing the acquisition. In default of a decision within three months, the transaction may proceed.

7–80   Section 44(1) of the 1995 Act requires the Bank to refuse approval where:

(a)   it is not satisfied as to the suitability of the person proposing the acquiring transaction; or

---

[83a] See below para 13–12 *et seq.*
[84]   s.39(4).
[85]   Or the date of request of further information under section 39(4).

(b) where it considers that the acquiring transaction is likely to be prejudicial to the sound and prudent management of an authorised member firm; or

(c) where it considers that the acquiring transaction is likely to be prejudicial to the proper and orderly regulation of an authorised investment business firm.

Section 44(2) authorises the Bank to issue directions under section 21 to the directors and managers of an authorised investment business firm where it refuses approval, or where it has not been notified of the acquiring transaction, as required under section 39. These directions may extend to requiring the investment business firm to suspend business for up to 12 months. However, no direct penalty is imposed on the proposed purchaser for failure to notify. Section 45(1) allows an appeal to the High Court against a refusal of approval or against the imposition of conditions or requirements on any approval. Where the appeal is successful, the High Court remits the matter to the Bank directing it to make a decision in accordance with the determination of the High Court.

(4) Implementation of the Acquiring Transaction

7–81   Section 41 of the 1995 Act allows the Bank to specify a period for the implementation of an acquiring transaction. Section 42(1) provides that approval of the acquiring transaction shall be subject to any conditions or requirements or both as the Bank may impose. The only limitation on this power is that these conditions and requirements must, in the Bank's opinion, be necessary for the orderly and proper regulation of investment business firms. Any conditions imposed may be amended or revoked at any time under section 42(2).

(5) Validity of Certain Acquiring Transactions

7–82   Section 43 of the 1995 Act invalidates any acquiring transactions which are: (a) unapproved (b) not entered into within 12 months of the receipt of approval in writing or (c) in the case of approval by default, not entered into within 12 months of the end of the three month period. The effect of this invalidity is that title to any shares or other interest shall not pass and any consequential purported exercise of powers relating to such shares or other interest will be invalid.

(6) Ongoing Obligations

7–83   In keeping with paragraph 2 of Article 9(4) of the ISD, section 47 of the 1995 Act requires authorised investment business firms to inform the Bank at least one a year of the names of direct shareholders and members possessing qualifying holdings and the size of such holdings. Furthermore, they must make best efforts to ascertain the identity of all indirect shareholders and members possessing qualifying holdings and notify the Bank of the names of such persons at least once a year. This section recognises the difficulty of obtaining information about indirect shareholders. In the ISD, it is suggested that such information may be obtained at annual general meetings of shareholders or as a result of compliance with the regulations applicable to listed companies. For example, both the Irish Stock Exchange Listing Rules and the Companies Act, 1990 contain disclosure requirements for acquisitions of interests in companies.[86]

(7) Sections 201 and 203 of the Companies Act 1963

7–84 Sections 201 and 203 enable acquisitions and disposals to be effected by means of a court order. Section 48(2) of the 1995 Act prohibits the making of any such order in respect of a proposed amalgamation which is an acquiring transaction until the Bank has been notified and given its approval to the acquiring transaction or until the expiry of the default period. This ensures that the Bank is aware of such transactions and is given the opportunity to supervise their suitability. Section 48(3) which has no correspondent in the Stock Exchange Act 1995 allows the Bank, having consulted with the Minister for Finance, to exempt certain types of firms from the notification and approval requirements of this Part of the Act or specify circumstances in which firms will be so exempted. The criteria for exercising this discretion is the proper and orderly regulation and supervision of investment business firms, the protection of investors and the requirements of the ISD.

C. Insurance Firms

7–85 Until 1976, the basic supervisory laws for all insurers in Ireland were contained in the Assurance Companies Act 1909, the Insurance Act 1936 and the Insurance Act 1964. In 1976, the first EEC Non-Life Establishment Directive[86a] was implemented into Irish law by the European Communities (Non-Life Insurance) Regulations 1976.[87] The effect of these Regulations was to update the supervisory laws for non-life insurers. The supervisory laws for life assurers were updated in 1984 when the European Communities (Life Assurance) Regulations 1984[88]

---

[86] See below para. 13–87 *et seq.*
[86a] Directive 73/239/EEC [1973] O.J. L228/3.
[87] S.I. No. 115 of 1976.
[88] S.I. No. 57 of 1984.

implemented the 1979 EEC Life Establishment Directive.[89] The Insurance Act 1989 was subsequently introduced in order to protect consumers. This latter Act has three objectives: to add to the Minister for Industry and Commerce's powers of supervision of insurance companies; to regulate insurance commissions paid by insurance companies to intermediaries; and finally to regulate insurance intermediaries.[90]

I. THE INSURANCE ACT 1989

7–86 Part II of the Insurance Act 1989 deals with the Minister's supervisory powers over insurers. An "insurer" is defined in section 2(1) of that Act as the holder of an authorisation under the European Communities (Non-Life Insurance) Regulations 1976 or the European Communities (Life Assurance) Regulations 1984.

7–87 Section 36 of the Insurance Act 1989 sets out the powers of the High Court in respect of the amalgamation of insurance companies or the transfer of insurance business. Section 36(1) provides that whenever the Court sanctions under section 13 of the Assurance Companies Act 1909 (i) the amalgamation of two or more insurance companies or (ii) the transfer of insurance business of any class from one insurance company to another, the Court should provide for certain specified matters by the order granting the sanction. Section 13 of the 1909 Act requires the sanction of the High Court for the amalgamation of two or more insurance companies or the transfer of insurance business other than in the area of motor, fire and accident insurance. Section 36(1) also provides that whenever an amalgamation or transfer as aforesaid is to be effected which does not require the Court's approval under section 13, upon application being made to it, the Court should also provide for the same specified matters. The matters specified in section 36(1) are:

"(a) the transfer to the transferee company of the whole or any part of the undertaking and of the property or liabilities of any transferor company;
(b) the allotting or appropriation by the transferee company of any shares, debentures, policies or other like interests in that company which under the amalgamation or transfer are to be allotted or appropriated by that company to or for any person;
(c) the continuation by or against the transferee company of any legal proceedings pending by or against any transferor company;
(d) the dissolution, with winding up, of any transferor company;
(e) such incidental, consequential and supplementary matters as are necessary to secure that the amalgamation or transfer shall be fully and effectively carried out."

---

[89] Directive 79/267/EEC [1979] O.J. L63/1. Ellis and Wiltshire (eds.) *Regulation of Insurance in the United Kingdom and Ireland* (Kluwer Publishing).
[90] 387 *Dáil Debates* Col. 1074.

Section 36 (2) provides that where an order is made under subsection (1) which provides for the transfer of property or liabilities, the effect of the order will be to transfer the property to and vest it in the transferee company and to transfer the liabilities to and render them the liabilities of the transferee company. If the order so directs, any property so transferred may be freed from any mortgage or charge which is invalidated by virtue of the amalgamation or transfer. Where an amalgamation is sanctioned or approved under subsection (1), the transferee company must deposit office copies of the order with the Minister.[91]

II. THE 1994 REGULATIONS

7–88   The European Communities (Non-Life Insurance) Framework Regulations 1994[92] give effect to the Third Non-Life Insurance Framework Directive (Directive 92/49/EEC)[93] which institutes a single authorisation system of supervision of non-life insurance undertakings operating throughout the European Communities. This single system ensures that insurance undertakings transacting business on either a cross-border or branch basis will be subject to overall supervisory control of the supervisory authority where their head offices are located.

An "insurance undertaking" is defined in Article 2(1) as meaning:

(a) for the purpose of carrying on insurance business in the State by way of establishment, the holder of an authorisation under these Regulations or, as the case may be, under Article 6 of Council Directive 73/239/EEC as inserted by Article 4 of Directive 92/49/EEC or the holder of an authorisation under Article 23 of Council Directive 73/239/EEC;

(b) for the purpose of carrying on insurance business by way of services, the holder of an authorisation under these Regulations or, as the case may be, under Article 6 of Council Directive 73/239/EEC as inserted by Article 4 of Directive 92/49/EEC.

7–89   The European Communities (Life Assurance) Framework Regulations 1994[94] give effect to the Third Life Assurance Framework Directive (Directive 92/96/EEC)[95] which initiates a single authorisation system of supervision of life insurance undertakings operating throughout the European Communities.[96] It too seeks to ensure that insurance

---

[91] s.36(3).
[92] S.I. No. 359 of 1994.
[93] O.J. No. L228/1.
[94] S.I. No. 360 of 1994.
[95] O.J. L360/1.
[96] These regulations also implement relevant provisions of the Second life Assurance Freedom of Services Directive (Directive 90/619/EEC) O.J. L330.

undertakings transacting business on either a cross-border or branch basis will be subject to overall supervisory control of the supervisory authority where their head offices are located. An "insurance undertaking" is defined in Article 2(1) as meaning:

(a) for the purpose of carrying on insurance business in the State by way of establishment, the holder of an authorisation under these Regulations or, as the case may be, the holder of an authorisation under Article 27 of Council Directive 79/267/EEC;

(b) for the purpose of carrying on insurance business by way of services, the holder of an authorisation under these Regulations or, as the case may be, under Article 6 of Council Directive 79/267/EEC as inserted by Article 3 of Directive 92/96/EEC;

Identical provisions are set out in Articles 20 and 40 of The European Communities (Non-Life Insurance) Framework Regulations 1994 and The European Communities (Life Assurance) Framework Regulations 1994 respectively in relation to qualifying holdings in insurance undertakings. For the purposes of convenience, Article 40 of the European Communities (Life Assurance) Framework Regulations 1994 will be described.

7–90 Article 40(1) provides that any person who proposes to acquire, either directly or indirectly, a qualifying holding in an insurance undertaking must firstly notify the Minister indicating the size of the proposed qualifying holding. A "qualifying holding" is defined by Article 9(4) as:

> "a direct or indirect holding in an insurance undertaking which represents 10 per cent. or more of the capital or of the voting rights or which makes it possible to exercise a significant influence over the management of the undertaking in which a holding subsists."[96a]

A second obligation imposed by Article 40(1) requires any person who proposes to acquire, either directly or indirectly, a qualifying holding in an insurance undertaking to notify the Minister where it is proposed to increase such qualifying holding so that the percentage level of the voting rights or capital held by that person reaches or exceeds certain percentage levels. The relevant percentage levels are 20 per cent, 33 per cent or 50 per cent.[97]

7–91 Once the Minister is notified by a person in accordance with Article 40(1), the Minister has three months to oppose the proposed

---

[96a] A similar definition is contained in Art. 9(4) of S.I. No. 359 of 1994.
[97] Art. 40(4).

acquisition where he is not satisfied as to the suitability of that person.[98] The Minister must make this decision on the basis of ensuring the sound and prudent management of the insurance undertaking in question. If the Minister forms the opinion that the control exercised by the persons referred to in Article 40(1) is "likely to operate against the prudent and sound management of an insurance undertaking", the Minister may seek a Court order pursuant to Article 40(6) to terminate that situation. This may be done either by way of injunction, suspension of the exercise of the voting rights attaching to the shares held by the persons in question or otherwise. The Court is authorised to make such order in relation to this matter as it deems necessary.[99] Article 40(8) authorises the Minister to make an application under Article 40(6) where a person fails to comply with the notification requirements referred to in Article 40(1). If a holding is required contrary to the provisions of this Article the Court may, on the application of the Minister, in addition to any other order which it may make, order the suspension of the corresponding voting rights or the nullity of votes cast. This acts as a sufficient form of deterrent to ensure enforcement.

7–92 The Regulations also impose obligations on the insurance companies themselves in these circumstances. Where the insurance undertaking becomes aware of any acquisitions or disposals of holdings in its capital so that such holdings exceed or fall below these percentage levels, the undertaking must inform the Minister.[100] In addition, the insurance undertaking must submit regular[101] notifications to the Minister of the names of shareholders or members possessing qualifying holdings and the size of such holdings by reference, for example, to information received at annual general meetings of shareholders or as a result of compliance with the Companies Acts 1963 to 1990.[102] The Minister is also entitled at any time to seek information concerning all shareholders irrespective of the size of their shareholding.

---

[98] Art. 40(2).
[99] Art. 40(7).
[100] Art. 40(5).
[101] At such times as may be specified by the Minister and at least once a year.
[102] See paras 13–87–13–100.

PART 3

ACQUISITIONS OF PUBLIC COMPANIES

CHAPTER 8

ACQUISITION OF THE BUSINESS OF A PUBLIC COMPANY

8–01   One of the main advantages to acquiring the assets of a company, rather than its shares, is that one may choose to acquire only some of the assets, leaving what is undesirable behind. With an acquisition of the shares of a company, one acquires a share in all the assets of the company. The down-side of this however, is that each asset acquired must be identified and then vested in the transferee, the offeror. Stamp duty is then payable on these assets. Stamp duty on the transfer of assets is 6 per cent as opposed to the stamp duty payable on a transfer of shares which is 1 per cent. In addition, the transferor will be subject to a corporation tax charge on any capital gain. If the proceeds of the sale are passed on to shareholders, the shareholders may themselves be subject to tax in the form of income tax on dividends or capital gains tax on a deemed winding up. The tax implications of such a transfer were considered in Chapter 1, para. 1–09.

The acquisition may be effected either by the offeree's management selling the business directly to the offeror, by a single vesting order under section 201 of the Companies Act 1963 or by way of a merger where the assets and liabilities of the acquired company are simultaneously transferred to the acquiring company.

A. Offer to Acquire the Assets of the Offeree

8–02   When a offeror makes an offer to acquire the whole or part of the assets of an offeree, the offer is put initially to the management of the company. The reason for this is that the business is owned by the company not by the shareholders. If the management is agreeable, the offeror will then acquire the assets from the target company. A number of issues arise for consideration.

I. POWER TO ACQUIRE AND DISPOSE OF ASSETS

8–03   Where the offeror decides to acquire the business or assets of the offeree, the directors of the offeror must ensure that they are authorised to acquire assets under the objects clause in the memorandum of association or in the articles of association. Similarly, before the offeree's directors may sell the assets of the target to the offeror, they must ensure that they are empowered to do so under its own memorandum or articles of association. If the memorandum or articles of association allow, management may sanction the acquisition or disposal of assets without recourse to shareholders. Often the objects clause will be drafted sufficiently broadly to allow management to make any such decision in the interests of the company. Once the directors make this decision bona fides in what they consider to be the best interests of the company, shareholders cannot generally interfere. Of course, if the sale involves a breach by the directors of their fiduciary duties or minority oppression under section 205 of the Companies Act 1963 ("the 1963 Act"), the shareholders will be in a position to complain to the courts.[1]

8–04   If the objects clause or the articles of association does not vest the directors with the power to acquire or dispose of assets, they may be altered to give directors these powers. A company's objects clause may be altered by a special resolution.[2] This alteration may be challenged by:

(a)   the holders of not less in the aggregate than 15% in nominal value of the company's issued share capital or any class thereof or,

(b)   by the holders of not less than 15% of the company's debentures, entitling the holders to object to alterations of its objects.[3]

A company is also entitled to amend its articles of association or any part of them by special resolution.[4] A shareholder cannot restrain an amendment of the articles unless it amounts to a breach of contract or unless the alteration was not made bona fides in the best interests of the company as a whole.[5]

8–05   Even if the power to dispose of assets is not granted to the offeree's directors in the articles of association, where the offeror acquires the assets in good faith, the agreement must be honoured. Section 8(1) of the 1963 Act provides that:

> "any act or thing done by a company which if the company had been empowered to do the same would have been lawfully and effectively done, shall, notwithstanding that the company had no power to do such act or thing, be effective in favour of any person relying on such act or thing who is

---

[1]   See paras 19–23–19–52.
[2]   Companies Act 1963, s.10(1).
[3]   *ibid.,* s.10(3).
[4]   *ibid.,* s.15.
[5]   *Allen v. Gold Reefs of West Africa* [1900] 1 Ch. 656, *Clark v. Workman* [1920] 1 I.R. 107.

not shown to have been actually aware, at the time when he so relied thereon, that such act or thing was not within the powers of the company . . .".[6]

In such a case, any director or officer to the offeree who was responsible for the disposal would be liable to the offeree for any loss or damage suffered by the company as a consequence.

Where the offeree is a listed company, depending on the classification of the disposal under the Stock Exchange Listing Rules, certain announcements may have to be made and a circular and the approval of the offeree's shareholders may be required. Where the entire undertaking or the majority of the assets is being acquired, the listing will normally be suspended. Similarly, where the offeror is a listed company, the Stock Exchange Listing Rules may require that the offeror's shareholders be notified of the acquisition and their approval sought. These Listing Rules were considered in Chapter 5.[6a]

II. CONSIDERATION FOR THE ACQUISITION

8–06 An important decision which must be made at an early stage is whether the consideration for the acquisition will take the form of a cash payment, the exchange of shares or some combination of both. Other issues will then flow from this decision.

(1) Power to Issue Shares

8–07 Where the offeror intends paying for the assets with its own shares, the directors of the offeror must ensure that they are entitled to issue shares. Indeed, even where consideration takes the form of a cash payment, if insufficient liquid cash is available, the offeror may obtain the extra cash by issuing and marketing shares. A rights issue is typically used to raise cash from existing shareholders for an acquisition. The option of issuing shares as consideration or as a source of finance is likely to be more limited in the case of a private company as a private company is restricted from issuing shares to the public.[7]

8–08 The right to issue shares is normally vested in directors either by the articles of association or by a special resolution of the company.[8] Section 20 of the Companies (Amendment) Act, 1983 seeks to ensure that director's powers in this respect are not abused. Section 20 prohibits directors from exercising any power of the company to allot relevant

---

[6] See generally, Forde, *Company Law* (Mercier Press, 1992), 427–433; Ussher, *Company Law in Ireland* (Sweet & Maxwell, 1986), pp. 123–134.
[6a] See above paras 5–33–5–47.
[7] See paras 14–03–14–11.
[8] See Companies Act 1963 First Schedule, Table A, Part I Art. 5.

securities, unless they are authorised to do so by the company in general meeting or by the articles of association of the company. Authority, for the purposes of the section, may be given for a particular exercise of that power or for the exercise of that power generally. Authority may also be given subject to certain conditions.[9] Furthermore, any such authority must state the maximum amount of relevant securities that may be allotted thereunder and the duration of the authority. As authority may not be given for a period of more than five years,[10] the directors will have to apply to the company in general meeting to have this authority renewed at regular periods. The company is entitled to decide, by ordinary resolution, to give, vary, revoke or renew this authority.[11] It is obvious therefore, that directors who are deemed by the shareholders to have abused their authority, risk having it revoked or not renewed.

8–09   Where the offeror is a listed company, certain additional Stock Exchange Listing Rules apply. Circulars issued in connection with a resolution proposing to grant directors authority to allot relevant securities must include:

> "(a) a statement of the maximum amount of relevant securities which the directors will have the authority to allot and the percentage which that amount represents of the total ordinary share capital in issue as at a date not more than one month prior to the date of the circular;
> (b) a statement by the directors as to whether they have any present intention of exercising the authority, and if so, for what purpose; and
> (c) a statement as to when the authority will lapse."[12]

Where the authorised share capital of the company is insufficient to effect the acquisition, it may be necessary to increase it. To do this, the approval of shareholders in general meeting must be sought.[13]

8–10   In certain circumstances, the right of a private company to issue shares may also be restricted by a shareholders agreement.[14] In *Russell v. Northern Bank Development Corporation*,[15] a number of shareholders entered into a shareholders' agreement providing *inter alia* that "no further share capital shall be created or issued in the company . . . without

---

[9] Companies (Amendment) Act 1983 s.20(2).
[10] *ibid.* s.20(3). In the case of an authority contained in the articles of association at the time of the original incorporation of the company, the five year period commences on the date of incorporation. In all other cases, the five year period commences on the date on which the resolution giving the directors authority is passed.
[11] *ibid.* s.20(6).
[12] Stock Exchange Listing Rules, Chap. 14 para. 14–7.
[13] Companies Act 1963 s.68(1); Companies Act 1963 Table A, Part I First Schedule, Art. 44.
[14] paras 15–06–15–12.
[15] [1992] 1 W.L.R. 588.

the written consent of each of the parties." The company was joined as a party to this agreement. The Court of Appeal determined that this provision was an unlawful fetter on the company's statutory power to increase its ordinary share capital by ordinary resolution and was thus invalid. The House of Lords held, however, that although a provision in the company's articles restricting its statutory power to alter its articles would be invalid, as would a restriction on the company's powers to increase its share capital, individual shareholders were entitled to enter into a private agreement as to the exercise of their voting rights. They could thus agree privately that they would not allow the articles to be altered or the share capital to be increased. However, the aspects of the agreement involving the company agreeing to restrict its own powers was unenforceable as a fetter on the company's statutory powers.

8–11   Where the offeror is a listed company, the Stock Exchange Listing Rules state that if the offeror needs to increase its authorised share capital to generate sufficient shares, circulars issued in connection with such a resolution must include:

(a)   a statement of the proposed percentage increase in the authorised share capital of the relevant class; and

(b)   a statement of the reason for the increase.

In addition, the offeror must notify the Company Announcements Office without delay, of the proposed change in its capital.[16]

(2) Pre-emption Rights

8–12   Pre-emption rights oblige companies when they first issue new equity securities to do so by giving their shareholders a first option on the shares in proportion to their existing holding. The advantage for shareholders is that it avoids a dilution of shareholdings, and thus of voting strength. Although there is no common law principle requiring it,[17] sections 23 and 24 of the Companies (Amendment) Act 1983 makes pre-emption compulsory for every company.

8–13   Pre-emption rights will not apply, however, in the case of an acquisition of an undertaking or a business for shares. This is because the shares will be issued for a non-cash consideration. Section 23(4) of the Companies (Amendment) Act 1983 provides that pre-emption rights do not apply:

---

[16]   Stock Exchange Listing Rules, Chap. 9, para. 9–10(a) and para. 14–9..
[17]   *Mutual Life Assurance Co. of NY v. Rank Organisation Ltd.* [1985] B.C.L.C. 11.

> "in relation to a particular allotment of equity securities if the securities are, or are to be, wholly or partly paid up otherwise than in cash"

8–14 However, if the acquisition is being paid for by cash and the offeror intends to issue shares to finance the purchase, pre-emption rights become important and the company may be obliged to market its shares by means of a rights issue. Section 23(1)(a) states that subject to the provisions of sections 23, 24 and 25, a company proposing to allot any equity securities:

> "shall not allot any of those securities on any terms to any person unless it has made an offer to each person who holds relevant shares or relevant employee shares to allot to him on the same or more favourable terms a proportion of those securities which is as nearly as practicable equal to the proportion in nominal value held by him of the aggregate of relevant shares and relevant employee shares."

The offer need not be exactly mathematically pro rata, a proportion that is as "near as practicable" equal suffices. An offer which is required under section 23(1) must remain open for at least 21 days.[18] During this period, any shareholder may renounce his pre-emption rights in favour of anyone else, subject to any restrictions in the companies regulations against admitting new shareholders into the company.

8–15 Section 23(10) provides that a private company can exclude or vary the pre-emption rights in its memorandum or articles of association. In addition, section 24(1) provides that where authority exists under the Act to make an allotment,[19] then the directors may be empowered by the articles or by a special resolution at a general meeting to waive either wholly or partly the pre-emption requirement. In order that such a waiver be effective, the authority to allot must exist and the waiver must have been recommended by the directors. In addition, the notice proposing the special resolution must be accompanied by a written statement from the directors setting out:

(a) their reasons for making the recommendation;

(b) the amount to be paid to the company in respect of the equity securities to be allotted; and

(c) the directors' justification of that amount.[20]

It is an offence to knowingly or recklessly permit the inclusion in any such statement of any matter which is misleading, false or deceptive in a material particular.[21]

---

[18] s.23(8).
[19] s.20.
[20] s.24(5).
[21] s.24(6).

8–16 The Irish Association of Investment Managers (IAIM) Guidelines warns that existing shareholders would be exposed to significant dilution of control if cash placings replaced rights issues.[22] It also points out that if cash is to be raised in overseas markets, shares could find their way back to the Irish market with overseas investors taking a quick profit. The IAIM thus suggests that listed companies should obtain shareholder approval annually for a special resolution to disapply the rights. It also suggests that they apply for a disapplication only where: "the individual or combined issues do not exceed the greater of £1million or 5 per cent of the issued equity share capital at the time the authority is sought". In all other circumstances, it states the company should use a traditional rights issue, underwritten or at a deep discount or it should obtain specific shareholder approval for a placing for cash. The IAIM advises their members not to oppose proposals for combination issues where the non-pre-emptive issue does not represent more than 5 per cent of share capital.

As noted in Chapter 5, where the offeror is a listed company, the Stock Exchange Listing Rules reaffirms the general principle that companies should offer their shares to shareholders before offering them to the market. However, shareholders may authorise the disapplication of these rights, in accordance with section 24 of the Companies (Amendment) Act 1983.[23]

(3) Listing Particulars

8–17 If the offeror intends allotting shares of the same class as shares already listed, a listing will need to be obtained for these shares. The application for listing such further shares must be made not more than one month after allotment.[24] As noted in Chapter 5, the offeror may be exempt from the obligation to publish listing particulars as these additional shares are "securities which have been issued in connection with a merger involving the transfer of all or part of an undertaking's assets and liabilities or as consideration for the transfer of assets other than cash".[25] This exemption will apply if a document containing equivalent information to listing particulars has been published in the previous 12 months.

(4) Share Premiums

8–18 Where a company issues shares at a price above its nominal share price, the difference is known as a "share premium". Strict rules regulate how a share premium must be dealt with by the company.[26]

---

[22] Issued in March 1989 and updated in October 1991.
[23] Stock Exchange Listing Rules, paras 5–58–5–60 and 9–20.
[24] *ibid.*, Chap. 9, para. 9–33
[25] *ibid.*, Chap. 5, para. 5–23A (a) (ii).
[26] Companies Act 1963, s.62 as amended by the Companies (Amendment) Act 1983 Schedule One, para. 11 and the Companies Act 1990, s.231(1).

Section 62(1) of the 1963 Act states that where a company issues shares at a premium, whether for cash or otherwise, a sum equal to the aggregate amount or value of the premiums on those shares must be transferred to "the share premium account".

8–19   When a offeror acquires the assets of a company in return for the exchange of its own shares, if the value of the assets acquired exceed the nominal value of the shares, a share premium results and this must be transferred to the share premium account. Even where the acquisition is to be paid for in cash, the offeror may decide to issue further shares and market them to raise this cash. In such a case, if the shares are being marketed at a price in excess of their nominal share price, again a share premium results which must be transferred to the share premium account.

8–20   The share premium account is treated as if it were paid up share capital for the purposes of the provisions relating to the reduction of share capital.[27] Section 62(2) sets out the purposes for which the share premium account may be applied. The account may be applied in paying up unissued shares of the company to be allotted to members of the company as fully paid bonus shares, in writing off either (a) the preliminary expenses of the company, or (b) the expenses of, or the commission paid or discount allowed on, any issue of shares or debentures of the company. Alternatively, the account may be used in providing for the premium payable on the redemption of any redeemable preference shares[28] or on the repayment of any debentures.

(5) Independent Valuation

8–21   One of the central principles of capital maintenance is that shares may not be issued at a discount on the nominal value.[29] Where shares are being issued for a non-cash consideration, it is important to determine that no hidden discounts are being offered in the form of inadequate consideration for those shares.

(a) Allotment of Shares Otherwise than for Cash

8–22   Section 30(1) of the Companies (Amendment) Act 1983 provides as follows:

---

[27] Companies Act 1963, ss.72–77
[28] Companies Act 1990, s.220.
[29] Companies (Amendment) Act 1983 s.27. See also *Ooregum Gold Mining Company of India v. Roper* [1892] A.C. 125.

> "Subject to subsection (2), a public limited company shall not allot shares as fully or partly paid up (as to their nominal value or any premium payable on them) otherwise than in cash unless –
> (a) the consideration for the allotment has been valued in accordance with the following provisions of this section;
> (b) a report with respect to its value has been made to the company by a person appointed by the company in accordance with those provisions during the six months immediately preceding the allotment of the shares; and
> (c) a copy of the report has been sent to the proposed allottee of the shares."

The requirements of section 30(1) are applicable only where shares have been allotted "otherwise than in cash". A share is deemed to have been allotted for cash:

> "if the consideration for the allotment . . . is cash received by the company or is a cheque received by the company in good faith which the directors have no reason for suspecting will not be paid or is the release of a liability of the company for a liquidated sum or is an undertaking to pay cash to the company at a future date".[30]

8–23　Ussher suggests that the section 30(1) requirement will not apply where the share issue has been arranged by two separate contracts and a set-off is operated.[31] In such a situation, the offeror would allot shares for cash to the offeree, the offeree then separately agrees to sell its assets for cash and the reciprocal debts are then set-off against each other. The reason such a transaction would not need a valuation, is that the definition of "cash" in section 2(3) above does not expressly reject the long-established principle that set-off is the equivalent of a cash payment.[32]

Where no set off is operated and an undertaking is being acquired in return for shares in an offeror which is a public limited company, an independent valuation of the undertaking will be required.

(b) Independent Valuation

8–24　A report detailing this valuation must be given to the offeree and to the offeror before allotment. Such a valuation should be carried out by an "independent person". Such a person is normally "a person qualified at the time of the report to be appointed or to continue to be auditor of the company".[33] However, if the auditor believes that it would be reasonable to have another person make the valuation because that other person has the requisite knowledge and experience and is not an officer or employee of the company, that independent

---

[30]　Companies (Amendment) Act 1983, s.2(3)(a).
[31]　See Ussher, *op.cit.*, above, n.6, 312–313.
[32]　*Re Gibson, Little & Co. Ltd.* (1880–81) 5 L.R. Ir.139
[33]　Companies (Amendment) Act 1983, s.30(5).

person may choose to accept such a valuation together with a report that will enable the independent person to make his or her own report.

(c) Consequences of a Breach of Section 30

8–25 Where shares are allotted in contravention of subsection (1) and the allottee has not received a report, or where there has been some other contravention of this section and the allottee should have known that this amounted to a contravention, the allottee will be liable to pay the company "an amount equal to the nominal value of the shares, together with the whole of any premium or, if the case so requires, such proportion of that amount as is treated as paid up by the consideration". In addition, the allottee will have to pay interest at the appropriate rate on the amount payable.[34]

8–26 Any person who becomes the holder of any shares in respect of which there has been a contravention under section 30 and by virtue of that contravention another person is liable to pay this amount, that person will also be liable to pay this amount unless they are a bona fide purchaser for value without notice or he derived title, directly or indirectly, from a person who became a holder of them after the contravention and was not so liable.[35] Where a company contravenes section 30, the company and also any officer of the company in default will be guilty of an offence.[36] The undertaking, however, to provide the non-cash consideration is still enforceable.[37]

(d) Exemptions

8–27 An exemption to the section 30(1) requirement to obtain a valuation exists in two specified situations set out in section 30(2). Firstly, section 30(1) will not apply to the allotment of shares by a company "in connection with a proposed merger of that company with another company".[38] Section 30(4) provides that for this purpose:

> "there is a proposed merger of two companies when one of them proposes to acquire all the assets and liabilities of the other in exchange for the issue of shares or other securities in that one to shareholders of the other, with or without any cash payment to those shareholders".

An independent valuation is unnecessary thus where the offeror proposes to acquire all the assets and liabilities of the offeree in exchange for the issue of its shares or other securities *to the offeree's shareholders*. This exemption will not thus apply where only part of the assets of the target

---

[34] *ibid.*, s.30(10).
[35] *ibid.*, s.30(11).
[36] *ibid.*, s.36(1).
[37] *ibid.*, s.36(2).
[38] *ibid.*, s.30(2)(b).

are being acquired, nor will it apply where the shares are being allotted to the target company itself, rather than its shareholders.

8–28 Secondly, section 30(1) will not apply to the allotment of shares by a company "in connection with:

> "an arrangement providing for the allotment of shares in that company on terms that the whole or part of the consideration for the shares allotted is to be provided by the transfer to that company or the cancellation of all or some of the shares of a particular class, in another company (with or without the issue to that company of shares, or of shares of any particular class, in that other company)".[39]

A valuation will be unnecessary thus where the allotment is made "in connection with an arrangement" which involves, as either whole or part of the consideration, a transfer to the offeror, or the cancellation of all or some of the shares, or of all or some of the shares of a particular class in another company. Section 30(1) does not thus apply to takeovers or mergers by exchange of shares in connection with an arrangement under section 201 or 260 of the 1963 Act considered below

(6) Payments to Offeree's Directors

8–29 Where the agreement to acquire the offeree's assets involve a "sweetener" to directors offering to compensate them for their ensuing job loss, sections 186 and 187 of the 1963 Act may apply. Section 186 makes it unlawful for a company to make a payment to a director as "compensation for loss of office" or "in connection with his retirement from office" without the payment being disclosed to shareholders and approved by them in general meeting. Section 187(1) states that disclosure and shareholder approval are also necessary where any payment is made to a director as compensation for loss of office or in connection with his or her retirement "in connection with the transfer of the whole or any part of the undertaking or property of a company". This latter section would obviously include a payment by either the offeror or the offeree.[40] Where a director receives a payment in contravention of section 187, the payment shall be deemed to have been received "on trust" for the company.[41] Accordingly, the director will be liable to turn over such a payment to the company if and when he or she is requested to do so.

---

[39] *ibid.*, s.30(2)(a).

[40] Companies Act 1963, s.189(3) provides that bona fide payments by way of damages for breach of contract or by way of pension in respect of part services are not included under sections 186 or 187.

[41] *ibid.*, s.187(2).

(7) Rule 9 of the Takeover Rules

8–30   Where an offeree is offered shares in the offeror in return for the transfer of its assets, the offeree must be aware that in certain circumstances an obligation may be imposed upon it under Rule 9 of the Irish Takeover Panel Act 1997, (Take over) Rules, 1997 ("The Takeover Rules"). This rule imposes a duty on a person who acquires shares carrying 30 per cent or more of the voting rights of a company to extend the offer to the holders of all the outstanding shares in that company. If the offeror seeks to acquire the assets of a relatively large offeree, and the consideration to be paid takes the form of shares, the offeree may end up owning shares carrying more than 30 per cent of the offeror's voting rights. This would give rise to a curious situation where Rule 9 would require that the intended target make a general offer for the original offeror. To avoid this, the approval of the offeree's shareholders at an independent vote at a shareholders meeting would be obtained and an application would be made to the Panel for a dispensation from this rule.[42] The Irish Takeover Panel Act, 1997 (Substantial Acquisition) Rules, 1997 ("the SARs") are unlikely to be relevant to an acquisition of shares by the offeree in this context. Even where the offeror is a relevant company, the acquisition of new voting shares will not be tested as an acquisition of voting securities for the purposes of Rule 3 of the SARs which defines a "substantial acquisition of securities".

(8) Borrowing

8–31   Where the offeror is paying for the assets with cash, an alternative to marketing shares to raise the cash is to borrow the cash. As noted, the power to borrow may already be given to directors in the articles of association. Even where this is so, the offeror may need to amend its articles of association in order to permit the directors to exceed the original limits imposed on the their power to borrow.

III. INVOLVEMENT OF DIRECTORS

8–32   Where a director in the offeree has an interest in the offeror[43] or a director in the offeror has an interest in the offeree, shareholder approval may be necessary to effect the transfer of assets.

8–33   Section 29(1)(b) of the Companies Act 1990 requires the prior approval of shareholders at general meeting before an offeror buys one or more non-cash assets of the "requisite value" from a director or connected

---

[42] See para. 11–75.
[43] See paras 18–20–18–26, and 18–41–18–47.

person. A body corporate may be deemed to be connected with a director of a company, if it is controlled by that director.[44] Therefore, if the offeree is controlled by one of the offeror's directors, shareholder approval would be necessary. Section 29 also applies where an offeree sells to a company which is controlled by one of its directors. Thus, such a disposal would also require the approval of the offeree's shareholders at general meeting.[44a] The "requisite value" is stated in section 29(2) to be more than £50,000 or 10 per cent of net assets, with a *de minimis* value of £10,000. Section 29(3) provides that any transaction which is not approved in the correct manner is voidable at the company's instance unless:

(a) restitution of the money or property is no longer possible or the company has been indemnified for the loss or damage;

(b) a *bona fide* third party for value without notice of the contravention would be affected by its avoidance; or

(c) the arrangement is affirmed by the company in general meeting within a reasonable time.

A party to an arrangement in contravention of the section is liable to account to the company for any resulting gain made whether directly or indirectly and is liable to indemnify the company for any loss or damage it suffered. Any other director of the company who authorised the transaction is similarly liable.[45] A connected director may however be exempted from liability if he or she shows that he or she took "all reasonable steps to secure the company's compliance" with section 29. In addition a connected person and any other director who authorised the transaction will be exempted from liability if they can show that at the time the arrangement was entered into, they did not know the relevant circumstances constituting the contravention.[45a]

8–34 As noted in chapter 5,[45b] chapter 11 of the Stock Exchange Listing Rules deals with transactions with related parties. Where a transaction is being proposed between a listed company and a related party, a circular must be issued and the prior approval of the company in general meeting will be required. A "related party" for the purposes of chapter 11, includes a director or shadow director[46] of the company, its parent, subsidiary or a fellow subsidiary of its parent. The definition

---

[44] Companies Act 1990, s.26(2).

[44a] Companies Act, 1990 s.29(1)(a). However, s.29(8) provides that s.29(1)(a) will not apply if the director is also a member of the company and the acquisition of the asset from the company is made in his or her character as member rather than as director.

[45] Companies Act 1990, s.29(4).

[45a] Companies Act 1990, s.39(5).

[45b] See paras 5–43–5–47.

[46] Or a person who held this title within the previous 12 months.

also includes an associate of a related party, which could include any company controlled by a director or his or her family.

IV. SECTION 260 OF THE COMPANIES ACT 1963

8–35 If, as a result of the acquisition of the offeree's business in return for shares in the offerer, the offeree will be placed in voluntary liquidation and its shares in the offerer distributed amongst its own shareholders, section 260 of the 1963 Act may apply.

(1) The Arrangement

8–36 Section 260(1) provides as follows:

> "Where a company is proposed to be, or is in course of being, wound up voluntarily, and the whole or part of its business or property is proposed to be transferred or sold to another company, whether a company within the meaning of this Act or not (in this section referred to as 'the transferee company'), the liquidator of the first-mentioned company (in this section referred to as 'the transferor company') may, with the sanction of a special resolution of that company, conferring either a general authority on the liquidator or an authority in respect of any particular arrangement, receive in compensation or part compensation for the transfer or sale, shares, policies or other like interests in the transferee company for distribution among the members of the transferor company, or may enter into any other arrangement whereby the members of the transferor company may, in lieu of receiving cash, shares, policies or other like interests, or in addition thereto, participate in the profits of or receive any other benefit from the transferee company".

Any sale or arrangement in pursuance of section 260 is binding on members of the transferor company.[47]

8–37 A change of control may occur therefore by proposing the voluntary winding-up of the offeree (the transferor) and the transfer of the whole or part of its business or property to another company (the transferee company) in return for compensating the target's liquidator for the transfer. This compensation may take the form of cash, shares, policies or other like instruments in the transferee company for distribution among the offeree's shareholders.[48] Alternatively, the liquidator may enter into any other agreement whereby the offeree's shareholders instead of or in addition to receiving cash, shares, policies or other like interests, participate in the profits of or receive any other benefit from the transferee company.

---

[47] Companies Act 1963, s.260(2).
[48] Section 271 of the Companies Act 1963 provides that section 260 shall apply in the case of a creditor's voluntary winding up as in the case of a members' voluntary winding up, with the modification that the powers of the liquidator under section 260 shall not be exercised except with the sanction either of the court or of the committee of inspection.

(2) Special Resolution

8–38　In order to effect such an arrangement, section 260(1) makes it clear that the liquidator must obtain a special resolution from the offeree conferring either a general authority on the liquidator or an authority in respect of any particular arrangement.

As noted previously, a special resolution must be passed by not less than three-fourths of the votes cast by such members as, being entitled to vote, vote in person or, where proxies are allowed, by proxy at a general meeting. In general, at least 21 days notice of this meeting should be given to the relevant shareholders, specifying the intention to propose the resolution as a special resolution.[49]

(3) Court Order

8–39　Section 260(3) provides that any shareholder who does not exercise their voting rights in favour of the special resolution may express their dissent in writing to the liquidator within seven days of the passing of the special resolution requiring the liquidator either to abstain from effecting the arrangement or to purchase that part of their interest which those shares represent.[50] The price to be paid for these shares must be determined either by agreement or by arbitration.[51] Where there are a number of dissenting shareholders and the demands on the liquidator to purchase shares are likely to be high, the company may prefer to initiate a scheme of amalgamation under section 201 of the Companies Act 1963. However, this may not always be allowed by the court.[52]

8–40　Section 260(5) provides that if a court order is made within a year for winding up the company by the Court, the special resolution will not be valid unless it has been sanctioned by the court. This section allows creditors to stop the reconstruction by seeking a compulsory winding up where they believe that their interests are being jeopardised. In addition, shareholders can seek to have the court stop the reconstruction by making a compulsory order to wind up the company. Such an application is likely to be granted where the arrangement is eminently unfair to the independent minority shareholders and is only passed by means of a large majority of shares held by another company which alone benefits from the scheme. In *Re Consolidated South Rand Mines Deep Ltd.*,[53] the Court found that in the circumstances it would have

---

[49]　*ibid.*, s.141(1).
[50]　*Re Demerara Rubber Co. Ltd.* [1913] 1 Ch. 331.
[51]　Section 260(6) provides that the provisions of the Companies Clauses Consolidation Act 1845 shall be incorporated with the Companies Act 1963.
[52]　See para. 8–41 *et seq.*
[53]　[1909] 1 Ch. 491.

been a positive injustice to the minority shareholders to allow the voluntary winding-up to continue. A compulsory winding up order was thus made with the effect that the reconstruction could not go through unless it was sanctioned by the court. According to Swinfen Eady J. some advantage should accrue to shareholders as a result of making the compulsory winding up order which would not be available if they were merely bought out as dissentient shareholders.

B. Section 201 Arrangement

8–41   An alternative method of acquiring an undertaking is through an arrangement under section 201 of the 1963 Act. This section provides for the transfer of the assets and liabilities of the offeree to the offeror by means of a single vesting order. Shares in the offeror will then be issued to the offeree's shareholders in compensation for the disposal of the net assets. The offeree will then be wound up. The main advantage of this method of acquiring assets is that the offeror's shares are left widely dispersed in the hands of the offeree's shareholders rather than vesting them all in the offeree. The offeror does not thus have to contend with a single strong voting block of shares.

Section 201(1) provides as follows:

> "Where a compromise or arrangement is proposed between a company and
> its creditors or any class of them or between the company and its members
> or any class of them, the court may, on the application of the company or of
> any creditor or member of the company, or, in the case of a company being
> wound up, of the liquidator, order a meeting of the creditors or class of
> creditors, or of the members of the company or class of members, as the case
> may be, to be summonsed in such manner as the court directs."

I. SHAREHOLDER APPROVAL

8–42   Where such an arrangement is proposed between the offeree and the offeree's shareholders, the High Court may, on the application of the company, or on the application of any member of the company, order a meeting of shareholders. The scheme must then be approved by the shareholders.

Section 201(3) requires the approval of a majority in number representing three-fourths in value of the creditors or class of creditors or members or class of members, as the case may be, present and voting either in person or by proxy. If such a majority vote in favour of a resolution agreeing to any compromise or arrangement, the resolution will be binding if it is sanctioned by the Court.

8–43   In *Sovereign Life Assurance v. Dodd*,[54] Bowen L.J. noted that all those whose rights would be affected by the scheme must be given the opportunity of voting at a meeting and in addition, each meeting must be properly constituted to include only "those persons whose rights are not so dissimilar as to make it impossible for them to consult together with a view to their common interest . . .". In *Re Hellenic & General Trust Ltd.*,[55] a scheme was proposed which involved the cancellation of all existing ordinary shares in a company and the allotment of a like amount of new shares to Hambros Bank and the payment of compensation by Hambros Bank to the former ordinary shareholders. 53 per cent of these ordinary shares in the company were held by a wholly owned subsidiary of Hambros Bank which naturally voted in favour of the scheme. If the scheme went through one of the other shareholders, NBG, would become liable to a very substantial tax liability. The Court held that the shares owned by Hambros Bank formed a separate class from other ordinary shareholders for the purpose of the class meeting under the UK equivalent of section 201. Accordingly the class meeting having consisted of two classes of shareholders was not properly constituted.

II. COURT APPROVAL

8–44   As noted above, High Court approval is then necessary to sanction the scheme and make it binding on all the shareholders and on the company.[56] In *Re Alabama, New Orleans, Texas and Pacific Junction Railway Co*,[57] Lindley L.J. set out the tests to be used by a court in determining whether a scheme of arrangement ought to be sanctioned. These tests were subsequently approved by the Supreme Court in *Re John Power & Son Ltd.*[58] First, the court must be satisfied that the provisions of the 1963 Act have been observed. Secondly, those voting at the meeting must have exercised their vote bona fide in the interests of the class. On this point, Lindley L.J. stated: "the Court must look at the scheme, and see whether . . . the majority are acting bona fide, and whether they are coercing the minority in order to promote interests adverse to those of the class they purport to represent."[59] Thirdly, the arrangement must be objectively reasonable. This latter requirement means showing that the arrangement is one which "a fair and impartial mind" would sanction.[60]

---

[54]   [1892] 2 Q.B. 573 at 583.
[55]   [1975] 3 All E.R. 382.
[56]   s.201(3). See Ussher, *op. cit.*, above, n.6, 289–297.
[57]   [1891] 1 Ch. 213.
[58]   [1934] I.R. 412.
[59]   *op. cit.*, n.57 at 239.
[60]   *Re John Power & Son Ltd. per* Murnaghan J., above, n.58 at 432.

8–45   In *Re Anglo-Continental Supply Co. Ltd.*,[61] the reconstruction of an existing company by the winding-up and sale of its entire undertaking and assets for shares in a new foreign company was effected as an arrangement under the equivalent of section 201. Astbury J. stated that where a scheme of arrangement is really a sale under the equivalent of section 260, the provisions of section [260] must be complied with and cannot be evaded by calling it a scheme under section [201]. Where a scheme cannot be carried through under section [260] although it involves *inter alia* a sale to a company within that section for "shares, policies and other like interests" and for liquidation and distribution of the proceeds, Astbury J. stated that the court can sanction it under section [201] if it is fair and reasonable in accordance with the principles upon which the court acts in these cases. In addition, he opined that the court may, if it thinks fit, insist as a term of its sanction on the dissentient shareholders being protected in a similar manner to that provided for in section [260]. Even where a scheme or arrangement is outside section [260], Astbury J. stated that the court could also impose a similar sanction.

8–46   In *Re Hellenic & General Trust Ltd.*,[62] the Court also found that even if the class meeting had been properly constituted, the application for an order under the equivalent of section 201 would have failed. This is because the scheme could have been brought under the equivalent of section 204. However, Templeman J. noted that the fact an arrangement under section [201] produces a result which is the same as a takeover under section [204] is not necessarily fatal stating that: "It is not always so unfair as to preclude the court from exercising its discretion in favour of the scheme".[62a] Reference was made to *Re National Bank Ltd.*[63] where Plowman J. stated that it would involve imposing a limitation either on the generality of the word "arrangement" in section [201] or else on the discretion of the court under that section. Since the legislature had not imposed any such limitation, the Court was unwilling to apply one. In addition, Plowman J. pointed out that the two sections involve quite different considerations and approaches:

> "Under section [201] an arrangement can only be sanctioned if the question of its fairness has first of all been submitted to the court. Under section [204], on the other hand, the matter may never come to the court at all. If it does come to the court then the onus is cast on the dissenting minority to demonstrate the unfairness of the scheme. There are, therefore, good

---

[61]   [1922] 2 Ch. 723.
[62]   [1975] 3 All E.R. 382.
[62a] *ibid.*, at p. 387.
[63]   [1966] 1 All E.R. 1006.

reasons for requiring a smaller majority in favour of a scheme under section [201] than the majority which is required under section [204] if the minority is to be expropriated."[64]

Whilst Templeman J. accepted this, he stated that the present proposals placed the company in an "inescapable dilemma". It could not succeed under section [204] because of the express provisions of that section and the size of the shareholdings of the objectors. It could only succeed under section [201] by using the votes of the Hambros Bank subsidiary to secure the majority. In the circumstances, Templeman J. decided that the Court should not exercise its discretion in favour of authorising the arrangement against the wishes of NBG. In support of this proposition, Templeman J. referred to the *Anglo-Continental Supply Co.* case.

8–47 In order to be effective, an office copy of the court order must be delivered to the registrar of companies for registration.[65] A copy of every order must also be annexed to every copy of the memorandum of the company issued after the order has been made. Failure to comply with these procedural requirements will render the company and every officer of the company who is in default to a fine not exceeding £100.[66]

III. SECTION 203 ORDER

8–48 Where an application has been made to the court for an order under section 201 of the 1963 Act in connection with a reconstruction scheme or an amalgamation scheme under which the whole or part of the undertaking or the property of any company concerned in the scheme is to be transferred to another company, the petition for the sanctioning of the arrangement will also ask for an order under section 203(1). This latter subsection gives the court wide powers to make orders facilitating the full and effective carrying out of the merger. It provides:

"Where an application is made to the court under section 201 for the sanctioning of a compromise or arrangement proposed between a company and any such persons as are mentioned in that section, and it is shown to the court that the compromise or arrangement has been proposed for the purposes of or in connection with a scheme for the reconstruction of any company or companies or the amalgamation of any two or more companies, and that under the scheme the whole or any part of the undertaking or the property of any company concerned in the scheme (in this section referred to as 'a transferor company') is to be transferred to another company (in this section referred to as 'the transferee company'), the court may, either by the

---

[64] *ibid.* at 1013.
[65] Companies Act 1963, s.201(5).
[66] *ibid.*, s.201(6).

order sanctioning the compromise or arrangement or by any subsequent order make provision for all or any of the following matters –

(a) the transfer to the transferee company of the whole or any part of the undertaking and of the property or liabilities of any transferor company;

(b) the allotting or appropriation by the transferee company of any shares, debentures, policies or other like interests in that company which under the compromise or arrangement are to be allotted or appropriated by that company to or for any person;

(c) the continuation by or against the transferee company of any legal proceedings pending by or against any transferor company;

(d) the dissolution, without winding up, of any transferor company;

(e) the provision to be made for any persons who, within such time and in such manner as the court directs, dissent from the compromise or arrangement;

(f) such incidental, consequential and supplemental matters as are necessary to secure that the reconstruction or amalgamation shall be fully and effectively carried out."

8–49 Where an order under section 203 provides for the transfer of property or liabilities,[67] the property will be transferred to and vested in the transferee company and the liabilities will be transferred to and become the liabilities of the transferee company by virtue of the order. If the order so directs property may also be freed from any charge which is to cease to have effect by virtue of the compromise or arrangement.[68]

Every company in relation to which an order is made under section 203 must cause an office copy of the order to be delivered to the registrar of companies for registration within 21 days after the making of the order. Any company and every officer of a company in default of this requirement will be subject to a maximum fine of £125.[69]

C. European Communities (Mergers and Division of Companies) Regulations 1987

8–50 The European Communities (Mergers and Division of Companies) Regulations 1987[70] ("the Regulations"), implement the Third Council Directive 78/855 concerning mergers of plcs[71] and the Sixth Council

---

[67] The term "property" in this section includes "property, rights and powers of every description" and the term "liabilities" includes "duties". (s.203(4)).

[68] Companies Act 1963, s.203(2).

[69] *ibid.* s.203(3).

[70] S.I. No. 137 of 1987.

[71] [1978] O.J. L295/36.

Directive 82/891/EEC concerning the division of plcs.[72, 73] The objectives of these Directives are to co-ordinate the laws of Member States relating to mergers and divisions of public limited companies in order to ensure:

– the communication of objective information to shareholders and creditors;

– the extension of safeguards afforded to members and third parties to cover certain legal practices similar to mergers; and

– the limitation of cases in which nullity may arise.

8–51   It is important to note that in cases where the Regulations apply, sections 201 to 204 of the 1963 Act are expressly disapplied. The Regulations apply where the assets and liabilities of a public limited company are being acquired by another public limited company. Since the Regulations apply only where the transferor and transferee are public companies,[74] by converting a public company into a private company before proceeding to a merger or division, Gore Browne has suggested that the Regulations could be avoided.[75] Furthermore, the Regulations will not apply where one company acquires merely a controlling interest in the share capital of another company. In such a case, no company is dissolved and a "merger" or "disposal" as defined in the Regulations will not have occurred.

I. MERGERS

8–52   Where a company is being wound up, Regulation 5(2) provides that the company is given the option of becoming a party to a "merger by acquisition" or a "merger by formation of a new company" or of availing of the provisions of sections 201–204 (arrangements and reconstructions), 260 (sale of property in a members voluntary winding-up) and 271 (sale of property in a creditor's voluntary winding-up) of the 1963 Act. The first two options are only available if the distribution of the company's assets to its shareholders has not begun at the date on which the draft terms of merger have been

---

[72] [1982] O.J. L378/47.
[73] The proposed tenth directive on cross border Mergers (O.J. 28 C23/11) was designed to extend the co-ordination effected by the Third Directive to mergers involving companies governed by the laws of different Member States. This directive would not, however, have appeared to have been on the agenda for discussion for some time.
[74] And to certain unregistered companies defined in Reg. 2(1).
[75] See *Gore-Browne on Companies*, para. 30–11B on the Companies (Mergers and Divisions) Regulations 1987 (S.I. No. 1991 of 1987) which implement the two Directives into UK law.

signed by the directors of the relevant companies.[76] A "merger by acquisition" is defined as:

> "an operation whereby an existing company (the acquiring company) acquires all the assets and liabilities of another company or companies in exchange for the issue to the shareholders of the company or companies being acquired of shares in the acquiring company, with or without any cash payment, and with a view to the dissolution of the company or companies being acquired".[77]

A "merger by formation of a new company" is defined as:

> "a similar operation where the acquiring company has been formed for the purpose of such acquisition."[78]

Subject to Regulation 5(2), sections 201 to 204, 260 and 271 of the 1963 Act will not apply to mergers by acquisition or by the formation of new companies.[79]

II. DOCUMENTATION

8–53   In the event of a merger under the Regulations, three categories of documents must be prepared. Firstly, the directors of the merging companies must draw up draft terms of the merger in writing.[80] These draft terms which must be signed and dated and must contain certain basic information concerning the merger. They must include, at least:

(a) the names and registered offices of each of the merging companies;

(b) the nature of each of such companies i.e. whether it is a public company limited by shares, a public company limited by guarantee and having a share capital or a company to which section 377(1) of the 1963 Act relates;

(c) the proposed share exchange ratio and the amount of any cash payment;

(d) the proposed terms relating to the allotment of shares in the acquiring company;

(e) the date from which the holders of such shares may participate in profits of the acquiring company;

(f) the date in the accounts from which the company will be treated as acquired;

---

[76] Reg. 6(4).
[77] Reg. 5(1)(a).
[78] Reg. 5(1)(b).
[79] Reg. 5(3).
[80] Reg. 6(1).

(g) any special conditions applying to the securities issued as consideration; and

(h) any additional payments or benefits conferred on directors or independent persons.[81]

8–54   The second category of report which must be drawn up is an explanatory report. A separate explanatory report must be prepared by the directors of each of the merging companies.[82] The explanatory report should detail and explain:

(a) the draft terms of merger;

(b) the legal and economic grounds for and implications of the draft terms of merger;

(c) the methods used to arrive at the proposed share exchange ratio and the reasons for the use of these methods; and

(d) any special valuation difficulties which have arisen.[83]

8–55   The third category of document which is needed is an independent person's report. Each of the merging companies must appoint an independent person to prepare a written report to the shareholders of the company concerned.[84] The person appointed by the company must also be authorised by the Minister for the purposes of the proposed merger.[85] This report is required to:

(a) state the method(s) used to arrived at the proposed share exchange ratio;

(b) give the opinion of the person making the report as to whether the proposed share exchange ratio is fair and reasonable;

(c) give the opinion of the person making the report as to whether the method(s) used are adequate;

(d) indicate the values arrived at using each such method;

(e) give the opinion of the person making the report as to whether the relative importance attributed to such methods in arriving at the values decided on;

(f) describe any special valuation difficulties which have arisen.[86]

---

[81] Reg. 6(2).
[82] Reg. 7(1).
[83] Reg. 7(2).
[84] Reg. 8(1).
[85] Reg. 8(2).
[86] Reg. 8(7).

A fourth document which will be needed if the accounts are more than six moths old is an accounting statement to update the company's financial position.[87]

8–56　These documents together with the audited annual accounts for the preceding three financial years of each company[88] should be available for inspection at the company's registered offices.[89] In addition, a copy of the draft terms of the merger should be delivered for registration in the register of companies and notice of this delivery should be published in at least two daily newspapers[90] and in *Iris Oifigiúil*.[91]

III. LIABILITY FOR BREACHES OF THE REGULATIONS

8–57　The Regulations provide for the civil liability of directors or authorised independent persons guilty of misconduct in the preparation or implementation of the merger.[92] Liability is also imposed for untrue statements in the draft terms of the merger, the explanatory report, the independent person's report or the accounting statement.[93] The usual defences apply to these charges. Thus, a director will not be held civilly liable where (a) the documents were published without the director's knowledge or consent and that on becoming aware of their issue he or she informed the shareholders of this fact, or (b) the director had reasonable grounds, having exercised all reasonable care and skill for believing that the statement was true and the director believed the statement was true up to the time the merger took effect.[94]

8–58　An independent person may also be civilly liable for an untrue statement in his or her report.[95] It shall, however, be a defence for such a person to claim that (i) on becoming aware of the statement, he or she informed the company concerned and the shareholders of the untruth or (ii) he or she was competent to make the statement and had reasonable grounds for believing and did up to the time the merger took effect that the statement was true.[96]

---

[87] Reg. 9(1).
[88] Where the company has not traded for three years, the audited annual accounts for the period it has traded will be sufficient.
[89] Reg. 12(1).
[90] Circulating in the district where the registered office or principal place of business of the company is situated.
[91] Reg. 11(1).
[92] Reg. 22(1).
[93] Reg. 22(2).
[94] Reg. 22(3).
[95] Reg. 22(1).
[96] Reg. 22(4).

8–59   Criminal liability is imposed on directors and other persons who authorised the issue of the draft terms of the merger, the explanatory report or the accounting statement for untrue statements therein.[97] Criminal liability is also imposed on the independent person and any person who authorised the issue of the independent person's report where the report contains an untrue statement.[98] It will be a defence for any person on a criminal charge to show that, having exercised all reasonable skill and care, he or she had reasonable grounds for believing and did believe, up to the time of the issue of the documents, that the statement was true.[99]

IV. SECTIONS 30 AND 31 OF THE COMPANIES (AMENDMENT) ACT 1983

8–60   The provisions of sections 30 and 31 of the Companies (Amendment) Act 1983 will not apply to the issue of shares by any company formed for the purposes of a merger by formation of a new company.[100] As noted above, these sections require that expert's reports be obtained before shares are allotted for a non-cash consideration. This ensures that shares are not issued at a discount. Section 30(2)(b) exempts the allotment of shares by a company in connection with a proposed merger of that company with another company. Section 30(4) defines a merger for the purposes of section 30(2)(b) as a situation whereby one company proposes to acquire all the assets and liabilities of the other company in exchange for the issue of shares or other securities in that one to shareholders of the other, with or without any cash payment to those shareholders. Many mergers which fall under the Regulations would thus be excluded anyway.

V. APPROVAL

8–61   The Regulations provide for a procedure for approving mergers at meetings. The draft terms of the merger must be approved by a special resolution of each of the merging companies.[101] In addition, where the merger is a merger by formation of a new company, the memorandum or draft memorandum and articles or draft articles of association should also be approved by special resolution.[102] However, in certain circumstances, approval by special resolution may not be necessary in the case of:

---

[97]   Reg. 23(1).
[98]   Reg. 23(2).
[99]   Reg. 23(3).
[100] Reg. 10.
[101] Reg. 13(1).
[102] Reg. 13(2).

(a) a merger by acquisition, or;

(b) an operation whereby one or more companies are acquired by another company which holds at least 90 per cent, but not all, of their shares and securities conferring voting rights, or;

(c) an operation whereby the acquiring company acquires all the assets and liabilities of another company or companies and the acquiring company is the holder of all of the shares and other securities conferring voting rights of the company being acquired.[103]

The voting rights referred to in the above two paragraphs include voting rights held either by the acquiring company together with or solely by other persons in their own name but on behalf of that company.

VI. COMPULSORY PURCHASE OF SHARES

8–62 In addition to requiring shareholders consent to the merger, another shareholder protection provided by the Regulations is the obligation to purchases the shares of shareholders to do not agree to the merger. Unlike section 204 of the 1963 Act, there is however no reciprocal right enjoyed by the company to acquire the shares of the dissenting shareholders. Regulation 15(1)(a) provides that a shareholder in any of the merging companies who voted against the special resolution of the company concerned relating to the draft terms of merger may demand that the acquiring company acquire his shares for cash. Such a request must be made not later than 15 days after the shareholders meeting. A similar right to be bought out is provided for under Regulation 15(1)(b) to any shareholder (other than the acquiring company) in the case of an operation whereby one or more companies are acquired by another company which holds at least 90 per cent, but not all, of their shares and securities conferring voting rights.

VII. COURT APPROVAL

8–63 All the merging companies must apply jointly to the court for an order confirming the merger.[104] In the application, the court must be informed of the size of the shareholding of any shareholder who has requested the purchase of his shares and also the measures proposed to accommodate the request. Creditors may object to the confirmation by the court of the merger and the courts are given wide powers to ensure that the interests of any genuine creditors are protected.[105] Holders of

---

[103] Reg. 13(4).
[104] Reg. 16.
[105] Reg. 17.

securities other than shares with special rights are also protected by being entitled to at least equivalent rights in the acquiring company.[106] Once the court is satisfied that the requirements of the Regulations have been complied with and that proper provision has been made for any dissenting shareholder, other security holder and creditor, it may make an order confirming the merger with effect from some appointed date.[107] On this date, all the assets and liabilities of the company or companies being acquired shall stand transferred to the acquiring company in accordance with the draft terms of merger; all the shareholders of the company or companies being acquired will become shareholders in the acquiring company in accordance with the draft terms of merger; the company or companies being acquired shall be dissolved; and all legal proceedings pending by or against the dissolved companies shall be continued by or against the acquiring company.[108]

8–64 The Regulations also entrust the court with a wide discretion to make orders making provisions for "such matters as the Court considers necessary to secure that the merger shall be fully and effectively carried out."[109] In particular, the court may order the acquiring company to comply with the request of dissenting shareholders and purchase their shares. In such a case, the consideration for these shares shall be fixed by the court but may not be less than the market sale price of the shares on the appointed date.[110] In addition, section 41(1) of the Companies (Amendment) Act 1983 which prohibits a company from acquiring its own shares will not apply to these purchases by the company.[111]

8–65 One limitation is imposed on the court's power to make orders. No order should be made until the merger is cleared by the Minister under the Mergers, Takeovers and Monopolies (Control) Act 1978.[112] Such clearance may take the form of:

(a) a written statement by the Minister that he or she has decided not to make an order prohibiting the merger;

(b) conditional approval of the merger or;

(c) the elapsing of the relevant three month period without the Minister making a prohibiting order.

---

[106] Reg. 18.
[107] Reg. 19(1).
[108] Reg. 19(2).
[109] Reg. 19(3).
[110] Reg. 19(4).
[111] Reg. 19(5).
[112] Reg. 20. See Chap. 6.

VIII. DIVISIONS

8–66   Part III of the Regulations apply to divisions by acquisition and divisions by formation of new companies. A division by acquisition is defined as:

> "an operation whereby two or more companies ('the acquiring companies') of which one or more but not all may be a new company acquire between them all the assets and liabilities of another company in exchange for the issue to the shareholders of that company of shares in one or more of the acquiring companies with or without any cash payment and with a view to the dissolution of the company being acquired."[113]

A "division by formation by new companies" is defined as:

> "a similar operation whereby the acquiring companies have been formed for the purposes of such acquisition".[114]

Where a company is being wound up it may choose to become a party to a division by acquisition or by formation of new companies, provided that the distribution of its assets to shareholders has not begun at the date of the draft terms of a division.[115] Alternatively, the company may choose to avail of the provisions of sections 201 to 204, 260 and 271 of the 1963 Act.[116] Subject to this, the aforementioned provisions will not apply to the division by acquisition or by formation of new companies.[117] Similar provisions to the provisions which apply to mergers apply to divisions in respect of the necessary documentation, shareholder approval, shareholder, creditor, and security holder protection, court confirmation and civil and criminal liability.

---

[113]   Reg. 25(1)(a).
[114]   Reg. 25(1)(b).
[115]   Reg. 25(2)(a).
[116]   Reg. 25(2)(b).
[117]   Reg. 25(3).

CHAPTER 9

TRANSFER OF UNDERTAKINGS REGULATIONS

9–01 Where a takeover involves a purchase of shares in the offeree, the employees remain employed under their existing contracts of employment with the offeree. However, where a takeover involves the sale or transfer of the business as a going concern, the new employer is entitled under common law to re-employ selectively. The new employer has no common law obligation to offer the employees employment on their existing contract terms and the employees have no common law right to insist on transferring across with the business to the new employer. The reason for this is that a contract for personal services cannot be unilaterally transferred without the consent of the employee.[1]

9–02 This common law situation was substantially altered by Council Directive 77/187[1a] on the approximation of the laws of the Member States relating to the safeguarding of employees' rights in the event of transfers of undertakings, businesses or parts of undertakings or businesses. This Directive was implemented in Ireland by the European Communities (Safeguarding of Employees' Rights on Transfer of Undertakings) Regulations 1980[2] ("the Regulations"). These Regulations have had significant implications for the relationship between employers and employees.[3] The basic effect of the Regulations is that where an undertaking is transferred from one party to another, all the transferor's rights and obligations arising from the employment contract or employment relationship will be transferred to the transferee. Thus, where a company decides to acquire the assets of a target, it must be aware that certain of the undertaking's liabilities in this regard will automatically be transferred.

---

[1] In *Nokes v. Doncaster Amalgamated Collieries Ltd.* [1940] 3 All E.R. 549 at 556, Lord Atkin stated: "I had fancied that ingrained in the personal status of a citizen under our laws was the right to choose for himself whom he would serve, and that this right of choice constituted the main difference between a servant and a serf."

[1a] 1977 O.J. L61/26.

[2] S.I. No. 306 of 1980.

[3] *Mythen v. EAT, Buttercrust Ltd and Joseph Downes & Sons Ltd* [1990] 1 I.R.

9–03   Council Directive 98/50[4] of June 29, 1998 introduced a number of amendments to Council Directive 77/187 ("the Directive"). This amending Directive sought to clarify the legal concept of a "transfer", an "undertaking" and an "employee" in light of certain case-law of the European Court of Justice ("ECJ"). It also amended earlier provisions pertaining to the information, consultation and participation of employees during the transfer process. Article 2 of Council Directive 98/50 requires Member States either to implement regulations to comply with Directive 98/50 by July 17th 2001 or alternatively, to ensure that employers' and employees' representatives have introduced the required provisions by means of agreement. In the latter case however, Member States are required to take the necessary steps to guarantee the results imposed by Council Directive 98/50.

A. The Scope of the Directive and Regulations

9–04   The Directive and implementing Regulations apply where an undertaking or part of an undertaking has been sold to a different employer.

I. SHARE SALES

9–05   The original proposal for a Directive, submitted by the Commission in May 1974, dealt with "the harmonisation of the legislation of Member States on the retention of the rights and advantages of employees in the case of mergers, takeovers and amalgamations".[5] It referred to the necessity to safeguard workers in the event of changes in undertakings' structure in order to afford them, as far as possible, stability and security of employment and preservation of working conditions and entitlements previously enjoyed. The Recitals stated that changes in undertakings' structures adversely affect conditions for workers especially as regards preservation of the workers entitlements and benefits and stated that "the same problems arise irrespective of the precise form of the takeover". Despite the Commission's express recognition of this fact, the Directive as introduced only applies where there has been a transfer of an undertaking or part of an undertaking. It does not apply where a limited company is taken over by the acquisition of its share capital. In such circumstances, the Directive and the implementing Regulations will be of no use to employees.[6]

---

[4]   [1998] O.J. L201/88.
[5]   [1974] O.J. C104/1.
[6]   Contrast this to the Mergers, Takeovers & Monopolies Act 1978 which includes share and asset purchases.

McMullen has pointed to the value of certain of the protections afforded to workers by the Directive in a share sale situation.[7] He states that when a company is taken over there is, in reality, a change of identity of employer. Clearly, a change in share ownership can be just as important to an employee as a change in the identity of the employer following a transfer of a company's undertaking to another. Two aspects of the Directive which McMullen indicates would be useful to employees in such cases are the right to be notified of the sale and the provision for automatic unfairness of dismissals in connection with the takeover. While the proposed Takeover Directive provides for the former, it does not provide for the latter.[8] Neither is this latter matter addressed by legislation on unfair dismissal. A dismissal following a takeover is not one of the forms of dismissal considered under section 5 of the Unfair Dismissals Act 1977[9] to be automatically unfair.

II. TRANSFERS DURING INSOLVENCY PROCEDURES

9–06 Case-law provided that the original Article 1 did not apply to the transfer of an undertaking where the transferor has been adjudged insolvent and the undertaking in question forms part of the assets of the insolvent transferor.[10] It has been applied, however, to transfers effected during procedures prior to a winding up. In, *Mythen v. EAT, Buttercrust Ltd and Joseph Downes & Sons Ltd.*,[11] the Regulations were deemed to apply to a transfer affected by a receiver appointed by a debenture holder. In *Dethier Équipement*,[12] the ECJ held that the Directive applies in the event of the transfer of an undertaking which is being wound up by the court if the undertaking continues to trade. In particular, it observed that where the undertaking continues to trade while it is being wound up by the court, continuity of the business is assured when the undertaking is transferred. There is accordingly no justification for depriving the employees of the rights which the Directive guarantees them on the conditions it lays down. In *Europièces SA, in liquidation v. Wilfried Sanders, Automotive Industries Holding Company SA, declared insolvent*,[13] the ECJ held that the reasons which led

---

[7] McMullen, Business Transfers and Employee Rights (3rd.,) Butterworths, 1992, chap. 1.
[8] See Chap. 4.
[9] As amended by the Unfair Dismissals (Amendment) Act 1993 s.4.
[10] *Abels v. Bedrijfsuereniging Voor de Metaalindustrie en de Electrotechnische Industrie* [1985] E.C.R. 469. See also *Hugh Cooney as official court liquidator of Castle Brand Ltd* unreported, High Court, Hamilton P., March 25, 1985.
[11] [1990] 1 I.R. 98.
[12] Case C–319/94 [1998] E.C.R. I–1061.
[13] Case C–399/96.

the court to hold in *Dethier Équipement* that the Directive can apply to transfers that occur while an undertaking is being wound up by the court are all the more pertinent where the undertaking transferred is being wound up voluntarily.

9–07   Article 4a(1) which was added to the original Directive by Article 1 of Directive 98/50 expressly states that Articles 3 and 4 on the transfer of rights and automatic unfairness of dismissals will not apply to any transfer of an undertaking, business or part of an undertaking or business:

> "where the transferor is the subject of bankruptcy proceedings or any analogous insolvency proceedings which have been instituted with a view to the liquidation of the assets of the transferor and are under the supervision of a competent public authority (which may be an insolvency practitioner authorised by a competent public authority)."

Member States are given the power, however, to apply otherwise. Article 4a(2) provides that where Articles 3 and 4 apply to a transfer during insolvency proceedings in relation to a transferor (whether or not these proceedings have been instituted with a view to liquidating the transferor's assets) and provided the proceedings are supervised by a competent public authority (which may be an insolvency practitioner determined by national law), a Member State may provide that:

(a)   the transferor's debts arising from any contracts of employment or employment relationship and payable before the transfer or before the opening of proceedings shall not be transferred provided the employees are sufficiently protected;[14] and, or alternatively, that

(b)   the transferee, transferor or person exercising the transferor's functions, on the one hand, and the employees' representatives on the other hand may agree alterations, insofar as current law or practice allows, to the employees' terms and conditions of employment designed to safeguard employment opportunities by ensuring the survival of the undertaking, business or part of the undertaking.

Paragraph (b) above may also be applied by Member States to any transfers where the transferor is in a state of serious economic crisis provided that the situation is declared by a competent public authority and open to judicial supervision.[15] Article 4a(4) requires Member States to take appropriate measures to ensure that insolvency proceedings are not abused in such a way as to deprive employees of their rights under the Directive.

---

[14] At least equivalent protection to that provided for in situations covered by Council Directive 80/987/O.J. L283/23 on the approximation of laws of the Member States relating to the protection of employees in the event of insolvency of their employer.
[15] Art. 4a(3).

III. TRANSFERS OF NON-PROFIT MAKING UNDERTAKINGS

9–08 The original Directive did not make any distinction between undertakings with a commercial purpose and others. In the case of *Dr Sophie Redmond Stichting v. Bartol*,[16] the ECJ emphasised that the Directive applies equally to non-profit making bodies such as charities or foundations. The first sentence of Article 1(c) as amended clarifies matters absolutely by providing that the Directive shall apply, "to public and private undertakings engaged in economic activities whether or not they are operating for gain".

B. What Constitutes a "Transfer"?

9–09 In order for the Directive to apply, Article 1(1)(a) provides there must be "a transfer of an undertaking, business or part of an undertaking or business to another employer as a result of a legal transfer or merger".

I. TRANSFER OF PART OF AN UNDERTAKING

9–10 As the Directive applies to the transfer of "part" of an undertaking, it becomes necessary to consider whether the part of the undertaking transferred is capable of standing as a separate and identifiable part of the whole undertaking. If it is not, the Directive and Regulations will not apply. Both the national courts and tribunals and the ECJ have provided further elucidation on this issue.

9–11 A transfer within the meaning of the Directive involves a transfer of the business not a mere transfer of assets. The established test to decide whether a business or an asset has been transferred is to answer the question "Has there been a transfer of a going concern?"[17] The first significant ruling of the ECJ on this question was *Spijkers v. Gebroeders Benedik Abattoir CV*. The essential question according to Advocate General Slynn was:

> "whether the transferee has obtained a business or an undertaking (or part thereof) which he can continue to operate."[18]

In this case, having totally ceased activity and dissipated the goodwill of the business, the vendor sold the assets of the undertaking including the slaughter house. After a six weeks break, the purchaser commenced

---

[16] Case C–29/91 [1992] E.C.R. 1–3189. See also case C–382/92 *Commission v. United Kingdom* [1994] E.C.R. 1–2435.

[17] See *Lloyd v. Brassey per* Denning [1969] 1 All E.R. 382.

[18] [1986] E.C.R. 1119 at 1121.

operations continuing to use the premises as an abattoir. New customers were attracted and the business employed all but two of the original employees. One of these two individuals sued the purchaser claiming back wages from the date of the sale. Advocate General Slynn recommended avoiding technical rules and recommended looking instead at the "substance" rather than the form. He stated that the essential question was whether the purchaser had obtained a business which he could continue to operate. He noted:

> "That at the time of transfer the business is still active, that machinery is being used, customers supplied, workers employed and that all the physical assets and goodwill are sold are strong indicators that a transfer within the meaning of the article has taken place. But these are not all necessary prerequisites of a transfer in every case."

The ECJ noted that the concept of a transfer assumed that the transferor's activities are actually continued by the transferee in the same framework in the same undertaking:

> "It is clear from the scheme of the Directive and from the terms of Article 1(1) thereof, that the Directive is intended to ensure the continuity of employment relationships existing within a business, irrespective of any change of ownership. It follows that the decisive criterion for establishing whether there is a transfer for the purposes of the Directive is whether the business in question retains its identity . . . it is necessary to consider, in a case such as the present, whether the business was disposed of as a going concern."

9–12　In *Woodhouse v. Peter Brotherhood Ltd.*,[19] the owner of a factory which made diesel engines sold the factory to the defendant who made turbines and spinning machines. As part of the sale arrangements, the vendor asked the purchaser to complete five unfinished diesel engines for the vendors customers. This work was completed under a contract with the vendor. The employee applicant, who had worked for the vendor, started to work for the purchaser. For a period, he worked on exactly the same equipment in the same environment. The Court of Appeal held, however, that the purchaser did not take over the business as a going concern, but only the physical assets using them in a different business. This finding was made despite the fact that some of the same employees were employed using the same tools. The Court held that the applicant's previous employment could not be considered in a redundancy claim against the purchaser as the transfer was merely a transfer of assets.

---

[19] [1972] 3 All E.R. 91. See also *Melon v. Hector Powe Ltd* [1981] 1 All E.R. 313.

9–13   These cases clearly emphasise the distinction between business transfers and asset sales. The sale of machinery, premises and stock will not be enough on its own, the purchaser must be put in a position of running the business as a going concern. Strong indicators of a transfer under the Directive and the Regulations will be: the use of the assets by the purchaser, the transfer of the premises, stock and equipment, the transfer of goodwill,[20] the transfer of customers, the transfer of stock and contracts, the use of the same name and the transfer of the workforce.

Article 1.1(b) as amended gives effect to this caselaw by providing that there is a transfer within the meaning of the Directive:

> "where there is a transfer of an economic entity which retains its identity, meaning an organised grouping of resources which has the objective of pursuing an economic activity, whether or not that activity is central or ancillary."

9–14   In *Farmer v. Danzas (UK) Ltd.*,[21] the UK Employment Appeals Tribunal [EAT] considered a situation where the business acquired, a transport business, was merged into the transport operations of the transferee. It stated that:

> "There is nothing in any European decision to suggest that an economic activity ceases to retain its identity merely because the economic activity is subsumed into the transferee's business . . . It is possible to identify the work being done by the employees engaged in that business before and after the transfer. That is sufficient to satisfy the [Regulations]. Whether or not the transferee intended to integrate the acquired business into its own operation is neither here nor there. Immediately after the moment of transfer the economic activity was the same as it had been immediately before, and it retained its identity. That is the crucial moment; what happened later does not alter the position."

II. LICENSES AND FRANCHISES

9–15   The Directive will apply to licences or franchises even though there is no change in legal ownership, merely a change in management. Cases involving the termination of licences or franchises are often problematic as the employers are not the absolute owners of their businesses. In a number of cases, the ECJ has stressed that the Directive applies to business transfers which involve a change in the natural or

---

[20] In *Minister for Labour v. De Voy* [1985] 4 J.I.S.L.L. 76 Kenny J. emphasised the transfer of goodwill may not be enough on its own to amount to a "transfer". However, in *Ward v. Haines Watts* [1983] I.C.R. 231, the transfer of goodwill alone of a professional practice where no other assets were sold came within the scope of the Directive.

[21] Unreported, UK E.A.T. 858/93.

legal person responsible for operating the undertaking not just a change in ownership. In *Landsorganisationen i Danmark fur Tjenerforbundet i Danmark v. Ny Moelle Kro*,[22] the owner of a restaurant leased it to a woman who concluded an agreement with her employees. Three months later, the lessor rescinded the lease due to non-compliance with certain of its terms. The restaurant was closed for three months and then opened for business again under the operation of its original owner. A waitress claimed under the original agreement maintaining that her rights under it were transferred to the lessor. The ECJ held that Article 1(1) of the Directive applied to the proprietor's resumption of the running of an undertaking, because of the lessee's infringement. It explained the rational for this decision as follows:

> "[T]he purpose of the directive is to ensure, so far as possible, that the rights of employees are safeguarded in the event of a change of employer by enabling them to remain in employment with the new employer on the terms and conditions agreed with the transferor. The directive is therefore applicable where, following a legal transfer or merger, there is a change in the legal or natural person who is responsible for carrying on the business and who by virtue of that fact incurs the obligations of an employer vis-à-vis employees of the undertaking, regardless of whether or not ownership of the undertaking is transferred. Employees of an undertaking whose employer changes without any change in ownership are in a situation comparable to that of employees of an undertaking which is sold, and require equivalent protection."

9–16 In *Foreningen Af Arbejdsledere i Danmark v. Daddy's Dance Hall A/S*,[23] the ECJ held that the Directive applies as long as the "economic unit retains its identity". This view was reiterated in *P. Bork international A/S v. Foreningen Af Arbejdsledere i Danmark*[24] where a lessee leased a wood veneer factory from the lessor in April 1980. The lease expired in December 1981. The lessee dismissed all the employees and the undertaking ceased operating on December 22. On December 30th, a new company bought the factory from the lessor and it entered possession on January 4th, 1982 bringing the factory back into operation and retaining 50 per cent of the staff. The closure of the factory coincided with the Christmas holidays. The issue arose as to whether the lessee's obligations were transferred to the new owner. The ECJ held that Article 1(1) of the Directive could apply to a situation where a lessee ceases to be an employer at the end of a lease and a third party subsequently acquires this capacity under a contract of sale concluded with the owner. It stated:

---

[22] Case 287/86 [1987] E.C.R. 5465.
[23] [1998] E.C.R. 739 at para. 10.
[24] [1988] E.C.R. 3057.

> "The Directive ... applies whenever within the framework of contractual relations there is any change in the natural or legal person responsible for operating the undertaking who enters into contractual obligations as an employer with the employees of the undertaking."[24a]

9–17 In *Berg and Busschers v. I M Besselsen*,[25] the applicants were employed in a Dutch bar owned by Besselsen. In February 1983, the operation of the business was transferred by Besselsen to a commercial partnership by means of a lease purchase agreement. Under such an agreement ownership does not pass until the total price is paid. The two employees then transferred to the new operation. In November 1983, the lease purchase agreement was dissolved due to breach and the business returned to Besselsen. The ECJ held that the transfer under the lease purchase and the re-transfer came within the scope of the Directive.

III. CONTRACTING OUT OF SERVICES

9–18 In *Bannon v. Employment Appeals Tribunal*,[26] Bannon, a security guard employed by Drogheda Town Centre Ltd. ("DTC") to carry out security duties at Drogheda town centre, was given redundancy as a result of DTC's contracting out of security services to an outside firm. Bannon was offered employment by the outside firm but on different terms and refused. He sued DTC for unfair dismissal. The High Court was asked to determine when the Directive and Regulations applied to contracting out of services. Having referred to *Landsorganisationen i Danmark fur Tjenerforbundet i Danmark v. Ny Moelle Kro*[27] and *Spijkers v. Gebroeders Benedik Abattoir CV*,[28] Blayney J. stated that it was clear that where there had been a legal transfer of a business or part of a business, the Directive applies if the business retains its identity or if there is a change in the legal or natural person who is responsible for carrying on the business regardless of whether or not ownership of the business is transferred. Having decided that both criteria were satisfied in the case at hand, the Directive was deemed to apply and the dismissal was deemed unlawful. Blayney J. emphasised that the fact that the contracting out was a temporary measure in the sense that no absolute transfer of ownership took place did not alter the position.

[24a] [1988] E.C.R. 3057 at para. 13.
[25] [1988] E.C.R. 2559. See also *Mercks v. Ford Motors Co. Belgium SA* [1996] I.R.L.R. 467.
[26] [1993] 1 I.R. 500.See also *Cunningham and O'Connor v. Oasis Stores Ltd.* [1995] E.L.R. 183.
[27] [1989] I.R.L.R. 37.
[28] [1986] E.C.R. 1119.

9–19   Although the earlier ECJ cases on contracting out of services also suggest that the Directive applies to the contracting out of services which involves the transfer of an activity upon which employees are working to a new legal entity,[29] a more restrictive approach has recently been adopted by the ECJ on this point. In *Henke v. Gemeinde Schirke and Verwaltungsgemeinschaft "Brocken"*,[30] the ECJ held that the Directive did not apply to the transfer of administrative functions from a municipality to an administrative collectivity. Henke had been employed as a secretary by a municipality. When a number of municipalities joined together to form a new entity to provide for the collective administration of the various areas, the separate municipal administrations were dissolved. The ECJ held that neither the re-organisation of the structures of a public administration nor the transfer of administrative functions between public administrative authorities constitute a transfer.

9–20   In *Ayse Suzen v. Zehnacker Gebaudereinigung GmbH Krankenhaus-service*,[31] a German Court sought a ruling from the ECJ as to whether the Directive applied in the case of a cleaner employed by a company to clean a school. The school had terminated its contract with the cleaning company and had awarded the contract to another company which had not re-employed any of the original cleaners. The ECJ held that for the Directive to be applicable, the transfer had to relate to "a stable economic entity" whose activity was not limited to performing one specific works contract. The term "entity" thus referred to an organised grouping of persons and assets facilitating the exercise of an economic activity which pursued a specific objective. To determine whether the conditions of the transfer of an entity were met, the Court stated that it was necessary to consider all the circumstances of the transaction and in particular:

– the type of undertaking or business concerned;

– whether its tangible assets were transferred;

– the value of its intangible assets at the time of the transfer;

– whether the majority of employees were taken over by the new employer;

– whether its customers were transferred;

---

[29] See *Dr Sophie Redmond Stichting v. Bartol* [1992] E.C.R. 1–3189; *Rask v. ISS Kantineservice A/S* [1993] I.R.L.R. 133; *Christel Schmidt v. Spar-und Leihkasse der Fruheren Amter Bordesholm, Kiel und Cronshagen* [1994] I.R.L.R. 302; *Bannon v. EAT & Drogheda Town Centre* [1992] E.L.R. 203.

[30] [1996] I.R.L.R. 701.

[31] [1997] I.R.L.R. 255.

– the degree of similarity between the activities carried on before and after the transfer;

– the length of any suspension of those activities.

The Court emphasised that an entity was not defined merely by the activity entrusted to it. The mere loss of a service contract to a competitor could not therefore, of itself, indicate the existence of a transfer within the meaning of the Directive. As a result, the Directive was deemed not to apply to the factual circumstances in hand.[32]

9–21 The *Ayse Suzen* case was applied by the Irish Employment Appeals Tribunal in *Cannon v. Noonan Cleaning Ltd. & CPS Cleaning Services Ltd.*[33] where it was held that there was no transfer of an undertaking when the contract for the cleaning of a particular garda station was lost to CPS Cleaning. No tangible assets were transferred between the two contractors and CPS Cleaning were deemed entitled to refuse to employ the claimant. However, the *Ayse Suzen* case was applied with contrary results in the UK in *Marie Power v. St. Pauls Nursing Home and T & M Cleaning Ltd.*[34] In that case, the claimant had been employed by St. Paul's Nursing Home until the cleaning was contracted out to T & M Cleaning. In this case, however, the cleaning equipment used by St. Pauls was transferred to the contractor and the contractor had originally indicated their intention to rehire the cleaning staff. The Employment Appeals Tribunal determined that the cleaning operations at St. Pauls were capable of forming a separate economic entity.

9–22 Article 1(1)(c) as amended, clarifies the "transfer" concept to some extent. It provides that:

> "an administrative reorganisation of public administrative authorities, or the transfer of administrative functions between public administrative authorities is not a transfer within the meaning of the Directive."

This does not, however, go as far as the draft revision[35] of the Directive adopted by the Commission in late 1995 to clarify the "transfer" concept. It stressed that a clear distinction had to be made between transfers of undertakings, businesses or parts of businesses and the transfer of only an activity of an undertaking:

---

[32] See also *Ledernes Hovedorganisation (Rygaard) v. Dansk Arbejdsgiverforening (Stro Molle Akustik AS* [1996] I.R.L.R. 51. *Francisco Hernandez Vidal SA v. Gomez Perez* [1999] I.R.L.R. 132 and *Sanchez Hidalgo v. Asocicion De Servicos Aser* [1999] I.R.L.R. 136.

[33] RPP 324/97, UD 200/97 and MN 591/97.

[34] U/D 611/97.

[35] Proposal for a Revised Directive 94/C274/08 COM(94) 300 final, 94/0203(CNS) (O.J. C274/10).

"The transfer of an activity which is accompanied by the transfer of an economic entity which retains its identity shall be deemed to be a transfer within the meaning of this Directive. The transfer of only an activity of an undertaking business or part of a business whether or not it was previously carried out directly does not in itself constitute a transfer within the meaning of the Directive."

C. What is being Transferred?

9–23   Regulation 3 of the 1980 Regulations provides that:

"The rights and obligations of the transferor arising from a contract of employment or from an employment relationship existing on the date of a transfer shall, by reason of such transfer be transferred to the transferee."

This echoes Article 3(1) of the Directive.

Regulation 3 amounts thus to a statutory novation of the contract of employment transferring the rights and obligations of the original employer to the new employer. Such obligations would include wages and unpaid statutory holidays. Similarly, all contractual liabilities arising under the contract of employment are transferred. A purchaser must examine the terms of the employment contracts carefully thus to ascertain the extent of the liabilities. Although, in all probability, restrictive covenants are included in the transfer, the effect of the transfer may have implications for its enforceability. The terms may not be considered reasonable in the light of the changed identity of the new employer.[36] Regulation 4 provides that after the transfer, the purchaser should continue to observe terms and conditions in any collective agreement on the same terms applicable to the transferor until the date of termination or expiry of the collective agreement or until the date of entry into force or application of a new collective agreement. This may present difficulties for the employees as traditionally such agreements could not be enforced in Ireland unless they were incorporated into individual contracts or unless the employees possessed a written confirmation that the agreement is enforceable.[37]

9–24   Article 3(2) as amended, introduces a new provision obliging Member States to adopt appropriate measures:

"to ensure that the transferor notifies the transferee of all the rights and obligations which will be transferred to the transferee under this Article, so far as those rights and obligations are or ought to have been known to the transferor at the time of the transfer."

---

[36] See *Morris Angel Ltd v. Hollande* [1993] I.R.L.R. 169.
[37] *NCB v. Galley* [1958] 1 W.L.R. 16. See also Clark, *Contract Law in Ireland* (4th ed., Round Hall Sweet & Maxwell, 1998), pp. 79–82.

This provision will be particularly welcomed by potential purchasers. It clearly places an obligation on the transferor to notify the transferee of all relevant rights and obligations. The Directive, however, gives Member States discretion as to how this liability may be imposed. In all likelihood, civil liability will be imposed for a breach of this obligation to notify. However, in order to protect employees, Article 3(2) continues to state that:

> "A failure by the transferor to notify the transferee of any such right or obligation shall not affect the transfer of that right or obligation and the rights of any employees against the transferee and/or transferor in respect of that right or obligation."

Despite this, the purchaser would still be best advised to make careful enquiries and seek far reaching warranties and indemnities against possible claims. In addition, an agreement should be sought in advance to determine which party is to bear any liability for any employment claims which arise after the transfer.

D. What is Not Transferred?

9–25 Originally the Directive stated that Article 3 did not apply to employees' rights to old-age, invalidity or survivors' benefits under supplementary company or inter-company pension schemes outside the statutory social security schemes in Member States. Regulation 4.2 made the same provision in respect of Regulation 3. The amended version of Article 3(4)(a) allows Member States to provide otherwise and to include these rights. However, even where Member States choose not to apply the protective provisions of the Directive to old-age, invalidity or survivors' benefits, Article 3(4)(b) imposes an obligation on Member States to:

> "adopt the measures necessary to protect the interests of employees and of persons no longer employed in the transferor's business at the time of the transfer in respect of rights conferring on them immediate or prospective entitlement to old age benefits, including survivors' benefits under supplementary schemes referred to in subparagraph (a)."

This obligation has been interpreted as meaning that Member States have to protect any pension scheme's rights which crystallise at the time of the transfer. In *Adams and Others v. Lancashire County Council & BET Catering Services Ltd.*,[38] the plaintiffs worked part-time for the

---

[38] [1997] ICR 834.

County Council in its school catering service. The catering service was then contracted out to BET and the plaintiffs' contracts were transferred under the implementing regulations. BET did not offer the plaintiffs membership of their pension scheme. The Court of Appeal held that the plaintiffs were not entitled to comparable rights to an occupational pension from BET as the Directive excluded all pension rights. However, the Court held that the Directive required Member States to protect the interests of employees "in respect of rights conferring on them immediate or prospective entitlement to old age benefits including survivors benefits". This was interpreted as meaning that BET had to ensure that rights accrued up to the time of the transfer were honoured. This imposed a duty on them to ensure that the transferor has a properly funded pension scheme. The British Government has indicated that transferees should still be encouraged to replicate pension rights.[39] Failure to do so may also leave the transferor open to a case of constructive dismissal on the grounds that the transferor cannot honour future rights. In Ireland, Regulation 4(2) requires the transferee to ensure that the interests of employees and ex-employees in respect of rights conferring on them immediate or prospective entitlement to old-age benefits under supplementary company pension schemes are protected.

E. What Employees are Affected?

9–26   An important factor to be determined is which employees will be transferred with the undertaking where only part of the assets are being acquired.[40] In *Botzen v. Rotterdamsche Droogdok Maakschappij BV*[41] the ECJ held that:

> "an employment relationship is essentially characterised by the link existing between the employee and the part of the undertaking or business to which he is assigned to carry out his duties."

The court held the Directive did not require the transfer of those employees of the vendor who are not engaged in the part of the business sold but merely use its assets, or the transfer of employees who work in one of the vendors departments providing services to various parts of the business including the business sold. This latter category could include employees providing administration services or

---

[39] The Government Guide to Market Testing (HMSO, 1993), 26.
[40] For transfer of part of a group, see *Michael Peters Ltd v. Farnfield and Michaels Peters Group Ltd* [1995] I.R.L.R. 190 and *Sunley Turriff Holdings Ltd. v. Thompson* [1995] I.R.L.R. 184.
[41] [1985] E.C.R. 519 at para. 15.

legal advice. The *Botsen* case was followed by the Employment Appeals Tribunal in *Ebbs and Healy v. Oasis Stores plc*.[42]

9–27 In *Duncan Webb Offset (Maidstone) Ltd v. Cooper*,[43] the UK Employment Appeals Tribunal stated that in such cases, one might consider *inter alia*:

> "the amount of time spent on one part of the business or the other; the amount of value given to each part by the employee; the terms of the contract of employment showing what an employee could be required to do; how the cost to the employer of the employee's services had been allocated between the different parts of the business."

Article 2.2 as amended, prohibits Member States from excluding contracts of employment or employment relationships solely because:

(a)   of the number of working hours performed or to be performed;

(b)   they are relationships governed by a fixed-duration contract within the meaning of Directive 91/383;[43a] or

(c)   they are temporary relationships within the meaning of Directive 91/383/EEC.

F. Dismissals

I. THE PROHIBITION

9–28   A genuine concern existed that employees would be dismissed just before the transfer in order to allow the transferee freedom to re-engage certain employees selectively after the transfer without the acquisition of previously accrued rights.[43b] To prevent this happening, Article 4(1) provides *inter alia* that:

> "the transfer of an undertaking, business or part of a business shall not in itself constitute grounds for dismissal by the transferor or the transferee."

Regulation 5.1 repeats this provision and adds that:

> "a dismissal, the grounds for which are such a transfer, by a transferor or a transferee is hereby prohibited."

---

[42]   U.D. 82/94 and U.D. 1020/94.
[43]   [1995] I.R.L.R. 633, at para. 15.
[43a]   O.J. L206/19.
[43b]   For a general discussion of dismissals see, Byrne, *Transfer of Undertakings* (Blackhall, 1999), Part 6, Reorganisation and Rationalisation.

9–29 In *P. Bork International v. Foreningen etc.*,[44] the ECJ were asked to decide whether the closure of a factory and dismissal of its staff on December 22, 1981 followed by a takeover of the factory with effect from January 4, 1982 constituted the transfer of an undertaking. The ECJ stated:

> "In order to determine whether the employees were dismissed solely as a result of the transfer, contrary to Article 4(1), it is necessary to take into consideration the objective circumstances in which the dismissal took place and, in particular, in a case such as this, the fact that it took effect on a date close to that of the transfer and that the employees in question were taken on again by the transferee."[44a]

Where the main ground for the dismissal is the transfer itself, the provisions of Article 4(1) and Regulation 5(1) are clearly breached. The effect of such a dismissal was also discussed by the ECJ in the *P. Bork* case:

> "Whether or not such a contract or relationship [of employment] exists at [the time of the transfer] must be assessed on the basis of national law subject, however, to compliance with the mandatory provisions of the directive concerning protection of employees from dismissal as a result of the transfer. Accordingly, the employees of the undertaking whose contract of employment or employment relationship was terminated with effect from a date prior to that of the transfer, contrary to Article 4(1) of the directive, must be regarded as still in the employ of the undertaking on the date of the transfer, with the result, in particular, that the employer's obligations towards them are automatically transferred from the transferor to the transferee in accordance with Article 3(1) of the Directive."[44b]

9–30 In *Litser v. Forth Dry Dock & Engineering Co. Ltd.*,[45] the receiver of FDD sold all the assets of the business to FEE at 4.30 pm on February 6th, 1994. One hour beforehand, FDD dismissed the employees. The House of Lords held that the relevant Regulations and the Directive apply, not only to employees employed "immediately before the transfer", but also to employees who would have been so employed if they had not been unfairly dismissed. Lord Oliver stated:

> "Because the relationship between employer and employee is of an essentially personal nature, the repudiation severs the factual relationship resulting from the contract, since the primary obligations on both sides are no longer capable of being performed. The contract itself, however, is not, strictly speaking, terminated but remains in being and undischarged so far as the enforcement of secondary obligations are concerned."[45a]

---

[44] Case C–101/87 [1988] E.C.R. 3057.
[44a] *ibid.* at para. 18.
[44b] *ibid.* at paras 17 and 18.
[45] [1990] 1 A.C. 546.
[45a] *ibid.* at p. 568.

9–31   The question of whether a dismissal in breach of Article 4(1) was a nullity or not and thus whether the employment continues, was discussed by the House of Lords in *British Fuels Ltd v. Baxendale and Wilson v. St Helen's Borough Council.*[46] Two similar cases arose for consideration. In the first case, employees of BCC and its subsidiary NFD were given notice of dismissal on grounds of redundancy effective from August 28th, 1992. The employees received redundancy pay. When the undertakings of NFD and of BFL (another subsidiary of BCC) merged, the employees were offered jobs by BFL with effect from September 1, 1992 on less favourable terms. These offers were accepted and a number of employees subsequently claimed that they were employed on the terms applicable to their employment with NFD. In the second case, a community home controlled by Lancashire County Council was taken over by St Helen's Borough Council on the condition that it would not affect the latters' resources. Employees were offered jobs by St Helen's under new terms. They were also notified by Lancashire County Council that their contracts were terminated with effect from the September 30th, 1992. The new contracts started in October 1992 and in March 1993 one of the employee's unions asked for the restoration of old terms. Proceedings commenced to recover lost wages. The House of Lords was asked to determine whether the dismissals by the transferor took effect or were nullities, *i.e.* whether the dismissed employees could compel the transferee to employ them. Lord Slynn stated:

> "Where the transferee does not take on the employees who are dismissed on transfer the dismissal is not a nullity though the contractual rights formerly available against the transferor remain intact against the transferee. For the latter purpose, an employee dismissed prior to the transfer contrary to Article 4(1), i.e. on the basis of the transfer, is to be treated as still in the employment of the transferor at the date of transfer . . . The Court has said that the employees' rights are safeguarded by 'enabling them to remain in employment with the new employer on the terms and conditions agreed with the transferor' (*Bork*) or by 'making it possible for them to continue to work for the new employer on the same conditions as those agreed with the transferor' (*Katsikas*), or, so far as possible, safeguarding employees' rights by 'allowing them to remain in employment with the new employer on the terms and conditions agreed with the transferor' (*Daddy's Dance Hall*, paragraph 9). The emphasis is on the same terms and conditions applying if the employment is continued. I do not read, however, any of these expressions as meaning that the transferee is bound actually to take on an employee who has been dismissed, whether because of the transfer or for independent reasons, and to give him the same work as he had before. They mean that if he does take the

---

[46]   [1998] I.R.L.R. 706.

employee he takes him on the terms of the employment with the transferor, *i.e.* there is a deemed novation by the two willing parties. If the transferee does not take the employee because the latter has already been dismissed by the transferor, or because he himself dismisses the employee on the transfer, then he must meet all of the transferor's contractual and statutory obligations unless (a) the employee objects to being employed by the transferee or (b) the principal reason for dismissal is an economic, technical or organisational reason entailing changes in the workforce when the employee is not to be treated as unfairly dismissed and when for the purposes of the 1978 Act and the 1976 Order the employee is to be regarded as having been dismissed for a substantial reason justifying the dismissal as fair."[46a]

Lord Slynn held that if the dismissal is unfair, the working relationship ends so that there is nothing of that to pass to the transferee. The contract of employment is deemed to be kept alive only for the purpose of enforcing rights for breach of it or for enforcing statutory rights dependent on the contract of employment and not for the purpose of creating an obligation which did not exist under domestic law to continue with the working relationship to the transferee.

9–32 Section 15 of the Unfair Dismissals (Amendment) Act 1993 provides that a transfer of a business does not break continuity of service for the purpose of unfair dismissal and minimum notice unless the employee has received and retained a redundancy payment from the transferor. In *Brett, Drury and Others v. Niall Collins Ltd. (in receivership) and Oyster Investments Ltd t/a Fotoking,*[47] the EAT had to consider whether the receipt of a redundancy payment made by a transferor in circumstances where the employee subsequently transferred to the transferee terminates the continuity of employment. The EAT determined that there was a transfer under the Regulations. Because the dismissal contravened Regulation 5 due to its connection with the transfer, it was deemed to be a nullity and because redundancy requires a dismissal, the payment was deemed not to be a redundancy payment.

9–33 Although, Article 3(1) of the Directive allows Member States to provide that "after the date of the transfer, the transferor and the transferee shall be jointly and severally liable in respect of obligations which arose before the date of the transfer from a contract of employment or an employment relationship existing on the date of the transfer", Ireland did not avail of this provision. The transferor is thus discharged from its obligations after the date of the transfer.[48] The concept of joint liability only arises in Ireland thus, where the transferor dismisses the

---

[46a] [1998] I.R.L.R. 706 at paras 73 and 74.
[47] [1995] E.L.R. 69.
[48] *Berg and Busschers v. I M Besselsen* [1988] E.C.R. 2559.

employees prior to the transfer as was the case in *Mythen v. EAT, Buttercrust Ltd and Joseph Downes & Sons Ltd.*[49] There Barrington J. stated:

> "[I]t appears to me that the scheme of the Directive contemplates that an employee who has lost his job as a result of a transfer of a business or part of a business may claim against either the transferor or transferee or against both of them."[49a]

Barrington J. also stated that the fact an employee claims relief against either the transferor or transferee will not estopp him from claiming relief against the other.

9–34 Regulation 5(2) provides that if a contract of employment or an employment relationship is terminated because a transfer involves:

> "a substantial change in working conditions to the detriment of the employee concerned, the employer concerned shall be regarded as having been responsible for the termination of the contract of employment or of the employment relationship."

Clearly, this provision would allow an employee claim constructive dismissal against the transferee where his or her working conditions had been altered by the transferee after the transfer. Possibly, it may also allow an employee to claim constructive dismissal before the transfer in order to anticipate the substantial alteration to his or her working conditions.[50]

II. "ECONOMIC, TECHNICAL OR ORGANISATIONAL REASONS"

9–35 Regulation 5(1) provides that nothing in the Regulation will be construed as prohibiting dismissals for "economic, technical or organisational reasons entailing changes in the work-force." A similar statement is made in Article 4(1) of the Directive.

In *Wheeler v. Patel*,[51] the UK Employment Appeals Tribunal held that the word "economic" had to be construed *ejusdem generis* with the words "technical and organisational" and the word "economic" had to be given a limited meaning relating to the conduct of the business. It did not include broader "economic" reasons for dismissal such as the achievement of an agreement for sale. The need for dismissals, under this decision, has to relate to the conduct of the business. Thus,

---

[49] [1990] 1 I.R. 98.
[49a] *ibid.* at p. 108.
[50] See McMullen, Business Transfer and Employee Rights (Butterworths, 1992), pp. 87–91.
[51] [1987] I.R.L.R. 211. This case was followed by the EAT in Scotland in *Gateway Hotels Ltd v. Stewart* [1988] I.R.L.R. 287.

objective criteria are necessary to justify pre-transfer redundancies. If the supposed economic reason amounts to no more than a desire to obtain an enhanced price, or achieve a sale, this is not a reason which relates to the conduct of the business. This is a significant decision which increases the potential of employers for unfair dismissal liability, if the dismissal is at the behest of the purchaser and for no other reason.

9–36   The ECJ view of Article 4 would appear to be consistent with that of the court in *Wheeler* in *H.B.M. Abels v. Administrative Board of the Bedrijfsvereniging voor de Metaalindustrie en de Electrotechnische Industrie*,[52] Attorney General Slynn dealing with Article 4(1) noted:

> "It is said that this exception will always be open on economic grounds in a liquidation, so that Article 4(1)'s first sentence is otiose. That does not seem to me to follow, since if a viable part of a business in liquidation is sold off, there may be no valid economic grounds for dismissing any of the staff employed in that part of the business."

This seems to suggest that the reason for the dismissal must be established as an objective fact.

9–37   It would seem that a genuine redundancy within the meaning of section 7(2) of the Redundancy Payments Act 1967 as amended, will be regarded as following within the scope of this proviso. In *Powell & McHugh v. Bewleys Manufacturing Ltd and Felwood Manufacturing Ltd.*,[53] O'Malley J. in the Circuit Court was satisfied that the redundancies created were done for the purposes of shedding an uneconomic operation and saving money and whereas, there were difficulties with the workforce, these difficulties were settled fairly. Because the transferor was loosing £20,000 per month, a reorganisation was deemed essential as far as the bakery was concerned. It was held that if the transfer were part of this, it was done for sound economic technical and organisational reasons.[54] In *Cunningham and O,Connor v. Oasis Stores Ltd.*[55] two senior executives responsible for the management of a retail clothes business were not re-hired when the business was sold to the defendant. The EAT determined that their dismissals were for an economic, technical or organisational reason because the business was being operated under a new organisational structure which no longer used senior executives in these posts.

---

[52] [1985] E.C.R. 469; at 472.
[53] [1990] E.L.R. 68. See also *Morris, Brennan, Cooney, Christie, Walsh, Sargent and Dunne v. Smart Bros. Ltd.* EAT688/739/740/741/1045/1046/1047 U.D. 688/93 and *Trafford v. Sharpe & Fisher (Building Supplies) Ltd* [1994] I.R.L.R. 325.
[54] The Unfair Dismissals (Amendment) Act 1993, s.15 is consistent with O'Malley J.'s reasoning here.
[55] [1995] E.L.R. 183.

III. OBJECTION TO NEW EMPLOYER

9–38 Because Article 3(1) provides that the transferor's rights and obligations arising from contracts of employment or employment relationships existing at the date of the transfer "shall, by reason of such transfer, be transferred to the transferee", the question arose as to whether the employees could object to and prevent this transfer. In *Foreningen a.f. Arbejdsledere i Danmark v. Danmols Inventar*,[56] the ECJ noted that:

> "The protection which the directive is intended to guarantee is however redundant where the person concerned decides on his own accord not to continue the employment relationship with the new employer after the transfer. That is the case where the employee in question terminates the employment contract or employment relationship of his own free will with effect from the date of the transfer, or where that contract or relationship is terminated with effect from the date of the transfer by virtue of an agreement voluntarily concluded between the worker and the transferor or the transferee of the undertaking. In that situation Article 3(1) of the directive does not apply."

9–39 In *Katsikas v. Konstantinidis and Others*,[57] the ECJ was asked about the compatibility with Article 3(1) of the Directive with a particular provision of German law which provided that where a part of an undertaking is transferred, the objection of an employee in that part of the undertaking prevents the transfer of his employment relationship such that the employment relationship with the transferor continues. The ECJ ruled:

> "The Directive does not, however, require Member States to provide that, in the event of the employee deciding of his own accord not to continue with the contract of employment or employment relationship with the transferee, the contract or relationship should be maintained with the transferor. Neither does the Directive preclude this. In such a case, it is for the Member States to determine what the fate of the contract of employment or employment relationship with the transferor should be."

In *British Fuels Ltd v. Baxendale and Wilson v. St Helen's Borough Council*,[58] the House of Lords also accepted that in the event of a transfer of an undertaking, the employee is entitled to refuse to transfer.

9–40 Because, the Irish Regulations do not expressly specify the fate of an employee who objects to the transfer, it is unclear whether the

---

[56] [1985] E.C.R. 2639 at para. 16.
[57] [1992] E.C.R. 6577. See also Europièces *SA, in liquidation v. Wilfried Sanders, Automotive Industries Holding Company SA, declared insolvent, op.cit.,* above, n.13.
[58] [1998] I.R.L.R. 706.

contract of employment with the transferor continues or whether the contract is terminated. It is likely, however, that the contract will be terminated and the employee will be deemed redundant.

9-41   In *Photostatic Copiers (Southern) Limited v. Okuda and Japan Office Equipment Limited,*[59] the UK Employment Appeals Tribunal held that since employees have a right to refuse to be transferred, they cannot exercise this right if they do not have the necessary information. Thus, the tribunal said there was no transfer where the employee was unaware of the fact of transfer and the identity of the transferee. In this case, the employee had worked for two years without realising that a transfer has occurred. He was held entitled to sue the transferor when the transferee went into liquidation. However, in *Secretary of State for Trade and Industry v. Cook,*[60] the UK Employment Appeals Tribunal refused to follow the *Photostatic* decision on the basis that it would undermine the very protection which the Directive is supposed to provide. Mr Justice Morrison stated that:

> "If the employee needs to know in advance, the identity of the transferee before his contract is transferred, unscrupulous employers would simply refuse to disclose what was happening. It is partly because workers are often not told what is happening that the Regulations were designed to take effect in a way which would guarantee continuity of employment for them."[60a]

IV. VARIATION AND WAIVER OF RIGHTS

9-42   In the *Daddy's Dance Hall* case,[60b] the ECJ was asked whether an employee who concludes a contract with a purchaser waives rights conferred by the Directive. The Court said that the ability to waive these rights depended upon whether the reason for the waiver was the transfer. In that case, new management altered terms after a transfer and the court had to decide whether employees could accept these new terms notwithstanding the mandatory effect of the Directive in preserving employees' rights. The Court held that the protection of workers is a matter of public policy and as such outside the control of the parties to the employment. Therefore the provisions in the Directive, in particular those relating to the protection of workers against dismissal because of the transfer, must be considered as mandatory and may not be waived by an employee even if the overall advantages to him outweigh the disadvantages. However, the ECJ then referred to its judgment in

---

[59]   [1995] I.R.L.R. 11.
[60]   [1997] I.R.L.R. 150. See also *MRS Environmental Services Ltd. v. Dyke* UK EAT 93/96.
[60a] *ibid.* at para. 12
[60b] *op. cit.,* n.23.

Forenin gen af Arbejeds'edere i Danmark v. Danmols Inventar[60c] and went on to say that:

> "[The Directive] is intended to achieve only partial harmonisation, essentially by extending the protection guaranteed to workers independently by the laws of the individual Member States to cover the case where an undertaking is transferred. It is not intended to establish a uniform level of protection throughout the Community on the basis of common criteria. Thus the Directive can be relied on only to ensure that the employee is protected in his relations with the transferee to the same extent as he was in his relations with the transferor under the legal rules of the Member State concerned.
>
> Consequently, in so far as national law allows the employment relationship to be altered in a manner unfavourable to employees in situations other than the transfer of an undertaking, in particular as regards their protection against dismissal, such an alternative is not precluded merely because the undertaking has been transferred in the meantime and the agreement has therefore been made with the new employer. Since by virtue of Article 3(1) of the directive the transferee is subrogated to the transferor's rights and obligations under the employment relationship, that relationship may be altered with regard to the transferee to the same extent as it could have been with regard to the transferor, provided that the transfer of the undertaking itself may never constitute the reason for that amendment."

Therefore, if national law allows the employer to alter the relationship, the fact that there is a transfer is irrelevant once it is not the cause of the alteration.

9–43 The ECJ confirmed this view in *Rask*,[61] stating:

> "[I]n so far as national law allows the employment relationship to be altered in a manner unfavourable to employees in situations other than the transfer of an undertaking, in particular as regards their terms and conditions of remunerations, such an alteration is not precluded merely because the undertaking has been transferred in the meantime and the agreement has therefore been made with the new employer. Since by virtue of Article 3(1) of the Directive the transferee is subrogated to the transferor's right and obligations under the employment relationship, that relationship may be altered with regard to the transferee, to the same extent as it could have been with regard to the transferor, provided that the transfer of the undertaking itself may never constitute the reason for that amendment."

9–44 In *British Fuels Ltd v. Baxendale and Wilson v. St Helen's Borough Council*,[62] the House of Lords was asked to determine whether a

---

[60c] *op. cit.*, n.56.
[60d] paras 16 and 17.
[61] [1992] E.C.R. I–5755 at para. 28.
[62] [1998] I.R.L.R. 706. See above, para. 9–31.

variation of the terms of employment could lawfully be agreed between the parties. Despite the fact that it was not strictly necessary to deal with this issue because of its findings that the dismissals were effective, Lord Slynn agreed to consider the matter. An argument was made by B.F.L. to the effect that if the dismissals were nullities and the contracts of employment were transferred to B.F.L. then those contracts were varied when the employees accepted B.F.L.'s offer or when they continued to work on B.F.L.'s terms for two years. They argued that the Directive could not have intended to rule out genuine agreements as to variations taking place in the context of the transfer. Lord Slynn stated:

> "[W]here there is a transfer of an undertaking and the transferee actually takes on the employee, the contract of employment is automatically transferred so that, in the absence of a permissible variation, the terms of the initial contract go with the employee, who though he may refuse to go, cannot as a matter of public policy waive the rights which the Directive and the Regulations confer on him."[62a]

On the issue of an permissible variation Lord Slynn continued:

> "Although on a transfer, the employees' rights previously existing against the transferor are enforceable against the transferee and cannot be amended by the transfer itself, it does not follow there cannot be a variation of the terms of the contract for reasons which are not due to the transfer either on or after the transfer of the undertaking. It may be difficult to decide whether the variation is due to the transfer or attributable to some separate cause. If, however, the variation is not due to the transfer it can, in my opinion, on the basis of the authorities to which I have referred, validly be made."[62b]

Having accepted that certain variations are effective once not connected to the transfer, Lord Slynn turned to the question of conduct amounting to a variation:

> "The question as to whether and in what situations, where there has been a transfer and employees have accepted the dismissal, claimed compensation based on it and worked for a long period after the transfer, there can be a valid variation by conduct is not an easy one. I do not accept the argument that the variation is only invalid if it is agreed on or as a part of the transfer itself. The variation may still be due to the transfer and for no other reason even if it comes later. However, it seems that there must, or at least may, come a time when the link with the transfer is broken or can be treated as no longer effective."[62c]

[62a] *ibid.* at para. 73.
[62b] *ibid.* at para. 93.
[62c] *ibid.* at para. 90.

G. Consultation with Employees

9–45 Article 6(1) imposes an obligation on the transferor and the transferee to inform their respective employee representatives of the following:

– the date or proposed date of the transfer;

– the reasons for the transfer;

– the legal, economic and social implications of the transfer for the employees; and

– any measures envisaged in relation to the employees.

The information must be given by the transferor to its employee representatives "in good time before the transfer is carried out". The transferee's representatives must receive their information from the transferee also "in good time" but it must be received before the employees are directly affected by the transfer as regards their conditions of work and employment. Where either the transferor or transferee envisages measures in relation to their employees, Article 6(2) requires that the employee representatives be consulted in good time on such measures with a view to reaching agreement. Clearly, however, such agreement need not be reached. These provisions are implemented into Irish law by Regulation 7(1) and (2). To avoid doubt, Article 6(4), as amended, provides that these obligations are stated to apply to transfers irrespective of whether the decision resulting in the transfer was taken by the employer or an undertaking controlling the employer. Similarly, failure by the controlling company to provide the necessary information will not constitute a good defence to a claim that the informational obligations have been breached.

9–46 Where, through no fault of their own, no employee representatives exist, Article 6.6 as amended provides that the employees concerned must be given the same information as would have been given to the employee representatives if they existed. Previously, Article 6 merely required that the employees be informed in advance when a transfer was about to take place.[63] In *Case C–382/92 Commission v. UK*,[64] this had been interpreted by the ECJ as meaning that if there were no representatives, a statement should be given to each employee and notices should be put up.

---

[63] The original Art. 6(5) of Directive 77/187.
[64] [1994] I.R.L.R. 392.

9–47   There is no clear explanation of the phrase "in good time". In *Griffin and Others v. South Western Water Services Ltd.*,[65] the English High Court considered a similar consultation "in good time" principle in the E.C. Collective Redundancies Directive.[65a] The Court said that the obligation to consult only arises when the employer's contemplation of redundancies has reached the point where the employer is able to identify the workers likely to be affected and can supply the information which the Article requires be supplied. This situation is unlikely to be reached at an early stage in the process.

Failure to comply with Regulation 7 may lead to an action by an employee or a union to obtain injunctive relief.[66] Failure to comply with the provisions of the Regulations in general may be punished by a maximum fine of £500 on summary conviction. No successful prosecutions have taken place to date. In addition, it is submitted that this figure is wholly inadequate and is unlikely to act as a deterrent.

---

[65] [1995] I.L.R.L. 15.
[65a] Directive 75/129 as amended by Directive 92/56.
[66] See *Maybury v. Pump Services Ltd and Eldea Ltd* unreported, High Court, Blayney J., May 2, 1990.

CHAPTER 10

PARTIES TO A TAKEOVER

Introduction

10–01 Section 8 of the Irish Takeover Panel Act 1997 ("the 1997 Act") authorises the Irish Takeover Panel ("the Panel") to make rules to ensure that takeovers and other relevant transactions comply with the General Principles set out in the schedule to the 1997 Act. The purpose of these rules is to provide an orderly framework within which takeovers are conducted. The rules introduced by the Panel pursuant to section 8 are the Irish Takeover Panel Act 1997, Takeover Rules, 1997 ("the Rules").

10–02 The Rules set out the rights and responsibilities of the various parties to the takeover or other relevant transaction. In addition, as will be discussed in Chapter 13, dealings by these parties during the offer period will be strictly regulated.[1] The Panel is entitled to give a direction to these parties to do or refrain from doing anything which the Panel specifies in the direction in order to ensure compliance with the General Principles and the Rules.[2]

10–03 Section 1(1) of the 1997 Act contains a list of persons who are deemed to be "parties to a takeover or other relevant transaction" for the purposes of the 1997 Act. This list which is long and broad ranging includes the following:

"(a) the offeror;
(b) any person acting in concert with the offeror;
(c) the directors of the offeror if the offeror is a company
(d) the offeree;
(e) the holders of the securities to whom the offer is made;
(f) the directors of the offeree;

---

[1] Dealings by a related party may have consequences under R. 4 (restrictions on dealings), R. 5 (restrictions on acquisitions), R. 6 (purchases above the offer price), R. 7 (consequences of certain dealings), R. 8 (disclosure of certain dealings), R. 9 (mandatory offers) and R. 11 (obligation to offer cash). In addition, relevant parties may be required to disclose shareholdings and dealings under R. 24 and R. 25. See Chap. 13.
[2] Irish Takeover Panel Act 1997, s.9(2)(a).

(g) any person acting as an adviser to any of the foregoing persons in relation to the takeover or other relevant transaction

(h) any person who, following a request made of him or her to do so by the offeror pursuant to rules under section 8, confirms that they are available to the offeror resources of such an amount as will enable the offer, if it is fully accepted, to be implemented;

(i) such other persons as are specified in rules under section 8 for the purposes of this definition or whom the Panel deems in the circumstances of a particular takeover or other relevant transaction to be parties to that takeover or transaction."

10–04   Clearly, paragraph (i) of section 1(1) gives the Panel enormous discretion to bring other persons within their jurisdiction. The Panel has utilised this authority and Rule 3.2 of Part A. of the rules sets out a number of additional parties to a takeover or other relevant transaction. These parties are:

"(a) an associate of an offeror or an offeree;

(b) an underwriter of an offer;

(c) a person acting as receiving agent to an offer;

(d) a person acting as registrar of an offeree;

(e) a relevant company which enters into a reverse takeover transaction;

(f) the directors of a relevant company which enters into a reverse takeover transaction;

(g) a person, or persons acting in concert, who makes or make a substantial acquisition of securities;

(h) the company securities of which are the subject of a substantial acquisition of securities;

(i) the persons from whom the securities the subject of a substantial acquisition of securities are acquired;

(j) a person or persons acting in concert, who seeks or seek to acquire securities pursuant to a tender offer;

(k) the company securities of which are the subject of a tender offer;

(l) the holders of securities to whom a tender offer is addressed; and

(m) a person who is privy to confidential price-sensitive information concerning an offer or contemplated offer."

In this Chapter, the concepts offeror, offeree, concert parties and advisers will be examined. These parties will be defined and the role they play in the takeover process identified. The responsibilities of these various parties will then be set out in the following three Chapters.

A. Offeror and Offeree

10–05   Section 1(1) of the 1997 Act defines an offeror as:

"a person who makes, or intends or is required to make, an offer or does any act in contemplation of making an offer".

Similarly, the definition of an "offeree" is defined as

"a relevant company –
(a) any securities of which are the subject of an offer that has been made or is intended or required to be made, or
(b) in respect of which, or in connection with which, a person does any act in contemplation of making an offer to holders of securities in that company."

Not only do these definitions include companies who have actually made an offer or for whom an offer has actually been made, but they also include companies intending to make an offer and companies for whom an offer is intended to be made. The definitions of the terms "offeror" and "offeree" in the Irish Takeover Panel Bill 1996 as first introduced, were amended in order to ensure that the provisions of the Act would apply equally to parties at certain stages prior to the making of an offer. For example, where a person intends to make an offer for the shares of a company, the shareholders of the intended offeree need the protection of the Takeover Rules in order to ensure that a false market is not created at this time leading to the inequitable treatment of shareholders.

10–06 The definitions of offeror and offeree also include persons who are required to make offers or relevant companies for whom offers are required to be made. Thus, where a person acquires or consolidates control in a company such that a general offer will be required for all the shares in the company under Rule 9, the company which must make this offer qualifies immediately as an "offeror" and the company in which control has been acquired or consolidated qualifies as the "offeree".

10–07 Finally, the definition of "offeror" also includes persons who do any act in contemplation of making an offer and the definition of "offeree" also includes companies in respect of which a person does any act in contemplation of making an offer. Such an act might include for example, an approach to a number of financiers to raise the necessary funds to make the acquisition. Thus, where negotiations and discussions concerning the offer are about to be extended to include more than a very restricted number of people, Rule 2.2(e) requires an announcement by the "offeror".

B. Concert Parties

10–08 "Concert parties" is the term used to describe persons who are deemed to be "acting in concert". A definition of "acting in concert" is provided in section 1(3) of the 1997 Act. It states that, for the purposes of the Act:

> "two or more persons shall be deemed to be acting in concert as respects a takeover or other relevant transaction if, pursuant to an agreement or understanding (whether formal or informal) between them, they actively co-operate in the acquisition by any one or more of them of securities in the relevant company concerned or in the doing, or the procuring of the doing, of any act that results in an increase in the proportion of such securities held by any one or more of them."

Three integral elements of this definition merit emphasis. Firstly, in order to qualify as concert parties, an agreement or understanding must exist between the parties. This agreement may either be formal, for example a legally binding contract, or informal, for example an informal under-standing. Secondly, these parties must pursuant to this agreement or understanding "actively co-operate" in either the acquisition by one of them in securities of the relevant company or the doing or procuring of the doing of an act which results in an increase in one or more of the parties holding of relevant securities. The issue of active co-operation is interesting if rather ambiguous. For example, if the acquisition by one person is the result of an unintentional or unsought action of a third party, it would not be clear that the first person would be deemed to be acting in concert with a related party. Rule 3.3 of Part A of the Rules provides clarification of the Panel's understanding of this term. The third element of the definition which must be considered is that it is not necessary that the acquisition lead to the obtaining or consolidating of control. It is important to note that the term "acting in concert" in the City Code on Takeovers and Mergers refers to something substantially different. The term "persons acting in concert" is defined in the City Code as:

> "persons who, pursuant to an agreement or understanding (whether formal or informal), actively co-operate, through the acquisition by any of them of shares in a company, to obtain or consolidate control."

The effect of the parties actions under this definition must be to obtain or to consolidate control.[2a]

I. RULE 3.3 CONCERT PARTIES

10–09   Rule 3.3 of Part A of the Rules provides that certain persons are presumed for the purposes of the 1997 Act to be acting in concert with other persons as respects a takeover or other relevant transaction, until the contrary is established to the satisfaction of the Panel. Thus:

[2a] It should also be noted that for this reason the Rules governing the Substantial Acquisitions of Shares ("SARs") administered by the London Panel on Takeovers and Mergers do not refer to "concert parties". Instead, Rule 5 of the SARs provides that persons acting by agreement or understanding in the acquisition of shares carrying voting rights will have their holdings and acquisitions aggregated and

(a) a company, its holding company, its subsidiaries and any sub-sidiaries of its holding company, any associated company of such companies and companies of which such companies are associated companies are all presumed to be acting in concert with each other.

(b) a company and each company with which it is presumed to be acting in concert according to paragraph (a) above is presumed to be acting in concert with
  (i) each of the directors of the first mentioned company
  (ii) any spouse, parent, brother, sister or child of such director, and
  (iii) any trustee of a trust (including a discretionary trust) of which such a director or any spouse, parent, brother, sister or child of such a director is a beneficiary or potential beneficiary.

(c) a company and each company with whom it is presumed to be acting in concert according to paragraph (a) above is presumed to be acting in concert with the trustees of any pension scheme (other than an industry-wide scheme) in which the first mentioned company participates.

(d) a fund manager (including an exempt fund manager) is presumed to be acting in concert with any collective investment scheme or other person whose investments the fund manager manages on a discretionary basis in respect of the relevant investment accounts.

(e) a financial or other professional adviser (including a stockbroker) is presumed to be acting in concert with its clients in respect of securities held by the adviser and by persons controlling, con-trolled by or under the same control as such adviser[3]

(f) directors of a company will be presumed to be acting in concert with each other in relation to the company at certain times. These are (i) during the course of an offer in respect of a relevant company (ii) whilst the directors of a relevant company have reason to believe that an offer in respect of that company may be made in the near future (iii) whilst a relevant company is in the course of redeeming or purchasing its own securities or (iv) whilst the directors of a relevant company propose that the company redeem or purchase its own securities. At other times, directors will not be presumed to be acting in concert in relation to the control of their company.

---

treated as a holding or acquisition by one person for the purpose of the SARs. Because the definition of the term in the Act does not refer to the acquisition or consolidation of control, the term "acting in concert" is used in the Irish Takeover Panel Act, 1997 (Substantial Acquisition) Rules, 1997.

[3] Except in the case of an exempt market maker.

In addition, where an offeree's directors have advised against an offer, shareholders who have indicated their support for the offeree's directors may be presumed by the Panel to be acting in concert with the directors if they subsequently buy securities to frustrate the offer.[4]

10–10   Rule 7.2(a) provides that discretionary fund managers connected to the offeror dealing in respect of investment accounts managed by them on a discretionary basis will be presumed to be acting in concert with the offeror during the offer period after the identity of the offeror is publicly known until the contrary is established to the satisfaction of the Panel. Similarly, according to Rule 7.2(b), discretionary fund managers connected with the offeree will be presumed to be acting in concert with directors of the offeree who are also shareholders of the offeree during the offer period in respect of investment accounts managed by them on a discretionary basis. The result of this is that dealings by a fund manager may then give rise to an infringement of Rule 5 or Rule 9. If this is likely, the fund manager should consult the Panel in advance of the dealing. These presumptions will not apply to an exempt fund manager which is connected with the offeror or offeree only insofar as the fund manager is controlled by, controls or is under the common control of a financial or other professional adviser acting in relation to the offer.[5]

10–11   As will be seen in Chapter 13, concert parties are subject to more onerous dealing restrictions and disclosure requirements than other investors. In addition, the definition of concert parties is particularly important in terms of Rule 9 which requires an offer for all shares where certain shareholdings are acquired by a person or by persons acting in concert with them.[6] It may often arise that a mandatory offer is triggered because of the aggregation of holdings between concert parties. Indeed, it could happen that persons unaware of the purchases of concert parties may unknowingly trigger this requirement. Special rules apply to concert parties in this respect.[7]

Once the Panel has ruled a group of persons to be acting in concert, clear evidence must be presented to the Panel in order for the Panel to become satisfied that the concert party status should no longer apply.[8]

II. ASSOCIATES

10–12   Certain parties which are close to the offeror or offeree are deemed "associates". A person may be an associate of the offeror or

---

4   R. 9, note 3.
5   R. 7.2(b).
6   paras 11–64–11–75.
7   See Chap. 11, para. 11–65
8   Note 1(a) on R. 2.1 of Part A.

offeree irrespective of whether they are acting in concert with the offeror or offeree. Rule 2.2 of Part A of the Rules defines the term "associate" for the purpose of the Rules as:

(a) a holding company, a subsidiary or a subsidiary of the holding company of the offeror or offeree;

(b) an associated company of the offeror, the offeree or an associate of either the offeror or offeree as described in paragraph (a);

(c) a company of which the offeror, offeree or an associate of either the offeror or offeree as described in paragraph (a) or (b) is an associated company;

(d) a bank or a financial or other professional adviser (including a stockbroker) which is acting for the offeror or offeree or for an associate of either as described in paragraphs (a),(b) or (c) in relation to the offer;[8a]

(e) a person controlling, controlled by, or under the same control as an associate described in paragraph (d);

(f) a director of the offeror or offeree or any associate of either as described in paragraphs (a),(b) or (c)
  – or a spouse, parent, brother, sister or child of such a director
  – or a trustee of a trust[9] of which such a director or relation of a director is a beneficiary or potential beneficiary;

(g) a trustee of any pension scheme(other than an industry wide scheme) in which the offeror or offeree or any associate of either as described in paragraphs (a), (b) or (c) participates;

(h) a collective investment scheme or other person whose investments the offeror or offeree or any associate of the offeror or offeree manages on a discretionary basis in respect of the relevant investment accounts;

(i) a person who owns or controls alone or with concert parties at least 5 per cent of any class of relevant securities[10] of the offeror or offeree;

(j) a party to any indemnity or option arrangement[11] with any offeror or with an associate of any offeror in respect of relevant securities of that offeror or offeree or with the offeree or an associate of the offeree in respect of relevant securities;

[8a] A Bank which is merely engaged in the provision of normal commercial banking services or which merely confirms that cash is available or handles acceptances and other registration work is not included in this definition.
[9] Including a discretionary trust.
[10] As described in R. 8.9(a)–(d).

(k) a person with a material business relationship with the offeror or
      offeree; or

(l) a person who directly or indirectly owns or deals in securities of an
      offeror or the offeree who has, in addition to a normal interest as
      security holder, an interest or potential interest, whether com-
      mercial, financial or personal in the outcome of the offer.

This classification is wider than that of a concert party. It should be
noted that all associates may not necessarily be concert parties whereas
all concert parties will be associates. As will be seen in Chapter 13,[11a]
associates are subject to more onerous dealing disclosure requirements
than other investors.

III. EXEMPT MARKET MAKERS

10–13   In 1986, the London Stock Exchange abandoned its minimum
commission rule, allowing brokers to act as jobbers and vice versa and
allowing foreign firms to become members. This deregulation was
known as "Big Bang" and its effect on the structure of the London
market was substantial. It lead to a number of UK and foreign banks
entering the securities industry in the City of London and led to the
common ownership within single organisations of brokers, market-
makers, fund managers and corporate finance operations. As a result of
the development of these multi-function organisations, the likelihood
increased that organisations acting as advisers to clients in a takeover
would also wish to deal as a principal, in the role of market-maker or
broker/dealer, in the shares of companies involved in the takeover. It
became important thus to establish whether the dealings of the market-
making arm of the adviser should be deemed to be actions in concert
with the companies involved in the takeover.

10–14   The creation of Chinese walls[12] or internal procedures to prevent
the communication of information between the corporate finance
department and other divisions helped to solve the difficulties of dealing
before the possibility of an offer is known. The situation changes,
however, when the takeover offer is made and the involvement of the
corporate finance department becomes public. At this stage dealings by a
related party may have consequences under the Rules. The London
Panel decided that when a multi-service financial institution is advising
an offeror, whether as banker stockbroker or otherwise, all principal

---

[11] Under R. 8.7.
[11a] See paras 13–106–13–109.
[12] See paras 10–59–10–69.

dealings in relevant securities by any part of the organisation would be presumed to be in concert with the offeror. An exception to this was dealings by "an exempt market maker". An organisation qualifying as an exempt market maker must operate their market-making operations wholly independently and without regard to the interests of clients of the corporate finance department of the organisations.

10–15 The main rational for offering exempt status to market makers is the fear that if the restrictions in the rules were extended to market makers, the liquidity of the market in the relevant securities would be damaged by the withdrawal of a market maker because of its connection with the offeror.

10–16 In the Dublin market, there are no market makers for equities.[13] However, the London market makers who have exempt status for the purpose of the City Code may apply to be so recognised in Ireland. The Rules thus provide a definition and Rule 38 is concerned solely with exempt market makers. An "exempt market maker" is defined in Rule 2 of Part A as a person who, in relation to the securities concerned,

(i) is registered as a market-maker in those securities by the London Stock Exchange Ltd. or is accepted by London Panel on Takeovers and Mergers as a market-maker in those securities

(ii) has applied to and been recognised by the Panel as an exempt market maker for the purposes of the Rules

(iii) has been notified in writing by the Panel of this recognition, and

(iv) has not been notified by the Panel of the withdrawal of such recognition.

IV. EXEMPT FUND MANAGERS

10–17 The advent of Big Bang also caused problems for fund managers whose connections with corporate finance advisers in certain takeovers would have constrained their operations substantially. Changes were introduced in 1986 to the City Code to provide that the London Panel could grant to a discretionary fund manager an exemption such that the fund manager, if connected with the offeror through the advisory side of the operation, would not be presumed to be acting in concert with regard to discretionary investment accounts. This allows the manager to deal for discretionary clients in securities relevant to the takeover without regard to any City Code restrictions affecting the offeror.

---

[13] However, six primary dealers or market makers operate in respect of government bonds.

10–18 The Irish Rules also recognise the position of exempt fund managers. The term "exempt fund manager" is defined in Rule 2 of Part A as a discretionary fund manager who:

(i) has applied to the Panel to be recognised by the Panel as an exempt fund manager for the purposes of the Rules

(ii) has been notified in writing by the Panel of this recognition, and

(iii) has not been notified by the Panel that recognition has been withdrawn.[14]

10–19 Approval may be absolute or it may be subject to the fulfilment by the applicant of any requirements imposed by the Panel. The Panel will seek to establish that the day to day business of fund management is conducted wholly independently of the corporate finance side of the company. The establishment of Chinese walls will be essential. Fund managers connected with the offeror or offeree who do not have the benefit of exempt status must have regard to Rule 7.2 after the involvement of the advisory side in the offer is publicly known. They will be presumed to be concert parties unless the contrary is established to the satisfaction of the Panel.

V. CONNECTED MARKET-MAKER OR FUND MANAGER

10–20 Rule 2.3 of Part A defines a connected market-maker or fund manager as one which is controlled by, controls or is under the same control as:

(a) the offeror;

(b) the offeree;

(c) any bank or any financial or other professional adviser (including a stockbroker) which is acting for the offeror or offeree in relation to the offer.[14a]

(d) an investor in a consortium formed for the purpose of making an offer.

Where a market-maker or fund manager is connected with either the offeror or offeree, the exempt status is relevant only where the firm is only connected because it is controlled by, controls or is under the same

---

[14] R. 2.1 of Part A

[14a] A bank which is merely engaged in the provision of normal commercial banking services or which merely confirms that cash is available or handles acceptances and other registration work is not included in this definition.

control as a financial or other professional adviser acting in relation to the offer for the offeror or offeree.[15] Dealings by a connected market-maker in a market making capacity will not normally be considered to fall within the acting in concert presumptions. Clearly, however, dealings by such a market maker in any other capacity will.[16]

C. Advisers

10–21   The role of an adviser in a takeover is essentially a co-ordinating and facilitating role. Advisers are normally merchant banks or corporate finance houses who provide financial, tactical and corporate planning advice but the term also applies to other professional advisers such as accountants, stockbrokers or solicitors. Advisers collectively are responsible for advising their clients on regulatory and tactical matters, on the financing of the offer and on its presentation to the market. They are also responsible for ensuring that all the documentation is properly prepared and that all regulatory requirements including those contained in the Rules are satisfied. In addition to advising parties of their responsibilities under the Rules, certain obligations are imposed specifically on advisers under the Rules. In addition, because of their relationship with their clients, certain dealing restrictions and disclosure restrictions apply to advisers.

10–22   It should be noted that "advice to undertakings relating to mergers and the purchase or sale of undertakings" is not deemed to be "investment advice" for the purposes of the Investment Intermediaries Act 1995.[17] Thus, firms exclusively offering such advice do not need to be authorised for the purposes of that Act. However, many of the firms offering these services will be credit institutions, stock brokers or investment intermediaries and as noted in Chapter 7, will be regulated under the Central Bank Acts, the Stock Exchange Act 1995 or the Investment Intermediaries Act 1995.

I. DEALINGS AND DISCLOSURE OF DEALINGS

10–23   A "bank or a financial or other professional adviser, including a stockbroker, which is acting in relation to the offer for the offeror or

---

[15]   Note 5(b) on R. 2.1 of Part A.
[16]   Note 5(c) on R. 2.1 of Part A.
[17]   Section 2(1) of the Investment Intermediaries Act 1995 as amended by section 52(a)(i) of the Investor Compensation Act 1998.

offeree or for an associate[18] of the offeror or offeree" is itself deemed pursuant to rule 2.2(d) of Part A of the Rules to be an associate of the offeror or offeree, as the case may be. In addition, a financial or other professional adviser, including a stockbroker, will be presumed to be acting in concert with its clients in respect of securities held by the adviser and by persons controlling, controlled by or under the same control as such adviser.[19] Because of this status, certain additional restrictions on dealings will be imposed and certain additional disclosure requirements will be imposed under the Rules. Disclosure of dealings by the advisers will also be required in the offer document and the board circular.[20] In addition, in certain circumstances dealings by advisers may trigger an obligation to make a mandatory offer[21] or an obligation to offer a minimum level of consideration.[22]

II. COMMUNICATION

10–24 In addition to advising their clients on the relevant standards of care to be adopted in relation to documents issued in connection with the takeover, the advisers will be restrained in terms of their own publications during this period. Advisers are prohibited generally from issuing statements which might mislead shareholders.[23] In addition, if the advisers propose to issue a statement which includes "an estimate of the anticipated financial effects of a takeover" the Panel must be consulted in advance and the statement must include:

  (i) the basis of the belief (including sources of information and any assumptions made) supporting the estimate;

 (ii) reports by financial advisers and auditors that the estimates have been made with due care and consideration;

(iii) an analysis and explanation of the constituent elements of the estimate;

(iv) a base figure for any comparisons drawn and

 (v) a disclaimer.[24]

An estimate of a resulting change in profit, cash flow, operating costs or earnings per share will also be included in this restriction.

---

[18] An associate described in paragraph (a),(b) or (c) of the definition of "associate" in R. 2.2 of Part A of the R.s.
[19] Except in the capacity of an exempt market-maker. See Rule 303 of Part A of the Rules.
[20] R. 24.3 and R. 25.3. See paras 12.37–12.38 and 12.46–12.48.
[21] R. 9 and R. 37. See paras 11.64–11.75 and 20.69–20.71.
[22] R. 6. See paras 11.50–11.53.
[23] R. 19.3(a).
[24] R. 19.3(b).

10–25 Meetings during the offer period between the advisers and shareholders of either the offeror or the offeree, analysts, stockbrokers or other investment managers or advisers are strictly regulated to ensure that no material new information is disclosed.[25] To avoid doubt, parties are advised of the usefulness of recording the proceedings.[26] While the advisers (and brokers or other associates of an offeror or offeree) may issue circulars during the offer period to their own investment clients, these circulars must be approved in advance by the Panel.[27] If the circulars contain information on the companies involved in the offer, the advisers must ensure that the information does not include "any statement of fact or opinion derived from information which is not generally available".[28] In particular, the information must not include any profit forecast unless the forecast has already been included, and only to the extent that it has been included, in the offer documents or offeree circulars.

III. THE ROLE OF ADVISERS

10–26 Advisers to the offeror and offeree play a distinct role in the takeover process. Often the adviser to the offeree will be the first party approached by an offeror intending to make an offer for their client. Rule 1(a) obliges any adviser notified by an offeree of an intention to make an offer for its client to notify the offeree board immediately.

10–27 Even before this, however, the adviser to the offeror will have become involved. This person will play a large role in structuring the offer and in financing it. General principle 3 provides that:

> "No offer shall be made and no announcement of a proposed offer shall be made safe after careful and responsible consideration of the matters by the offeror and any advisers of the offeror and only if the offeror and any advisers of the offeror are satisfied that the offeror will be able to implement the offer if it is accepted."

Rule 2.5(a) prohibits an offeror from announcing a firm intention to make an offer until both the offeror and its financial adviser are satisfied that the offeror is able and will continue to be able to implement the offer. The Notes to Rule 2.5(a) counsel the advisers to undertake a careful review of the offeror's current and prospective financial position and of any assumptions upon which the offeror's prospective financial position is predicated. Rule 1(c) obliges the offeror, if so

---

[25] R. 20.1(b). See para. 12–25.
[26] Note 3 on R. 20.1.
[27] R. 20.1(c).
[28] R. 20.1(c).

requested by the board of the offeree, to satisfy it that it has, or will have at the time it announces the offer, sufficient resources to enable it to implement the bid in full. Furthermore, the announcement of an offer under Rule 9 or Rule 37 must include confirmation by the offeror's financial adviser or by another appropriate third party that the offeror has sufficient resources to satisfy full acceptance of the offer. Except with the consent of the Panel, an offer made under Rule 9 and Rule 37 must be in cash or accompanied by a cash alternative offer.[29] If this confirmation subsequently proves to be inaccurate, the person who gave it may be required to provide the necessary resources.[30] Clearly, this could be a substantial undertaking with serious financial implications for the adviser. Such cover will not be necessary, however, if the Panel is satisfied that the adviser or third party acted responsibly and took all reasonable steps to assure itself that the cash was available and would continue to be available at all relevant times.

10–28   Before the offeree board is approached, the offeror is responsible for monitoring the market for any untoward movement in the offeree's share price and for any rumour or speculation concerning the offeree.[31] This is an extremely onerous responsibility. A similar obligation rests on offeree board after the approach.[32]

The advisers to the offeror and offeree will be required under Rule 2.10 to furnish the Panel in writing with an address within the State at which notices, directions and other documents may be served or given. The number of a facsimile machine located at that address must also be furnished. This duty must be fulfilled as soon as practicable after their appointment as advisers.

IV. THE PROVISION OF INDEPENDENT ADVICE

10–29   The offeree board is required to obtain competent independent advice on every offer in respect of the offeree and to convey this advice to its shareholders.[33] This requirement is stated to be particularly important where the offer is a management buy-out or similar transaction or is being made by the existing controlling shareholder or group of shareholders. In such cases, the independence of the adviser must be "beyond question". Since the responsibility born by the adviser in such cases is considerable, the offeree is advised to appoint an independent adviser as soon as it becomes aware that an offer should be made.[34]

---

[29] R. 9.4(a) and R. 37.1(c).
[30] R. 2.5(c).
[31] R. 2.3(a).
[32] R. 2.3(b).
[33] R. 3.1(a).
[34] Note 1 on R. 3.1.

10–30 Where directors of the offeror are faced with a conflict of interest in respect of the offer, the board of the offeror must also obtain competent independent advice.[35] The offeror board is also required to obtain independent advice if it proposes to enter a reverse takeover transaction.[36] The substance and source of the advice which the offeror board receives in these circumstances must be conveyed to their shareholders.[37] Where the Rules provide that competent independent advice must be obtained by the offeror board, this advice must be obtained before announcing the offer concerned or any revision of the offer or the reverse takeover. The advice obtained must deal with the issue of whether the making of the offer or the entering of the transaction would be in the shareholders' best interests. In addition, shareholders must be given sufficient time to consider this advice before being called upon to approve the implementation of the offer or the reverse takeover transaction.[38]

10–31 Rule 3.3 deems certain persons to be disqualified advisers for the purpose of giving independent advice, except where the Panel rules otherwise. A person will be deemed disqualified from giving advice to the offeree board "if such person controls, is controlled by or is under the same control as the financial or other professional adviser (including a stockbroker) to an offeror".[39] Similarly, a person will be deemed disqualified from giving advice to the offeror board or a relevant company proposing to enter a reverse takeover transaction "if such person controls or is controlled by or is under the same control as the financial or other professional adviser (including a stockbroker) to the board of the offeree or the other party to the reverse takeover". A person may not give advice to any such board if the person has a significant interest in or financial connection with the offeror, the offeree or (as the case may be) any other party to the transaction concerned "of such a kind as to cause a conflict of interest".[40] For the purposes of this Rule, the Panel has indicated that a shareholding of 20 per cent or more will normally be considered to constitute a "significant interest".[41]

10–32 In order to ensure that the advice is properly objective, a person who has had a recent advisory relationship with the offeror may be considered inappropriate to give advice to the offeree. The views of the

---

[35] R. 3.2(a)(i).
[36] R. 3.2(a)(ii). See para. 11–89–11–96.
[37] R. 3.2(a)(iii).
[38] R. 3.2(b).
[39] R. 3.3(a).
[40] R. 3.3(b).
[41] Note 3 on R. 3.3.

offeree board will obviously be important in this respect.[42] For the same reason, a person who manages, or is part of the same group as the investment manager of an investment trust company, may not be the appropriate person to give advice to that company.[43]

V. LIABILITY OF ADVISERS

10–33 It has been established that a duty of care can arise where there is a professional relationship between the parties. Where the relationship is contractual, a duty of care will generally be imposed by the contract itself, but a duty imposed by the general law and giving rise to liability in tort may also exist.[44]

(1) Duty of Care in Contract

10–34 The contract entered into between the adviser and the client may contain express terms concerning the standard of duty and the extent of the adviser's liability. More commonly, however, the nature of these duties will be implied.[45]

Terms may be implied into a contract in circumstances where the terms have been tacitly agreed.[46] In *Kavanagh v. Gilbert*,[47] an auctioneer who undertook to sell property for his client was deemed to be subject to an implied obligation to use skill and care in concluding the contract for sale. Terms may also be implied into a contract with the object of giving the transaction such efficacy as both parties must have intended.[48] In *Butler v. McAlpine*,[49] the Irish Court of Appeal held that there was an implied duty on a wharf owner to take reasonable care that the berth was reasonably safe for barges to dock to unload cargo.

10–35 Where duties of care are implied into a contract, the duties imposed will require performance with reasonable care rather than an

---

[42] Note 1 on R. 3.3.
[43] Note 2 on R. 3.3.
[44] See *Finlay v. Murtagh* [1979] I.R. 249. *Midland Bank Trust Co Ltd. v. Hett, Stubbs and Kemp* [1979] Ch. 384 and *Henderson v. Merrett Syndicates Ltd* [1995] 2 A.C. 145.
[45] For a detailed discussion of implied terms see Clark, *Contract Law in Ireland* (Roundhall Sweet & Maxwell, 1998), Chap. 6 *Implied Terms* and Clark & Clarke, *Contract Cases and Materials* (Gill and Macmillan,1994), chap. 7.
[46] This is termed the "officious bystanders test" and was established in the case of *Shirlaw v. Southern Foundries* (1926) Ltd. [1939] 2 K.B. 206. This test was approved by the Supreme Court in *Tradax (Ireland) Ltd. v. Irish Grain Board Ltd.* [1984] I.R. 1.
[47] (1875) I.R. 9 C.L. 136.
[48] This is termed the "business efficacy test" and was established initially by Bowen L.J. in *The Moorcock* (1889) 14 P.D. 64. This test is considerably wider than the officious bystander test.
[49] [1904] 2 I.R. 445.

obligation to achieve a specified result. In *Greaves & Co. (Contractors) Ltd v. Baynham, Meikle & Partners*, Lord Denning M.R. stated:

> "The law does not usually imply a warranty that he [the professional] will achieve the desired result, but only a term that he will use reasonable care and skill. The surgeon does not warrant that he will cure the patient. Nor does the solicitor warrant that he will win the case".[50]

10–36 In addition to terms implied in fact, terms may be implied under statute. For example, section 39 of the Sale of Goods and Supply of Services Act 1980 implies a term into a contract to the effect that a supplier of services has the necessary skill to render the service and will supply the service with due skill, care and diligence. This section applies to contracts where the supplier is acting in the course of a business.

(2) Common Law Duty of Care – Negligence

10–37 The notion of a Common Law "duty of care" was explained by Lord Atkin in the seminal case of *Donoghue v. Stevenson* as follows:

> " . . . in English law there must be, and is, some general conception of relations giving rise to a duty of care . . . You must take reasonable care to avoid acts or omissions which you can reasonably foresee would be likely to injure your neighbour. Who, then, in law, is my neighbour? The answer seems to be – persons who are so closely and directly affected by my act that I ought reasonably to have them in contemplation as being so affected when I am directing my mind to the acts or omissions which are called in question."[51]

In *Hedley Byrne & Co. Ltd. v. Heller and Partners Ltd*,[52] the House of Lords held that a person giving advice could owe a duty of care to a person who relied on the advice and suffered economic loss as a consequence. Although the *Hedley Byrne* case involved economic loss resulting from misstatements, subsequent case law has shown that the *Hedley Byrne* principle is not so confined.[53] It can permit recovery of economic losses for professional misfeasance.

In *Esso Petroleum Company v. Marden*,[54] Lord Denning M.R. stated:

> "If a man, who has or professes to have a special knowledge or skill, makes a representation by virtue thereof to another – be it advice information or

---

[50] [1975] 3 All E.R. 99 at 103.
[51] [1932] A.C. 562 at 580. This principle was followed in the Irish case *Kirby v. Burke (and Holloway)* [1944] I.R. 207.
[52] [1964] A.C. 465.
[53] *Henderson v. Merrett Syndicates Ltd.* [1995] 2 A.C. 145. *Williams v. Natural Life Health Foods Ltd.* [1998] 1 WLR 830.
[54] [1976] 2 All E.R. 5 at 16.

opinion – with the intention of inducing him to enter into a contract with him, he is under a duty to use reasonable care to see that the representation is correct, and that the advice, information or opinion is reliable."

(a) UK Developments

10–38   A revised version of the neighbour test was suggested by Lord Wilberforce's in *Anns v. Merton London Borough Council*.[55] A two-stage test was suggested. First, one had to prove a sufficient relationship of proximity such that, in the reasonable contemplation of the defendant, carelessness on his or her part would be likely to cause damage to the plaintiff. Secondly, one had to consider whether there were any considerations which should negative or limit the scope of the duty or the class of person to whom the duty is owed.

10–39   In the ensuing period, however the *Anns* test fell out of favour in the UK.[56] It was argued that it led to the imposition of "liability in an indeterminate amount for an indeterminate time to an indeterminate class".[57] A three stage test was subsequently applied by the House of Lords in *Caparo Industries plc v. Dickman*[58] in order to establish a duty of care:

> "What emerges is that, in addition to the foreseeability of damage, necessary ingredients in any situation giving rise to a duty of care are that there should exist between the party owing the duty and the party to whom it is owed a relationship characterised by the law as one of "proximity" or "neighbourhood" and that the situation should be one in which the court considers it fair, just and reasonable that the law should impose a duty of a given scope on the one part for the benefit of the other."[59]

Clearly, in many cases these three criteria will overlap. The criterion of reasonable foreseeability is based on the knowledge that a person, in the defendant's position, is likely to possess. Proximity focuses on the particular relationship between the parties. In the *Caparo* case, Lord Oliver stated:

> "What can be deduced from the *Hedley Byrne* case, therefore, is that the necessary relationship between the maker of a statement or giver of advice (the adviser) and the recipient who acts in reliance upon it (the advisee) may typically be held to exist where
> (1) the advice is required for a purpose, whether particularly specified or generally described, which is made known, either actually or inferentially, to the adviser at the time when the advice is given,

---

55   [1978] A.C. 728 at 751.
56   *Murphy v. Brentwood District Council* [1991] 1 A.C. 398.
57   *Ulltramares v. Touche* [1931] 174 NE 441 at p. 444 per Cardoza J.
58   [1990] 2 A.C. 605.
59   *ibid.*, 617–618 *per* Lord Bridge.

(2) the adviser knows, either actually or inferentially, that his advice will be communicated to the advisee, either specifically or as a member of an ascertainable class, in order that it should be used by the advisee for that purpose,

(3) it is known, either actually or inferentially, that the advice so communicated is likely to be acted on by the advisee for that purpose without independent inquiry and

(4) it is so acted on by the advisee to his detriment."[60]

10–40   In *Galoo Ltd. v. Bright Grahame Murray*,[61] a firm of auditors were sued for breach of a duty of care in relation to a purchase of shares. The auditor in this case was aware that the price of the shares to be sold by the company was based on the financial figures in the accounts which they were producing. The auditor's knowledge of the purpose of the accounts led to the imposition of a duty in this case. A further claim based upon losses resulting from subsequent purchases of additional shares was not accepted as the auditors could not have been aware that their accounts would be relied on for these purchases.

10–41   Except where the adviser has communicated the advice directly to the plaintiff in response to a direct request,[62] the knowledge of the adviser that the advice will be communicated to the representee may be difficult to prove. It has been argued that the fear of floodgates being opened and of defendants being held to owe a duty of care to an indeterminate class of individuals has exerted a great influence at this point.[63] A professional person will not thus, be held to owe a duty of care in respect of public documents prepared or advice publicly communicated to any member of the public who places reliance on it. In *Caparo v. Dickman* itself, no duty of care was held to be owed by an auditor to members of the public who relied on public accounts to buy shares in the company. Furthermore, no duty was said to be owed to individual shareholders who wished to increase their shareholdings.[64]

10–42   In *Morgan Crucible Co v. Hill Samuel Bank Ltd.*,[65] the court at first instance determined that the directors and financial advisors of an offeree in a contested takeover bid owed no duty to a known offeror in respect of the accuracy of profit forecasts, financial statements and defence documents prepared for the purpose of contesting the bid. It was accepted that the purpose of these documents was to advise the

---

[60] *op. cit.*, n.58.
[61] [1995] 1 All E.R. 16.
[62] *Candler v. Crane Christmas & Co.* [1951] 2 K.B. 164.
[63] Dugdale and Stanton, *Professional Negligence* (Butterworths, 1998) 122.
[64] See also *Al-Nabik Investments (Jersey) Ltd v. Longcroft* [1990] 3 All E.R. 321.
[65] [1991] 1 All E.R. 148.

offeree's shareholders, not to guide the offeror. However, the Court of Appeal distinguished *Caparo* on the basis that all the representations relied on in *Caparo* were made before an identified offeror emerged. It was accepted that since some of the representations in this case were made after the offeror emerged, a secondary purpose of the defence document issued by a company to its own shareholders advising them to reject the offer could have been to persuade the offeror to increase the value of its offer. In *Barings plc v. Coopers & Lybrand*,[66] the Court of Appeal allowed service out of the jurisdiction on the grounds that an arguable case had been established that the defendant auditors owed a duty of care to the plaintiff holding company because they were retained to audit the accounts of a subsidiary in circumstances where they knew their accounts would be used to enable the plaintiff to produce accounts relating to the entire group. This was one of a number of cases resulting from the collapse of Barings Group 1995 as a consequence of the unauthorised dealings of Nick Leeson for a subsidiary company in Singapore.

10-43   The knowledge of the impact of the advice may also be difficult to prove. In *James McNaughton Papers Group Ltd v. Hicks Anderson*,[67] auditors were sued for breach of a duty of care by the offeror who had relied on draft accounts prepared by the auditors for the offeree and on the answer to an inquiry furnished by the auditors to the effect that the company was breaking even or doing marginally worse. The Court of Appeal held that the accountants owed no duty to the offeror as the accounts were not produced for the offeror, they were merely draft accounts, and the auditors could not have reasonably foreseen that the plaintiffs would treat them as final. In this case, the auditors did not participate in the negotiations. The Court stated that as the plaintiffs were aware that the company was in a poor state, they should have consulted their own accountants. On this point, Neill L.J stated:

> "In cases where the existence of a duty of care is in issue it is always useful to examine the matter from the point of view of the plaintiff . . . One should therefore consider whether and to what extent the advisee was entitled to rely on the statement, whether he did or should have used his own judgment and whether he did or should have sought independent advice. In business transactions conducted at arms length it may sometimes be difficult for an advisee to prove that he was entitled to act on a statement without taking any independent advice."[68]

---

[66] [1996] I.B.C.L.C. 427. See also *Bank of Credit and Commerce International (Overseas) Ltd. v. Price Waterhouse* [1998] 15 LS Gaz. R. 32.
[67] [1991] 1 All E.R. 134.
[68] *ibid.*, at 145.

10–44   In *Ginora Investments Ltd v. James Capel & Co Ltd.*,[69] the Court considered the duty of a merchant bank to a client in the context of a hostile takeover bid made by the client. The defendant was retained to advise Priest Marian Holdings plc ("PMH") three days before it launched a bid. PMH subsequently sued the defendant for damages for alleged misrepresentation and negligence. PMH alleged that it should not have been advised to proceed with the acquisition, that the value per share advised was incorrect, and finally that the defendant negligently failed to advise PMH that the transaction involved a high level of risk and that liabilities might emerge after the acquisition. The defendant acknowledged that it had a duty to give "competent and objective advice on the pros and cons of the deal." However, Rimer J. stated that whether or not the defendant had been negligent had to be determined in the light of the circumstances obtaining at the time rather than with the benefit of hindsight. Thus, the question of the attractiveness of the acquisition and the share price paid was a question essentially of judgment at the time. Furthermore, Rimer J. stated that the existence of an element of risk was "blindingly obvious" as such risks are inherent in a decision to proceed by way of a hostile bid. He stated that the board of PMH was a sophisticated board with a high degree of business acumen and it could be expected to have anticipated this risk.

(b) Irish Developments

10–45   The Irish courts have adopted a slightly different approach to the imposition of a duty of care than their UK counterparts. The "neighbour test" which has been applied by the Irish courts is based on the *Anns* case rather than on the *Caparo* case. In *Ward v. McMaster*,[70] the Supreme Court affirmed the *Anns* test viewing it as "a confirmation of the long established principles of the law of tort contained in *Donoghue v. Stevenson*".[71] Consequently, the Irish Courts tend to approach cases of negligence by asking:

 (i) whether a relationship of proximity exists between the parties;

 (ii) if so, whether the relationship was such that in the reasonable contemplation of the defendant, carelessness on his or her part would be likely to cause damage to the plaintiff; and

(iii) if these questions are answered affirmatively, are there any considerations which ought to negative or reduce the scope of the common law duty of care.

---

[69]   unreported, Chancery Division, Rimer J., 10 February, 1995.
[70]   [1988] I.R. 337.
[71]   Per Costello J. in *HMW (nee F) v. Ireland* unreported, High Court, Costello J. , April 14, 1997 at p. 17.

10–46 The *Hedley Byrne* principle was accepted by the High Court in *Securities Trust Ltd v. Hugh Moore & Alexander Ltd.*[72] In that case, an action for negligent misstatement was based on a printing error in the articles of association of the defendant company which were sent out to the plaintiff shareholder. The Court held that it could not have been intended that the defendant company owed a duty to the world at large to take care to avoid mistakes and printing errors in their reprints. Similarly, in *McSweeney v. Bourke*,[73] a financial consultant who advised a group of companies in financial difficulties on methods of raising finance was sued by the plaintiffs who were majority shareholders in the group. Their action failed, as the duty of care was deemed to be owed to the client rather than to the third party. Although the courts have accepted that auditors can owe a duty both to the shareholders of the audited company and to prospective investors, the foreseeability of the auditors must be very immediate.[74] In *Kelly v. Haughey, Boland & Co.*,[75] Lardner J. discussed whether the defendants knew or should have reasonably foreseen at the time the accounts were audited that a person might rely on those accounts for the purposes of deciding whether or not to take over the company and therefore could suffer loss if the accounts were inaccurate. In the circumstances, no liability was found.

10–47 Three recent cases merit attention. In *Doolan v. Murray & Others*,[76] Keane J. approved the dictum of Lord Denning M.R. in the *Esso Petroleum Company* case quoted above. In the *Doolan* case, a one-time owner of property who had created a right of way over that property was held liable to a subsequent owner for negligent misrepresentation. The case in *O'Donnell & Co. Ltd. v. Truck & Machinery Sales Ltd.*,[77] was arguably more clear cut. An experienced dealer of earth moving equipment was held liable to a purchaser in relation to inaccurate misrepresentation made with a view to inducing sales. In *Doran v. Delaney*,[78] the Supreme Court held that while the primary duty of a solicitor acting for the vendor in a contract for the sale of property is to protect his or her own client, that obligation is perfectly consistent with the existence of a duty of care in certain circumstances to the purchaser. The Court based its decision on the *Hedley Byrne* principle. Interestingly, it then went on to note, however, that the transmission of inaccurate information by a solicitor to a third party and the subsequent reliance by the third party

---

[72] [1964] I.R. 417.
[73] unreported, High Court, Carroll J. Nov 24th, 1980.
[74] McMahon and Binchy, *Irish Law of Torts* (2nd ed., Butterworths, 1990), 152.
[75] [1989] I.L.R.M. 373.
[76] unreported, High Court, December 21, 1993.
[77] unreported, High Court, Moriarty J., June 7, 1996.
[78] [1998] 2 I.L.R.M. 1.

does not of itself, afford a cause of action in negligence to the injured party. Other necessary factors to give rise to liability were stated to be the four factors set out in *Midland Bank plc v. Cameron, Tong, Peterkin and Duncans*[79] to the effect that:

(1) the solicitor must assume responsibility for the advice or information furnished;

(2) the solicitor must let it be known to the third party expressly or impliedly that he claims, to have the requisite skill or knowledge to give the advice or furnish the information;

(3) the third party must have relied on that information as a matter for which the solicitor has assumed personal responsibility; and

(4) the solicitor must have been aware that the third party was likely to rely.

The idea of a personal assumption of responsibility is clearly an onerous burden to prove.

(3) Deceit

10–48 A professional adviser may be liable for the tort of deceit if he or she makes a false statement of fact. In *Derry v. Peek*,[80] the directors of a company issued a prospectus intimating that they could use steam/mechanical power for their trams. The Board of Trade refused to allow them permission to do so. The Court held that no action in deceit lay as the directors held an honest belief that their statements were true. Lord Herschell stated:

> "First, in order to sustain an action of deceit, there must be proof of fraud, and nothing short of that will suffice. Secondly, fraud is proved when it is shown that a false representation has been made [1] knowingly, or [2] without belief in its truth, or [3] recklessly, careless whether it be true or false . . . [but there may be cases where] the fact that an alleged belief was destitute of all reasonable foundation would suffice of itself to convince the court that it was not really entertained." [81]

It is important to note that the recklessness referred to by Lord Herschell in *Derry v. Peek* cannot be divorced from "the heart of the tort of deceit".[82] Lord Herschell himself stated:

---

[79] 1988 SLT 611.
[80] [1889] 14 A.C. 337
[81] At 375–376. This principle was accepted by the Irish Court of Appeal in *Delany v. Keogh* [1905] 2 I.R. 267.
[82] *Witter Ltd. v. TBP Industries* [1996] 2 All E.R. 573 at 587 *per* Jacob J.

"... there always has to be present, and regarded as an essential element, that the deception was wilful either because the untrue statement was known to be untrue, or because belief in it was asserted without such belief existing ... I cannot assent to the doctrine that a false statement made through carelessness and which ought to have been known to be untrue, of itself renders the person who makes it liable to an action for deceit".[83]

10–49 Damages cannot thus be claimed on the basis of recklessness alone. In *Witter Ltd. v. TBP Industries*,[84] the purchasers of a company were deemed to have been negligent rather than dishonest in not disclosing to the purchasers that the management accounts submitted contained deferred expenditure and also in stating that the accounts contained a once-off expense of £120,000 when they had obtained only a rough estimate of that expense.

10–50 The distinguishing line between recklessness and dishonesty may, however, in certain circumstances be a fine one. In *Arkerheilm v. De Mare*,[85] the Privy Council held that:

"the meaning placed by the defendant on the representation made, may be so far removed from the sense in which it would be understood by any reasonable person as to make it impossible to hold that the defendant honestly understood the representation to bear the meaning claimed by him."

In making the representation the defendant must have intended the representee to have acted upon it. Thus in *Peek v. Gurney*,[86] a person who, in reliance on statements made in a company prospectus, bought shares in the market could not sue the directors as the prospectus is not normally designed to induce persons to buy shares on the market but rather to encourage persons to apply to and buy from the company itself.

(4) Limitations on Liability

10–51 In order to avoid liability, the adviser will seek to include an exemption clause in the contract of appointment, exempting the adviser from any liability incurred as a result of its breach. Alternatively, an attempt may be made to limit or define the circumstances in which the adviser will be liable.

(a) Common Law

10–52 In order to exempt liability under the law of contract, the exemption clause must be incorporated into the contract and it must as

---

[83] At 369.
[84] [1996] 2 All E.R. 573
[85] [1959] A.C. 789 at 805. See also *Angus v. Clifford* [1891] 2 Ch. 449.
[86] (1873) LR 6 (H.L.) 377.

a matter of construction cover the event which has occurred. Generally, in commercial contracts, an exemption clause will be incorporated by the parties signing a contract. In such a case, the clause will be binding despite the fact that the plaintiff may not have read it or comprehended its meaning.[87] Exemption clauses may also be incorporated by giving reasonable notice[88] or by a course of dealing.[89] Depending on the nature of the risk being displaced, however, the clause may need to be brought specifically to the attention of the other party. For example, in *Thornton v. Shoe Lane Parking,*[90] Lord Denning stated that certain exemption clauses are so wide and so destructive of rights that they should only be binding if brought to the other party's notice in an explicit way. Similarly, in *Western Meats Ltd. v. National Ice and Cold Storage Co Ltd.*[91] Barrington J. stated:

> "It appears to me that a businessman, offering a specialist service, but accepting no responsibility for it, must bring home clearly to the party dealing with him that he accepts no such responsibility".

10–53 Liability in negligence may be excluded by an express clause in the contract clearly exempting liability from negligence. In addition, a general clause broad enough to include liability for negligence will suffice "if the logic of the clause and contract otherwise compels such a construction".[92] This will be the case, *e.g.* where negligence is the only possible head of damage in respect of which the exemption clause could apply.[93] In *Regan v. Irish Automobile Club Ltd.,*[94] a clause exempting the RIAC from "liability arising out of accidents howsoever caused" was deemed sufficiently clear to exempt them from liability for negligence. Where the breach of warranty amounts to a fundamental breach of contract (i.e. a breach which goes to the root of a contract), whether the clause is applicable or not depends on the true construction of the contract.[95]

---

[87] *L'Estrange v. Graucob* [1934] 2 K.B. 394, *Slattery v. CIE* 106 I.L.T.R. 71. Exceptions will be allowed in rare circumstances however where the signature was given as a result of fraud, misrepresentation or mistake or where the defence of *non est factum* is available.

[88] *Parker v. S.E. Railway* (1877) 2 C.P.D. 416, *Ryan v. Great Southern & Western Railway* 32 I.L.T.R. 108.

[89] *Spurling v. Bradshaw* [1956] 1 W.L.R. 461.

[90] [1971] 2 Q.B. 163. See also *Interfoto Picture Library Ltd. v. Stiletto Visual Productions Ltd.* [1989] Q.B. 433.

[91] [1982] I.L.R.M. 99 at 102.

[92] *Deepak Fertilisers and Petrochemicals Corporation v. ICI Chemicals & Polymers Ltd.* [1998] 2 Lloyds Law Reports 139 *per* Rix J at 159.

[93] *Canada Steamship Lines Ltd. v. The King* [1952] A.C. 192, *Hollier v. Rambler Motors (AMC) Ltd.* [1972] 1 All E.R. 399, *Deepak Fertilisers and Petrochemicals Corporation v. ICI Chemicals & Polymers Ltd. op. cit.,* n.92.

[94] [1990] 1 I.R. 278.

[95] *Suisse Atlantique Societe d'Armement Maritime S.A. v. N.V. Rotterdamsche Kolen Centrale* [1967] 1 A.C. 361, *Photo Production Ltd. v. Securicor transport Ltd.* [1980] 2 W.L.R. 283. *Clayton Love v. B&I Transport* (1970) 104 I.L.T.R. 157

(b) Section 40 of the Sale of Goods Act 1980

10–54   Section 40 of Sale of Goods and Supply of Services Act 1980 allows any term implied into a contract pursuant to section 39 to be negatived or varied by an express term of the contract or by a course of dealing between the parties or by usage. However, where the recipient of the service deals as a consumer, the exemption or variation term must be shown to be fair and reasonable and it must have been brought specifically to his attention. A party to a contract deals as consumer in relation to another party if:

(a)   he neither makes the contract in the course of a business nor holds himself out as doing so; and

(b)   the other party does make the contract in the course of a business; and

(c)   the goods or services supplied under or in pursuance of the contract are of a type ordinarily supplied for private use or consumption.[96]

In *O'Callaghan v. Hamilton Leasing (Ireland) Ltd.*,[97] the owner of a takeaway outlet who leased a drinks vending machine for use in his outlet was deemed not to have acted as a consumer because the machine was provided for his business use. Clark has pointed out that the appellate courts in the UK have tended to find that a degree of regularity in dealing is necessary before a buyer looses the status of a consumer.[98] In the case of an acquisition by a company of the assets of a business, this would obviously be an important distinction as the transaction would generally be a once-off transaction and yet the company would be purchasing the assets for business use.

10–55   In determining whether a term is fair and reasonable, "the test is that it shall be a fair and reasonable one to be included having regard to the circumstances which were, or ought reasonably to have been, known to or in contemplation of the parties when the contract was made".[99] Matters which will be taken into account in making this decision include:

(a)   the relative strength of the bargaining positions of the parties;

(b)   whether the customer received an inducement to agree to the term, or in accepting it had an opportunity of entering into a similar contract with other persons, but without having to accept a similar term;

---

[96] s.3(1).
[97] [1984] I.L.R.M. 146.
[98] Clark, *Contract Law in Ireland* (Roundhall Sweet & Maxwell, 1998), p. 182.
[99] Schedule to the Sale of Goods and Supply of Services Act 1980.

(c)   whether the customer knew or ought reasonably to have known of the existence and extent of the term having regard among other things, to any custom of the trade and any previous course of dealing between the parties;

(d)   where the term excludes or restricts any relevant liability if some condition is not complied with, whether it was reasonable at the time of the contract to expect that compliance with the condition would be practicable; and

(e)   whether any goods involved were manufactured, processed or adapted to the customer's special order.

(c) Unfair Terms Regulations

10–56   Exemption clauses will be subject to the test of reasonableness under the European Communities (Unfair Terms in Consumer Contracts) Regulations 1995[100] where the plaintiff is defined as a consumer under the Regulations. A consumer is defined as "a natural person who is acting for purposes which are outside his business." These Regulations do not apply, however, where the term has been individually negotiated.[101] They only apply where the contract has been drafted in advance and the consumer has been unable to exert any influence on its content. A contractual term is regarded as unfair for the purpose of the Regulations

> "if, contrary to the requirement of good faith, it causes a significant imbalance in the parties' rights and obligations under the contract to the detriment of the consumer, taking into account the nature of the goods or services for which the contract was concluded and all circumstances attending the conclusion of the contract and all other terms of the contract or of another contract on which it is dependant."[102]

Schedule 2 to the Regulations sets out certain non-exhaustive guidelines for the application of the good faith test. It states that particular regard should be had to:

> "– the strength of the bargaining positions of the parties;
> – whether the consumer had an inducement to agree to the term;
> – whether the goods or services were sold or supplied to the special order of the consumer; and
> – the extent to which the seller or supplier has dealt fairly and equitably with the consumer whose legitimate interests he has to take into account."

Examples of unfair terms are given in Schedule 3 and include exemption clauses for total or partial non-performance and terms allowing the

---

[100]   S.I. No. 27 of 1995.
[101]   Art. 3(1).
[102]   Art. 3(2).

vendor unilaterally alter the terms of the contract without a specified reason.[102a]

(d) Contributory Negligence

10–57 Contributory negligence may also be used as a defence to an action for negligence.[103] If the defendant succeeds in proving that the plaintiff was partially at fault, the quantum of damages awarded may be reduced accordingly. This common law approach was put on statutory footing with the enactment of the Civil Liability Act 1961. Section 34(1)(b) of the Act states that if contributory negligence is proven, "the damages recoverable in respect of the said wrong shall be reduced by such amount as the court thinks just and equitable having regard to the degrees of fault of the plaintiff and defendant". Where it is not possible to establish different degrees of fault, liability will be apportioned equally. Another defence to an action for negligence is the voluntary assumption of risk. This common law position has been altered by section 34(1) of the Civil Liability Act 1961 which allows a more equitable defence argument. A defence may now be entered that "the plaintiff, before the act complained of, agreed to waive his legal rights in respect of it".

(e) Section 200 of the Companies Act 1963

10–58 Section 200 of the Companies Act 1963 renders void any provision in the articles of a company or in any contract with a company or otherwise which exempts an officer of the company, an auditor employed by the company from any liability or which indemnifies them against any liability which by virtue of any rule of law would otherwise attach in respect of any negligence, default, breach of duty or breach of trust of which he or she might be guilty in relation to the company.[104] Although directors may avoid this through use of an appropriate article of association defining their duties to the company, an auditor, whose duties are fixed by statute may not.[105] Section 391(1) of the Companies Act 1963 provides some degree of defence, however. It provides that if in any proceedings for negligence, default, breach of duty or breach of trust against an officer of the company or an auditor "employed by the company as auditor", the court believes that the officer or auditor has "acted honestly and reasonably, and that having regard to all the circum-

---

[102a] In *AEG (UK) Ltd. v. Logic Resource Ltd.* [1995] CCH Commercial Law Reports 265, the majority of the Court of Appeal invoked the common law to strike out a clause in a sale of goods contract as unreasonable. The clause provided that the purchaser should return any defective parts at his own expense.

[103] See generally, McMahon and Binchy, *Irish Law of Torts* (Butterworths, 1990), Chap. 20.

[104] Exceptions are provided in paragraphs (a) and (b) of section 200.

[105] See Ussher, *Company Law in Ireland* (Sweet & Maxwell, 1985) p. 238.

stances of the case, including those connected with his appointment, he ought fairly to be excused", the court may relieve him, either wholly or partly from his liability on such terms as the court deems fit. One difficulty, however, in utilising this defence is that generally where negligence has been established, it will be hard to imagine circumstances in which the auditor could still maintain that he acted "reasonably".

(5) Chinese Walls

10–59 "Chinese walls" is the term given to the set of internal procedures designed to prevent confidential information obtained by persons in one part of a firm's operations being transmitted to persons in another part of the firm. The object of Chinese walls therefore is to restrict the flow of information. In their Consultation Paper on Fiduciary Duties and Regulatory Rules, the UK Law Commission[106] describes Chinese walls as:

> "normally involving some combination of the following organisational arrangements:
> (a) the physical separation of the various departments in order to insulate them from each other – this often extends to such matters of detail as dining arrangements;
> (b) an educational programme, normally recurring, to emphasis the importance of not improperly or inadvertently divulging confidential information;
> (c) strict and carefully defined procedures for dealing with a situation where it is felt that the wall should be crossed and the maintaining of proper records where this occurs;
> (d) monitoring by compliance officers of the effectiveness of the wall; and
> (e) disciplinary sanctions where there has been a breach of the wall."

In addition to the physical separation procedures referred to in paragraph (a) above, strategies such as the use of code names and password protected computer data can also help to maintain the confidentiality of information.

(a) Existence of Chinese Walls

10–60 Section 37 of the Investment Intermediaries Act 1995 obliges the Central Bank to design and issue a code of conduct for investment business firms, unless it is satisfied that the firm is one of a class regulated in this respect by an approved professional body or otherwise. Seven principles are set down as expressing basic standards of business conduct.[107] The sixth principle states that investment business firms

---

[106] (1992) (Law. Com. No. 124).
[107] These seven principles are repeated in article 11 of the Investment Services Directive. They are derived from the ten principles drawn up by the Securities and Investments Board in the UK in March 1990.

should make "a reasonable effort" to avoid conflicts of interest and when they cannot be avoided, firms should ensure that their clients are treated fairly. In June 1996, the Central Bank issued a Code of Conduct for Investment Business Firms. Rule 20 provides that:

> "Firms shall ensure that there are effective Chinese walls in place between the different business areas of the firm, and between the firm and its connected parties and that all procedures relating to the maintenance of Chinese walls are in writing and are notified to all employees of the firm."

Chinese walls are defined in the Code as:

> "an arrangement within the organisation of a firm, or between a firm and any associate of that firm, which requires information obtained by the firm or, as the case may be, an associate in the course of carrying on one part of its business of any kind to be withheld in certain circumstances from persons with whom it deals in the course of carrying on another part of its business of any kind".

The Central Bank's Code of Conduct for Investment Managers, published at the same time, contains, in Rule 19, a similar requirement for investment managers.

10–61 The Irish Association of Investment Managers Code of Best Practice on Insider Dealing also provides for Chinese walls. It states that:

> "all companies, stockbroking firms, advisers, corporate finance houses and institutional investors should have Chinese walls/written arrangements in place to ensure that (i) price sensitive information is not communicated, directly or indirectly, to individuals who should not be in receipt of such information and (ii) activities such as broking and investing can be carried out even if other individuals in the firm or group hold unpublished price sensitive information."[108]

10–62 Section 38 of the Stock Exchange Act 1995 obliges the Central Bank to design and issue a code of conduct for stock exchange member firms, unless the stock exchange has introduced its own code. The same seven principles set out in the Investment Intermediaries Act 1995 are set down in section 38 as expressing basic standards of business conduct. The Irish Stock Exchange has introduced in its Rules ten General Obligations in this respect. One of these obligations requires a member firm to:

> "make all reasonable efforts to avoid conflicts of interest and, when they cannot be avoided, ensures that its clients are fairly treated."

---

[108]   para. 2–4. July 1991.

Rule 4.24.1 of the Stock Exchange's Conduct of Business Rules deals specifically with Chinese walls. It states as follows:

> "Member firms shall ensure that there are effective Chinese walls in place between the different business areas of the member firm, and between the member firm and its connected parties where there is potential, in the absence of Chinese walls, for the spread of any unpublished information which might reasonably be expected to materially affect the price of an investment instrument throughout the member firm, and that all procedures relating to the maintenance of Chinese walls are in writing and are notified to all employees of the member firm."

(b) Section 108(7) of the Companies Act 1990

10–63 The existence and the effectiveness of Chinese walls was given statutory recognition by section 108(7) of the Companies Act 1990. Although companies are precluded under section 108(6) from dealing in any securities at a time when an officer of the company is precluded from dealing in those securities by the insider dealing provisions of that Act, an exception is provided in subsection (7). A company is not precluded from entering into a transaction at any time by reason only of information in the possession of an officer of the company if:

> "(a) the decision to enter into the transaction was taken on its behalf by a person other than that officer;
> (b) it had in operation at that time written arrangements to ensure that the information was not communicated to that person and that no advice relating to the transaction was given to him by a person in possession of the information; and
> (c) the information was not so communicated and such advice was not so given".

It seems clear thus that the presumption exists that where Chinese walls are in place, they will prevent information from passing.

(c) Common Law Approach

10–64 Despite this, the acceptance of Chinese walls by the courts has not been as unequivocal. The issue of Chinese walls generally arises in action for breach of confidence[109] or breach of fiduciary duties. In *Rakusen v. Ellis, Munday and Clarke*,[110] a small firm of solicitors operated with only two partners who carried on, what amounted to, separate practices, each with his own clients, without any knowledge of the other's clients and with the exclusive services of certain of the clerks. The plaintiff consulted one of the partners in this firm in relation to a

---

[109] See para. 14–20.
[110] [1912] 1 Ch. 831.

particular contentious matter. After the plaintiff had terminated this solicitor's retainer, the other partner, who had never met the plaintiff and was not aware that he had consulted his partner, was retained by the opposite party in the same matter. The trial judge granted an injunction to restrain the solicitor from acting in breach of confidence. The Court of Appeal however, found that there is no absolute bar on a solicitor acting in a case where one partner in a firm of solicitors has acted for one side and another partner in that firm wishes to act for the other side in litigation. It was stated that the court will only intervene to stop such a practice if it is satisfied that the continued acting of one partner in the firm against a former client of another partner is likely to cause real prejudice to the former client. Unfortunately, the test for disqualification was expressed in different terms by each of the three members of the Court. Sir H.H. Cozens-Hardy M.R. laid down the test as being that a court must be satisfied that "real mischief and real prejudice will, in all human probability, result if the solicitor is allowed to act".[110a] Fletcher-Moulton L.J. said that "as a general rule the court will not interfere unless there be a case where mischief is rightly anticipated."[111] Finally, Buckley L.J. said the court would interfere where" there exists, or, I will add, may exist, or may be reasonably anticipated to exist, a danger of a breach of that which is a duty, an enforceable duty, namely the duty not to communicate confidential information."[112]

10–65　In *David Lee & Co (Lincoln) Ltd. v. Coward Chance (a firm)*,[113] the Chinese walls operating within a firm were not as obvious as in the previous case. The liquidators of two companies brought actions against certain parties alleging a fraudulent breach of trust. During the preparation of this action, the firm of solicitors advising the liquidators and the firm of solicitors which had formerly acted in the actions for some of the principal defendants amalgamated. The liquidators wanted their solicitors to continue to act for them but the defendants objected on the basis that confidential information about their defence had been given to one or more of the partners in this new firm and that any leakage of the information would be highly damaging. The amalgamated firm offered undertakings to the court to keep separate and confidential the information relating to the separate cases. Referring to the *Rakusen* case, Sir Nicolas Browne-Wilkinson V-C in the High Court opined that the differing expressions of the tests were difficult to reconcile and that the preferred expression of the test in his mind was "whether mischief was rightly anticipated". He continued:

[110a] [1912] 1 Ch. 831 at 835.
[111]　*ibid.*, at 841.
[112]　*ibid.*, at 845.
[113]　[1991] Ch. 259.

> "When one has sensitive information in a firm or in any other group of people, there is an element of seepage of that information through casual chatter and discussion, the letting slip of some information which is not thought to be relevant but may make the link in a chain of causation or reasoning . . . I am afraid that on the information that I have I am not satisfied that the amalgamated firm has demonstrated that the Chinese walls that they are proposing to erect will be sound-proof. Experience in this court demonstrates that the maintenance of security on either side of Chinese walls in the context of the city does not always prove to be very easy."[113a]

Not being satisfied on the evidence submitted that there was no real risk of leakage of information in the amalgamated firm, the Court held that it would not be lawful for the amalgamated firm to continue to act for the liquidators.

10–66 In the Court of Appeal decision *Re a firm of Solicitors*,[114] it was proposed that a large law firm should act in commercial litigation for one party, although it possessed confidential information concerning the other party to the litigation which it had obtained from acting for a client which was independent of, but closely associated with that other party. Parker J. analysed the judgments in *Rakusen* and suggested :

> " . . . the proper approach is to consider whether a reasonable man informed of the facts might reasonably anticipate such a danger . . . If a reasonable man with knowledge of the facts would say "If I were in the position of the objector I would be concerned that, however unwittingly or innocently, information gained while the solicitor was acting for me, might be used against me," the court, in my judgment, can and should intervene."[114a]

Despite the firm's promise to erect Chinese walls, the Court decided that some confidential information might permeate the walls. Parker J. concluded by stating:

> "Save in a very special case such as *Rakusen's* I doubt very much whether an impregnable wall can ever be created".[114b]

10–67 The issue of Chinese walls was considered recently by the House of Lords in *Prince Jefri Bolkiah v. KPMG (A Firm)*.[115] This case involved a potential breach of confidentiality not by a solicitor but by an accountancy firm. An action for breach of confidence was brought by the plaintiff against KPMG, essentially seeking an order to restrain KPMG from acting for the Brunei Investment Agency ("the BIA"). The BIA held and

---

[113a] At 268 and 270.
[114] [1992] 1 Q.B. 959.
[114a] At 969.
[114b] At 971.
[115] [1999] 2 W.L.R. 215.

managed the General Reserve Fund and the external assets of the Government of Brunei and, for many years, operated under the chairmanship of Prince Jefri. In addition to being auditors of the BIA, KPMG had been retained by one of Prince Jefri's companies over a period of 18 months between 1996 and 1998, to undertake a substantial investigation in connection with major litigation in which he was personally involved. The investigation, which was given the code name Project Lucy, was mainly conducted by KPMG's London forensic accounting department. This department provided extensive litigation support services. In the course of Project Lucy, KPMG was entrusted with or acquired extensive confidential information concerning Prince Jefri's assets and financial affairs. In June 1998, a governmental task force was appointed to investigate the activities of the BIA following Prince Jefri's departure. KPMG was appointed to assist the task force in carrying investigations into the destination of large sums of money which had been transferred out of the BIA's funds. This further assignment, which was given the code name Project Gemma, was again carried out by members of the forensic accounting department. It was accepted that as a result of this investigation, civil and even criminal proceedings might be initiated against Prince Jefri. Although, a number of the KPMG staff working on Project Gemma had previously been engaged on work for Project Lucy, KPMG contended that none of these persons were in possession of confidential information. Instructions were given by KPMG that Chinese walls should be put in place within the forensic accounting department, and special arrangements were established to protect the confidentiality of information in the possession of KPMG which related to Prince Jefri.

10–68   In the House of Lords, Lord Millett (with whom the other judges unanimously agreed) stated that where the court's intervention is sought by an existing client, the basis of the courts jurisdiction is the "inescapable conflict of interest" which is inherent in the situation. It was stated that a fiduciary cannot act at the same time both for and against the same client unless the client consents. However, this consent may on occasion be inferred. His lordship gave as an example a large accountancy firm whose audit clients are publicly identified. In such cases, clients are taken to consent to their auditors acting for competing clients, although the auditors must maintain the confidentiality of the information obtained from their clients. In the case of an application by a former client however, the position is different and the court's jurisdiction is based on the continuing duty to preserve the confidentiality of information imparted during its subsistence. Lord Millett stated:

> "[T]he duty to preserve confidentiality is unqualified. It is a duty to keep the information confidential, not merely to take all reasonable steps to do so . . . The former client cannot be protected completely from accidental or

inadvertent disclosure. But he is entitled to prevent his former solicitor from exposing him to any avoidable risk."[115a]

The degree of risk accepted by the court in the *Rakusen's* case, *i.e.* "a reasonable probability of real mischief", was rejected by Lord Millett as imposing an unfair burden on the former client. Instead, Lord Millett suggested that a court should intervene unless it is satisfied that there is no risk of disclosure. Whilst his Lordship qualified this by stating that that risk must be a real risk and not merely fanciful or theoretical, he stated that the risk did not need to be substantial.[116] Thus, once the former client has established that the defendant firm is in possession of information which was imparted in confidence and that the firm is proposing to act for another party with an interest adverse to his in a matter to which the information is or may be relevant, the evidential burden shifts to the defendant firm to show that despite this there is no risk that the information will come into the possession of those now acting for the other party. Lord Millett stated:

> "Even in the financial services industry, good practice requires there to be established institutional arrangements designed to prevent the flow of information between separate departments. Where effective arrangements are in place, they produce a modern equivalent of the circumstances which prevailed in *Rakusen's* case. The Chinese Walls which feature in the present case, however, were established ad hoc and were erected within a single department."[117]

Lord Millett declared himself unsatisfied thus that on the evidence that KPMG had discharged the heavy burden of showing that there was no risk that the relevant confidential information in their possession might unwittingly or inadvertently come to the notice of those working on Project Gemma. This case indicates the very onerous burden of proof imposed by the courts on financial or legal service providers.

10–69 The most recent case to consider this issue is *Young and Others v Robson Rhodes (A Firm) and Another*.[117a] In this case, two accountancy partnerships, Robson Rhodes ("RR") and Pannell Kerr Foster ("PKF"), announced their intention to merge. Members of RR had been retained as experts on behalf of the plaintiffs who were engaged in major litigation against PKF. The plaintiffs sought an injunction to enjoin the merger until after the trial of their actions against PKF and also sued RR for breach of confidence. In the latter claim, the plaintiffs sought to rely on the *Prince Jefri* case on the basis that members of RR possessed

---

[115a] [1999] 2 W.L.R. 215 at 225.
[116] Lord Millett referred approvingly of the test formulated by Lightman J. in *Re a Firm of Solicitors* [1997] Ch. 1 and adopted by Pumfrey J., the trial judge in this case.
[117] At 228.
[117a] Unreported decision of Laddie J., Chancery Division, *The Times* May 11, 1999.

crucial information relating to the action against PKF and should not thus subject the plaintiff to the risk of any of the information leaking to PKF. In response to RR's undertaking to the plaintiffs to set up Chinese walls within the newly merged group, the plaintiffs argued that this was insufficient and referred to the following passage from Lord Millett's judgment in the *Prince Jefri* case:

> "In my opinion an effective Chinese wall needs to be an established part of the organisational structure of the firm, not created ad hoc and dependant on the acceptance of evidence sworn for the purpose by members of staff engaged on the relevant work".

Laddie J. disagreed with this interpretation of the case and stated:

> "As I understand the *Prince Jefri* case, the court must ensure that there is no additional risk to the client. It must be satisfied that barriers are in place which are effective to prevent disclosure of confidential information. The crucial question is 'will the barriers work?' If they do, it does not matter whether they were created before the problem arose or are erected after-wards. It seems to me that all Lord Millett was saying was that Chinese walls which have become part of the fabric of the institution are more likely to work than those artificially put in place to meet a one-off problem."

Laddie J. stated that the plaintiffs were at risk of inadvertant leakage of confidential information if relevant members of the RR firm worked alongside or were in regular professional contact with members of PKF connected with the action. However, undertakings were accepted by the court from RR and PKF as to: the non-disclosure by RR of infor-mation relating to the litigation, the physical separation of the working places of the relevant members of RR and employees of PKF working on the litigation, the removal of all RR's relevant documents to their solicitor's office and the deletion by RR of all relevant electronic information, save for one copy on discs to be held by their solicitor. In these circumstances, Laddie J. refused the application for an injunction on the basis that it would inflict unwarranted harm on both RR and PKF and would be of no legitimate benefit to the plaintiffs.

10–70   In practice, the offeror and offeree in takeover situations are unlikely to question whether confidential information is being passed to other parties by their own advisers. They are free to choose their own advisers. Dissenting shareholders might perhaps argue that the existence of conflicts of interest has sullied the takeover process in some way. It is more likely, however, to be the regulators who will be anxious to ensure that confidential price-sensitive information does not pass between different operations within the same firm or that different operations are not deemed to be acting together for the purpose of aggregating or disclosing dealings.

CHAPTER 11

ACQUISITION OF THE SHARES OF THE PUBLIC COMPANY

11–01   A number of options are available to an offeror who wishes to acquire control of a public company through the acquisition of its shares. Where the offeree is a "relevant company" for the purposes of the Irish Takeover Panel Act 1997,[1] the Irish Takeover Panel Act 1997 (Takeover) Rules 1997 ("the Takeover Rules") will play an important part in regulating the acquisition. An offer may be made directly to all the offeree's shareholders to acquire all or part of their shareholding in the offeree. Alternatively, an offer may be made to the controlling shareholders only to acquire their shares. Instead of approaching shareholders directly, the offeror may decide to have its broker or agent acquire the shares on the Stock Exchange. Less direct methods of acquiring control available to the offeror would include organising for the offeree to issue sufficient of its shares to the offeror to give it effective control or organising to have the offeree's shares transferred to the offeror under a section 201 arrangement. A final means of acquiring control to be considered in this Chapter is a reverse takeover.

A. A Takeover Offer to the Shareholders
of the Offeree

11–02   One of the most common methods of acquiring control of a company is through the making of a successful general offer to all of the offeree's shareholders to acquire all their shares in return for a specified consideration. A partial offer, by contrast, is an offer to acquire merely a portion of shares in the offeree. Under the rules, partial offers must be made to all shareholders. Special rules govern partial offers because they may lead to the isolation of existing shareholders in circumstances where the offeror acquires a controlling interest without giving minority shareholders the opportunity to accept the offer in respect of all their shares.

---

[1]   para. 3–18.

I. AN OFFER FOR ALL THE OFFEREE'S SHARES

11–03   The actual decision to make an offer to acquire the offeree may be made by the directors of the offeror alone without recourse to their shareholders.[2] However, shareholder approval may be required under the Stock Exchange Listing Rules if either the offeree or offeror is a listed company and the transaction is classified as a Class 1 Transaction or a Transaction with Related Parties.[3]

(1) Compulsory Acquisition of Shares – Section 204

11–04   An offer to acquire all the equity shares of the offeree is normally made conditional upon its acceptance, by a specified date, by the holders of at least 80 per cent in value of the shares. Acceptance by this percentage allows the offeror to compulsorily acquire the remaining shares under section 204 of the Companies Act 1963 ("the 1963 Act"). If the offeror does not signal its intention to acquire the remaining shares, the remaining shareholders may demand to be bought out. The advantage of this section from the shareholder's perspective is that it prevents oppression of the minority by the majority. From the offeror's perspective it has a positive effect in that it allows the entire shareholding to be acquired in circumstances where it may not be possible to trace a small number of shareholders or where a small number of shareholders are apathetic.

Section 204(1) states that:

> "Subject to subsection (2), where a scheme contract or offer involving the acquisition by one company, whether a company within the meaning of this Act or not (in this section referred to as "the transferee company") of the beneficial ownership of all the shares (other than shares already in the beneficial ownership of the transferee company) in the capital of another company, being a company within the meaning of this Act (in this section referred to as "the transferor company") has become binding or been approved or accepted in respect of not less than four-fifth in value of the shares affected not later than the date 4 months after publication generally to the holders of the shares affected of the terms of such scheme, contract or offer, the transferee company may at any time before the expiration of the period of 6 months next following such publication give notice in the prescribed manner to any dissenting shareholder that it desires to acquire the beneficial ownership of his shares, and when such notice is given the transferee company shall, unless on an application made by the dissenting shareholder within one month from the date on which the notice was given, the court thinks fit to order otherwise, be entitled and bound to acquire the

---

[2]   See Chap. 8, paras 8–03–8–06.
[3]   See Chap. 8, paras 5–37–5–47.

beneficial ownership of those shares on the terms on which under the scheme, contract or offer, the beneficial ownership of the shares in respect of which the scheme, contract or offer has become binding or been approved or accepted is to be acquired by the transferee company."

(a) Level of Shareholder Approval

11–05 Section 204(1) provides that where at least 80 per cent in value of offeree shareholders accept a general offer by the offeror to acquire the beneficial ownership of all its shares, the offeror is entitled to expropriate the remaining 20 per cent or less on the same terms as the other offeree shareholders received. There are two important pre-requisites to the operation of the section 204 compulsory purchase machinery. Firstly, the offer must be made to all the shareholders to acquire all the shares of the company. It is not available to partial offers. Secondly, the 80 per cent threshold must be reached within four months of the publication of the terms of the offer. In calculating this 80 per cent, shares already in the beneficial ownership of the offeror prior to the offer period are ignored.

11–06 Section 204(2) provides that if at the date the terms of the offer are published, the offeror (or transferee company) is the beneficial owner of shares in the offeree (or transferor company) to a value greater than 20 per cent of the aggregate value of those shares and the shares affected, section 204(1) will not apply unless the assenting shareholders, as well as holding not less than 80 per cent in value of the shares affected, constitute not less than 75 per cent in number of the holders of those shares. In order to ensure equality of treatment of different classes of shareholders, where the offer is being made for a particular class or classes of shares, these requirements will apply to each class in question.[4]

(b) Procedure for Buying Out the Offeree's Shareholders

11–07 Within six months of the publication of the offer, section 204(1) allows the offeror to give notice to dissenting shareholders that it wishes to acquire the remaining shares.[5] Provision is made for a dissenting shareholder to apply to the court to prevent the acquisition of the remaining shares. Such an application must be made, however, within one month of the date on which notice was given. Unless the court, upon the application of a dissenting shareholder, orders otherwise,

---

[4] Companies Act 1963, s.204(11).
[5] If an offer is extended, the 6 month period will probably commence on the date of the original offer, but if the offer is revised, the 6 month period could technically start again from the date of the "new offer".

the offeror becomes bound and entitled to acquire the outstanding shares. Section 204(5) provides that if the offeror gives notice of its' intention to acquire the remaining shares and the court has not, on the application of a dissenting shareholder, ordered otherwise, the offeror must transmit to the offeree a copy of the notice together with an instrument of transfer of the shares of the dissenting shareholders. The transferee must transmit these documents on the expiration of one month from the date the notice was given. If an application by a dissenting shareholder to the court is pending at this time, the documents must be transmitted after the application has been disposed of by the court.

11–08   The instrument of transfer of the shares of the dissenting shareholder should be executed on behalf of that shareholder, as transferor, by any person appointed to the transferee and by the transferee (being either the transferee company, a subsidiary of the transferee or a nominee of either).[6] The transferee must also pay to or vest in the transferor the consideration payable by the transferee for the shares being acquired. The transferor is then required to register the person who executed the instrument as the transferee as the holder of those shares.[7] The transferor must pay these sums into a separate bank account to be held on trust for the persons entitled to the outstanding shares.[8] Where shares in the transferee are issued as consideration, the transferor company cannot exercise any voting rights conferred by those shares unless instructed to do so by the shareholders in respect of whom the shares were issued.[9]

(c) The Consideration

11–09   Section 204(1) provides that the dissenting shareholders are entitled to sell their shares on the same terms as their fellow shareholders received. Section 204(10) provides that if the original offer allowed assenting shareholders to elect between two or more sets of terms for the acquisition, this same choice must be available to dissenting shareholders, and details of the terms must be sent to them in a notice. The notice must also state which set of terms will be given to shareholders who do not indicate a choice within 14 days from the date of the giving of the notice. This requirement to offer the same consideration may place

---

[6]   An instrument of transfer is not required for any share for which a share warrant is, for the time being, outstanding.
[7]   Companies Act 1963, s.204(5).
[8]   *ibid.*, s.204(6).
[9]   *ibid.*, s.204(7).

a heavy burden on the offeror where for example it may have to keep a cash offer open for this extended period of time.

(d) Court Intervention

11–10   As noted above, section 204(1) allows a dissenting shareholder to apply to the court upon notification of an intention to expropriate his or her shares, and the court if it thinks fit may order otherwise.

11–11   Where the entire transaction is at arms length the burden of proving that the acquisition should not be allowed rests on the dissenting shareholder. Since at least 80 per cent of shareholders will have already deemed the offer acceptable, this will be a difficult burden to overcome. In *Re Grierson, Oldham and Adams Ltd.*,[10] Plowman J. said that it is not enough to show that the scheme is "open to criticism" or is "capable of improvement". In *Re Sussex Brick*,[11] Vaisey J. said that the courts would only interfere if the scheme was "obviously unfair, patently unfair, unfair to the meanest intelligence". In the past, the courts have taken into account the number of shareholders dissenting, the proportion of shares held by such shareholders, the views of the directors and any independent advisers, whether the offer represented a premium on market prices, the views of the creditors and the fact that the offer has been accepted by the majority of other shareholders.[12]

11–12   The situation is likely to be reversed however, if the transaction is not at arms length. In *Re Bugle Press*,[13] two controlling shareholders attempted to oust a third shareholder by forming a bidding company, and making an offer. The offer was accepted as 90 per cent of the acceptances came from the controlling shareholders themselves. The court said this was a "barefaced attempt to expel" the third shareholder. It would thus appear that if the offeror and the shareholders are in economic fact the same, mere proof of this fact may constitute a prima facie case for the court to allow the application by the dissenting shareholders. At the very least, it would place on onus of proving that the transaction was fair on the directors of the offeror.

(e) Right of the Dissenting Shareholders to be Bought Out

11–13   Having acquired 80 per cent or more of the share capital of the offeree, the offeror may decide not to acquire the remaining shares. This

---

[10]   [1968] Ch. 17.
[11]   [1961] Ch. 289.
[12]   *Gower's Principles of Modern Company Law* (1997, Sweet & Maxwell) pp. 811–812; Ussher, *Company Law in Ireland* (1986, Sweet & Maxwell) pp. 297–301; Forde, *Company Law* (1992, The Mercier Press) pp. 413–415.
[13]   [1961] Ch. 270.

is particularly likely, where only a very small minority remain. In such circumstances, section 204(4) entitles the minority shareholders to demand to be bought out. This subsection requires the offeror who has acquired 80 per cent of all the shares in the offeree to notify all shareholders in the offeree which have not accepted the offer of this fact within one month of the date of acquisition. A dissenting shareholder has three months from the giving of this notice to insist on being bought out. Where a shareholder makes such a request, the offeror is entitled to and obliged to acquire the beneficial ownership of those shares.

The terms which will apply are the original terms offered to the assenting shareholders, or alternatively, such other terms as may be agreed, or as the court on the application either of the offeror or a shareholder thinks fit to order. Thus, it is clear that some element of discretion exists here which may alleviate the financial burden otherwise imposed on the offeror.

(2) Minimum Acceptance Condition – Rule 10

11–14 As noted above, where an offeror makes an offer to acquire all the shares in the offeree, the offer is normally made conditional upon its acceptance by a specified date by the holders of at least 80 per cent in value of the shares. However, the offeror will normally reserve the right to declare the offer "unconditional as to acceptances"[14] notwithstanding that acceptances may relate to a lower percentage of shares than originally sought. There is, however, a minimum level above which acceptances must be received in order to fulfil the acceptance condition.

11–15 Rule 10 of the Takeover Rules requires certain voluntary bids to contain a minimum acceptance condition, unless the Irish Takeover Panel ("the Panel") consents otherwise. This rule only relates to a voluntary offer for equity share capital conferring voting rights, which, if accepted in full, could result in the offeror holding securities conferring more than 50 per cent of the voting rights in the offeree. It must be a condition of any such offer, that the offer will not become or be declared unconditional as to acceptances unless the offeror has acquired or agreed to acquire shares[15] conferring:

---

[14] "Declaring" an offer "unconditional as to acceptances" means signifying that all conditions in respect of acceptances are deemed fulfilled. By contrast, an offer "becomes" unconditional as to acceptances, when all the conditions have actually been fulfilled.

[15] Either pursuant to the offer or not.

(a) more than 50 per cent of the voting rights in the offeree conferred by the equity share capital alone; and

(b) more than 50 per cent of the voting rights in the offeree conferred by the equity share capital and the non-equity share capital combined.

In certain exceptional cases, subject to prior consultation and appropriate safeguards, the Panel may consider waiving this requirement. Such a waiver may be available where the offeree would not be controlled by any one person following maximum potential acceptance of the offer, unless such a person or a concert party held the interest prior to the offer. This will usually only be the case where the offer is made on behalf of a group of investors not otherwise connected with each other who are not acting in concert with each other or with offeree shareholders. Such an exceptional case might arise for example where, following a major change of management policy, it becomes desirable to give shareholders an opportunity of disposing of their shares in circumstances where the offer is made on behalf of a group of unconnected investors whose purpose is not to gain control.[16] Rules 10.3 and 10.4 set out the circumstances in which an acceptance of an offer and a purchase of shares by an offeror or its nominee may be counted towards fulfilling an acceptance condition of the offer. Rule 10.5 then sets out the acceptances and purchases which may be counted in determining whether an acceptance condition of an offer has been satisfied prior to the final closing date. An offer cannot become or be declared unconditional as to acceptances until the offeror's receiving agent has issued a certificate to the offeror or its financial adviser stating the number of acceptances that have been received which comply with Rule 10.3 and the number of shares acquired which comply with Rule 10.4, and, in each case, if appropriate, Rule 10.5. Copies of this certificate must be sent to the Panel and to the offeree's financial adviser as soon as possible after it is issued.[16a]

(3) Other Terms of the Offer

11–16 Rule 12 of the Takeover Rules deals with offers which constitute proposed mergers or takeovers to which the Mergers, Takeovers & Monopolies (Control) Act 1978[17] ("the 1978 Act") applies by virtue of section 2 of that Act.[18] Voluntary offers must be made subject to a

---

[16] Note on rule 10.1.
[16a] R. 10.6.
[17] As amended by the Competition Act 1991 and the Competition Amendment Act 1996.
[18] Chap. 6, paras 6–42–6–51.

condition which will be satisfied if the Minister for Enterprise, Trade and Employment ("the Minister") indicates that he or she has decided not to make an order under section 9 of the 1978 Act in relation to the proposed merger or takeover.[19] Furthermore, the offeror may elect to provide in the conditions of the offer that the condition may be satisfied either: if the Minister states in writing that he or she has made an order under section 9 prohibiting the proposed acquisition except on certain specified conditions; or if the relevant period under the 1978 Act elapses without the Minister making any order under section 9. In the former situation, the offeror may stipulate in the offer that the conditions set out by the Minister must be acceptable to the offeror.[20]

11–17 Similarly, if the offer could give rise to a concentration with a Community dimension under the European Merger Regulation[21], it must be a term of the offer that it will lapse if the European Commission initiates proceedings under Article 6(1)(c) of that Regulation or if the Commission refers the concentration to a competent authority of a Member State under Article 9(1) of that Regulation before the first closing date of the offer or the date when the offer becomes or is declared unconditional as to acceptances, whichever is the later.[22] In addition, the offeror may make the offer conditional on the European Commission deciding that there will be no such initiation of proceedings or referral and if the offeror chooses, it may stipulate that any terms to which such a decision is subject may be acceptable to it.[23] Following the lapse of an offer on an initiation of proceedings by the European Commission or a referral by the European Commission, it should be noted that General Principle 6 and Rule 21 prohibiting frustrating action except with the consent of the shareholders will continue to apply.[23a]

11–18 Except as permitted under Rule 12 or allowed by the Panel, offers should not be made subject to any condition the satisfaction of which depends solely on subjective judgments by the offeror's directors or conditions whose fulfilment is within the control of the directors.[24] Such conditions would allow directors absolute control to cause an offer to lapse at any stage before it has been accepted. It is noted however, that the Panel may be prepared to accept an element of

---

[19] R. 12(a)(ii).
[20] R. 12(a)(ii).
[21] Council Regulation 4064/89/EEC [((1989) O.J. L395/1)] as amended by Reg. 1310/97 [(1997) O.J. L180/1)]. See Chap. 6, para. 6–19–6–39.
[22] R. 12(b)(i).
[23] R. 12(b)(ii).
[23a] Note on R.12(b). See also R. 19.8 and Note 1 on R. 35.1.
[24] R. 13.

subjectivity, in certain special circumstances, where it is not practicable to specify all the factors on which satisfaction of a particular condition depends. This is particularly evident in cases involving official authorisations, the granting of which may be subject to additional material obligations for the offeror. Furthermore, in an announcement of an offer, it would normally be acceptable for the offer to be expressed as conditional on statements or estimates being appropriately verified.[25] The offeror is also advised against invoking any condition in order to cause the offer to lapse unless the circumstances which give rise to the right to revoke the condition are materially significant to the offeror in the context of the offer.[26]

11–19 Rule 16 prohibits special arrangements which could confer benefits on certain shareholders which are not available to other shareholders unless they are made with the consent of the Panel. The offeror and any concert parties are prohibited from making any arrangement with any shareholder or intending shareholder of the offeree which involves a dealing in, or acceptance of an offer for, or otherwise relates to, shares in the offeree, if there would be attached to such arrangement a term favourable to such shareholder or intending shareholder or any other person which is not being extended under the offer to all shareholders of the offeree. This prohibition applies during an offer period or when an offer is reasonably in contemplation. If special arrangements are entered into in breach of this rule, the Panel may direct the offeror or any concert party to make available to all acceptors of the offer such additional consideration as the Panel decides is "fair". The Panel may make a direction of this kind where it believes, having regard to the General Principles, that it is appropriate to do so. The purpose of this rule is to ensure that all shareholders of the same class are treated equally.

(4) Different Classes of Share Capital

11–20 Where an offer is made for any class of voting equity share capital, comparable offers should be made for each class of equity share capital unless the Panel agrees otherwise.[27] It should be noted, however, that a "comparable" offer need not necessarily be an identical offer. The method for assessing the comparability of offers is based on the value of the shares on the Stock Exchange.[28] This is the case irrespective of whether such capital carries voting rights or not. Furthermore, where

---

[25] Note 1 on R. 13.
[26] Note 2 on R. 13.
[27] R. 14.1.
[28] Note 1 to R. 14.

an offer is made for more than one class of shares the offeror must make separate offers for each such class.[29]

The obligation to make a comparable offer does not apply where an offer is made only for a class of shares which does not confer voting rights.[30] This is because the Panel is primarily concerned with monitoring the acquisition of voting control.

If an offer is made for equity share capital of a relevant company and the offeree has outstanding securities convertible into, or rights or options to subscribe for, shares of the class the subject of the offer, Rule 15 requires that an "Appropriate" offer must also be made to those security holders.

(5) Announcement of Acceptance Levels – Rule 17

11–21 The announcement of acceptance levels is strictly regulated. Rule 17.1 requires the offeror to make an announcement as to the total number of:

(i) shares in the offeree for which acceptances of the offer have been received;

(ii) securities of the offeree held before the offer period; and

(iii) securities of the offeree acquired or agreed to be acquired during the offer period.

This announcement should be made by 8.30 a.m. on the business day following the day on which: an offer is due to expire, an offer becomes or is declared unconditional as to acceptances, or an offer is revised or extended.

The consequences of failing to make such an announcement are significant. Rule 17.2 provides that the Panel may ask the Stock Exchange to suspend the quotation of the offeree's shares and, if appropriate, the offeror's shares until an announcement is made. If the offeror has already announced that the offer is unconditional as to acceptances and yet fails to make an announcement in accordance with Rule 17.1 by 3.30 p.m. on the relevant day, each shareholder who has accepted the offer becomes entitled to withdraw his or her acceptance. These consequences are so detrimental to the offeror that compliance with Rule 17.1 is ensured.

This notice serves to inform the shareholders whether the offer has been accepted in sufficient levels to be declared unconditional as to acceptances. As *Weinberg and Blank* note: "once the offeror announces that it has become entitled, whether pursuant to acceptance of the offer or otherwise, to place itself in a position of owning more than 50 per cent of the voting rights of the offeree, most remaining shareholders will normally submit their acceptances with alacrity".[31]

---

[29] R. 14.2.
[30] R. 14.3.
[31] Weinberg & Blank on Takeovers & Mergers (Sweet & Maxwell), Part II Chap. 2 para. 2–19

(6) Timeframe of the Offer – Rule 31

11–22   Rule 31.1 requires an offer to be open for acceptances initially for a period of at least 21 days following the date on which the offer document is posted. If the offeror does not receive acceptances representing 80 per cent of the shareholding by this time, it may decide to wait until it does so before declaring the offer unconditional as to acceptances in order to give it access to the section 204 machinery.[32] It may decide therefore to extend the closing date further. Unless a "no extension statement" is included in the documents sent to the offeree shareholders, this is generally possible.[33] However, the offeror runs the risk of reducing the number of its overall acceptances in this case. The reason for this is that a shareholder who accepts initially is entitled from the date which is 21 days after the first closing date to withdraw his or her acceptance if the offer has not become or been declared unconditional as to acceptances.[34] This entitlement to withdraw is exercisable until either the offer becomes, or is declared, unconditional as to acceptances or until the final time for lodgment of acceptances under Rule 31.6, whichever is earlier. Alternatively, the offeror may decide to declare the offer unconditional as to acceptance once it has acquired shares conferring more than 50 per cent of the voting rights in the offeree and leave the offer open for a further period. In such a case shareholders of the offeree who have accepted the offer will not be entitled to withdraw their acceptances.

11–23   Rule 31.6 states that unless the Panel agrees otherwise, an offer will lapse unless it has become, or been declared, unconditional as to acceptances by 5 p.m. on the 60th day after the day the initial offer document was posted or on any "relevant earlier date". Such a "relevant earlier date" is a date beyond which the offeror has stated that the offer will not be extended unless it is unconditional as to acceptances by this date and in respect of which the offeror has not withdrawn the statement.

Although there is in general no obligation to extend an offer where the conditions are not met by the first or any subsequent closing date, the Panel may order an extension if it believes that this is appropriate having regard to the General Principles.[35]

---

[32]   Weinberg & Blank note that often, in highly leveraged bids, the providers of finance may require the 80 per cent condition be strictly adhered to in order to ensure that the company is not seen to breach section 60 of the Companies Act 1963 by giving financial assistance for the purchase of its own shares. (Part 2, Chap. 2, para. 2–019, note 28a).

[33]   R. 31.5.

[34]   R. 34.

[35]   R. 31.3.

(7) Restrictions Following Offers

11–24 According to Rule 35.1(a), where an offeror has announced a firm intention to make an offer or has posted an offer (not being a partial offer) and that offer has been withdrawn or has lapsed, the offeror, any party who acted in concert with the offeror as respects the offer and any person who following the expiry of the offer period is acting in concert with the offeror will be subject to certain restrictions for a period of 12 months from the date on which the original offer lapsed or was withdrawn, unless the Panel agrees otherwise. These persons are prohibited from:

 (i) making a fresh offer in respect of the offeree;

 (ii) acquiring any securities of the offeree which would give rise to a requirement to make a mandatory offer under Rule 9; or

 (iii) acquiring any securities of the offeree, if the offeror and any of the concert parties hold securities conferring in the aggregate more than 49 per cent but not more than 50 per cent of the voting rights in the offeree.

11–25 Except with the Panel's consent, these restrictions also apply to persons who make announcements concerning a relevant company which, although not amounting to a firm intention to make an offer (not being a partial offer), raises or confirms the possibility that such an offer may be made, and then a firm intention to make or not to make an offer is not announced within what the Panel deems to be a reasonable period. The restriction will also apply to persons acting in concert with the offeror at the time of the announcement and persons who are subsequently acting in concert with the offeror.[36]

In addition, a six month moratorium is imposed on acquisitions above the offer value where the original offer (not being a partial offer) was for more than 50 per cent of the voting rights of the company.[37] The purpose of this rule is to ensure companies do not have to endure prolonged sieges by the same offeror after a failed bid. This would be an unreasonable distraction for the offeree's management. Dispensations are available from this rule, where for example the offeree recommends the new offer or where the new offer follows the announcement by a third party of a firm intention to make an offer in respect of the offeree.[38] In addition, the Panel may consider granting its consent if the previous offer lapsed in accordance with Rule 12(b) because the European Commission initated proceedings or referred the concentration to a competent authority of a

---

[36] R. 35.1(b).
[37] R. 35.2.
[38] Note 1 on R. 35.1.

Member State under the Merger Regulation and the new offer follows the issuing of a decision by the European Commission or by the competent authority. However, any such offer would normally need to be announced within 21 days of the announcement of the decision. Similarly, the Panel may also consider granting consent in circumstances where it is impossible or it is likely to be impossible to obtain governmental or regulatory clearances relating to an offer within the timetable laid down by the Rules.

II. A PARTIAL OFFER

11–26 A partial offer is defined by Rule 2.1 of Part A as:

> "an offer made to holders of a class of securities of a relevant company to acquire some but not all of that class of securities".

Rule 9, which will be discussed below, requires a mandatory offer for all the shares of the offeree where an offeror acquires or consolidates control. The objective of this rule is to safeguard minority shareholders. As partial offers could not be viewed as a means of avoiding Rule 9, only in very exceptional and unusual situations will partial offers be allowed.

(1) The Prohibition – Rule 36.1

11–27 Except with the Panel's consent, partial offers to acquire the voting securities of a relevant company are prohibited under Rule 36.1. The purpose of this prohibition in the case of offers for a majority of the offeree's shares is to ensure that existing shareholders are not isolated as a minority interest in circumstances where a person acquires a controlling interest without giving all shareholders an opportunity to sell their shares. In the U.S., this process is referred to as a "freeze-out". In the event of a partial offer for a minority of the offeree's shares, Rule 36 allows the Panel to impose tailored conditions to suit each particular case.

11–28 If the offer could not result in the offeror and concert parties holding securities carrying more than 30 per cent of the voting rights, consent is likely to be granted. This is because the offeror will not be deemed to be acquiring control. The notes to the Rules warn that if an offer could result in the offeror and concert parties holding securities conferring 30 per cent or more but less than 100 per cent of the voting rights in a relevant company, Panel consent may not be granted for the acquisition in certain circumstances. The examples given by the Panel of such circumstances are where the offeror and concert parties have acquired the offeree's voting securities, selectively or in significant numbers, during the previous 12 months, or where the securities have been purchased after the Panel deems that the partial offer was reasonably in contemplation.[39]

(2) Restrictions on Acquisitions During and After a Partial Offer

11–29   Where Panel consent is given to the making of a partial offer, restrictions are imposed on the acquisition of securities in the offeree during and after the making of a partial offer. The purpose of these restrictions is to prevent an offeror acquiring effective control without paying the full price. Again, however, Panel consent may be sought to allow these acquisitions.

Rule 36.2(a) prohibits purchases of securities of the offeree by the offeror and any concert parties during the offer period.

11–30   If a partial offer ("the original offer") becomes unconditional as to acceptances, Rule 36.2(b) prohibits the offeror from (i) making any offer in respect of the offeree or (ii) acquiring any securities of the offeree during a specified period. The same prohibition applies to any persons who acted in concert with the offeror as respects the original offer and any persons who following the expiry of the offer period are acting in concert with the offeror or any such person. The specified period commences at the time at which the original partial offer is declared unconditional as to acceptances and ends on the date at which the offer either lapses (if unsuccessful) or on the date which is 12 months after the date on which it becomes or is declared unconditional in all respects (if successful).

If a person has announced a firm intention to make a partial offer or has posted a partial offer which, if accepted in full, could result in the offeror and persons acting in concert with it holding securities conferring in the aggregate at least 30 per cent of the voting rights in the offeree and the offer has been withdrawn or lapsed, a delay of 12 months is required by Rule 36(2)(c) before certain acquisitions are possible. These are the same restrictions which are set out in Rule 35.1(a) as applying after an unsuccessful non-partial offer.

11–31   Rule 36.2(d) provides that if an offeror makes an announcement concerning a relevant company which although not amounting to an announcement of a firm intention to make such an offer, raises or confirms the possibility that the offeror may make a partial offer which, if accepted in full could result in the offeror and any persons acting in concert with it holding securities conferring in aggregate 30 per cent or more of the voting rights in the offeree, and the offeror does not announce a firm intention either to make or not to make the offer within a reasonable time the restrictions in Rule 35.1 (a) will apply to

---

[39]   Note to R. 36.1.

the offeror for a specified period. The period in this case is 12 months commencing from the expiry of that reasonable period. These restrictions apply not only to the offeror but also to any person who was acting in concert with the offeror at the time of the announcement and any person who is subsequently acting in concert with the offeror or any such person. The Panel will be responsible for determining what constitutes a "reasonable" period in this context.

11–32   Because Rule 9 applies only to acquisitions which bring a person's shareholding in a company to 30 per cent or more or to acquisitions of more than 1 per cent where a person already holds securities conferring between 30 per cent and 50 per cent of the voting rights, where a partial offer is made, which, if accepted in full, could result in the offeror and any concert parties holding securities conferring more than 49 per cent of the voting rights in the offeree, the offeror will be free, subject to Rule 36.2 to acquire further securities. For this reason, the offer document in such a case must contain specific and prominent reference to this fact in order to warn shareholders of the consequences of accepting the offer.[40]

(3) Comparable Partial Offers

11–33   Where a partial offer is made for shares in a relevant company with more than one class of equity share capital, and the offer if accepted, could result in the offeror and any concert parties holding securities conferring in the aggregate 30 per cent or more of the voting rights in the offeree, comparable partial offers must be made for each class of equity share capital.[41] Again, the purpose of this requirement is to ensure that different classes of shareholders are treated equally.

(4) Acceptances

11–34   A minimum acceptance condition applies to certain partial offers. If a partial offer could result in the offeror and any concert parties holding securities conferring in the aggregate between 30 per cent in aggregate and 50 per cent of the voting rights in the offeree, the offer may not be declared unconditional as to acceptances unless acceptances are received for at least the number of shares for which offers are made. The precise number of shares for which the offer is made must be stated in the offer document.[42]

11–35   In addition, Rule 36.4 provides that if an offer could result in the offeror and any concert parties holding shares conferring in the

---

[40]   R. 36.5.
[41]   R. 36.7(a).
[42]   R. 36.3.

aggregate 30 per cent or more of the voting rights in the offeree, the offer must normally also be conditional on the approval of the offer by shareholders holding securities conferring in the aggregate more than 50 per cent of the voting rights in the offeree not including voting rights conferred by securities held by the offeror and any concert parties. As Rule 36.4 requires the approval of more than 50 per cent of the exercisable votes, rather than 50 per cent of the votes cast, this is an extremely onerous requirement. Such approval may be given by share-holders, even though the shareholders in question do not necessarily accept the offer. This is normally done by putting a separate box on the offer document for shareholders to indicate their approval to the partial offer. Thus, shareholders who choose not to accept the offer themselves may agree to allow others accept the offer. The Panel has indicated the possibility of waiving this particular requirement if over 50 per cent of the voting rights are held by one shareholder.[43]

11–36 Partial offers must be made to all shareholders of the relevant class and arrangements must be made by the offeror for shareholders to accept in full for the relevant percentage of their holdings. If shares are tendered in excess of this percentage, they must be accepted by the offeror from each shareholder in proportion to the number tendered, to the extent necessary to enable it to obtain the total number of shares for which it has offered.[44] This ensures that all shareholders are treated equitably and given an equal opportunity to participate in the offer.

III. CONSIDERATION FOR THE ACQUISITION

11–37 In addition to making a decision as to the size of the share-holding for which the offer is to be made, the offeror must determine the type of consideration to be offered to the offeree shareholders. This decision will have significant implications for both parties. Consideration may take the form of cash, an exchange of shares or some combination of each.

(1) Power to Issue Shares

11–38 If the offeror decides to offer its own shares as consideration for the shares in the offeree, the offeror's directors must ensure that they have authority to issue shares. Generally, directors are empowered to issue shares only if authorised by the articles or by a shareholder resolution.[45] If sufficient shares are not already in issue, the authorised

---

[43] Note 2 on R. 36.4.
[44] R. 36.6.
[45] Chap. 8 paras 8–07–8–11.

share capital may have to be increased. It is not uncommon to make an offer subject to a condition that the capital will be increased. In issuing shares to the offeree's shareholders in exchange for their own shares, the offeror does not need to concern itself with pre-emption rights as pre-emption rights do not apply to non-cash consideration.[46]

11–39 Where the offeror issues shares to the offeree's shareholders in return for their shares in the offeree, this will constitute an issue of shares for a non-cash consideration. However, a valuation will not be required pursuant to section 30(1) of the Companies (Amendment) Act, 1983. Section 30(2)(a) of that Act allows an exemption where shares are allotted in return for all or some of the shares, or of all or some of the shares of a particular class in another company.[47]

11–40 Section 62 of the 1963 Act requires a company which issues shares at a premium whether for cash or a non-cash consideration, to transfer the "premium" to a share premium account for restricted use. In *Shearer v. Bercain Ltd.*,[48] an acquisition of a company by a holding company involved a share for share exchange. Because the shares issued by the offeror were lesser in value than the shares acquired in the offeree, a premium resulted and a share premium account was created. In the UK, section 131 of the Companies Act, 1985 provides relief from this require-ment in cases of mergers by exchange of shares once certain conditions are satisfied.[49] No similar provision exists in Irish legislation.

(2) Listing Requirements

11–41 If, as is likely, the offeror intends to use listed shares as con-sideration, it must seek a listing for the new shares issued. As already noted,[50] the Listing Rules are generally relaxed in these situations. Chapter 5, paragraph 23A(a)(ii) and (iii) states that the Stock Exchange may exempt issuers from the obligation to publish listing particulars where the securities, for which admission to listing is applied, are securities which have been issued in connection with a takeover offer or "a merger involving the acquisition of another company, or the formation of a new company, the division of a company, the transfer of all or part of an undertaking's assets and liabilities or as consideration for the transfer of assets other than cash". This exemption will only

---

[46] Chap. 8 paras 8–12–8–16.
[47] Chap. 8 paras 8–21–8–28.
[48] [1980] 3 All E.R. 295. See Ussher, "Doubts remain on Shearer v. Bercain" (1982) 3 *Company Lawyer* 28.
[49] *Gore-Browne on Companies*, (Jordans UK) para. 13.5.3.
[50] Chap. 5 para 5–48 *et seq.*

apply if a relevant document (within the meaning of the Prospectus Regulations) was published in Ireland not more than 12 months before the admission of the securities. Such a document should contain equivalent information to that which would be otherwise required to be included in listing particulars by the Exchange. Chapter 10, paragraphs 46.49 of the Listing Rules deal with the listing particulars which may be required in relation to takeovers and mergers.

(3) Section 60 of the Companies Act 1963

11–42 If the offeror decides to make a cash offer, a decision of the offeror's directors to this effect is normally all that is required.[51] However, if the offeror does not have sufficient cash to finance the bid itself, shareholder approval may be needed in order to borrow money beyond the limits imposed upon the directors by the articles of association.

11–43 A difficulty may subsequently arise, where the offeror attempts to sell off some of the assets of the offeree when acquired, in order to pay off its own borrowings. This may be viewed as the giving of financial assistance for the purchase of own shares contrary to section 60 of the 1963 Act. The prohibition in the 1963 Act was based on the findings of the *Jenkins Committee* that:

> "If people who cannot provide the funds necessary to acquire control of the company from their own resources, or by borrowing on their own credit, gain control of a company with large assets on the understanding that they will use the funds of the company to pay for their shares, it seems to us all to likely, that in many cases the company will be made to part with its funds either on inadequate security or for an illusory consideration. If the speculation succeeds, the company and therefore its creditors and minority shareholders may suffer no loss, although their interests will have been subjected to an illegitimate risk . . . "[52]

To avoid such a situation, section 60(1) provides as follows:

> "Subject to subsections (2), (12) and (13), it shall not be lawful for a company to give, whether directly or indirectly, and whether by means of a loan, guarantee, the provision of security or otherwise, any financial assistance for the purpose of or in connection with a purchase or subscription made or to be made by any person of or for any shares in the company, or, where the company is a subsidiary company, in its holding company."

---

[51] Chap. 8, paras 8–03–8–05.
[52] 1962: Cmnd. 1749 para. 173.

11–44   It may not always be easy to determine whether in a complex commercial arrangement, a company has assisted in the purchase of its own shares. Denning M.R. in *Wallersteiner v. Moir*[53] advised that

> "The transactions are extremely complicated, but the end result is clear. You look to the company's money and see what has become of it. You look to the company's shares and see into whose hands they have got. You will soon see if the company's money has been used to finance the purchase."

Similarly, in *Charterhouse Investment Trust Ltd. v. Tempest Diesels Ltd.*,[54] Hoffmann J. stated that:

> "one must examine the commercial realities of the transaction and decide whether it can properly be described as the giving of financial assistance by the company".

11–45   While section 60(2) provides an exception to the prohibition where the company has passed a special resolution not more than 12 months previously and obtained a statutory declaration from its directors, the use of this subsection by public limited companies is severely restricted. Section 60(15A) provides that the exemption in subsection (2) only applies to a public limited company if the special resolution was passed before the company's application for registration or re-registration. The only other available exceptions to section 60 are contained in section 60(12) and (13). Section 60(12) provides that the payment of a properly declared dividend or the discharge of a lawfully incurred liability will not be included in the general prohibition. Section 60(13) provides a further three exemptions for companies.[55] Firstly, the lending of money by a credit institution in the ordinary course of business will not be excluded.[56] Secondly, the prohibition will not cover the provision by a company of money for the purchase of, or subscription for, fully paid shares in the company or its holding company under an existing employee share scheme. Under such a scheme, the shares must be held by or for the benefit of employees or former employees of the company or any of its subsidiaries.[57] Directors or former directors holding salaried employment or office in the company or any of its subsidiaries will also be included in this

---

[53] [1974] 3 All E.R. 217 at 238.
[54] [1986] B.C.L.C. 1 at p. 10.
[55] The Companies Act 1963 s.60(15B) allows public limited companies to give financial assistance under section 60(13) only if the company's net assets are not thereby reduced or, to the extent that those assets are thereby reduced, if the financial assistance is provided out of profits which are available for dividend.
[56] *ibid.*, s.60(13) (a). This sub para. refers to a company "where the lending of money is part of the ordinary business of the company".
[57] *ibid.*, s.60(13)(b).

exemption. Finally, the making of loans to employees of the company or any of its subsidiaries, other than directors, with a view to allowing them to purchase or subscribe for fully paid shares in the company or its holding company is also allowed where the shares are to be held by those employees as beneficial owners.[58] Acquisitions by subsidiaries of shares in their holding companies are permitted subject to the provisions of section 224 of the Companies Act 1990 and the European Communities (Public Limited Companies Subsidiaries) Regulations, 1997.[58a]

11–46 Section 60(14) provides that any transaction in breach of this section is voidable at the instance of the company against any person who had notice of the facts which constitute the breach. Actual notice of the facts is however required. In *Bank Of Ireland Finance Limited v. Rockfield Ltd.*, the defendant company created an equitable mortgage over its assets in the Bank's favour as security for a loan made to two persons. The money lent by the plaintiff was used by these two persons to buy the issued shares in the defendant company and thus to obtain control of it. The Supreme Court determined that the mortgage was valid. In respect of section 60(14), it was held that the onus of proving that the money was advanced for the purchase of shares in the defendant company lies on the person who alleges this. Kenny J. stated:

> "The plaintiffs do not have to prove that they had no notice of facts which constituted a breach of section 60. What has to be established is that the plaintiffs had notice when lending the money that it was to be used for the purchase of shares in the defendant company . . . If they got notice of this subsequently, that is irrelevant. The notice referred to in subsection 14 of section 60 is actual notice and not constructive notice . . . I use the term "actual notice" as meaning in this case that the plaintiff bank, or any of its officials, had been informed, either verbally or in writing, that part of the advance was to be applied in the purchase of shares in the defendant company, or that they knew facts from which they must have inferred that part of the advance was to be applied for this purpose."[59]

In addition, any officer of the company who is in default shall be liable to a maximum penalty of a £500 fine or a six month prison sentence for a summary conviction or a £2,500 fine or a two year prison sentence for a conviction on indictment.[60] The purpose of this section is to safeguard the interests of creditors and minority shareholders.

---

[58] *ibid.*, s.60(13)(c).
[58a] S.I. No. 67 of 1997. See also para. 20–07.
[59] [1979] I.R. 21 at 36–37. See also *In Re CH (Ireland) Inc (in liquidation) v. Credit Suisse Canada*, unreported, High Court, McCracken J., December 12, 1997.
[60] *ibid.*, s.60(15).

(4) Mandatory Cash Consideration

11–47 In certain circumstances, the offeror may have to make an offer in cash or provide a cash alternative offer. Such an obligation is imposed in order to ensure that all shareholders are treated fairly and offered equivalent consideration. This obligation is based on General Principle 1 which requires that all shareholders of the same class of a offeree company must be treated similarly by an offeror.

11–48 Firstly, if a mandatory offer is required under Rule 9, unless the Panel consents otherwise, Rule 9.4 requires that the offer be in cash or that it be accompanied by a cash alternative at a minimum price. This is dealt with in paragraphs 11–71–11–72 below. Rule 9.4 also applies with certain modifications to offers made pursuant to Rule 37.1(a) which requires a mandatory offer be made in circumstances where a person acquires or consolidates control as a result of the redemption or purchase by a company of its own securities.[61] A cash offer or cash alternative is required at a price which is not less than either (a) the highest price at which the offeree redeemed or purchased shares in the offeree of that class during the period beginning 12 months prior to the commencement of the offer period and ending on the date of the redemption or purchase by the offeree of its own shares or (b) the highest price paid by the offeror or any concert party for shares in the offeree of that class during the period beginning 12 months prior to the commencement of the offer period and ending on the expiry of the offer period.

11–49 Secondly, Rule 11 requires a voluntary offer to be in cash or accompanied by a cash alternative in two specified circumstances unless the Panel consents otherwise. These circumstances are as follows:

(a) where the offeror or any concert party has purchased for cash during the relevant period securities of any class under offer in the offeree which confer in the aggregate 10 per cent or more of the voting rights in the offeree exercisable at a class meeting of holders of securities of that class; or

(b) where the offeror or any concert party has purchased for cash during the relevant period securities of any class under offer in the offeree which confer in the aggregate less than 10 per cent of the voting rights in the offeree exercisable at a class meeting of holders of securities of that class in circumstances where the Panel feels such a course is necessary having regard to the General Principles.[62]

---

[61] R. 37.1(c)(i).
[62] R. 11(a).

The "relevant period" for the purposes of Rule 11 is the period beginning 12 months prior to the commencement of the offer period and ending on the expiry of the offer period.

(5) Minimum Level of Consideration

11–50   In certain circumstances, unless the Panel consents otherwise, a minimum level of consideration may have to be paid to the offeree's shareholders. As noted above, where a cash offer or a cash alternative is required a minimum consideration is stipulated. In addition, Rule 6 specifies certain purchases which may lead to the imposition of an obligation on the offeror to offer a minimum level of consideration. It is specifically provided however, that without prejudice to the obligations imposed by Rules 9 and 11, Rule 6 shall not oblige an offeror to make available a cash offer by reason of the offeror or any concert party having purchased for cash securities of the offeree of a class for which an offer has been made.[63]

11–51   Rule 6.1 provides that if, in the case of a voluntary offer, the offeror or any concert party has purchased securities of the offeree of a class which is the subject of the offer within the period beginning three months prior to the commencement of the offer period and ending at the time of the announcement of the offeror's firm intention to make an offer, the offer made by the offeror to offeree shareholders of that class must be "on terms no less favourable".[64] The same obligation is imposed on the offeror where the purchase takes place within the period beginning 12 months prior to the commencement of the offer period and ending at the time of the announcement of the offeror's firm intention to make an offer, if in the Panel's view, having regard to the General Principles, this is a more appropriate period and the Panel so directs.[65] Rule 6.1 provides that the Panel may give its consent to the avoidance of this obligation. In the case of an offer, the consideration for which includes the issue of securities, Rule 6.1 also provides that the consideration must have, at the time of the announcement of the firm intention to make an offer, a value at least equal to the highest price paid in respect of any such purchase.

11–52   Rule 6.2 provides that if the offeror or any concert party, during the offer period, but after the announcement of a firm intention to offer, purchases securities of the offeree of a class which is subject to the offer, at a price above the current offer price, the offer must be increased in

---

[63] R. 6.3(a).
[64] R. 6.1(a).
[65] R. 6.1(b).

respect of that class of securities to at least the highest price paid for the securities so purchased.[66] Immediately after any such purchase is made, the offeror must thus announce that a revised offer will be made in accordance with Rule 6.2.[67] This announcement must state the number of securities so purchased and the price paid. It should also include the details prescribed by Rule 2.5(b) which sets out the contents of an announcement of a firm intention to make an offer.

11–53   For the purpose of Rule 6, the price at which the offeree's securities will be deemed to have been purchased is the price at which the bargain between the purchaser or his or her broker and the vendor (or market maker) is struck.[68] However, stamp duty and the commission payable to the broker by the purchaser will not be regarded as part of the purchase price for this purpose. These requirements ensure that all shareholders are treated equally and none receive a better price during this period.

(6) Requirement to Make an Announcement

11–54   Where an offeror becomes obliged to increase the offer price (under Rule 6, Rule 9 or Rule 37) or to make a cash offer (under Rule 11), Rule 7.1(a) requires the offeror to make an immediate announcement to this effect. The announcement should disclose the number of securities purchased, the price paid and the details required by Rule 2(5)(b).

An immediate announcement will also be required under Rule 7.1(b) in the case of an announced possible offer (i) where a public indication of the amount of its probable offer price has been made and the offeror or any concert parties purchase securities of the offeree at a price above that amount or (ii) where a third party has already made an offer in respect of the same offeree and the first mentioned offeror or any concert parties purchases securities of the offeree at a price above the price of that offer.

(7) Payments to Offeree Directors

11–55   If the terms of the offer put to shareholders would involve the making of a payment to the directors of the offeree company, the approval of the offerees' shareholders may be necessary.[69] As noted in Chapter 8, section 186 of the 1963 Act makes it unlawful for a company to make a payment to a director as "compensation for loss of office" or "in connection with his retirement from office" without the payment

---

[66]   R. 6.2(a).
[67]   R. 6.2(b).
[68]   s.6.3(b).
[69]   Chap. 8, para. 8–29.

being disclosed to and approved by shareholders in general meeting. Section 187 states that shareholder approval is also necessary where any payment is made to a director as compensation for loss of office or in connection with his retirement in connection with the transfer of the whole or any part of the undertaking or property of a company. This latter section would obviously include a payment by either offeror or offeree company.[70] Furthermore, section 188 requires that where payment is made to a director as "compensation for loss of office" or "in connection with his retirement from office", in connection with the "transfer" to any persons of all or any of the shares in a company, the director should ensure that the payment is disclosed in the offer document. The "transfer" in question is:

> "a transfer resulting from –
> (a) an offer made to the general body of shareholders, or
> (b) an offer made by or on behalf of some other body corporate, with a view to the company becoming its subsidiary or a subsidiary of its holding company; or
> (c) an offer made by or on behalf of an individual with a view to his obtaining the right to exercise or control the exercise of not less than one-third of the voting power at any general meeting of the company; or
> (d) any other offer which is conditional on acceptance to a given extent;"

These provisions ensure that shareholders of the offeree will be informed of, and given the opportunity to vote on, payments to their directors in connection with their loss of office.

B. An Offer to the Existing Controllers of the Offeree

11–56 Instead of offering to acquire shares from all the offeree's shareholders, the offeror may offer to acquire shares privately from the offeree's existing controllers. In such a case, the offeree's controlling shareholders may decide to sell their shares without referring to the remaining shareholders or considering their needs. This could lead to a situation where the offeror gains control without having to make a general offer to the offeree's shareholders. For this reason, such acquisitions are strictly controlled by the Takeover Rules.

---

[70] Section 189(3) provides that bona fide payments by way of damages for breach of contract or by way of pension in respect of part services are not included under sections 186, 187 or 188.

I. POWER TO ACQUIRE SHARES – RULE 5

Rule 5 imposes restrictions on the ability of a offeror to acquire shares in the offeree.

(1) The Prohibitions

11–57 Where a person holds voting securities or rights over voting securities of a relevant company which, when aggregated with any voting securities held, or rights over such securities held by persons acting in concert with that person, confer less than 30 per cent of voting rights in the company, that person may not acquire any voting securities or rights over such securities of that company which when aggregated with voting securities or rights over voting securities already held by that person or any person acting in concert would confer 30 per cent or more of the voting rights.[71] In other words, a person in possession of securities conferring less than 30 per cent of the voting rights of a company should not increase their interests beyond this 30 per cent threshold.

In addition, if a person holds voting securities or rights over voting securities of a relevant company which when aggregated with any voting securities or rights over such securities held by persons acting in concert confer 30 per cent or more but not more than 50 per cent of voting rights in that company, that person may not acquire voting securities or rights over voting securities which when aggregated with any voting securities or rights over voting securities acquired by that person or any concert party in the previous 12 months confer more than 1 per cent of the voting rights in that company.[72] This provision is known as "the creeper provision" because it allows for the gradual consolidation of control. A similar provision was abolished by the London Panel on Takeovers and Mergers in August 1998 and may similarly be removed following the review of the Irish Takeover Rules in 1999.

11–58 These restrictions are not relevant to a person who already holds securities conferring more than 50 per cent of a company's voting rights. Nor will they apply to certain acquisitions under established share option schemes or to the receipt of bona fide gifts or inheritances.[73] However, acquisitions of voting securities or rights over such securities for discretionary clients by fund managers connected with an offeror (who are not exempt fund mangers) will be included in the aggregation of securities, unless the Panel directs otherwise.[74] An obligation is

---

[71] R. 5.1(b)(i).
[72] R. 5.1(b)(ii). However, voting securities acquired by a person before or during a previous mandatory R. 9 offer will not be treated as additional voting securities for this purpose.
[73] R. 5.1(c)(i)&(ii).
[74] R. 5.1(d).

imposed on the offeror, the offeror's financial adviser and the relevant fund manager to ensure that this obligation is observed. It should be noted that, subject to the above exemptions, all acquisitions of voting securities of the relevant company and rights over voting securities of that company are agregable for the purposes of Rule 5.1. This includes acquisitions of rights over voting securities which do not entitle their holders to exercise or control the exercise of the voting rights conferred by the underlying securities, provided, however, that no voting right may be counted more than once in any aggregation.[74a] This is in marked contrast to Rule 9 where only such rights carrying control of the associated votes are taken into account.[74b]

(2) Exemptions

11–59 Certain exemptions from these restrictions are provided for by Rule 5.2 in circumstances where the offeree's shareholders interests are not in such serious need of protection.

Rule 5.2(a)(i) disapplies the restrictions in the case of an acquisition of voting securities or of rights over such securities from a single holder of securities[75] where it is the only such acquisition within a period of seven days. The acquisition from the single shareholder should be disclosed to the company, the Stock Exchange, the Panel and the press not later than 12 noon on the business day following the date of the acquisition.[76] Where this exemption applies, the offeror should not make any further acquisitions of voting securities of that company or rights over voting securities of that company unless in accordance with Rule 5.2(a)(ii)–(v) below.[77] It should be noted that this exception will not apply if the person making the acquisition has announced a firm intention to make an offer in respect of the company and the posting of the offer is not subject to a pre-condition.[78]

11–60 Rule 5.2(a)(ii) disapplies the restrictions in the case of an acquisition which immediately precedes the announcement by that person of a firm intention to make an offer in respect of the company, provided either that the offer will be publicly recommended for acceptance by the offeree board or that the acquisition is made with the agreement of the offeree board. In addition, the acquisition must be conditional upon the announcement of the offer.

[74a] R. 5.1(a).
[74b] See para. 11–65.
[75] R. 5.2(c) provides that except with the consent of the Panel, a market-maker will not be considered to be a single holder of securities for the purposes of R. 5.2.
[76] R. 5.4.
[77] R. 5.3(a).
[78] R. 5.2(a)(i).

11–61 Rule 5.2(a)(iii) disapplies the restrictions in the case of an acquisition made immediately after the person has announced a firm intention to make an offer, provided that the acquisition satisfies a precondition of the posting of the offer. In addition, here too the offer must either be recommended by the offeree board or the acquisition must be made with the agreement of the offeree board.

11–62 Rule 5.2(a)(iv) disapplies the restrictions in the case of an acquisition made after the person has announced a firm intention to make an offer in respect of the company, provided that the posting of the offer is not at the time of the acquisition subject to a precondition. In addition, to qualify for an exemption under this paragraph:

(1) the acquisition must be made with the agreement of the offeree board; or

(2) the offer or any competing offer must have been publicly recommended by the offeree board; or

(3) either:

> the first closing date of the offer must has passed without any "constraint on the implementation" of the offer being outstanding under section 3 of the Mergers, Takeovers and Monopolies (Control) Act, 1978 and no other governmental or regulatory authorisation or clearance is outstanding in any jurisdiction. Furthermore, it must be established either that no action will be taken in respect of the offer by the European Commission or any competent authority of a Member State under the European Merger Regulation or that the offer does not come within the scope of the Regulation.

> or

> the first closing date of any competing offer must have passed without any "constraint on the implementation" of the competing offer being outstanding under section 3 of the Mergers, Takeovers and Monopolies (Control) Act, 1978 and no other governmental or regulatory authorisation or clearance is outstanding in any jurisdiction. Furthermore, it must be established either that no action will be taken in respect of the competing offer by the European Commission or any competent authority of a Member State under the European Merger Regulation or that the competing offer does not come within the scope of the Regulation; or

(4) the offer is unconditional in all respects.

11–63 Finally, Rule 5.2(a)(v) disapplies the restrictions in the case of an acquisition which is by way of acceptance of an offer made in accordance with the Takeover rules. At present, an anomaly exists in the rules in that whilst an acceptance of an offer is thus exempted from Rule 5.1 an undertaking to accept an offer is not. Currently, rights over shares arising on foot of an irrevocable undertaking to accept an offer are aggregable for Rule 5 as such "rights" are defined in Part A of the Rules as "interests in securities" as defined in section 1 of the Act. This anomaly may be removed following the review of the Takeover Rules in 1999.

An acquisition of securities permitted by Rule 5.2 will normally result in an obligation to make a mandatory offer under Rule 9, in which case an immediate announcement of such an offer must be made.[79]

II. THE RULE 9 MANDATORY OFFER[80]

11–64   Section 8(3)(a)of the Irish Takeover Panel Act 1997 imposes a duty on the Panel:

> "to make rules requiring that where
> (i) a person, or persons acting in concert, acquire control of a relevant company (other than in circumstances referred to in paragraph (b)(i),[81] or
> (ii) a person, or persons acting in concert, who control a relevant company, acquire, within a specified period, a specified amount of additional securities in that company
>
> that person, or, as the case may be, such one or more of those persons as the Panel shall determine pursuant to the rules, shall make an offer or offers to acquire all or a specified class or classes of the remaining securities in that company upon or subject to such terms (including consideration) as the Panel specifies in the rules or in a direction given by it for the purpose pursuant to the rules."

The Panel satisfied this obligation by the introduction of Rule 9 of the Takeover rules. The purpose of this rule is to ensure equality between shareholders by requiring all shareholders to be given an opportunity to dispose of their shares at the highest price paid by the new controller. Rule 9 gives shareholders an opportunity to chose not to remain in a company under the control of a new person. There are a number of reasons why shareholders would not wish to remain with the company. For example, shareholders may not have confidence in the new controller's ability to run the company properly or successfully or they may not like the new controller's reputation. A further rational for Rule 9 is that it allows all shareholders to participate in the premium paid to acquire control.

---

[79] Note 1 on R. 5.2.
[80] It should be noted that R. 37 also imposes a requirement to make a mandatory offer. See paras 20–69–20–71.

(1) Requirement for a General Offer to All Shareholders

11–65 Rule 9.1 states that, unless the Panel agrees otherwise, where a person or any concert party acquires control of a relevant company (otherwise than in the circumstances referred to in Rule 37.1(a)(i)),[82] such person or persons shall be required to extend the offer to the holders of each class of equity share capital of the relevant company and also to the holders of each class of non-equity share capital conferring voting rights of which such person or persons hold shares.[83] Offers made by the offeror for different classes of equity share capital of the offeree must be comparable. This rule applies whether control is acquired by a series of transactions over a period of time or otherwise. "Control" in relation to a relevant company is defined in section 1(1) of the Irish Takeover Panel Act 1997 as:

> "the holding, whether directly or indirectly, of securities of the company that confer, in aggregate, not less than 30 per cent (or such other percentage as may be prescribed) of the voting rights in that company."[84]

A general offer is also required where a person or any concert party holding securities in a relevant company conferring between 30–50 per cent of the voting rights acquires in any 12 month period additional securities[85] conferring in the aggregate more than 1 per cent of the voting rights in that company.[86] Because of the application of Rule 9 to concert parties, the Notes on Rule 9.1 set out the manner in which the term "acting in concert" is interpreted by the Panel in this context. Firstly, the Notes provides for a situation where a party which has acquired securities independently subsequently comes together with other holders of securities in order to acquire or consolidate control. Even though the aggregate holdings of this group confer 30 per cent or more of the voting rights, a general offer will not be required by reason only of the earlier acquisition. However Rule 9 will apply to further acquisitions by any members of the group. Secondly, it is noted that the actions of shareholders voting together on particular resolutions may

---

[81] Section 8(3)(b) allows the Panel make rules regulating the acquisition of control by reason of a redemption or purchase by a company of its own shares. This is dealt with in R. 37.

[82] R. 37.1(a)(i) deals with a situation where a person acquires or consolidates control as a result of the purchase or redemption by a company of its own shares. This is dealt with in paras 20.69–20.71.

[83] R. 9.1(a).

[84] Rule 2.1 defines control as having the meaning assigned to it by s.1(1) of the Irish Takeover Panel Act 1997.

[85] Rule 9.1 expressly provides that securities of the offeree acquired before or during a previous R. 9 offer, or acquired with the consent of the Panel under R. 9.1 will not be treated as "additional securities" for the purposes of para. (b).

[86] R. 9.1(b).

not of itself give rise to a mandatory offer. However, such joint action may, in certain circumstances, be interpreted by the Panel as an indication that the shareholders are concert parties with the result that purchases by any of the shareholders could give rise to an obligation. Thirdly, directors of an offeree will be presumed to be acting in concert during an offer period or when they have reason to believe that a bona fide offer may be made in the near future. At all other times, no such presumption exists. Where a hostile offer has been made, shareholders of the offeree who have indicated their support for the directors and purchase securities in order to frustrate the offer, may also be deemed to be concert parties. Finally, it is noted that whilst a concert party is recognised as a single unit, there will be circumstances in which the acquisition of securities by one member of a concert party from another member will give rise to a mandatory offer. If the concert party holds securities conferring 30 per cent or more of the voting rights and as a result of such an acquisition, a single member acquires securities holding 30 per cent or more of the voting rights (or acquires more than 1 per cent in any 12 month period if already holding over 30 per cent), the Panel will be required to consider whether a waiver of Rule 9 is justified. In making this decision, the Panel will consider whether the leader of the group or the largest individual holding has changed and whether the balance between the holdings in the group has changed significantly. The Panel will also consider the price paid for the securities acquired, the relationship between the concert parties and the duration of the concert party. If the group holds between 30 per cent– 49 per cent of the voting rights, a mandatory offer will arise if there are acquisitions from non-members of more than 1 per cent in the aggregate in any 12 month period. Where more than 49 per cent is held, no obligations normally arise from acquisitions by members of the group. However acquisitions by a single member of the group of securities sufficient to increase his or her voting rights to 30 per cent or more (or if her or she already has 30 per cent or more, by more than 1 per cent in any 12 month period) may give rise to an obligation under Rule 9. The factors taken into account by the Panel in considering a waiver are as mentioned above.

(2) Resources

11–66   General Principle 10 states that:

> "Where an acquisition of securities is contemplated as a result of which a person may incur an obligation to make an offer, he or she must, before making the acquisition, ensure that he or she can and will continue to be able to implement such an offer".

Rule 9.2(a) gives effect to this principle by prohibiting a person from making an acquisition which would give rise to a requirement to make a general offer under Rule 9 unless they are satisfied that they are able and will continue to be able to implement the offer. The offeror's financial advisers must also be satisfied on this point.

(3) Minimum Acceptance Condition

11–67   Rule 9.2(b)(i) provides that a mandatory offer must contain a minimum acceptance condition unless the Panel agrees otherwise. Subject to Rule 12, the mandatory bid must be conditional only upon acceptances being received in respect of shares which, together with securities acquired or agreed to be acquired before or during the offer, will result in the offeror and any concert parties holding in the aggregate securities conferring more than 50 per cent of the voting rights in the offeree. Where the offeror and any concert parties hold securities conferring more than 50 per cent of the voting rights before the offer is made, the offer under Rule 9 must be unconditional except as provided in Rule 12.[87]

In certain circumstances, the Panel may grant dispensations from this rule.[88] An example of such a situation would be where any governmental or regulatory clearance other than that referred to under Rule 12 is required. Examples of such situations are set out in Chapter 7. A further example given of a situation which might merit a dispensation is when the necessary cash consideration is to be provided, wholly or partly, by an underwritten cash alternative offer or another issue of securities which is conditional on the obtaining of a quotation for the new securities.

(4) Merger Approval

11–68   A person is prohibited from making an acquisition which would give rise to a requirement to make a mandatory offer under Rule 9, if the making or implementation of such offer would or might be conditional upon the passing of a resolution at a meeting of the offeror's shareholders or upon any other condition, consent or arrangement.[89]

An exception to this is that the offer may be dependent upon a condition required by Rule 12.[90] Indeed, Rule 9.3(a) specifically states that where applicable, every mandatory offer should be made subject to the conditions required by Rule 12(a) & (b). As noted above, Rule 12

---

[87]   Note 1 on R. 9.2.
[88]   Note 3 on R. 9.2.
[89]   R. 9.2(b((ii).
[90]   R. 9.2(b)(ii).

deals with proposed mergers or takeovers to which the Mergers, Takeovers and Monopolies (Control) Act 1978 ("the 1978 Act") or the European Merger Regulation applies.[91]

11–69 Rule 12(a)(i) requires that mandatory offers under Rule 9 or Rule 37 must be made subject to a condition which will be satisfied if:

- the Minister for Enterprise and Employment ("the Minister") states in writing that he or she does not intend to make an order under section 9 of the 1978 Act in relation to the proposed merger or takeover; or

- the Minister states in writing that he or she has made an order under section 9 prohibiting the proposed acquisition except on certain specified conditions but the offeror may stipulate under the order that such condition be acceptable to the offeror; or

- the relevant period under the 1978 Act elapses without the Minister making any order under section 9.

If this condition is not then satisfied and the offer lapses, the Panel may direct the offeror or any concert party to reduce their aggregate holdings to below the 30 per cent threshold or to its original percentage level before the acquisition was made.[92] If this condition is not satisfied by the first closing date, it should be noted that Rule 31.7(b) may apply. This rule provides that if an offer under Rule 9 or Rule 37 has become or been declared unconditional as to acceptances but remains subject to a condition under Rule 12(a) or any other condition permitted by the Panel under Rule 9.2 which will be satisfied by the issue in the State or any other jurisdiction of any governmental or regulatory authorisation or clearance, the Panel may direct the offeror to extend the offer period. The Panel is authorised to make such a direction where it is of the opinion that, having regard to the General Principles, "it is just and proper so to direct". It is important that the Panel should have this power because it would defeat the whole purpose of Rule 9 if the mandatory offer requirement could be frustrated by the failure of the Minister to give the necessary clearance in time.

11–70 Rule 12(b) states that if an offer would give rise to a concentration with a Community dimension within the scope of the European Merger Regulation, it shall be a term of the offer that it will lapse if the European Commission initiates proceedings under Article 6(1)(c) of that Regulation or refers the concentration to a competent authority in a Member State under Article 9(1) of the Regulation before the later of

---

[91] By virtue of section 2 of that Act. See Chap. 6, para. 6–42–6–51.
[92] R. 9.3(b).

the first closing date of the offer or the date the offer becomes uncon-ditional as to acceptances. If an offer lapses for this reason, the obligation under Rule 9.1 to make an offer shall nonetheless continue, and if the transaction is subsequently allowed by the European Commission or the competent authority, the offeror must reinstate the offer on the same terms and not less than the same price as soon as practicable. If the proposed transaction is eventually prohibited, the Panel may again direct the offeror or concert parties to reduce their aggregate holdings below the 30 per cent threshold or to its original percentage level before the acquisition was made if that was 30 per cent or more.[93]

It should be noted that while the European Commission or any competent authority is considering the case following an initiation of proceedings or a referral, neither the offeror or any concert parties may acquire further securities of the offeree without the Panel's consent.[94]

(5) Consideration

11–71 Rule 9.4(a) provides that, unless the Panel agrees otherwise the offer must be in cash or be accompanied by a cash alternative offer at a price which is not less than the highest price paid by the offeror or any concert party for shares in the offeree of that class during the offer period and within 12 months prior to its commencement. Even where shares have been acquired for a consideration other than cash, Rule 9.4(b) provides that the offer must nevertheless be in cash or be accompanied by a cash alternative of at least equal value, which must be determined by an independent valuation. If the acquisition involved an exchange of securities in return for the offeree's shares, Rule 9.4(c) provides that the Panel may require the offeror, in addition to making a cash offer, to offer such securities to all the offeree's shareholders on whatever terms the Panel deems appropriate.

11–72 Rule 9.4(f) provides that the Panel may impose an obligation to make an offer at a price it determines to be fair. The Panel may do this in the circumstances where neither the offeror nor any concert parties have acquired shares of the class which is the subject of the offer. In addition, the Panel may also do this if, in any other circumstances, the Panel is of the opinion that, having regard to the General Principles, it would be just and proper to do so. Thus, if a dispensation would not lead to unequal or unfair treatment of shareholders, it may be granted. The offeror is advised therefore to consult the Panel where it believes that the highest price should not apply. In considering an application by the offeror for an

---

[93] R. 9.3(c).
[94] R. 9.3(d).

adjusted price, the Panel may take into account the following factors: the size and timing of the relevant purchases, the attitude of the offeree board; whether securities had been purchased at high prices from directors or other persons closely connected with the offeror or offeree; and the number of securities purchased in the preceding 12 months.[95]

(6) Offeree's Directors

11–73 An additional responsibility is placed on the directors of a relevant company who intend to sell securities of that company in circumstances which would give rise to an obligation on the purchaser to make a general offer. The directors must ensure as a condition of sale of those securities that the purchaser undertakes to fulfil its obligations under Rule 9.[96] Except with the consent of the Panel, these directors may not resign from the board of the offeree until the first closing date of the offer, or until the offer becomes or is declared unconditional in all respects or lapses, whichever is the later. This rule ensures a continuity of management at this crucial period. It is important to note that the term "directors" is defined by Rule 2.1 of Part A of the rules as including both directors and shadow directors, *i.e.* persons in accordance with whose directions or instructions any one or more of the directors are accustomed to act unless such director or directors are accustomed so to act by reason only that he or she or (as the case may be) they do so on adivce given by a person in a professional capacity. In addition, the term "directors" would clearly include both executive and non-executive directors.

Unless the Panel consents, neither the person obliged to make a mandatory offer under Rule 9 nor any person acting in concert with that person may appoint or nominate a nominee to the board of that company until the offer document has been posted. In addition, until that time such persons are prohibited from exercising the voting rights conferred by the securities held in the company.[97]

(7) Voluntary Offers

11–74 It is always possible that a Rule 9 obligation will be triggered during a voluntary offer. Where this is likely, the offeror should consult the Panel in advance.[98] Once the obligation is triggered, the offeror should make an immediate announcement of its obligation to make a general offer under Rule 9.

Neither the offeror or any concert party in a voluntary offer should make an acquisition which could give rise to a requirement to make an

---

[95] R. 9.4(f), note on R. 9.4.
[96] R. 9.5.
[97] R. 9.6.
[98] R. 9.7.

offer under Rule 9, unless it is possible to leave the offer open for acceptance for a further 14 days following the date on which the amended offer document is to be posted.

If no change in the consideration is required, it will suffice for the offeror, following its announcement of the mandatory offer, to notify the offeree shareholders in writing:

– of the total shareholdings in the offeree held by the offeror and concerted parties as a result of the acquisition;

– that subject to Rule 9.2 and Rule 12 the acceptance condition is the only remaining condition of the offer; and

– of the period for which the offer will remain open.

(8) Exemptions from the Rule 9 Obligation

11–75 It is accepted that, in certain circumstances, it will not be necessary to require a mandatory bid in order to satisfy the equality of treatment principle. Indeed, on occasion, it may even be inequitable to require a mandatory bid. The notes on dispensations from Rule 9 therefore list several examples of situations in which dispensations are likely to be granted by the Panel.

(1) Where new securities are issued as consideration for an acquisition and the issue would otherwise trigger a Rule 9 bid, the Panel may waive the obligation if there is an independent vote at a shareholders' meeting. The same will apply to a cash subscription or the underwriting of an issue of shares. This dispensation is called a "Whitewash" and a Whitewash Guidance Note is contained in the notes to Rule 9 and summarised in paragraphs 11–84–11–85 below.

(2) The Panel may consider waiving the obligation, if it has resulted from the enforcement of a security for a loan. This may occur where a holding of securities is charged as security for a loan and as a result of enforcement, the lender exceeds the Rule 9 thresholds. In deciding whether to allow this waiver, the Panel will consider whether the security was given at a time when the lender believed enforcement likely.

(3) In rescue operations, where the relevant company is in such a serious financial position that its only means of survival involves the issue of new shares or the acquisition of existing securities by the rescuer, the Rule 9 obligation may be waived.

(4) Where the obligation is triggered as a result of an inadvertent mistake which is remedied by the sale of a sufficient number of shares to unconnected persons, the obligation may also be waived.

(5) The Panel may consider waiving the obligation where the holder exceeds the 30 per cent threshold as a result of the enfranchisement of non-voting shares. Such a waiver is unlikely however, where the shares were purchased at a time when the purchaser had reason to believe that enfranchisement would take place.

(6) The obligation may be waived where the approval of independent shareholders to the transfer of existing securities from one share-holder to another is obtained or where the threshold is breached as a result of a gift or inheritance.

(7) A waiver will normally be given to a person who acquires voting securities by way of a bona fide gift or inheritance. Such a person would however be subject to Rule 5.1(b)(ii) in respect of further acquisitions.[99]

In deciding whether to waive the Rule 9 requirement, the Panel may take into account a statement by the holders of securities conferring 50 per cent or more of the voting rights that they would not accept such an offer or the fact that securities conferring 50 per cent or more of the voting rights are already held by one other person.

III. IRREVOCABLE UNDERTAKINGS

11–76 The offeror should be aware that the acquisition of irrevocable undertakings for a sufficiently large block of shares may in certain circumstances be regarded as an offer for the offeree as a whole. For example, the acquisition by Pernod-Ricard of irrevocable undertakings in Irish Distillers in 1988 was considered an offer by the London Panel.[100] Rule 4.3 now states that anyone proposing to contact a private individual or small corporate shareholder with a view to seeking an irrevocable commitment to accept or refrain from accepting an offer or contemplated offer must contact the Panel. The Panel will expect that the financial adviser to the offeror has ensured that all relevant legislative and regulatory requirements are complied with when irrevocable commitments are being sought.

IV. THE SUBSTANTIAL ACQUISITION RULES

11–77 In addition to Rule 5, the Irish Takeover Panel Act 1997 (Substantial Acquisition) Rules, 1997 will apply unless there has been an announcement by the offeror of a firm intention to make an offer in

---

[99] Note 4 on R. 5.1.
[100] Panel Statement, Sept. 5, 1988.

respect of the company the posting of which is not, or has ceased to be, subject to the fulfilment of any condition.[101] These rules will be discussed in greater detail in Chapter 13.[101a]

C. Purchase of Shares on the Stock Exchange

11–78 Instead of putting an offer directly to the offeree's shareholders, the offeror may decide to have its' broker purchase the shares on the market at the market price. The decision to purchase shares on the Stock Exchange is normally a matter only for the offeror's directors and the shareholders of the offeree who decide to sell.[102] In many cases, the identity of the offeror may not be known to the shareholders who decide to sell, nor may they be aware that the offeror has intentions to acquire ultimate control of the offeree.

I. RESTRICTIONS ON DEALING IN SHARES

11–79 Both Rule 5[103] and Rule 9[104] apply to market purchases. Subject to these restrictions, the offeror is free to deal in the offeree's shares until there is a reason to suppose that an approach or an offer is contemplated. At this stage Rule 4.2 becomes relevant. It imposes restrictions on dealings in securities by the offeror and concert parties. If the offeror is in possession of unpublished price sensitive information, the provisions of Part V. of the Companies Act, 1990 relating to insider dealing may also prevent any dealing in the shares of the offeree. These restrictions are examined in greater detail in Chapter 13.[104a]

II. DISCLOSURE OF DEALINGS

11–80 A variety of statutory and regulatory provisions restrict a offeror's ability to surreptitiously build up large stakes in the offeree.

Part IV chapter 1 of the Companies Act 1990 ("the 1990 Act") deals with the disclosure requirements of directors, shadow directors, company secretaries and their families. Part IV Chapter 2 of the 1990 Act deals with individual and group acquisitions. In addition, sections 90 to 96 of the 1990 Act give statutory effect to Directive 88/627/EEC which provides for the publication of information concerning the

---

[101] Note 5 on R. 5.1.
[101a] See Chap. 13, paras 13–111–13–137.
[102] See Chap. 8, paras 8–03–8–05.
[103] paras 11–56–11–63.
[104] paras 11–64–11–75.
[104a] See Chap. 13, paras 13–03–13–86.

acquisition or disposal of a major holding in a company which is officially listed on the Stock Exchange. In addition to the Companies Acts requirements, one of the ongoing obligations imposed on listed companies under the Stock Exchange Listing Rules is to notify the Company Announcements Office without delay of major interests in shares.[105] These disclosure requirements will be examined further in Chapter 13.[105a]

III. RULES GOVERNING SUBSTANTIAL ACQUISITIONS OF SHARES

11–81   The Irish Takeover Panel Act 1997 (Substantial Acquisition) Rules, 1997 ("the SARs") provide a further impediment to a offeror who wishes to acquire control through the acquisition of shares on the Stock Exchange. The SARs, which are administered by the Panel, are designed primarily to restrict the speed with which a person may increase a holding of voting securities and rights over voting securities of a relevant company[106] to an aggregate of between 15 per cent and 30 per cent of the voting rights of that company. In addition, the SARs require accelerated disclosure of acquisitions of shares or rights over shares relating to such holdings. The SARs are examined in greater detail in chapter 13.[106a]

D. Procuring the Issue of Shares to the Offeror

11–82   If the offeree company agrees to issue sufficient new voting shares to the offeror, the offeror may acquire control in this manner. This process avoids the necessity to approach the offeree shareholders directly.

I. POWER TO ISSUE THE SHARES

11–83   The directors of the offeree must be authorised under the company's articles of association to issue these shares. If they are not so authorised, a resolution may be passed allowing them to do so. A resolution will also be necessary if the offeree's authorised share capital needs to be increased.[107] The directors of the offeree will have to consider the issue of pre-emption rights as shares are being offered to

---

[105]   Stock Exchange Listing rules, Chap. 9, paras 9–11–9–14.
[105a] See Chap. 13, para. 13–87 *et seq.*
[106]   A "relevant company" for the purposes of the SARs is the same as a "relevant company" for the purposes of the takeover rules and is defined in section 2 of the Act.
[106a] See Chap. 13, paras 13–111–13–137.
[107]   Chap. 8, paras 8–07–8–11.

the offeror for a cash consideration.[108] Share premiums will also become relevant.[109] If a minority of the offeree's shareholders are unhappy at the prospect of a change of control being effected in this manner, they may apply to the court under section 205 of the Companies Act 1963 claiming that the directors are exercising their powers in an oppressive manner or in disregard of their interests as members.[110]

Where the offeror is a listed company, certain requirements may be incurred by the offeror's directors under the Stock Exchange Listing Rules, depending on the classification of the transaction.[111] The requirements in the Listing rules on notifications relating to capital may also apply.[112]

II. MANDATORY OFFER – RULE 9

11–84 If as a result of the issue, the offeror or any concert party acquires shares carrying 30 per cent or more of the voting rights, a Rule 9 obligation will be incurred requiring the making of a cash offer to other shareholders. As noted,[113] the Panel may waive this obligation where new securities have been issued as consideration for a cash subscription and the issue is approved in an independent vote by the offeree shareholders in general meeting ("a whitewash").

In granting such a waiver, the Panel will generally insist on certain conditions being met as follows:

– no "disqualifying transactions" having been undertaken during the preceding 12 months. Such a transaction would include the purchase by the offeror or concert parties of securities of the offeree in the 12 month period prior to the posting to shareholders of circulars in respect of the proposals but subsequent to the commencement of negotiations with the offeree directors in relation to the issue. A waiver may actually be withdrawn if purchases are made on behalf of such persons during the period between the posting of the circular and the meeting of the shareholders.

– prior consultation having taken place with the Panel at an early stage and compliance with any of the Panel's directions or rulings.

– obtaining the prior approval of the proposals by an independent vote, on a poll, at a separate meeting of the holders of each relevant class of shares.

---

[108]   Chap. 8, paras 8–12–8–16.
[109]   Chap. 8, paras 8–18–8–20.
[110]   Chap. 19, paras 19–23–19–39.
[111]   Chap. 5, paras 5–37–5–47.
[112]   See paras 5–30–5–31.
[113]   para. 11–75.

– disenfranchising at each such meeting the person(s) seeking the waiver and any related parties.[114]

11–85 The Panel sets out certain information and statements which should be contained in the circular to the shareholders. Shareholders should be given, for example, competent legal advice regarding the proposed transaction, details of the potential controlling shareholders' maximum holding of securities and arrangements in connection with the proposal. Following the consideration of the proposals at a shareholders meeting, an announcement must be made by the offeror giving the outcome of the meeting and the number of securities of the offeree to which the controlling shareholders have thereby become entitled. The offeror should also announce the percentage of the total voting rights in the offeree represented by those securities.

III. FRUSTRATING ACTIONS

11–86 In cases where the offeree is already the subject of a competing offer or where the offeree has reason to believe that a bona fide offer might be imminent, the issue of shares to a friendly offeror may be viewed as a frustrating action by the Panel. General Principle 6 sets out the views of the Panel in respect of such actions. It states:

> "It is the duty of the directors of an offeree when an offer is made or when they have reason to believe that the making of an offer is imminent to refrain from doing anything as respects the conduct of the affairs of the offeree which might frustrate that offer or deprive shareholders of the opportunity of considering the merits of the offer, except upon the authority of those shareholders given in general meeting."

Rule 21 gives effect to this Principle by prohibiting any actions by the offeree which might frustrate the making or implementation of a bid unless the actions are sanctioned by the Panel or approved of by the offeree's shareholders in a general meeting. The allotment or issuance of any authorised but unissued shares is specifically included as an example of behaviour which might frustrate such a bid.

For this reason, before a offeree may issue shares to a offeror in circumstances where a competing bid is likely to be made or has actually been made, the approval of the offeree's shareholders should be obtained.[114a]

---

[114] Whitewash Guidance Notice in the notes on R. 9.
[114a] See Chap. 20, paras 20–08–20–12.

E. A Section 201 Arrangement

11–87   The offeror may acquire control of the offeree by organising to have shares in the offeree transferred to it by means of a single vesting order under section 201 of the 1963 Act. This scheme would obviously require the agreement of the management of the offeree.

Such a scheme involves having all the shares in the offeree which are held by its' existing shareholders cancelled. Shares in the offeror are then transferred to the offeree's shareholders to compensate them for their loss. Although, in theory, the offeree's shareholders could be offered cash instead of shares, this would be less usual. The reserve created in the offeree by the share cancellation is then capitalised and applied in paying up further shares in the offeree. These new shares may then be issued to the offeror, in place of those cancelled. The eventual outcome of this arrangement is that the offeree becomes a wholly owned subsidiary of the offeror and all the offeree's shareholders become shareholders in the offeror.[115]

11–88   As noted previously,[116] such a scheme requires the approval of 75 per cent in value of the shareholders present and voting. Court approval is also necessary to sanction the scheme and a copy of the court order must be delivered to the registrar of companies for registration.

The main advantage of this approach over a straightforward offer to the offeree's shareholders is that it requires the agreement of only 75 per cent of the offeree's shareholders to acquire control. With a straightforward offer, the agreement of 80 per cent of the offeree's shareholders is required to allow the offeror compulsorily acquire the remainder of the shares under section 204 of the 1963 Act. Also, in the case of a section 201 arrangement, it is 75 per cent of those shareholders who are present and voting who must consent rather than a percentage of all shareholders. The offeror will benefit thus from shareholder apathy. Additionally, it is possible to determine at the meeting whether the transaction will be acceptable rather than having to wait until the offer period closes (and possibly an extended period closes) to determine whether the shareholders have accepted the offer. The main drawback of this method, however, is that control will not pass until the court order is filed. This delay may allow a rival offeror an opportunity to intervene.

Depending on the classification of this transaction in Chapter 10 of the Stock Exchange Listing Rules, certain requirements relating to announcements, circulars and shareholder approval may be imposed.[117]

---

[115]   See Weinberg & Blank, *op.cit.*, above, n.31, Part 2, Chap. 3, para. 2–066.
[116]   Chap. 8, para. 8–42.
[117]   Chap. 5, paras 5–37–5–47.

F. A Reverse Takeover Offer

11–89 Where a company ("B Ltd.") seeks control of a desired offeree ("T Ltd."), an alternative to making an offer for T Ltd. is to organise for T Ltd. to make an offer for B Ltd. The directors of B Ltd. thus orchestrate a share for share offer by T Ltd. for all the outstanding capital of B Ltd..

This indirect method of acquiring control may be used where B Ltd. wishes to acquire control of a smaller company, and the offer is acceptable to the directors of that company. Since T Ltd. is a smaller company, in order for it to acquire control of the larger B Ltd., it will have to offer shareholders in B Ltd. a greater number of its own shares as consideration for every share in B Ltd. acquired. Thus, for example, it may give shareholders in B Ltd. four shares in T Ltd. for every share in B Ltd. acquired. This will require T Ltd to increase its issued share capital and probably its authorised share capital.[118]

11–90 A "reverse takeover transaction" is defined in Rule 3.2(c) as:

> "a transaction entered into by a relevant company whereby the relevant company acquires securities of another company, a business or assets of any other kind and pursuant to which the relevant company will or may be obliged to increase by more than 100 per cent its existing issued share capital that confers voting rights".

The outcome of this share for share exchange is that the original shareholders of B Ltd. will end up as majority shareholders of the enlarged capital of T Ltd., and the pre-existing shareholders of T Ltd. will end up with a minority interest. B Ltd. will then become a wholly owned subsidiary of T Ltd.

I. ATTRACTIONS OF A REVERSE TAKEOVER

11–91 Although the economic effect of a reverse takeover will be the same for the shareholders of B Ltd. as if B Ltd. had made the bid itself exchanging its shares for shares in T Ltd., there may be certain attractions for B Ltd. If B Ltd. is unlisted and T Ltd. is a listed company with a well established name and reputation, the directors of B Ltd. may wish to ensure that the holding company retains the title of the listed company.

11–92 A reverse takeover may also prove useful, where the shareholders of B Ltd. are more likely to be receptive to the proposal than shareholders in T Ltd. The success of an ordinary share for share offer

---

[118] Chap. 8, paras 8–08–8–11.

by a offeror for a offeree depends on the offeror's shareholders approving the issue of shares and possibly the increase of authorised share capital. The offerors shareholders must also give their approval under the Stock Exchange Listing Rules.[119] For the offeror to be in a position to compulsorily acquire all the shares in the offeree under section 204 of the 1963 Act, at least 80 per cent of the offeree's shareholders must approve of the bid. During this process, the bid may be frustrated by shareholders of either company. To defeat a bid, the offeror's shareholders could refuse to approve the resolution to increase the issued or authorised share capital or they could withhold their approval under the Listing Rules. In theory, this would need more than 50 per cent of shareholders in the offeror to vote against the proposals. As Weinberg and Blank point out, apathy and the tendency of shareholders to follow the recommendations of their board would operate against the interests of those who wished to defeat the bid.[120] On the other hand, to defeat a bid, the offeree shareholders would only have to ensure that 20 per cent of the shareholders did not accept the offer. In this way shareholder apathy would actually work in favour of the opponents of the takeover bid. Thus, if it seems likely that the offerors shareholders would be more receptive than those of the offeree to an acquisition, and if the offerees management agrees, it might make sense that the desired offeree initiate the offer.

11–93 A further reason why a reverse takeover might be the desired method of acquiring control would be where B Ltd. is prohibited from acquiring the shares of T Ltd. An example of this was seen in 1999 in the merger of Irish Life and Irish Permanent by way of a reverse takeover offer by Irish Permanent for the shares in Irish Life. Because of a provision in the Building Societies Act 1989,[121] which prohibited the acquisition of 15 per cent or more of the securities of Irish Permanent for five years following its conversion, an offer by Irish Life for Irish Permanent would not have been feasible. By organising to have Irish Permanent make the offer however, this prohibition could be avoided.

II. POWER OF THE DIRECTORS TO MAKE THE ACQUISITION

11–94 Although the directors of a company are generally entitled to make a decision to make an acquisition without recourse to their shareholders,[122] a court may intervene if directors are deemed to have breached their fiduciary duties or if an action under section 205 of the 1963 Act for

---

[119] Chap. 5, para. 5–42.
[120] *op. cit.*, no. 31, Part II, Chap. 3, para. 2–063.
[121] s.102.
[122] Chap. 8, paras 8–03–8–05.

oppression of a minority is initiated.[123] In blatant cases, directors may be found to have infringed General Principle 8 requiring directors to disregard their own interests and to consider the interests of the shareholders as a whole or General Principle 9 prohibiting the oppression of a minority and requiring the exercise of control in good faith.

III. INDEPENDENT LEGAL ADVICE

11–95 The Takeover Rules will apply to reverse takeovers as to any other form of takeover. An additional rule also applies. Where a company proposes to enter into a reverse takeover transaction, Rule 3.2(a)(ii) requires the board of T Ltd. to obtain competent independent advice before announcing its proposals. This advice should involve a consideration as to whether or not the entry into the reverse takeover transaction is in the interests of its shareholders. The board of the T Ltd. must then allow its shareholders sufficient time to consider this advice before calling a meeting to implement the transaction. Every document issued by the board in such circumstances must include a responsibility statement by the directors as set out in Rule 19.2.

IV. STOCK EXCHANGE LISTING RULES

11–96 For the purposes of the Listing rules, a reverse takeover is defined as:

> "an acquisition by a listed company of a business, an unlisted company or assets where any percentage ratio[124] is 100 per cent or more or which would result in a fundamental change in the business or in a change in board or voting control of the listed company".[125]

Upon the announcement of a reverse takeover which is agreed or in contemplation, the Stock Exchange will suspend listing of the company's securities. The company must prepare a Class 1 circular for shareholders and obtain their approval for the transaction. If the company wishes to be listed following completion of the transaction, it must also prepare listing particulars as if it were a new applicant. One exception to this is that audited accounts need only be in respect of one year rather than three years. If the shareholders approve the transaction and it is completed, the existing listing will be restored on publication of the circular and listing particulars.[126]

---

[123] Chap. 19, paras 19–23–19–52.
[124] Chap. 5, para. 5–37.
[125] Chap. 10, para. 4(d).
[126] Chap. 10, para. 39.

CHAPTER 12

PROCEDURAL REQUIREMENTS FOR THE TAKEOVER OF A PUBLIC COMPANY

Introduction

12–01   In this Chapter, the procedure by which a "relevant company"[1] is acquired is considered in greater detail. An examination is undertaken of the Irish Takeover Panel Act 1997, Takeover Rules, 1997 ("the Takeover Rules") pertaining to the different stages in the acquisition process – from the approach by the offeror to the offeree board up until the payment of consideration to the offeree shareholders upon successful completion of the offer.

A. Approach to the Offeree

12–02   Rule 1 governs the approach to the offeree board. Where the offeror intends making an offer for an offeree, it should disclose this intention, in the first instance, to the board of the offeree or to its advisors. Where the advisers are notified initially, they are responsible for immediately notifying the offeree board. The offeror must make this notification before any announcement concerning the offer is made. The amount of notice given to the offeree board will depend on the nature of the offer and the reaction it is likely to provoke. For example, in the case of a friendly bid, the offeree board will be notified well in advance of the announcement and their approval and co-operation will be sought. In the case of a hostile bid, the offeree board will probably be notified only hours before the announcement is to be made to the shareholders of the offeree.

12–03   Where the offeree board or its advisers are approached by the offeror (or by some person on the offeror's behalf) with a view to making an offer or disclosing an intention to make an offer, the identity of the offeror and, if applicable, the identity of the ultimate controlling interests in the offeror should be disclosed.[2] This ensures that the

---

[1]   Irish Takeover Panel Act 1997, s.2.
[2]   R. 1(b).

offeree board is not negotiating in a vacuum. In order to ensure that it's time is not diverted unnecessarily, the offeree board may ask the offeror to satisfy it that it has "sufficient resources to enable it to implement the offer in full." The offeror must comply with any such request.[3] This provision relates to the consideration to be provided for the acquisition. It does not, however, mean that the offeror must satisfy the offeree that sufficient working capital is in place to ensure the future success or viability of the company once the acquisition has been made.

12–04   Whilst the restrictions governing dealing during the course of the offer are set out in the next Chapter,[3a] Rule 4.1 merits a brief mention in this context. Rule 4.1(a) specifically prohibits dealings in the offeree's securities by persons, other than the offeror, in possession of inside information concerning the offer or contemplated offer during the period commencing when an offer is contemplated and ending at the announce-ment either of the approach or the announcement of an offer or the termination of discussions. A second prohibition on dealing is introduced during this same period by Rule 4.1(c). Persons, other than the offeror, in possession of inside information concerning an offer or contemplated offer, are prohibited from dealing in any way in securities of the offeror during this period. This latter prohibition will not, however, apply where the offer is not price-sensitive in relation to such securities. Arguably an offer for a pure cash consideration could be said to be insensitive to the price of the offeror's securities. In reality, however, an offeror's ability to raise cash or to borrow cash will be directly related to it's share price. Two issues are worth emphasising in respect of the aforementioned two prohibitions. Firstly, the prohibition on dealing in securities also includes dealing in traded and other options and derivatives in respect of or referenced to such securities. Secondly, the prohibitions do not apply to dealings by the offeror. The rational for exempting the offeror from these dealing prohibition is that dealing by the offeror in offeree securities or possibly even the offeror securities may facilitate the making of the bid. For example, once, the offeror forms an intention to make an offer, it may want to consolidate its position in the offeree before it approaches the company and makes the offer. Recommending persons to deal in securities in such circumstances is similarly prohibited by Rule 4.1(b). In order to further facilitate the takeover, Rule 4.1(d) allows the offeror organise for concert parties to acquire securities in the offeree on condition that "the offeror bears all the risks and receives all the benefits". In addition, persons, other than the offeror, in possession of

---

[3]   R. 1(c).
[3a]   See Chap. 13, paras 13–03–13–86.
[4]   R. 4.1(c).

unpublished price sensitive information concerning the bid, are prohibited from dealing in the offeror's securities during the same period.[4]

12–05 Prior to the making of an announcement under Rule 2, a duty is imposed on the offeror, the offeree and their associates and advisers to observe "absolute secrecy" in respect of the offer or contemplated offer. Confidential information may be passed on to other persons only if this is absolutely necessary and only then, if the recipient accepts the need for maintaining the secrecy of the information. Furthermore, all parties are obliged to conduct themselves in such a way as to minimise the possibility of an accidental leak of information.[5]

B. Announcements

12–06 In order to ensure that shareholders are kept informed at all times, the Rules require that announcements be made on certain occasions. In addition, the Rules also specify the parties responsible for making the announcements, the mode of announcements and the content of such announcements.

I. THE OBLIGATION TO MAKE AN ANNOUNCEMENT

12–07 The Irish Takeover Panel ("the Panel") has absolute discretion to direct a party to make an announcement where it considers it appropriate. In addition, unless the Panel agrees otherwise, Rule 2.2 requires an announcement concerning an offer or a possible offer in the following circumstances:

(a) immediately after the offeree board has been notified of a firm intention to make an offer the making of which is not, or has ceased to be, subject to any pre-condition;

(b) immediately after a transaction which gives rise to an obligation to make an offer to all shareholders under Rule 9 or Rule 37;[6]

(c) when, following an approach to the offeree, the offeree is the subject of rumour and speculation or if there is an untoward movement[7] in its share price;

---

[5] R. 2.1.
[6] Or which, subject only to the issue in the State of a governmental or regulatory authorisation, consent, approval or clearance, will give rise to such an obligation.
[7] The note on Rule 2.2 explains that a movement of the order of 10 per cent would normally be regarded as "untoward". This is likely to be the subject of review by the Panel in the future. The application of a single percentage figure to stocks of law and

(d)   when, before an approach has been made to the offeree, the offeree is the subject of rumour and speculation or if there is an untoward movement in its share price and there are "reasonable grounds" for attributing these events to the offeror's own actions or intentions;

(e)   when negotiations or discussions concerning the offer are about to be extended to include more than a very restricted number of people;

(f)   when a purchaser is being sought for a holding, or aggregate holdings, of securities conferring 30 per cent or more of the voting rights in a relevant company, or when the board of the offeree is seeking potential offerors and (i) the company is the subject of rumour and speculation or (ii) there is an untoward movement in its' share price or (iii) the number of potential purchasers or offerors approached is about to be increased to include more than a very restricted number of persons; or

(g)   when, after an announcement has been made to the effect that offer discussions are taking place or that an approach or offer is contemplated, the discussions are terminated or the offeror decides not to proceed with the offer.

12–08   Where the offeree is the subject of rumours and speculation or there is an unusual level of speculative activity in its shares, the market price of the shares is affected. This situation may be explicable by publicly known facts. Where there are no such facts and where there has been no approach to the offeree, it is possible that the acts of the potential offeror, have created the situation. In such circumstances, in order to avoid the creation of a false market, an announcement should be made. In practice, speculation and resultant price movements can occur at a very early stage of a contemplated offer. This may occur even where the offeror is confident about its security. If the offeree is the subject of such rumour and speculation or if there is an untoward movement in its share price, and the person responsible for making the announcement does not consider that the circumstances require an immediate announcement, they are required to consult the Panel without delay.[8]

12–09   As soon as practicable after an announcement is made of an offer or possible offer under Rule 2.2, each of the offeror, its directors and its concert parties and each of the offeree and its directors are

---

high monetary value and to stocks subject to both frequent and infrequent trading is capable of producing anomalous results. In the UK, reference is also made to a rise of 5 per cent in the course of a single day.

[8]   R. 2.2, final para.

required to furnish the Panel in writing with an address within the State for service of documents and with a number of a facsimile machine at the address.[9] Similar obligations are imposed upon the advisers to both the offeror and offeree as soon as practicable after their appointment. In addition, the Panel may impose a similar requirement on any other person.

II. THE RESPONSIBILITY FOR MAKING AN ANNOUNCEMENT

12–10   Before the offeree board is approached, the offeror is responsible for making the necessary announcements.[10] This is rather an onerous duty as it involves monitoring the market to determine if there has been any speculation concerning the offer or if there has been an untoward price movement in the offeree's shares. In addition, if it proves necessary, the offeror is responsible for making an announcement under Rule 2.2(b) and an announcement of a firm intention to make an offer under Rule 2.5.

12–11   After the approach, the offeree board generally assumes the responsibility for making the relevant announcements.[11] This includes responsibility for making an announcement under Rule 2.2(g). If the offeree board intends to recommend the offer to its shareholders, and the offeree's quotation is likely to be suspended temporarily, instead of making an immediate announcement, the offeree board may instead obtain a suspension at the time the announcement would normally have been made and then make an announcement.[12] Where the offeree board expects to recommend an unannounced proposed offer and the offeror intends to provide a cash underwritten alternative offer, the offeree board must request a suspension before the proposed offer is disclosed by the offeror to any sub-underwriters. However, if the offer is not to be recommended by the offeree board, a suspension would be impracticable and the offeror is entitled to inform a limited number of underwriters and sub-underwriters of the offer immediately before the announcement. Such persons must however be advised of the confidential nature of the information and of their status as insiders resulting from the disclosure.[13]

12–12   The responsibility for making an announcement under Rule 2.2(f) to the effect that a purchaser for a holding of securities conferring more than 30 per cent of the voting rights or potential offerors are being

---

[9] R. 2.10.
[10] R. 2.3(a).
[11] R. 2.3(b).
[12] R. 2.3(b).
[13] R. 2.3(d).

sought rests with the potential vendor or the board of the relevant company.[14]

After the offer period commences, the offeree is also responsible for circulating copies of the relevant announcement or a circular summarising the terms of the offer to its shareholders and to the Panel.[15] If it is appropriate the offereee board may also explain the implications of the announcement.

III. THE MODE OF ANNOUNCEMENT

12–13   Except as otherwise provided by the Rules, announcements must be made in writing and delivered either by hand or by facsimile to the Stock Exchange (Company Announcements Office) and the Panel.[16]

IV. THE CONTENT OF AN ANNOUNCEMENT

12–14   Until a firm intention to make an offer has been notified, a brief announcement that talks are taking place is normally sufficient.[17] There is no requirement to name the offeror in such an announcement. In special circumstances or in the case of a mandatory offer under Rule 9 or Rule 37, a more detailed announcement may be required.

Where an announcement is required in circumstances where a person is being cited as a potential offeror, that person may decide to make a statement to the effect that they do not intend to make an offer in respect of the relevant company. However, if that person makes such a statement, they are then prohibited from making an offer for that company for 12 months.[18] Where such a statement is made, it should be as clear an unambiguous as possible in order to ensure that the market is not misled.

V. THE ANNOUNCEMENT OF A FIRM INTENTION TO MAKE AN OFFER

12–15   The making of an announcement of "a firm intention to make an offer" marks an important turning point. From this time on, the offeror must generally proceed with the offer unless the Panel agrees otherwise. However, the Takeover Rules allow the offeror to discontinue the offer either where the posting of the offer is subject to some condition which has not been fulfilled or where a higher offer has already been posted for the offeree by another offeror.[19]

---

[14]   R. 2.3(e).
[15]   R. 2.6.
[16]   R. 2.9.
[17]   R. 2.4
[18]   R. 2.8.
[19]   R. 2.7.

12–16   It is important to note that before the offeror may announce a firm intention to make an offer, Rule 2.5(a) requires both the offeror and its financial advisers to be satisfied that the offeror is capable and will continue to be capable of implementing the offer. The offeror's financial advisers are required to take all necessary steps to verify the offeror's capacity to implement the offer, in particular by a careful review of the offeror's current and prospective financial position and of any assumptions upon which the offeror's prospective financial position is predicated.[20] This rule reflects General Principle 3 which states:

> "No offer shall be made and no announcement of a proposed offer shall be made save after careful and responsible consideration of the matter by the offeror and any advisers of the offeror and only if the offeror and any advisers to the offeror are satisfied that the offeror will be able to implement the offer if it is accepted."

The purpose of this rule is to avoid the creation of a false market which might result from the making of an offer which ultimately is incapable of being completed. In the case of a mandatory bid, the offeror's financial advisor will be required to confirm the offeror's capacity to complete the offer in the announcement of an offer. In order to ensure enforcement, Rule 2.5(c) provides that if this confirmation proves to be inaccurate, the Panel may require the person who gave the confirmation to provide the necessary resources. Such an obligation will not however be imposed where the Panel is satisfied that the person acted responsibly and took all reasonable steps to verify its confirmation.

12–17   When a firm intention to make an offer is announced, the announcement must contain:

  (i) the terms of the offer;

 (ii) the identity of the offeror and, if applicable, of the ultimate controlling interests in the offeror;

(iii) details of any existing holdings of securities of the offeree:

    (1) owned or controlled by the offeror;
    (2) owned or controlled by any person acting in concert with the offeror;
    (3) in respect of which the offeror has received an irrevocable commitment to accept the offer;
    (4) in respect of which the offeror or any concert party holds an option to purchase;

---

[20] Note on Rule 2.5(a).

(iv) details of any options to subscribe for new securities of the offeree held by the offeror or any concert party;

(v) details of any outstanding derivative referenced to any securities of the offeree entered into by the offeror or any concert party;

(vi) all conditions (including normal conditions relating to acceptances, quotation and increase of capital) to which the offer or the posting of it is subject; and

(vii) details of any indemnity or option arrangement relating to the offeree's securities.[21]

12–18   For reasons of secrecy, it may not be possible for the offeror to make enquiries about its interests in the offeree's securities. In such a case, the offeror is allowed to obtain this information after the making of the announcement and communicate it to the Panel. If the holdings are significant, the Panel may require the offeror to publish the information in a subsequent announcement. It should also be noted that an announcement under Rule 2.2(b) should not be delayed while full information is being obtained. Any information not included in the first announcement may be published in a subsequent supplementary announcement.

C. Conduct During the Offer Period

12–19   The Takeover Rules set out guidelines relating to the conduct of parties during the offer period. This is a particularly crucial period in the course of the offer and the conduct of the offeror, the offeree and their associates and advisers is strictly regulated during this time. The Takeover Rules cover dealings by the parties during the offer period, communications issued by the parties in connection with the offer or potential offer and also any actions taken by the offeree which might lead to the frustration of the offer.

I. DEALINGS DURING THE OFFER PERIOD

12–20   Certain dealings in securities by parties to the takeover are restricted or prohibited by the Takeover Rules. Other dealings are allowed, but must be publicly or privately disclosed. These dealings are examined in greater detail in the next Chapter.[21a]

---

[21] R. 2.5(b).
[21a] See Chap. 13, paras 13–69–13–86 and 13–106–13–110.

II. COMMUNICATIONS

12–21 Rule 19.1(a) imposes an obligation on both the offeror and the offeree to ensure that each document, advertisement and statement in connection with the offer which is issued or made by it or on its behalf during the course of the offer satisfies the same standards of accuracy, completeness and fair presentation as would be required of a prospectus. The language used should be unambiguous reflecting clearly and concisely the position being described.[22] The Panel has stated that it regards financial advisers as being responsible for guiding their clients, any relevant public relations advisers and any other relevant persons employed by their clients in connection with the offer in respect of any information released during the course of an offer in connection with the offer.[23] Any material facts contained in such documentation should be accompanied by a statement of their source unless such facts have already been included in previous documentation sent to shareholders.[24] Similarly, although quotations may be included, once they are in context, details of their source should also be included.[25] In addition, the board of the company which issues the document containing the quotation must be prepared, where appropriate, to corroborate or substantiate the contents of the quotation and the document must contain a directors' responsibility statement. Where the offeror or offeree intends to use televised, video or taped materials in connection with the offer, the Panel must be consulted in advance in order to ensure that they are appropriate.[26]

12–22 All documents issued to shareholders of the offeree and almost all advertisements published in connection with the offer by either the offeror or offeree or on their behalf during the course of the offer are required to include a responsibility statement.[27] Press announcements are deemed to be advertisements for the purposes of Rule 19.2. In this statement, the directors should accept responsibility for the information contained in the document or advertisement. They should also state that, "to the best of their knowledge and belief (having taken all reasonable care to ensure that such is the case)," the information contained in the document or advertisement is factually correct and does not contain anything likely to affect the import of such information. This statement is regarded by the Panel as embracing expressions of opinion in the document or advertisement.[28] Unless the Panel allows otherwise, all of

---

[22] Note 2 on Rule 19.1.
[23] Note 1 on Rule 19.1.
[24] R. 19.1(b).
[25] R. 19.1(c).
[26] R. 19.1(e).
[27] R. 19.2(a).
[28] Note 2 on Rule 19.2.

the directors should be included in this responsibility statement.[29] The only advertisements which do not need a directors' responsibility statements are product advertisements or corporate image advertisements not bearing on the offer or potential offer, advertisements which are notices relating to court schemes and advertisements which contain only information already published in a circular which contained a directors' responsibility statement.[30]

12–23 Although, most advertisements connected with an offer or potential offer are prohibited, certain advertisements containing non-controversial information such as reminders of closing dates, product advertisements or corporate image advertisements not bearing on an offer or potential offer are allowed.[31] Even where advertisements are allowed, the content, format and publication schedule must be approved by the Panel. Telephone campaigns[32] and media interviews[33] are carefully regulated in order to ensure that no new information is disclosed and no information is conveyed which is inaccurate or misleading.

12–24 Where any documents or announcements bearing on the offer or any advertisements are released to shareholders of the offeree or to the media, copies should be made available at the time of release to the Panel and to the advisers of all other principals concerned with the offer or competing offer.[34] In addition, if the material is released outside normal business hours, the person making the release is subject to two obligations. Firstly, he or she must inform the advisers of the release immediately. In order to bring this information to their attention, it may be necessary to telephone the advisers. Secondly, the person making the release must deliver the material to the Panel and to the advisers, if necessary making special arrangements to ensure this is done. In addition, Rule 4.3 states that anyone proposing to contact a private individual or small corporate shareholder with a view to seeking an irrevocable commitment to accept or refrain from accepting an offer or contemplated offer must contact the Panel *e.g.* if an offeror intends launching a telephone campaign to gather irrevocable commitments, the Panel must be notified.

12–25 Rule 20.1(a) requires that information about companies involved in an offer which is tendered by or on behalf of either the offeror or offeree must be made equally available by it to all the

---

[29] R. 19.2(b).
[30] R. 19.2(a).
[31] R. 19.4.
[32] R. 19.5.
[33] R. 19.6.
[34] R. 19.7.

shareholders in the offeree of the class or classes which are the subject of the offer. This information should be released "as nearly as possible at the same time and in the same manner". The purpose of this rule is to ensure equality of treatment of all shareholders. This is in keeping with General Principle 2 which states:

> "Where information is tendered by the offeror or offeree or their respective advisers to shareholders of the offeree in the course of any offer, it shall be made available equally to all of the shareholders who may accept the offer".

Rule 20.1 will not prevent brokers or advisers to or other associates of an offeror or offeree from issuing circulars during the offer period to their own investment clients.[35] The issues must, however, be approved in advance by the Panel. In addition, these circulars should not include any statement derived from non-public information or any profit forecast unless such a forecast is contained in the offer documents or offeree board circulars. If representatives of the offeror or offeree or their advisers hold meetings with shareholders of the offeror or offeree or with analysts, stockbrokers or other investment intermediaries during the offer period, no material new information should be disclosed. If this proves unavoidable and new information is disclosed, the offeree's shareholders must be circularised with this information "as soon as possible thereafter".[36] Unless the Panel consents otherwise, an appropriate representative of the financial adviser or corporate broker to the offeror or, as the case may be, the offeree must be present at the meeting and must confirm to the Panel in writing that no material new information was disclosed and no material new opinion was expressed at the meeting. This confirmation must be submitted to the Panel not later than 12.00 noon on the business day following the date of the meeting.

12–26   Finally, although an offeree may prefer one offeror to another, information provided to one offeror should be provided to other offerors who have made announcements. The difficulty with this provision from the other offerors perspective is that the information must only be provided where it has been "specifically requested".[37] Thus, if competing offerors are not aware of the correct questions to ask, they will not obtain equivalent information.

---

[35] R. 20.1(c).
[36] R. 20.1(b).
[37] R. 20.2.

III. FRUSTRATING ACTIVITIES

12–27 Except with the Panel's consent or with the approval of share-holders in a general meeting, the offeree should not engage in actions likely to frustrate a bid during the course of an offer or at any earlier time when an offer is believed to be imminent.[38] Examples of the type of activities likely to frustrate the making of the offer or the offer itself include: allotting or issuing shares, issuing or granting options in respect of unissued shares, creating or issuing securities with convertible rights; acquiring or disposing of material assets or entering into unusual contracts. This rule gives effect to General Principle 6 which states:

> "It is the duty of the directors of the offeree when an offer is made or when they have reason to believe that an offer is imminent to refrain from doing anything as respects the conduct of the affairs of the offeree which might frustrate the offer or deprive shareholders of the opportunity of considering the merits of the offer, except upon the authority of those shareholders given in general meeting".

Frustrating activities will be considered further in Chapters 19 and 20.

D. The Making of the Offer and the Offeree's Response

12–28 Rule 23(a) imposes obligations on the offeror to give sufficient information and on the board of the offeree to give sufficient infor-mation and advice to the offeree's shareholders in order to allow them to reach a properly informed decision as to the merits or demerits of an offer. The obligation of the offeror in this respect towards the offeree's shareholders is said to be no less than its duty towards its own share-holders. In addition to being accurate, the information must be timely, in order to enable the offeree shareholders to make a decision in good time. The emphasis on the timeliness of information is met by the rules setting out the strict timetable to be adhered to by the parties.[39] Rule 23(a) is entirely consistent with General Principle 4 which states:

> "Shareholders to whom an offer is made shall be entitled to receive such information and advice as will enable them to make an informed decision on the offer. For that purpose the information and advice should be accurate and adequate and be furnished to the shareholders in a timely fashion."

Rule 23(b) provides that any documents issued to shareholders of the offeree by or on behalf of the offeror or the offeree must include

---

[38] R. 21.
[39] See paras 12–54–12–62.

information in respect of any material change in any information previously published by it or on its behalf during the offer period.[40] Furthermore, Rule 24.14 requires an offeror to announce without delay details of any material change which occurs during the offer period in any information previously published by it or on its behalf. If required by the Panel to do so, the offeror must issue a circular to the offeree's shareholders containing details of any such material change. Rule 25.7 imposes a similar requirement on the offeree.

I. OFFEROR DOCUMENTS

12–29   If the making of the offer has been announced to be subject to a pre-condition relating to action by the offeree shareholders (including the rejection of a proposed acquisition or disposal by the offeree), the first major circular sent by the offeror to the offeree shareholders must include the information which would be required by Rule 24 to be included if that circular were an offer document.[41] The purpose of this is to ensure that the shareholders do not have to make an important decision without being in full possession of all the relevant facts.

12–30   Rule 24 sets out the contents of the offer document. On the offeror's part, the general obligation to provide adequate and timely information is normally fulfilled by the issuing of this document. The offer document must include a heading stating:

> "If you are in any doubt about this offer, you should consult an independent financial adviser who, if you are taking advice in Ireland, is authorised or exempted under the Investment Intermediaries Act 1995".[42]

Normally, the heading will provide for a UK adviser and so the above sentence will continue with words to the following effect "or if you are taking advice in the UK, is authorised under the Financial Services Act 1986 of the United Kingdom". The first page of the offer document will also generally contain the date the document is dispatched, the name and address of the offeror and, if appropriate, of the person making the offer on behalf of the offeror.[43]

(1) The Terms of the Offer

12–31   The document must provide details of the shares for which the offer is made and inform the shareholders whether the shares will be

---

[40] If there have been no such changes, this fact must be stated.
[41] R. 23(c).
[42] R. 24.2(b)(i).
[43] R. 24.2(b)(ii).

transferred *ex div* or *cum div*.[44] The former term means that the shares are being transferred without the dividend and the latter term means that the shares are being transferred with the dividend still included. Market price quotations will also be required for the shares for which the offer is made, and in the case of a securities exchange offer for the securities offered.[45] This will allow the offeree shareholders to assess the value of the offer. In the case of a securities exchange offer, certain particulars of the new securities being issued as consideration should be included.[46] These details should include, for example, particulars of the first dividend or interest payment, the ranking of the securities for dividends or interest, capital and repayment. Any significant effects of full acceptance of the offer upon the offeror's assets, profits and business must also be identified in the case of a securities exchange offer.[46a] If the offer document compares the value of the offer with previous prices of the offeree's shares, the document must include a comparison between the current value of the offer and the price of the offeree's shares on the last business day prior to the commencement of the offer period.[47] This is to ensure that the comparison is fair and meaningful.

12–32   The total consideration to be offered must be clearly stated.[48] The offer document must also describe how the offer is to be financed and the source of finance. The principal lenders or arrangers of such finance must be identified. If the offeror intends that the payment of interest on, repayment of or security for, any liability will depend to any significant extent on the business of the offeree, the arrangements proposed must be described in the offer document. If the offeror has no such intention, this should be clearly stated.[49] If the consideration under the offer is in the form of cash or includes any element of cash, the offer document must contain a confirmation by an appropriate third party, usually the offeror's commercial bank or financial adviser, that the offeror has sufficient resources to satisfy full acceptance of the offer.[50] The giving of this confirmation is a significant undertaking for the third party because, in the event the conformation proves to be inaccurate, they may be required to provide the necessary capital. It will however be a defence to prove that, in giving the confirmation, they acted responsibly and took all reasonable steps to ensure that the cash was available at all relevant times. If part or all of the consideration to be offered is comprised

---

[44]   R. 24.2(b)(iii).
[45]   R. 24.2(b)(vi).
[46]   R. 24.2(b)(vii).
[46a] R. 24.2(b)(viii).
[47]   R. 24.2(e).
[48]   R. 24.2(b)(iv).
[49]   R. 24.2(d).
[50]   R. 24.7.

of securities and the offeror intends to apply for a quotation on the Irish Stock Exchange or on a regulated market in another jurisdiction, the relevant quotation will become a condition of the offer. Unless the Panel consents otherwise, this condition should be structured in such a way as to ensure that it is capable of being accepted only when the stock exchange grants the quotation.[51] If the consideration includes the issue of unquoted securities, the offer document should provide an appropriate adviser's estimate of their value.[52] An estimate should also be provided in any subsequent circulars from the offeror. Unless the Panel agrees, the offeree shareholders are entitled to receive the consideration free of any lien, right of set-off, counterclaim or other analogous right to which the offeror may be entitled against any shareholder. A statement to this effect must be included in the offer document.[53]

The offer document must incorporate language reflecting the timing obligations or restrictions on the offeror and the rights of shareholders of the offeree in respect of the acceptance conditions.[54]

(2) Procedure for Accepting the Offer

12–33 The offer document must inform shareholders of the particulars of all documents required and the procedures to be followed for acceptances of the offer.[55] Shareholders will be asked to return their completed acceptance forms to the receiving agent. In the case of shares held in certificated form, they will be asked to return the relative share certificates, other documents of title, letters of indemnity and any supporting documentation. Letters of indemnity may be necessary where any of the certificates or documents of title have been lost or mislaid by their owners. Where shares are held by any shareholders in uncertified form (*i.e.* Crest), the shareholders will be required to provide their participant identity and member account identity under which the shares are held in Crest. In addition, shareholders will be required to take certain steps to ensure that their shares are transferred to an escrow balance specifying a particular escrow agent. Appendix 1 of the Takeover Rules sets out the procedures for receiving agents. Rule 22 requires the offeree and its registrar to comply with these procedures. The offeree must also ensure that transfers of securities of the offeree are registered promptly during the course of an offer.

12–34 If there is a cash underwritten alternative offer provided by a third party in connection with the offer, this may in certain circumstances be shut off in accordance with Rule 33.2. Thus, the procedure

---

[51] R. 24.9.
[52] R. 24.10.
[53] R. 24.11.
[54] R. 24.6.
[55] R. 24.2(b)(v).

for accepting this offer must be prominently stated in the relevant documents and acceptance forms. The offer document, the acceptance form and any subsequent documents must make clear whether shareholders are required to lodge their certificates as well as their completed acceptance forms by the closing date of the cash underwritten alternative offer in order to receive cash.[56]

(3) Financial & Other Information on the Offeror and the Offeree

12–35 If the offeror is a company incorporated under the Companies Acts 1963 to 1990, an "existing company" as defined in those Acts or an unregistered company to which section 377(1) of the Companies Act 1963 applies and its shares are quoted on the Irish Stock Exchange, Rule 24.2(a)(i) requires the following information on the offeror:

(1) turnover, net profit or loss before and after tax, the tax charge, extraordinary items, minority interests, the amount absorbed by dividends and earnings and dividends per share for the last three financial years for which the information has been published;

(2) a statement of the assets and liabilities specified in the last published audited accounts;

(3) a cash flow statement if provided in the last published audited accounts;

(4) all known material changes in the financial or trading position of the company subsequent to the last published audited accounts;[57]

(5) details relating to items referred to in sub-paragraph (1) in respect of any interim statements or preliminary announcements made since the last published audited accounts;

(6) significant accounting policies together with any points taken from the notes to the accounts which are of major relevance to an appreciation of the figures;

(7) if figures are not comparable to a material extent because of a change in accounting policy, this should be disclosed and the approximate amount of the resultant variation should be stated;

(8) the names of the offeror's directors;

(9) the nature of the offeror's business and its financial and trading prospects;

(10) a summary of the principal contents of each material contract entered into by the offeror or any of its subsidiaries during the

---

[56] R. 24.13.
[57] If there were no changes a statement to this effect should be included.

period commencing two years before the commencement of the offer period.

The offer document should also contain information on the offeree on the same basis as set out in sub-paragraphs (1) to (7) above.[58] This is mandatory whether the offeree is quoted on the Stock Exchange or not.

12–36 If the offeror is not a company incorporated under the Companies Acts 1963 to 1990, an "existing company" as defined in those Acts or an unregistered company to which section 377(i) of the Companies Act 1963 applies or if its shares are not quoted on the Irish Stock Exchange, Rule 24.2(a)(ii) requires the following information to be included concerning the offeror:

(1) the information described in Rule 24.2(a)(i) so far as it is appropriate and such further information as the Panel may require in the particular circumstances of the case;

(2) details of the identity and interests in the offeror held by any person who has made (or proposes to make or increase) an investment in the offeror for the purposes of the offer such that they will have a potential interest in any part of the equity share capital or potential equity share capital of the offeree and such other information as the Panel requires about this person;

(3) similar details as is required in the previous sub-paragraph concerning any person whose pre-existing interest in the offeror is such that they have an interest of 5 per cent or more in any part of the equity share capital or potential equity share capital of the offeree.

(4) Shareholdings and Dealings

12–37 It is important that shareholders of the offeree are aware of the level of shares already held in their company by the offeror and certain related parties. In addition, shareholders are entitled to be informed of the level of recent dealings of such parties. In the case of a successful securities exchange offer, the shareholders in the offeree will become shareholders in the offeror. In such a case, they will then become interested in the shareholdings of related parties to the offeror in the offeror. In addition, they will be anxious to ensure that the offeror's current price has not been artificially inflated by heavy dealing by related parties.

---

[58] R. 24.2(c).

12–38 Rule 24.3(a) requires the offer document to state:

(i) the shareholdings[59] of the offeror in the offeree;

(ii) the shareholdings in the offeror (in the case of a securities exchange offer only) and in the offeree in which directors of the offeror are interested;

(iii) the shareholdings in the offeror (in the case of a securities exchange offer only) and in the offeree which any persons acting in concert with the offeror own or control (with the names of such persons acting in concert);

(iv) the shareholdings in the offeror (in the case of a securities exchange offer only) and in the offeree owned or controlled by any persons who, prior to the posting of the offer document, have irrevocably committed themselves to accept the offer, together with the names of such persons; and

(v) the shareholdings in the offeror (in the case of a securities exchange offer only) and in the offeree owned or controlled by any persons with whom the offeror or any person acting in concert with the offeror has any arrangement to which Rule 8.7 applies.

If there are no shareholdings in any of the above categories, this should be clearly stated.[60] In addition, any person required by Rule 24.3 to disclose shareholdings, must disclose details of any dealings for value in the securities concerned during the period beginning 12 months prior to the commencement of the offer period and ending with the last practicable date prior to the posting of the offer document. If no dealings have taken place, this fact must be stated.[61]

(5) Profit Forecasts and Asset Valuations

12–39 Rules 28 and 29 deal with profit forecasts and asset valuations issued by or on behalf of either the offeror or offeree during the offer period. Rule 28.1 provides that all profit forecasts must be compiled with care, accuracy and objectivity by the directors of the offeror or offeree. In addition, it requires the financial advisers to the offeror or offeree to satisfy themselves that the forecast has been prepared in this manner. Rule 28.2(a) provides that if a profit forecast appears in any document addressed by the directors of the offeror or offeree to shareholders of the offeree in connection with the offer, the document must state the assumptions upon which it is based in order to allow shareholders to

---

[59] As defined by Rule 24.3(f).
[60] R. 24.3(b). This will not apply to categories (iv) or (v) above if there are no such irrevocable commitments or arrangements.

form a view as to the reasonableness and reliability of the forecast. The shareholders' attention must be drawn specifically to those uncertainties which could materially disturb the ultimate achievement of the forecast. The document must also indicate any limitations on the accuracy of the forecast in order to assist shareholders in their review. A description of the general nature of the business should be included with an indication of any major hazards of forecasting in the particular business. Rule 28.2(b) provides that if the offeror or the offeree, after posting the offer document or the first major offeree board circular, makes a profit forecast in a public statement, the statement must include the information required by Rule 28.2(a). The advice of the financial advisers and accountants to the offeror and offeree must be made available and these persons must satisfy themselves that the forecasts have been made with care. Rule 28.3(a) provides that reports may also be required from the auditors, consultant accountants or in certain cases independent valuers in respect of these forecasts.[62] If, after the commencement of the offer period, a profit forecast is made by an offeror before the offer document is posted, or by an offeree before the first major offeree board circular is published, Rule 28.4 provides that the reports required by Rule 28.3 should be included in the document. If the profit forecast is not made until after the posting of these documents, a document containing the requisite reports should be sent to shareholders with a minimum of delay after the publication of the forecast. Rule 28.5 requires that any documents sent out by the offeror or offeree in connection with the offer must comment on the continuing validity of the forecast. Examples of statements which will be treated as profit forecasts are set out in Rule 28.6 and include: estimates of minimum or maximum profits for a particular period; estimates of profit by an offeror or offeree of profit for a period which has expired; most unaudited profit figures published by the offeror or offeree during the offer period; a profit forecast for a limited period; a profit warranty published by the offeror or offeree; and a statement published by or on behalf of the offeror or offeree of the anticipated effects of a takeover on the profits or earnings per share of either company, or from which such effects can be inferred unless accompanied by a appropriate disclaimer.

12–40   Rule 29.1(a) provides that unless the Panel consents otherwise, the offeror and offeree or a person acting on behalf of the offeror or offeree should not provide any asset valuation during the offer period in

---

[61] R. 24.3(c).

[62] Such a requirement may not apply to a profit forecast made by an offeror where the consideration under the offer consists entirely of cash or, with the consent of the Panel, where the consideration consists entirely of (a) a non-convertible debt instrument or (b) a combination of cash and a non-convertible debt instrument.

connection with an offer unless it is supported by the opinion of a named independent valuer. The opinion of value should be contained in the document containing the asset valuation. This document should also state that the valuer has given and not withdrawn his or her consent to the publication of the valuation certificate.[63] The basis of valuation shall be clearly stated in the valuation.[64] The document sent to the offeree shareholders should also include a statement regarding any potential tax liability that would arise if the assets were to be sold for the amount stated.[65] Shareholders should also be informed as to whether the valuation is current and in general, outdated valuations should be updated.[66] Rule 29 of the City Code on Asset Valuations was significantly amended in July 1998 to reflect changes to the UK Royal Institute of Chartered Surveyors' Appraisal and Valuation Manual. It is likely that this rule will also be the subject of review by the Irish Panel.

(6) The Offeror's Intentions

12–41 The offer document is required to inform the offeree's shareholders of the offeror's intentions regarding the continuation of the business of the offeree and its subsidiaries.[67] If any major changes are intended to be introduced in the business, this should also be stated.[68] The shareholders should also have explained to them the long-term commercial justification for the offer.[69]

The intentions of the offeror with regard to the continued employment of the employees of the offeree and its subsidiaries should also be stated.[69a] The Company and Commercial Law Committee of the Law Society of Ireland have made the valid point that it would be difficult, if not impossible in the case of a hostile bid for the bidder to give any indication of any changes in the conditions of employment in the offeree as it is unlikely to be aware of such conditions. As seen in Chapter 4, the draft 13th Directive places a greater emphasis on safeguarding the rights of employees in takeovers by consulting them and notifying them of the likely impact of the takeover on them.

(7) Recommendations or Opinions of Financial Advisers

12–42 Generally, the offer document will contain a recommendation from the offerees financial adviser for or against acceptance. Rule

---

63 R. 29.5.
64 R. 29.2.
65 R. 29.3.
66 R. 29.4.
67 R. 24.1(a).
68 R. 24.1(b).
69 R. 24.1(c).
69a R. 29.1(d).

24.2(f) provides that any such recommendation or opinion must be accompanied by a statement that the adviser has consented to the issue of the document with the inclusion of the recommendation or opinion in the form and context in which it is included.

(8) Directors' Emoluments

In the case of a securities offer, the offer document must state whether the emoluments of the offeror directors will be affected by the acquisition or by any other associated transaction.[70] If they will, the manner in which they will be affected must be stated. If, they will not be affected, a statement to this effect must be included.

(9) Special Arrangements

12–43   Unless the Panel consents otherwise, if there are any special arrangements existing between the offeror or any person acting in concert with it or any associate of it and the offeree's directors or security holders or recent directors or security holders having any connection with or dependence upon the offer, this fact must be disclosed in the offer document.[71] Details of any such arrangement must also be included. This will ensure that the offeree shareholders are aware of any additional incentive the offeree's directors may have to recommend the offer or the offeree's security holders may have to accept the offer. If no such agreements exist, this must also be stated.

12–44   Rule 24.12 provides that the offer document must also disclose the existence of any arrangements between the offeror or any person acting in concert with the offeror and any other person in relation to dealings to which Rule 8.7 applies. If no such agreements exist, this must also be stated. If the directors or the financial advisers are aware of any such arrangement between any other associate of the offeror and any other person, this should be disclosed. A Rule 8.7 arrangement means:

> "an indemnity or option arrangement, and any other arrangement or understanding, formal or informal, of whatever nature between two or more persons, relating to relevant securities[72] which is or may be an inducement to one or more of such persons to deal or refrain from dealing in such securities".

---

[70]   R. 24.4.
[71]   R. 24.5.
[72]   The term "relevant securities" is defined in Rule 8.9 and includes *inter alia* the equity share capital of the offeree or an offeror.

II. OFFEREE BOARD CIRCULARS

(1) Views of the Offeree Board

12–45   For its part, the offeree board is required to communicate its' own views on any offer together with the views of an independent adviser to its shareholders.[73] If there is not unanimity of views on the offeree board in respect of the offer, the views of any minority of directors should also be circulated.[74] Directors with a conflict of interest should not be joined with the other directors in expressing their views and the nature of any conflict should be explained clearly to the shareholders in any document issued by the offeree.[75] If any document issued by or on behalf of the offeree board to shareholders in connection with the offer contains a recommendation or an opinion of a financial adviser for or against acceptance of the offer, the document must contain a statement by the adviser agreeing to consent to the issue of the document with the inclusion of the recommendation or opinion in the form and context in which it is included.[76] If the document is issued by the financial adviser itself, this will not be necessary. The offeree board is required to comment upon the statements made by the offeror in the offer document in respect of its intentions regarding the offeree and its employees.[77]

(2) Shareholdings and Dealings

12–46   Many of the requirements of Rule 24.3 in respect of share-holdings and dealings of the offeror and related parties are repeated in Rule 25.3 in respect of the offeree. Rule 25.3(b) requires the first major circular from the offeree board advising on the offer to state:

"(i) the shareholdings of the offeree in the offeror;

(ii) the shareholdings in the offeree and in the offeror in which directors of the offeree are interested;

(iii) the shareholdings in the offeree and in the offeror owned or controlled by a subsidiary of the offeree, by the trustees of a pension scheme (other than an industry-wide scheme) in which the offeree or a subsidiary of the offeree participates, or by an associate of the offeree as specified in paragraph (d) or (e) of the definition of "associate"[78] but excluding exempt market makers;

---

[73] R. 3.1 & R. 25.1(a).
[74] R. 25.1 (c).
[75] R. 25.1(d).
[76] R. 25.1(b).
[77] R. 25.2.
[78] See Chap. 10, para. 10–12.

(iv) the shareholdings in the offeree and in the offeror owned or controlled by a person who has an arrangement to which Rule 8.7 applies with the offeree or with any person who is an associate of the offeree by virtue of any of the paragraphs (a) to (g) of the definition of "associate";

(v) except with the consent of the Panel, the shareholdings in the offeree and (in the case of a securities exchange offer only) in the offeror which are managed on a discretionary basis by fund managers (other than exempt fund managers) connected with the offeree (the beneficial owner need not be named); and

(vi) whether the directors of the offeree intend, in respect of their own beneficial shareholdings, to accept or reject the offer."

Rule 25.3(c) provides that if in any of the above categories, with the exception of category (v), there are no shareholdings, this fact should be stated in the circular. However, this shall not apply to category (iv) above if there are no arrangements of that kind in place.

12–47   In addition to disclosing shareholdings, dealings must also be disclosed. Rule 25.3(d)(i) provides that persons whose shareholdings must be disclosed under Rule 25.3(b)(i) or (ii) above, must also disclose any dealings for value in the securities concerned during the period beginning 12 months prior to the commencement of the offer period and ending with the latest practicable date prior to the posting of the circular. Details such as the number of securities, the dates of dealing and the prices should all be included. For the persons required to disclose shareholdings under Rule 25.3(b)(iii) to (iv), disclosure of dealings is also required but disclosure relates to dealings during the offer period and ending with the latest practicable date prior to the posting of the circular.[79] In all cases, if no dealings have taken place, the circular is required to make this fact clear.[80]

12–48   Rule 25.5 provides that the first major circular to shareholders from the offeree board advising them on the offer must disclose any arrangement between the offeree or any person who is an associate of the offeree by virtue of any of paragraphs (a) to (g) of the definition of "associate"[81] and any other person to which Rule 8.7 applies. If no such agreements exist, this must also be stated. If the directors or the financial advisers are aware of any such arrangement between any other associate of the offeror and any other person, this should be disclosed.

---

[79]   R. 25.3(d)(ii).
[80]   R. 25.3(d)(iii).
[81]   Chap. 10, para. 10–12.
[82]   R. 25.4(a).

(3) Directors' Service Contracts

12–49　The first major circular to shareholders from the offeree board advising them on the offer must disclose particulars of all service contracts of any director or proposed director of the offeree with the offeree or any of its subsidiaries or associated companies where such contracts have more than 12 months to run.[82] If no such contracts exist, this must be clearly stated in the circular. If any such contract has been entered or amended[83] within the previous six months, the circular should also contain particulars in respect of the earlier contracts (if any) which have been amended or replaced.[84] Again, if there has been no earlier contract, this should be stated.

The particulars which must be disclosed[85] in respect of these contracts are:

"(i) the name of the director under contract;
(ii) the expiry date of the contract;
(iii) the amount of fixed remuneration payable under the contract (irrespective of whether received as a director or for management);
(iv) the amount of any variable remuneration payable under the contract (including *inter alia*, commission on profits) with details of the basis for calculating such remuneration; and
(v) arrangements for company payments in respect of a pension or similar scheme."

(4) Material Contracts

12–50　The first major circular to shareholders from the offeree board advising them on the offer must contain a summary of the principal contents of each material contract entered into by the offeree or any of its subsidiaries during the period beginning two years before the commencement of the offer period.[86] Only material contracts which are not entered into in the ordinary course of business will be relevant. Disclosure is required *inter alia* of the dates, terms and conditions of the contracts, the parties to the contracts and any consideration passing to or from the offeree or any of its subsidiaries.

(5) Profit Forecasts and Asset Valuations

12–51　As noted above, Rules 28 and 29 deal with profit forecasts and asset valuations issued by or on behalf of the offeree as well as the offeror or during the offer period.

---

[83]　According to Rule 25.4(d), an increase in the remuneration of a director who has a service contract with more than 12 months to run, made within the previous six months shall be treated as an amendment of a service contract.
[84]　R. 25.4(b).
[85]　R. 25.4(c).
[86]　R. 25.6.

III. DOCUMENTS ON DISPLAY

12–52   Unless the Panel agrees otherwise, the offeror and offeree are each required to put certain documents specified in Rule 26(b) on display at an address in Dublin or such other location as the Panel allows. The documents specified are as follows:

(i) the memorandum and articles of association of the offeror or offeree, as appropriate;

(ii) audited consolidated accounts of the offeror or offeree, as appropriate, for the last two financial years for which these have been published;

(iii) in the case of the offeree, all service contracts of offeree directors with more than 12 months to run;

(iv) any report, letter or valuation or other document, any part of which is exhibited or referred to in any document issued by the offeror or offeree, as appropriate;

(v) written consents of the financial advisers (as required by Rules 24.2(f) and 25.1(b));

(vi) all material contracts (as required by Rules 24.2(a) and 25.6);

(vii) where a profit forecast has been made, reports of the auditors or consultant accounts and of the financial advisers and also the letters of consent from the auditors or consultant accounts and of the financial advisers (as required by Rules 28.4 and 28.5);

(viii) where an asset valuation has been made, the valuation certificate and associated schedule and a letter of consent from the valuer (as required by Rule 29.5);

(ix) any document evidencing an irrevocable commitment to accept an offer;

(x) if the Panel has consented to the aggregation of dealings, a full list of all dealings;

(xi) in the case of the offeror, documents relating to the financing arrangements for the offer if such arrangements are described in the offer document;[87] and

(xii) all derivative contracts which have been disclosed in accordance with the Rules.[88]

---

[87]   In compliance with the third sentence of rule 24.2(d).
[88]   Under Rule 24.3(a), Rule 24.3(c), Rule 25.3(b), Rule 25.3(d) or in accordance with Rule 8.1.

IV. DOCUMENTS SUBSEQUENTLY SENT TO SHAREHOLDERS

12–53   After the initial offer document and response, there is likely to be a succession of documents from both sides containing further arguments and information. Each document sent to the offeree's shareholders by either the offeree or the offeror must contain details of any material change in the information which it has previously published.[89] Certain information which was previously published must be updated in subsequent documents. This latter requirement relates to information concerning changes in material contracts, shareholdings and dealings, directors emoluments, special arrangements, the ultimate owner of shares acquired under the offer, arrangements in relation to dealings and changes to directors' service contracts. If a profit forecast has been made by either party in a document sent to offeree shareholders, the continuing validity of the forecast should be confirmed in subsequent documents by that party.[90]

E. The Timetable for the Offer

12–54   The timetable of an offer is strictly regulated. It is important to ensure that the offeree's shareholders are given adequate time to consider an offer and the implications of its acceptance. The offeror too is entitled to have its offer receive a fair opportunity for acceptance. It is equally important, however, that the offeree's management's time is not diverted for too long from the running of the business. General Principle 11 states that: "an offeree ought not to be disrupted in the conduct of its affairs beyond a reasonable time by an offer for its securities". The Rules setting out the timetable thus attempts to strike a balance between the interests of all parties.

I. POSTING OF THE OFFER DOCUMENT AND THE OFFEREE CIRCULAR

12–55   An offer cannot be posted until a firm intention to make an offer has been announced under Rule 2.5.[91] Once such an announcement has been made, unless the Panel consents otherwise, the offer document must be posted within 28 days after this date.[92] The offeree board circular is also subject to a strict timetable. Unless the Panel consents otherwise, a circular containing advice for the shareholders of

---

[89] R. 27.1.
[90] R. 27.2.
[91] R. 30.1.
[92] R. 30.2.

the offeree must be posted within 14 days after the date of publication of the offer document.[93] In the case of offers which are unanimously recommended by the offeree board, the circular is often dispatched to shareholders together with the offer document.

II. TIMEFRAME OF THE OFFER

12–56 In order to give shareholders adequate time to consider the offer, the offer must remain "open for acceptance" for a period of at least 21 days following the date on which the offer document was posted.[94] After the offer has become or has been declared unconditional as to acceptances, it must be kept open for a further period of at least 14 days following the date on which it would otherwise have expired.[95]

However, to ensure that the bid is not prolonged excessively, Rule 31.6 introduces the "final day rule". The offer cannot be extended, without the Panel's consent, beyond 60 days from the date the offer is posted, unless it has previously become or been declared unconditional as to acceptances.[96] Thus, unless the Panel consents otherwise, the offer will lapse unless it has been declared or become unconditional as to acceptances by 5 p.m. on the 60th day after the day on which the initial offer document was posted. Where the offeror has stated that its offer will not be extended unless it is unconditional as to acceptances by such date, the offer will similarly lapse by this "relevant earlier date" unless the statement has been withdrawn by the offeror. The Panel may consent to a waiver of this final day rule where a competing offer has been announced. In this case, the Notes to Rule 31.6(a) note that unless the Panel determines otherwise, both offerors will be bound by the timetable established by the posting of the competing offer document. Other situations in which an extension may be allowed is where the offeree board consents to an extension, where the offeror's receiving agent seeks an extension to comply with Rule 10.6 and produces a certificate, or as provided in Rule 31.3 or Rule 31.9.

In order to inform shareholders of the current situation, the offeror must make an announcement on the 60th day (or if applicable, any relevant earlier date) as to whether the offer is unconditional as to acceptances or has lapsed.[97] A statement as to the current position in the count of acceptances should also be made. In determining the level

---

[93] R. 30.3.
[94] R. 31.1.
[95] R. 31.4. In the unusual case where the offer is unconditional as to acceptances from the outset, such an extension will not be required and the offeror must make this fact clear and obvious in the offer document.
[96] R. 31.6(a)(i).
[97] R. 31.6(b).

of acceptances, the offeror is only permitted to take into account acceptances or purchases of shares in respect of which all relevant documents have been received by its receiving agent[98] before the last time for acceptance set out in the offeror's relevant document or announcement. This time may not be later than 1.00 p.m. on the 60th day or any relevant earlier date.[99] However, Rule 31.6(a)(iii) provides that if there is a matter involving the Takeover Rules outstanding on the final closing date for acceptance and it is inappropriate for the offer to lapse or become or be declared unconditional as to acceptances, the Panel may extend the time period within which the offer may become or be declared unconditional. Such an extension may be granted if the Panel is of the opinion that, having regard to the General Principles, it is just and proper to do so. This extension will not, however, permit any extension of the time by which all relevant documents in respect of acceptances, withdrawals of acceptances and purchases must be received for the purposes of the acceptance condition.

12–57 Unless the Panel agrees otherwise, all conditions of the offer other than the acceptance condition must be satisfied within 21 days after the first closing date for acceptance or after the date on which the offer becomes or is declared unconditional as to acceptances, which ever is the later.[100] If this does not happen, the offer will lapse. This is a very short period, particularly if approval must be obtained from the Minister under the Mergers Act. For this reason, it may become necessary to seek an extension of this period from the Panel. The Takeover Rules themselves provide one exception to this deadline. In the case of a mandatory offer under Rule 9 or Rule 37, if the offer has become or been declared unconditional as to acceptances but remains subject to a condition under Rule 12(a) in respect of the Mergers, Takeovers and Monopolies (Control) Act 1978 Act or any other condition permitted under Rule 9.2 which will be satisfied by the issue of any governmental or regulatory authorisation, consent, approval or clearance, the Panel may direct the offeror to extend the period within which the offer must either become or be declared unconditional in all respects or lapse.[101] The Panel will only make this direction if it is satisfied that, having regard to the General Principles, it is just and proper so to direct.

12–58 A person who accepts an offer is allowed to withdraw his or her acceptance from the date which is 21 days after the first closing date of the initial offer unless by this date the offer has become or is declared uncon-

---

[98] In accordance with Rules 10.3 and 10.4.
[99] R. 31.6(a)(ii).
[100] R. 31.7(a).
[101] R. 31.7(b).

ditional as to acceptances.[102] This entitlement to withdraw acceptances lasts until the offer becomes or is declared unconditional as to acceptances or until the final time for lodgement of acceptances of the offer which can be taken into account in accordance with Rule 31.6, whichever is the earlier. Thus, if the offer has not proven successful, shareholders who originally decided to accept the offer may choose to retain their shares. This allows them to make the decision as to whether to sell the shares or not on the basis of their true assessment of the offer rather then on their view as to whether other shareholders will accept or not.

12–59   The offeree board is prohibited from announcing trading results, a profit or dividend forecast, an asset valuation or a proposal for a dividend payment, unless the Panel agrees otherwise, after the 39th day following the posting of the initial offer document.[103]

12–60   Unless the Panel agrees otherwise, where an offer becomes or is declared unconditional in all respects, the consideration relative to an acceptance must be posted within 14 days after (a) the first closing date for acceptance of the offer or (b) the date on which the offer becomes or is declared unconditional in all respects or (c) the date of receipt of that competed acceptance, whichever is the later.[104] On the other hand, if an offer lapses, all documents must be returned to shareholders within 14 days after the lapsing of the offer.[105]

III. EXTENSION OF THE OFFER PERIOD

12–61   In general, an offeror is not obliged to extend an offer where the acceptance condition has not been satisfied by the first or any subsequent closing date for acceptance. If, however, the Panel considers that an extension is necessary having regard to the General Principles, it may direct the offeror accordingly.[106] The Panel might decide to do this, for example, where it believed that for some reason the shareholders had not been given a proper opportunity to consider the offer. Such an extension might be necessary if a postal strike had prevented the delivery of many of the offer documents. Where the offeror decides to extend the period during which the offer will remain open for acceptances, an announcement to this effect must be made. Such an announcement must state (a) the next closing date for acceptances, or

---

[102] R. 34.
[103] R. 31.9.
[104] R. 31.8.
[105] R. 31.10.
[106] R. 31.3.

(b) if the offer is unconditional as to acceptances, that the offer will remain open for acceptance until further notice. In the latter case, before closing the offer, the offeror must give 14 days' written notice to the shareholders who have not accepted the offer.[107]

12–62   Often, when making the offer, the offeror will state in a document sent to shareholders of the offeree, that the offer period will not be extended beyond a specified date unless it is unconditional as to acceptances by that date. Such a statement is termed a "no extension statement". It may be designed by the offeror with the objective of encouraging the offeree's shareholders to accept the offer quickly and not to expect the offer period to be extended giving them further time to make up their minds and possibly allowing a competitor time to make an alternative offer. In order to encourage certainty, unless the Panel agrees otherwise, "no extension statements" are normally binding unless in the "no extension statement" the offeror has expressly reserved the right to extend.[108] The same rule applies where a "no-extension statement" is otherwise made by or on behalf of an offeror or its directors, officers or advisers and not withdrawn immediately if incorrect. However, if a competing offer is made, particularly a new offer which is to be recommended by the board of the offeree, the offeror may wish to extend the offer period. This is allowed provided that: (i) notice to this effect is given as soon as possible[109] and shareholders are informed in writing at the earliest opportunity; and (ii) any shareholders of the offeree who accepted the offer on or after the date of the "no-extension statement" are allowed withdraw their acceptances during the period of eight days following the date of posting of the notice.[110] The notice must inform shareholders about this entitlement in an appropriate and prominent manner. An offeror may also choose not to be bound by a "no-extension statement" which would otherwise prevent it from posting an increased or improved offer which is recommended for acceptance by the offeree board.[111] In the aforementioned cases, however, the offeror may choose not to be bound by the "no-extension statement" only if it has specifically reserved the right to do so in such circumstances at the time the statement was made.[112]

---

[107] R. 31.2.
[108] R. 31.5(a).
[109] Such notice must be given within four business days after the day of the announcement of the relevant competing offer.
[110] R. 31.5(b).
[111] R. 31.5(c).
[112] R. 31.5(d).

F. Revision of an Offer and Alternative Offers

12–63 An offer may need to be revised if the offeror buys shares above the offer price, or if it becomes obliged to make a cash offer or to increase an existing cash offer. Alternatively, the offeror may wish to revise and increase the offer if a competing offer is made. Where an offer is revised, the Rules seek to ensure that the shareholders of the offeree are given adequate time to consider the revised offer. Thus Rule 32.1(a) provides that if an offer is revised, it must be kept open for acceptance for at least 14 days following the date on which the revised offer document is posted.[113] This means that an offeror cannot post a revised offer document during the 14 days ending on the last day on which the offer is capable of becoming unconditional as to acceptances. Similarly, the offeror should not place itself in a position in which it would be required to revise the offer during the 14 day period.

12–64 Often, when making the offer, the offeror will state in a document sent to shareholders of the offeree that the value of the offer will not be increased. Like a "no-extension statement", such a statement may be used as a strategy in the negotiations with shareholders. The rules governing "no-increase statements" are very similar to the Rules governing "no-extension statements". In order to encourage certainty, unless the Panel agrees otherwise, "no increase statements" are normally binding unless the offeror has expressly reserved the right to increase the offer. Indeed, the offeror is prohibited from amending the terms of its offer in any way notwithstanding that the amendment would not result in an increase in the value of the offer, including, *inter alia*, the introduction of a securities exchange alternative offer with a lower value. The same rule applies where a "no increase statement" is otherwise made by or on behalf of an offeror or its directors, officers or advisers and not withdrawn immediately if incorrect. Similarly, the offeror is prohibited from placing itself in a position in which it would be required to revise the offer, unless the Panel has consented.[114] However, if a competitive situation arises after a "no increase statement" has been made, the offeror may revise the offer if:

(i) notice to this effect is given as soon as possible[115] and shareholders are informed in writing at the earliest opportunity; and

(ii) any shareholders of the offeree who accepted the offer on or after the date of the no increase statement are allowed withdraw their

---

[113] R. 32.

[114] R. 32.2(a).

[115] Such notice must be given within four business days after the day of the announcement of the relevant competing offer.

acceptances during the period of eight days following the date of posting of the notice.[116]

The notice must inform shareholders about this entitlement in an appropriate and prominent manner. An offeror may also choose not to be bound by a no increase statement" which would otherwise prevent it from posting an increased or improved offer which is recommended for acceptance by the offeree board.[117] In the aforementioned cases, however, the offeror may choose not to be bound by the no-increase statement only if it has specifically reserved the right to do so in such circumstances at the time the statement was made.[118] To ensure equality of treatment, in the case of a revised offer all shareholders who accepted the original offer are entitled to the revised consideration.[119]

12–65 Where an offer has been revised so as to increase or improve the consideration, the offeror may find it necessary in order to implement the revised offer to introduce new conditions of the offer. Such conditions may include for example obtaining shareholder approval to the increase or obtaining a quotation for new shares. Such new conditions may only be introduced where the Panel consents.[120]

12–65A An "alternative offer" is defined in Rule 2.1 of Part A of the Takeover Rules as:

> "a right granted under an offer by the offeror, or by a third party at the request of the offeror, to acceptors of the offer to elect to receive, instead of the whole or part of the basic consideration available under the offer, a consideration different from that basic consideration."

Rule 33.1 deals with the timing and revision of alternative offers. An arrangement made by the offeror under which the offeree shareholders can elect, subject to the election of other offeree shareholders, to vary the proportion in which they are to receive different forms of consideration under the offer will not be treated as an alternative offer. As a result, an arrangement of this kind may be closed at any time in keeping with its terms as set out in the offer document.[120a]

The provisions of Rule 31 on the timeframe of an offer (other than Rules 31.6, 31.7 and 31.8 and the exception to Rule 31.3) and Rule 32 on revision of an offer apply *mutatis mutandis* to alternative offers including

---

[116] R. 32.2(b).
[117] R. 32.2(c).
[118] R. 32.2(d).
[119] R. 32.3.
[120] R. 32.4.
[120a] R 33.1(b).

cash offers.[120b] If an offer becomes or is declared unconditional as to acceptances, all subsisting alternative offers must remain open for acceptance for at least 14 days in accordance with Rule 31.4.[120c] However, if the value of a cash underwritten alternative offer provided by a third party is, at the time of the announcement of that alternative offer, more than half the maximum value of the offer, the offeror shall not be obliged to keep the alternative offer open in accordance with Rule 31.4 or Rule 33.1 if it has given notice in writing to the offeree shareholders that it reserves the right to close it on a stated date or to extend it on that stated date. The stated date should not be less than 14 days after the date on which the written notice is posted. Such notice should not be given, however, during the period between the time at which a competing offer is announced and the end of the resulting competitive situation.[120d] If the offeror makes a firm statement to the effect that an alternative offer will not be extended or reintroduced and the offer has ceased to be open for acceptance, it may not subsequently be reintroduced and the offeror may not make any substantially similar offer. If no such statement is made, the offeror may reintroduce that alternative offer at a later date.[120e]

G. Renewal of an Offer

12–66 According to Rule 35.1(a), where an offeror has announced a firm intention to make an offer or has posted an offer (not being a partial offer) and that offer has been withdrawn or has lapsed, the offeror, any party who acted in concert with the offeror as respects the offer and any person who, following the expiry of the offer period, is acting in concert with the offeror will be subject to certain restrictions for a period of 12 months from the date on which the original offer lapsed or was withdrawn, unless the Panel agrees otherwise. These persons are prohibited from: (i) making a fresh offer in respect of the offeree; (ii) acquiring any securities of the offeree which would give rise to a requirement to make a mandatory offer under Rule 9; or (iii) acquiring any securities of the offeree, if the offeror and any of the concert parties hold securities conferring in the aggregate more than 49 per cent but not more than 50 per cent of the voting rights in the offeree. These restrictions also apply, except with the Panel's consent, to persons who make announcements concerning a relevant company which although not amounting to a firm intention to make an offer (not being a partial offer), raises or confirms the possibility that such an offer may be made by the offeror, and then a firm intention to make or not to

---

[120b] R. 33.1(a)]
[120c] R. 33.1(c).
[120d] R. 33.2(a)
[120e] R. 33.3.

make an offer is not announced within what the Panel deems to be a reasonable period.[121] In addition, a six month moratorium is imposed on acquisitions above the offer value where the original offer was for more than 50 per cent of the voting rights of the company.[122] Such a moratorium applies to the offeror, any person acting in concert with it as respects the original offer, and any person who following the expiry of the offer period is acting in concert with the offeror or any such person. The purpose of this rule is to ensure companies do not have to endure prolonged sieges by the same offeror after a failed bid. This would be an unreasonable distraction for the offeree's management. Dispensations are available from this rule, where for example the offeree recommends the new offer or where a third party has become involved and has announced an intention to make an offer.[123]

12–67 Similar delays apply to both successful and unsuccessful partial offers under Rule 36. If a partial offer becomes unconditional as to acceptances, neither the offeror, nor any party who acted in concert with the offeror as respects the offer nor any person who following the expiry of the offer period is acting in concert with the offeror, is allowed to make any offer in respect of the offeree or to acquire any securities of the offeree during a specified period.[124] This period commences at the time at which the original offer is declared unconditional as to acceptances and ends, if the offer subsequently lapses, on the date on which it lapses. If the offer becomes or is declared unconditional in all respects, the period ends on the date which is 12 months after the date on which it becomes or is declared unconditional in all respects. If a person has announced a firm intention to make an offer or has posted a partial offer which, if accepted in full, could result in the offeror and any concert parties holding securities conferring in the aggregate not less than 30 per cent of the voting rights in the offeree and that offer has been withdrawn or has lapsed, the restrictions in Rule 35.1(a) will apply during the 12 months after the date of the withdrawal or lapse.[125] These restrictions also apply to persons who make announcements concerning a relevant company which although not amounting to a firm intention to make a partial offer, raises or confirms the possibility that such an offer may be made, and then a firm intention to make or not to make an offer is not announced within what the Panel deems to be a reasonable period.[126]

---

[121]   R. 35.1(b).
[122]   R. 35.2.
[123]   Note 1 on Rule 35.1.
[124]   R. 36.2(b).
[125]   R. 36.2(c).
[126]   R. 36.2(d).

CHAPTER 13

DEALING RESTRICTIONS AND DISCLOSURE REQUIREMENTS DURING THE COURSE OF THE OFFER

13–01 In considering an offer, making an offer or implementing an offer, the offeror must be aware of the many rules which would restrict its ability to deal in either its own or the offeree's securities or which would require disclosure. An offeree may find itself similarly restricted. In addition, individual members of either company, advisers, associates and concert parties must all be aware of the rules and the implications of dealing.

13–02 Many of the dealing restrictions and disclosure rules which follow apply at all times. For example, the disclosure provisions of Part IV of the Companies Act 1990 apply at any time when a relevant transaction is entered. Some of the restrictions and rules apply only during the course of an offer or during an offer period. For example, disclosure requirements under Rule 8 of the Irish Takeover Panel Act 1997 (Takeover) Rules ("the Takeover Rules") apply during the offer period. The standard of care imposed by Rule 19 applies to the offeror or offeree during the course of an offer. The term "offer period" in relation to an offer is defined in Rule 2.1 of Part A of the Takeover Rules as:

> "the period commencing with the time of the announcement of such offer as a proposed or possible offer (with or without terms) and ending at the time of the first closing date or, if later, the time at which the offer becomes or is declared unconditional as to acceptances or lapses whichever first occurs provided that if, in the case of a proposed or possible offer, an announcement is made to the effect that the offer will not be made, the period shall end at the time of such announcement".[1]

The term "the course of an offer" is defined as:

> "the period commencing with the commencement of the offer period and ending at the time at which the offer ceases to be open for acceptance or

---

[1] For the purposes of this definition, an announcement that a holding, or aggregate holdings, of securities conferring 30% or more of voting rights in a relevant company is for sale or that the board of a relevant company is seeking potential offerors shall be deemed to be the announcement of a possible offer in respect of that company.

> lapses whichever first occurs (provided that if an announcement is made to the effect that an offer will not be made, the period shall end at the time of such announcement)".

Yet other restrictions apply for a period after an offer lapses or is declared unconditional in all respects. For example, Rule 35 requires a delay of 12 months after the lapsing of an unsuccessful offer before a new offer may be made.

A. Dealing Restrictions

I. INSIDER DEALING

(1) Theory

13–03 It appears to be a commonly accepted view that insider dealing is inequitable, damaging and morally reprehensible. Critics of insider dealing have used a wide array of arguments to denounce insider dealing. Arguments based on equity have been used to suggest that information should be made available to all market participants at the same time. The fear is that inequality of access to information may enable informed investors to increase their wealth at the expense of the less well informed. This may lead to decreased public confidence in the market and an unwillingness to invest. Public confidence in the securities market is generally regarded as an essential condition for the fulfilment of their role in the economy.[2] As the recitals to the Insider Dealing Directive state:

> "... the smooth operation of [the secondary market in transferable securities] depends to a large extent on the confidence it inspires in investors ... by benefiting certain investors as compared with others, insider dealing is likely to undermine that confidence ...".[3]

13–04 However, empirical evidence suggests that many investors trade on inside information and expect other to do so too.[3a] It may even be argued that the price outsiders pay reflects the risk of insider dealing.[4] Indeed, it has been suggested that the growth in institutional investment has been assisted by the realisation of small shareholders

---

[2] Suter, *The Regulation of Insider Dealing in Britain* (1989), p. 37.
[3] Directive 89/592/O.J. L334/30.
[3a] Baesel and Stein "The Value of Information: Inferences from the Profitability of Insider Dealing" 14 J. Fin. & Quantitative Analysis 553 (1979). Finnerky "Insiders and Market Efficiency", 31 J. Fin. & Quantitative Analysis 1141 (1976).
[4] Scott "Insider Trading: Rule 10b–5, Disclosure and Corporate Privacy" (1980) 9 J. Legal Stud. 801 at p. 807.

that they are at an informational disadvantage.[5] A second criticism of insider dealing is that it involves a relaxation of ethical standards and is unprofessional and possibly immoral. This argument suggests that insider dealing jeopardises investor protection, the existence of a level playing field, and honest markets.[5a] A third criticism put forward is that insider dealing creates a moral hazard by allowing insiders to profit on bad news. This might reward entrepreneurs for bad work or might encourage insiders to disseminate false information about the company or to delay disclosure.[6] These negative views of insider dealing are the underlying basis for many of the disclosure rules which follow.

13–05   One of the few commentators suggesting that insider dealing is not as harmful as suggested and indeed is capable of yielding positive results is Henry Manne. Manne argues that:

> "just because the phrase 'insider dealing' raises a spectre of dishonesty, fraud, exploitation, and greed is not a sufficient basis for assuming that the fact must be so or that the practice must, ipso facto, be outlawed".[7]

Manne is credited with being the first person in the current literature to explore the subject of insider dealing thoroughly and to present a logical argument to suggest that insider dealing is desirable from the standpoint of the market and society itself.[8] Manne argues that there are at least three reasons for defending insider dealing. First, he described it as a "victimless crime". He noted that:

> "manipulation differs dramatically from insider trading, just as a reliable tip on a winning horse differs from having the race 'fixed'".[9]

The only situation in which it can be said that the purchases of insiders harm others, he claims, is where the purchases cause a price rise and persons sell in response to this who would not otherwise have done so. Secondly, he argues that insider dealing makes the stock market function more efficiently. Arguments based on efficiency suggest that market prices should reflect all available information. Only in this way can scarce resources be directed to their most productive uses. Manne

---

[5]   Suter, ibid., at 38.

[5a] Brudney, "Insiders, Outsiders and Informational Advantages under the Federal Securities Laws" 93 Harv. L. Rev. 322 (1979). Scheppele "It's Just Not Right; Ethics of Insider Trading" (1993) 56 *Law and Contemporary Problems 123*; *Justices Report on Insider Trading* (London 1972).

[6]   Lever, "Securities and Secrets: Insider Trading and the Law of Contract" (1982) 68 Van. L. Rev.117 at 149 and Schotland, "Unsafe; At Any Price; A Reply to Manne, Insider Trading and the Stock Market" 53 Van. L. Rev. 1245 (1967) at 1451.

[7]   Manne, "Insider Trading and the Law Professors" (1970) 23 Van. L. Rev. 547. See also Manne, *Insider Trading and the Stock Market* (The Free Press, New York, 1966).

[8]   Hetherington, "Insider Trading and the Logic of the Law" (1967) Wis. L. Rev. 720 at 720.

[9]   Manne, "Insider Trading and the Law Professors" (1970) Van. L. Rev. 547 at 575.

also argues that stock market prices serve to allocate management and the control of corporations more efficiently because share prices are the best indicators of the performance record of management and the potential profitability of a takeover.[10] Manne argues that insider dealing promotes efficiency because it increases the speed and accuracy with which the market integrates information. Delay in the reflection of new information or the inaccurate reflection of new information is detrimental to the market as it causes uncertainty and irrational trading. Disclosure cannot fully fill this role, Manne argues, as it is incomplete, costly and in some cases might destroy the value of the information. He cites as an example confidential information.[11] Manne's third argument is that insider dealing provides a meaningful form of compensation in large companies for the entrepreneurial function. Manne argues that while capitalist investors are compensated by dividends, share price appreciation and interest and managers are compensated by salaries, entrepreneurs should be compensated by insider dealing.[12] Manne claims that such compensation would provide an adequate incentive for further innovational activity. Since the process of innovation results in inside information, the entrepreneur's reward is then directly linked to the value of his contribution.

Despite the logical attractiveness of Manne's arguments, they have not found general approval. The general view still denounces insider dealing as wrongful.

(2) The Common Law

13–06   In *Percival v. Wright*,[13] the members of a company approached their directors and offered to sell their shares. Although the directors were aware that a takeover bid was imminent and that the bid, if successful, would lead to a substantial share price increase, they did not inform the shareholders of the negotiations and accepted the offers. Subsequently, the shareholders sought to have the contracts set aside. Swinfen Eady J. held that the directors owed no duty to the shareholders to inform them of the negotiations. He stated as follows:

> "I am therefore of the opinion that the purchasing directors were under no obligation to disclose to their vendor shareholders the negotiations which ultimately proved abortive. The contrary view could place directors in a most invidious position as they could not buy or sell shares without disclosing negotiations, a premature disclosure of which might well be against

---

[10] See Chap. 2 paras 2–11–2–14.
[11] Carlton & Fischel, "The Regulation of Insider Trading" 35 Stan. L. Rev 867.
[12] *cf.* Schotland, "Unsafe At Any Price: A Reply To Manne, Insider Trading and The Stock Market", 53 Va.L. Rev. 1425 Suter.
[13] [1902] 2 Ch. 421.

the best interests of the company. I am of the opinion that the directors are not in that position."[13a]

It is clear from this decision that a director owes no liability to shareholders at common law for buying or selling shares without disclosing confidential price sensitive to the shareholders. Subsequent cases sought to mitigate the strictness of this rule.

13–07   In *Coleman v. Myers*[14] the New Zealand Court of Appeal found that there were special circumstances which created a quasi fiduciary relationship between the directors and shareholders such that the directors were obliged to disclose price sensitive information during the negotiations. This case concerned the purchase of members' shares by the directors of a small family company. The court held that a fiduciary relationship stemmed from the trust and confidence which the members placed in the directors not to abuse their inside knowledge of the company's affairs. In the lower court Mahon J. described the decision in *Percival v. Wright* as "opposed . . . to prevailing notions of correct commercial practice" and "wrongly decided".[14a] The Court of Appeal was less direct. Woodhouse J. stated that:

> "it is not the law that anybody holding the office of director of a limited liability company is for that reason alone to be realised from what otherwise would be regarded as a fiduciary responsibility owed to those in the position of shareholders of the same company".[14b]

Instead, Woodhouse J. was of the view that:

> "the standard of conduct required from a director in relation to dealings with a shareholder will differ depending upon all the surrounding circumstances and the nature of the responsibility which in a real and practical sense the director has assumed towards the shareholder."[14c]

He elaborated on this by stating:

> "While it may not be possible to lay down any general test as to when the fiduciary duty will arise from a company director or to prescribe the exact conduct which will always discharge it when it does, there are nevertheless some factors that will usually have an influence upon a decision one way or the other".[14d]

[13a] *ibid.*
[13a] *ibid.* at p. 426.
[14] [1977] 2 N.Z.L.R. 298.
[14a] [1977] 2 N.Z.L.R. 255 at p. 268.
[14b] *op. cit.*, no. 14 at p. 324.
[14c] *ibid.* at p. 324.
[14d] *ibid.* at p. 325.

The factors cited by Woodhouse J. were: the existence of a relationship of confidence; the significance of some particular transaction for the parties; and the extent of any positive action taken by or on behalf of the director to promote it.

13–08   The Irish courts have also had an opportunity to consider this issue. In *Securities Trust Ltd v. Associated Properties Ltd*,[15] McWilliam J. stated that:

> "although, a director is not a trustee for the shareholders, directors are to some extent in a fiduciary position".

In the circumstances, the learned judge felt that shareholders of a target company in a takeover situation were entitled to be given reasonable particulars of the takeover which was to be financed by the company itself. From these cases, Ussher deduced that one could discern:

> "an emerging fiduciary duty owed by directors to members to disclose material facts when the members' rights are to be directly affected by proposals to which the directors are party or privy, provided that the directors are trusted and relied upon to actually do so by the members, which will not, of course, always be the case".[16]

13–09   In the recent case of *Crindle Investments, Roche and Roche v. Wymes and Wood*,[17] Murphy J. referred to Woodhouse J.'s comments in *Coleman v. Myers* as "correct" and "instructive" and accepted the principle that "duties may be imposed or accepted by parties above and beyond those derived from particular offices or status". However, the learned judge also stated:

> "the presumption must be that parties who elect to have their relationship governed by corporate structures . . . intend their duties – and where appropriate their rights and remedies – to be governed by the legal provisions relating to such structures and not otherwise. It would require, in my view, reasonably clear evidence to impose obligations on directors or shareholders above and beyond those prescribed by legislation or identified by long established legal principles".[18]

On the facts of the case, Murphy J. held that the requisite evidence was not available to support the existence of a fiduciary duty to the shareholders.

13–10   Directors owe a fiduciary duty to the company to account for any profits they make as a result of using corporate information for their own gain. Their liability to account arises from the fact of a profit being made. As such, there does not have to be fraud, bad faith or even damage to the beneficiary.

---

[15] Unreported, High Court, November 19, 1980 at p. 10.
[16] Ussher, *Company Law in Ireland* (Sweet and Maxwell 1986) p. 206.
[17] Unreported, High Court, March 27, 1997.
[18] *ibid.*, at 11.

(3) Part V Companies Act 1990

13–11   Part V of the Companies Act 1990 ("the 1990 Act") implements Council Directive 89/592[19] on Insider Dealing ("the Directive") into Irish law. As noted above, the purpose of the Directive is to ensure the smooth operation of the market by ensuring that investors are confident that they are placed on an equal footing in the market and will be protected against the improper use of information. The Directive sets out the minimum standards and permits Member States to adopt more stringent or additional provisions.[20]

(a) Inside Information

13–12   Although the term "inside information" is typically used to describe the information the subject of Part V of the 1990 Act, the term is not actually used in the text of the sections of the Act. The term "inside information" is, however, defined in Article 1 of the Directive as:

> "information which has not been made public of a precise nature relating to one or several issuers of transferable securities or to one or several transferable securities, which, if it were made public, would be likely to have a significant effect on the price of the transferable security or securities in question."

Section 108(1) of the 1990 Act refers simply to:

> "information that is not generally available, but, if it were, would be likely materially to affect the price of those securities".

A number of prerequisites must thus be satisfied before information can be proven to be of the type referred to in the Act.

13–13   It seems clear that the information should be of a class which could materially or significantly effect the price of the securities in question. While there is no definition of "materiality" in the 1990 Act, the Irish Association of Investment Managers Guidelines, which are considered in the next section, refer to information which would lead to the price of the security being less than 95 per cent or more than 105 per cent of the market price on the day that dealing occurred. In the US, the Supreme Court has stated that the issue of materiality depends not on price effect but on whether there is a substantial likelihood that a reasonable shareholder would consider it important in deciding how to act.[21]

---

[19]   O.J. L334/30
[20]   Art. 6.
[21]   TSC *Industries Incorp v. Northway Inc* 426 US 438 (1976).

13–14 The nature of the information is also important. The Directive requires the information to be "information . . . of a precise nature" relating to the issuers of securities or the securities themselves. Hopt stated that the term "precise" was introduced in order to exclude mere rumours and speculations at the Stock Exchange.[22] A statement of fact rather than a statement of opinion is thus required. By contrast, the definition in the 1990 Act is much broader. Any confidential information which would affect the price of a company's securities is included. This might lead to persons feeling uncertain as to whether a piece of information, especially on a general matter, is or is not inside information. Clearly, unpublished information concerning a takeover or a potential takeover of the company would constitute such price sensitive information. However, if a person were to become aware of a Central Bank interest rate increase prior to that information becoming public, that information could arguably be said to be information which would affect the price of securities. It would not however, constitute precise information relating to securities under the Directive. Similarly, confidential opinions could in certain circumstances give rise to price fluctuations under the definition in the Act particularly if the source was influential and well regarded. Yet such opinions would not suffice under the Directive.

13–15 In terms of the confidentiality of the information, the 1990 Act refers to information which is "not generally available." This differs slightly from the Directive which refers instead to information "which has not been made public". If the information has been made public thus no action will lie. At first glance, this might appear to be a very easy test for a defendant to satisfy. In the law of defamation for example, publication means communication to any other third party. It would thus seem that if a small number of directors have been given price-sensitive information, they could act upon it on the basis that it had been made public. This is however, a particularly narrow interpretation of the phrase "made public". Under the 1990 Act such persons would however be prohibited from dealing, on the basis that the information had not been made generally available. A similar definition is contained in section 58 of the Criminal Justice Act 1993 implementing the Directive in the UK. Under that Act, the information is deemed to have been made "public" if it was:

[1] officially published as required by the market;

[2] contained in statutorily required records;

---

22 Hopt, "The European Insider Dealing Directive" (1990) 27 CML Rev. 51.

[3] readily available to those likely to deal in the relevant securities; or

[4] derived from information that has been made public.

The concept of information which is not "generally available" is based on the Australian regulations. In *Kinwat Holdings Ltd v. Platform Ltd.*,[23] information was deemed "generally available" because it was pleaded in court proceedings and published in a newspaper. In *Johnson v. Wiggs*[24], information was deemed to be in the public arena because it had been reported in the newspapers and on a local television station. In *SEC v. Texas Gulf Sulphur Co.*,[25] the U.S. Court of Appeals, took matters a step further and suggested that not only should the information be communicated to the public but that there should be a time lapse so that the information could be assimilated. Although that case was decided in 1968 in advance of the substantial developments in information technology, it may still be necessary to give other investors time to assimilate the information when it comes on screen. Ashe and Murphy suggest that the Directive too requires a period of delay to allow the information be absorbed:

> "It would be odd to think that it was the intention of the Directive to allow insiders to deal at the instant after the news had been released since they would still have the trading advantage which the measure is seeking to strip from them".[26]

Arguably, such a delay might be necessary to achieve the Directive's intention of placing investors on an equal footing. On the other hand, this idea would seem to run contrary to the efficient market theory which suggests that information is immediately assimilated into share prices such that it is not possible to make a profit on information. As was noted in Chapter 2, however, it is generally accepted that the market is not efficient in terms of unpublished information.[26a]

(b) The Prohibitions – Primary Insiders:

(i) Section 108(1)
13–16 The central prohibition on insider dealing in the 1990 Act is contained in section 108(1) which provides that:

> "It shall not be lawful for a person who is, or at any time in the preceding six months has been, connected with a company to deal in any securities of that company if by reason of his so being, or having been, connected with that

---

[23] 1982 6 A.C.L.R. 398.
[24] 443 F.2d 803.
[25] 312 F. Supp. 77 (S.D.N.Y. 1970) Aff'd, 446 F.2d 1301, (2d Cir. 1971).
[26] Ashe and Murphy, *Insider Dealing* (Roundhall Press, 1992) 47.
[26a] See Chap. 2, para. 2–08.

company he is in possession of information that is not generally available but, if it were, would be likely materially to affect the price of those securities".

This subsection prohibits persons who have received inside information as a result of their connection with the company from dealing in securities of the company. Two issues thus require further clarification – first, the nature of the connection which gives rise to the prohibition and secondly, the effect of the restriction.

Connected with the Company
13–17 Section 108(11) provides that a person is "connected" with a company if:

"being a natural person –
(a) he is an officer of that company or of a related company;
(b) he is a shareholder in that company or in a related company;[27]
(c) he occupies a position (including a public office) that may reasonably be expected to give him access to [inside] information . . . by virtue of –
  (i) any professional, business or other relationship existing between himself (or his employer or a company of which he is an officer) and that company or a related company; or
  (ii) his being an officer of a substantial shareholder[28] in that company or in a related company."

For the purposes of Article 2 of the Directive, a person is similarly connected if he possesses inside information:

"– by virtue of his membership of the administrative, management or supervisory bodies of the issuer,
 – by virtue of his holding in the capital of the issuer, or
 – because he has access to such information by virtue of the exercise of his employment, profession or duties."

13–18 Ashe makes a distinction between receiving information "by virtue of ones employment" and receiving information "incidentally in the course of ones employment".[29] A person who receives inside information by virtue of his employment, *e.g.* the legal adviser to an offeror, will thus be included in this prohibition. On the other hand, a person who receives the information incidentally in the course of his employment, for example, the cleaner in the legal adviser's office, would not be included in this prohibition. Such a person may, however, be prohibited as a secondary insider from dealing under section 108(3).

---

[27] In the U.S. reference is made in section 16 of the Securities Exchange Act 1934 to a "controlling shareholder" which makes more sense since it is unlikely an ordinary shareholder would have access to confidential information.

[28] Defined in section 108(12) as "a person who holds shares in a company, the number of which is above the notifiable percentage for the time being in force under section 70."

[29] Ashe, "Who is an Insider" in *The Fiduciary, the Insider and the Conflict* Ed Rider and Ashe (Roundhall Sweet & Maxwell, 1995), 77.

Dealing in Securities

13–19 Under section 108(1), certain persons are prohibited from "dealing" in "securities" of the company. The term "securities" is defined by section 107 of the 1990 Act as meaning:

> "(a) shares, debentures or other debt securities issued or proposed to be issued, whether in the State or otherwise, and for which dealing facilities are, or are to be, provided by a recognised stock exchange[30];
>
> (b) any right option or obligation in respect of any such shares, debentures or other debt securities referred to in paragraph (a);
>
> (c) any right option or obligation in respect of any index relating to any such shares, debentures or other debt securities referred to in paragraph (a); or
>
> (d) such interests as may be prescribed."

The term "dealing" in relation to securities is stated in section 107 to mean:

> "(whether as principal or agent) acquiring, disposing of, subscribing for or underwriting the securities, or making or offering to make, or inducing or attempting to induce a person to make or to offer to make, an agreement –
>
> (a) for or relating to acquiring, disposing of, subscribing for or underwriting the securities; or
>
> (b) the purpose or purported purpose of which is to secure a profit or gain to a person who acquires, disposes of, subscribes for or underwrites the securities or to any of the parties to the agreement in relation to the securities."

This paragraph appears to be drafted very awkwardly. It might seem at first glance that "dealing" must have as its purpose or purported purpose the securing of a profit. However, read properly, it is submitted that paragraph (a) and (b) do not apply to the first part of this sentence, *i.e.* to the acquiring, disposing of, subscribing for or underwriting of the securities.

13–20 It is important to note that mere possession of the information is not prohibited under section 108(1), only dealing whilst in possession of the information. Such dealing is prohibited even if the person does not make use of the inside information. In addition, in order to breach section 108(1) positive action is required. Thus, a decision not to acquire or dispose of securities is not prohibited.

13–21 The definitions of "securities" and "dealing" appear to mean that if there are dealing facilities for a security, even if the actual trade in the security takes place off the Stock Exchange, there will be a deal in

---

[30] Section 107 defines a "recognised stock exchange" as "any exchange prescribed by the Minister which provides facilities for the buying and selling of rights or obligations to acquire stock".

securities for the purposes of the Act. Thus, all off-market trades would appear to be included. The situation regarding shares whose listing is suspended is interesting in this regard. Arguably, a dealing facility is not available during the period of suspension and the parties are thus free to deal. The Irish Company Law Review Committee have accepted the view that the prohibition in section 108(1) should include off-market transactions. It did however, consider that certain exceptions might be possible, *e.g.* if a person in possession of price sensitive information were to deal with another person in possession of the same information. The fear in such a case, however, would be that the market would be distorted as a result.[30a]

(ii) Section 108(2)

13–22 The second restriction on insider dealing is contained in section 108(2). This subsection provides that:

> "It shall not be lawful for a person who is, or at any time in the preceding six months has been, connected with a company to deal in any securities of any other company if by reason of his so being, or having been, connected with the first mentioned company he is in possession of information that –
> (a) is not generally available but, if it were, would be likely materially to affect the price of those securities, and
> (b) relates to any transaction (actual or contemplated) involving both those companies or involving one of them and securities of the other, or to the fact that any such transaction is no longer contemplated."

This subsection prohibits a person who is, or at any time in the previous six months has been, connected with a company from dealing in the securities of another company if his connection with the first company has given him access to inside information and the information relates to a transaction involving both companies or one of the companies and securities of the other, or to the fact that the transaction is no longer contemplated. In the context of a takeover, this subsection would prevent a party connected with the offeror from dealing in securities of the offeree where he was aware that a takeover offer was imminent or that takeover discussions had broken down.

(iii) The Prohibitions – Secondary Insiders

13–23 Persons who receive the information directly or indirectly from a primary insider are termed "secondary insiders" or "tipees". The Act prohibits such persons from dealing. Thus, section 108(3) provides:

> "Where a person is in possession of any such information as is mentioned in subsection (1) or (2) that if generally available would be likely materially to

---

[30a] Company Law Review Group, first report, December 1994, Chap. 5, para. 5–13.

affect the price of securities but is not precluded by either of those sub-sections from dealing in those securities, it shall not be lawful for him to deal in those securities if he has received the information, directly or indirectly, from another person and is aware, or ought reasonably to be aware, of facts or circumstances by virtue of which that other person is then himself precluded by subsection (1) or (2) from dealing in those securities."

The prohibition on dealing applies where the tipee "receives" the information from the primary insider. No positive action is thus acquired on the tipee's behalf. A tipee does not need to have "acquired" the information which might involve more direct contact. In addition, once in possession of the information, the prohibition on dealing applies. Again, it is irrelevant whether the tipee intends to make use of that information or not in his dealing.

Unlike a primary insider, a tipee does not need to have, or have had, a connection with the company. Receiving the information from a person who is so connected is all that is required. The tipee must however be aware that the information is "inside information" and that the person from whom they have received the information is precluded from dealing.

(iv) Other Prohibitions

13–24　In addition to being precluded from dealing, both primary and secondary insiders are also prohibited from causing or procuring other persons to deal in the relevant securities. Section 108(4) provides that:

"It shall not be lawful for a person at any time when he is precluded by subsection (1), (2) or (3) from dealing in any securities, to cause or procure any other person to deal in those securities."

This restriction will apply even if the inside information is not revealed to the other person. It is sufficient that the person is encouraged to deal.

13–25　Primary and secondary insiders are also precluded from com-municating the information to persons they know, or ought reasonably to know, will deal, or will procure others to deal. Section 108(5) thus provides that:

"It shall not be lawful for a person at any time when he is precluded by subsection (1), (2) or (3) from dealing in any securities, by reason of his being in possession of any information, to communicate that information to any other person if he knows, or ought reasonably to know, that the other person will make use of the information for the purpose of dealing, or causing or procuring another person to deal, in those securities."

13–26　Article 3(a) of the Directive provides that each Member State shall prohibit any person subject to the prohibition laid down in Article 2 who possesses inside information from disclosing that information to any third party, "unless such disclosure is made in the normal course of the exercise of his employment, profession or duties . . . ". There is however no similar exclusion in the Act. Furthermore, it would seem that the Directive seeks to prohibit communication *per se*. Some commentators suggest that the Act appears to link communication of information with subsequent use of the information in dealing.[31] However, it is submitted that on a literal interpretation of the subsection, dealing by the recipient is not required in order to make the insider liable.

(v) The Position of Companies

13–27 Whilst section 108(1), (2) and (3) sets out the dealing restrictions which apply to individuals, section 108(6) sets out the position in relation to dealings by companies. It states that a company may not deal in any securities:

> "at a time when any officer of that company is precluded by subsection (1), (2) or (3) from dealing in those securities".[32]

However, section 108(7) sets out certain exceptions to the prohibition contained in section 108(6). A company is not precluded from entering into a transaction at any time:

> "by reason only of information in the possession of the officer if –
> (a) the decision to enter into the transaction was taken on its behalf by a person other than the officer;
> (b) it had in operation at that time written arrangements to ensure that the information was not communicated to that person and that no advice relating to that transaction was given to him by a person in possession of the information; and
> (c) the information was not so communicated and such advice was not so given."

Thus, where Chinese Walls as discussed in Chapter 10[33] are in place, a company may deal. Such an exception is essential in order to allow financial institutions to continue to operate different departments such as fund management and corporate finance.

13–28 The recitals to the Directive provide that:

> "since the acquisition or disposal of transferable securities necessarily involves a prior decision to acquire or to dispose taken by the person who undertakes

---

[31] McCormack for example suggests that liability may only arise if use is made of the information. See McCormack, *The New Companies Legislation* (1991), Chap. 19 p. 1.

[32] It is unclear whether companies are persons for the purposes of section 108(4) and (5). Ashe & Murphy, *op. cit.*, n.26 at p. 88 state that the existence of an insider dealing provision for companies and the wording of the two subsections suggest that they are probably not intended to be included.

[33] See Chap. 10, paras 10–59–10–69.

one or other of these operations, the carrying-out of this acquisition or disposal does not constitute in itself the use of inside information".

This is particularly relevant in the context of a takeover. Often, the offeror who decides to make a general offer to the company to acquire all its shares may intend to build up its stake in the company in advance. Yet the fact that it intends to make an offer is obviously price-sensitive information. It is important that the offeror be allowed to do this without breaching Part V of the 1990 Act. Section 108(8) provides that a company is not precluded from dealing in the securities of another company at any time:

> "by reason only of information in the possession of an officer of the first-mentioned company, being information that was received by the officer in the course of the performance of his duties as an officer of the first-mentioned company and that consists only of the fact that the first-mentioned company proposes to deal in securities of that other company."

Such an exception ensures that the possession of knowledge of the acquisition by an officer of the offeror will not prevent the offeror from dealing in securities of the offeree.

(vi) Exemptions from the Prohibitions in section 108

13–29 Two absolute exempt transactions are allowed under section 110(1); where shares are acquired under a will or under a Revenue Commissioners' approved employee profit sharing scheme.

13–30 Transactions entered into in good faith attract exemptions in four other situations set out in section 110(2):

(a) the obtaining by a director of a share qualification under section 180 of the Companies Act, 1963;

(b) a transaction entered into by a person in compliance with his obligations under an underwriting agreement;

(c) a transaction entered into by a personal representative of a deceased person, a trustee, a liquidator, receiver or examiner in the performance of the functions of his office;

(d) a transaction arising out of a mortgage of or charge on securities or a mortgage, charge, pledge or lien on documents of title to securities.

Section 4 of the Companies (Amendment) Act, 1999 amends section 110 of the 1990 Act in order to incorporate into primary legislation changes which were previously made by the Companies Act, 1990 (Insider Dealing) Regulations, 1991.[34] A new subsection (2A) is added to section

---

[34] S.I. No. 151 of 1991.

110 providing that a person will be regarded as having entered in good faith into a transaction to which section 110(2)(b) relates if he enters in good faith into:

(a) negotiations with a view to entering an agreement to which paragraph (b) or (c) would relate, or

(b) an agreement to underwrite securities, or

(c) an agreement, in advance of dealing facilities being provided by a recognised stock exchange for securities, to acquire or subscribe for a specified number of those securities, or

(d) a transaction in accordance with such person's obligations under an agreement to which paragraph (b) or (c) relates.

Section 6 of the Companies (Amendment) Act, 1999 then revokes the Companies Act, 1990 (Insider Dealing) Regulations, 1991.

Section 2 of the Companies (Amendment) Act, 1999, in effect, provides a further exception to section 108 of the 1990 Act in respect of stabilising activity in relation to the issue or sale of securities.[34a] The purpose of such stabilisation is to protect investors from sharp falls in the price of their securities in the aftermath of a public offering. Section 2 provides that section 108 will not be contravened:

> "by reason of –
>
> (a) anything done in the State for the purposes of stabilising or maintaining the market price of securities if it is done in conformity with the Stabilisation Rules, or
>
> (b) any action taken during the stabilising period by a person in any jurisdiction other than the State for the purpose of stabilising or maintaining the market price of securities, but only if the action is taken is, in all material respects, permitted by or is otherwise in accordance with all relevant requirements applicable to such actions in the jurisdiction where such action is effected, including, if those securities are also listed on a stock exchange in that jurisdiction, the rules or other regulatory requirements governing that stock exchange."

This provision allows for the taking of action to support share prices during a specified period referred to as the "stabilising period". This action is generally taken by the investment bank making the offer or the Bank managing this issue. This Bank will then be referred to as the "stabilisation manager". If the stabilising action is undertaken outside

---

[34a] The introduction of this provision obviated the need for the Companies Act, 1990 (Insider Dealing) Regulations, 1992 (S.I. No. 131 of 1992) which were promulgated to facilitate stabilising action outside the State. These Regulations are thus revoked by section 6 of the Companies (Amendment) Act, 1999.

the State, it must conform with all relevant regulatory requirements in the relevant jurisdiction. If such action is undertaken in the State, it must conform with the Stabilisation Rules set out in the Schedule. The stabilisation period in relation to action undertaken in the State[34b] is defined in the Stabilisation Rules as:

> "the period beginning with the date on which the earliest public announcement of the issue or offer for sale which states the issue price or offer price, as the case may be, is made and ending with the relevant day, save that, in relation to an issue of relevant securities which are debentures or other debt securities, the stabilising period means the period beginning with the date on which the earliest public announcement of the issue is made (whether or not that announcement states the issue price) and ending with the relevant day."

The "relevant day" is defined in the Stabilisation Rules as:

(a) the 30th day after the date the issuer receives the proceeds of the issue or the offerer receives the proceeds of the offer for sale (or the first instalment of the proceeds, if applicable);

(b) any previous time, if the stabilisation manager determines and has notified the Irish Stock Exchange accordingly.

The action permitted by the Stabilisation Rules is the purchase, agreement to purchase or offer to purchase of certain "relevant securities" or securities defined in the Stabilisation Rules as "associated securities". The Stabilisation Rules provide that "relevant securities" are securities:

(a) issued for cash;

(b) offered for case in circumstances where dealing facilities are not already provided by a recognised stock exchange;[34c]

(c) offered for case in circumstances where dealing facilities are already provided by a recognised stock exchange, if the total cost of the securities which are the subject of the offer is at least £15 million;

and at a specified price, where the securities may be dealt in on a recognised stock exchange without a formal application or where an application has been made to a recognised stock exchange for the securities to be dealt in on that exchange.

However, in order for the Rules to apply, such issues and offers must not be made in connection with a takeover offer. The term "takeover offer" is defined in this context as:

[34b] A slightly different definition of the term "stabilising period" set out in section 1(1) applies to stabilising action undertaken outside the State.

[34c] As defined by section 107 of the 1990 Act.

> "an offer made generally to holders of shares in a company to acquire those shares or a specified proporation of them, or to holders of a particular class of those shares to acquire the shares of that class or a specified proporation of them."

The Stabilisation Rules also set out certain preliminary steps which must be taken and certain price limits which apply. They also require the recording of the details of any stabilising actions and the notification of the Stock Exchange. Although the Companies (Amendment) Act, 1999 was introduced prior to the flotation of Telecom shares in July 1999, due to the strong market for Telecom Shares, price stabilisation proved unnecessary.

13–31 Section 108(9) provides exemptions for agents. This is necessary as the definition of "dealing" set out in section 107 includes dealing "whether as principal or agent". There are, however, two preconditions to the exemption set out in section 108(9). Firstly, the agent must enter into the transaction "as agent for another person pursuant to a specified instruction of that other person to effect that transaction". Secondly, the agent must not have given "any advice to the other person in relation to dealing in securities, or rights or interests in securities, of that company that are included in the same class as the first-mentioned securities." These conditions are consistent with the Recitals to the Directive which provide that:

> "the mere fact that market makers, bodies authorised to act as *contrepartie*, or stockbrokers with insider information confine themselves, in the first two cases, to pursuing their normal business of buying or selling securities or, in the last, to carrying out an order should not in itself be deemed to constitute use of such inside information; whereas likewise the fact of carrying out transactions with the aim of stabilising the price of new issues or secondary offers of transferable securities should not in itself be deemed to constitute use of inside information".

Section 113 of the 1990 Act introduces a new offence however, in respect of agents. It prohibits a person from dealing on behalf of another person if he has reasonable cause to believe or ought to conclude that the deal would be unlawful within the meaning of section 108.

13–32 Section 108(10) has proved to be a controversial one. It states that section 108 will not preclude a person from dealing in securities if: "while not otherwise taking advantage of his possession of information referred to in subsection (1)":

(a) he gives at least 21 days' notice to the Stock Exchange of his intention to deal, within the allowed period, in the securities of the company concerned; and

(b) the dealing takes place within a period beginning 7 days after the publication of the company's interim or final results, as the case may be and ending 14 days after such publication; and

(c) the notice given to the Stock Exchange is published by the Stock Exchange immediately upon its receipt.

This subsection was added into the Companies (No. 2) Bill 1987 just before the enactment of the 1990 Act and has been criticised as not being consistent with the overall philosophy of the 1990 Act. It was included to clarify when a person privy to information about a company's results can deal in shares after the publication of those results without fear of liability. The phrase "while not otherwise taking advantage of his possession of such information," is, however, ambiguous. It is clearly not intended to mean that an insider may deal on inside information provided that he does so at a specific time of year. Instead, it was intended to allow a person deal during this period on information which is restricted to information about the results.

(vii) Penalties

13–33 The Directive is silent as to the sanctions to be imposed for insider dealing only stating that they should be "sufficient" to promote compliance. Whilst, the UK government introduced only criminal sanctions, the 1990 Act imposes both civil and criminal liability.

Section 109(1) provides that a person who deals in or causes or procures another to deal in securities contrary to section 108 or who communicates information in any such manner shall be liable. Such persons may be required:

> "to compensate any other party to the transaction who was not in possession of the relevant information for any loss sustained by that party by reason of any difference between the price at which the securities were dealt in in that transaction and the price at which they would have been likely to have been dealt in in such a transaction at the time when the first-mentioned transaction took place if that information had been generally available".

In addition, the person held liable must

> "account to the company that issued or made available those securities for any profit accruing to the first-mentioned person from dealing in those securities."

It is important to note that the obligation to compensate individuals relates only to compensating the counter parties to the transactions. The obligation does not extend to compensating persons dealing contemporaneously on the market, although such persons may have been indirectly affected by the insider dealing.

13–34 The amount of compensation or profit for which a person is liable is the amount of the loss sustained by the person claiming the compensation or the amount of the profit accruing to the first-mentioned person from dealing in those securities.[35] The compensation to the company yields the company a windfall that it could not otherwise have obtained because it could never have acted on the information.

13–35 Section 109(2)(b) expressly limits the amount of compensation for which the first-mentioned person will be liable where several claims arise out of the same transaction. It provides:

> "if the person so liable has been found by a court to be liable to pay an amount or amounts to any other person or persons by reason of the same act or transaction, the amount of that loss or profit less the amount or the sum of the amounts for which that person has been found to be liable."

If the first-mentioned person has been found by a court to be liable to pay an amount or amounts to others by reason of the same act or transaction, the compensation or profit which is thus due is the amount of that loss/profit less the amount or the sum of the amounts for which that person has been found liable. The onus of proving that the liability of a person to pay another person arose from the same act or transaction from which another liability arose lies on the person liable to pay the amount.[36]

The claimant has two years after the date of completion of the transaction in which the loss or profit occurred, to initiate an action for recovery of a loss or profit.[37] It would seem that the claimant has to prove both the fact of loss and the price differential. The former is likely to be particularly difficult.

13–36 Section 111 of the 1990 Act provides that a person who deals in securities in a manner declared unlawful by section 108 will be guilty of an offence. The penalties provide for a term of imprisonment not exceeding 12 months and/or a fine not exceeding £1,000 upon summary conviction. On conviction on indictment, a term of imprisonment not exceeding 10 years and/or a fine not exceeding £200,000 may be imposed. In addition, a person found criminally liable under section 111 is prohibited from dealing for a 12 month period from the date of the conviction.[38] However, if the person convicted has initiated a transaction before the date of his conviction, he may complete the

---

[35] s.109(2)(a).
[36] s.109(3).
[37] s.109(4).
[38] Section 112(1).

transaction where the Stock Exchange has indicated in writing to the parties to the transaction that it is satisfied the transaction was initiated but not completed before the date of the conviction, that failure to complete would prejudice the rights of an innocent third party and that the transaction would not be unlawful under any other provision of this part of the Act. The completion of the deal cannot thus amount to dealing on inside information contrary to section 108.

13–37 The 1990 Act is silent as to whether or not a transaction in breach of the insider dealing laws is void and unenforceable. In *Crafter v. Singh*,[39] the Supreme Court of Western Australia held that a transaction was not void and unenforceable. However, in *Chase Manhattan Equities Ltd. v. Goodman*,[40] the opposite result ensued. In the latter case, a director was deemed to be in possession of price sensitive information at the time of the sale of the shares to a third party who re-sold them to Chase Securities. The information consisted of the fact that the director was about to resign and also the existence of a dispute as to the existence of a large company debt. Accordingly, in selling his shares, the court found that the director was in breach of the Company Securities (Insider Dealing) Act 1985. The transaction between the director and Chase Equities was held to have been brought into effect as a direct result of the director's illegal act and the English High Court would not in the circumstances assist the director in enforcing it: Knox J. stated:

> "The sale agreement was in itself an entirely lawful contract and its implementation today would involve no illegality. But it was brought into being as a direct result of an illegal act by [the director] and if the law lends its assistance to its completion [the director] will benefit, in the sense of avoiding loss, as a direct result of his illegal act."[41]

Since the transfer of the shares had not been effected, there was no difficulty about unscrambling the transaction and the Court simply directed that the transaction was unenforceable against Chase Equities.

(viii) *Role of the Stock Exchange*
13–38 The relevant authority of a recognised stock exchange[42] ("the Stock Exchange") must report on any suspected offences under Part V. of the 1990 Act to the Director of Public Prosecutions ("the DPP").[43] The DPP should be given information and access to and facilities for

---

[39] (1990) 2 A.C.S.R. 1.
[40] [1991] B.C.L.C. 897.
[41] *ibid*. at p. 933.
[42] Section 107 defines the "relevant authority" as (a) the board of directors, committee of management or other management body or (b) the manager of the Stock Exchange.
[43] s.115(1).

inspecting and copying documents in the possession of the Stock Exchange which relate to the matters in question. Similarly, where a member of the Irish Stock Exchange suspects that a person has breached the provisions of Part V, he must report the matter to the Stock Exchange who then become bound to investigate and report on the matter to the DPP.[44] Where a court, in any proceedings, suspects that an offence has been committed and a report has not been made to the DPP, the court may on its own initiative or, on the application of any interested party, direct the Stock Exchange to make such a report.[45]

13–39 Where the DPP receives a report and decides to institute proceedings, the Stock Exchange, every officer of the company whose securities are concerned and any other person believed by the DPP to be in possession of relevant information (other than any defendants in the proceedings) are obliged to give all assistance they reasonably can.[46]

13–40 The Minister for Enterprise, Trade and Employment also plays an important role in relation to enforcement. If a complaint has been made to the Stock Exchange concerning an alleged offence under Part V. and the Minister believes that the Stock Exchange should use its powers under this Part but has not, the Minister may direct the Stock Exchange to use its powers.[47] Similarly, a direction may be given where the Minister believes that a report should be sent to the DPP and has not yet been sent. In such cases, the Stock Exchange must communicate the results of its investigations or a copy of its report to the Minister.[48]

13–41 Section 115(7) grants the Stock Exchange immunity from liability in damages in respect of actions or omissions of the Stock Exchange in connection with its exercise of its functions under Part V. An exception to this immunity is where the acts or omissions complained of are done or omitted to be done in bad faith.

13–42 The Stock Exchange's investigations are generally carried out by an authorised person who will be the manager of the Stock Exchange or a person nominated by the Stock Exchange pursuant to section 117 of the Act.[49] The Stock Exchange is obliged to ensure that potential conflicts of interest are avoided on the part of any such person.[50] The authorised person has wide investigative powers and may require a

---

[44] s.115(2).
[45] s.115(3).
[46] s.115(4).
[47] s.115(5).
[48] s.115(6).
[49] s.117(1).
[50] s.117(2).

person who is reasonably believed to have dealt in securities or to have information about such dealings, to furnish information on the securities concerned, the issuer of the securities, his dealings in the securities and any other information the authorised person reasonably requires in relation to such securities or such dealings.[51] Both the authorised person and anyone required by the authorised person to furnish information may apply to the court for a declaration.[51a] The court may decide that the exigencies of the common good do warrant or do not warrant the exercise by the authorised person of the powers conferred by section 117.[51b] In the latter case, the authorised person should withdraw the requirement as soon as possible.[51c] In the former case, the information must be furnished as soon as may be.[51d] Where a person fails to comply with the requirement in such circumstances, the authorised person will certify the refusal to the court. After hearing any statements from the defence, the court will punish the offender as if the party in breach had been guilty of contempt of court.[51e]

13–43   Section 118(1) provides that information obtained by the Stock Exchange, an authorised person or an employee or former employee by virtue of the exercise of the Stock Exchange of its functions under the Act shall not be disclosed "save in accordance with the law". This provision does not however, prevent the Stock Exchange furnishing information to the Minister or to a similar authority in another EU Member State.

(ix) Co-operation between Relevant Authorities
13–44   As a significant proportion of share dealing involves cross border transactions, it is important that stock exchanges in different Member States co-operate with each other to identify and eliminate insider dealing. Section 116 of the 1990 Act imposes an obligation on the Stock Exchange to co-operate with similar authorities in other Member States when it receives a request for information in relation to the exercise by the foreign authority of its functions under any enactment of the European Communities relating to unlawful dealing. This applies whether the dealing has taken place within the State or elsewhere. This co-operation extends to making use of its powers under the Act to obtain and supply the information requested by the foreign authority.

---

[51] s.117(3)
[51a] s.117(5).
[51b] s.117(6).
[51c] s.117(7).
[51d] s.117(8).
[51e] s.117(9).

13–45 The Stock Exchange must, however, inform the Minister of the request and the Minister may direct the Stock Exchange not to communicate this information.[51f] The Minister may decide to direct a refusal where communication of the information requested might adversely affect the "sovereignty, security or public policy of the State". A refusal may also be directed where civil or criminal proceedings in the State have already been commenced against a party in respect of any acts to which the request for information has been received or where any person has already been convicted in the State of a criminal offence in respect of any such acts.[51g]

(x) Territorial Scope

13–46 Article 5 of the Directive requires each Member State to ensure that the Directive applies "at least to actions undertaken within its territory to the extent that the transferable securities concerned are admitted to trading on a market of a Member State". It continues by stating that "each Member State shall regard a transaction as carried out within its territory, if it is carried out on a market as defined in Article 1(2) *in fine*, situated or operating within that territory." The Companies Act, 1990 (Insider Dealing) Regulations 1992[52] confined the application of section 108 to securities dealings which took place within the State. While this was obviously intended to exempt price stabilisation which took place abroad, it meant that dealings outside the State were thus not relevant for the purposes of section 108. In 1994, the Company Law Review Group recommended that the legislation be amended to cover attempts to circumvent the application of Part V by the conduct of all or part of the dealings outside Ireland.[52a] The aforementioned regulations were revoked by section 6 of the Companies (Amendment) Act 1999. During the course of the Dáil Debates on the Bill, reference was made to the fact that IBEC had drawn attention to the fact that the revocation of the regulations would lead to the application of the 1990 Act to dealings outside the State in Irish securities.

13–47 A further recommendation of the Company Law Review Group was that dealings which take place in the State in the securities of foreign incorporated companies quoted on the Irish Stock Exchange should be included within the scope of Part V. Such companies are not currently included because the definition of "company" in the Act does not include companies which are not incorporated in the State.[52b]

[51f] s.116(3).
[51g] s.116(4).
[52] S.I. No. 131 of 1992.
[52a] *op. cit.*, n.30a at para. 5–17.
[52b] *ibid.*, at para. 5–16.

(4) Irish Association of Investment Managers Code of Best Practice

13–48   A Code of Best Practice ("the Code") was developed by the Irish Association of Investment Managers ("the IAIM") in July 1991 to meet the following objectives:

(a)   to facilitate participants in the market in complying fully with the insider dealing provisions contained in Part V. of the 1990 Act;

(b)   to ensure that the Irish stock market is an informed and fair market; and

(c)   to ensure that investors, and potential investors, have confidence that some participants in the market do not have an unfair advantage over others through dealing on the basis of unpublished price sensitive information.

13–49   Part 2 of the Code provides a working definition of "unpublished price sensitive information" for the purpose of facilitating compliance with the 1990 Act.

> "In general, unpublished price sensitive information is that information which companies are required to announce through the Stock Exchange's Regulatory News Service. Information constructed by an investor or analyst from a number of pieces of information, such as details of industry circumstances, interpreting accounting policies and analysing merger and acquisitions policy, be they received from the company and/or from other research sources, shall not be considered unpublished price sensitive information for the purposes of the Code of Best Practice."

This is a particularly useful definition given that the 1990 Act itself fails to define this term. The IAIM also explains the term "materially affected" which is used in the 1990 Act in relation to share prices:

> "It is considered by market participants that the price of a liquid equity security would be likely to have been materially affected if, had the information been generally available (and in the absence of any specific announcement, general sectoral influence or market movement), the price of the security would have been less than 95 per cent or more than 105 per cent of the then market price on the day(s) on which the dealing(s) occurred."

13–50   The Code proceeds then to set out the responsibilities of companies. Companies whose shares are quoted on the Stock Exchange should observe, insofar as price sensitive information is concerned, the Stock Exchange's continuing requirements for listed companies. Care should be taken to ensure that price sensitive information is not released selectively to investors or analysts at meetings, presentations or company visits. If information is released in this manner, the IAIM requires the company to inform the recipient of the dealing and communication restrictions which apply and to give serious consideration to making the information generally available through the Stock Exchange's Regulatory News Service ("RNS"). Where companies intend making price sensitive announcements at general meetings of shareholders, the IAIM recommends that they should first ensure that the information has been notified to the Company's Announcements Office ("the CAO") in the Stock Exchange and published by the RNS. When publishing preliminary and interim results, companies should publish details of any information which would be price sensitive. This serves to ensure a fair market in the company's securities because the information is disseminated in an equitable manner. For the same reason, if the company is preparing summaries of lengthy or complex price sensitive announcements in accordance with the Stock Exchange Listing Rules, the IAIM requires that all price sensitive information be included in the summary. Finally, to facilitate the general availability of potentially price sensitive information, companies should include in their annual reports a schedule of dates for the making of regulatory or statutory filings.

13–51   The Code sets out the responsibilities of investors and analysts who meet companies on a group or individual basis. During the sensitive periods immediately preceding the preliminary announcement of the company's annual and interim results, such meetings should be avoided. Investors and analysts are asked to respect the fact that companies cannot release information selectively in such circumstances and not to interpret a refusal as being indicative of their position and thus price sensitive in itself. Where the analysts or investors do come into possession of unpublished price sensitive information, the IAIM suggests that they should adhere to the dealing and communication restrictions set out in the 1990 Act. It is also recommended that institutional investors and stockbrokers should have internal authorisation procedures regarding participation by analysts in company visits organised by brokers or companies.

13–52   Like the 1990 Act, the Code accepts the necessity of giving advance information in certain circumstances to specified institutional investors. An example of such an occasion would be where information is communicated to a potential underwriter of a rights issue in order to enable an accurate assessment of the risk to be made. In the absence of Chinese Walls, such institutions should not, however, deal in the company's shares until the price sensitive information is generally available. Similarly, the persons in receipt of the price sensitive information should adhere to the dealing and communication restrictions until the information has been published by the RNS or until it is agreed that the matter under discussion is closed. In order to avoid inadvertent communication of sensitive information, institutional investors are advised to publish a list of persons designated to deal with any issues which may arise involving unpublished price sensitive information. A dealer who receives unpublished price sensitive information from an in-house researcher in the same investment house is subject to the usual dealing and communication restrictions and must ensure that his or her compliance officer is aware of the breach. This rule also applies to a stockbroker within a stockbroking firm who receives such information from an in-house researcher.

13–53 Because stockbrokers in the course of their normal duties may come into possession of unpublished price sensitive information which is not directly linked to a company, it becomes more difficult to determine how the restrictions apply to them. For example, a stockbroker may become aware that a particular investor wishes to buy or sell a large amount of a particular company's shares. Obviously such an acquisition or disposal could have a significant effect on that company's share price. A stockbroker is prohibited under section 113 of the 1990 Act from dealing on behalf of another person, if they have reasonable cause to believe or ought to conclude that the deal would be unlawful.

13–54 The Code recommends that stockbroking firms, corporate finance houses, advisers and institutional investors should establish rules and procedures in accordance with the Code and which cover dealings in securities by employees and persons which are under the control or influence of employees. Compliance with such rules should be a requirement of the employee's contract of employment. Furthermore, the Code recommends that both directors and key employees should comply with the Model Code for Securities Transactions by Directors of Listed Companies.

(5) The Stock Exchange Listing Rules "Model Code"

13–55 Listed companies are required to adopt and apply a code of dealing based on the Model Code set out in the Appendix to chapter 16 of the Stock Exchange Listing Rules. The Model Code imposes restrictions which are different to, and in some instances more restrictive than, those imposed by law. In addition, the Listing Rules emphasise that the Model Code contains minimum requirements and that companies may impose more rigorous restrictions upon dealings.[53] The stated purpose of the Model Code is to ensure that directors, certain employees and persons connected with them do not abuse, and do not place themselves under suspicion of abusing, price sensitive information that they may have, or be thought to have, especially in periods leading up to an announcement of results.

---

[53] Listing Rules, para. 16–19.

13–56   The Model Code must be complied with by:

– the directors;

– relevant employees, *i.e.* any employee of the listed company or any director or employee of a subsidiary or parent undertaking of the listed company who, because of his office or employment in the listed company or subsidiary or parent is "likely to be in possession of unpublished price sensitive information in relation to the listed company".[54]

(a) Definitions

13–57   The term "unpublished price-sensitive information" is defined as meaning:

> "information which:
>   (i) relates to particular securities or to a particular issuer or to particular issuers of securities and not to securities generally or issuers of securities generally (and, for these purposes, information shall be treated as relating to an issuer of securities which is a company not only were it is about the company but also where it may affect the company's business prospects);
> (ii) is specific or precise;
> (iii) is not generally available within the meaning of section 108 of the Companies Act 1990; and
> (iv) if it were generally available would be likely materially to affect the price of any securities."

Under the Model Code, such persons are restricted from "dealing" in "securities of the company."

13–58   The term "securities" means:

> "any listed securities and, where relevant, securities which have been listed or admitted to dealing on, or have their prices quoted on or under the rules of, NASDAQ or any investment exchange in a Member State which provides facilities for the buying and selling of securities."

This is clearly more extensive than the definition in Part V. of the 1990 Act. The term "dealing" includes:

> "any sale or purchase of, or agreement to sell or purchase, any securities of the company and the grant, acceptance, acquisition, disposal, exercise or discharge of any option (whether for the call, or put, or both) or other right or obligation, present or future, conditional or unconditional, to acquire or dispose of securities, or any interest in securities, of the company".

---

[54] Listing Rules, para. 16–18.

Paragraphs 19 and 20 of the Listing Rules provide guidance on actions which constitute dealings for the purposes of the Model Code and those that do not. For example, off-market dealings and dealings between directors and/or relevant employees of the company constitute dealings. However, the taking up of entitlements under a rights issue, the giving of an undertaking to accept, or the acceptance of, a takeover offer are not included. Finally, the term "recognised stock exchange" is defined as:

> "any recognised stock exchange defined as such under section 107 of the Companies Act 1990."

(b) Restrictions on Dealing

13–59 There are four main restrictions imposed on dealings by directors and relevant employees. First, directors and relevant employees are prohibited from dealing in any securities of the listed company on considerations of a short term nature. In addition, they must take reasonable steps to prevent any dealings by or on behalf of connected persons in any securities of the listed company on considerations of a short term nature.

13–60 Secondly, directors and relevant employees must not deal in any securities of the listed company during a "close period". Such a period is a period which precedes the announcement of the company's results. The term is thus defined in paragraph 3 as:

> "(a) the period of two months immediately preceding the preliminary announcement of the company's annual results or, if shorter, the period from the relevant financial year end up to and including the time of the announcement; and
>
> (b) if the company reports on a half-yearly basis, the period of two months immediately preceding the publication of the half-yearly report . . . or, if shorter, the period from the relevant financial period end up to and including the time of such publication; and
>
> (c) if the company reports on a quarterly basis, the period of one month immediately preceding the announcement of the quarterly results or, if shorter, the period from the relevant financial period end up to and including the time of the announcement (save that for the final quarter paragraph 3(a) of this Model Code applies)."

13–61 The third restriction prohibits directors and relevant employees dealing in securities of the listed company at any time when they are in possession of unpublished price-sensitive information in relation to those securities.

The final restriction prohibits directors and relevant employees from dealing in securities of the listed company where clearance to deal is not given under paragraph 7 of the Model Code.

(c) Clearance to Deal

13–62 Before dealing in any securities of the listed company, the director or relevant employee must advise the chairman or a designated director or directors and receive clearance. Where the chairman or designated director wishes to deal, he must advise and receive clearance from the board in advance at a board meeting or he must advise another designated director.

13–63 Paragraph 7 prohibits the giving of clearance to deal during a "prohibited period". The following periods are prohibited periods:

(a) any close period;

(b) any period when there exists any matter which constitutes unpublished price sensitive information in relation to the company's securities (whether or not the director or relevant employee has knowledge of such matter) and the proposed dealing would (if permitted) take place after the time when it has become reasonably probable that an announcement will be required in relation to that matter; or

(c) any period when the person responsible for the clearance otherwise has reason to believe that the proposed dealing is in breach of the Model Code.

13–64 In exceptional circumstances, paragraph 9 allows clearance be given to a director or relevant employee to sell securities when he would otherwise be prohibited if "it is the only reasonable course of action available" to the director or relevant employee. An example given of such an exceptional circumstance would be one where a pressing financial commitment could not otherwise be satisfied.

Furthermore, paragraphs 13 to 18 sets out specific circumstances during which certain dealings by directors or relevant employees is allowed. These include the granting of options under employee share schemes and the exercise of options under an employees' share scheme where the final date for the exercise of such option falls during any prohibited period and the director could not reasonably be expected to have exercised it at an earlier time.

(d) Responsibilities of Directors and Relevant Employees

13–65 Paragraph 11 provides that directors and relevant employees must seek to prohibit any dealing in securities of the listed company during a close period or a period when they are in possession of unpublished price-sensitive information in relation to those securities by connected persons or by investment managers dealing on their behalf or on behalf of connected persons.[55] Any steps they take to prohibit such dealings must, however, be consistent with their duty of confidentiality to the company. Care should be taken for example to avoid signalling confidential matters in this way.

In order to prohibit such dealing paragraph 12 requires directors and relevant employees to advise all such connected persons and investment managers:

(a) of the name of the relevant company;

(b) of the close periods;

(c) of any other periods when the director or relevant employee knows he is not free to deal (unless such disclosure would itself amount to a breach of confidentiality); and

(d) that they must advise him immediately after dealing in securities of the company (except under a discretionary personal equity plan or authorised unit trust or where the dealing is on behalf of a trust of which the director is a trustee but not a beneficiary).

(e) Enforcement

13–66   As noted in Chapter 5,[55a] failure to comply with the Listing Rules may lead to censure and the suspension or cancellation of a listing. If the Committee determines that any contravention is due to a failure of any of the issuer's directors to discharge their responsibilities under the Listing Rules, the director may be censured and the censure may be published. Where the director wilfully or persistently fails to discharge his responsibilities following such a censure, the Committee may recommend the removal of the director from his or her office, and they may suspend or cancel the issuer's listing if the director remains in office.

13–67   In *Chase Manhattan Equities Ltd. v. Goodman,*[56] Mr Goodman, a director of Unigroup plc, transferred shares to his common-law wife Mrs Fitzgerald subject to a charge to the Bank without informing the board of directors of Unigroup plc of the transfer as he should have done in accordance with the Model Code. Chase Manhattan Securities Ltd. ("Chase Securities") acted as brokers to Unigroup plc and Chase Manhattan Equities Ltd. ("Chase Equities") acted as market makers in the Unigroup plc's shares. Soon afterwards, Mrs Fitzgerald sold the shares to Chase Equities through brokers who were members of the Stock

---

[55] This applies whether the funds are discretionary funds or not.
[55a] See Chap. 5, paras 5–68 and 5–69.
[56] [1991] B.C.L.C. 897.

Exchange. At the time of the sale, Mr Goodman resigned from the board of Unigroup plc. Before the transfer of the shares from Mrs Fitzgerald to Chase Equities was actually effected, it was discovered that the shares had originally been held by Mr Goodman. Chase Equities claimed that it was entitled to repudiate the transaction for the purchase of the shares on the grounds that the gift of the shares by Mr Goodman to Mrs Fitzgerald was a sham and therefore, as the beneficial owner, Mr Goodman should have disclosed to Chase Equities that he was the seller pursuant to the obligations contained in the Model Code. The Court held that the transaction between Mr. Goodman and Mrs Fitzgerald was indeed a sham in the sense that it did not deprive Mr. Goodman of the beneficial interest in the shares. However, it held that although Mr. Goodman had been in breach of the provisions of the Model Code by failing to report the sale of the shares to his fellow directors, this did not give rise to any remedy on the part of Chase Equities. Knox J. in the English High Court held that:

> "the obligations, which the listing rules impose, are obligations on the companies concerned and the obligations which the companies in turn are required to impose on their directors are obligations to the companies of which they are directors. There is no direct obligation imposed upon a director towards any other person."[56a]

The Court held that there was too long and tenuous a chain of legal obligation between the duty of a director to make disclosure under the Model Code and a market maker in that security:

> "The director's duty is to the company under a code which the Stock Exchange is empowered to require and does require the company to impose on its directors as a condition of the listing of the securities in question. A market maker is only one category of persons who would have an interest in the due observance of the model code, and I see no sufficient justification for implying a duty to speak in favour of that category. Indeed there are arguments in favour of the proposition that it is ordinary investors rather than market makers who are more likely to suffer from buying on a false market that is too low than are market makers because, as the evidence of this case shows, market makers do not as a rule go either long or short on large amounts of stock but prefer to be sure that they have a buyer before they themselves deal in substantial holdings."[56b]

In addition, the Court found that on the facts of the case, Chase Equities did not rely on the fact that the seller of the shares was a director and therefore it was not in any way influenced by Mr. Goodman's duty to make disclosure under the Model Code.

[56a] *ibid.* at p. 928.
[56b] *ibid.* at p. 929.

(f) Restriction on Dealing by the Company

13–68 Paragraph 9.38 prohibits dealings in any securities by, or on behalf of the company, or any other member of its group at a time when a director of the company would be prohibited from dealing in its securities under the Model Code. There are two exceptions to this prohibition. Firstly, dealings entered into in the ordinary course of business by a securities dealing business are not prohibited. Secondly, dealings entered into on behalf of third parties by the company or any other member of its group are allowed.

(6) Rule 4.1 of the Takeover Rules

13–69 Rule 4.1 was originally introduced in the City Code Mergers and Takeovers at a time when there was no statutory prohibition on insider dealing. Thus to a large extent, the rule has been superseded by legislation prohibiting insider dealing which covers the same ground. However, the prohibitions on insider dealing contained in Rule 4.1 continue to have force and the Irish Takeover Panel ("the Panel") is responsible thus for supervising the market to ensure that no insider dealing takes place.

13–70 Rule 4.1(a) of the Takeover Rules prohibits dealings by persons, other than the offeror, privy to confidential price-sensitive information concerning an offer or potential offer. It should be remembered at this point that the definition of "offeror" includes not just a person who makes an offer but also a person who intends to make an offer. Such a prohibition applies during the "relevant period" which commences from the time that the person first believes that an offer, or an approach with a view to making an offer, is contemplated until the offer or approach is announced or until the termination of the discussions is announced. The prohibition in paragraph (a) relates to dealing in any securities of the offeree including traded and other options and derivatives in respect of or referenced to such securities. This prohibition seeks to restrict both primary insiders and secondary insiders from dealing.

13–71 Rule 4.1(b) seeks to prevent the information being passed to secondary insiders. It prohibits persons who are privy to confidential price-sensitive information concerning an offer or potential offer from making any recommendations during the relevant period to any other person as to dealings of any kind in securities of the offeree. The offeror is included in this prohibition.

13–72 Rule 4.1(c) prohibits any person who is privy to confidential price-sensitive information concerning an offer or contemplated offer, other than an offeror, from dealing during the relevant period in securities of the offeror. Again the prohibition extends to dealing in options and derivatives in respect of or referenced to the offeror's securities. An exception to this latter prohibition is allowed where the offer is not price sensitive in relation to such securities.

13–73   It is important to note the exception made in Rule 4.1(a) and (c) allowing the offeror to deal in the relevant securities. This concession is given because it is accepted that the offeror may choose to engage in such dealing in order to facilitate the bid. It may for example wish to build up its stake in the company prior to making an offer. As noted in paragraph 13.28, such dealing would also be exempt under section 108(8) of the 1990 Act.

II. OTHER RESTRICTIONS ON DEALING

13–74   In addition to restricting dealing on the basis of inside information, the Takeover Rules impose certain general restrictions in dealing during the offer period. These restrictions are detailed below. In addition, it should be remembered that certain Rules, whilst not restricting dealing, impose certain requirements on parties as a result of the dealing. For example, whilst the Rules allow a person acquire through dealing more that 30 per cent of the shares conferring the voting rights of the company, that person is then required to make a mandatory offer for all the remaining shares under Rule 9.[57] These Rules were examined in Chapters 11 and 12.[57a]

(1) Rule 4.2

13–75   Rule 4.2 imposes restrictions on dealings in securities by the offeror and concert parties. Under Rule 4(2)(a), the offeror and any concert parties are prohibited from selling securities of the offeree during an offer period without the consent of the Panel. In addition the offeror, or the concert party must make an announcement at least 24 hours before the dealings to the effect that such sales may be made. After making such an announcement, the offeror and concert parties are prohibited from purchasing any of the offeree's securities during the remainder of the offer period without obtaining the consent of the Panel. In addition, such dealing prevents the offeror revising the offer, except with the consent of the Panel.

13–76   Under Rule 4(2)(b), the offeror and any concert parties are also prohibited from dealing in the offeree's securities before an announcement

---

[57] Rr. 6, 7, 11 and 37 also confer certain obligations on parties as a result of dealing.
[57a] See Chap. 11, paras 11–47–11–54, 11–64–11–75 and Chap. 12, para. 12–04.

of an offer if the offeree has supplied them with confidential information. The purpose of this rule is to prevent offerors from dealing when in possession of an unfair advantage over ordinary investors. If, after an announcement has been made that negotiations are taking place or that an approach is contemplated, negotiations cease or the offeror decides not to proceed any further, dealing by the offeror or anyone privy to this information is prohibited until a new announcement is made.[58] This prevents the offeror from dealing when the share price is inflated by bid speculation.

13–77   The restrictions extend to directors of and financial advisers to either an offeror or offeree. If such persons own securities of that company, they may not deal without the consent of the Panel in such securities in a manner inconsistent with the advice they have given to their shareholders or with any advice with which they were reasonably associated.[59] Therefore, if the directors of the offeree recommend that shareholders should reject an offer of 80 pence per share, they are prohibited from selling their own shares for 80 pence or less. If the Panel consents to any dealing, it may require the directors to make an announcement giving advance notice of their intention to deal together with an appropriate explanation.

(2) Rule 4(3)

13–78   There is no prohibition on any person seeking irrevocable commitments to accept or refrain from accepting a contemplated offer. However, the Panel should be consulted in advance. Each of the shareholders contacted should be provided with adequate information as to the details of the proposal and the nature of the commitment sought. In addition, each shareholder should be afforded a realistic opportunity to consider the offer and to obtain independent advice.

13–79   The potential importance of irrevocable undertakings was evident during the Irish Distillers takeover in 1988. This case involved a hostile takeover bid by GC&C Brands for Irish Distillers. GC&C Brands offered shareholders 400p for their shares. Pernod Ricard, which was regarded by management as a "friendly suitor", then announced an interest in acquiring Irish Distillers. Together with Irish Distillers' directors, Pernod Ricard management approached Irish Distillers' shareholders with a proposal to make an offer of 450p per share. This approach was made during the course of one particular

---

[58] R. 4.2(c). Dealing in options and derivative in respect of, or referenced to, such securities is also prohibited.
[59] R. 4(2)(d).

weekend. Shareholders were informed, however, that Pernod Ricard would only make this offer if they could obtain in advance irrevocable commitments to accept its proposed offer from the holders of shares which, in addition to shares already purchased by Pernod Ricard, would represent over 50 per cent of the total shares in Irish Distillers. The shareholders were faced with a dilemma. If they did not give the undertakings required, the higher bid would not be made and they would not have the opportunity to accept the higher price. If they did give the undertakings, they would not then be free to accept any higher offer that GC&C might subsequently make. On the Sunday, the London Panel met and agreed that these approaches to shareholders by Pernod Ricard constituted a competing offer. GC&C were thus allowed to increase their original offer to shareholders to 525p which they did the same day. However, Pernod Ricard then announced its bid of 450p per share, contending that it had received sufficient irrevocable undertakings to bring its stake in Irish Distillers to more than 50 per cent. Pernod Ricard were ultimately successful in this offer. The London Panel later stated that the gathering of irrevocable undertakings in such circumstances required "particular care". However, despite a number of breaches of the Code, the Panel stated that none was sufficiently serious nor of such significant effect on shareholders as to make it appropriate to release shareholders from their irrevocable undertakings. Thus "the competing equities" did not require the position to be disturbed.[60]

(3) Rule 5

13–79A   Rule 5 restricts the manner in which a person, together with any concert parties, may increase a holding of voting securities or rights over voting securities through 30 per cent. It also restricts a person's ability to acquire voting securities, or rights over voting securities, representing more than 1 per cent of the company's securities if holding between 30 per cent and 50 per cent of these securities. The exceptions to Rule 5 are contained in Rule 5.2. For example, an acquisition from a single shareholder will be permitted where it is the only acquisition within a seven day period. Failure to comply with Rule 5 will give rise to a Rule 9 obligation. Rule 5 is examined in greater detail in Chapter 11.[60a]

(4) Rule 7.3

13–80   Rule 6.2 prevents an offeror or concert parties from buying securities of the offeree at a price above its offer price without the

---

[60] The Panel on Takeover and Mergers Irish Distillers Group plc, November 11, 1988.
[60a] See Chap. 11, paras 11–56–11–63.

offeror increasing its offer price. In the case of a securities exchange offer, the price of the offer is determined by reference to the market price of the relevant offeror securities. It would thus, clearly be in the offeror's best interests to inflate its own share price in order to increase the apparent worth of the offer. This would allow it to raise the level at which it could purchase the offeree's securities. One way in which the offeror might increase its share price is by buying or getting sympathetic parties to acquire its own securities. The effect of this would be to create a false market in the securities. Rule 7.3 is designed to ensure that any such potential manipulation is disclosed before the offeror can reap the benefits of its artificially high share price. Thus, it provides that, in the case of a securities exchange offer, if, at any time during the offer period, the offeror or concert parties purchase relevant securities of the offeror, neither the offeror or any concert parties may purchase any further securities of the offeree until 8.30 a.m. on the business day following disclosure of their purchases. This disclosure is required by Rule 8. If the offeror makes any statements concerning the value of the offer, prior to disclosure of the dealings, the statement must include details of the amount of securities acquired and the price paid.

(5) **Rule 35**

13–81   According to Rule 35.1(a), where an offeror has announced a firm intention to make an offer or has posted an offer (not being a partial offer) and that offer has been withdrawn or has lapsed, the offeror, any party who acted in concert with the offeror as respects the offer and any person who following the expiry of the offer period is acting in concert with the offeror will be prohibited from making a fresh offer in respect of the offeree for a period of 12 months from the date on which the original offer lapsed or was withdrawn. Provision is however made for the Panel to agree otherwise. In addition, these persons will be prohibited from acquiring any securities of the offeree which would give rise to a requirement to make a mandatory offer under Rule 9 or acquiring any securities of the offeree, if the offeror and any of the concert parties hold securities conferring in the aggregate more than 49 per cent but not more than 50 per cent of the voting rights in the offeree.

13–82   These restrictions also apply, except with the Panel's consent, to persons who make announcements concerning a relevant company which although not amounting to a firm intention to make an offer, raises or confirms the possibility that such an offer may be made, and then a firm intention to make or not to make an offer is not announced within what the Panel deems to be a reasonable period.[61]

---

[61] R. 35.1(b).

13–83   In addition, a six month moratorium is imposed on acquisitions above the offer value where the original offer was for more than 50 per cent of the voting rights of the company.[62] The purpose of this rule is to ensure companies do not have to endure prolonged sieges by the same offeror after a failed bid. This would be an unreasonable distraction for the offeree's management. Dispensations are available from this rule, where for example the offeree recommends the new offer or where a competing offeror has become involved.[63]

Similar delays apply to both successful and unsuccessful partial offers under Rule 36.[64]

(6) Rule 38

13–84   As noted in Chapter 10,[64a] a market maker is required to satisfy the Panel as to its independence from connected corporate finance operations before it will be granted exempt status by the Panel. Because such status provides generous exemptions for the market maker in terms of dealing and disclosure, Rule 38 restricts what an exempt market-maker may do.

13–85   Rule 38.1 prohibits exempt market-makers from dealing with the purpose of assisting any offeror or offeree with whom they are connected. Breaching this rule could lead to the withdrawal of exempt status for a period deemed appropriate by the Panel.

13–86   Rules 38.2–38.4 contain further restrictions on exempt market-makers to restrict their ability to help the corporate clients with which they are connected. Rule 38.2 prohibits an offeror or concert party dealing as principal during the offer period with a connected market-maker in securities of the offeree. This provision ensures that the exempt market-maker does not use its status to covertly acquire offeree securities. Rule 38.3 prohibits an exempt market-maker connected with the offeror from accepting the offer prior to the time it is declared unconditional as to acceptances. Finally Rule 38.4 prohibits an exempt market-maker connected with either the offeror or offeree from exercising the voting rights conferred by any securities of the offeror or offeree either during the offer period or at an earlier time at which it has reason to believe that an offer is imminent.

---

[62] R. 35.2.
[63] Note 1 on Rule 35.1.
[64] See Chap. 11, paras 11–30 and 11–31.
[64a] See Chap. 10, para. 10–16.

B. Disclosure Requirements

I. COMPANIES ACTS DISCLOSURE REQUIREMENTS

13–87   Part IV of the 1990 Act deals with the disclosure of interests in shares. The objective of Part IV is to provide shareholders with as complete information as possible concerning the shareholdings of directors and their families and large shareholders.

(1) Share Dealings by Directors, Secretaries and their Families

13–88   Chapter 1 of the 1990 Act[65] deals with the disclosure requirements of directors, shadow directors, company secretaries and their families. Once a person becomes a director[66] or secretary of a company, section 53 provides that he must notify the company of all his interests in the shares or debentures of the company or the company's subsidiary or holding company or a subsidiary of the company's holding company.[67] Notification is also required when a director or secretary: becomes interested in such shares or debentures or when he ceases to become so interested; enters a contract to sell any such shares or debentures; assigns a right granted to him by the company to subscribe for shares or debentures of the company; or is granted, exercises or assigns a right to subscribe for such shares or debentures granted by the company's subsidiary, holding company or a subsidiary of the company's holding company.[68] A strict timetable applies and the notification must be made within five days of the acquisition or disposal.[69]

13–89   Every company is required to keep a register of these interests.[70] Disclosure in the directors' report or the notes to the company's accounts is also required.[71] Section 54 sets out the provisions which apply in determining whether a person has an interest in shares or debentures for the purposes of section 53. Section 55 then sets out the interests which are to be disregarded for the purposes of section 54 and sections 56 to 58. For example, an interest of a director accruing by virtue of his holdings in a registered unit trust scheme or a UCITs scheme will not require disclosure as an interest under section 53.

---

[65] ss. 53–66.
[66] s.53(9) provides that s.53 applies to shadow directors as to directors.
[67] s.53(1).
[68] s.53(2).
[69] s.56.
[70] s.59. s.59(5) provides that s.59 applies to shadow directors as to directors.
[71] s.63.

13–90　　A person who fails to notify the company within the proper period will be guilty of an offence.[72] More importantly, where a person fails to fulfil, within the proper period, a notification obligation pursuant to section 53, no right or interest of any kind whatsoever in respect of the shares or debentures concerned shall be legally enforceable by him, whether directly or indirectly, by action or legal proceedings.[73] This is generally sufficient to ensure compliance with the Act. (It should be noted, however, that the restriction does not apply in respect of a disposal of shares or debentures.[74]) A person affected by the restriction may apply to the court for relief. If the court is satisfied that the default was accidental, or due to inadvertence or some other sufficient cause, or that on other grounds, it is just and equitable to grant relief, it may grant such relief.[75] Relief may not be granted however, if it appears that the default has arisen as a result of a deliberate act or omission on the part of the applicant for relief.[76] The relief granted may be general or it may be granted as respects a particular right or interest on such terms and conditions as the court deems fit.

13–91　　Where a person authorises an agent to acquire or dispose of shares in or debentures of a company on his behalf, he must ensure that the agent notifies him immediately of any acquisitions or disposals which would give rise to an obligation to notify under this Chapter.[77]

13–92　　If the securities of the company enjoy dealing facilities on a recognised Stock Exchange, the company must notify the Stock Exchange if it is notified of any interests or change in interests by directors or secretaries relating to shares or debentures for which such dealing facilities are provided.[78] This notification must be made before the end of the next day following notification to the company.[79] The Stock Exchange is given discretion as to whether to publish this information.

(2) Individual and Group Acquisitions

13–93　　Chapter 2 of Part IV of the 1990 Act[80] deals with individual and group acquisitions. Any person who acquires or disposes of an interest

---

[72]　s.53(7).
[73]　s.58(3).
[74]　s.58(6).
[75]　s.58(4).
[76]　s.58(5).
[77]　s.58(1).
[78]　s.65(1). A recognised Stock Exchange is defined in section 3(2) of the 1990 Act as an exchange prescribed by the Minister for the purposes of the section of the Act in question.
[79]　s.65(2).
[80]　ss.67–96.

in voting shares in a public limited company must notify the company if the acquisition or disposal brings their interest above or below 5 per cent in nominal value of the "relevant nominal capital".[81] The meaning of the term "relevant nominal capital" is the issued share capital of a class carrying voting rights at general meetings. Section 68(5) provides that the obligation to notify also arises under Section 67(1)(b) when at any time a person holding more than the notifiable percentage increases or decreases their holding by at least one percent. Sections 77 and 78 set out the interests in shares which are to be notified and those that are to be disregarded. In determining what constitutes a notifiable interest in shares, section 77(2) provides that an interest is to be read as including an interest of any kind whatsoever in the shares. It provides thus, that any restraints or restrictions to which the exercise of any right attached to the interest is or may be subject should be disregarded. Section 77(4)(a) provides that a person will be deemed to have an interest in shares if he enters into a contract for their purchase by him. It may be argued thus that "an interest" for these purposes includes acceptances under a takeover offer, whether the offer is unconditional as to acceptances or not.

The same strict timetable applies here and the notification must be made within 5 days.[82] The notification must specify the share capital to which it relates. It must also state the number of shares comprised in that share capital in which the person making the notification was aware that he was interested immediately after the time when the obligation arose. Alternatively, in the case where the person no longer has a notifiable interest in shares comprised in that share capital, the person must state that he no longer has that interest.[83]

13–94 For the purposes of these notification obligations, a person is taken to be interested in any shares in which his spouse or any minor child of his is interested.[84] In addition, a person is taken to be interested in shares for those purposes if a company whose directors act in accordance with his instructions is interested or if a company in which he is entitled to control the exercise of at least one-third of the voting rights is interested.[85]

It should be noted that the Companies (Amendment) Act, 1999 introduced a new exemption from the disclosure requirements contained in sections 67 to 79 of the 1990 Act. Section 3 (1) of the 1999 Act exempts stabilising action undertaken in the State in conformity with the Stabilisation Rules or undertaken outside the State in accordance

---

[81] ss. 67–70.
[82] s.71.
[83] s.71(2).
[84] s.72(1).
[85] s.72(2).

with all relevant regulatory requirements in the jurisdiction in question. Section 3(2) of the 1999 Act provides that any interest in relevant share capital acquired by a person during the stabilisation period in order to stabilise or maintain the market price and which remains in their ownership at the end of the stabilisation period will be treated for the purposes of sections 67–79 as having been acquired on the first business day following the end of the stabilisation period. These Rules are discussed at para. 13–30 above.

13–95 Sections 73 to 76 deal with agreements by concert parties to acquire interests in a public limited company. Section 73(1) provides that:

> "an agreement between two or more persons which includes provision for the acquisition by any one or more of the parties to the agreement of interests in shares comprised in relevant share capital of a particular public limited company ('the target company') is an agreement to which this section applies if –
> (a) it also includes provisions imposing obligations or restrictions on any one or more of the parties to the agreement with respect to their use, retention or disposal of interests in that company's shares acquired in pursuance of the agreement (whether or not together with any other interests of theirs in that company's shares to which the agreement relates); and
> (b) any interests in the company's shares is in fact acquired by any of the parties in pursuance of the agreement."

An agreement which is not legally binding is included only if it involves mutuality in the undertakings, expectations or understandings of the parties to it. Agreements to underwrite or sub-underwrite any offer of shares in a company are, however, excluded provided that the agreement is confined to that purpose and to any matters incidental to it.[86] For the purposes of disclosure, each party to an agreement to which section 73 applies will be deemed to be interested in all shares in the target company in which any other party to it is interested apart from the agreement.[87] Each concert party in making a notification must include:

(a) a statement to the effect that the person making the notification is a party to such an agreement;

(b) the names and addresses of the other concert parties, identifying them as such;

(c) a statement as to whether or not any of the shares to which the notification relates are shares in which he is so interested by virtue of section 53 and section 74 and if so, the number of those shares.[87a]

---

86 s.73(5).
87 s.74(1).
87a s.74(4).

Where the notification is to the effect that the person has ceased to be interested in any shares by virtue of the fact that he or any other person has ceased to be a party to the agreement, the notification must include a statement that he or the other party has ceased to be a party to the agreement and in the latter case, the name and address of that other person.[88] In addition to being subject to the notification requirements, each concert party will be obliged to keep the other parties informed of the relevant particulars of his interests in shares of the company.[89] In addition to committing an offence under section 79(7), section 79(3) provides that where a person fails to fulfill a notification obligation imposed by Chapter 2 within the proper period, or knowingly makes a false statement or fails to fulfill an obligation to give any other person notice as required, no right or interest of any kind whatsoever in respect of any shares in the company concerned, held by that person will be enforceable. This subsection does not apply, however, in the case of a disposal of shares. Section 79(4) allows for the making of an application to the court to grant relief by that person or any other person affected. Such relief may be granted where the court is satisfied that the default was accidental or inadvertent or that there are other grounds which make the granting of such relief just and equitable in the circumstances. If the court believes that the applicant defaulted from his or her obligations as a result of their own deliberate act or omission, relief will not be forthcoming. Furthermore, section 79(8) provides that it shall be a defence for a person charged with an offence under section 79(7) to prove that it was impossible to make proper notification within the proper period and that either the situation has not changed or that notice was given as soon as it became possible to do so.

13–96 Where the acquisition or disposal of shares is made through a broker or other agent, the person must ensure that the agent notifies them immediately of acquisitions or disposals of interests in shares effected on their behalf. This, then allows them to make any required notification.[90] Every public limited company must keep a register showing all such notifications received.[91] Where a public limited company knows or reasonably suspects that a person has an interest in voting shares of the company, it may serve a notice in writing on that person requesting particulars.[92] These particulars may include details of the persons' past or present interest in the shares and where the interest is a past interest, particulars about the identity of the person to whom the shares were sold. This is a useful power as it ensures that companies are aware of the identity of their shareholders at all times.

---

[88] s.74(5).
[89] s.75.
[90] s.79(1).
[91] s.80.
[92] s.81.

Sections 90 to 96 of Chapter 2 give statutory effect to Council Directive 88/627.

Directive 88/627/EEC

13–97 Council Directive 88/627 ("the Directive") regulates the information to be published when a major holding in a listed company is disposed of or acquired. By providing adequate information to investors, the objective was to increase investors' confidence in securities market and as a result ensure that securities markets function correctly. In addition, by making such protection equivalent throughout the E.U., the desired result is "greater inter-penetration of the Member States' transferable securities markets" and the establishment of "a true European capital market". The type of information required to be provided by the Directive is information on major holdings and of changes in those holdings in Community companies listed within the Community.

The Notification Requirement

13–98 Member States are obliged to apply the Directive to acquisitions and disposals involving changes in the holdings of voting rights in companies incorporated under their law whose shares are officially listed on a stock exchange or stock exchanges situated or operating within one or more of the Member States.[93] Acquisitions or disposals of major holdings in collective investment undertakings are excluded from the scope of the Directive.[94] Section 91(1) of the Act applies the provisions to interests in shares of public limited companies listed on the Irish Stock Exchange. It should be noted that the Directive allows Member States discretion to impose on persons more strict requirements or additional requirements, provided that such requirements apply generally to all those acquiring or disposing of holdings and all companies or to all those falling within a particular category acquiring or disposing of holdings or of companies.[95] According to Article 4(1), notification is required where following an acquisition or disposal by a person, the proportion of voting rights held by that person reaches, exceeds or falls below one of the thresholds of 10 per cent, 20 per cent, $1/3$, 50 per cent and $2/3$. Instead of applying a threshold of $2/3$, a threshold of 75 per cent may be applied. Similarly, instead of applying thresholds of 20 per cent and $1/3$, a single threshold of 25 per cent will suffice. Section 91(3) utilises this option and the relevant thresholds under the Act are 10 per cent, 25 per cent, 50 per cent and 75 per cent.

---

[93] Art. 1(1).
[94] Art. 1(3).
[95] Art. 3.

13–99 Section 91(2) provides that where a person becomes aware that, following an acquisition or disposal, the percentage level of his interest in the company's share capital exceeds or falls below the thresholds, in addition to disclosing this to the company as required under section 67,[96] he must notify the Stock Exchange of his interest in the shares following the acquisition or disposal. Unlike, Article 4(1), the obligation only arises when the party becomes aware of the acquisition. A further difference between the Act and the Directive is that the Act does not include situations where the thresholds are reached but not crossed.

Procedure for Notification

13–100 The Directive requires that notification be made both within seven days to the company itself and the competent authorities. In Ireland, the maximum period is five days.[97] This notification must set out the proportion of voting rights held by the person following the acquisition or disposal. Member States are given the option under Article 4(2) of requiring that a company be informed in respect of the proportion of capital held by a natural person or legal entity. The Directive allows the competent authorities to grant exemptions from the notification requirement in respect of acquisitions or disposals of major holdings by authorised professional dealers[98] acting in that capacity without intending to intervene in the management of the company concerned.[99] It would not appear that Ireland has availed of this option. Within three days of the receipt of a notification of the acquisition or disposal, section 91(5) requires the competent authority to disclose it to the public.[100] The Stock Exchange may exempt companies from this disclosure obligation pursuant to section 91(6) where it considers that the disclosure of such information would be contrary to the public interest" or "seriously detrimental to the company or companies concerned".[101] However, the omission of this information must not lead to the misleading of the public leading to the creation of a false market.

II. IAIM GUIDELINES

13–101 In January 1992, the IAIM produced a set of guidelines for members on how some aspects of the disclosure requirements con-

---

[96] Under section 67, the person is obliged to disclose his interests to the company. See para. 11–93.
[97] s.91(4) states that the provisions of Chapter 2 shall apply as regards the interests which are to be notified to the Exchange, and the manner in which they are to be so notified, as they apply to the interests to be notified to a company under Chapter 2. Therefore, see section 71(1).
[98] Art. 9(2).
[99] Art. 9(1).
[100] See also Art. 10(1).
[101] See also Art. 11.

tained in the 1990 Act should be operated. Advice was obtained from the IAIM's solicitors and from senior counsel on the interpretation of the 1990 Act. On this basis, the IAIM was advised that the interpretation of some of the disclosure requirements is not free from doubt.

13–102 The IAIM recommends that an investment manager, regardless of whether or not he is the beneficial owner, should aggregate and disclose shareholdings at the levels required by the 1990 Act, if he is entitled to exercise any rights conferred by the holding of the shares or he is entitled to control the exercise of any such right. This applies to funds which are in the beneficial ownership of an investment manager and to segregated pension funds, unit trusts etc.

13–103 Where shares are held in the name of a nominee, the responsibility for disclosure lies with the investment manager. Nominee companies which are bare nominees should not disclose an interest since they are excluded by section 78(i)(a) of the 1990 Act. The IAIM maintains that disclosure of convertible shares and warrants is only required if they carry voting rights as described in section 67(2). Shareholdings in unquoted public limited companies need not be disclosed to the Company in accordance with section 67(2) of the 1990 Act.

13–104 On the question of the treatment of percentage movements, the IAIM provides that for the purpose of disclosure to companies, the aggregated percentage shareholding should be rounded down to the nearest whole percentage. They also note that each transaction above or around the 5 per cent level is not necessarily notifiable. The test is whether the holding has changed from one percentage (rounded down) to another percentage (rounded down). Thus, an increase in a holding from 6.00 per cent to 6.9 per cent does not require notification because the holding when rounded down has not increased from 6 per cent. In contrast, an increase from 6.99 per cent to 7 per cent does result in a notification requirement because the holding when rounded down has increased from 6 per cent to 7 per cent. Regardless of the percentage movements however, a reduction in the shareholding to below the 5 per cent level must be notified to the company. It is noted that the same requirements apply for calculating whether notification to the Stock Exchange is required under section 91 of the 1990 Act.

13–105 As to the format for notifying shareholdings, the IAIM states that investment managers with a notifiable interest are required to give the number of shares held in a particular company along with details of the registered owners and the number of shares held by each registerable owner. It is up to the investment manager to disclose whether or not he has a beneficial rather than a notifiable interest in the shareholding.

III. TAKEOVER RULES

(1) Rule 8

13–106 Rule 8 of the Takeover Rules provides for public and private disclosure by the parties to the takeover, their associates and large shareholders of dealings in "relevant securities during the offer period. The term "relevant securities" is defined by Rule 8.9 to mean:

"(a) securities of the offeree which are the subject of the offer or which confer voting rights;

(b) equity share capital of the offeree or an offeror;

(c) securities of an offeror which confer on their holders substantially the same rights as are conferred by any securities to be issued by the offeror as consideration under the offer;

(d) securities of the offeree or an offeror conferring on their holders rights to convert into or subscribe for any of the foregoing securities; and

(e) options (including traded options) in respect of any of the foregoing securities and derivatives referenced to any of the foregoing securities."

Rules 8.1(a) and (b)(i) requires the public disclosure of all dealings in relevant securities by the offeror or offeree or an associate for their own account or for the account of discretionary investment clients during the offer period. An exemption in Rule 8.1(b)(ii) allows dealings by an associate for the account of discretionary investment clients be privately disclosed if the associate is an exempt fund manager connected with the offeror or offeree. (However, public disclosure will still be necessary, if the exempt fund manager (i) is an associate by virtue of owning or controlling, together with concert parties, 5 per cent or more of the relevant securities of the offeror or offeree or (ii) owns or controls 1 per cent or more of any class of relevant securities of the offeror or offeree.) In addition, Rule 8.1(c) exempts a recognised market maker from making disclosure at all under Rule 8.1 if (i) it is an associate only by virtue of owning or controlling, together with concert parties, 5 per cent or more of the relevant securities of the offeror or offeree and (ii) it acts solely in a market making capacity in relation to the securities concerned.

13–107 Rule 8.2 obliges the offeror, offeree or their associates to privately disclose all dealings for non-discretionary investment clients in relevant securities during an offer period unless the Panel agrees otherwise. The offeror, offeree and their associates may not be classified as non-discretionary investment clients in this respect.

13–108 The third disclosure requirement of Rule 8 is contained in Rule 8.3(a) which requires a person who owns or controls 1 per cent or more of any class of relevant securities[102] of the offeror or offeree to publicly

---

[102] Not including options and derivatives.

disclose all of their dealings during an offer period in securities of that company of that class or in relevant options or derivatives. Similar disclosure is required if the person will as a result of any transaction own 1 per cent or more of any such class. Rule 8.3(a) does not however apply to a recognised market maker acting in that capacity. Where two or more persons act in concert to acquire or control relevant securities, they will be treated as a single person for the purposes of Rule 8.3(a).[103] Similarly, a discretionary fund manager will be deemed to be controlling the relevant securities so managed.[104] It is likely that where disclosure is required under Chapter 2 of Part IV of the 1990 Act in respect of a notifiable interest in shares and a dealing occurs during an offer period, disclosure will also be necessary under Rule 8.3.

13–109   Dealings in relevant securities during the offer period for the account of discretionary investment clients by an associate which is an "exempt fund manager" connected with the offeror or offeree generally requires only private disclosure to the Panel.[105] Where investment decisions are made by discretionary fund managers, the securities are treated by the Panel as controlled by the manager rather than the person on whose behalf the fund is managed. If the dealings are for the account of non-discretionary investment clients, private disclosure to both the Stock Exchange and the Panel is required.[106] Such disclosure will not be published by the Stock Exchange on the Regulatory News Service. Stockbrokers, banks and other persons who deal in relevant securities on behalf of clients during an offer period are required to ensure that their clients are aware of these disclosure requirements and are willing to comply with them.[107] By contrast, public disclosure must be made under Rules 8.1(a), 8.1(b)(i) and 8.3. to the Stock Exchange, the Panel and the Press. Dealings in this case are disclosed to the CAO of the Stock Exchange and the Panel by means of a written notification delivered by facsimile or hand. Separate disclosure to the Press is not required. The disclosures in this case should be made by the person who deals or by an agent acting on its behalf.

In addition to disclosing dealings to the Stock Exchange and the Panel, certain dealings must also be disclosed in the offer document. These requirements are set out in Chapter 12.[107a]

---

[103] R. 8.3(b).
[104] R. 8.3(c).
[105] R. 8.1(b)(ii).
[106] R. 8.2 and R. 8.5(b).
[107] R. 8.8.
[107a] See Chap. 12, paras 12–37–12–38.

(2) Rule 38.5

13–110   Rule 38.5 requires compliance with certain disclosure requirements in respect of dealing by an exempt market maker connected with an offeror or the offeree. Dealings should be aggregated and disclosed by the exempt market maker to the Stock Exchange, the Panel and the media by 12 noon on the business day following the date of the dealing. Certain details should be contained in this disclosure such as the total purchases and sales, the highest and lowest price paid and received, the connected party and the market in which the dealing took place. In the case of dealings in options and derivatives, sufficient details must be given to allow the transactions to be understood.

IV. SARs

13–111   General Principle 12 states that:

> "a substantial acquisition of securities (whether such acquisition is to be effected by one transaction or a series of transactions) shall take place only at an acceptable speed and shall be subject to adequate and timely disclosure".

The importance of this principle was recognised further in section 8(2) of the Irish Takeover Panel Act 1997 which imposes an obligation on the Panel to make rules specifying the conditions under which an acquisition by a person "including a person acting pursuant to an agreement or understanding with another person" of securities conferring voting rights in a relevant company should to be regarded as a substantial acquisition of securities for the purposes of the Act. Section 8(2) provides further that these conditions must be, "specified by reference to:

> (a) the proportion which the amount of securities conferring voting rights acquired, or as the case may be, to be acquired bears to the total amount of such securities held in the relevant company concerned;
> (b) the extent to which the acquisition of securities carrying voting rights increases or will increase any existing holding of such securities in the relevant company concerned;
> (c) in the case of a series of acquisitions of such securities, the periods of time that elapse between each such acquisition being effected.

13–112   The Panel drafted rules in compliance with its obligation under section 8(2) and the rules were approved by the Minister[108] and introduced as the Irish Takeover Panel Act, 1997 (Substantial Acquisition) Rules 1997. The Rules, which are known as "the SARs", provide a further impediment to an offeror who wishes to acquire control

---

[108]   As required by section 8(5) of the 1997 Act.

through the acquisition of shares on the Stock Exchange. The SARs, which are administered by the Panel, are very similar to the Rules Governing Substantial Acquisitions of Shares issued on the authority of the London Panel.

13–113   The SARs are designed primarily to restrict the speed with which a person may increase a holding of voting securities and rights over voting securities of a relevant company[109] to an aggregate of between 15 per cent and 30 per cent of the voting rights of that company. In addition, the SARs require accelerated disclosure of acquisitions of shares or rights over shares relating to such holdings. The original purpose of the SARs was to regulate dawn raids *i.e.* offers to acquire shares which were not extended to non-professional shareholders

(1) The General Prohibition

13–114   Rule 4(a) of the SARs prohibit persons[110] making a substantial acquisition of shares, except as permitted by Rule 4(b) or Rule 5.

(2) Definition of a Substantial Acquisition of Shares

13–115   Rule 3(a) of the SARs defines a "substantial acquisition of securities" as "an acquisition or a series of acquisitions by a person of voting securities of a relevant company or of rights over voting securities of that company" where:

"(i)   any voting securities so acquired by that person and the voting securities the subject of any rights so acquired by that person confer in the aggregate 10 per cent or more of the voting rights in the company; and

(ii)   any voting securities so acquired by that person and the voting securities the subject of any rights so acquired by that person, when aggregated with any voting securities already held by that person and any voting securities over which that person already holds rights, confer 15 per cent or more, but less than 30 per cent, of the voting rights in the company; and

(iii)   in the case of a series of acquisitions of securities, all of such acquisitions are made within a period of 7 days."[111]

The effect of this rule is that it will be necessary for a person, before making an acquisition of voting securities of a relevant company, to

---

[109]   A "relevant company" for the purposes of the SARs is the same as a "relevant company" for the purposes of the Takeover Rules and is defined in section 2 of the Irish Takeover Panel Act, 1997.

[110]   SARs, R. 8(a).

[111]   The acquisition of new voting securities, subscription rights (other than rights under a rights issue), convertibles or options are not treated as acquisitions for the purposes of this rule.

identify and aggregate the acquisitions of such securities of that company made by them or a concert party in the preceding six days with the acquisition about to be made and any other acquisitions already made that day. If the aggregate figure is less than 10 per cent of the total voting rights, the SARs do not apply and the proposed acquisition may be made. If the aggregate figure is 10 per cent or more, and when aggregated with the voting rights already possessed by that person or a concert party would confer 15 per cent or more, but less than 30 per cent, of the voting rights in the company, the acquisition may not be made, unless it falls within one of the exemptions permitted under Rule 5 of the SARs as discussed below.

13–116 The SARs do not apply to an acquisition by a person of voting securities or rights over voting securities of a relevant company if the voting rights conferred by the acquisition, when aggregated with voting rights already possessed by that person or a concert party, would amount to 30 per cent or more of the total voting rights in the company.[112] Such a person will be subject to the provisions of Rule 5 of the Takeover Rules and will, if appropriate, be obliged to make a mandatory offer under Rule 9 of the Takeover Rules.

13–117 Rule 3(b)(i) of the SARs provides that

> "any two or more persons who are acting in concert shall together be deemed to constitute one person and accordingly every acquisition by, and every holding of, such persons or any of them of voting securities of the relevant company concerned or of rights over voting securities of that company shall be aggregated with every other such acquisition by or (as the case may be) holding of such persons or any of them and shall be deemed to be an acquisition by, or (as the case may be) a holding of, one person."

It should also be noted that under Rule 3(b)(iii), any acquisitions or holdings by a person managing investment accounts on a discretionary basis for those accounts will be treated as acquired or held by that person and not the persons on whose behalf the holdings are managed. In addition, a discretionary fund manager will be deemed to be acting in concert with any company controlling, controlled by or under the same control as the fund manager. Rule 8(a) of the SARs provides that where any obligation is imposed by the SARs on a person (the "obligor") and by virtue of Rule 3 of the SARs two or more persons who are acting in concert are together deemed to constitute the obligor, each of the persons acting in concert will be bound by that obligation.

---

[112] Note 1 on Rule 5 of the SARs.

(3) Rule 4(b)

13–118   The prohibition set out in Rule 4(a) prohibiting the making of substantial acquisitions of securities will not, however, apply to certain substantial acquisition of securities made by dealers[113] pursuant to Rule 4(b).

13–119   A substantial acquisition by a dealer from a single holder of securities will not be prohibited if the dealer makes the acquisition with the intention of selling a sufficient number of the securities to persons who are not associates of the dealer[114] before 12 noon on the following business day.[115] In order to avoid the prohibition, the dealer must sell such numbers of the voting securities or of the rights over voting securities, comprised in the substantial acquisition as will reduce the aggregate percentage of the voting rights conferred by the remainder of those voting securities and by the voting securities the subject of the remainder of those rights to less than 10 per cent.[116] Alternatively, if the dealer holds voting securities and voting securities the subject of the rights conferring less than 15 per cent of the voting rights immediately prior to the acquisition, the dealer must sell such number of the voting securities (if lesser) or rights over the voting securities comprised in the substantial acquisition as will reduce the aggregate percentage of the voting rights conferred by the remainder of those voting securities and by the voting securities the subject of the remainder of those rights to less than 15 per cent.[117]

13–120   Once a dealer makes a substantial acquisition, it must notify the Panel immediately.[118] Unless sufficient securities are then disposed of in accordance with the preceding paragraph, certain sanctions may be imposed. The dealer may be required by the Panel to notify the acquisition to the company and the Stock Exchange in accordance with Rule 6 of the SARs. The Panel may also require the dealer to reduce its holding of voting securities, or of rights over voting securities of the relevant company as soon as it is practicable to do so. Finally, the Panel may impose restrictions on further acquisitions by the dealer of securities of that company and on the exercise by the dealer of the voting rights in that company conferred by the securities held by it.

---

[113] A dealer is defined in Rule 4(b)(i) as a person whose business is dealing in securities.
[114] R. 4(b)(iii).
[115] R. 4(b)(i).
[116] R. 4(b)(i)(1).
[117] R. 4(b)(i)(2).
[118] R. 4(b)(i).

13–121   If a dealer inadvertently makes a substantial acquisition as a result of buying a portfolio of securities without knowledge of its contents, it must notify the Panel immediately. In such a case, the prohibition will not apply if, before 12 noon the following business day, the dealer disposes of a "sufficient" quantity of securities as set out above.[119] The effects of failing to comply with this requirement is similar to that outlined in the previous paragraph.

(4) Exceptions to the Restriction

13–122   Rule 5 of the SARs contains four exemptions to the prohibition in Rule 4(a) on acquiring substantial acquisitions of shares. The principle underlying these exemptions is that a potential offeror should not be prohibited from building up a stake in the company once all shareholders of the same class are treated equally.

13–123   Firstly, Rule 5(a)(i) of the SARs provides that an acquisition from a single holder of securities is permitted once it is the only acquisition of voting securities or of rights over voting securities, of the company concerned made by that person within any seven day period. There is therefore, no maximum limit under the SARs on acquisitions made in the seven day period from a single shareholder as long as no other acquisitions are made in that period. This is necessary in order to allow a large shareholder dispose of its holdings as a single bloc and thereby realise the true value of his holding.

13–124   Holdings of two or more holders of securities acting in concert[120] will not be considered to be the holding of a single holder for the purposes of the exemption in Rule 5(a)(i) unless the holders concerned fall within Rule 5(b).[121] This latter paragraph provides that acquisitions from two or more persons will only be regarded as acquisitions from a single holder if:

(i)   one of such persons is a spouse, parent, brother, sister or child of the other such person, or of each of the other such persons; or

(ii)   one of such persons is (1) a subsidiary (2) the holding company or (3) a subsidiary of a company which is the holding company, of the other such person or of each of the other such persons.

---

[119]   R. 4(b)(ii).
[120]   Deemed by Rule 3 to be one person.
[121]   Note 2 on Rule 5.

Furthermore, except with the consent of the Panel, a market maker will not be considered to be a single holder of securities for the purpose of this exemption.[122]

13–125   The second exemption provided for by Rule 5(a)(ii) allows a substantial acquisition if it is made pursuant to a tender offer in accordance with Rule 7 of the SARs as set out below.

13–126   The third exemption set out in Rule 5(a)(iii) allows a substantial acquisition which immediately precedes the announcement of a firm intention to make an offer in respect of the company, provided either that the offer will be recommended by the offeree board or the acquisition is made with the agreement of the offeree board. In addition, to qualify for this exemption, the acquisition must be conditional upon the announcement of the offer.

13–127   The final exemption set out in Rule 5(a)(iv) allows a substantial acquisition which follows immediately upon an announcement of a firm intention to make an offer in respect of the company, provided that the posting of the offer is not subject to a pre-condition. A person who makes such an announcement is subject to the Takeover Rules and not the SARs.

(5) Disclosure

13–128   Rule 6(a) provides for the accelerated disclosure of certain acquisitions of voting securities or rights over voting securities of a relevant company. Disclosure of the acquisition and the person's total holdings of voting securities and rights over voting securities must be notified to the company, the Stock Exchange and the Panel not later than 12 noon on the business day following the acquisition. This accelerated disclosure requirement will not, however, apply to a substantial acquisition which falls within Rule 5(a)(ii)(iii) or (iv).[123]

13–129   The accelerated disclosure requirement will apply to an acquisition in two situations. Firstly, it will apply if the voting rights in the company conferred by any voting securities already held by that person, and by any voting securities over which that person already holds rights, confer in the aggregate less than 15 per cent of the voting rights, and that percentage is increased to or beyond 15 per cent when aggregated with the voting rights conferred by the voting securities, or

---

[122] R. 5(c).
[123] R. 6(b).

by the voting securities the subject of the rights, so acquired.[124] The same rule applies if the percentage will be increased subject only to the issue in the State of a governmental or regulatory authorisation, consent, approval or clearance. Secondly, the accelerated disclosure requirement will apply if the voting rights in the company conferred by any voting securities already held by that person and by any voting securities over which that person already holds rights confer in the aggregate 15 per cent or more but less than 30 per cent of the voting rights, and that percentage is increased to or beyond any whole percentage figure when aggregated with the voting rights conferred by the voting securities, or by the voting securities the subject of the rights, so acquired.[125] Again, this same rule applies if the percentage will be increased subject only to the issue in the State of a governmental or regulatory authorisation, consent, approval or clearance.

(6) Tender offers

13–130   A "tender offer" is defined as:

> "an invitation made by a person by public advertisement to holders of a class of securities of a relevant company to tender securities of that company, up to a stated number, for purchase by that person, on terms stipulated in the advertisement".[126]

As noted above, Rule 5(a)(ii) of the SARs provides that the prohibition in Rule 4(a) on substantial acquisitions does not apply to a substantial acquisition of securities by a person pursuant to a tender offer in accordance with Rule 7. A tender offer is permitted because unlike a dawn raid it provides equal opportunities for all shareholders. In the case of a tender offer, there is no requirement to issue a circular. The Panel will, however, scrutinise the advertisement to ensure compliance with the SARs.

13–131   Rule 7.1(a) of the SARs provides that the maximum number of securities of a relevant company that are the subject of any tender offer under this rule, must be less than the number which would give the purchaser and any concert party control on the date the tender offer closes, if the tender offer was fully subscribed. In other words, they should not lead to the purchaser and any concert parties holding voting securities or rights over voting securities which securities would confer in the aggregate 30 per cent or more of the voting rights in that company.

---

[124]   R. 6(a)(i).
[125]   R. 6(a)(ii).
[126]   R. 2.1 Part A of the Takeover Rules.

13–132   Rules 7.2 to 7.6 which follow apply only to a tender offer which if fully subscribed would constitute a substantial acquisition of securities by the purchaser.[127] The person who publishes the tender offer must do so by paid advertisement in two national newspapers. The person is also required to notify the Panel, the Stock Exchange Listing department and the relevant company itself of certain information at least seven days before the day on which the tender offer closes.[128] If the offer is made through the Stock Exchange, the content and the publication of the advertisement is subject to the prior approval of the Listing department. If the offer is not made through the Stock Exchange, the Panel's prior approval will be needed.[129]

13–133   The purchaser must consult the Panel in advance if a tender offer is proposed in relation to the securities of a relevant company which is the subject of an outstanding offer under the Takeover Rules.[130] In such a case the Panel will consider *inter alia*:

(i) an extension of the offer period in respect of the offer under the Takeover Rules;

(ii) the circulation of the tender advertisement to all shareholders; and

(iii) disclosure of dealings by the person making the tender offer and any of that person's associates in the manner set out in Rule 8 of Part B of the Takeover Rules.

13–134   A tender offer must be for cash only. While a fixed price or a maximum price may be stipulated, top-up arrangements are not permitted.[131] All security holders who tender their securities must be treated on equal terms.[132] Therefore, if a fixed price is stipulated and the tenders exceed the number of securities sought, the tenders must be scaled down pro rata.[133] If a maximum price is stipulated and the tenders exceed the number of securities sought, the striking price for the offer will be the lowest price at which the number of securities sought is met. All security holders who tender at or below this price must receive that price.[134] If the tender offer is under-subscribed, all security holders who tendered must receive the same price, which will

---

[127] R. 7.1(b).
[128] R. 7.2(a).
[129] R. 7.2(d).
[130] R. 7.2(f).
[131] R. 7.2(c).
[132] R. 7.2(b).
[133] R. 7.2(c)(i).
[134] R. 7.2(c)(ii). Where appropriate, tenders made at the striking price will be scaled down pro rata or balloted.

be either the maximum or the fixed price, unless fewer securities are tendered then the percentage below which the tender is void.

13–135 Rule 7.3(a) of the SARs sets out the informational requirements of the advertisement of a tender offer as including: the purchaser's name; the name of the purchaser's broker or agent; the name of the relevant company; the maximum number of securities and the corresponding proportion of voting capital offered for; a statement that, if tenders totalling less than 1 per cent of the voting rights of the company are received, the tender offer will be void;[135] a statement that subject to the minimum acceptance condition, a tender by security holders will be irrevocable; the fixed or maximum price as the case may be; the purchaser's current holding of securities of the relevant company; the closing day and time for the tender offer; and the arrangements for tendering securities and for delivery and settlement. Apart from the minimum acceptance condition, a tender offer should not be subject to any conditions.[136] The advertisement may also include a statement by the purchaser about its future intentions but this statement must be explicit and unambiguous and in any case, the Panel must be consulted in advance.[137] A statement may also be made comparing the value of the tender offer with the market value of the securities.[138] Apart from the above information and any information required by law or by any rule of a regulatory authority or by a Panel ruling or direction, no other information should be contained in the advertisement.[139] This restriction is strictly enforced and the Panel warns that "no form of argument or persuasion is allowed".[140] Consequently, the Panel warns that neither the purchaser nor its advisers may make any statement or otherwise make public any information in connection with the tender offer which is not already contained in the tender offer advertisement itself. If the purchaser includes a statement which expressly states or implies that it does not intend to make an offer in respect of the company concerned, it will not normally be permitted by the Panel to make such an offer within the following 12 month period. An exception may be allowed, however, where a third party announces an offer within this period.[140a]

---

[135] If the Stock Exchange approves, a higher percentage than 1 per cent may be stipulated by the purchaser. The Stock Exchange has indicated that, in tender offers on the market, it will not normally permit any figure higher than 5 per cent.

[136] R. 7.3(b).

[137] R. 7.3(c).

[138] R. 7.3(d).

[139] R. 7.3(e).

[140] Note 3 on Rule 7.3.

[140a] Note 2 on Rule 7.3 of the SARs.

13–136   Copies of the tender announcement may be circulated by the purchaser or its agent to all holders of the class of securities of the relevant company. A copy of any such circular must also be lodged with the Listing department and the Panel at the same time. Where the relevant company sends any documents to its security holders in connection with the tender offer, these documents must be lodged with the Panel.[141]

13–137   The result of the tender offer must be announced by 8.30 a.m. on the business day following the close of the tender offer.[142] Between the time the tender offer is announced and the time the result is announced, a purchaser is prohibited from acquiring or disposing of any securities of the relevant company, other than pursuant to the tender offer.[143]

V.   STOCK EXCHANGE LISTING RULES DISCLOSURE REQUIRE-MENTS

13–138   As noted in Chapter 5, a general obligation of disclosure is imposed on companies as one of the continuing obligations imposed on listed companies under the Stock Exchange Listing Rules.

(1)   General Disclosure Obligation

13–139   Paragraph 9.1 of the Listing Rules imposes a general obligation on the issuer to disclose any information in respect of substantial new developments in its sphere of activity which are not public knowledge and which may lead to substantial movements in the price of its listed securities.[144] In the case of a company with debentures listed, any unpublished information in respect of substantial new developments in its sphere of activity which may significantly affect its ability to meet its commitments must be disclosed.[145] The issuer must notify the CAO without delay of all relevant information concerning the change. Where the company's directors are aware that there is such a change in the company's financial condition, in the performance of its business or in the company's expectation of its performance, and knowledge of that fact is likely to lead to substantial movements in the price of its listed securities, paragraph 9.3 provides that the company must notify the CAO immediately. All relevant information concerning the change should be notified.

13–140   Certain information need not be disclosed in the above manner. Information about impending developments or matters in the course of

---

[141]   R. 7.4.
[142]   R. 7.5.
[143]   R. 7.6.
[144]   See also Sched. C to the Admissions Directive, para. 5(a).
[145]   See also Sched. D to the Admissions Directive, para. 4(a).

negotiation need not be notified. Such information may be given in confidence to recipients within the following categories:

(a)   the company's advisers and advisers of any other person who is or may be involved in the development or matter in question;

(b)   persons with whom the company is negotiating or intends to nego- tiate any commercial, financial or investment transaction, including prospective underwriters or placees of securities of the company;

(c)   representatives of the company's employees or trade unions acting on their behalf;

(d)   any government department, the Bank of England, the Central Bank,[146] the Competition Authority or any other statutory or regulatory body or authority.

Clearly thus, during the negotiating stage prior to the announcement of a takeover offer, notification will not be required once the information is not passed to a wider range of people.[147] The company must be satisfied that these recipients appreciate the confidential nature of the information and the dealing restrictions thus imposed. If the company believes that a breach of this confidence has occurred or is likely to occur, and that this breach would be likely to lead to substantial movement in the price of its listed securities, the CAO must be notified at least with a warning to the effect that the company expects to release information which may lead to a price movement.

13–141   Where a company proposes to announce price sensitive information at any meeting of holders of a company's listed securities, the CAO must be notified in time to ensure that the market is appraised of this information at least as early as the security holders.[148] It is important to note that companies listed on the Irish Stock Exchange and also on any other Stock Exchanges must ensure that equivalent information is made available at the same time to the market at the Irish Stock Exchange and to the market at each of the other Stock Exchanges.[149]

---

[146]   Although para. (d) of the London Stock Exchange Listing rules refers to the Bank of England and not the Central Bank of Ireland, it would seem obvious that the latter should be included in the Irish Stock Exchange Listing rules. Unusually, the Green Pages do not specifically make this change. In any case, the Central Bank would be included as a statutory or regulatory authority.

[147]   Rule 2.2(e) of the Takeover Rules requires an announcement to be made when negotiations or discussions concerning an offer are about to be extended to include more than a very restricted number of people.

[148]   Para. 9–7.

[149]   Para. 9–9 of the Listing Rules and Sched. C & D to the Admissions Directive, paras 6 & A5, respectively.

Where the disclosure of this information might prejudice the company's legitimate interests, paragraph 9–8 provides that the Stock Exchange may grant a dispensation from this disclosure requirement.

(2) Notification of Major Interests in Shares

13–142   Acquisitions or disposals of major interests in shares disclosed to the company in accordance with sections 67 to 79 of the 1990 Act must be notified by the company itself to the CAO without delay.[150] The CAO should be informed of the date on which the information was disclosed to the company and the date on which the transaction was affected if this is known by the company.

In addition, if the company itself obtains any information under section 81 of the 1990 Act, this should also be disclosed without delay to the CAO. This obligation is only incurred where it becomes apparent that an interest exists or has been increased or reduced or has ceased to exist and its existence, increase or reduction should have been disclosed under sections 67 to 79 of the 1990 Act but has not been so disclosed.[151]

The aforementioned two obligations to notify the CAO will be deemed to have been discharged if the relevant interest has been notified to the CAO pursuant to the requirements of the Takeover Rules or the SARs.

(3) Notification of Interests of Directors and Connected Persons

13–143   Paragraph 16.13(a) of the Listing Rules provides that the CAO must be notified of any information relating to interests in listed securities or securities which are to be listed which is disclosed to the company in accordance with section 53 as extended by section 64 of the 1990 Act.[151a] Notification to the CAO is also required of any such information entered in the company's register in accordance with section 59 of the 1990 Act. In such cases, the CAO should also be informed of:

 (i) the date on which the disclosure was made to the company;

 (ii) the date on which the transaction giving rise to the interest or cessation of interest was effected;

(iii) the price, amount and class of securities concerned;

(iv) the nature of the transaction; and

 (v) the nature and extent of the director's interest in the transaction.

---

[150] Listing Rules, para. 9–11. See also paras 13–93–13–96 above.
[151] Listing Rules, para. 9–12.

Paragraph 16.13(b) provides that the CAO must also be notified of information relating to any interest of a connected person of a director in listed securities or securities which are to be listed which, if the connected person were a director, would be required to be disclosed by him to the company or entered in the company's register. The notification should give the particulars specified above plus the identity of the director and connected parson, the nature of the connection and the nature and extent of the director's interest (if any) in the transaction. Paragraph 16.13(c) provides that the CAO must be given details of the grant to, or acceptance by, a director or connected person of any option relating to the company's securities or of any other right or obligation to acquire or dispose of securities in the company which are or will be listed or any interest of whatever nature in such securities. Details must also be given of the acquisition, disposal, exercise or discharge of, or any dealing with, any such option, right or obligation by a director or connected person. In these cases, the notification should identify the director or connected person and the nature of the connection between them, state the nature and extent of the directors' interest (if any) and give the particulars specified in para. 16.13(a)(i)–(iv) of the Listing Rules.

13–144 In order to comply with these obligations, paragraph 16.17 requires companies to oblige each of its' directors to disclose all the relevant information as soon as possible and not later than the fifth business day following the day on which the existence of the interest comes to the director's knowledge. The duty extends to information which is known to the director or could, with reasonable diligence, be ascertained by the director. The company is thus directed to require each of its directors to confirm that he has made due enquiry of persons connected with him. Such confirmation should be obtained at such times as the company deems necessary or desirable. In order to protect, companies it is expressly stated that a company is not required to notify the CAO of information which, despite compliance with paragraph 16.17, it does not have.

[151a] See paras 13–88–13–92 above.

PART 4

ACQUISITION OF PRIVATE COMPANIES

CHAPTER 14

INTRODUCTION & PRE-CONTRACTUAL NEGOTIATIONS

14–01 As with the acquisition of a public company, a decision must be taken as to whether to acquire the business of the target from the company itself or whether to acquire the shares of the target from the shareholders. The advantages and disadvantages of these different methods were examined in Chapter 1.[1] Where the purchaser makes a decision to acquire the business of the company but decides to leave the liabilities behind, obviously the due diligence exercise would not need to cover the same range of issues. In addition, the warranties would not need to be as extensive because as the company would still be in existence, it would retain responsibility for the liabilities which might subsequently arise. For these reasons, the acquisition of the business or the assets of a company rather the acquisition of its shares is likely to be the preferred choice of acquisition for the purchaser.

Once a decision is made as to the form the acquisition will take, the purchaser must organise its finances to ensure that it will be able to make and to implement the offer.

A. Financing the Acquisition

14–02 Where the acquisition is being made by a public listed company, it will have the option either to offer its shares as consideration to the target company shareholders or to raise cash by a placing or rights issue.

A private company will find it more difficult to finance an acquisition because these options are not available to a private company which must pay for its acquisition by cash. Neither can it avail of a share issue to raise this cash. It must thus rely on internal funds, the shareholders own funds, grants or borrowings.

In the case of the acquisition of the shares of the target company, the company seeking to make the acquisition must also take care to ensure that the target company does not assist it in the purchase of its shares.

---

[1] See Chap. 1, para. 1–09.

I. PROHIBITION ON OFFERING SECURITIES TO THE PUBLIC

14–03   Section 33(1) Companies Act 1963 ("the 1963 Act") defines a "private company" as a company which has a share capital and which, by its articles:

(a)   restricts the right to transfer its shares; and

(b)   limits the number of its members to 50;[1a] and

(c)   prohibits any invitation to the public to subscribe for any shares or debentures of the company.

Both the prohibition on offering securities to the public and the requirement to limit the number of members to 50 imposes severe restrictions on a private company in its attempts to raise capital. The prohibition on the issuance of shares to the public is reinforced by section 21(1)(a) of the Companies (Amendment) Act 1983 ("the 1983 Act") which prohibits a private company offering to the public any shares in or debentures of the company. Section 21(1)(b) prohibits a company from allotting or agreeing to allot any shares in or debentures of the company with a view to all or any of those shares or debentures being offered for sale to the public. These prohibitions apply whether the securities are offered or allotted for cash or otherwise. In addition regulation 2(c) of Part II of Table A provides that any invitation to the public to subscribe for any shares or debentures of the company is prohibited.

(1) Enforcement

14–04   A private company and any officer of the company in default of the prohibitions in section 21 of the 1983 Act will be guilty of an offence and liable on summary conviction to a fine not exceeding £500.[2] A fine of this magnitude is not likely to act as a significant deterrent. Moreover, section 21(4) provides that nothing in section 21 will affect the validity of any allotment or sale of shares or debentures or any agreement to allot shares or debentures.

14–05   However, the main incentive for the directors or promoters of a private company to ensure that no offer to the public is made stems from the fact that Part III of the 1963 Act imposes both civil[3] and

---

[1a]   Not including persons who are in the employment of the company and persons who, having been formerly in the employment of the company, were, while in that employment, and have continued after the determination of that employment to be, members of the company.

[2]   s.21(4).

[3]   s.49.

criminal[4] liability for misstatements in the prospectus. A prospectus is defined in section 2(1) of the 1963 Act as "any prospectus, notice, circular, advertisement or other invitation, offering to the public for subscription or purchase any shares or debentures of a company". Every prospectus issued by or on behalf of a company or a company promoter must comply with the onerous informational obligations of the Third Schedule.[5] The Prospectus Directive[6] also sets out detailed information which must be included in the prospectus. Section 44(3) renders it unlawful to issue any form of application for shares in or debentures of a company, unless the form is issued with a prospectus complying with the requirements of Part III of the 1963 Act and a fine not exceeding £500 may be imposed for non-compliance. An exception is made under section 44(4)(b), if the shares or debentures are not offered to the public.[6a]

Section 49(1) of the 1963 Act renders directors, promoters and every person who authorises the issue of a prospectus to be liable to pay compensation to all persons who subscribe for any shares or debentures on faith of the prospectus. Such persons will be liable for any loss or damage sustained by the subscribers by reason of any untrue statement included in the prospectus.[7] Private companies are not generally subject to this provision because they are prohibited from offering shares to the public. If a private company does, however, make an offer to the public in contravention of section 21 of the 1983 Act, the offer document or advertisement will be treated as a prospectus for the purposes of section 49 of the Act.

(2) Statutory Definition of "Public"

14–06 Section 61(1) of the 1963 Act provides that a reference to offering shares or debentures to the public in the 1963 Act[8] shall, subject to any provision to the contrary contained therein, be construed as including:

> "a reference to offering them to any section of the public, whether selected as members or debenture holders of the company concerned or as clients of the person issuing the prospectus or in any other manner . . ."[9]

---

[4] s.50.

[5] Section 44(1) of the 1963 Act subject to the provisions of section 45.

[6] Council Directive 89/298 which is implemented into Irish law by S.I. No. 202 of 1992, European Communities (Transferable Securities and Stock Exchange) Regulations 1992.

[6a] Exceptions are also provided in s.44(4)(a) and s.45 of the Companies Act, 1963. In addition, defences are set out in s.44(5).

[7] Section 49(3) sets out a number of defences to any action under section 49(1).

[8] Section 21(2) of the Companies (Amendment) Act 1983 provides that sections 51(1) and 61 of the Companies Act 1963 applies for the purpose of section 21 as they apply for the purposes of the Companies Act 1963.

[9] Section 61(1) provides that references in the Companies Act 1963 or in a company's articles to invitations to the public to subscribe for securities are to be construed accordingly.

It is important to note that, on the basis of this definition, offering shares to existing shareholders could constitute an offer to the public.

14–07 Because a private company may not make an offer to the public, it becomes important to distinguish an offer to the public from a private offer which a private company may make. Section 61(2) of the 1963 Act provides a little further clarification. It states:

> "Subsection (1) shall not be taken as requiring any offer or invitation to be treated as made to the public if it can properly be regarded, in all the circumstances, as not being calculated to result, directly or indirectly, in the shares or debentures becoming available for subscription or purchase by persons other than those receiving the offer or invitation, or otherwise as being a domestic concern of the persons making and receiving it, and in particular –
> (a) a provision in a company's articles prohibiting invitations to the public to subscribe for shares or debentures shall not be taken as prohibiting the making to members or debenture holders of an invitation which can properly be regarded as aforesaid, and
> (b) the provisions of this Act relating to private companies shall be construed accordingly."

14–08 It would seem thus, that a private company would be entitled to offer shares to persons if the shares could not become available to other persons who were not amongst the original offerees. Where the shares are offered to a limited number of persons to be held by them for long term investment purposes, an offer to the public may thus not be deemed to have arisen. Care must be taken to ensure that the offer is available for acceptance only by the original offerees. Determining whether this has been the case is not always easy. Grey areas may arise where for example shares are offered to 30 strangers by way of a non-renounceable letter of allotment. In such a situation, it is not immediately clear whether the offer could be deemed to be of "domestic" concern only. In an attempt to avoid the prohibition on offering shares or debentures to the public, private companies seeking investors under BES schemes ensure that copies of the information booklet offering the securities, which could otherwise be deemed to be a prospectus, are addressed specifically to named individuals who have previously been identified as potentially interested investors. Such persons may be asked to return the document to the company in the event they decide not to make an investment. Although there has been no attempt to prosecute such persons for failing to comply with the prospectus regime of the 1963 Act, the success of such measures in exempting persons from liability under section 49 has yet to be tested in the courts.

(3) Common Law Definition of "Public"

14–09 Caselaw has offered some elucidation on this subject. In *Nash v. Lynde*,[10] the directors of a private company prepared a document which was in the form of a general offer for shares. Although the offer was not advertised, a copy was shown to one person with a view to his subscribing to the company and becoming a director. The House of Lords held that this did not constitute an offer to the public. Viscount Sumner stated:

> "The Public" in the definition section . . . is of course a general word. No particular numbers are prescribed. Anything from two to infinity may serve: perhaps even one, if he is intended to be the first of a series of subscribers but makes further proceedings needless by himself subscribing the whole. The point is that the offer is such as to be open to anyone who brings his money and applies in due form, whether the prospectus was addressed to him on behalf of the company or not. A private communication is thus not open . . . [to being deemed to be made to the public.]"[11]

In *Government Stocks etc. v. Christopher*, Wynn Parry J. stated that the test is "not who receives the circular, but who can accept the offer put forward".[12]

14–10 In *Lee v. Evans*,[13] a company promoter approached individually a handful of strangers who had apparently been selected at random and offered them shares. The majority of the Australian High Court held that, in the circumstances, the offerees were "individuals in the general mass of citizens" and that there had been no offer to the public. Barwick C.J. stated that:

> "Whether the question is whether the invitation is ex facie an invitation to the public or whether an invitation has become an invitation to the public by reason of the nature or extent of its issue, the basic concept is that the invitation, though maybe not universal, is general; that it is an invitation to all and sundry of some segment of the community at large. This does not mean that it must be an invitation to all the public either everywhere, or in any particular community. How large a section of the public must be addressed in a general invitation for it to be an invitation to the public in the relevant connexion must depend on the context of each particular enactment and the circumstances of each case."[14]

---

[10] [1929] A.C. 158. See also *Sleigh v. Glasgow and Transvaal Options* (1904) 6 F 420; *Sherwell v. Combined Incandescent Mantles Syndicate (Ltd.)* (1907) 23 T.L.R. 482 *and Re South of England Natural Gas and Petroleum Co. Ltd.* [1911] 1 Ch. 573.

[11] *ibid.* at 169.

[12] [1956] 1 W.L.R. 237 at p. 242.

[13] (1964–65) 112 C.L.R. 276.

[14] *ibid.* at 285–286.

Kitto J. stated that an offer was not an offer to the public unless it was "an invitation made to the public generally and capable therefore of being acted upon by any member of the public".[14a] His lordship stated that the size of the immediate audience is not necessarily conclusive of the question whether the offer is a public offer or not. Rather, he stated:

> "That is a question of the true scope of the invitation. While it may be answered conclusively in one case by the terms in which the invitation was expressed, it may require in another case a consideration both of the words in which it was expressed and of the circumstances in which they were used. I see no reason to doubt that the statement of an invitation even to one person only may be seen when considered in the light of all the surrounding circumstances, to be part of, even though only the first step in, the communication of the invitation to the public generally, so that if the lone hearer were to tell some stranger of it the stranger would be right in treating it open to acceptance by him no less than the hearer."[15]

However, Kitto J. suggested that it was going too far to say that proof of an invitation given to a person as a member of the public is necessarily proof of an invitation to the public. He stated:

> "It remains, I think, a question of fact whether his invitation is to the public or to the selected individual only . . . and in considering the answer the distinction must not be overlooked between the case of an invitation which in itself is open to acceptance by any member of the public who may be interested and the case of an invitation which itself is open to acceptance by a specific individual only but, if declined by him, is likely to be followed by similar invitations to other specific individuals in succession until an acceptor is found. The first of these is a case of an invitation to the public; the second, in my opinion, is not"[16]

The above extract from the judgment of Kitto J. was subsequently relied upon by the High Court of Australia in *Australian Softwood Forests Pty. Ltd. v. AG (NSW); Ex Rel Corporate Affairs Commission.*[17]

14–11   It would seem to follow, from these cases, that the essence of an invitation to the public is not the manner of its communication or the number of persons to whom it is communicated. Instead, the pertinent question is – are the offerees a select group of whom and to whom the invitation alone is addressed so that if an outsider sought to respond to it, he would be told that he was not so entitled.

[14a] *ibid.* at 286.
[15] *ibid.* at 287.
[16] *Loc. cit.* at 287.
[17] (1981) 148 C.L.R. 121. See also *Corporate Affairs Commission (S.A.) v. Australian Central Credit Union* (1985) 157 C.L.R. 201.

II. PROHIBITION AGAINST GIVING FINANCIAL ASSISTANCE

14–12   One possible source of finance for a private company is to seek financial assistance from the target itself. This may be done, for example, by using the assets of the target as security for any borrowings. As noted in Chapter 11,[17a] the ability of a company to do this is severely restricted.

Section 60(1) of the 1963 Act prohibits a company from giving, whether directly or indirectly:

> "any financial assistance for the purpose of or in connection with a purchase or subscription made or to be made by any person of or for any shares in the company".

Where the company is a subsidiary company, the prohibition extends to giving any financial assistance for the purchase of shares in its holding company.[17b] Examples of such prohibited financial assistance are loans, guarantees and the provision of security.

(1) General Exceptions to the Prohibition

14–13   A number of transactions are specifically excluded from the prohibition by the Act. Section 60(12) provides that the payment of a properly declared dividend or the discharge of a lawfully incurred liability will not be included in the general prohibition. Section 60(13) provides a further three exemptions for private companies.[18] Firstly, the lending of money by a credit institution in the ordinary course of business will not be prohibited.[19] Secondly, the prohibition will not cover the provision by a company of money for the purchase of, or subscription for, fully paid shares in the company or its holding company under an existing employee share scheme. Under such a scheme, the shares must be held by or for the benefit of employees or former employees of the company or any of its subsidiaries.[20] Directors or former directors holding salaried employment or office in the company or any of its subsidiaries will also be included in this exemption. Finally, the making of loans to employees of the company or any of its subsidiaries, other than directors, with a view to allowing them to

---

[17a] See Chap. 11, paras 11–42–11–36. See also Courtney, *The Law of Private Companies* (Butterworths, 1994) paras 12–027–12–045.

[17b] See para. 20–07.

[18] Section 60(15B) allows public limited companies to give financial assistance under section 60(13) only if the company's net assets are not thereby reduced or, to the extent that those assets are thereby reduced, if the financial assistance is provided out of profits which are available for dividend.

[19] Companies Act 1963, s.60(13)(a). This sub-paragraph refers to a company "where the lending of money is part of the ordinary business of the company".

[20] *ibid.* s.60(13)(b).

purchase or subscribe for fully paid shares in the company or its holding company is also allowed where the shares are to be held by those employees as beneficial owners.[21]

(2) Exception for Private Companies

14–14   In the case of private companies, section 60(2) provides that the prohibition in section 60 will not apply if shareholders pass a special resolution authorising the giving of this financial assistance and a copy of a statutory declaration is sent to shareholders and delivered to the registrar of companies.[22] The special resolution must be passed by not less than three-fourth of the votes cast by shareholders[23] at a meeting not more than 12 months before the giving of the financial assistance.[23a] In general, at least 21 days notice must be given of any meeting at which a special resolution is to be proposed. However, a shorter notice period is allowed if a majority holding not less than 90 per cent in nominal value of the shares conferring voting rights in number of the shareholders entitled to vote at any such meeting.[24] Every member of the company will be entitled to receive notice of and attend this meeting.[25]

14–15   When notice of the meeting is being sent to shareholders, a copy of a statutory declaration should accompany the notice. The statutory declaration must be made by all or the majority of the directors at a meeting of directors held not more than 24 days before the meeting at which the special resolution will be proposed.[26] This declaration must state:

(a)   the form which the financial assistance is to take;

(b)   the persons to whom the financial assistance is to be given;

(c)   the purpose for which the company intends those persons to use the financial assistance; and

(d)   that the directors making the declaration have made a full enquiry into the affairs of the company and that, having done so, they have

---

[21] *ibid*. s.60(13)(c).
[22] Section 60(15A) provides that section 60(2) and section 60(11) will not apply to a public limited company originally incorporated as such or to a company registered or re-registered as a public limited company under the Companies (Amendment) Act 1983 unless a special resolution as provided for under subsection (2) was passed before the company's application for registration or re-registration.
[23] Companies Act 1963, s.141(1).
[23a] *Re Northside Motors Company*, unreported, High Court, July 24, 1985.
[24] Companies Act 1963, s.141(2).
[25] *ibid*. s.60(6).
[26] *ibid*. s.60(3).

formed the view that after the giving of the financial assistance the company will still be able to pay its debts as they fall due.

Clearly, the objective of this declaration is to ensure that the financial assistance will not be given where it would jeopardise the viability of the company. In order to ensure that the directors take their duties seriously in this respect, criminal liability is imposed on a director who makes a statement without having reasonable grounds for believing that the company's solvency will not be affected.[27] If the company is wound up within the period of 12 months after the making of the declaration and the company's debts are not paid or provided for in full within 12 months of the commencement of the winding up, it will be presumed that the directors did not have reasonable grounds for their opinion. The onus of proving that sufficient reasons existed to substantiate their view will thus lie on the directors.

14–16   Once the resolution is made sanctioning the financial assistance, a period of 30 days must generally be allowed before the transaction whereby the assistance is to be given is carried out. Where all the members of the company entitled to vote, vote in favour of the resolution, this delay will not however be necessary.[27a] In such a case, there is obvious unanimity. In all other cases, the 30 day period will be necessary in order to allow the persons who did not consent to or vote in favour of the resolution an opportunity to apply to the court under section 60(8) of the Act for the cancellation of the special resolution.[28] If such an application is made to the court, section 60(8) provides that the special resolution will not take effect except to the extent that it is confirmed by the court. Such an application may be made by the holders of not less, in the aggregate, than 10 per cent in the nominal value of the company's issued share capital or any class thereof. In addition, the application must be made within 28 days after the date on which the special resolution was passed.[29]

(3) Consequences of Breach

14–17   A transaction entered into whereby assistance is given in breach of section 60 of the Act will be voidable at the instance of the company against any person who had notice of the facts which

---

[27]   *ibid.* s.60(5).
[27a]   *ibid.* s.60(7).
[28]   Under section 60(10) , an application may not be made under subsection (8) by any person who has consented to or voted in favour of the special resolution.
[29]   *ibid.* s.60(11).

constitute the breach.[30] This sanction will apply whether the person was a party to the transaction or not.

In addition, every officer of a company who acts in contravention of section 60 will be held criminally liable. If the officer is convicted on indictment, a maximum sentence of a term of imprisonment not exceeding two years or a fine not exceeding £2,500 may be imposed or both. If the officer is convicted summarily, a maximum sentence of a term of imprisonment not exceeding six months or a fine not exceeding £500 or both may be imposed.

B. Negotiation

I. CONFIDENTIALITY AGREEMENT

14-18   During the course of negotiations either for the acquisition of the undertaking or the acquisition of shares, a significant amount of non-public information is likely to be disclosed to the potential purchaser. Such disclosure is necessary in order to allow the purchaser to determine the suitability of the acquisition and to determine an appropriate price. In order to safeguard this information, the potential purchaser is likely to be asked to sign a confidentiality letter agreeing not to pass on this information to other persons and to return any documentation supplied to the vendor at the conclusion of negotiations. In addition to keeping this information secure and confidential, the potential purchaser may also be asked not to disclose the fact that negotiations are in progress. The potential purchaser's advisers are also likely to be asked to sign this document.

14-19   The advantage to the potential vendor of contractually guaranteeing confidentiality of information is that, in the event of negotiations proving unsuccessful, it can be assured that sensitive business information will not be passed on to competitors. (As will be seen in Chapter 16,[30a] the issue of protecting commercially sensitive information will become relevant to the purchaser subsequent to the acquisition in seeking to restrain the vendor from using this information to compete with the company or business acquired.)

14-20   As the target company is a private company, the insider dealing provisions contained in Part V of the Companies Act 1990 will not

---

[30] *ibid.* s.60(14). For a discussion of the consequences of a breach on the bank lending money to a purchaser of shares on terms allowing the bank take security from the company itself, see Breslin, *Banking Law in the Republic of Ireland*, (Gill & Macmillan, 1998) pp. 689–692.

[30a] See Chap. 16, paras 16–42–16–56.

apply. However, sensitive information may be protected by Competition legislation which allows contracts to be drafted including clauses restricting the use of such information in certain circumstances[31] and by copyright law. In addition, the information may be protected by the common law right of action for breach of confidence.[32]

14–21 In the event that a confidentiality letter is not signed, it is always possible that the vendor has a right of action against the potential purchaser for breach of confidence. In *Coco v. Clarke (AN) Engineers Ltd.*,[33] Megarry J. set out the three prerequisites to instituting such an action:

> "First the information itself . . . must have the necessary quality of confidentiality about it. Secondly that information must have been imported in circumstances importing an obligation of confidentiality. Thirdly there must be an unauthorised use of that information to the detriment of the party communicating it."[34]

Similarly, in *Private Research Ltd. v. Brosnan*,[34a] McCracken J. in the High Court referred to *Coppinger and Skone James on Copyright*[35] where the elements of an action for breach of confidence are stated as follows:

> "In order to succeed in an action for breach of confidence, the Plaintiff must establish, to the satisfaction of the Court, three elements: firstly, that the information which he is seeking to protect is of a confidential nature; secondly, that the information in question was communicated in circumstances importing an obligation of confidence; and, thirdly, that the Defendant is about to make, or has made, an unauthorised disclosure or use of that information."

14–22 The use by a competitor of sensitive information received in strict confidence during takeover negotiations would clearly constitute such a breach.[36] Such an action may either be contractual or equitable in nature. It is contractual, where the relationship between the parties is contractual. For example, in *Lamb v. Evans*,[37] Bowen L.J. stated that an obligation of confidentiality could be implied into a contract in order to give it efficacy. However, during the negotiations preceding an acquisition, unless a confidentiality letter or binding heads of agreement is executed, the parties are unlikely to be contractually bound and an action based on

---

[31] *ibid.*
[32] Lavery, *Commercial Secrets: An Action for Breach of Confidence in Ireland* (Roundhall Sweet & Maxwell, 1996), Clark & Smyth, *Intellectual Property Law in Ireland*, (Butterworths 1997) Chap. 23.
[33] [1969] R.P.C. 41.
[34] *ibid.* at 47.
[34a] unrep. 1 June 1995.
[35] Coppinger and Skone, *Copyright* (Sweet & Maxwell (11th ed.,)) para. 90.
[36] See Ashe & Murphy, *Insider Dealing* (Roundhall Press, 1992), 64–67 .
[37] [1893] 1 Ch. 218.

contract is thus unlikely to arise. An action based on equity is therefore more likely. In *House of Spring Gardens v. Point Blank Ltd.*[38] the High Court's equitable jurisdiction was invoked in relation to the law of confidence in circumstances where a licensee misused confidential information relating to the design and manufacture of bullet proof vests in order to manufacture its own vests. In *Oblique Financial Services Ltd. v. The Promise Production Co. Ltd.,*[39] an injunction was granted by the High Court to prevent a third party publishing information it had received from a person who was contractually bound to maintain absolute confidentiality.

As noted in Chapter 10,[39a] the House of Lords have recently stated that "the duty to preserve confidentiality is unqualified. It is a duty to keep the information confidential, not merely to take all reasonable steps to do so . . . ".[40]

II. HEADS OF AGREEMENT

14–23   In the case of the acquisition of the shares of the company, a "Heads of Agreement" or a "Letter of Intent" is likely to be drawn up. This involves making a written note of the terms agreed by the parties to the sale. This is a useful record of the salient issues agreed prior to the drawing up of a share purchase agreement. It is also useful for pinpointing areas of potential conflict and highlighting areas to be covered by the due diligence exercise.

In order to determine the contractual impact, if any, of the agreement itself, it is necessary to consider two prerequisites of any binding contract – an intention to enter into legal relations and certainty.

(1) Contractual Intent

14–24   In the case of commercial agreements regulating business arrangements, it is presumed that the parties intend the agreement to be binding and to lead thus to the creation of legally enforceable rights and obligations.[41]

14–25   However, this presumption may be rebutted. In *Cunard Steam Ship Co. Ltd. v. The Revenue Commissioners,*[42] a booking arrangement was held not to be a contract because it was intended that a subsequent

---

[38]   [1984] I.R. 611.
[39]   [1994] 1 I.L.R.M. 74.
[39a] para. 10–68.
[40]   *Prince Jefri Bolkiah V. KPMG (A Firm)* 1999 2 W.L.R. 215. See Chap. 10, paras 10–67–10–68.
[41]   *Rose & Frank Co. v. Crompton* [1923] 2 K.B. 261, *Commodity Broking Co. Ltd. v. Meehan* [1985] I.R. 12.
[42]   [1931] I.R. 287.

contract be made. A similar finding was reached in *Cadbury Ireland Ltd. v. Kerry Co-operative Creameries Ltd and Dairy Disposal Ltd.*[43] This case involved an agreement by Dairy Disposals Ltd. to supply the plaintiff with milk in the event of its expansion. This promise was intended to and did encourage the plaintiff to proceed with its plans for expansion. Subsequently, when Dairy Disposal Ltd. was negotiating the sale of certain of its creameries to Kerry Co-op, it emphasised that adequate supplies to the plaintiff would have to be ensured. In a subsequent agreement between Dairy Disposal Ltd. and Kerry Co-op, the latter undertook (in clause 19 of the agreement) to continue supplying the plaintiff subject to price and total supply stipulations. Barrington J. stated:

> "It appears to me that the imprecision of the language in clause 19 is explained by the fact that the clause was concerned with policy considerations and that the draughtsman assumed that clause 19 would be supplemented by a bilateral agreement between the plaintiffs and the first named defendants in which the precise rights and duties of both parties would be set out. Put another way one could say that clause 19 contemplated a further agreement between the plaintiffs and the first-named defendants to give it business efficacy."[44]

An obvious finding in the case of heads of agreement would appear to be that the parties did not intend to enter into contractual obligations because they intended to enter into a legally binding sales agreement at a later stage. At this preliminary stage, inevitably a number of issues remain to be settled and further negotiation is necessary. These outstanding issues may have an impact on the price to be paid.

14–26 Another possibility, however, is that the parties may wish to be contractually bound at the time they enter into the heads of agreement so that neither party can withdraw from the agreement. In such a case issues may still remain outstanding. In *Pagnan SpA v. Feed Products*,[45] Lloyd L.J. noted that:

> "[T]here is no legal obstacle which stands in the way of the parties agreeing to be bound now while deferring important matters to be agreed later. It happens every day when parties enter into so-called 'heads of agreement'."[46]

In such a case, the issue of certainty, discussed below, becomes particularly relevant.

14–27 Rather than leave the matter unsettled, the parties may decide to expressly negate contractual effect. In *Rose and Frank Co. v. J R*

---

[43] [1982] I.L.R.M. 77.
[44] *ibid.* at p. 85.
[45] [1987] 2 Lloyds Rep. 601.
[46] *ibid.* at 619.

Crompton & Bros. Ltd.,[47] an agreement between the parties contained the words "this arrangement is not entered into, nor is this memorandum written, as a formal or legal agreement, and shall not be subject to legal jurisdiction in the law courts either of the United States or England, but it is only a definite expression and record of the purpose and intention of the three parties concerned . . . ". The House of Lords stated that the intention to avoid legal relations may be either expressed by the parties or implied from the subject-matter of the agreement. In this case, the House of Lords held that the words used clearly expressed such an intention. "Honour clauses" may thus be used by the parties to specifically label heads of agreements as "gentleman's agreements" without contractual effect. Parties who wish to avoid contractual relationships in this way should do so clearly to avoid any doubt. In one recent case, the words "my board have agreed in principle" was not deemed sufficient to prevent a concluded agreement coming into existence.[48]

(2) Certainty

14–28   An agreement which is incomplete may indicate an intention on the part of the parties not to enter into a legally binding contract. It may also lead to a finding that the agreement is void for uncertainty. An agreement may be held not to be binding because it itself is vague or it contains terms which are ambiguous or illusory. In *Electricity Supply Board v. Newman*,[49] an agreement by the defendant to indemnify Dublin Corporation against loss sustained by reason of a customer's default in discharging her electricity "accounts" was deemed unenforceable *per se* because the term "accounts" could refer either to periodic accounts in respect of one premises or accounts due in respect of a number of premises.[50] Similarly, in *Gould v. Gould*,[51] a promise to pay a sum of money every week as long as the promisor could "manage it" was deemed too vague to give rise to contractual obligations.

14–29   Where the parties have failed to reach agreement on important issues, an agreement may be held to be unenforceable on the grounds of uncertainty. In *Central Meats v. Carney*,[52] an agreement to supply cattle to a meat factory was deemed incomplete as agreement had not been reached on the number of cattle or the quality of cattle to be

---

47 [1923] 2 K.B. 261.
48 *Irish Mainport Holdings Ltd v. Crosshaven Sailing Centre Ltd.*, Unreported, High Court, Keane J., October 14, 1980.
49 (1933) 67 I.L.T.R. 124.
50 In this case, parol evidence was admitted in order to explain the term.
51 [1969] 3 All E.R. 728.
52 [1944] 10 Ir. Jur. Rep. 34.

supplied or the price to be paid. In the absence of these essential details, the Court found that no contract had come into existence. Occasionally, the courts may become involved in gap-filling or in interpreting terms in order to give effect to the intention of the parties. Clearly, this can only be done where the parties intend to enter a binding contract. Thus, in *Hillas & Co. v. Arcos*,[53] an agreement to purchase a quantity of timber "of fair specification" was deemed enforceable by the House of Lords. Lord Wright noted:

> "Business men often record the most important agreements in crude and summary fashion; modes of expression sufficient and clear to them in the course of their business may appear to those unfamiliar with the business far from complete or precise. It is accordingly the duty of the court to construe such documents fairly and broadly without being too astute or subtle in finding defects . . . "[54]

The House of Lords resolved the uncertainty in this case by reference to the previous dealings between the parties and the custom of the timber trade. In *Sudbrook Trading Estate Ltd. v. Eggleton*,[55] tenants were given an option under a lease to buy the premises at a price to be agreed by two valuers, one appointed by the tenants, the other by the landlord. When the tenants attempted to exercise the options, the landlord refused to appoint a valuer and claimed that the options were void for uncertainty as no price had been agreed. The House of Lords determined that the options were legally enforceable as agreements to sell at a reasonable price which price was to be determined by the specified procedure. However, as the procedure specified was merely subsidiary and non-essential to the main purpose of the clause which was to provide for the sale of the property at a fair and reasonable price, the Court could substitute its own machinery to prevent the contract from being unenforceable. On other occasions, where a meaningless clause is included in an otherwise complete contract, the court may be able to sever the meaningless clause and enforce the remainder of the agreement.[56]

14–30 In certain other cases where terms are omitted, the court may decide instead that the parties intended to avoid contractual effect until the matters are resolved. In *CPC Consolidated Pool Carriers Gmbh v. CTM CIA Trans-Mediterranea SA*,[57] negotiations for the shipment of a jet foil were stated to be "subject to details/logical amendments". Potter J. found that in this instance, there was no concluded contract and that a

---

[53] [1932] All E.R. 494.
[54] *ibid.* at 504.
[55] [1982] 3 All E.R. 1.
[56] *Nicolene v. Simmonds* [1953] 1 Q.B. 543.
[57] [1994] 1 Lloyds' Rep. 68.

formal contract was intended to be drawn up later. In *Pagnan SpA v. Feed Products*[58] by contrast a binding contract was deemed already to exist. Lloyd L.J. summarised as follows the principles which he derived from the authorities relating to the question whether parties have created a binding contract:

"(1) In order to determine whether a contract has been concluded in the course of correspondence, one must first look at the correspondence as a whole.

(2) Even if the parties have reached agreement on all the terms of the proposed contract, nevertheless they may intend that the contract shall not become binding until such further condition has been fulfilled. That is the ordinary 'subject to contract' case.

(3) Alternatively, they may intend that the contract shall not become binding until some further term or terms have been agreed; see . . . *Hussey v. Horne-Payne* (1879) 4 App Cas 311 where Lord Selborne said at p. 323:

'. . . The observation has often been made, that a contract established by letters may sometimes bind parties who, when they wrote those letters, did not imagine that they were finally settling the terms of the agreement by which they were to be bound; and it appears to me that no such contract ought to be held established, even by letters which would otherwise be sufficient for the purpose, if it is clear, upon the facts, that there were other conditions of the intended contract, beyond and besides those expressed in the letters, which were still in a state of negotiation only, *and without the settlement of which the parties had no idea of concluding any agreement.*' [my emphasis]

(4) Conversely, the parties may intend to be bound forthwith even though there are further terms still to be agreed or some further formality to be fulfilled . . .

(5) If the parties fail to reach agreement on such further terms, the existing contract is not invalidated unless the failure to reach agreement on such further terms renders the contract as a whole unworkable or void for uncertainty.

(6) It is sometimes said that the parties must agree on the essential terms and that it is only matters of detail which can be left over. This may be misleading, since the word 'essential' in that context is ambiguous. If by 'essential' one means a term without which the contract cannot be enforced then the statement is true: the law cannot enforce an incomplete contract. If by 'essential' one means a term which the parties have agreed to be essential for the formation of a binding contract, then the statement is tautologous. If be 'essential' one means a term which the Court regards as important as opposed to a term which the Court regards as less important or a matter of detail, the statement is untrue. It is for the parties to decide whether they wish to be bound and, if so, by what terms, whether important or unimportant. It is the parties who are, in the

---

[58] [1987] 2 Lloyds' Rep. 601.

memorable phrase coined by the Judge, 'the masters of their contractual fate'. Of course the more important the term is the less likely it is that the parties will have left it for future decision. But there is no legal obstacle which stands in the way of the parties agreeing to be bound now while deferring important matters to be agreed later. It happens every day when parties enter into so-called 'heads of agreement'.[59]

In this case, the parties had agreed on the price, identity and quality of goods and the terms of shipment although they had not, however, agreed on a loading rate, demurrage and dispatch and carrying charges. Despite this, they were deemed to have entered into a binding contract.

(3) Agreements to Negotiate

14–31   Where the parties have agreed to be bound but not yet finalised all the material terms, they may insert a clause into the agreement agreeing to negotiate these remaining terms in good faith. The enforceability of this category of clause has been the subject of much debate.

(a) Enforceability of Agreements to Negotiate

14–32   Earlier indications appeared to suggest that an agreement to negotiate could be deemed to be a binding contractual agreement. In *Hillas & Co Ltd v. Arcos Ltd*,[60] Lord Wright in the House of Lords stated *obiter*:

> "If, however, what is meant is that the parties agree to negotiate in the hope of effecting a valid contract...There is then no bargain except to negotiate, and negotiations may be fruitless and end without a contract ensuing; yet even then, in strict theory, there is a contract (if there is good consideration) to negotiate, though in the event of repudiation by one party the damages may be nominal, unless the jury thinks that the opportunity to negotiate was of some appreciable value to the injured party . . . The conclusion of [the Court of Appeal] would in very many cases exclude in law the possibility of business men making big forward contracts for future goods over a period, because in general in such contracts it must be impossible, as I have already indicated, to specify in advance all the details of a complicated performance . . . [but] it must always be a matter of construction of the particular contract whether any essential terms are left to be determined by a subsequent contract."[61]

However, in *Courtney & Fairbairn Ltd v. Tolaini Brothers (Hotels) Ltd*,[62] the Court of Appeal maintained that the law cannot recognise a contract to

---

[59]   *ibid.* at 619.
[60]   [1932] All E.R. 494.
[61]   *ibid.*, at 505 and 507.
[62]   [1975] 1 W.L.R. 297. *Courtney* was applied by the Court of Appeal in *Mallozzi v. Carapelli S.p.A* [1976] 1 Lloyds' Rep 407.

negotiate. Lord Denning considered Lord Wright's opinion ill founded. He stated:

> "If the law does not recognise a contract to enter into a contract (where there is a fundamental term yet to be agreed) it seems to me it cannot recognise a contract to negotiate. The reason is because it is too uncertain to have any binding force. No court could estimate the damages because no one could tell whether the negotiations would be successful or would fall through: or if successful what the result would be. It seems to me that a contract to negotiate, like a contract to enter into a contract, is not a contract known to the law."[63]

14–33 In *Walford v. Miles*,[64] the House of Lords stated that agreements to negotiate lacked sufficient certainty to be enforceable. Lord Ackner stated:

> "The reason why an agreement to negotiate, like an agreement to agree, is unenforceable is simply because it lacks the necessary certainty . . . How can a court be expected to decide whether, subjectively, a proper reason existed for the termination of negotiations? The answer suggested depends upon whether the negotiations have been determined 'in good faith'. However, the concept of a duty to carry on negotiations in good faith is inherently repugnant to the adversarial position of the parties when involved in negotiations. Each party to the negotiations is entitled to pursue his (or her) own interest, so long as he avoids making misrepresentations. To advance that interest he must be entitled, if he thinks it appropriate, to threaten to withdraw from further negotiations or to withdraw in fact in the hope that the opposite party may seek to reopen the negotiations by offering him improved terms. [Counsel], of course, accepts that the agreement upon which he relies does not contain a duty to complete the negotiations. But that still leaves the vital question: how is a vendor ever to know that he is entitled to withdraw from further negotiations? How is the court to police such an 'agreement'? A duty to negotiate in good faith is as unworkable in practice as it is inherently inconsistent with the position of a negotiating party. It is here that the uncertainty lies. In my judgment, while negotiations are in existence either party is entitled to withdraw from those negotiations, at any time and for any reason. There can be thus no obligation to continue to negotiate until there is a 'proper reason' to withdraw. Accordingly, a bare agreement to negotiate has no legal content."[65]

The decision in *Walford v. Miles* was referred to recently in *The Martel Building Limited v. Her Majesty The Queen*,[66] before the Canadian Federal Court of Appeal which held that it was not possible yet to conclude that a tort of failure to negotiate in good faith has emerged.[67]

---

[63]   *ibid.*, at 301.
[64]   [1992] 2 W.L.R. 174.
[65]   *ibid.* at 181–182.
[66]   1998 D.L.R. Lexis 642, 163 D.L.R. 4th 505.
[67]   *cf. Canada Steamship Lines v. Canadian Pacific Ltd.* (1979), 7 B.L.R. 1 (Ont. S.C.) and *Lac Minerals Ltd. v. International Corona Resources Ltd.* [1989] 2 S.C.R. 574.

14–34 Early Irish caselaw appeared to suggest that an agreement to negotiate could be considered enforceable. In *Guardians of Kells Union v. Smith*,[68] nominal damages were awarded for breach of a contract to enter into a contract. In that case, the plaintiff advertised seeking tenders for the supply of meat. The advertisement stated that a formal contract would be signed on a fixed day. Although the defendant was told that his tender was successful, he decided against entering into a contract and purported to withdraw the contract. The Court stated that although no contract to supply meat existed, the defendant was liable for breaching a contract to enter into this formal contract. However, in *Cadbury Ireland Ltd. v. Kerry Co-op Creameries Ltd.*,[69] Barrington J. referred to a particular clause disparagingly as unenforceable because it involved at best "a commitment to enter into honest negotiations".[70]

14–35 The strict rule will not apply, however, where an enforceable contract already exists. In *Donwin Productions v. EMI Films*,[71] the Court implied a term that the parties would negotiate in good faith because an enforceable contract already existed, although certain other covenants existed which lacked precision. Pain J. said that the *Courtney* decision did not stop him implying such a term "once a firm agreement has been made and a further agreement is in contemplation".

(b) Applicability

14–36 Distinguishing between an agreement to negotiate which is likely to be unenforceable and an agreement to sell at a fair and reasonable price to be ascertained by the parties is not always easy. In *Black Country Housing Association Ltd v. Shand*,[72] the defendants argued that they had agreed with the Council that they would not object to the Council purchasing part of their property under a compulsory purchase order in return for the Council agreeing to convey certain disputed land to them. The trial judge found that the Council had agreed to transfer the land at a price to be agreed and stated that if no agreement was reached within a reasonable time, the parties would not be bound by it. In the Court of Appeal, it was necessary to determine whether an agreement in those terms could properly be regarded as an agreement to agree or to negotiate, in which case the Court stated, on the basis of *Walford v. Miles*, it would not be sufficiently certain to be enforceable at

---

[68] (1917) 52 I.L.T.R. 65.
[69] [1982] I.L.R.M. 77.
[70] *ibid.* at 85.
[71] Unreported, *The Times*, March 9, 1984. See also *Dalgety Foods Holland BV v. Deb-ITS Ltd.* [1994] F.S.R. 125.
[72] Court Of Appeal (Civil Division) May 22, 1998. Available on *Lexis*.

law. The alternative was that the agreement could be regarded as an agreement to sell at a fair or reasonable price to be ascertained, which the Court stated, would be enforceable on the basis of *Sudbrook Trading Estate Ltd v. Eggleton*. Chadwick L.J. stated that the applicable principles are as follows:

> "If the agreement between the parties is to sell at a price which is to be agreed between them in the future, then the agreement is unenforceable because it lacks the necessary certainty. The court cannot tell whether the parties will agree any, and if so what, price. The uncertainty is not removed by any implication of a term that the parties will negotiate in good faith for the reasons explained by Lord Denning MR in *Courtney & Fairbairn Ltd v. Tolaini Brothers (Hotels) Ltd* . . . and by Lord Ackner in *Miles v. Walford* . . . But, where the agreement between the parties is to sell at a fair and reasonable price — albeit a price not then ascertained — there is sufficient certainty. That is because the court will, if necessary, direct an inquiry in order to ascertain what the fair and reasonable price is . . . As Lord Diplock pointed out in *Sudbrook Trading v. Eggleton*: "A contract is complete as a contract as soon as the parties have reached agreement as to what each of its essential terms is or can with certainty be ascertained: for it is an elementary principle of the English law of contract *id certum est quod certum reddi potest*[73]."[74]

Chadwick L.J. then considered what test would be applied in order to distinguish agreements of the first type from those of the second type in circumstances in which the parties contemplate that the price will be determined in the future but do not provide any machinery for arriving at such a determination and do not provide in express terms that the price shall be such as may be agreed. He referred to Lord Scarman in *Sudbrook Trading v. Eggleton* and stated:

> "What, upon the true construction of the words which they had used and having regard to the circumstances in which they made their agreement, is the true nature or object of their bargain? Was it of the essence of their contract that neither party was to be bound to pay or to accept a price which had not been fixed by future agreement? Or was the true nature of the contract that the property would be transferred at a price which represented a fair and reasonable value having regard to their respective interests; a price which they expected to be able to agree in the future but which, if determined objectively, would be acceptable to each of them? In the latter case the actual price is not of the essence of their contract. The essential bargain is that the transaction should take place at a price which is objectively fair and reasonable. The true nature or object of their bargain is a matter to be determined by construing the words used in the light of the surrounding circumstances. Like many questions of construction, it is largely a matter of impression."[75]

---

[73] This literally means "that is certain which can be made certain".
[74] *ibid*. at 22.
[75] *ibid*. at 23.

The substantial benefit to the Council by the defendants not raising any objections to the compulsory purchase order or the price offered was emphasised by the Court. Chadwick L.J. opined that it would have been a matter of astonishment to either side to have been told that the bargain was worthless because either of them might in the future refuse to agree a transfer price for the disputed land. He thus decided that this case fell into the second category of cases:

> "The essence of the bargain between the parties was that the disputed land would be transferred at a price which would represent a fair and reasonable value having regard to their respective interests. That price would be fixed in the future. No doubt the parties expected to be able to agree that price; but agreement as to price was not essential to the transaction."[76]

The agreement was thus held to be binding.

(c) Agreements to Use Reasonable Endeavours

14–37   The distinction referred to above is relevant also to the consideration of agreements to use reasonable endeavours. It may appear confusing at first glance that agreements to make "reasonable endeavours" are enforceable whilst "agreements to negotiate" are not. In *Rooney v. Byrne*,[77] the plaintiff agreed to purchase a particular house from the defendant subject to getting an advance on the property. O'Byrne J. held that the purchaser was bound to make reasonable efforts to secure the necessary advance. Similarly, in *Queensland Electricity Generating Board v. New Hope Collieries Pty. Ltd.*,[78] the Privy Council stated that an agreement to use "reasonable endeavours" was enforceable. The agreement there stipulated "the base price and provisions for variations in prices . . . shall be agreed by the parties . . . ". The Court interpreted this as meaning that "the parties undertook implied primary obligations to make reasonable endeavours to agree on the terms of supply . . . and failing agreement to do everything reasonably necessary to procure the appointment of an arbitrator." This was held to be acceptable.

14–38   It is difficult to determine why an agreement to negotiate in good faith has not met with judicial approval when an agreement to use reasonable endeavours has been readily accepted. Such agreements do not appear to have raised any difficulties in terms of policing. In *Walford v. Miles*,[79] Lord Ackner attempted to explain the difference between the two agreements on the grounds that the latter, unlike the former, does not

---

[76]   *ibid* at 25.
[77]   [1933] I.R. 609.
[78]   [1989] 1 Lloyd's Reports 205.
[79]   [1992] 2 W.L.R. 174.

lack the necessary certainty.[80] Such an explanation would not appear to be altogether satisfactory. The principle in *Walford v. Miles* was considered and clarified by the Court of Appeal in *Little v. Courage.*[81] In that case, an option to renew a lease of a public house was expressed to be conditional upon the tenant and landlord agreeing a business plan and business agreement. One of the arguments put forward by the tenant was that the landlord was under an implied obligation to use its best endeavours to reach agreement with the tenant on the business plan and business agreement. Reliance was then placed on the observation of Lord Ackner in *Walford v. Miles* that an agreement to use best endeavours does not suffer from the defect of uncertainty as an agreement to negotiate. Millett L.J., giving the judgment of the Court said:

> "An undertaking to use one's best endeavours to obtain planning permission or an export licence is sufficiently certain and is capable of being enforced: an undertaking to use one's best endeavours to agree, however, is no different from an undertaking to agree, to try to agree, or to negotiate with a view to reaching agreement; all are equally uncertain and incapable of giving rise to an enforceable obligation."[82]

An agreement to use reasonable or best endeavours will thus be treated similarly to an agreement to negotiate where the object which the best endeavours is to be used to achieve is left wholly indefinite.

(d) Reform

14–39   A slight change of approach to the issue of an agreement to negotiate may be perceived in the decision of the Irish High Court in *Bula Ltd. & Others v. Tara Mines & Others.*[83] Although Murphy J. referred to the decisions in *Courtney* and *Cadbury Ireland*, he also stated that "consideration must still be given to the observations of Lord Wright in *Hillas & Co Ltd. v. Arcos Ltd."*. He stated that "it does offer the bones of an argument which, as I understand it, the plaintiffs seek to couple with the arbitration clause in the present case."[84]

14–40   In *Coal Cliff Colleries Pty Ltd. v. Sijehama Pty. Ltd.,*[85] the majority of the New South Wales Court of Appeal while accepting that the law will not enforce an agreement to agree, rejected the principle that every promise to negotiate in good faith is unenforceable. Kirby P. noted:

---

80   See above para. 14–33.
81   (1994) 70 P & CR 469. See also *Phillips Petroleum Cork Ltd. v. Erron Europe Ltd.* (C.A.) 10/10/96, available on *Lexis*.
82   *ibid.*
83   [1987] I.R. 95.
84   *ibid.* at 102.
85   (1991) 24 N.S.W.L.R. 1.

> "I agree with Lord Wright's speech in *Hillas* that, provided there was consideration for the promise, in some circumstance a promise to negotiate in good faith will be enforceable depending on its precise terms . . . Nevertheless . . . I believe that the proper approach to be taken in each case depends upon the construction of the particular contract . . . In many contracts it will be plain that the promise to negotiate is intended to be a binding legal obligation to which the parties should then be held. The clearest illustration of this class will be cases where an identified third party has been given the power to settle ambiguities and uncertainties . . . But even in such cases, the court may regard the failure to reach agreement on a particular term as such that the agreement should be classed as illusory or unacceptably uncertain . . . In that event, the court will not enforce the arrangement. In a small number of cases, by reference to a readily ascertainable external standard, the court may be able to add flesh to a provision which is otherwise unacceptably vague or uncertain or apparently illusory. Finally, in many cases, the promise to negotiate in good faith will occur in the context of an "arrangement" (to use a neutral term) which by its nature, purpose, context, other provisions or otherwise makes it clear that "the promise is too illusory or too vague and uncertain to be enforceable."[86]

This approach would appear to be superior and more in keeping with the commercial realities of such agreements. In *Con Kallergis Pty Ltd (T/A Sunlighting Australasia Pty Ltd) v. Calshonie Pty Ltd (Formerly Cw Norris Pty Ltd)*,[87] an agreement between Norris and Sun Lighting obliged Norris to pay (and Sun Lighting to accept) a price for the variation of a building contract that was to be determined in a particular way – by negotiation between Norris and the builder. It was argued that Norris was obliged by its agreement with Sun Lighting to conduct the negotiations with the builder in good faith (or honestly and reasonably). The Supreme Court of Victoria held that although there may be difficult questions of fact and degree about whether evidence of particular conduct reveals a lack of good faith or lack of honesty or reasonableness, the obligation to act in good faith or honestly or reasonably is an obligation that is certain:

> "Where, as I assume may be the case here, B and C must negotiate (B because it is bound to A to do so and C because it is bound to B to do so) and there is a process for resolving any disagreement between B & C, I consider that the obligation 'to negotiate' the price is certain. The contract considered in *Walford v. Miles* was held to be uncertain because either party could break off negotiations at any time and for any reason. It was held that the implication of an obligation to negotiate in good faith did not cure the difficulty because a negotiator, acting in good faith, might nevertheless always break off negotiations. But unlike the kind of contract considered in *Walford v. Miles*, a contract of the kind now under consideration (in which I assume there is a

---

[86] *ibid.* at 26.
[87] 1997 Vic Lexis 175; Available on *Lexis*.

provision for resolution of disputes between the negotiators) does provide for an end to the negotiation other than the parties to it retreating to their offices to nurse their pride and their rejected bargaining position. If one party withdraws from the negotiations, whether in the hope that the opposite party will re-open them with an improved offer or for any other reason, the impasse between the parties can be resolved by one or other setting in train arbitration of the dispute or whatever other process of dispute resolution has been agreed. The matter will not stop with the breaking off of negotiations. Thus, even if *Walford v. Miles* is to be regarded as good law in Australia (and there are indications in some of the authorities that I have mentioned[88] that suggest there is at least room for doubt about the width of some of the propositions advanced in that case), I consider that on the assumptions I have mentioned the present contract does not suffer from the difficulties identified by their Lordships."

14–41   There has been much criticism in the UK of the decision of the Court of Appeal in *Walford v. Miles*. Lord Steyn has written suggesting that if the question of the enforceability of an obligation to negotiate in good faith was to arise again, that he hoped the concept of good faith would not be rejected out of hand.[89] While the question did arise again recently in *UK News Ltd v. Mirror Group plc and another*,[90] Thomas J. in the English High Court referred to the criticisms but apparently reluctantly stated that he was bound by the earlier decisions to hold that there could not be an enforceable obligation to use best endeavours to negotiate.

(e) Quantum Meruit

14–42   Although an agreement to negotiate may prove fruitless and pre-contractual negotiations may fail, a party who has produced work during the negotiations may be awarded a *quantum meruit*. Such an award involves paying a person, literally "as much as he has earned".[91] In *British Steel Corporation v. Cleaveland Bridge & Engineering Co. Ltd.*[92] the defendant had successfully tendered for the fabrication of steel-work to be used in the construction of a building. It then entered into negotiations with the plaintiff for the supply by the plaintiff of steel nodes which would form part of the relevant steelwork. It was proposed that this sub-contract would be in a standard form used by the defendant. The defendant requested the plaintiff to commence work on

---

[88]   The cases referred to previously were *Trawl Industries of Australia Pty Ltd v. Effem Foods Pty Ltd* (1992) 27 N.S.W.L.R. 326; *Hooper Bailie Associated Ltd v. Natcon Group Pty Ltd* (1992) 28 N.S.W.L.R. 194 and *Elizabeth Bay Developments Pty Ltd v. Boral Building Services Pty Ltd* (1995) 36 N.S.W.L.R. 709.

[89]   113 L.Q.R. 433. See also by 108 L.Q.R. 406 per Lord Neill.

[90]   March 19, 1998. Available on *Lexis*.

[91]   Clark, *Contract Law in Ireland* (Roundhall Sweet and Maxwell, 1998) pp. 509–512; Treitel. *The Law of Contract* (Sweet and Maxwell, 1995) pp. 951–954.

[92]   [1984] 1 All E.R. 504.

the steel nodes immediately 'pending the preparation and issuing to you of the official form of sub-contract'. The intended formal contract was not entered into, because the parties failed to agree certain terms to go into it. The plaintiff produced and delivered to the defendant all but one of the steel nodes. The plaintiff then sued for the value of the nodes it had supplied by way of *quantum meruit*. In considering the plaintiff's *quantum meruit* claim, Robert Goff J. in the English High Court stated:

> "In my judgment, the true analysis of the situation is simply this. Both parties confidently expected a formal contract to eventuate. In these circumstances, to expedite performance under that anticipated contract, one requested the other to commence the contract work, and the other complied with that request. If thereafter, as anticipated, a contract was entered into, the work done as requested will be treated as having been performed under that contract; if, contrary to their expectation, no contract was entered into, then the performance of the work is not referable to any contract the terms of which can be ascertained, and the law simply imposes an obligation on the party who made the request to pay a reasonable sum for such work as has been done pursuant to that request, such an obligation sounding in quasi contract or, as we now say, in restitution. Consistently with that solution, the party making the request may find himself liable to pay for work which he would not have had to pay for as such if the anticipated contract had come into existence, e.g. preparatory work which will, if the contract is made, be allowed for in the price of the finished work (c.f. *William Lacey (Hounslow) Ltd. v. Davis* [1957] 2 All E.R. 712, [1957] 1 W.L.R. 932)."[92a]

14–43 This case was distinguished, however, in *Regalian Properties plc v. London Dockland Development Corp.*[93] where the English High Court held that while *quantum meruit* is possible where one party to an expected contract expressly requests the other to perform services or supply goods that would have been performable or suppliable under the expected contract, the situation is different where parties entered into negotiations with the intention of concluding a contract but on express terms that each party was free to withdraw from the negotiations at any time. In such a case Rattee J. determined, it is clear that, pending the conclusion of a binding contract, any costs incurred by one of the parties in preparation for the intended contract are incurred at his own risk in the sense that he will have no recompense for these costs if no contract results. His Lordship stated:

> "The costs for which Regalian seeks reimbursement were incurred by it not by way of accelerated performance of the anticipated contract at the request of LDDC, but for the purpose of putting itself in a position to obtain and then perform the contract."[93a]

[92a] *ibid.* at 511.
[93] [1995] 1 W.L.R. 212.
[93a] *ibid.* at 230.

It should be noted that even where no benefit accrues to one of the parties to the negotiation as a result of the work performed by the other party, *quantum meruit* may still be awarded. In *Folens & Co. v. Minister for Education*,[94] the Department of Education which had entered into negotiations with the plaintiff with a view to the publishing company producing a children's encyclopaedia for the Department, were found liable to the plaintiff for expenses incurred in preparatory work carried out with the Department's approval.

(4) Lock-Out Agreements

14–44   Agreements to negotiate are often accompanied by lock-out agreements. A lock-out agreement involves an undertaking given to a potential purchaser to the effect that the vendor will not negotiate to sell to a third party for a period of time. Such an agreement is useful in the early stages of negotiating a takeover. It gives the potential purchaser exclusive negotiating rights for a period, thus allowing time to carry out due diligence. It thus allows the potential purchaser an opportunity to negotiate without the pressures of a competitive bid situation. Lock-out agreements are legally enforceable, subject to certain requirements.

14–45   In *Walford v. Miles*,[95] the respondents entered into discussions with the appellants with a view to selling them their beneficial interest in a company. The appellants orally agreed to provide a "letter of comfort" in return for the respondents agreeing to break off negotiations with any third party, and to deal exclusively with the appellants. No time limit was provided for this exclusive opportunity to negotiate. Although the letter of comfort was provided and a draft share-purchase agreement drawn up, the respondents subsequently decided not to proceed with the negotiations and sold their interest to someone else. The appellants sued for breach of contract. The respondents argued that the agreement implied an undertaking to negotiate in good faith which was unenforceable. The trial judge found that the oral agreement was a separate and collateral agreement which the respondents had repudiated. The Court of Appeal deemed the collateral agreement merely an agreement to negotiate and thus unenforceable. Lord Ackner in the House of Lords stated that agreements to negotiate lacked sufficient certainty to be enforceable. On the subject of the lock-out agreement itself, Lord Ackner agreed that a lock-out agreement for a limited period was enforceable. He said:

---

94   [1984] I.L.R.M. 265.
95   [1992] 2 W.L.R. 174.

"There is clearly no reason in the English contract law why A, for good consideration, should not achieve an enforceable agreement whereby B, agrees for a specified period of time, not to negotiate with anyone except A in relation to the sale of his property. There are often good commercial reasons why A should desire to obtain such an agreement from B. B's property, which A contemplates purchasing, may be such as to require the expenditure of not inconsiderable time and money before A is in a position to assess what he is prepared to offer for its purchase or whether he wishes to make an offer at all. A may well consider that he is not prepared to run the risk of expending such time and money unless there is a worthwhile prospect, should he desire to make an offer to purchase, of B, not only then still owning the property, but of being prepared to consider his offer. A may wish to guard against the risk that, while he is investigating the wisdom of offering to buy B's property, B may have already disposed of it or, alternatively, may be so advanced in negotiations with a third party as to be unwilling or for all practical purposes unable, to negotiate with A. But I stress that this is a negative agreement – B by agreeing not to negotiate for this fixed period with a third party, locks himself out of such negotiations. He has in no legal sense locked himself into negotiations with A. What A has achieved is an exclusive opportunity, for a fixed period, to try and come to terms with B . . . I therefore cannot accept [counsel's] proposition . . . that without a positive obligation on B to negotiate with A, the lock-out agreement would be futile".[96]

However, Lord Ackner felt that as the lock-out agreement here for was an unspecified duration, it necessarily implied a duty to negotiate in good faith. He referred to Bingham L.J. in the Court of Appeal who had suggested that in such a case the obligation would end once the parties acting in good faith were unable to come to mutually agreeable terms. As this would impose a positive duty on the respondents to negotiate in good faith, a duty which, as noted above, he believed was unenforceable, Lord Ackner held that the agreement was unworkable.[97]

14–46   A lock-out agreement for a finite period has, however, been held to be enforceable. In *Pitt v. PHH Management Ltd.*,[98] a vendors promise in a contract to sell property, not to negotiate with third parties for a specified duration, was deemed sufficient to satisfy the requirement of certainty and thus to give rise to a collateral contract.

14–47   It is submitted that the Irish courts may take a different view to the House of Lords in respect of lock-out agreements for an indefinite

[96] *ibid.* at 182–183.
[97] For an analysis of this case, see Neill, "A Key to Lock-Out Agreements ?" (1992) 109 L.Q.R. 405.
[98] [1993] 4 All E.R. 961.

period. An Irish court is unlikely to infer an obligation to negotiate in good faith into such an agreement. Implying such a term would destroy the agreement as agreements to negotiate in good faith are unenforceable. In *Karim Aga Khan v. Firestone,*[99] Morris J. stated that "it cannot . . . be logical to ask the court to imply into a contract a term so as to give it business efficacy when it would have the contrary effect".

Gower notes that a more challenging attack on lock-out agreements may be based on the duty of directors not to fetter their discretion.[100] This duty will be examined in greater detail in Chapter 19.[101]

---

[99] [1992] I.L.R.M. 31.
[100] *Gower's Principles of Modern Company Law* (Sweet & Maxwell, 1997), 608–610 786–788.
[101] See Chap. 19, paras 19–47 and 19–48.

CHAPTER 15

DUE DILIGENCE

15–01 Before the purchaser enters into a share purchase agreement or a contract to purchase the undertaking, it will carry out a due diligence exercise to confirm the details given to it by the vendor and to satisfy itself as to the state of affairs of the company. This exercise is likely to uncover a number of issues for which warranties and indemnities may subsequently be needed. In very serious cases, it may even lead to an abandonment of the purchase.

15–02 A number of parties will be involved in the due diligence exercise, each providing their own particular expertise and skill. Typically, lawyers, accountants, tax advisers and actuaries will play a role and depending on the nature of the firm or business being acquired, environmental engineers, information technology experts and other industry specialists may also be required. In order to ensure efficient communication between these parties and in order to avoid duplication of work, a schedule will generally be devised setting out the respective functions of the various participants. The purchaser's corporate finance advisers will general be responsible for co-ordinating all these parties.

15–03 This Chapter considers some of the main issues which will be examined during the due diligence exercise. In certain cases, the purchaser's team will be responsible for seeking out the relevant information and analysing it. In other cases, the information will be obtained directly from the vendor. Because most of this information will not be in the public domain, the vendor will seek to ensure that the confidentiality of the information is maintained. As noted in the previous Chapter,[1] a confidentiality agreement will generally be drafted to protect the vendor in this regard.

---

[1] See Chap. 14, paras 14–18–14–19.

A. Shares

15–04 Where the purchaser is acquiring the shares of the target company rather than the undertaking, it should be satisfied that the vendor possesses the title to the shares proposed to be transferred and is free to transfer those shares to the purchaser. In addition, the purchaser should ensure that no other persons possess any rights or options to acquire shares.

I. TITLE TO SHARES

15–05 The purchaser should satisfy itself that the vendor possesses the title to the shares proposed to be transferred. In order to ensure this, it may be necessary to trace the transferor's title back to the original allotment in order to ensure that no defect exists. Section 79 of the Companies Act 1963 ("the 1963 Act") states that:

> "the shares or other interest of any member in a company shall be personal estate, transferable in manner provided by the articles of the company, and shall not be of the nature of real estate".

Shares in private companies are transferred by the execution of a share transfer form by the registered owner in favour of the purchaser.[1a] The transferee must then be registered as a member of the company.[1b] According to section 81 of the 1963 Act, notwithstanding anything in the articles of the company, it shall not be lawful for the company to register a transfer of securities in the company unless a "proper instrument of transfer" has been delivered to the company. This does not however prejudice the power of the company to register as a sharehlder or debenture holder any person to whom the right to shares in, or debentures of the company has been transmitted by operation of law. Section 83 of the 1963 Act provides that upon the application of the transferor of the shares, the company must register the transferee's name in its register of members, in the same manner and subject to the same conditions, as if the application were made by the transferee. Until the transferee is registered as a member of the company in this way, the transfer is not legally complete.[2] The purchaser should be aware, however, that inclusion on the register is not conclusive evidence of membership, because provisions in the company's articles of association may prevent a registered person from becoming a member. In addition, the register provides no evidence of the identity of the beneficial owner of the shares.

[1a] See *Re Greene* [1949] 1 All E.R. 167.
[1b] *Kinsella v. Alliance and Dublin Consumers' Gas Company*, unreported, (Barron J.) Oct. 5, 1982.
[2] *Tangney v. The Clarence Hotels Co Ltd et al* [1933] I.R. 51.

II. REFUSAL TO REGISTER THE TRANSFER OF SHARES

15–06 The director of a private company may refuse to register the transfer of shares. Regulation 3 of Part II of Table A of the 1963 Act suggests the following form of restriction:

> "The directors may, in their absolute discretion, and without assigning any reason therefor, decline to register any transfer of any share, whether or not it is a fully paid share."

The directors' powers in this respect are extremely broad and, in general, no reason need be given to the transferee for the refusal to register the shares. Obviously, however, this discretion should be exercised bona fides in what directors consider to be for the benefit of the company as a whole.[3] Section 84(1) of the 1963 Act provides that if a company refuses to register a transfer of shares or debentures, the transferee must be notified of this fact within two months of the transfer date. Failure to do so will lead to the loss by the directors of their right to refuse registration.[3a] Where the directors refuse to register a transfer and the purchase price has been paid, the transferor remains the legal owner of the shares but is a trustee of the shares for the transferee who is the equitable owner.[4] This means in effect that the transferee will be entitled to direct the transferor as to the manner in which the voting rights attached to the shares should be exercised.[4a] The power to decline to register a transfer will also apply to a transfer of shares to a mortgagee in order to effect a legal mortgage or to a transfer made by a legal or equitable mortgagee in pursuance of his power of sale. However, this power has been strictly construed. Unless the articles specifically provide, it will not prevent a shareholder renouncing his or her right to subscribe for shares which are allotted with a right to renounce. Similarly, the power will not apply to an assignment of a right to subscribe for shares.[4b] While this form of restriction on registration which gives directors absolute discretion is quite extreme, other less extreme forms of restriction may be adopted without jeopardising private company status.[5]

---

[3] *Re Smith and Fawcett Ltd.* [1942] 1 Ch. 304, *Re Hafner* [1943] I.R. 426, *Re Dublin North City Milling Co* [1909] 1 I.R. 179.

[3a] *Re Inverdeck Ltd.* [1998] 2 B.C.L.C. 242.

[4] Courtney, *The Law of Private Companies* (Butterworths, 1994), paras 10–045–10–047. See also *Stevenson v. Wilson* (1907) S.C. 445.

[4a] *Musselwhite v CH Musselwhite & Son Ltd.* [1962] Ch 964, *JRRT (Investments) Ltd. v Haycraft* [1993] BCLC 401.

[4b] Stedman & Jones, *Shareholders' Agreements*, (Longman Group UK Ltd., 1986) pp. 21–22.

[5] Ussher, *Company Law in Ireland* (Sweet & Maxwell, 1986), 188.

III. RESTRICTION ON THE RIGHT TO TRANSFER SHARES

15–07   A private company is defined in section 33(1)(a) of the 1963 Act inter alia as a company which, by its articles, restricts the rights to transfer its shares. One common form of restriction on the transfer of shares in private companies is a pre-emption right.[6] Typically, pre-emption rights are included in the articles of association although they may also be contained in a private contract between the shareholders. Such a private contract is enforceable in accordance with the general principles of the law of contract. The consideration for such an agreement, where it is not under seal, will be the mutual obligations of the parties. A pre-emption right imposes an obligation on shareholders who desire to sell their shares to offer the shares in the first instance to existing shareholders in proportion to their existing shareholding.[7] It thus allows the remaining shareholders an opportunity to increase their interest in the company and prevents any other party from acquiring the shares. If the other shareholders do not want to acquire any additional shares, the shares may then be offered to a third party, although they may not generally be offered at a lower price. In *Tangney v. Clarence Hotels Co. & Others,*[8] Johnston J. describes a pre-emption right as follows:

> "That device has been adopted by company draftsman in many different forms – that is, to place no restriction upon the circulation of the shares among the members of the company, but to enable the heavy hand of the Directors to come down when a stranger seeks to enter into the charmed circle".[9]

15–08   In addition to placing restrictions on the persons to whom the shares may be transferred, the articles or the contract may also place restrictions on the consideration payable. In order to value a shareholding, a pro rata basis may be used, although often a premium is added to reflect a majority holding or a discount is used to reflect a minority holding. Alternatively, the articles or the contract may provide that a "fair price" must be determined.[9a] A mechanism will then be provided for the parties, their auditors or other experts to agree this price. In the latter case, the expert's determination will be final unless there is manifest error or evidence of bad faith.[10]

15–09   In many private companies, existing shareholders, their families and employees are given preferential treatment in terms of the transfer

---

[6] These are different to the pre-emption rights on the allotment of shares which are discussed in Chap. 5, paras 5–58–5–60 and Chap. 8, paras 8–12–8–16.

[7] See Hannigan, "Share Transfer Problems in the Private Company", Vol. 11 *The Company Lawyer* No. 9, 170.

[8] [1933] I.R. 51.

[9] *ibid.* at 63.

[9a] *AG for Ireland v. Jameson* [1904] I.R. 644.

[10] *Johnston v. Chestergate Hat Manufacturing Co Ltd* [1915] 2 Ch. 338.

of shares. In *AG v. Jameson*,[11] the pre-emption rights clause under consideration stated "A share may be transferred or bequeathed to any person who is already a member, but no share shall, save as hereinafter provided, be transferred to a person who is not a member, so long as any member is willing to purchase the same at 'fair value'." A further clause provided that, subject to the approval of the directors, "any share might be transferred by a member to any son or brother of such member, or to any son or brother of any existing member, and that any share of a deceased member might be transferred by his executors or administrators to any son or brother of such deceased member, or to any son or brother of any existing member". Although these clauses in the articles severely restricted the shareholder's right to transfer the shares, they were deemed to be valid.

15–10 In addition to restricting the transfer of existing shares, shareholders' agreements may restrict or prohibit any increase in a company's share capital. Section 68 of the 1963 Act empowers a company to increase its share capital if it is so authorised by its Articles. Regulation 44 of Table A empowers a company to do so by ordinary resolution. Shareholders may decide, however, to restrict the exercise of these powers. In *Russell v. Northern Bank Development Corporation*,[12] a number of shareholders entered into a shareholders' agreement providing *inter alia* that "no further share capital shall be created or issued in the company . . . without the written consent of each of the parties." The House of Lords held that individual shareholders are entitled to enter into a private agreement as to the exercise of their voting rights. Where shareholders agree not to transfer their shares, that agreement will thus be binding on those shareholders and an injunction will be granted to enforce the agreement. The Court indicated that the company could not, however, be a party to an agreement of this kind as it would involve fettering its statutory powers under the equivalent of section 68 to alter its share capital. Lord Jauncey indicated that the shareholders agreement was binding only on those who executed it and would not bind future shareholders. In order to avoid such a finding, Courtney suggests excluding Regulation 44 from the companies articles. In this way, the power of a company to increase its share capital pursuant to section 68 on condition that the company is authorised to do so in its articles would not be relevant. The company could then be prevented from increasing its share capital.[12a]

---

[11]   [1904] 2 I.R. 644.
[12]   [1992] 1 W.L.R. 588.
[12a] *op. cit.* n.4 at para. 5–034.

15–11   Where the purchaser is seeking to acquire shares from a controlling shareholder but a number of other shareholders exist, the existence of pre-emption rights should be established at an early stage. In order to do this, the purchaser should ensure that the memorandum and articles of association are examined and copies of any share-holder's agreements are obtained. Unlike the memorandum and articles of association, a shareholders agreement is unlikely to be filed in the Companies Registration Office.[12b] Any resolutions attaching rights or restrictions to any share or varying such rights or restrictions will however be registered with the registrar of companies.[13]

15–12   Although pre-emption clauses are enforced by the courts,[14] the purchaser should be aware that they tend to be strictly construed contra proferens. Where a company wishes to apply pre-emption rights to the assignment of the equitable title, it must do so expressly and clearly in the pre-emption provisions.[14a] In considering the pre-emption rights, the purchaser should be also be aware that terms may be implied in order to give efficacy to the intentions of the parties. In *Lyle & Scott Ltd. v Scotts Trustees*,[14b] the company's articles of association required any shareholder who was "desirous" of transferring his shares to serve a transfer notice. The respondents were approached by a third party who wished to buy their shares. The respondents agreed that in the event of the offer becoming unconditional, the purchaser's nominee would be authorised to use general proxies, that the respondents would deliver their share certificates in respect of all the shares to be sold and, finally, that they would execute transfer deeds when called upon to do so. The purchaser paid for the shares but the company argued that the respondents were bound to adhere to pre-emption rights. The House of Lords determined that since the respondents agreed to the sale, it was not open to them, as long as that agreement was subsisting, to deny that they were desirous of transferring their shares. In *Safeguard Industrial Investments Ltd. v. National Westminster Bank Ltd.*,[15] the articles of

---

[12b] It has been argued that section 143(4)(c) of the 1963 Act imposes an obligation to register shareholders' agreements. This would appear to be true only where the agreement amounts to an agreement to alter the articles. For further discussion on this point, see Stedman & Jones, *op. cit.*, n.4b at pp. 49–53.

[13] Companies Act 1963, ss.143(4)(f) and (g). See also McGovern "Shareholders Agreements – their Nature and Effect" (1995) CLP 113.

[14] *Lee and Company (Dublin) Ltd v. Egan (Wholesale) Ltd.* unreported, High Court, Kenny J., April 27, 1978.

[14a] Stedman & Jones, *op. cit.*, n.4b, at pp. 23–25. See also *Hunter v. Hunter* [1936] AC 222, *Hawks v. McArthur* [1951] 1 All ER 27, *Tett v. Phoenix Property and Investment Co.* [1986] B.C.L.C. 149 and Courtney, *op. cit.* n.4 at paras 10–057–10–059.

[14b] [1959] 2 All ER 661.

[15] [1980] 3 All E.R. 849.

association of a company provided that members proposing to "transfer" shares were required to notify the company which was required to offer the shares to other shareholders. The Court of Appeal held that the term "transfer" only embraced the transfer of the legal title not the transferee of beneficial interests.

If the pre-emption mechanism is triggered, the vendor must then notify the company who will notify shareholders entitled under the pre-emption provision to make an offer.[16] If express provision is not made in the articles or shareholders agreement in respect of this obligation, it will be implied. In *Tett v Phoenix Property & Investment Company*,[16a] the Court of Appeal stated that a term could be implied into the articles of a company in order to give it efficacy requiring a shareholder wishing to transfer his shares to an outsider to take reasonable steps to give notice of his intention to persons to whom notice should be given. Such notice was deemed to be essential in order to give persons entitled to notice a reasonable opportunity to buy the shares. The Court of Appeal in this case also accepted that the notification acts as an invitation to treat informing other shareholders that they may make an offer for the shares.

IV. OPTIONS

15–13 The existence of any share options should be determined. Often options will be granted to directors or other key employees as part of their remuneration. These options are likely to be exercisable within a certain time period or upon the happening of a particular event. The company's share register and minute book should be searched in order to determine the extent of the outstanding share options and the identity of the holders of those options.

B. Financial Performance

15–14 A financial due diligence exercise is necessary in order to ensure that the company's financial position is as stated by the vendor. A firm of accountants will conduct this part of the due diligence exercise. It is essential that the purchaser instructs independent auditors to verify the company's financial position. As was seen in Chapter 10,[16b] little recourse will be available at common law to a purchaser who suffers loss as a result of relying on the company's own auditor's reports.

---

[16] B.C.L.C. 149. See Courtney, *op. cit.*, no. 4, at paras 10–053–10–057.
[16a] [1986] B.C.L.C. 149.
[16b] See Chap. 10, paras 10–37–10–47.

15–15   A review of the company's audited accounts should be undertaken in order to verify that the balance sheet, profit & loss figures and cash flows statements are consistent with the financial position of the company as represented by the vendor. This verification process will usually involve an appraisal of the company's accounts rather than an independent examination of the company's assets and liabilities. The company's accounting policies should be noted and any unusual accounting practices should be identified. In addition to the audited accounts, the purchaser should seek access to the unaudited management accounts.

The accountants will generally prepare some form of profit forecasts and cash flow projections. An attempt is also likely to be made to conduct some form of sensitivity analysis in order to identify the factors which might influence these projections.

C. Tax

15–16   The purchaser's tax advisers will normally be required to investigate the company's tax situation. The purchaser should be confident that the company has met all its past tax liabilities fully and that no potential tax liabilities may arise after completion.

The tax advisers will review tax returns, computations and accounts for the previous three years and will examine the results of any Revenue audits. Ideally, the purchaser's tax adviser should work in conjunction with the company's financial controller in order to produce the necessary information for the purchaser.

15–17   Liabilities to corporation tax, VAT, PAYE, PRSI, capital gains tax and stamp duty, etc., must be determined. Where the company has claimed the benefit of certain forms of tax relief such as manufacturing relief, the tax adviser should ensure that these benefits were correctly claimed and received and will continue to be available after completion of the acquisition.

As a result of the tax adviser's work, a tax indemnity will normally be drafted in favour of both the purchaser and in the case of a share sale, the company itself, in respect of any tax payable by the company other than that provided in the disclosure letter. Rather than include this tax indemnity in the share sale agreement, a separate tax deed of indemnity will normally be used.[17]

---

[17] See Chap. 16, para. 16–40.

D. Liabilities

15–18 The purchaser of the shares of a company should conduct a search of the Companies Registration Office to determine whether the company is up to date with its annual returns. Section 125 of the 1963 Act requires the company to make a return to the Registrar of Companies at least once a year and a fine not exceeding £1000 may be imposed for failure to make adequate and timely returns. The Fifth Schedule to the 1963 Act sets out the contents and form of the annual return and sections 7 to 12 of the Companies (Amendment) Act 1986 set out the documents which must be annexed to the annual return. The purchaser should thus have access to a copy of the balance sheet, the profit and loss account, the auditors report and the directors report.[18]

15–19 A search should also indicate whether any charges have been registered against the company. Sections 99(1) and section 100(1) of the 1963 Act require companies to register certain specified charges with the Registrar of Companies within 21 days of their creation. These relevant charges are set out in section 99(1) and comprise:

(a) a charge for the purpose of securing any issue of debentures;

(b) a charge on uncalled share capital of the company;

(c) a charge created or evidenced by an instrument which, if executed by an individual, would require registration as a bill of sale;

(d) a charge on land, wherever situate, or any interest therein, but not including a charge for any rent or other periodic sum issuing out of land;

(e) a charge on book debts of the company;

(f) a floating charge on the undertaking or property of the company;

(g) a charge on calls made but not paid;

(h) a charge on a ship or aircraft or any share in a ship or aircraft;

(i) a charge on goodwill, on a patent or licence under a patent, on a trademark or on a copyright or a licence under a copyright.

If any of the aforementioned charges are not registered, they will be deemed void against the liquidator and any creditor of the company.

---

[18] Companies classified as "small" and "medium sized" are subject to a number of exceptions on the documents to be annexed to the annual returns. In certain cases, for example, abridged accounts may be acceptable.

This means that the purchaser can be confident of identifying any valid charge to which the section applies.

15–19A By contrast, sections 101 and 102 of the 1963 Act[19] which require the registration of certain other charges not created by the company do not allow their charges to be avoided by non-registration. Section 101(1) requires a company to register a charge where it acquires any property which is subject to a charge of any such kind as would, if it had been created after the acquisition of the property, have been required to be registered under the Act. Section 102(1) requires the company to register judgment mortgages affecting any property of the company of which it has been notified by the judgment creditor.

15–20 Section 103(1) provides that the registrar of companies is required to maintain a register in respect of each company detailing all the charges requiring registration. This register will include details such as the date of creation of the charge or the judgment mortgage, the amount secured by the charge, short particulars of the property charged, the persons entitled to the charge, and if the charge was a charge on property acquired by the company, the date of the acquisition of the company.[20] This register is available for inspection by any person on payment of the prescribed fee.[21] A search may be done personally or a professional company may be employed to provide this service.

The purchaser should also search all the statutory books to verify that no promissory notes or share options are outstanding.

In order to assess other liabilities, copies of the facility letters in respect of all bank borrowings and other financial arrangements must be obtained. Where any inter-company debt exists, this must be identified by the purchaser.

E. Assets

I. REAL ESTATE

15–21 The purchaser should investigate title to the property being acquired. One way of doing this is to send the vendor either the Incorporated Law Society's standard form Requisitions on Title or a list of the vendor's solicitor's own requisitions.

15–22 A search of the Registry of Deeds will determine whether any documents under seal or other "instruments affecting land" have been

---

[19] As amended by section 122 of the Companies (Amendment) Act 1990.
[20] Companies Act 1963, s.103(1)(b).
[21] *ibid.*, s.103(2).

registered.[22] The latter term includes judgments, decrees and court orders which affect land. Land actions which are pending may also be registered in the Registry of Deeds.[23] Certain documents such as judgment mortgages will be ineffective unless they are registered.[24] Other documents will merely loose their priority if they are not registered. If the title to an estate or an interest in land is registered under the Registration of Title Act 1964, the registry of documents system ceases to apply to the estate or interest.[25]

15–23 The purchaser should also undertake a search of the Register of Title.[26] Three separate registers are available dealing with freehold interests in land, leasehold interests in land and incorporeal hereditaments. These registers record not only titles to interests which are recorded compulsorily or voluntarily but also certain other interests which appear as burdens against the title of other interests. The Land Registration Rules 1972[27] requires the register to be maintained in folios. The first folio contains: a description of the property the title to which is registered; easements, covenants and other rights for the benefit of the property; ownership of mines and minerals; and the boundaries of the property. The second folio contains: the name and a description of the owner of the property; the classes of owner and the classes of the titles by which they hold; the devolution of the property; special entries where there are co-owners, limited owners under the Settled Land Acts and infants; and cautions and inhibitions restricting the registration of dispositions of the property. The third folio contains: burdens protected by registration under section 69 of the Registration of Title Act 1964[28]; registered charges not separately registered; notes of burdens protected without registration under section 72 of the Registration of Title Act 1964,[29] or exemptions from them; and cautions and inhibitions against dealing with registered burdens.

---

[22] Under the Registration of Deeds Acts 1707, 1709, 1721 and 1785; Registry of Deeds (Amendment)(Ireland) Acts 1822, 1832 and 1864; Land Transfer (Ireland) Act 1848; Judgment Mortgage (Ireland) Acts 1850 and 1858. See generally Lyall, *Land Law in Ireland* (Oak Tree Press, 1994), Chap. 5; Wylie, *Irish Land Law*, Chap. 22.

[23] Alternatively, they may be registered as *lites pendentes* in the High Court.

[24] Judgment Mortgage (Ireland) Act 1850, ss. 6–8.

[25] Registration of Title Act 1964, s.116.

[26] See generally Lyall, *op. cit.*, n.22, Chap. 24, pp. 794–795.

[27] S.I. No. 230 of 1972.

[28] These interests include restrictive covenants or conditions as to the use of land, judgment mortgages, court judgements or orders, a charge on land created after first registration, incumbrances existing at the time of first registration, a power to charge land with the payment of money, a trust for securing money, a vendor's lien on land for unpaid purchase money and a lease for a life.

[29] The purchaser should be aware that these burdens may not appear on the register.

15–24   Lyall notes that the basic principle behind registration of title is that the registration should be a mirror of the title, reflecting all the interests which affect the land in question so that a purchaser does not have to go behind the register to discover interests binding on him.[30] However, he warns that in practice, this principle is qualified by a number of exceptions. Firstly, section 72 interests are binding regardless of registration. These interests include land improvement charges, public rights of way, certain easements, and rights of persons in actual occupation of the land of the Registration of Title Act 1964.[31] Secondly, the possibility always exists that the register will subsequently be rectified due to a fraud or an error. Thirdly, the nature of the transferee is also relevant. Where the transferee has not provided valuable consideration, it takes the title subject to unregistered charges which bound the transferor.

15–25   In addition to ensuring that the vendor possesses title to the property, the purchaser should examine all the title deeds to ensure that there are no onerous requirements. For example, when a leasehold interest is being acquired, there may be covenants included which impose onerous repair requirements or restrictive use conditions. In addition, the assignment of a leasehold interest will normally be subject to the landlord's prior written consent. Section 67 of the Landlord and Tenant (Amendment) Act 1980 provides that in so far as any covenant in a lease of a tenement absolutely prohibits a change of user, it is to have effect as if it were a covenant prohibiting change without the consent of the lessor. Furthermore, such consent may not be "unreasonably withheld". Often the contract will contain warranties by the vendor regarding use of the premises and other matters. These should be strictly noted by the purchaser.

15–26   Instead of conducting a search, the purchaser may decide to accept a certificate of title from the vendor's solicitor. If a difficulty subsequently emerges, the purchaser will be entitled to sue the solicitor for negligence. Alternatively, it may rely upon warranty protection.[32]

15–27   The purchaser should ensure that all buildings constructed or developed on the property acquired, or involving a material change of use since October 1, 1964 comply with the relevant planning permission under the Local Government (Planning and Development) Act 1963. In addition, certain large or intensive types of development may

---

[30] *op. cit.*, n.22 at p. 795.
[31] Unless inquiry is made of such persons and they do not disclose their rights.
[32] See Chap. 16, paras 16–11–16–13.

have required an environmental impact statement under the European Communities (Environmental Impact Statement) Regulations 1989[33] to accompany an application for planning permission. The existence of any special amenity orders should be identified where the orders could require the preservation of parts of the property which might be considered to be an area of outstanding beauty, an area of special recreational value or an area in need of conservation.[34] This could affect the purchaser's ability to expand the premises. Areas with special views and areas of ecological or archaeological interest may similarly be protected.[35] Any agreements restricting or regulating the development or use of the land, either permanently or for a specific period of time[36] should be identified in advance of the acquisition. Fortunately, planning authorities are required to maintain a register which records planning information, including planning permissions granted and the conditions attaching to them.[37]

15–28 Site plans should be examined to determine whether any boundary disputes are likely and whether any access problems exist which would affect the value of the property.

II. MACHINERY

15–29 The purchaser must determine whether the company's assets are owned outright. Where any of the machinery is leased or has been acquired under a hire purchase agreement, these contracts should be examined. Where the undertaking is being acquired rather than the company, the consent of the owners to the assignment of interest may need to be obtained. Even where it appears that the company has purchased the assets outright, reservation of title clauses may mean otherwise and must be identified in advance.

15–30 The purchaser should ensure that the premises and machinery are in a proper state of repair. The purchaser should consider the age of the machinery and its relative modernity in terms of current technology. Details of service and maintenance history should be obtained for plant and machinery.

15–31 Where the purchaser is acquiring the undertaking, the Sale of Goods and Supply of Services Acts 1893–1980 may apply to the plant,

---

[33] S.I. No. 349 of 1989
[34] Local Government (Planning and Development) Act 1963, s.42.
[35] *ibid.*, s.77.
[36] *ibid.*, s.38 as amended by the Local Government (Planning and Development) Act 1976.
[37] *ibid.*, s.8.

machinery and stock which is being acquired.[38] These statutes modify the normal rules of contract law for contracts falling within their scope. A "contract for the sale of goods" is defined as a contract whereby the seller transfers or agrees to transfer the property in goods to the buyer for a monetary consideration, called the price. "Goods" are said to include all chattels personal other than things in action and money. Section 12 of the Sale of Goods and Supply of Services Acts 1893–1980 implies a condition into every contract of sale on the part of the vendor that it has a right to sell the goods and an implied warranty that the goods are free from any charge or encumbrance. This rule will not apply if the vendor makes it clear that it is transferring only such title as it or a third person may have. In such a case, an implied warranty exists that all known charges and encumbrances have been disclosed, and that neither the seller, a third person with title or anyone claiming through them, should disturb the buyers quiet possession. Any clause purporting to exempt the buyer from liability under section 12 is deemed void. The European Communities (Unfair Terms in Consumer Contracts) Regulations 1995[39] apply to terms in a contract concluded between a vendor of goods or supplier of services and a consumer which have not been individually negotiated. These Regulations prohibit terms which are deemed unfair as defined by the Regulations.[40]

III. STOCK

15–32   Since the value of stock may be a substantial part of the assets of the company, a full inventory of stock including work in progress may need to be carried out in order to verify the figures in the accounts. Delivery documents and dispatch documents may need to be examined. A physical check of the materials may also be necessary. In many cases however, the time and expense involved in such a check would be prohibitive. Furthermore, despite due diligence exercises, it is often very difficult to value stock because the possibility exists that it might be run down just before completion. Often a specified minimum or maximum stock will thus be stated in the sale agreement.

IV. INTELLECTUAL PROPERTY

15–33   The purchaser should check any intellectual property rights owned or used by the company. If the company owns certain intellectual property, the purchaser should ensure that it is sufficiently

---

[38] Clark, *Contract Law in Ireland* (Round Hall Sweet & Maxwell, 1998), 171–187.
[39] S.I. No. 27 of 1995. See para. 10–56 above.
[40] Clark, *op. cit.*, above, n.38, 194–196.

protected. If the company uses another person's intellectual property by license, it is important to ensure that the license is valid and does not contain any overly restrictive clauses. It is important also to ensure that the company is not exceeding its rights under this agreement.

15–34 Both patents and trademarks are registered with the Controller of Patents, Designs and Trademarks and a search of the Register of Patents will thus be necessary to ensure the patent is valid and up-to-date. The Register of Patents in the Patents Office will disclose certain important details such as the date of the application, the details of the priority claim, the date on which notice of the grant of the patent is published, particulars of the patentee and particulars of any interest or title in a patent. Under section 36 of the Patents Act 1992, a patent may remain in force for twenty years from the date of filing the patent application, subject to the payment of renewal fees. The fact that a patent is a personal property right means that it may be assigned to the purchaser of an undertaking. It also means that it may be licensed or charged by way of mortgage.[41] Section 85(1) of the Patents Act 1992 imposes an obligation on the new owner or interest holder to record changes of ownership or an interest in a patent. In addition, section 99 of the Companies Act 1963 requires a company to register certain charges with the Registrar of Companies. A search of both Registers should thus satisfy the purchaser that the vendor still has title.

15–35 Trademarks will be registered in the Register of Trade Marks which is located in the Patents Office. Under section 47 of the Trade Marks Act 1996, the duration of a trade mark registration is ten years from the date of filing. It is renewable for successive ten year periods. Unlike a patent, a trademark registration may remain in force indefinitely upon payment of the renewal fees. A registered trade mark is also a personal property right and may thus be assigned in the same way as personal property. It will generally be assigned with the goodwill of an undertaking.

15–36 Rather than owning the trademark or patent, the vendor may merely be licensing it from its proprietor. The purchaser should ensure that the licence is valid and signed by or on behalf of the grantor. As a license is also a registrable transaction,[42] it will be in the licensee's interests to insist on recordal. Otherwise, the purchaser of the trademark may not be bound by the terms of the license.[43]

---

[41] See Clark & Smyth, *Intellectual Property Law in Ireland* (Butterworths, 1997), 103.
[42] Trade Marks Act 1996, s.29(2)(c).
[43] See Clark & Smyth, *op. cit.* above, n.41, 626.

15–37   Where the company uses special brand names, trade names or logos, the purchaser should ensure that the company is entitled to use them and will continue to be so entitled after the acquisition. Any agreements in relation to the use of these brand names, logos etc must be obtained and examined. Licences in relation to material protected by copyright under the Copyright Act, 1963 should also be acquired.[43a]

15–38   Finally, product designs may be registered and protected under the Industrial and Commercial Property (Protection) Act 1927. Designs which last for a period of 25 years will be registered with the Patent's Office.

15–39   Where the undertaking is being acquired rather than the shares, provision should be made for existing agreements such as licenses or leases to be either novated or assigned to the purchaser with the agreement of the third party and for completion to be conditional upon such novation or assignment.

V. DEBTORS

15–40   The figure for debtors should be examined. In a share sale, this may be an important determinant of the price offered. The purchaser should also check the length of time given to the debtors to meet their debts. Excessive concessions may cause capital to be tied up inefficiently for excessive periods of time. If possible, the purchaser should attempt to assess the credit worthiness of the debtors and the likelihood of their default.

VI. GOODWILL

15–41   Where the undertaking is being acquired, a figure will generally be paid for goodwill. In *Cruttwell v. Lye*,[44] goodwill was defined by Lord Eldon as "the probability that the old customers will resort to the old place". Goodwill is an extremely important asset of the company and the vendor should ensure ensure that it is correctly valued.[45]

[43a] The Copyright and Related Rights Bill 1999 has been initiated at the time of writing.
[44] (1810) 1 Rose 123.
[45] See Chap. 1, para. 1–16.

F. Employees

I. CONTRACTS OF EMPLOYMENT

15–42 Where the purchaser acquires the shares of the company, it will become directly responsible for the employees as there will be no change in their employer and thus their employment contracts. Where the purchaser acquires the undertaking, The European Communities (Safeguarding of Employees' Rights on Transfer of Undertakings) Regulations 1980[46] provides that the rights and obligations of the transferor arising from a contract of employment or from the employment relationship will be transferred to the purchaser. For this reason, it is equally important for the purchaser of the assets of a company as for the purchaser of the shares of the company to be aware of the employees' rights under their existing employment contracts.

15–43 Full details of all employees should be obtained including their age, length of service, salaries, bonuses, benefits in kind and pension entitlements. Details of profit sharing schemes and employee share schemes should also be acquired. In addition to identifying full and part time employees, contracts with independent contractors and consultants should be examined. The cost to the purchaser of maintaining all their employees should be assessed accurately. Where the purchaser intends to dismiss some of these employees, the potential cost to the company of redundancy payments or other compensatory payments should be assessed. All the directors' and senior managers' employment contracts should be examined in order to determine whether compensatory payments are provided for in the event of an acquisition. "Golden handshakes" may provide additional payments to directors or enhanced pension rights where a director looses his office as a result of a change of control. Alternatively, covenants may entitle employees who might otherwise be retained to receive lump-sum payments where they chose to leave within a specified period of the change of control.[47] Because of the importance of trade unions, it is essential that the purchaser identifies all the relevant unions to which the employees belong and obtains details of any collective agreements or informal agreements with non-unionised employees.

15–44 A due diligence exercise may be useful for a purchaser in determining which employees are essential to the continued success of the business. The purchaser may then choose to tie these persons into the business for a period of time. Alternatively, the purchaser may need

---

[46] S.I. No. 306 of 1980. See Chap. 9.
[47] Chap. 20, paras 20–33–20–46 will examine these provisions in greater detail.

to enforce an existing restrictive covenant in that persons' employment contract in order to prevent them departing to work for a competitor or to establish their own business. The common law view of such covenants is that they generally acceptable where they are reasonable in terms of duration, geographical coverage and scope and where they serve to protect a legitimate interest of the employers. Restrictive covenants of this type are now governed by the Competition Act 1991.[48]

II. PENSIONS

15–45 It is imperative that the purchaser conduct a thorough investigation of the vendor's pension scheme.[49] Normally, an actuary will be employed to give a professional assessment of its value. The existence and value of such a scheme is relevant both to the price being paid for the company and to the warranties to be obtained from the vendor. The purpose of a pension scheme is to provide death and retirement benefits for employees. The scheme may be a contributory one which requires both its members and their employers to contribute or it may be a non-contributory one to which only employers contribute. Almost all private occupational pension schemes are exempt approved schemes.[49a] Such schemes approved by the Revenue Commissioners benefit from tax relief on contributions[49b] and the investment yield is exempt from income[49c] and capital gains tax.[49d]

(1) Defined Benefit and Defined Contribution Schemes

15–46 Pension schemes are divided into two main categories, defined benefit and defined contribution schemes.

In a defined contribution scheme, the liabilities to members on retirement are determined by the contributions paid by and in respect of members and the investment yielded on that return. Such a scheme is defined in section 2(1) of the Pensions Act 1990 as:

> "a scheme which, under its rules, provides long service benefit,[50] the rate or amount of which is in total directly determined by the amount of the

---

[48] See Chap. 16, paras 16–45–16–56.
[49] For an examination of current pensions law, see Finucane and Buggy, *Irish Pensions Law & Practice* (Oak Tree Press, 1996).
[49a] Taxes Consolidation Act, 1997 pt 30; Chap. 1.
[49b] *ibid.*, s.744–775.
[49c] *ibid.*, s.744.
[49d] *ibid.*, s.613.
[50] A "long service benefit " is defined in section 2(1) as "the benefits which will be payable under a scheme in accordance with an obligation to or in respect of a member of a scheme on the assumption that he remains in relevant employment until such time as he attains normal pensionable age".

contribution paid by or in respect of the member and includes a scheme the contributions under which are used, directly or indirectly, to provide

(a) benefits, other than long service benefit, and

(b) long service benefit the rate or amount of which is in total directly determined by the part of the contributions aforesaid that is used for the provision of the long service benefit;"

Defined contribution scheme tend to be more popular with employers because they have lower administration and compliance costs and also are subject to less onerous regulatory requirements.

15–47 With defined benefit schemes, by contrast, the retirement benefits are not determined by the contributions made. Instead, the liabilities of such schemes are defined in the provisions of the scheme in terms of pensionable service and salaries at, or near, retirement. Actuaries determine the rates of contributions payable based on an estimate of the likely amount required to service the pension expectation. There is thus a guaranteed level of pension benefit payable to each member of the scheme. This type of scheme is defined rather basically in section 2 of the Pension Act 1990 as "a scheme which is not a defined contribution scheme". With contributory schemes, the employees contribute a fixed percentage of their wages and the required balance is contributed by the employers.[51] The investment risk is then born by the employer.

(2) Share Sales

15–48 If a takeover involves the acquisition of the shares of the company, the entire pension scheme will transfer with the company. The employees will be working for the same company, albeit that the company is now owned by someone else. Thus, the target continues as employer and the employees as scheme members. The purchaser will assume all responsibility for employees. For this reason, it will be in the purchaser's interests to ensure that the scheme is adequately funded before it assumes responsibility.

15–49 If the existing scheme is a defined benefit scheme, the purchaser should ensure that it will be able to meet its liabilities when they arise. An actuary is generally hired to confirm this fact. Schemes are likely either to be in deficit or in surplus when acquired. It is rare for a scheme to have perfectly matched its assets to the level of total past service reserves. This discrepancy will need to be reflected in the purchase price. For example, if the purchase price is based on profits

---

[51] This is referred to as the "balance of cost basis".

and the scheme is under-funded, the figure attributed to past profits will have been overstated. Similarly, if the price is based on the company's net asset value, then the value of the company being acquired can be reduced to reflect the extent of the under-funding. If the target has been over-funded, the actual profit figure is likely to be greater than the figure in the accounts. An accurate assessment of the pension scheme will effect the consideration which the purchaser is willing to give. Depending on the rules of the company's pension scheme, the employees might be entitled to transfer to the purchaser's scheme. If the purchaser's scheme provides additional benefits, pressure is likely to be put on the purchaser to equalise these benefits. This may give rise to certain industrial relations problems for the purchaser.

15–50 If the existing scheme is a defined contribution scheme, matters are more straightforward and the purchaser merely has to ensure that all contributions due before the sale have been paid in full. This is normally the subject of a warranty in the sale agreement. The purchaser should ensure that the terms of the scheme are fair and do not discriminate between the sexes. Again, from a public relations perspective, the purchaser should ensure that the employees are treated equally favourably after the transfer. Often, the vendor will seek an undertaking to this effect.

15–51 If the target does not have its own separate scheme, it being part of a group scheme for example, there will have to be a transfer of part of the group scheme's fund. Depending on the trust rules, this may involve a partial winding up of the vendor's scheme with respect to those employees being transferred. Alternatively, a transfer payment may be made. The employees will then be transferred to a newly set up company or to the purchaser's existing scheme. The amount transferred will have to be agreed and can be the subject of much negotiation and compromise. If the group scheme is in the deficit, the trustees will not want to pay out more than a proportionate share of the assets. However, if the scheme is over-funded they may not wish to pay out a proportion of the excess. The employees then have a number of options under their trust deed and rules and under Part III of the Pensions Act 1990. Employees with preserved entitlements may elect to leave their benefits in the old scheme, or to have them transferred by the trustee to a life office buy out bond which may take the form of an annuity or investment policy or alternatively have them transferred to the new scheme.

(3) Acquisition of Undertakings

15–52   If the entire undertaking or business is sold, the situation is relatively similar. The purchaser will replace the vendor as sponsoring employer of the scheme. This scheme will then be operated by the new employer. However, if only a part of the business is sold, only a portion of the pension fund will have to be transferred. This is likely to prove more complicated. Determining the proportion to be transferred is very important and the details will be set out in the sale and purchase agreement. A new scheme will have to be established to receive the transfer. Again, the employees have options in relation to their entitlements. The European Communities (Safeguarding of Employees Rights on Transfer of Undertakings) Regulations 1980 S.I. No. 306 of 1980 would appear to require a purchaser to maintain the employees accrued pension entitlements but not to continue the pension arrangements enjoyed by the employees with the vendor.[51a]

(4) The Role of the Actuary

15–53   Because of the importance of the value of the pension scheme in calculating the consideration to be paid for the acquisition, the purchaser will generally employ an actuary to examine the pension scheme. The actuary's role will be to place a value on the pension scheme. As noted above, this will be particularly important in the case of a defined benefit scheme.

15–54   The first way to measure a pension scheme's liabilities is to determine the total value of all members' leaving service benefits at a point in time. Leaving service benefits are generally based on pensionable service completed to the date of leaving and pensionable salaries at that date. This represents a scheme's liabilities if every member choose to leave on that particular date. Since this is unlikely, when recommending contribution rates, actuaries factor in the expectation that members will remain. This is done by targeting a level of funding for accrued benefits which allows for salary increases in the future to the date of expected retirement or departure. The total liability under this scenario is normally greater than the leaving service benefits and is termed "the past service reserve" for all members. The purchaser's actuary will seek copies of the audited accounts of the scheme and actuarial valuations.

15–55   Private occupational pension schemes are generally established under trusts administered by trustees who hold the assets of the scheme

---

[51a] See Chap. 9, para. 9–25.

("the trust fund") in trust for the employees. The scheme is not thus an asset of the employer and will not be available to shareholders upon a winding up. The trustees are appointed initially by the employer and may include, the employer itself, a company established by it for this purpose, a professional trustee company or certain named individuals. The rights and duties of the trustees will be set out in the trust documentation. Trustees are generally given full investment powers with respect to the scheme's funds. They are under a duty, however, to act in the beneficiaries best interests. Other duties of a trustee include ensuring contributions and benefits are paid, keeping the assets secure and ensuring that the terms of the scheme are carried out properly. Some of the decisions to be made by the trustee will require the employer's consent, for example the disposal of the surplus. The trust documentation normally consists of a trust deed which establishes the trust and rules which set out the actual benefit structure and provisions.[52] The trust rules should provide for members who leave service early.

15–56   The purchaser should obtain a copy of the trust deed and the rules. This documentation is important for a number of reasons. Firstly, it will inform the purchaser whether the consent of the trustees may be required for the transfer. It is not unusual for the purchaser to require the vendor to undertake to organise this consent. Secondly, provisions in the documentation may also deal with the consequences of a change of ownership possibly triggering a closure of the scheme or consent of members or consent of trustees. Thirdly, provisions in the trust documentation may deal with the transfer. It may, for example, provide for an apportionment of the fund on a partial winding-up or a bulk transfer in a particular way. Special provisions may also deal with partial wind-ups and bulk transfers.

15–57   One of the most important points *vis-à-vis* an acquisition is the question of entitlement to the surplus assets. Parties must determine whether the surplus should be distributed to members or returned to the original employer who contributed them. Finucane and Buggy suggest allowing the scheme actuary to determine the transfer amount. Ideally, this should be then be agreed by the actuaries representing both parties.[52a]

The outcome of this due diligence exercise will normally be the drafting of a pension schedule to be attached to the share purchase agreement or business sale agreement.

---

[52] The trust deed may generally be amended according to the terms of the deed itself.
[52a] *op. cit.*, n.49 at p. 572.

G. Environmental Issues

15–58 Environmental issues have become increasingly important. Often an environmental consultant will be employed to conduct an environmental audit. Part of the consultants task will be to ensure compliance with environmental regulations and part of their task will be to identify potential environmental liabilities. Failure to conduct a thorough due diligence into environmental issues may subsequently prove a very costly mistake.

I. INTEGRATED POLLUTION CONTROL LICENCE

15–59 The business being acquired and the premises used must then be considered. The concept of an integrated pollution control was introduced by the Environmental Protection Agency Act 1992 as a replacement for the pre-existing separate air and water pollution licensing systems for certain activities. Section 82 of the Environmental Protection Agency Act 1992 requires any person carrying on an activity listed in the First Schedule to the Act to have an integrated pollution control licence. These activities involve certain uses and treatments of minerals, energy, metals, mineral fibres, glass, chemicals, intensive agriculture, food and drink, wood, paper, textiles and leather, fossil fuels, cement, waste, surface coatings, engines, turbines, reactors, circuits, lime and ceramics.

15–60 The purchaser should ensure that the Environmental Protection Agency ("the EPA") has granted such a licence. In granting the licence pursuant to section 83 of the Environmental Protection Agency Act 1992, the EPA would have taken into account: any relevant air or water quality management plans or waste management plans[53]; any relevant noise regulations[54]; any special control area order;[55] and any other matters related to the prevention, limitation, elimination, abatement or reduction of environmental pollution. Since the EPA may have attached conditions to the license[56], compliance with these conditions must be verified. While section 91 of the Environmental Protection Agency Act 1992 provides that the validity of the license will be unaffected by any change in ownership of the asset, the license itself may provide otherwise. In any event, the change of ownership must be notified to the EPA.

---

[53] Air Pollution Act 1987, s.46 and the Local Government (Water Pollution) Act 1977, s.15, respectively.
[54] Environmental Protection Agency Act 1992, s.106.
[55] Air Pollution Act 1987, s.39.
[56] Environmental Protection Agency Act 1992, s.84.

II. LICENSES FOR UNSCHEDULED ACTIVITIES

15–61 If the activity is not listed in the First Schedule to the Environmental Protection Agency Act 1992, separate licenses may be necessary under the Local Government (Water Pollution) Act 1977[57] and the Air Pollution Act 1987. These Acts deal with discharges from the plant into rivers or sewers and emissions into the atmosphere respectively. If licenses exist, the purchaser should ensure that the vendor has been complying with all the terms and conditions imposed.

15–62 It should be noted that where a licence already exists under the Air Pollution Act 1987, that licence enures for the benefit of the industrial plant to which it applies. Therefore, a purchaser of that plant will not have to apply for a new licence. However, licences granted under the Local Government (Water Pollution) Act 1977[58] are personal in nature. Therefore, a purchaser of the business to which they relate must apply for new licences under those sections to the relevant local authority for the area in which the business is situate.

15–63 If any explosive or dangerous substances are used in the plant, a license may be required under the Dangerous Substances Act 1972. Again, any such licence should be obtained and examined.

III. WASTE

15–64 If the plant generates waste or has generated waste within the meaning of the Waste Management Act 1996,[59] the purchaser must examine the methods uses to dispose of the waste to ensure compliance with the Act. Section 32(1) of the Waste Management Act 1996 imposes a general duty on the holder of waste designed to prevent environmental pollution. "Waste" in this context includes hazardous waste. A person is prohibited from holding, transporting, recovering or disposing of waste in a manner that causes or is likely to cause environmental pollution.[60] In addition, section 32(2) prohibits a person from transferring the control of waste to any person other than an appropriate person. An "appropriate person" is defined as a local authority, the corporation of a borough that is not a county borough, the council of an urban district or a person otherwise authorised under and in accordance with the Waste Management Act 1996 or the Environmental Protection Agency Act 1992

---

[57] As amended by the Local Government (Water Pollution)(Amendment) Act 1990.
[58] Local Government (Water Pollution)(Amendment) Act 1977, ss. 4 & 16 are concerned with the granting of licenses to discharge into water and sewers, respectively.
[59] Waste Management Act 1996, First Sched. s.4(1)(a).
[60] Waste Management Act 1996, s.32(1).

to undertake the collection, recovery or disposal of the class of waste in question. An exception to section 32(2) is provided under section 32(4) where the Minister may, by regulations:

"(a) provide that the holder of a specified class or classes of waste shall effect and maintain a policy of insurance insuring him or her to a specified extent as respects any liability on his or her part to pay damages or costs on account of injury to person or property arising from the holding by him or her of the waste,

(b) provide that on the transfer of waste, in specified circumstances, the holder of the waste shall provide to the transferee specified particulars in writing of the waste so as to enable that person to avoid a contravention of the relevant provisions of this Act,

(c) provide that subsection (2) shall not apply in specified circumstances."

Where the purchase of the assets of the company finds itself in control of waste contrary to section 32, criminal sanctions may be imposed.[61] A greater incentive perhaps to ensure that section 32 is not breached is section 32(7). This subsection provides that where a person transfers the control of waste to another person in contravention of subsection (2):

"(a) any act done or instrument made by a person to transfer title in the waste for that purpose shall not operate to transfer the title,

(b) the first-mentioned person shall, for the purposes of this Act, be deemed to be a holder, in addition to the second-mentioned person, of the waste:"

15–65 If underground storage tanks are used on the site, the purchaser should check to ensure that there are no leaks of polluting matter from the tanks. Any such leaks may result in possible liability arising under the Local Government (Water Pollution) Act 1977, the Waste Management Act 1996 and the Environmental Protection Agency Act 1992. Liability in the latter case will arise if the leaks are in breach of an integrated pollution control licence.

IV. HEALTH AND SAFETY AT WORK

15–66 Finally, the purchaser should ensure that the vendor has complied with all the relevant provisions of the Safety, Health and Welfare at Work Act 1989.

15–67 Part II of that Act sets out the general duties of employers, employees and persons concerned with workplaces such as the manufacturers of machinery and the designers of the plants. The general duty

---

[61] s.32(6). A defence to such an offence arises from carrying out an activity in accordance with a waste collection or waste licence or a licence under the Environmental Protection Agency Act 1992.

of an employer is described by section 6(1) as a duty "to ensure, so far as is reasonably practicable, the safety, health and welfare at work of all his employees". Although criminal liability is provided for a breach of section 6, no right of action in civil proceedings arises.[62] The common law duties of employers and employees are however preserved.[63]

15–68   A general obligation is also imposed on an employer to prepare a safety statement specifying the manner in which safety, health and welfare at work are to be secured at work. This statement must be based on an identification of the possible hazards and assessment of the risks to safety and health.[64] This may involve for example the preparation of safety statements in respect of the plant or the provision of adequate training of employees in the safe use of machinery.

All the responsibility does not rest, however, on the employer. An employee is required by section 9(1) of the Safety, Health and Welfare at Work Act, 1989 to take reasonable care for his own safety, health and welfare and that of any other person who may be affected by his acts or omissions while at work.

H. Third-Party Consents

15–69   The consent of third parties may be necessary to effect the transfer of shares or of the undertaking. Where an acquisition involves an aspect of competition, the consent of the Minister for Enterprise, Trade and Employment or the Competition Authority may be required.[65] In the case of acquisitions involving a credit institution, prior authorisation to the acquisition may be required from the Central Bank.[66] In the case of an acquisition involving a company listed on the Irish Stock Exchange, the Stock Exchange Listing Rules may require that the approval of shareholders be obtained.[67]

15–70   In addition to these regulatory consents, the consent of the vendor's creditors may be necessary in order to maintain the current financing arrangements. If the purchaser is acquiring the undertaking, a written agreement or assignment will be necessary to transfer creditors as they will not transfer without consent. In other cases, financial documents may have a change of control clause. Such a clause will make

---

[62] s.60(1).
[63] s.60(3).
[64] s.12.
[65] See Chap. 6, paras 6–42–6–74.
[66] See Chap. 7, paras 7–06–7–18.
[67] See Chap. 5, paras 5–33–5–47.

the obtainment of the Bank's consent a condition precedent to the passing of control. Breach of this clause would activate an immediate repayment obligation. Similarly, if the company has received grant aid in the past, the consent of the granting authority may also be required to the change in control.

I. Litigation

15–71 Apart from the obvious liabilities disclosed in the accounts, the purchaser will be anxious to ensure that no contingent liabilities exist. The purchaser should attempt to discover, for example whether any civil or criminal legislation is pending which involves the company or its directors, officers or shareholders. As well as pending litigation, the purchaser should determine whether any arbitration proceedings are imminent. Any awards not anticipated may prove extremely costly for the purchaser.

J. Insurance

15–72 The purchaser should obtain a schedule of insurance from the vendor and certificates, where applicable. The purchaser should verify that each policy is up to date and that the principles liabilities are covered. These include: employers' liability, public liability, products liability, property cover (including fire and special perils risk), motor fleet, professional indemnity, personal accident, key person assurance and pecuniary losses (including fidelity guarantee and consequential loss).

15–73 The insurance cover may be provided on an individual basis or may be part of a collective package. The following issues should be determined:

– the identity of the insurer and their associated credit rating;

– the identity of the insurance intermediary;

– the period of insurance covered;

– payment of any premiums due;

– full details of cover to include risk addresses, plant, contingencies etc.;

– restrictions on cover such as exclusions on products liability cover in the U.S. or exclusion of flood cover for certain addresses; and

– the extent to which the risk may be self insured, either through agreed policy excess or deductibles.

15–74 The purchaser should also investigate the following details to form a view on future insurance cover: the company or businesses' previous claims history, the existence of any outstanding risk control recommendations, impending legislation and the status of current outstanding claims.

K. Contracts

15–75 In the case of an acquisition of the shares of the company, all onerous and long-term contracts should be examined carefully. This will obviously also apply where the purchaser of the undertaking is acquiring the contracts. In the latter case, the contracts will need to be novated. The purchaser should identify the potential liabilities which may result under guarantees and indemnities. Similarly, agency agreements should be scrutinised for the same reason.

15–76 The purchaser should be confident that the terms and prices offered to customers in long term contracts can be maintained. In addition, the purchaser will want to ensure that continuity of supply can be assured. If the purchaser finds that the company has been offering below cost products or unsustainable terms or guarantees, the turnover figures will have been unnaturally inflated. In addition, further liabilities may result at a later stage. The purchaser should also examine the contracts with suppliers. If any special arrangements have been made with suppliers which lead to reduced costs, this could have a negative effect on future profits. For example, the vendor may have negotiated special conditions as a result of bulk buying for other companies within the Group, owning a share in the supplier or being a subsidiary of the supplier. Such favourable conditions are unlikely to continue after the acquisition. Finally, an attempt should be made to identify major customers and suppliers on whom the company is particularly dependent. The effect of the loss of any such customer or supplier on the profits of the business should be calculated.

CHAPTER 16

THE SALE AGREEMENT

16–01 Having conducted a due diligence exercise and made the decision to proceed with the acquisition, the next step for the purchaser is to prepare the sale documentation.

The first part of this Chapter will examine the contents of the sale agreement.[1] In the case of an acquisition of the shares of the company, this contract will be "a share purchase agreement". In the case of an acquisition of the undertaking from the company, the contract will be "an agreement for the sale of the business". In reality, both sale agreements are likely to refer to many of the same issues and contain similar warranties and indemnities. This contract will be drafted by the purchaser's solicitor. Other documents which may be attached to the sale agreement or incorporated therein are the tax indemnity, the pension schedule and the completion agenda. The second part of this Chapter examines the remedies available to a purchaser for breach of a term of the sale agreement or for misrepresentation. The position of collateral warranties will also be examined in this context. The vendor may attempt to limit its liability or exempt liability totally through the use of exemption or limitation clauses in the sale agreement or through the device of disclosure. The third part of the Chapter will consider the effectiveness of such devices.

A. Contents of the Sale Agreement

The following issues are likely to be included in the sale agreement:

I. DETAILS OF THE SALE

16–02 The contract will commence with the recitals which set out the particulars of the company being acquired and recite the agreement for the vendor to sell and the purchaser to buy the shares or assets. In a

---

[1] See Wine, *Buying & Selling Private Companies & Businesses* (Butterworths, 1986); Sinclair, *Warranties and Indemnities on Share and Asset Sales* (FT Law & Tax, 1996); and *Due Diligence, Disclosures and Warranties in the Corporate Acquisitions Practice*, eds. Baker and Jillson, (Graham & Trotman, 1992).

share purchase agreement, the capacity in which the shares are sold will be stated. The vendor will normally transfer shares as "beneficial owner". A statement will also be included to the effect that the shares are sold free from charges and other encumbrances. A list of the contracting parties and the other parties involved[2] and a list of the definitions of the various terms found in the agreement usually follows.

16–03   In an agreement for the sale of a business, instead of the shares being transferred the assets and liabilities will be transferred. For this reason, the agreement must provide for the vesting of each individual item in the purchaser. Stamp duty is then payable on the transfer instrument. Under section 59 of the Stamp Act 1891, a contract for the sale of any property is a conveyance on sale and is dutiable. Included within the scope of the Stamp Act 1891 are intangibles such as goodwill, debt, cash in bank, trademarks, patents and designs, Land or property outside the State are excluded[2a] as are goods, wares and merchandise. In order to limit stamp duty, the purchaser will attempt to apportion consideration between assets on which duty is payable as a conveyance on sale or under the contract itself (as a deemed conveyance on sale) and assets which are not within the scope of section 59 and on which duty is not payable. The purchaser might thus be inclined to reduce the value attributed to fixed plant and machinery and correspondingly increase the value attributable to loose plant and machinery such as stock in trade where title passes upon delivery. It would also suit the purchaser to leave creditors, debtors and cash in bank with the vendor.

16–04   The consideration may be deferred until some future specified date or it may be deferred until the happening of some event such as the achievement of a certain profit or turnover or the flotation of the company. Some form of ratchet may be agreed by the parties particularly if the target had a low net asset value. Such an "earn out" clause may for example entitle the vendor to an agreed proportion of future profit or turnover. From the vendor's perspective, the main advantage of an earn out clause is that it allows the vendor participate in the future development of the company. From the purchaser's perspective, it acts as an incentive to the vendor to ensure that the company, when sold, is in a robust and viable state. Finally, a sale agreement may include a clause providing for further payment of consideration in the event that the inherent development value of property is realised or in the event that the company is substantially more profitable than envisaged at the time of the sale. Such a clause

---

[2]   The company itself is not normally a party to a share sale agreement.
[2a]   Finance Act 1992, s.209.

would be particularly common in the case of a management buy-out. It would be particularly desirable from the vendor's perspective in circumstances where the target was likely to go public within a relatively short time of the acquisition.

16–05   Such deferred payments may lead to difficulties in ascertaining tax liabilities. For example, a conveyance on sale which involves a consideration which cannot be ascertained (which can include a deferred consideration) will be charged to stamp duty based on the market value which could be obtained from a purchaser of the property paying full consideration. It is possible however, that the Revenue Commissioners may accept a down payment based on an estimate of 90% of the duty payable on presentation of the instrument of transfer for stamping and then the balance once the consideration has been ascertained.[2b] In addition to stamp duty, Capital Gains Tax ("CGT") must be considered. In *Marren v. Ingles*[2c] the method of calculating CGT in earn-out situations was considered. It was decided that where an earn-out formula applied, it would not be clear at the time the contract was concluded whether the vendor of the shares would ever receive the consideration determined according to the earn-out formula. At such a time, it would not be possible to predict how well or how poorly the company might perform. As a result it was agreed that an expert valuer should place a value, at the time the contract was concluded, on the possible additional consideration which might be received. The shareholders would then be regarded as having disposed of the shares for CGT purposes for a sum equivalent to the aggregate of any cash element received plus the sum calculated by an expert as the market value to the shareholders of the earn-out formula at the date of the contract. It should also be noted that the possible value to the shareholders of the additional consideration payable under the earn-out formula will be regarded as a separate asset (a chose in action) for CGT purposes. Each time the shareholders receive a payment of additional consideration under the agreed formula, the shareholders will be regarded as having made a part-disposal of the asset. Therefore, the original base cost will be apportioned on each occasion that a payment is received.

[2b] Finance Act, 1991 s.104 as amended by the Finance Act, 1992 s.213. See O'Connor "Stamp Duties and Deferred Consideration including Earn-outs" (1997) *Irish Tax Review* 151, Stamp Duties Work Manual and Practices of the Revenue Commissioners (The Revenue Commissioners, 1998); O'Connor & Cahill, *The Law of Stamp Duties*, (Institute of Taxation in Ireland, 1998) Chap. 19, Shardlow, "Taxing Deferred Consideration on Corporate Sales; A New Conflict?" (1999) 20 Co. Law. 1.4.
[2c] [1980] S.T.C. 500.

II. PRECONDITIONS

16–06 The sale contract will generally be made subject to certain third party approvals. As noted in the previous Chapter, the consent to the acquisition of third parties such as financiers, the Central Bank or the Stock Exchange may be needed.[2d] As it might not be possible to obtain these consents before the contract is signed, they may be specified in the contract as a condition precedent to the transfer. Other such conditions might include the obtaining of finance, shareholder approval or the retention of licences or contracts. In addition to specifying the preconditions, the agreement will generally set out the implications of a precondition not being satisfied by the completion date.

16–07 Typically, conditions may be classified as "conditions precedent" and "conditions subsequent".[2e] A "condition precedent" was defined by Costello J. in *Dorene Ltd. v. Suedes (Ireland) Ltd.*[3] as "a condition which must be satisfied before any legally binding contract comes into operation". If a condition precedent is not met, it may prevent the contract itself coming into existence. In *Pym v. Campbell*,[4] an agreement to sell an interest in a patent to the plaintiff was conditional upon a third party approving the project. Because this approval had not been obtained, no contract was deemed to exist upon which the plaintiff could base his claim.

16–08 A condition may also be precedent to liability under a contract. In such circumstances, the contract will be deemed to have come into existence and the parties will not thus be free to withdraw from the contract pending fulfilment of the condition.[5] In *Re Application of Butler*,[6] a condition of the applicant's insurance policy required the applicant to give the insurance company written notice of any accidents as soon as practicable after any accident. Fulfilment of the conditions in the insurance policy was expressed to be "conditions precedent to any liability". Although the insurance contract was a valid contract, the Supreme Court held that the applicant was not entitled to compensation for a particular accident as he had not notified the insurance company of the accident in question. Similarly, in *Macklin & McDonald v. Graecen & Co.*,[7] the defendants agreed to sell a licence attached to a particular public

---

[2d] See Chap. 15.
[2e] Treitel, *The Law of Contract* (Sweet and Maxwell, 1995), pp. 58–62; Clark and Clarke, *Contract Cases and Materials* (Gill and Macmillan, 1994), pp. 254–258; Clark, *Contract Law in Ireland* (Roundhall, Sweet and Maxwell, 1998), pp. 198–205.
[3] [1981] I.R. 312 at 324.
[4] (1856) 6 El & Bl 370
[5] *Smith v. Butler* [1900] 1 Q.B. 694.
[6] [1970] I.R. 45.
[7] [1983] I.R. 61.

house to the plaintiffs subject to the sale of the premises to the Northern Bank being completed. The defendants did not however promise that the Northern Bank would give its permission, and the Supreme Court determined that no liability under contract could be deemed to exist. It should be noted that although the main obligations may be inoperative in such cases until the relevant condition is fulfilled, subsidiary obligations may be enforceable relating to the fulfilment of the condition. These obligation may involve simply a duty not to prevent the condition being fulfilled[8] or they may involve a duty to use reasonable efforts to bring about the fulfilment of the contract.[9]

16–09   A condition is defined as a "condition subsequent" if it provides that a previously binding contract is to determine on the occurrence of the event.[10] In *Dorene Ltd. v. Suedes (Ireland) Ltd.*, Costello J. defined such a condition as "a condition which if not fulfilled, can result in the contract ceasing to be binding".[10a] In *Thompson v. ASDA-MFI Group plc*,[11] the plaintiff was a member of a Group pension scheme and contractually entitled to exercise an option to buy shares. A condition of this option agreement, however, was that the plaintiff's employer should be a member of the Group. When the employer was sold, the Court determined that the option ceased to be exercisable.

16–10   In terms of a sale agreement, this classification may be important as it may result in a determination that no contract exists and that both parties are entitled to withdraw at any time prior to the fulfilment of the condition. This would leave the vendor free to sell to another party. Alternatively, it may lead to a determination that the parties are contractually bound but that the assets or shares are not due to be transferred until the conditions are fulfilled.

III. WARRANTIES

16–11   The term *"caveat emptor"* means "let the buyer beware". In relation to an acquisition, this means that the purchaser must take the company or business as it finds it and cannot later claim to have been unaware of the poor state of the machinery, the limited stock, the excessive debts etc. In order to ensure additional protection, the purchaser will generally seek assurances or warranties from the vendor on important matters. If these warranties are breached, the purchaser will

---

[8]   *Mackay v. Dick* (1881) 6 App. Cas.251.
[9]   *Rooney v. Byrne* [1933] I.R. 609.
[10]   *op. cit.*, n.3 at p. 324.
[10a]   *op. cit.* n.3 at p.324.
[11]   [1988] 2 All E.R. 722.

generally be entitled to compensation for any loss suffered. The purchaser may also attempt to ensure that a condition is included in the contract providing that if an event occurs which renders the information contained in the warranties or disclosure letter untrue, the purchaser should be allowed to treat itself as discharged from its obligations under the contract. Alternatively, the contract may provide that if any breach of a warranty is discovered prior to completion, rescission is allowable.

16–12   In addition to transferring the risk on the items warranted back from the purchaser to the vendor, the process of determining and agreeing warranties is useful in forcing parties to investigate the true state of affairs of the company and to deal with all the relevant issues. There may thus be a number of warranties listed, breach of which will not entitle the vendor to damages or will only entitle the purchaser to nominal damages. The inclusion of such warranties functions more as a checklist for the parties.

16–13   Warranties are made in the form of statements concerning the current state of the target's business, assets, liabilities etc. All warranties must be expressly stated by the parties in a sale agreement as none will be implied. Often, the warranties will be set out in a separate schedule attached to the sale agreement.

(1) Matters to be Warranted

16–14   In an agreement for the purchase of the shares of the company, the warranties will cover a huge range of issues any of which could have an impact upon the present or future value of the business. In an agreement for the sale of a business, the warranties will relate only to the particular assets or liabilities acquired. In certain cases, for example where consideration is slight or in an asset sale, if the transfer is very straight forward, short form warranties will be used.

One of the first issues which the vendor will be asked to warrant is the accuracy of the warranties and any other information given to the purchaser by or on behalf of the company or the vendor.

Constitution and Share Capital

16–15   A general warranty is included to the effect that the shares being transferred constitute the entire allotted and issued share capital and that they are fully paid up. Issues such as ownership of shares and the non-existence of any encumbrances, claim or options will also be warranted by the vendor.

16–16   The vendor may warrant that the copy of the memorandum and articles of association accompanying the disclosure letter is accurate and complete, that the register of members has been accurately maintained and that the share capital is correctly stated.

Records

16–17 The vendor may warrant that all necessary books, registers and records have been properly completed and maintained and that all company documents which are required to be filed with the Registrar of Companies pursuant to the Companies Acts 1963 to 1990 have been duly filed.

The Accounts

16–18 The vendor may warrant that the latest accounts are true and accurate. It is important also to obtain a warranty to the effect that no substantial changes have taken place in the business or assets of the company and that no material contracts or commitments have been entered into since the accounts were prepared which would substantially affect net assets. The vendor may also warrant that the accounts of the business have been maintained in good order and according to the company's statutory duties. Finally, a warranty may be included to the effect that the books will be transferred to the purchaser upon completion.

Land and Interests in Land

16–19 Warranties under this heading relate to the title and ownership of the property, compliance with statutory obligations, the existence of valid and sufficient insurance, the condition of the property, the availability of access and the absence of encumbrances, adverse orders or tenancies.

Where the land being acquired is leasehold rather than freehold, warranties will be required to the effect that there are no unusual or onerous provisions in the lease which would affect the purchaser's ability to use or to develop the premises or which would allow the landlord terminate the lease without due cause.

The purchaser will require a warrant to the effect that any development carried out to the company's property complies with planning legislation and building regulations and has been carried out in accordance with any conditions or requirements imposed by the relevant regulatory body.

Other Assets

16–20 The vendor may warrant that it has good title to the assets and that the assets are free from any security interests, charges or other claims or restrictions. Other warranties included under this heading may relate to: the value of stock including work in progress; the existence of complete insurance; the state of repair and condition of the machinery; the terms of any leased assets; and the validity of intellectual property. If book debts are being acquired the vendor may be asked to warrant that they are collectible.

As the value of the company will be based on the assumption that contracts with suppliers and customers will continue after the acquisition, the vendor may be required to warrant the likelihood of ongoing business with existing customers and suppliers.

Liabilities

16–21 The vendor may warrant that there are no undeclared borrowings, no undisclosed contracts, no environmental liabilities and no subsisting guarantees or indemnities. In the case of a share sale, the purchaser is advised to ensure that all transactions between the vendor and the company are completed and all debts are discharged. A clause is usually drafted in the sale agreement to the effect that the vendor will procure that all monies owing by the vendor or the directors or any other related person to the company will be discharged and that guarantees given by the company for the benefit of the these persons will be released.

16–22 The vendor may also be asked to warrant that no insolvency proceedings have been initiated by any party against the company nor have any attachment orders or distress orders been entered against any of the company's assets.

16–23 In addition the purchaser will wish to ensure that no contingent liabilities exist. In this context, the vendor may be asked to warrant that the company is not involved in any litigation or dispute and that no such litigation or dispute is imminent or likely. In addition, a warranty will be sought to the effect that the company is not liable to make payments under any existing environmental or employment legislation. The vendor will be required to warrant that no investigations have been initiated under relevant legislation such as the Companies Acts 1963–1990 or the Competition Act 1991 which may give rise to future liability.

Employees

16–24 Warranties will be included to deal with employees, their terms of employment, their pension rights, the existence of any claims by the employees, the likelihood of any industrial disputes and the terms of any collective agreements. The vendor may, for example, warrant that the pension scheme is adequately funded, that the pension scheme is an exempt approved scheme and that all contributions due have been paid. A warranty should be included to the effect that all golden handshake agreements have been disclosed and that no redundancy payments are outstanding. The purchaser will seek a warranty to the effect that the company has complied with its statutory and contractual obligations. In addition, it would be important to ensure that the company has complied with any non-contractual obligation contained in collective agreements or any codes of conduct or best practice. Again, this is relevant in ensuring that the company is not subject to any unanticipated litigation in the future. The importance of having a clear warranty in respect of pension funding was highlighted recently in the action taken by UPM Kymmene Corporation, a Finnish company against BWG Limited. UPM claimed that a shortfall of £2.4 million existed in relation to the funding of the pension schemes in three companies acquired from BWG in 1981. UPM claimed that BWG warranted that the pension schemes of the three companies were fully funded and that it was entitled to be indemnified in respect of all payments it made in eliminating the shortfall. It argued that this shortfall would have been worth £17 million at 1998 investment value if it had been properly invested since 1981. Laffoy J. held that the plaintiff had not established a breach of warranty and that no assurances were given to UPM that the pension schemes were fully funded. It was noted that the purchaser had not retained an actuary or pension adviser in this jurisdiction and that the actuarial advice received by BWG indicated that the schemes were grossly underfunded.[11a]

Taxation

16–25   The vendor may warrant that the last accounts made full provision for all tax due and that all tax returns and payments due were made. Disclosure will normally be made against these warranties.[11b]

Disclosure

16–26   The vendor may be required to provide a warranty as to the accuracy of the disclosed information. This will be discussed further in paragraph 16–100–16–110.

General

16–27   The vendor may warrant that the affairs of the company were not conducted in a manner prejudicial to minorities, that there are no agency agreements or agreements restricting business and that the business has been conducted properly.

[11a] Unreported, High Court, Laffoy J., June 11, 1999 (*The Irish Times,* June 12, 1999).
[11b] For an excellent description of specific tax warranties which might be included, see Bohan "Buying a Business – Legal and Taxation Aspects: Part 2" (1998) *CLP* 10.

(2) Liability Under a Warranty

16–28   Usually, there will be a maximum amount specified in the agreement which can be claimed under a warranty. This tends to be the consideration paid for the target's shares. To avoid wasting time later on, a *de minimis* level should also be specified. A clause may be inserted at the purchaser's request giving the purchaser the option of choosing between the nominal measures of damages for breach of a contractual warranty and an indemnity basis.

(3) Duration of a Warranty

16–29   Normally, a time limit will be specified for suing under a warranty. This will usually be slightly shorter than the statutory limitation period. Under the Statute of Limitations 1957 and 1991, the time limit for actions relating to contract is six years from the breach, or twelve years if the contract is under seal. Claims under general warranties should normally become apparent on the audit following completion. The agreement will normally thus provide that the vendor should be notified and the claim proceeded with within a certain time.

(4) Joint and Several Liability

16–30   Where there is more than one shareholder selling shares under an agreement for the sale of the shares of a company, the liability for each shareholder under the contract will usually be expressed to be joint and several. Thus, whatever rights of contribution each share-holder will have against the other, the purchaser will be able to choose which shareholder to sue for the total liability under the contract. The vendor will generally provide in a separate agreement for rights of contribution between shareholders where there is not total identity between the vendors and the persons who give the warranties. In this way, vendors who are minority shareholders and who have not participated in management may attempt to limit their liability. They may give no warranties or they may give warranties as to the title of their shares only.

(5) Extent of the Warranty

16–31   The warranties may be absolute or just to the extent of the vendor's knowledge. The vendor will attempt to limit its liability by stating "so far as the seller is aware" after each warranty. Obviously, the purchaser will resist this. The warranties may also be limited by disclosure. In this way, liability will be excluded for all the matters disclosed in writing on or before the exchange of contract. This is done by including a clause in the agreement to the effect that the warranties are to apply "save as set out in the disclosure letter".[12] A disclosure letter will then list certain details in relation to warranted items. The disclosure letter may be attached as a schedule to the sale agreement or it may constitute a separate letter. In the latter case, the letter is normally addressed by the vendor's solicitors to the purchaser's solicitors.[13]

16–32 The vendor will attempt to disclose as many potentially controversial items as possible in order to reduce its liability under the warranties. The general principle is that a purchaser who enters into the agreement in full knowledge of the existence of certain issues cannot later claim loss incurred as a result of the breach. The extent to which disclosures reduce liability will depend upon the degree of accuracy and the specific nature of such disclosure. The effect of disclosure and any other attempted limitations on the warranties will be considered in Part C of this Chapter.

(6) Warrantor's Rights

16–33 From a Purchaser's point of view, it would not be satisfactory if, having successfully sued the warrantor, the warrantor was then in a position to claim to have been misled by a group company or its employees and commence legal action. Accordingly, the Dublin Solicitors Bar Association has recommended including the following clause in the sale agreement containing a waiver of such right of action:

> "None of the information supplied by any Group Company or its professional advisers to the Warrantor or his agents, representatives or advisers in connection with the Warranties and the contents of the Disclosure Letter, the Deed of Indemnity or otherwise in relation to the business or affairs of any Group Company, shall be deemed a representation, warranty or guarantee of its accuracy by the Group Company to the Warrantor and the Warrantor waives any claims against the Group Company (and its employees and agents) which he might otherwise have in respect of it."

(7) Management Buy-Outs

16–34 A difficulty may arise when it comes to agreeing the warranties to be included in a sale agreement in relation to the acquisition by management of a private company. Because of the separation of the ownership and control, the management are likely to be in a better position than the owners to determine the financial affairs of the

---

[12] See below paras 60–100–60–110.
[13] Where the disclosure letter is a separate letter, Sinclair suggests that it will not form part of the sale agreement for the purposes of registration if the disclosures are of a routine nature and are not likely to render the sale agreement misleading on its face (*op. cit.*, above, n.1, 239–240).

company and the veracity and accuracy of the financial statements. Yet, the owners are being asked to give them warranties on these issues. One suggestion as to the correct way to proceed in such cases is to divide the normal warranties into two broad categories:

- warranties which relate to matters independent of the activities of management; and

- warranties which relate to issues which would or should be the concern of management.[14]

The vendors would not then give warranties of the second category. This would not always be an easy distinction to make. For example while warranties in respect of bank balances clearly fall into the second category and warranties in respect of the title of the vendor to the shares into the first, the classification of warranties to the effect that the title to assets are free of charges is less clear.

(8) Sub-Purchasers

16–35 The purchaser may dispose of the undertaking or the shares to a new purchaser before a breach of a warranty becomes apparent. If, the purchaser has itself given warranties to the new purchaser, it will be liable to that new purchaser for the breach of those warranties and will in turn recover its losses from the original vendor. If, however, it has not itself provided any warranties to the new purchaser, the purchaser may not be able to claim damages as it will not have suffered any loss as a result of the breach. The doctrine of Privity of Contract provides that only a party to a contract may enforce rights under that contract.[15] The ability of a promisee to recover damages for losses sustained by a third party was denied in *Woodar Investment Development Ltd. v. Wimpey Construction UK Ltd.*[16] The effect of this case would be to prohibit a purchaser from suing a vendor for loss suffered by a third party to whom the purchaser has sold the company or the business acquired.

16–36 Certain decisions have considered the right of a promisee to recover more than nominal damages in respect of a third party's loss in other circumstances. In *Dunlop v Lambert*,[16a] the House of Lords held that the consignor of goods lost at sea could recover substantial damages even though the goods had become the property of the consignee by the time

---

[14] Sinclair, *op. cit.*, above, n.1, 12–13.
[15] *Dunlop Pneumatic Tyre Co. Ltd v. Selfridge & Co. Ltd* [1915] A.C. 847, *Murphy v. Bower* (1868) I.R. 2 C.L. 506. See generally Treitel, *op. cit.*, n.2e, Chap. 15; Clark and Clarke, *op. cit.*, n.2e, Chap. 15; and Clark, *op. cit.*, n.2e, Chap. 17.
[16] [1980] 1 All E.R. 571.
[16a] (1839) 6 C.L. & F. 600.

they were lost. The special contract which existed between the carrier and the consignor superseded the necessity of showing the ownership in the goods. This rule was confirmed in *The Albazero*[16b] as applying only where the contracts do not contemplate that the carrier will enter into separate contract with the eventual owner. This rule was applied to a building contract in the case of *St Martins Property Corporation Ltd. v. Sir Robert McAlpine Ltd.*,[17] where the plaintiffs were property developers who entered into a building contract with the defendant. In due course, they sold the development and assigned the building contract. The assignment was ineffective, however, as they had not obtained the defendant's consent. Later when defects were found in the construction, the plaintiffs sued for damages for the benefit of their assignees. The defendants argued that they were only entitled to nominal damages because they themselves had suffered no loss. Lord Browne-Wilkinson stated that a case like this fell within the rationale of the exception to the general rule that a plaintiff can only recover damages for its own loss.

> "The contract was for a large development of property which, to the knowledge of both Corporation and McAlpine, was going to be occupied, and possibly purchased, by third parties and not by Corporation itself. Therefore it could be foreseen that damage caused by a breach would cause loss to a later owner and not merely to the original contracting party, Corporation. As in contracts for the carriage of goods by land, there would be no automatic vesting in the occupier or owners of the property for the time being who sustained the loss of any right of suit against McAlpine. On the contrary, McAlpine had specifically contracted that the rights of action under the building contract could not without McAlpine's consent be transferred to third parties who became owners or occupiers and might suffer loss. In such a case, it seems to me proper, as in the case of the carriage of goods by land, to treat the parties as having entered into the contract on the footing that Corporation would be entitled to enforce contractual rights for the benefit of those who suffered from defective performance but who, under the terms of the contract, could not acquire any right to hold McAlpine liable for breach. It is truly a case in which the rule provides 'a remedy where no other would be available to a person sustaining loss which under a rational legal system ought to be compensated by the person who has caused it'[18]."[19]

The rule in *Dunlop v. Lambert* was also applied in the context of a building contract by the Court of Appeal in *Darlington BC v. Wiltshier Northern Ltd.*[19a] Unlike the St. Martins case where the plaintiff held a

[16b] [1977] A.C. 774.
[17] [1994] 1 A.C. 85. *Sub. nom. Linden Gardens Trust Ltd. v. Lenesta Shidge Disposals Ltd.*
[18] *The Albazero* [1977] A.C. 774 *per* Lord Diplock at 847.
[19] *op. cit.*, n.17 at 114–115.
[19a] [1995] 1 W.L.R. 68.

proprietary interest in the land at the date of the building contract, the employer in this case merely possessed a financial interest in the project and had agreed to assign all his rights and cause of action to the plaintiff which owned the land. The *St. Martins* decision was applied more recently by the Court of Appeal in *Alfred McAlpine Construction Ltd. v. Panatown Ltd.*[19b] In this case, the rationale for the rule in *Dunlop v. Lambert* was described by the Court as "contract-based" and it were stated that the promisees right to substantial damages arose because the parties to the contract had intended or, at the least, contemplated that such a right should exist. The intentions of the parties in this case were ascertained from the terms of the contract and the circumstances in which it was made in accordance with the general principles of the law of contract. Evans L.J. noted that the result of this case could be described either as an exception to the general rule that a plaintiff could not recover damages in respect of another person's loss or as "an equivalent to saying that the general rule can be modified by agreement, express or implied, between the parties concerned". The Court left open the question as to whether a similar contract-based approach to that in *Dunlop v. Lambert* could be adopted in other kinds of cases.

16–37 The purchaser may seek to avoid any difficulties with the doctrine of Privity by providing in the sale agreement that the original warranties enure for the benefit of any new purchaser. A clause providing that the benefit of the warranties and indemnities are assignable where any of the shares are sold or transferred avoids the problem of privity because an exception to the doctrine of privity exists where the benefit of a contract is assigned to a third party.[20] In such a case, the new purchaser, the assignee, may seek damages from the original vendor. The consent of the vendor to such an assignment is not generally required, although it must normally be notified of the transaction. In *Darlington Borough Council v. Wiltshier Northern Ltd.*,[21] a clause in a building contract allowed the third party the right to call for an assignment of such rights and this was deemed effective by the Court of Appeal. In this case, both parties to the contract were aware that the employer entered into the contract for the benefit of the third party and it was deemed foreseeable that damages caused by a breach would cause loss to the third party. Whilst accepting the *Woodar* decision as correct, the Court of Appeal emphasised the exception to the general rule recognised in that case where a party enters a contract as an agent or trustee for a third party who may

---

[19b] (1998) 58 Con. L.R. 47. See Coote, "More Light on *Dunlop v. Lambert*" 57 C.L.J. 250. In the UK, following a Law Commission Report (LawCom No. 242 (1996)), the Contracts (Rights of Third Parties) Bill, 1999 has been introduced. This bill allows third parties enforce contracts in certain specified circumstances.

[20] It should be noted that although chooses in action are not assignable at common law, they are assignable in equity.

[21] *op. cit.*, n.19a.

enforce the contract as the beneficiary. As was evident in the *St. Martins* case, to avoid this assignment, however, the vendor can include a clause in the original agreement prohibiting the purchaser from assigning those rights absolutely or prohibiting it from assigning them without consent. If a contract expressly provides that the rights arising under it (including the warranties) shall not be assigned, a purported assignment of such rights will amount to a breach of that contract and will be ineffective.[22]

IV. INDEMNITIES

16–38   The obligation to pay only arises in respect of warranties if there has been a breach of a duty imposed by law or by contract. In such a case, the purchaser is entitled to recover for any loss of bargain suffered as a result of the breach. In the case of an indemnity, liability arises not because of the breach but because the agreement provides that the vendor will be responsible for any loss incurred as a result of any matter arising in respect of the indemnity in question. This allows the purchaser to recover compensation for costs and expenses incurred by it in defending a successful claim as well as the claim itself. A further advantage is that while liability under a warranty may be affected by the purchaser's knowledge that the warranty is incorrect,[23] knowledge is not generally relevant to liabiltiy under an indemnity. As a result, the purchaser will attempt to include as many matters as possible in the agreement in the form of an indemnity. To limit liability, the vendor will typically attempt to ensure that the disclosures operate to qualify this deed. Such a restriction will clearly be opposed by the purchaser.

16–38A   The vendor should be asked to give an indemnity against any tax liabilities or clawback of tax reliefs resulting from any transaction before the completion date. A separate deed of indemnity will generally be drawn up for this purpose. Liabilities disclosed in the most recent accounts are usually excluded from the scope of the indemnity. A particular tax liability may be covered both by warranties and by indemnities. For this reason, it is common for the sale agreement to stipulate which claim should take priority. Where a tax warranty is breached, the damages available are measured by reference to the difference in the value of the shares as a result of the breach. Where a tax indemnity is given, the purchaser may claim compensation for the depletion of the company's net assets and all their associated costs. From the purchaser's perspective, it is thus more beneficial if liability arises under the indemnity.

---

[22] *Helstan Securities Ltd v. Hertfordshire CC* [1978] 3 All E.R. 262.
[23] See above paras 16–31–16–32.

16–39 In the case of an acquisition of the shares of the target, the purchaser will generally require that the indemnities are given in the form of covenants for the benefit of the purchaser as well as indemnities for the target. In the case of the sale of the business however, the purchaser does not take on the tax liabilities of the vendor company and tax indemnities in favour of the purchaser are not thus necessary.

A vendor's liability under a deed of indemnity is governed by the terms of the deed itself. These terms will be construed *contra proferens*.

Where the indemnities belong to the company acquired, they will remain unaffected if the company is re-sold. For this reason, the vendor may attempt to include a clause providing that the indemnity lapses if the target is re-sold.

V. RESTRICTIVE COVENANTS

16–40 It is not unusual to put a restrictive covenant in the sale agreement to the effect that the vendor will not compete with the company or business acquired following the acquisition. One obvious form of competition post acquisition would be for the vendor to establish a business making the same goods or providing the same service in competition with his former business or company. The vendor may even attempt to solicit its former customers or solicit its former employees as staff for its new business. In most types of business, goodwill would be unsaleable if the new purchaser could not place some restrictions on the vendor and could not enforce these obligations.

(1) Common Law

16–41 The traditional common law approach was that restraints of trade were contrary to public policy and therefore void. However, in *Nordenfelt v. Maxim Nordenfelt Guns and Ammunition* Co.[24] Lord MacNaghten noted that:

> "It is a sufficient justification, and indeed it is the only justification, if the restriction is reasonable - reasonable, that is, in reference to the interests of the parties concerned and reasonable in reference to the interests of the public, so framed and so guarded as to afford adequate protection to the party in whose favour it is imposed, while at the same time it is in no way injurious to the public".[25]

In recent times, the courts have tended to focus attention more on the reasonableness of the restrain *inter partes* rather than the public interest.[26]

---

[24] [1894] A.C. 535.
[25] *ibid.* at 565.
[26] *Esso Petroleum Co. Ltd v. Harpers Garage (Stourport) Ltd* [1968] A.C. 269.

16–42   Restraints of trade in sale agreements have been viewed by the Courts with less suspicion than those set out in ordinary employment contracts. In *John Orr Ltd. v. John Orr*,[27] Costello J. stated:

> "Greater freedom of contract is allowable in a covenant entered into between the seller and the buyer of the business than in the case of one entered into between an employer and an employee."[28]

In a contract for the sale of a business, the courts have accepted that interests exist in respect of the trade secrets, technical know-how and customer connections acquired which must be protected. However, the clauses used to protect these interests must also be reasonable and must not give excessive protection. Reasonableness will be judged in terms of the duration of the restraint, the geographic area covered by the restraint and the scope of the restraint. In *British Reinforced Concrete Engineering Co v. Schieff*,[29] Younger J. stated:

> "It is the business sold which is the legitimate subject of protection, and it is for its protection in the hands of the purchaser, and for its protection only, that the vendors restrictive covenant can be legitimately exacted . . . This covenant . . . must be judged by reference to the goodwill of the business sold, and so judged it is far wider than is necessary for the reasonable protection of the plaintiffs."[30]

In this case, the owners of a small business which supplied steel reinforcements for concrete roads, sold the business to a large company which made and supplied similar products to a bigger market. A three year non-competition clause on the manufacture and sale of reinforcements in any part of the UK was incorporated in the contract. The Court held that this clause was excessive on three counts. Firstly, it involved a restriction on manufacturing which was not within the scope of the vendors activities. Secondly, the clause also applied to the engagement of the vendors as mere servants with a rival. Finally, the geographic coverage was excessive as it extended throughout the UK, well beyond the area served by the vendor.

(2) Competition Act 1991

16–43   The Competition Act 1991[31] ("the 1991 Act") has largely superseded the common law in this area. Section 4(1) of the Act prohibits "all agreements between undertakings, decisions by associations of undertakings and concerted practices which have as their object or effect the

---

[27]   [1987] I.L.R.M. 702.
[28]   *ibid*. at 704
[29]   [1921] 2 Ch. 563.
[30]   *ibid*. at 574.
[31]   As amended by the Competition (Amendment) Act 1996.

prevention, restriction, or distortion of competition in trade in any goods or services in the State or in any part of the State". A restrictive covenant in a sale agreement restricting the vendors actions could, in certain circumstances, clearly be seen to be anti-competitive.

16–44 As noted in Chapter 6,[31a] the Competition Authority has stated that whilst mergers fall within the scope of section 4(1) of the 1991 Act, in many cases a merger or the sale of a business will not have any adverse effect on competition and so will not contravene the prohibition on anti-competitive agreements contained in section 4(1). In December 1997, the Competition Authority issued a certificate for Merger and/or Sale of Business Agreements ("the category certificate") defining the circumstances in which an agreement for a merger or sale of a business will not prevent, restrict or distort competition. The objective of such a certificate is to assist businesses and to reduce the need to notify agreements which are not anti-competitive.

(a) Restrictions on the Vendor Competing and Soliciting Employees or Customers

16–45 Article 4(a) of the category certificate provides that the certificate does not apply to a merger or sale of a business agreement which involves a post-sale restriction on the vendors competing with the purchaser unless the agreements are of a specific type. To benefit from the certificate, the agreement must include:

– the sale of the goodwill of the business; and

– the restriction on the vendor competing, soliciting customers, soliciting employees and/or doing any other things in competition with the purchaser must not:

  (a) exceed two years from the date of completion of the sale;

  (b) apply to any location outside the territory where the products concerned were manufactured, purchased or sold by the vendor at the time of the agreement; and

  (c) apply to goods or services other than those manufactured, purchased or sold by the vendor at the time of the agreement.

16–46 The first Competition Authority decision arose from the *Nallen & O'Toole (Belmullet)* case.[32] This case involved an agreement between the vendor and purchaser for the sale of an interest in a business in

---

[31a] See Chap. 6, para. 6–74 *et seq.*
[32] Competition Authority Decision No. 1 (April 2, 1992).

which they had both previously been partners. The vendor agreed not to engage in the business concerned within 20 miles of Belmullet for a period of three years, and also agreed not to, directly or indirectly, solicit any of the business. A certificate was requested under section 4(4) of the 1991 Act to the effect that the agreement was not in breach of section 4(1). The Competition Authority maintained that the agreement would not prevent, restrict or distort competition as it involved no reduction in actual numbers of competitors in the market, and did not reduce the threat of potential competition within the market in question. It stated that such an agreement is not a breach of section 4(1) once the restrictions are limited in terms of time, geographical coverage, and subject matter to those which are necessary to secure the adequate transfer of the goodwill. The Competition Authority accepted that such an agreement was essential for the transfer of goodwill to a purchaser. In making this decision, the Competition Authority referred to the guidelines set out by the E.U. Commission in the *Nutricia* case[33] where it indicated that among the factors to be taken into account in evaluating the duration of such clauses were:

"(I) how frequently consumers in the relevant market change brands and type (in relation to the degree of brand loyalty shown by them); and

(II) for how long, after the sale of the business, the seller, without a restrictive clause, would be able to make a successful comeback to the market and regain his old customers."

Finally, the Competition Authority noted that the area covered as a rule should be the market where the products concerned were manufactured, purchased or sold by the vendor at the time of the sale. Similarly, the market should be limited in terms of subject matter – the restraint should apply only to the line of business in which the vendor was previously engaged. The Authority indicated that a two year time period would normally be adequate for restrictions on dealing with or soliciting customers or employing or soliciting employees provided that the restrictions apply only to parties which have been customers of the firm at the time of the agreement or in the previous two years and apply only in respect of the business previously carried out by the vendor.

16–47 In *Woodchester Bank/UDT Bank*,[34] the Competition Authority accepted a three year non-solicitation restraint in respect of any

---

[33] Case 83/670 Nutricia/de Rooij and Nutricia/Zuid Hollandse Conservenfabriek (O.J. L376/22) and Case 42/84 *Remia BV and Verenigde Bedrijven Nutricia NV v. Commission* [1985] E.C.R. 2545.

[34] Competition Authority, Decision No. 6 (August 4, 1992).

customers or suppliers who were customers or suppliers in the 12 months prior to the transfer of the business as necessary in order to ensure the complete and effective transfer of the goodwill of the business. A three year non-solicitation of former employees clause was also deemed acceptable. In that case however, it was specifically provided that the clause would not prevent employees offering their services to the vendor or responding to non-directed job advertisements placed by the vendor. Nor would it prevent the vendor hiring employees who had been discharged by the new purchaser. This suggests that a prohibition on active recruitment is acceptable.

(b) Restrictions on the Vendor Competing, Soliciting Employees or Customers Where the Business Involves the Use of "Technical Know-How"

16–48 Notwithstanding Article 4(a) however, Article 4(b) of the category certificate provides that the certificate will apply to a merger or sale of business agreement which involves a post-sale restriction on the vendor's competing with the purchaser or soliciting customers for up to a maximum of five years from the date of completion where the business involves the use of "technical know-how". This latter term is defined in Article 4(a) as "a body of technical information that is secret, substantial and identified in an appropriate form". The restriction must, however, cease to apply once the know-how is in the public domain.

16–49 In *ACT/Kindle*,[35] the Competition Authority considered a three year non-compete restraint imposed on the vendors of Kindle's business by the purchaser, a UK software solutions company, which did not compete with Kindle in Ireland. Kindle's main business was the development and sale of software packages for banks and financial services companies. The Competition Authority accepted that the vendors, who were executives of Kindle, possessed technical know-how which justified the restraint. In *Phil Fortune/Budget Travel Limited*,[36] the Competition Authority emphasised that technical know-how does not include knowledge concerning a particular line of business. In that case, the Competition Authority held that confidential information about the business being transferred, while important as part of the value of the business, becomes eroded in value over time. Article 4(b) of the category certificate expressly provides that knowledge concerning a particular line of business is not included in the definition of technical know-how.

---

[35] Competition Authority, Decision No. 8 (August 4, 1992).
[36] Competition Authority, Decision No. 9 (September 14, 1992).

(c) Restrictions on the Vendor Disclosing Confidential Information

16–50 Article 4(c) of the category certificate provides that the certificate will apply to agreements which include restrictions on the vendor using or disclosing confidential information regarding the business for an unlimited period of time. The Competition Authority has pointed out that a restriction on the use or disclosure of such information for an unlimited period of time would not normally contravene the 1991 Act. An exception would exist where it could be shown that such a restraint would have the effect of preventing the vendor re-entering the market once a legitimate non-compete provision had expired.

16–51 In the Competition Authority's view, an unlimited restriction on the vendor using or disclosing confidential information is not acceptable where the information consists of technical know-how. In such cases, the vendor would clearly be at a disadvantage in re-entering the market if this know-how could not be utilised. In *ACT/Kindle*,[37] the Competition Authority also considered a clause restricting the disclosure or use of technical know-how for five years. This was accepted as valid by the Competition Authority which relied on the views expressed by the E.C. Commission in *Reuter/BASF* to the effect that "in no circumstances may an obligation to keep know-how secret from third parties, imposed on the transfer of an undertaking, be used to prevent the transferor, after the expiry of the reasonable term of a non-competition clause, from competing with the transferee by means of new and further developments of such know-how."[37a] In drawing the distinction between the know-how existing at the time of the sale and new or further developments of the know-how, the Commission indicated that a longer non-compete clause could apply in respect of the existing know-how. For this reason, Article 4(c) also provides that the certificate will not apply to an agreement which includes a restriction on the vendor using or disclosing technical know-how for a period exceeding five years. The Competition Authority in *ACT/Kindle* has stated, however, that the know-how must be substantial as a lengthy period of protection following a sale is not justified for worthless and trivial know-how. It also stated that the know-how must be "described or recorded" in such a manner as to make it possible to verify that the information is secret and substantial.

(d) Restrictions on a Vendor Still Engaged in the Business

16–52 In many cases, the vendor will remain engaged in the business as a shareholder, director or employee. The Competition Authority has

---

[37] Competition Authority, Decision No. 8 (September 4, 1992).
[37a] 76/743 (O.J. L254/40).

stated that in such cases, a restriction on the vendor of the business competing with the business or soliciting customers for the period of his continuing engagement with the company does not contravene the 1991 Act. Because of the longer restraint on competition permissible in such circumstances, the Competition Authority will scrutinise the arrangement carefully to ensure that it is not an artificial construction designed specifically for this purpose.

16–53   Article 5 of the category certificate provides that:

"(a) This certificate shall apply where, following completion, the vendor remains engaged in the business as a shareholder, director or employee and is prevented from competing with the business, soliciting customers and/or employees of the business for so long as s/he remains engaged in the business whether as a shareholder, director or employee.

(b) This certificate shall also apply where a vendor, who has retained a shareholding of not less than 10 per cent in the business following completion of the sale agreement, is prevented from competing with the business, soliciting customers and/or employees of the business for a period of up to two years from the date of any future sale of such shares."

16–54   The Competition Authority has indicated that where the vendor remains merely as a passive shareholder or holds the shareholding for purely investment purposes, the restriction would not be justified. In particular, it will not be justified if the vendor retains less than 10 per cent of the shares in the company and is not otherwise engaged in the firm whether as a director, employee or in any other capacity. However, where the vendor held more than 10 per cent and subsequently disposes of his shares, the Authority has opined that restrictions on competing with the business and/or soliciting customers or employees do not contravene the Competition Act provided that they:

– are for a maximum period of two years from the date of such sale;

– apply only to parties which have been customers of the firm at the time of the agreement or in the previous two years; and

– apply only in respect of the business previously carried on by the vendor.

Where the vendor of a business remains solely as a director or employee, a restriction on competing with the business following cessation of employment is, in the Competition Authority's opinion anti-competitive. A restriction on soliciting customers of the business for up to one year after cessation of employment is not however anti-competitive.[38]

---

[38] The actuarial assumptions are often set out separately in an actuary's letter.

VI. THE PENSION SCHEDULE

16–55   As noted in the previous Chapter, a myriad of important issues must be agreed concerning the company's or undertakings' pension arrangements prior to the acquisition. For this reason, a pension schedule is normally attached to the sale agreement.

Where there is a defined benefit scheme and where a transfer payment is to be made, the parties will have to agree: the details of how the pension scheme assets and liabilities will be valued, the underlying actuarial assumptions forming the basis of the calculations[38a] and the arrangements relating to the payment of the balancing sum where the scheme is in surplus or in deficit.

16–56   The sale and purchase agreement usually provides for warranties by both parties relating to pension arrangements.[39] Typically the vendor is required to warrant: that a defined benefit scheme is properly funded, that no pension promises have been made to employees which are not funded, that payment of contributions are accurate and up to date, that the scheme is exempt approved by the Revenue Commissioners, that the latest actuarial report is accurate, that no dispute or litigation is pending, that the Pension Act 1990 requirements have been met and that the scheme does not discriminate against the beneficiaries on grounds of sex. Following on from the study of the trust deeds during the due diligence exercise, the vendor may be asked to warrant that the trustees of the pension scheme will take certain action. Such action would include apportioning funds and transferring the amount agreed by the vendor and purchaser. Difficulties may arise if the trust deed documentation requires that the transfer amounts be determined by the trustee's on the advice of their own actuary. In such a case, the vendor may be asked to undertake to make payment out of its own resources if there is a disparity between the transfer value made by the trustees and the amount agreed by the vendor and purchaser.

16–57   The pension schedule should also address the transitional arrangements which apply. This is particularly likely in the transfer of part of a group scheme. The purchaser may, for example, wish the employees to continue to participate in the vendor's group scheme for a limited period after the acquisition until it organises the transfer arrangements. In such cases, the position of employees who joined the scheme after the acquisition but before the transfer would have to be determined.

[38a] Competition Authority, Decision No. 489, Certificates in Respect of Agreements Involving a Merger and/or Sale of Business, Explanatory Note, para. 37.

[39] For a detailed examination of the warranties in share purchase agreement, see Finucane & Buggy, *Irish Pensions Law and Practice* (Oak Tree Press, 1996), pp. 575–580.

VII. CHOICE OF LAW CLAUSE

16–58   A choice of law clause will generally be included in the agreement to the effect that Irish law applies in the event of any dispute. This is particular important where one of the parties is resident abroad or, in the case of a company, incorporated abroad or where all or part of the property is located abroad. Typically, the parties will also include a choice of jurisdiction clause to the effect that any disputes will be settled by the Irish Courts.

16–59   If no such choice of law clause is included in the contract, the Contractual Obligations (Applicable Law) Act 1991 applies. This Act implements the Convention on the Law applicable to Contractual Obligations ("the Rome Convention") which establishes uniform choice of law rules for contractual obligations in E.U. The Rome Convention will apply irrespective of whether either party to the contract is domiciled or resident in a Member State. It is sufficient in this respect that the dispute is tried in a Contracting State to the Convention. The basic rule of the Rome Convention is that parties are free to choose the applicable law to govern a contract.[40] However Article 1(2) of the Convention provides that the rules of the Convention will not apply to certain classes of agreement including arbitration agreements, obligations arising from negotiable instruments and the constitution of trusts. Also excluded by virtue of Article 1(2)(e) are "questions governed by the law of companies and other bodies corporate or unincorporate such as the creation, by registration or otherwise, legal capactity, internal organisation or winding up of companies and other bodies corporate or unincorporate and the personal liability of officers and members as such for the obligations of the company or body". The Rome Convention then sets out the circumstances in which the courts may override the parties' choice of law.[41] To the extent that the law applicable to the contract has not been chosen by the parties, the contract is to be governed by the law of the country with which it is most "closely connected".[41a] Certain presumptions are set out to aid the court in its determination of the country with the closest connection. Where the company being acquired is an Irish registered company or where the undertaking being acquired is located in Ireland, Irish law is likely to be applied.

---

[40]   Article 3 of the Rome Convention.
[41]   For example, Article 5 of the Rome Convention provides that a choice of law clause may not be effective in a consumer contract where it deprives the consumer of the protection afforded to him by the mandatory rules of law of the country in which ⊢ ⌐ is habitually resident.
[41a]   Article 4 of the Rome Convention.

VIII. DISPUTE RESOLUTION CLAUSES

16–60   A dispute resolution clause will normally be included in the sale agreement. Such a clause allows the parties to agree in advance an alternative forum to the courts for settling any disputes which arise in connection with the agreement. Generally, the parties will agree to refer the matter to arbitration. This may ultimately prove to be a speedier and less expensive solution to any ensuing difficulties. The agreement may refer to specific and agreed arbitrators.

IX. COMPLETION OBLIGATIONS

16–61   Normally, the completion of the contract does not take place simultaneously with the exchange of contracts. For this reason, a clause will be included in the contract whereby the purchaser agrees to buy and the seller agrees to sell the shares or the business on an agreed future date.

Restrictions may then need to be imposed on the way the company can be managed between contract and completion. Consent will generally be necessary for any material or unusual steps. For example, the company may be precluded from entering new contracts which are not in the usual course of business or from making large acquisitions or disposals without the purchaser's prior consent. The purpose of such restrictions is to ensure that the business eventually acquired is the same as that assessed by the purchaser in the due diligence exercise. The concern is that the vendor, having agreed a price, might make changes to withdraw value from the business either deliberately or as a result of apathy. Such changes could have a detrimental affect on the future profitability of the company.

16–62   In addition to requiring consent, warranties may be used to safeguard the purchaser's interests during this time. The vendor will often be asked to warrant that between the balance sheet date and the completion date: the overall financial position of the company will not have changed adversely in any material way, allowing for normal trade fluctuations; there will have been no material adverse change in the overall value of the net assets of the company on the basis of a valuation adopted in the balance sheet, allowing for normal trade fluctuations; and the business of the company will have been carried on in a similar manner as theretofore.

16–63   On a conveyance of land, in the absence of an agreement to the contrary, all terms of the contract of sale are deemed to be merged in the conveyance upon completion. To avoid the court applying a similar rule to the transfer of shares, a term may be incorporated into the contract to the effect that insofar as any term shall not be performed at completion, it shall remain in full force and effect. The main terms which will be outstanding at that stage will be the vendors warranties.

X. CONSOLIDATION OF AGREEMENTS

16–64 In order to ensure that the sale agreement and the deed of indemnity take priority over any previous agreements and are not joined to any previous agreement, a clause is generally inserted in the contract to the effect that the sale agreement and the deed of indemnity "supersede, cancel and replace" any previous agreements between the parties on this issue.

B. Remedies

I. BREACH OF A CONTRACTUAL OBLIGATION

16–65 Where an express or implied term of a contract is breached, the plaintiff will be entitled to initiate an action for breach of contract.

(1) Express Terms

16–66 Express terms in a contract may be classified as conditions, warranties or innominate terms. The precise classification of the terms is important in the context of the remedies available for their breach. The term "condition" in this context refers to a term which is regarded by the parties as essential, any breach of which allows the innocent party to treat itself as discharged from further performance and to claim damages. A "warranty" is a less important term, breach of which allows the innocent party merely to claim damages. The test for determining whether a term is a condition or a warranty is to determine, in the light of the surrounding circumstances, whether the parties intended the term to be treated as a condition or as a warranty.[42] Where the parties have expressly and clearly labelled a term as a condition or a warranty, the courts will give effect to this intention.[43] The category of an innominate term was recognised in 1962 in the *Hong Kong Fir Shipping Co Ltd. v. Kawasaki Kisen Kaisha Ltd* case.[44] An "innominate term" is a term the breach of which may lead to a right to terminate in

---

[42] *Bentsen & Son v. Taylor* [1893] 2 Q.B. 274, *Bunge Corporation v. Tradax S.A.* [1981] 1 W.L.R. 711.

[43] *Lombard North Central plc v. Butterworth* [1987] 1 All E.R. 267 and *Total Gas Marketing Ltd. v. Arco British Ltd. and Others* House of Lords, *The Times,* June 8th 1998. See also *Schuler AG v. Wickman Machine Tool Sales Ltd.* [1973] 2 All E.R. 39.

[44] [1962] 2 Q.B. 26. See also *Laird Brothers v. Dublin Steampacket* (1900) 34 I.L.T.R. 97.

addition to damages depending on the factual consequences of the breach. If the breach substantially deprives the injured party of substantially all the benefit which that party was intended to derive from the contract, it will be entitled to terminate the contract and treat itself as discharged from its obligations. In the *Hong Kong Fir Shipping Co Ltd.* case, a clause in the contract promising that a ship being chartered was "sea worthy" was deemed to be an innominate term, the breach of which was not, in the circumstances, serious enough to allow the charterer to treat the contract as at an end.

(2) Implied Terms

16–67   In addition to terms which are expressly included in a contract, terms may be deemed implied into a contract.[45] As noted in Chapter 10,[46] terms may be implied in fact in a contact based on one of two possible tests. MacKinnon J. stated that a term may be implied in circumstances where "if, while the parties were making their bargain, an officious bystander were to suggest some express provision for it in their agreement, they would testily suppress him with a common: 'Oh, of course'.[47] This test is known as the "Officious Bystander" test. The second test states that terms will be implied only where essential to give efficacy to the business consideration of the transaction. This is called the "Business Efficacy" test. This test was used *in Dundalk Shopping Centre v. Roof Spray Ltd.*[48] There, it was held to be an implied term of a contract to spray a waterproof substance over the roof of a shopping centre, that the roof would be rendered watertight as a result of the treatment.

16–68   In Chapter 10, it was also noted that terms may be implied under statute. In addition to section 39 of the Sale of Goods and Supply of Services Act 1980 which implies terms into a contract for the supply of services,[49] terms are implied into contracts for the sale of goods. Section 12 provides that every contract of sale contains an implied condition on the part of the seller that he or she has a right to sell the goods and an implied warranty that the goods are free from any charge or encumbrance. This rule will not apply if the seller makes it clear that he or she is transferring only such title as he or she or a third person may have. In such a case an implied warranty exists that all known

---

[45]   Clark, *Contract Law in Ireland* (Roundhall Sweet & Maxwell, 1998), Chap. 6; Clark and Clarke, *Contract: Cases and Materials* (Gill & Macmillan, 1994), Chap. 7; Treitel, *The Law of Contract*, (Sweet and Maxwell, 1995) Chap. 6.

[46]   para. 10–34.

[47]   *Shirlaw v. Southern Foundries (1926) Ltd* [1939] 2 K.B. 206 *per* MacKinnon L.J. at 227.

[48]   Unreported, High Court., Finlay P., March 21, 1979. See also *The Moorcock* (1889) 14 P.D. 64. and *Tradax (Ireland) Ltd. v. Irish Grain Board Ltd.* [1984] IR 1.

[49]   See Chap. 10, para. 10–36.

charges and encumbrances have been disclosed, and that neither the seller, a third person with title or anyone claiming through them, should disturb the buyers quiet possession. Section 13 provides that it is an implied term of every contract for the sale of goods by description that the goods will correspond with the description. Where the seller sells goods in the course of a business, section 14 provides that there is an implied condition that they will be of merchantable quality *i.e.* fit for the purpose for which they are commonly bought, or the specific purpose for which they are bought if this is made known to the seller.

(3) Remedies – Damages

16–69 The purpose of damages in contract law is to compensate a party for the loss suffered as a result of a breach of contract.[49a] The object of such an award is to put the injured party, so far as money can do it, in the same situation as if the contract had been performed. A party may be compensated for three main categories of loss. "Expectation loss" is loss of the interest which the claimant expected to gain from the promise. "Reliance loss" is the loss incurred by the claimant in reliance on the promise. Finally "restitution loss" is the loss of some benefit conferred by the claimant on the other party, *e.g.* a deposit paid. Recovery is subject to the overriding principle that the total amount recovered must not exceed the actual loss incurred.

16–70 In *Hadley v. Baxendale*,[50] the Court of Exchequer established the basic test for the recovery of damages for breach of contract. Damages are limited to:

> "such as may fairly and reasonably be considered either arising naturally
> i.e. according to the usual course of things, from such breach of contract
> itself, or such as may reasonably be supposed to have been in the con-
> templation of both parties, at the time they made the contract, as the
> probable result of the breach of it."[51]

What is considered to be "reasonably foreseeable" in any given case depends on the knowledge of the parties at the time of contracting. In *Victoria Laundry (Windsor) Ltd v. Newman Industries Ltd.*,[52] the Court of Appeal held that although each party is assumed to be aware of the loss liable to flow from a breach in the ordinary course of things:

> "there may have to be added in a particular case knowledge which he
> actually possesses of special circumstance outside the ordinary course of

---

[49a] Clark, *op. cit.*, n.45, Chap. 19; Clark & Clarke *op. cit.*, n.45; Treitel *op. cit.*, n.45 Chap. 21.
[50] (1854) 9 Exch. 341.
[51] *ibid.* at 342. This principle was accepted in Ireland in *Wilson v. Dunville* (1879) 6 L.R. (Ir.) 210.
[52] [1949] 2 K.B. 528.

things, of such a kind that a breach in those special circumstances would be liable to cause more loss."[53]

This means that if special circumstances do exist which are unknown to the party in breach, that party will only be liable for the amount of loss which would arise generally. If special circumstances do exist which may give rise to unusually high losses for the purchaser in the event of the vendor breaching a term of the contract, the purchaser must therefore ensure that the vendor is aware of this fact. In *Banque Bruxelles Lambert SA v. Eagle Star Insurance Company Ltd.*,[53a] a bank lent money on the basis of an assessement of the value of the property put up as security by a valuer employed by it for this purpose. The bank sought to recover damages from the valuer when the property failed to realise the amount owed, partly as a result of the negligent overvaluation of the property by the valuer and partly because property prices had fallen subsequent to the valuation. The House of Lords determined that the valuer was only liable for the loss attributable to the overvaluation and not for that part due to the decrease in property prices. Lord Hoffman noted that in order to succeed in its action the plaintiff would have to show that that the duty was owed to it and that it was "a duty in respect of the kind of loss which [it] suffered".[53b] His Lordship stated:

> "The scope of duty, in the sense of the consequences for which the valuer is responsible, is that which the law regards as best giving effect to the express obligations assumed by the valuer; neither cutting them down so that the lender obtains less than he was reasonably entitled to expect; nor extending them so as to improse on the valuer a liability greater than he could reasonably have thought he was undertaking."[53c]

His Lordship concluded that where someone is in breach of an implied obligation to take reasonable care in the provision of information on the basis of which another person will choose a course of action, the informant can be held responsible only for the consequences of the information being wrong. This, therefore, excludes any liability for losses which would have been incurred if the information had been correct.[53d]

16–71   The innocent party has a duty to take all reasonable steps to mitigate the loss consequent on the breach. Failure to do so may debar

---

[53]   *ibid.* at 539.
[53a]   [1997] 1 A.C. 191. See Oditah "Takeovers, Share Exchanges and the Meaning of Loss" (1996) 112 L.Q.R. 424.
[53b]   *ibid.* at p. 211.
[53c]   *ibid.* at p. 212.
[53d]   *ibid.* at p. 214. See also: Wightman "Negligent Valuations and a Drop in the Property Market: The Limits of the Expectation Loss Principle" 61 M.L.R. 69, Stapleton "Negligent Valuers and Falls in the Property Market" 113 L.Q.R. 1.

the innocent party from claiming in respect of any part of the damage which is due to his neglect to take such steps.[54]

(4) Remedies – Rescission

16–72 Where a contract is rescinded, the entire transaction is cancelled and the parties are returned, so far as possible, to their pre-contractual positions. Thus, in the case of a sale agreement, any purchase money would be refunded together with interest and expenses. As noted in paragraph 16.68, breach of a condition of a contract will allow the injured party to repudiate the contract.[55]

16–73 In addition, if the breach is fundamental, the injured party is also entitled to treat itself as discharged from its obligations under the sale contract. A fundamental breach is one which goes to the "root of the contract".[56] It is therefore a breach which affects the very substance of the agreement. The usual test to determine whether a breach has this effect is to consider the importance attached by the parties to the terms and the seriousness of the consequences which have resulted.[57] In *Taylor v. Smyth, Kape Investments Ltd., Calla Associates Ltd, and Northern Bank Ltd.,*[58] a contract for the sale of land included a term stipulating that the sale had to be completed by a certain date. When the sale was not completed by this date, the defendant purported to rescind the contract. The High Court found that in the circumstances the delay was an unreasonable one. Lardner J. stated that the correct principle to be applied in determining whether this allowed the other party rescind was:

> "to consider the effect of the breach upon the contract as a whole and whether the effect of the delay . . . deprived the innocent parties of substantially the whole benefit of the contract . . . If it had this effect the innocent parties in addition to any remedy in damages would be entitled to be discharged from any further obligation. But if the breach does not have this effect, its consequences can be remedied only by an award of damages."[59]

In the circumstances of this case, the Court was not of the view that the agreement could be treated as repudiated.

---

[54] *British Westinghouse Electric & Manufacturing Co Ltd v. Underground Electric Railways Co of London Ltd* [1912] A.C. 673 and *Lennon and Others v. Talbot Ireland Ltd*, unreported, High Court, Keane J., December 20, 1985.

[55] The injured party may, however, wish to waive its right to treat itself as discharged from its contractual obligations.

[56] *Karsales Harrow Ltd. v. Wallis* [1956] 1 W.L.R. 936 *per* Denning L.J. at 941.

[57] *Hong Kong Fir. Shipping Co. v. Kawasaki Kisen Kaisha* [1962] 2 Q.B. 26. See para. 16–68.

[58] [1990] I.L.R.M. 377. See also *Dundalk Shopping Centre Ltd. v. Roof Spray Ltd.* unreported, High Court, Finlay P., March 21, 1979.

[59] *ibid.* at 388.

16–74   Finally, a repudiatory breach also allows the innocent party to rescind the contract. Such a breach arises where one party intimates to the other an intention to abandon and altogether refuses to perform its obligations under the contract or an intention no longer to be bound by the contract.[60] This intimation may be given expressly or it may be implied by a party's actions. In *Lesson v. North British Oil and Candle Co.*,[61] a contract for the sale of a certain quantity of oil was deemed repudiated by a letter sent by the supplier before any orders were placed stating that no oil was available. In *House of Spring Gardens v. Point Blank Ltd.*,[62] the defendants entered a licensing agreement with the plaintiffs to manufacture bullet proof vests designed by the plaintiffs. The defendant's actions in manufacturing a similar product of its own and in suppressing information and dissimulating the origins of its product amounted to a repudiatory breach. In *Barry Hearn and Matchroom Boxing Ltd. v. Stephen Collins.*,[63] the High Court determined that the conduct of Mr. Hearn, the defendant's manager, constituted a repudiation of his management agreement with the defendant, a boxer. The conduct in question involved firstly, Mr. Hearn's conduct at a purse bids ceremony and secondly, a series of correspondence between Mr. Hearn and the World Boxing Organisation. At the ceremony, Mr. Hearn launched an attack on the credibility of Frank Warren and Sports Network, the defendant's promoter, suggesting that the latter should not be allowed bid. If Mr. Hearn had been successful in preventing the bid, the boxer would have been deprived of the £1.2 million purse. In the correspondence, Mr. Hearn attempted to interfere with the defendant's 75 per cent share entitlement to a particular match and he also suggested that the defendant was party to a spurious medical excuse in order to achieve a postponement of the match. The correspondence and the conduct at the purse bid ceremony were deemed to constitute fundamental breaches of Mr. Hearn's obligations to the defendant. It should also be noted that a contract may be repudiated during performance as in the *House of Spring Gardens* case or before the time for performance commences as in the *Lesson case.*

---

[60]   *Freeth v. Burr* (1874) L.R. 9 C.P. 208.
[61]   (1874) 8 I.R.C.L. 309. See also *Athlone Rural District Council v. AG Campbell & Son* (1912) 47 I.L.T.R. 142.
[62]   [1984] I.R. 611.
[63]   Unreported, High Court, O'Sullivan J., February 3, 1998.

II. MISREPRESENTATION

(1) Meaning of Representation

16–75   In order to initiate an action for misrepresentation, there must be a representation of existing fact. A mere puff will not fix liability.[64] Such a puff would not, however, be likely in a share sale agreement. While a statement of opinion or belief will have no legal effect, such a statement may however, by implication involve a statement of fact. In other words, it is a misrepresentation of fact for a person to say that he holds an opinion which he does not hold. This will be especially true where the facts are not equally well known to both parties. In *Smith v. Land and House Property Corporation*[65] Bowen L.J. stated:

> "It is often fallaciously assumed that a statement of opinion cannot involve the statement of a fact. In a case where the facts are equally well known to both parties, what one of them says to the other is frequently nothing but an expression of opinion. But if the facts are not equally well known to both sides, then a statement of opinion by the one who knows the facts best involves very often a statement of a material fact, for he impliedly states that he knows facts which justify his opinion."[66]

16–76   Similarly, while a representation as to the future does not, of itself, give rise to any cause of action for misrepresentation, in *Edginton v. Fitzmaurice*[67] Bowen L.J. commented:

> "The state of a man's mind is as much a fact as the state of his digestion. It is true that it is very difficult to prove what the state of a man's mind at a particular time is, but if it can be ascertained it is as much a fact as anything else. A misrepresentation as to the state of a man's mind is, therefore, a misstatement of fact."[68]

In that case, a prospectus inviting subscriptions stated that the money raised would be used to complete alterations to buildings and to buy vans and develop the company's supplies. The money was used instead to meet pressing liabilities. A shareholder succeeded in an action for misrepresentation against the directors.

16–77   While there is no civil remedy for a misrepresentation of law, a wilful misrepresentation of law may be ground for rescission in equity. Often however, in an action for recission the mistake will be held to be

---

[64] *Dimmock v. Hallett* (1866) LR 2 Ch. App. 21.
[65] (1884) 28 Ch. D 7.
[66] *ibid.* at 15.
[67] (1885) 29 Ch. D 459.
[68] *ibid.* at 483.

a mistake of fact rather than of law. In *Oakes v. Turquand & Harding*,[69] the Court held that a misrepresentation as to the contents of the company's memorandum and articles of association is a misrepresentation of fact not of law. Equity also gives relief for misrepresentation as to private rights, which are treated as representations of fact, *e.g.* a representation that the vendor possesses a patent in a certain invention would be deemed to be a representation of fact.

(2) Materiality and Reliance

16–78   In order to base an action on misrepresentation, the purchaser must also be able to prove that the representation was unambiguous. If the vendor makes an ambiguous statement, which is interpreted in a different sense by the purchaser, the vendor will only be liable if the court deems that the purchaser's interpretation is the correct one.[70] The representation must also be material. This has been interpreted as meaning that the representation must be one which would affect the judgment of a reasonable person in deciding whether, or on what terms, to enter into the contract.[71]

16–79   In order to prove misrepresentation, the purchaser must further prove that the representation induced the contract. Although reliance cannot exist where the representee was not aware of the representation, this is unlikely in a sale agreement which will be signed by both parties. Other circumstances in which reliance will not be deemed to exist are where the purchaser knew the truth, took a deliberate risk as to the truth, or relied on their own information.[71a]

(3) Remedies – Rescission

16–80   Where the purchaser is seeking rescission for misrepresentation, it is not necessary to prove fraud. A contract may be rescinded even where the misrepresentation is purely innocent. The general rule is that misrepresentation makes the contract voidable at the option of the representee. However, in certain circumstances, the representee may be deemed to have lost their right to rescind the contract.

16–81   Normally, where a person seeks to rescind a contract for misrepresentation, he or she will be required to restore any benefits received under the contract. If that person is for some reason unable to

---

[69]   [1867] L.R. 2 (H.L.) 325.
[70]   *McInerny v. Lloyds Bank Ltd.* [1974] 1 Lloyds' Rep. 246
[71]   *Dimmock v. Hallett* (1866) LR 2 Ch. App. 21. See Treitel, *op. cit.*, n.45, pp. 312–314.
[71a]   See below para. 16–106 *et seq.*

restore this benefit, this may bar his right to rescind. *Restitutio in integrum* may not be possible where property has changed hands and that property has been destroyed or altered. Rescission in equity is possible, however, on the basis of substantial restoration of the property and possibly a payment to compensate for the change.[72]

16–82   The rule in *Seddon v. N.Eastern Salt Co.*[73] states that an executed contract for sale will only be set aside in equity where there has been equitable fraud. In that case, the defendant purchased all the shares in a company relying on an innocent representation that the company was breaking even. In actual fact, the company was loosing money. The Court held that the defendant was not entitled to rescind the contract as the contract had been performed by the transfer of the shares and was thus complete. This rule was followed in the Irish High Court in *Lecky v. Walter.*[74] There, bonds were purchased on the belief that they were secured which was untrue. The Court held that in the circumstances the sale could only be set aside if there was fraud or a total lack of consideration. In the UK, the Misrepresentation Act 1967 has abrogated this restriction. Section 1(b) of that Act provides that a person who would otherwise be entitled to rescind a contract for misrepresentation without alleging fraud shall be entitled notwithstanding that the contract has been performed. As there is no similar statutory provision in Ireland, the rule in *Lecky v. Walter* still applies in Ireland. In *Smith New Court Securities v. Scrimgeour Vickers,*[75] Lord Browne-Wilkinson stated *obiter* that if the current law provides that there is no right to rescind the contract for the sale of quoted shares, once the specific shares purchased have been sold, the law will need to be closely looked at hereafter. The reason his Lordship gives for this doubt is that, since identical shares can be purchased on the market, the defrauded purchaser can offer substantial *restitutio in integrum* which is normally sufficient. Section 44 of the Sale of Goods and Supply of Services Act 1980 removes this bar to rescission for innocent misrepresentation. It provides as follows:

> "Where a person has entered into a contract after a misrepresentation has been made to him, and
> (a) the misrepresentation has become a term of the contract, or
> (b) the contract has been performed,
> or both, then, if otherwise he would be entitled to rescind the contract without alleging fraud, he shall be so entitled, subject to the provisions of this Part notwithstanding the matters mentioned in paragraphs (a) and (b)."

---

[72] *Erlanger v. New Sombrero Phosphate Co* (1878) 3 App. Cas. 1218.
[73] [1905] 1 Ch. 326.
[74] [1914] I.R. 378.
[75] [1996] 4 All E.R. 769.

This provision has only limited value to a purchaser because the term "contract" is defined for this purpose as a contract for the sale of goods, a hire-purchase agreement, an agreement for the letting of goods or a contract for the supply of services.[76] Shares which are choses in action are excluded as are contracts for the sale of real property.

16–83 In certain circumstances, the purchaser may be seen to have waived its right to terminate the contract. Waiver may take the form of some positive act or it may be implied by unreasonable delay in making use of the remedy. A positive act of affirmation may include for example, trying to sell the securities, accepting dividends or participating in general meetings.[77] Affirmation may also be inferred from a failure to rescind within a reasonable time. The right to rescind may also be lost where rescission would disrupt third party rights.[77a]

(4) Remedies – Damages

16–84 Damages may be awarded for fraudulent or negligent misrepresentation.[78] The purpose of damages in tort is to restore the plaintiff to the position which he or she occupied before the wrong was committed. Various types of damages may be available. "Nominal damages" will be awarded where the plaintiff suffered no actual loss. "Contemptuous damages" may be given where the court feels that the plaintiff though legally entitled to damages is not morally entitled. Damages may be classified further as "special" and "general". "General damages" are those that are presumed to arise naturally from such a wrong, and "special damages" are those that result from the particular circumstances of the case. Finally, "exemplary damages" may be also be awarded if the motives and conduct of the defendant were deemed to have aggravated the plaintiff's loss. For example, in *Garvey v. Ireland*[79] exemplary damages were awarded for wrongful dismissal, because the Government had acted in an oppressive and unconstitutional manner.

16–85 In *Smith New Court Securities v. Scrimgeour Vickers*,[80] the House of Lords considered the quantum of damages to award where a fraudulent misrepresentation had induced a plaintiff to enter into a contract to purchase shares. Lord Browne Wilkinson stated that the main purpose of damages in tort is to restore someone to the position they would have

---

[76] Sale of Goods and Supply of Services Act 1980, s.43.
[77] *Western Bank of Scotland v. Addie* (1867) L.R. 1 Sc. & Div. 145; *Sharpley v. Louth and East Coast Railway* (1876) 2 Ch. D 663.
[77a] *Anderson v. Ryan* [1967] I.R. 34.
[78] See Chap. 10, paras 10–37–10–50.
[79] [1979] 113 I.L.T.R. 61.
[80] [1996] 4 All E.R. 769.

been in if the wrong had not occurred. His Lordship affirmed the view of the court in *Doyle v. Olby (Ironmongers) Ltd.*[81] that the measure of damages where a contract has been induced by fraudulent misrepresentation is reparation for all the damage directly caused by entering the transaction. Lord Browne Wilkinson set down the following principles:

- the defendant must compensate the plaintiff for all damage directly flowing from the transaction;

- the damage does not have to be foreseeable but it has to have been directly caused by the transaction;

- in assessing damages, the plaintiff is entitled to recover the full price paid by him, but he must give credits for any benefits he has received as a result of the transaction;

- as a general rule, the benefits received by him include the market value of the property acquired at the date of the acquisition; but such general rule is not to be inflexibly applied where to do so would prevent him obtaining full compensation for the wrong suffered;

- although its not possible to state comprehensively the circumstances in which the general rule should not apply, it will normally not apply where either (a) the misrepresentation has continued to operate after the date of the acquisition of the asset so as to induce the plaintiff to retain the asset or (b) the circumstances of the case are such that the plaintiff is by reason of the fraud, locked into the property;

- in addition, the plaintiff may recover consequential loss.

16–86 In this case, the plaintiff bought Ferranti shares at 82 pence in July 1989 with the objective of holding the shares for investment purposes. This purchase was made on the basis of a misrepresentation that other firms were interested in acquiring the shares. If there had been no competition, the plaintiff would only have paid 78 pence for these shares. As a result of a major fraud in Ferranti (referred to as "the Guerin fraud"), Ferranti shares were suspended and when trading resumed, the share price had fallen significantly. In November, the plaintiff started to sell shares and by April 1990 it had sold them all at prices in the range of 30 to 49 pence. In December 1990, the plaintiff learned of the misrepresentation

---

[81] [1969] 2 Q.B. 158. The *Doyle* case was followed in *East v. Maurer* [1991] 1 W.L.R. 461and *Downs v. Chappell* [1996] 3 All E.R. 344. In both those cases the plaintiffs had purchased a business as a going concern in reliance on the defendants fraudulent misrepresentation. In each case after discovery of the fraud they sold the business at a loss and recovered by way of damages the difference between the original purchase price and the price eventually realised upon resale. See also *Banque Bruxelles Lambert SA v. Eagle Star Insurance Company Ltd., op. cit.,* n.53a.

and sought damages for deceit. What complicated matters in this case was the fact that the market value of the Ferranti shares at the transaction date in July was inflated, because the Guerin fraud had not yet been discovered. There was thus a false market, although this false market was not attributable to the fraud of the defendant. The House of Lords found that the plaintiff's loss was caused by the defendant's fraud, by reason of purchasing the shares which were "deadly". If the plaintiff was required to give credit for the shares having a value of 78p on July 21, 1989, the plaintiff would not be compensated for the actual loss suffered which was the difference between the contract price and the resale price. The House of Lords determined thus that this was one of the cases where the benefit the plaintiff ought to bring into account to be set against its loss for the total purchase price paid should be the actual resale price achieved by the plaintiff when eventually the shares were sold. In these circumstances damages of £11.3 million were awarded to the plaintiff.

16–87   Since the decision in *Salomon v. Salomon Ltd.*,[81a] it has been accepted that a company possesses a separate legal identity and separate legal responsibilities distinct from its members and directors. As a result, where a director acting within the scope of his or her authority causes a company to be involved in a tortious act, the company rather than any one individual will be responsible. Only in certain exceptional cases will a director be held personally accountable for a tort committed in the company's name.[81b] For example, in *Fairline Shipping Corporation v. Adamson*,[81c] a director was held personally liable for the performance of a negligent act because the director's dealings with the plaintiff had been on a personal rather than corporate footing. In this case, the director had clearly created an impression that he was accepting personal responsibility. One of the ways in which this impression was created was by the use of personal rather than company stationery for any correspondance. This issue was considered by the House of Lords recently in *Williams v. Natural Life Health Foods Ltd.*[81d] In this case, the plaintiff entered a franchise agreement for a health food shop with Natural Life Health Foods Ltd. in reliance on certain income projections provided by the defendant company. As a result of the inaccuracy of these projections, the plaintiff was forced to close the shop and incurred substantial losses. The plaintiff sought

---

[81a] [1987] A.C. 22.
[81b] Grantham & Rickett, "Directors' Tortious Liability: Contract, Tort or Company Law" 62 M.L.R. 133.
[81c] [1975] Q.B. 80.
[81d] [1998] 1 W.L.R. 830. See also Griffin "Company Directors' Personal Liability in Tort" 115 L.Q.R. 36 (1999).

damages from the company and when the company was wound up against Mr. Mistlin, the founder and managing director alleging that he owed a personal duty of care in respect of these provisions. Prior to setting up the company, Mr. Mistlin had previously run a similar shop on his own account. This argument was accepted by the Court of Appeal on the basis that the relevant knowledge and experience was entirely his qua Mr. Mistlin and not his qua director. The House of Lords reversed the decision of the Court of Appeal and held that the fact that knowledge underlying the advice was acquired by Mr. Mistlin in his personal capacity did not infer that as a director he had personally accepted responsibility for it. As a result, there was deemed to be no special relationship between the plaintiff and the defendant as required by Hedley Byrne. In addition, the House of Lords held that there was no clear evidence that the plaintiff had relied on Mr. Mistlin's personal responsibility and that it would not have been reasonable to do so in the circumstances.

It would appear that a shareholder who has been defrauded or otherwise mislead into entering the sale agreement will not be allowed claim damages against the company itself until he has rescinded the contract and ceased to be a member of the company. An action for damages may only be taken against the promoter, the directors or whoever wrongfully induced him to buy. This rule was laid down in *Houldsworth v. City of Glasgow Bank*.[82] In that case, the plaintiff claimed damages against the company because the directors fraudulently induced him to subscribe for shares. The Privy Council held that to award damages would be, inconsistent with the contract with the company into which the shareholder had entered. For the shareholder to try and sue is to try to "reconcile two inconsistent propositions, mainly, that of shareholder and that of creditor of the whole body of shareholders including himself".[82a] Critics of this rule argue that it runs against the fundamental principle of separate legal identity.[83] This principle has effectively been abolished in the UK by section 131 of the Companies Act 1989 which inserts a new section 111a into the Financial Services Act 1986 stating that a person is not debarred from obtaining damages or other compensation from a company by reason only of his holding shares in a company or a right to apply or subscribe for shares or to be included in the company's register.

16–88   No common law right to damages exists for a wholly innocent misrepresentation which has no contractual force. For a non-contractual misrepresentation, the representees may merely seek rescission.

---

[82]   (1880) 5 A.C. 317.
[82a] *ibid.* at 333.
[83]   Forde, *Company Law* (Mercier Press, 1992), pp. 202–203.

Although, section 45(1) of the Sale of Goods and Supply of Services Act 1980 provides for damages for innocent misrepresentation it is extremely limited in its application. For this reason, in cases of innocent misrepresentation, the plaintiff is likely to argue that the representation was a collateral warranty.

III. COLLATERAL WARRANTIES AND COLLATERAL AGREEMENTS

(1) Collateral Warranties

16–89   If a representation is deemed to have contractual force, the plaintiff may sue for damages for breach of a collateral contractual warranty and where the representation constitutes a condition, may even be able to claim itself as discharged from its contractual obligations. The test to determine whether a term has been incorporated into a contract or remains a mere representation is based on the intention of the parties as determined by the totality of the evidence. In *Oscar Chess Ltd. v. Williams*[84] Denning L.J. stated that:

> "The question whether a warranty was intended depends on the conduct of the parties, on their words and behaviour rather than on their thoughts. If an intelligent bystander would reasonably infer that a warranty was intended, that will suffice."[85]

Denning L.J added to this point in *Dick Bentley Productions Ltd. v. Smith (Motors) Ltd.*[86] stating:

> "It seems to me that if a representation is made in the course of dealings for a contract for the purpose of inducing the other party to act on it, and it actually induces him to act on it by entering into the contract, that is *prima facia* ground for inferring that the representation was intended as a warranty. It is not necessary to speak of it as being collateral. Suffice it that the representation was intended to be acted upon and was in fact acted upon."[87]

These cases were relied on by Kenny J. in *The Governor and Company of the Bank of Ireland v. Smith*[88] who noted that:

> "The modern cases . . . show a welcome tendency to treat a representation made in connection with a sale as being a warranty, unless the person who made it can show that he was innocent of fault in connection with it".[89]

The relative knowledge of the parties may be relevant in determining whether a statement is a warranty or a mere representation. In *Esso*

---

[84]   [1957] 1 W.L.R. 370.
[85]   *ibid.* at 375.
[86]   [1965] 2 All E.R. 65.
[87]   *ibid* at 67.
[88]   [1966] I.R. 646.
[89]   *ibid.* at 659.

Petroleum Co. Ltd. v. Mardon,[90] Mr. Mardon entered into a tenancy agreement with Esso in respect of a filling station on the basis of a representation made by one of Esso's agents. This agent calculated that the potential throughput was likely to reach 200,000 gallons by the third year of operation. When this figure proved incorrect, Mr. Mardon claimed damages for breach of this warranty as to throughput, or alternatively for negligent misrepresentation. The Court of Appeal held that Esso possessed special knowledge skill and experience which Mr. Mardon lacked. As a result Esso were held to have given a warranty that that they had made the forecast with reasonable skill and care.

16–90   A representation may be enforced thus as a "collateral warranty" which forms part of a single contract containing the main promise. The effect of the Parol Evidence rule on such a warranty must also be considered. This rule provides that parol testimony cannot be admitted to add to, vary or contradict a written contract or the terms in which the parties have deliberately agreed to record any part of their contract.[91] In *Heilbut, Symons & Co. v. Buckleton*,[92] Lord Moulton admitted that collateral contracts whose sole effect is to vary or add to the terms of the principal contract are viewed suspiciously by the courts and must be proven strictly. The presumption in such a case will be that the written agreement was intended to include all the terms of the contract. One important exception to the parol evidence rule, however, allows the admission of terms where the written agreement is not the whole agreement. In *Clayton Love v. B&I Transport*,[93] for example, the terms of a contract of carriage were found in the written contract between the parties and certain additional terms which had been agreed to in a telephone conversation between the parties. A representation which is viewed as a collateral warranty forming part of the contract may thus be acceptable.

(2) Collateral Agreements

16–91   It may be argued that the purchaser and vendor made two separate agreements, the main sale agreement and a second collateral agreement.[94] Such a collateral agreement must be intended to have contractual effect. In addition, consideration would be needed to effect such an agreement. However, often the purchaser's consideration for

---

[90] [1976] 1 Q.B. 801.
[91] *Bank of Australasia v. Palmer* [1897] A.C. 540. *Macklin & McDonald v. Greacen & Co.* [1983] I.R. 61.
[92] [1913] A.C. 30.
[93] (1970) 104 I.L.T.R. 157.
[94] Wedderburn "Collateral Contracts" (1959) C.L.J. 58, Treitel, *op. cit.*, above, n.45, 150, 165–166, 183–184 and 330–331, Clark, *op. cit.*, above, n.45 117–119.

this collateral agreement will be agreeing to enter into the sale agreement. In *Heilbut, Symons & Co. v. Buckleton*[95] Lord Moulton stated:

> "It is evident . . . that there may be a contract the consideration for which is the making of some other contract. 'If you will make such and such a contract I will give you one hundred pounds,' is in every sense of the word a complete legal contract. It is collateral to the main contract, but each has an independent existence, and they do not differ in respect of their possessing to the full the character a status of a contract."

However, Lord Moulton also opined that such collateral contracts must, from their very nature, be rare. Obviously, agreeing to enter into the main sale agreement could not constitute good consideration, if the parties have already concluded the sale agreement at the time the collateral agreement was made. The consideration would then be deemed past consideration and unacceptable.[96]

16–92 The parol evidence rule will not cause any difficulties where the collateral agreement is total independent of the sale agreement. Proving the existence of the collateral agreement will not involve varying or adding to the original agreement as it will be totally separate and independent. In *Mann v. Nunn*,[97] the plaintiff orally agreed to lease premises from the defendant and the defendant agreed to complete certain necessary repairs. The written agreement which was executed omitted any reference to the defendant's promise to complete the repairs. The plaintiff was able to enforce this promise, however, as a separate collateral contract. The Court determined that: "The parol agreement neither alters nor adds to the written one, but is an independent agreement."[98] Where a representation is viewed as a collateral agreement in the sense of being an independent agreement rather than an attempt to add to or alter the sale agreement, the parol evidence rule will not prohibit it. For this reason Murphy J. in *Cotter v. Minister for Agriculture*[99] stated that where a collateral contract exists "it is hardly an exception at all" to the parol evidence rule. However, if the term goes to the essence of the whole transaction, it may be difficult for a court to accept it merely as an independent agreement.[100]

16–93 There may be an advantage to claiming that a collateral agreement exists rather than a collateral warranty which forms part of

---

[95] *op. cit.*, n.92 at 47.
[96] *Roscorla v. Thomas* (1842) 3 Q.B. 234, *Provincial Bank of Ireland v. Donnell* (1932) 67 I.L.T.R. 142.
[97] (1874) 30 L.T. 526.
[98] *ibid.* at 527.
[99] Unreported, High Court, November 15, 1991.
[100] Treitel, *op. cit.*, above, n.45, pp 183–184.

the main agreement. Such an advantage would arise where the main contract contained an exemption or limitation clause.[101] In *Webster v. Higgin*,[102] the plaintiff, in order to persuade the defendant to enter into a hire purchase agreement, promised "If you buy the Hillman 10, we will guarantee that it is in good condition and that you will have no trouble with it." The defendant thereupon signed a written contract which contained a clause exempting liability for any "statutory or other warranty, condition, description or representation whether express or implied". The Court of Appeal held that by signing the document, the defendant had accepted the offer as a separate collateral agreement which, being broken, entitled him to avoid the main contract. Because the collateral agreement was a separate agreement, the exemption clause in the contract did not apply to it. In *Mitchelstown Co-operative Society Ltd. v. Societe des Produits Nestle SA, Chambourcy Food Company Ltd and Nestle (Ireland) Ltd.*,[103] Mitchelstown Co-operative Society Ltd ("the Co-op") entered into a licence and trade-mark user agreement with Nestle SA in 1984. A choice of law clause in this contract provided that the agreement should be deemed to be made under and to be governed by Swiss law. In addition, an arbitration clause was included referring any dispute to a board of arbitration sitting in Lausanne. At approximately the same time the Co-op entered into an agreement with Chambourcy Food Company Ltd., a UK based company, and Nestle SA which provided that until the Co-op had commenced to manufacture and market certain products under the Chambourcy trade-mark according to Nestle SA specifications, Chambourcy Food Company Ltd, would supply it with its own manufactured goods of a similar kind. This agreement also gave the Co-op sole distribution rights for these goods under Chambourcy's trademark in Ireland. Four years later, Nestle SA purported to repudiate its contract with the Co-op on the ground that the Co-op had not commenced the manufacture of its own products. Nestle (Ireland) Ltd. was then appointed by Nestle SA and Chambourcy Food Company Ltd to distribute Chambourcy products in Ireland. While the Co-op claimed that this amounted to a breach of the collateral agreement, the respondents denied the existence of any such collateral agreement. The Supreme Court held that the Co-op had established an arguable case for the existence of a collateral contract and granted an interlocutory injunction restraining Nestle (Ireland) Ltd. from distributing Chambourcy products in Ireland. Since this was a separate contract neither the choice of law clause or the arbitration clause was deemed to apply.

---

[101]   Clark, *op. cit.*, above, n.45, p. 118.
[102]   [1948] 2 All E.R. 127.
[103]   [1989] I.L.R.M. 582.

C. Exempting or Limiting Liability

I. EXEMPTING & LIMITING CLAUSES

16–94 Both the common law rules and the statutory rules which were referred to in Chapter 10[103a] as a means of incorporating and interpreting exemption and limitation rules apply to exemption or limitation clauses in sale agreements.

16–95 In addition to straight forward exemption or limitation clauses, a common practice has developed to include a clause in a contract emphasising that the written sale agreement constitutes "the whole agreement and understanding between the parties with respect to all matters therein referred to". These clauses are referred to as "entirety of contract clauses" or "whole agreement clauses". In *Alman and Benson v. Associated Newspapers Group Ltd.*,[104] Mr. Justice Browne-Wilkinson considered just such a clause. He accepted that it excluded any contractual claim based on a collateral understanding but not liability for misrepresentation. He stated:

> "If it were designed to exclude liability for misrepresentation it would, I think, have to be couched in different terms, for example, a clause acknowledging that the parties had not relied on any representations in entering into the contract."[105]

16–96 As a result of the *Alman* decision, entirety of contract clauses are drafted in conjunction with clauses acknowledging that the parties have not relied on any representations. However, in *Witter Ltd. v. TBP Industries*,[106] Jacob J. held that even where an entirety of contract clause goes on to provide for an acknowledgement that a party has not been induced to enter into a contract by any other than scheduled representations, this does not exclude liability in misrepresentation if the plaintiff can succeed evidentially in proving, despite the acknowledgement, that he was induced by it. He stated:

> "Unless it is manifestly made clear that a purchaser has agreed only to have a remedy for breach of warranty I am not disposed to think that a contractual term said to have this effect by a roundabout route does indeed do so. In other words, if a clause is to have the effect of excluding or reducing remedies for damaging untrue statements then the party seeking that

---

[103a] See Chap. 10, paras 10–51–10–56.
[104] Unreported, Ch. D. June 20th, 1980. Available on *Lexis*.
[105] *ibid.* p. 30. See also *Deerpak v. ICI* [1998] 2 Lloyd's Reports 139 where the entirety of contract clause was deemed to have excluded liability for collateral warranties.
[106] [1996] 2 All E.R. 573.

protection cannot be mealy-mouthed in his clause. He must bring it home that he is limiting his liability for falsehoods he may have told."[107]

16–97   The importance of drafting a properly worded exemption clause was emphasised recently in *British Sugar plc v. NEI Power Projects Ltd. & Another*.[108] In this case, the defendants agreed to design and supply electrical equipment for a consideration of £106,585. As the equipment was poorly designed and badly installed, the power supply to the plaintiffs broke down resulting in increased production costs and loss of profits totalling over £5 million. A clause was included in the contract which acknowledged the defendant's liability for loss and damage arising from the supply of unsuitable materials but limited the defendant's liability for "consequential loss" to the value of the contract. The defendants argued that any reasonable businessman would understand that loss of profits would be "consequential". The Court of Appeal, however, relying on two earlier decisions held that the word "consequential" does not cover any loss which directly and naturally results in the ordinary course of events from the supply of faulty products. Thus the exemption clause was not effective to avoid the plaintiff's action for £5 million.

II. THE DISCLOSURE LETTER

16–98   The disclosure letter will set out a substantial number of specific disclosures in relation to items warranted in the sale agreement. In addition, general disclosure is likely to be made in respect of all matters of public record. The disclosure letter serves a useful purpose for both parties to the transaction. From the vendor's perspective, it transfers the commercial risks to the purchaser. From the purchaser's perspective, it avoids informal disclosure being used as a defence in subsequent meetings. For example, a purchaser may literally be swamped with vast quantities of information most of it irrelevant. The objective in such a case would be to disclose a potentially important item in this manner whilst not actually bringing it to the attention of the purchaser.

(1) Quality of Disclosure

16–99   A breach of warranty would not normally be avoided merely by making known to the purchaser the means of knowledge which might enable him to determine certain facts and conclusions. In *Levison v. Farin*,[109] the owners of a company engaged in the fashion trade decided to sell the business to the defendants. Because the designer had been ill

---

[107]   *ibid.* at 596.
[108]   (1997) 87 Build L.R. 42.
[109]   [1978] 2 All E.R. 1149.

for a period of time, no autumn or spring collection had been produced. The purchasers were informed of this and also that the company was trading at a loss and was in a traded down state. They were not however told, because the owners did not know, exactly how much money was being lost. The agreement for the sale of the business contained, *inter alia*, a warranty by the owners that, "Save as disclosed, the vendors jointly and severally warrant to and undertake with the purchasers that between the balance sheet date and the completion date . . . there will have been no material adverse change in the overall value of the net assets of the company on the basis of a valuation adopted in the balance sheet allowing for normal trade fluctuations." Upon completing the acquisition the purchasers realised that there had been an adverse change in the overall net assets of the company to the value of £8,600. The English High Court decided that this constituted a material adverse change contrary to the warranty. The owners contended that they were not liable for breach of warranty by reason of the words "save as disclosed". Gibson J. held that to make the purchasers aware that the designer was ill and had not produced any collections was not the same as disclosing an adverse change in overall value of the net assets of the company within the meaning of the words "save as disclosed". In the first place, all that was disclosed was a possible cause of loss, not an actual drop in net assets. In addition, there was no purported disclosure for the purpose of or with reference to this clause. Gibson J. stated:

> "I do not say that facts made known by disclosure of the means of knowledge in the course of negotiation could never constitute disclosure for such a clause as this but I have no doubt that a clause in this form is primarily designed and intended to require a party who wishes by disclosure to avoid a breach of warranty to give specific notice for the purpose of the agreement and a protection by disclosure will not normally be achieved by merely making known the means of knowledge which may or do enable the other party to work out certain facts and conclusions."[110]

The owners were not deemed thus to have disclosed the adverse change so as to escape liability for breach of warranty.

16–100 Gibson J's observations were applied in *New Hearts Ltd. v. Cosmopolitan Investments Ltd.*[111] by Lord Penrose who took the opportunity to launch a vituperative attack on disclosures involving "the recitation of meaningless formulae which tend to confuse rather than enlighten". The disclosure letter in question, which was described as being "distinguished by the obscurity of its language", incorporated by reference a list of

[110] *ibid.* at 1157.
[111] [1997] 2 B.C.L.C. 249.

documents, including the latest accounts and the management accounts and purported to disclose their content and terms. The Court held that the "repetitive and omnibus approach" of an invitation to the purchasers to make what they wished of the documents with reference to which warranties had been given by the vendors could not "by any stretch of the imagination" be considered fair disclosure, with sufficient detail to identify the nature and scope of any matter purportedly disclosed:

> "Mere reference to a source of information, which is in itself a complex document, within which the diligent enquirer might find relevant information will not satisfy the requirements of a clause providing for fair disclosure with sufficient details to identify the nature and scope of the matter disclosed".[112]

Lord Penrose had to consider the effect of disclosure letters again in *Prentice and Another v. Scottish Power Plc.*[113] His Lordship noted that disclosure is seen as a means to limit the scope of wide and unqualified warranties either: by amendment or variation of the warranty provisions (as in the *New Hearts Ltd.* case); by waiver by the purchaser of a remedy for what would otherwise be breach; or by some other principle of contract law which must depend on the terms of the contract in question. Lord Penrose also stated that fairness of disclosures is only relevant to the extent that parties purport to make disclosure – "Fairness of disclosure is related to the content of what is disclosed, not to the decision whether to make disclosures at all".[113a]

16–101   A second issue which arose in the *Prentice* case was whether there was an implied term in the contract that the defendants would act reasonably in the exercising of their right to withdraw from the contact where there were disclosures which they deemed to involve unacceptable limitation of the warranties. This issue brought Lord Penrose back to the analysis of the disclosure process in the context of a concluded contract containing broad and unqualified remedies. Lord Penrose stated that it was difficult to avoid the conclusion that disclosure had become a tactical exercise with vendor's representatives seeking to offload responsibilities by the delivery of indigestible documents in quantity to purchasers' representatives who were put under pressure to investigate the material with inadequate time and facilities. His Lordship stated that there was nothing in general principle, nor in the language and structure of the contract, which implied that the purchasers had to exercise their rights to withdraw reasonably. There was no reason therefore why the purchaser should not be entitled to consult his own interests in deciding whether to be bound in the

---

[112]   *ibid.* at 259.
[113]   [1997] 2 B.C.L.C. 269.
[113a]   *ibid.* at 272.

altered circumstances brought about by the vendor's disclosures.[113b] The purchaser should however exercise care because many clauses are drafted in such a way as to deny the purchaser the ability to exercise any degree of judgment on this point.

(2) Accuracy of the Disclosures

16–102   Having made the disclosures, the vendor will then be asked to warrant their accuracy. This is normally done by warranting that the disclosures have been made "fully, fairly and accurately". In this way, the disclosures will themselves constitute representations, breach of which will entitle the purchaser to sue.

16–103   In *William Sindall plc v. Cambridgeshire CC*,[114] the Court of Appeal maintained that if the vendor is under a duty to make disclosures, a statement that the vendor is not aware of something implies that it has conducted such investigation as might reasonably be expected to be made. In that case also, certain responses given by the vendor setting out pertinent issues were prefaced with the words, "They are believed to be correct but the accuracy is not guaranteed and they do not obviate the need to make appropriate searches, inquiries and inspections." The vendor alleged that the effect of these words was to qualify all answers by reference to the vendor's knowledge or "reasonable means of knowledge". The Court refused to accept this argument maintaining that the words merely signify that the answers do not constitute collateral warranties but are instead mere representations.

(3) Knowledge of the Purchaser

16–104   In order to succeed in an action for misrepresentation, the purchaser must prove reliance on the representation. As noted in paragraph 16.81, reliance will be deemed not to exist where the representee already was aware of the truth. In such a case actual knowledge rather than constructive knowledge will be required. Thus in *Gahan v. Boland and Boland*,[115] Henchy J. in the Supreme Court stated:

> "I consider it to be well settled law that the only knowledge that will debar a purchaser from repudiating a contract he has been induced into by the vendor's misrepresentation is actual and complete knowledge of the true situation. It does not lie with a vendor, who has by his misrepresentation induced the purchaser to enter into a contract to purchase, to have his

---

[113b] *ibid.* at 277.
[114] [1994] 1 W.L.R. 1016.
[115] Unreported, Supreme Court, January 20th, 1984.

misrepresentation excused or overlooked and to have the purchaser deprived of a right to rescind because he did not ignore the misrepresentation and pursue matters further so as to establish the truth of what was misrepresented. That would be unconscionable and unfair."[116]

16–105   A person may be entitled to relief even though he or she had but did not take, the opportunity to test the accuracy of the representation. In *Smith v. Eric S Bush*,[117] the plaintiff bought a house using a mortgage based on a valuation which had been negligently conducted by the lender's surveyor. The plaintiff succeeded in an action for negligence against the surveyor despite the fact that an independent survey would have revealed the truth. The House Lords held that as the house was of modest value it was not likely to be the subject of an independent assessment and it was not reasonable to expect the purchaser to seek one. However, the House of Lords indicated that the position might be different in the case of the purchase of commercial or industrial premises or expensive residential property. Treitel states that the principle appears to be that failure to make use of an opportunity to discover the truth may defeat a claim for negligent misrepresentation where, but only where, it is reasonable to expect the representee to make use of the opportunity.[118] Where a commercial enterprise is making an expensive acquisition of the business or shares of another company, it is arguable however that it would be reasonable to expect it to use any reasonable opportunity available to verify the truth of a statement.

16–106   A person who actually avails of the opportunity to test the accuracy of the representation cannot however be said to have relied on the representation.[119] The exception to this is where the representation is fraudulent. In *S Pearson & Son Ltd. v. Dublin Corporation*,[120] the plaintiff entered into a contract to construct sewage works for a price which was calculated in reliance upon a misrepresentation. A clause in the contract stipulated that the plaintiff should satisfy itself as to the dimensions, levels and nature of all existing works and other things connected with the contract works and that the defendant did not hold itself responsible for the accuracy of the information as to the sections or foundations of existing walls and works. Lord Loreburn L.C. stated, however, that "it seems clear that no one can escape liability for his own fraudulent statements by inserting in a contract a clause that the

---

[116]   *ibid.* at p. 4.
[117]   [1990] 1 A.C. 831.
[118]   Treitel, *op. cit.*, above, n.45, p. 315.
[119]   *Attwood v. Small* (1838) 6 CL & Fin 232.
[120]   [1907] A.C. 351.

other party shall not rely upon them."[120a] Although it was contemplated that an innocent man might need to protect himself against the fraud of his agents Lord Loreburn noted that the clauses in question "contemplate honesty on both sides and protect only against honest mistakes."[120b]

16–107 In *Eurocopy plc v. Teesdale and others*,[121] the trial judge relied on *Pearson* to suggest that it was arguable that clauses could not be relied on by a party who knew that the disclosure letter was incomplete because to do so would be dishonest. The directors of a company, the shares of which were being sold, warranted that there were no material facts or circumstances in relation to the company which had not been disclosed in the disclosure letter and which if disclosed might have been expected to affect the decision of the plaintiff to enter into the agreement or the decision of any purchaser to purchase the shares or any of them. The plaintiff claimed that in breach of this warranty the defendants had failed to disclose material facts or circumstances and that as a result the shares were worth far less than the sum paid for them. The defendants countered by denying the materiality of the facts and alleging that in any case the plaintiff had acutal knowledge of the facts and circumstances which were said not to have been discussed. The plaintiff argued that the material terms of the agreement, namely clauses 3.3 and 4.1, precluded the defendants from relying on that defence and the plaintiff sought to strike out that part of the defence. Clause 3.3 of the agreement stated:

> "The Warranties are given subject to matters set out in the Disclosure Letter in accordance with Clause 4 below but no other information relating to the Company of which the Purchaser has knowledge (actual constructive or imputed) shall preclude or affect any claim made by the Purchaser for breach of any of the Warranties or reduce any amount recoverable."

Clause 4.1 of the agreement stated:

> "The purchaser shall not be entitled to claim that any fact omission circumstance or occurrence constitutes a breach of the Warranties if such fact omission circumstance of occurrence has been fairly disclosed to the Purchaser in the Disclosure Letter but no other information of which the Purchaser has knowledge (actual or constructive) shall prejudice any claim by the Purchaser under the Warranties or operate to reduce any amount recoverable and accordingly the Disclosure Letter contains all material details of the matters disclosed therein."

[120a] *ibid.* at 353, 354.
[120b] *ibid.* at 354.
[121] [1992] B.C.L.C. 1067.

The plaintiff maintained that the warranties were expressly qualified by reference only to the disclosure letter and that the attempt by the defendants to allege actual knowledge of facts and matters not disclosed in the disclosure letter was contrary to the contract the parties had made.

The Court of Appeal held that it could be argued that the words in clause 4.1 did not apply to a matter which the parties treated as immaterial. It was also decided on the facts, that it was not obvious that the defendants should be precluded from asserting that the plaintiff knew of the undisclosed facts. As a result, the Court of Appeal held that there was not a strong and arguable case for striking out. Lloyd L.J. also stated that in ascertaining the fair value of the shares, the value the parties themselves placed on the share was relevant.

16–108   The purchaser may try to protect itself against an allegation that it has waived any right to sue for breach of the warranties because it was aware of problems and failed to act. The purchaser may seek to include a clause in the contract providing that its remedies in respect of any breach of warranties will not be affected by an investigations made by the purchaser or by the rescinding, or the failure to rescind, the contract. The Dublin Solicitors Bar Association suggest the following wording:

> "The rights and remedies of the Purchaser in respect of any breach of the Warranties shall not be affected or extinguished by Completion, by any investigation made by it or on its behalf into the affairs of any Group Company, by its rescinding or failing to rescind this Agreement, or failing to exercise or delaying the exercise of any right or remedy, or by any other event or matter, except a specific and duly authorised written waiver or release, and no single or partial exercise of any right or remedy shall preclude any further or other exercise."

CHAPTER 17

COMPLETION

17–01 A completion agenda will generally be drawn up to organise the various matters which must take place following the execution of the sale agreement. This is especially important where the purchaser is acquiring the shares of a company as matters will be more complex. The agenda will also schedule the handing over of the consideration. In addition, if there is an interval between the finalisation of the contract and completion, the warranties and disclosures will generally be repeated at completion. The vendor will not normally be allowed disclose further matters at this stage unless the matters are trivial.

A. Shareholder Approval

17–02 Where the directors of the vendor company have an interest in the contract, the permission of the company's shareholders at general meeting may be required to approve the transaction. Such an interest would arise for example in the case of a management buy-out where the directors are involved in the purchasing company. This will be examined in greater detail in Chapter 18.

If the purchaser is a listed company, depending on the size of the acquisition, the shareholders of the purchaser may have to be circularised and possibly their approval may need to be sought.[1a]

B. Completion Board Meeting

17–03 A completion meeting of the outgoing directors of the vendor will be called. In the case of a share sale agreement, a board resolution approving the transfer of shares to the purchaser must then be passed. Any existing pre-emption rights applying to the transfer of shares will also need to be avoided.[1] The completion board must also register the purchaser or the purchaser's nominees under letters of allotment.

---

[1] See Chap. 15, paras 15–06–15–12.
[1a] See Chap. 5, paras 5–33–5–47.

17–04   The board will generally be required to pass a resolution agreeing the change of names which will be required for the company's bank mandate. The existing mandate will thus be revoked and new mandates will be issued giving authority to the purchaser's nominees. Finally, the completion board must appoint the purchaser's nominees as directors and resign their positions as directors or officers of the company and furnish their letters of resignation. The auditors and company secretary will generally furnish their resignations at this stage too. The purchaser should also seek written confirmation from these persons or firms to the effect that they have no claims against the company.

C. Delivery of Documents

17–05   In the case of a share sale, the purchaser must take delivery of the company's books, records and registers. These will include the company's certificate of incorporation, its common seal, the statutory books, the memorandum and articles of association, the title deeds to any of the company's properties, current bank statements, cheque books, insurance policies, contracts to which the company is a party and the deed of indemnity. In addition, the share certificates and the duly executed share transfer forms will be delivered to the purchaser. Where any of the share certificates have been lost or cannot be located, the purchaser will obtain an indemnity in lieu thereof. The share transfer forms must be stamped with the appropriate amount of stamp duty. An unstamped instrument will not be acceptable as proof of title in a property transaction so the purchaser must insist on these forms being duly stampled. Section 1(3) of the Stamp Act, 1891 directs that any instrumental chargeable with duty is, unless it is written upon duly stamped material, to be stamped within 30 days after it is first executed. Special rules apply to the stamping of certain instruments and it is important to note that in order to be enforceable, certain instruments, such as promissory notes, must be stamped prior to becoming operative. Section 17 of the Stamp Act 1891 provides that it is an offence for any person whose office it is to enrol or register upon any books or records any instrument chargeable with duty, to enter any instrument which is not duly stamped. A fine of £500 is payable for a breach of this provision. This section would apply in the case of the registration by a company secretary of an unstamped stock transfer form.[1b]

[1b]   See O'Connor & Cahill, *The Law of Stamp Duties*, (The Institute of Taxation in Ireland, 1998) Chap. 11, Goodman "Stamp Duty on Contracts for Sale" (1999) *Irish Tax Review* 60.

17–06   The letters of resignation from the outgoing directors will also be delivered to the purchaser. Where it has proven necessary to obtain the consent of third parties such as banks or grant agencies, including the IDA, to the acquisition, letters from these persons giving this consent if they have not already been obtained by the purchaser, must also be delivered at this stage.

D. Vesting of Assets

17–07   In the case of an asset sale, each asset must vest in the purchaser. Where property is being sold, a formal conveyance will be required. In addition, as the insurance for the assets acquired will be in the vendor's name, the purchaser must change the policy for these assets to its own name.

E. Completion Accounts

17–08   Completion accounts are generally prepared by an agreed person and made available to the other party who then has an agreed period to notify its approval of them. Normally, it is stated that if an agreement cannot be reached, the matter will be referred to an arbitrator.

F. Consideration

17–09   The purchaser will also agree to the time for delivery of the consideration. The entire amount due may be transferred after completion or, as noted in Chapter 16,[1c] a part of it may be deferred until some later agreed time. Typically a bank draft for the agreed amount will be delivered to the vendor's solicitors upon completion.

G. Consultation with Employees

17–10   Section 52(1) of the Companies Act 1990 provides that the directors "are to have regard in the performance of their functions..[to] the interests of the company's employees in general" as well as the interests of its members. Although this would seem to constitute an important development for employees, section 52(2) minimises the

---

[1c]   See Chap. 16, paras 16–04–16–05.
[2]   This rule was established in *Foss v. Harbottle* (1843) 2 Hare 461.

benefit of subsection (1) considerably. It states that the duty imposed on directors by this section, "shall be owed by them to the company (and the company alone) and shall be enforceable in the same way as any other fiduciary duty owed to a company by its directors". This means that the employees cannot themselves enforce this duty. The company alone is the correct plaintiff in any action.[2] Gower described the equivalent UK section 309 of the Companies Act 1985 as a "grudging recognition that the interests of the company include those of its workforce".[3] Thus, whilst employees might complain that directors have breached their duties by ignoring the interests of employees during a takeover situation, they will have to wait for the company to enforce their rights. Unlike shareholders who feel that directors have breached their duties, employees do not have access to the section 205 of the 1963 Act machinery as this is restricted to "members".[4]

Legislation has been introduced specifically to give employees rights in one specified area during the acquisition process – the right to be consulted.

I. TRANSFER OF UNDERTAKINGS

17–11   The consultation provisions set out in the Transfer of Undertakings Regulations are set out in Chapter 9, paragraphs 9–45 *et seq.*

II. THE PROTECTION OF EMPLOYMENT ACT 1977

17–12   The Protection of Employment Act 1977 ("the 1977 Act") provides certain informational benefits to employees where collective redundancies are anticipated. The 1977 Act was introduced to provide for the implementation of a Council Directive on the approximation of the laws of Member States relating to collective redundancies.[5] The 1977 Act seeks to protect employees where collective redundancies are effected in any period of 30 consecutive days for certain reasons stated in the Act.

17–13   The term "collective redundancies" is defined in section 6(1) of the Act as:

> "dismissals which are effected for a reason specified in subsection(2) (other than a reason related to the individual employees dismissed) where in any period of 30 consecutive days the number of such dismissals is –
> (a) at least five in an establishment normally employing more than 20 and less than 50 employees;

---

3   *Gower's Principles of Modern Company Law* (Sweet & Maxwell, 1997), 555.
4   Chap. 19, paras 19–23–19–39.
5   Directive 75/129. OJ L48/29.

(b) at least ten in an establishment normally employing at least 50 but less than 100 employees;

(c) at least ten per cent. of the number of employees in an establishment normally employing at least 100 but less than 300 employees; and

(d) at least 30 in an establishment normally employing 300 or more employees."

Dismissals of this proportion are quite likely in the wake of large scale acquisitions. For example, when Royal Sun Alliance merged with Royal Insurance in 1996 in a £15 billion deal, 5,000 employees in the UK were dismissed as part of a drive to save £175 million in costs.

17–14 Section 6(2) of the 1977 Act provides that the reasons for a dismissal referred to in section 6(1) are:

"(a) that the employer concerned has ceased, or intends to cease, to carry on the business for the purpose of which the employees concerned were employed by him, or has ceased or intends to cease, to carry on that business in the place where those employees were so employed;

(b) that the requirements of business for employees to carry out work of a particular kind in the place where the employees concerned were so employed have ceased or diminished or are expected to cease or diminish;

(c) that the employer concerned has decided to carry on the business with fewer or no employees, whether by requiring the work for which the employees concerned had been employed (or had been doing before their dismissal) to be done by other employees or otherwise;

(d) that the employer concerned has decided that the work for which the employees concerned had been employed (or had been doing before their dismissal) should henceforward be done in a different manner for which those employees are not sufficiently qualified or trained;

(e) that the employer concerned has decided that the work for which the employees concerned had been employed (or had been doing before their dismissal) should henceforward be done by persons who are also capable of doing other work for which those employees are not sufficiently qualified or trained."

Dismissals falling under paragraphs (c) would be common in a horizontal takeover where employees in the offeree perform the same tasks as employees in the offeror and are thus rendered redundant following the takeover. Similarly, dismissals falling under paragraph (b) would be common where an undertaking re-locates a part of its operations to create synergies in the aftermath of an acquisition.

17–15 Section 9(1) of the 1977 Act stipulates that where an employer proposes to create collective redundancies it shall, "with a view to reaching an agreement", consult with employees' representatives representing the employees affected by the proposed redundancies and supply them with all relevant information. The term "consultation" in this section is stated to include "the possibility of avoiding the proposed redundancies, reducing the number of employees affected by them or otherwise mitigating their consequences".[6] It should also include the basis on which it will be decided which particular employees will be made redundant.

17–16 For the purpose of consultations under section 9, section 10(1) of the 1977 Act requires the relevant employer to supply the employees' representatives with all relevant information relating to the proposed redundancies. This information should include the reasons for the proposed redundancies, the number of employees to be made redundant, the number of employees normally employed and the period during which it is proposed to effect the proposed redundancies.[7] Failure by the employer to initiate these consultations will render it liable to a fine not exceeding £500 on summary conviction.[8]

17–17 Section 12(1) also requires the employer to notify the Minister for Employment in writing of proposed redundancies at the earliest opportunity and in any event at least 30 days before the first dismissal takes effect. A copy of this notification should also be sent as soon as possible by the relevant employer to the employees' representatives who may then make submissions to the Minister on the notification.[9] An employer who fails to notify the Minister in accordance with this section will be liable to a maximum fine of £500 upon summary conviction.[10] Collective redundancies are prohibited from taking effect before the expiry of this 30 day period.[11] Where they are effected by an employer before this time, the employer will be guilty of an offence and liable on conviction on indictment to a fine not exceeding £3,000.[12] At the Minister's request, the relevant employer must enter consultations with either the Minister or an authorised officer for the purpose of seeking solutions to the problems caused by the redundancies.[13]

17–18 A number of problems render this legislation less than potent in safe-guarding employees' interests in a takeover. Firstly, it may be argued that even if a takeover likely to cause redundancies in a listed company is planned, details cannot be passed to employees prior to that information being published without breaching inside information

[6] Protection of Employment Act 1977, s.9(2)(a).
[7] *ibid.*, s.10(2).
[8] *ibid.*, s.11.
[9] *ibid.*, s.12(3).
[10] *ibid.*, s.13.
[11] *ibid.*, s.14(1).
[12] *ibid.*, s.14(2).
[13] *ibid.*, s.15(1).

regulations. There would exist in such circumstances a substantial like-lihood that the employees would deal on the basis of this information.[14] When the offer is actually published, there may be no point in the target directors consulting with employees as the former may have no control over those redundancies if the offer is successful. If the offer is successful, arguably it will be too late for employees or even the Minister to persuade the new controller not to cut their jobs. Any redundancies which are planned are likely to have already been factored into the cost of the acquisition. A final problem is that the maximum penalty for failing to initiate consultations is a fine of £500. This is unlikely to act as an adequate deterrent. In any case, the employer is offered a possibility of mitigating this penalty by pleading that "substantial reasons related to his business" made it "impracticable for him to comply" with his obli-gations.[15] The necessity of maintaining the confidentiality of certain information may provide just such an excuse. In July 1999, it was reported that the outgoing Irish Commissioner for Employment and Social Affairs, Mr. Padraig Flynn was sending Ireland a reasoned opinion complaining that the Directive had been inadequately transposed into Irish Law. One of the Commission's criticisms is that the penalties are inadequate to protect workers' rights to claim compensation for non-consultation by employers.[15a]

III. THE TRANSNATIONAL INFORMATION AND CONSULTATION OF EMPLOYEES ACT 1996

17–19 The Transnational Information and Consultation of Employees Act 1996 ("the 1996 Act") was introduced in order to implement Council Directive 94/45[15b] concerning the establishment of European Works Councils or procedures in community-scale undertakings and groups of undertakings for the purpose of informing and consulting employees. The Directive requires the establishment of European Works Councils in large enterprises operating across two or more Member States. It also provides for the establishment of special negotiating bodies ("SNBs") comprising of representatives from the undertakings operations in the countries concerned. It was anticipated that with the completion of the Single Market, mergers and takeovers across EU country borders would lead to the "transnationalisation of enterprises". In this environment, it was felt that community action was required to ensure that undertakings operating in more than one Member State were obliged to inform and to consult representatives of employees

---

[14] See Chap. 13, para. 13–25.
[15] Protection of Employment Act 1977, s.22.
[15a] *Irish Times*, July 22, 1999.
[15b] O.J. L254/64.

affected by their decisions. Although there is no specific reference to takeovers, decisions on the future prospects of the business could obviously be categorised as a decision affecting employees.

17–20 A "community-scale undertaking" is defined in section 3(1) of the 1996 Act as any undertaking with at least 1000 employees within the Member States and at least 150 employees in each of at least two Member States. A "community-scale group of undertakings" is defined in the same section of the Act as "a group of undertakings with (a) at least 1000 employees within the Member States and (b) at least one group undertaking with at least 150 employees in one Member State and at least one other group undertaking with at least 150 employees in another Member State." These thresholds are based on the average number of employees, including part-time employees, employed in the undertaking or group of undertakings during the two years immediately proceeding the request for the establishment of the SNB.[16]

17–21 Section 8 of the 1996 Act sets out the general obligations of community-scale undertakings and community-scale groups of undertakings as regards the information and consultation of employees. It provides that either a European Works Council or arrangements for the information and consultation of employees must be established in every such undertaking and group of undertakings. The central management of the undertaking or in the case of a group of undertakings, the central management of the "controlling undertaking" is given responsibility for "creating the conditions necessary for the setting up of an arrangement for the information and consultation of employees".[16a] The "controlling undertaking" is the undertaking which can exercise a dominant influence over another undertaking by virtue of ownership, financial participation or the rules which govern the controlled undertaking.[17] In order to facilitate the information and consultation process, the central management may on its own initiative establish a SNB to negotiate with the central management for the establishment of a European Employees' Forum or an information and consultation procedure. Where at least 100 employees or their representatives in at least two undertakings in at least two different Member States request in writing, the central management must establish the SNB.[18] The function of the SNB is to negotiate with the central management for a written agreement for the establishment of arrangements for the information and consultation of employees.[19] Both

---

[16] Transnational Information and Consultation of Employees Act 1996, s.4.
[16a] *ibid.*, s.9(1).
[17] *ibid.*, s.5(1).
[18] *ibid.*, s.10.
[19] *ibid.*, s.11.

the SNB and the central management are obliged to negotiate in a "spirit of co-operation" with a view to reaching an agreement to set out *inter alia* the structure, coverage, functions and procedures of the information and consultation arrangements.[20]

17–22 Members of the SNB's, the European Works Council or the European Employees Forum are required to maintain the confidentiality of sensitive information conveyed to them. In addition, the central management are authorised to withhold commercially sensitive information.[21] Such information would obviously include information to the effect that takeover negotiations are in process in circumstances where that information had not yet been published . Where there is a dispute as to whether information is commercially sensitive or not, the dispute will be referred to an arbitrator.[22]

17–23 This Act only provides a limited protection for employees in a takeover situation. Apart from the limited application of this Act to employees in general, other difficulties would stem from the confidential nature of the information to be disclosed and the fact that while the Act ensures that employees are informed of major changes in employment, their ability to affect the decisions being made would seem slight. In addition, an exemption from the provisions of the Act may be obtained by undertakings which by September 1996 are party to an agreement providing for the transnational information and consultation of employees and covering the entire workforce.[23] The majority of the employees must, however, have consented to this agreement. To date, the Labour Court has been asked on two occassions to arbitrate on disputes over European Works Councils.

IV. THE PROPOSED 13TH DIRECTIVE

17–24 Article 3(1) of the proposed 13th Directive on Company Law concerning takeover bids[24] sets out six general principles which must be respected in the rules introduced by Member States to implement the Directive. As noted in Chapter 4, in the original version of the proposal one of these principles imposed a duty on the board of the target company "to act in the interests of the company as a whole". An amended proposal in 1997 required the board "to act in all the interests of the

---

[20] *ibid.*, s.12.
[21] *ibid.*, s.15
[22] *ibid.*, s.20.
[23] *ibid.*, s.6.
[24] COM(97) 565 final (O.J. C 378/97).

company, including employment". The Company and Commercial Law Committee of the Law Society of Ireland noted that this principle would cause difficulties where there was a conflict between the interests of the shareholders and the interests of the employees. Such a conflict would arise for example where a generous offer had been made to shareholders but in circumstances where the bidder made clear its intention to dismiss a large portion of the workforce following the acquisition. Modern corporate theory would appear to suggest that the claims of the shareholders should be paramount.[25] Furthermore, the Committee pointed out that as the main focus of the Directive is on protecting shareholders, theirs would appear to be the overriding interest. The latest version of the proposed Directive refers again to a duty "to act in the interests of the company as a whole".

17–25 Article 6 sets out the informational requirements to be complied with by Member States in their rules. This Article imposes obligations on Member States to provide employees with certain relevant information. This is in keeping with a recommendation of the EU Economic and Social Committee.[26] Article 6(1) states that as soon as the bid has been made public, the board of the offeree must inform the representatives of its employees, or the employees themselves if there are no representatives. In addition, Article 6(2) requires that when the offer document has been made public the board communicate it to the employees' representatives or, where there are no representatives, to the employees. Article 6(3) sets out the minimum informational requirements to be included in the offer document. This document should contain *inter alia* details of the offeror's intentions with regard to the future business and undertakings of the offeree, its employees and its management. The 1997 proposal required that the document should also include "any change" in the conditions of employment. This would have involved an obligation to notify any intended change, no matter how trivial. It could include, for example, a delay of 10 minutes in the timing of a lunch break. The latest proposal is more pragmatic and requires notification of "any material change" in the conditions of employment. Notifying the employees of proposed redundancies as a consequence of a takeover would clearly be warranted under these provisions. However, although the employees may thus be entitled under the Directive to be informed of their plight, there would appear to be little they could do to avoid their fate.

---

[25] Clarke, "Corporate Responsibility In Light Of The Separation Of Ownership And Control" (1997) Vol. 19 *Dublin University Law Journal* 50.
[26] [1996] O.J. No. C295/1.

PART 5

MANAGEMENT BUY-OUTS

CHAPTER 18

MANAGEMENT BUY-OUTS

18–01 A management buy-out ("MBO") involves a part or all of the existing management of the offeree company becoming involved in a consortium set up to acquire the offeree.[1] A related concept is a leveraged buy-out or "LBO". This is an American term for an acquisition which has been initiated not by the management, but by a group of financiers. This type of transaction involves a heavily geared or leveraged company. The company being acquired may be either a public company or a private company. One of the most famous MBOs of a public company was the $25 billion buyout of RJR Nabisco in 1989. The consideration in this case amounted to a premium of $12 billion over the previous market value. The 1998 Chapman Flood survey records 12 MBOs being reported during 1998, an increase on the previous year when seven took place. However, the survey also reported that interest in MBOs was only slightly higher than in 1997. The largest of the deals was worth almost £12.7 million.[2]

18–02 Typically, an MBO involves a 100 per cent purchase of the offeree's shares or assets for cash. An MBO will normally be effected by either incorporating a new company for this specific purpose or by purchasing an "off the shelf" company to acquire the offeree. The new company is then capitalised in order to allow it meet the cost of the acquisition. Institutional investors are generally involved in order to fund the new company and to assist in the negotiations with the vendor. The management in turn brings to the new company expertise and experience, though generally only a small portion of the finance.

A. Attractions of an MBO

18–03 MBOs provide an attractive opportunity to existing private owners who wish to retire or to realise a profit from their investment.

---

[1] Another related transaction is a Management Buy-In Or "MBI". This involves the acquisition of a company by outside management with the help of a group of financial backers. Many deals involve an element of both MBOs and MBIs and are known as BIMBOs (a term coined by III). These are deals which involve both existing and external management.

[2] An MBO of Betatherm Corporation in April, 1998.

MBOs are also a useful means by which a parent company can dispose of a subsidiary which is no longer in keeping with the parent's development plans or which is under-performing. Alternatively, a parent may decide to sell a subsidiary in order to raise cash for other business ventures. Finally, where a company is in receivership, an MBO generally offers the receiver a more efficient alternative to a liquidation.

Because the existing management are very familiar with the operations of the company, its financial standing and its future prospects, they are often in a better position than other outside parties to assess the true value of the business. They are thus capable of putting a well priced offer to the company's shareholders in a relatively short period of time.

B. The MBO Vehicle

18–04   MBOs by their nature tend to involve a high level of gearing. One of the reasons for this is that the managements intending to acquire the company do not generally have access to a large amount of personal capital. A second reason is that managements seek to retain as much of the equity of the company as possible in order to maintain control. A further reason why debt financing is so popular at the moment is that the bull market has driven up the price of equity significantly and, as interest rates are low, debt may be perceived as better value.

Large companies may be acquired through the use of high yield bonds or "junk bonds". This market began in the United States in the latter half of the 1970s and was dominated by a single investment bank, Drexel Burnham Lamber, until the mid-1980s.[2a] Although these bonds were structured as term bonds paying a fixed interest at the outset, more complex bond stuctures are used now, particularly in the case of bonds issued for MBO financing. In order to avoid the interest rate burden becoming a severe restraint on the company's cash flow, bonds are issued with deferred interest structures or step-up bonds providing for low-interest payments for the initial period increasing to higher interest payments over time. These type of bonds are beginning to become popular in the UK and Irish markets. A popular source of finance for medium-sized MBOs is asset-backed financing. This involves the issuance of securities which have a pool of assets such as future cash flows as collateral. In this case, the company retains control of the management of debtors and an outside lender provides a lump sum based on a discount of invoice values. Generally, up to 80 per cent

---

[2a] Fabozzi (ed.), *The New High-Yield Debt Market*, (Harper & Row, New York, 1991) Chap. 2 – Madden and Balestrino, "Evolution of the High-Yield Market".

of the value of the approved invoices will be available to the company immediately. Subsequently, when all the debts are collected, the remaining 20 per cent, less the invoice discounting company's charges, are available to the company. The advantage of this source of finance is that it guarantees the company a constant and steady cashflow irrespective of the debtor's days figure. The principle of invoice-discounting can be extended to loans secured on other assets such as stock or even property. Another similar source of finance available to a company is factoring. By contrast with invoice-discounting, this involves handing over management of the company's debtors ledger to an independent factor who assumes responsibility for enforcing payment.

Management may seek a mix of debt and equity to finance their acquisition. In such a case, the new company which is used as a vehicle for the MBO, will have a complex share structure consisting of ordinary shares held by management and some form of Mezzanine debt held by the institutions. Mezzanine debt is a mix between straight debt and equity with characteristics of both. Like debt, it is typically subordinated to other borrowings, ranking just before share capital in a liquidation. Because of the higher risk associated with this category of finance, it typically bears a higher than average interest rate. Mezzanine debt possesses the characteristics of semi-permanent capital in that normally instead of providing for a phased repayment of the principal over time, it provides for a bullet payment at the end. Like equity, the instrument constituting the mezzanine debt entitles the provider of finance to acquire a pre-determined proportion of the company's share capital on preferential terms. This entitlement often takes the form of a warrant to subscribe for new shares in the company either on the occurrence of an "exit event" or at some future predetermined time. Unlike senior debt, mezzanine finance normally has a negative asset cover as it relies totally on future cashflows for reward and repayment. The reason that mezzanine finance is so useful in MBO situations is that it offers great flexibility to the MBO team in terms of structuring the finance and attracting investors with different degrees of risk aversity.

Often, the structure will provide a ratchet for management linking the percentage shareholding available to them overall to company performance. Because of the leveraged nature of the transaction, the provisions of section 60 of the Companies Act 1963 are particularly relevant.[3] The target company must ensure that it is not financing the purchase of its own shares.

18–05 The providers of finance will be particularly interested in the exit routes which will be available to them to allow them to recoup

---

[3] See Chap. 14.

their investment at some subsequent date. The most attractive route is through the eventual flotation of the company on the Stock Exchange. This is the ideal scenario as it generates huge profits for the financiers while allowing them to continue their relationship with the company if they so desire. Where an MBO is proposed by the management of a listed company who wish to take the company private, this exit route will obviously not be available. In such a case, much would depend on the ability of management to persuade financiers that the company has been seriously undervalued by the market, and that having freed itself from the shackles of its shareholders, it can increase performance and returns.

C. Regulation

18–06 Depending on whether the company to be acquired by management is a private company or a public company, the rules and regulations set out in Parts 3 and 4 of this text will apply. In addition, certain additional specific rules come into play when a company is being acquired by its management. Most of these rules constitute safeguards to protect shareholders against the conflict of interest situation which develops.

18–07 A director of a company who is also a participant in the MBO will obviously be placed in a situation in which his or her interests conflict with those of the shareholders. As a director of the offeree, he or she is obliged to act in the best interests of the shareholders and achieve the highest price for them if the sale goes ahead. In certain cases, it might be in the shareholders best interests to advise shareholders to reject the offer or to seek a higher offer. As a participant in the offeror, the director is obviously interested in expediting the sale at the lowest price possible. As long as he or she remains a director with fiduciary duties to the company and its shareholders, conflicts must be resolved in such a manner as best furthers the interests of the company and its shareholders.

I. COMMON LAW FIDUCIARY DUTIES

18–08 The courts have imposed a duty on directors to act for a proper purpose in the interests of the company and not to exercise their powers for some ulterior motive.[3a] As was noted previously, directors are often given a wide discretion in selling assets.[4] Furthermore, they

---

[3a] See generally Gower's *Principles of Modern Company Law* (Sweet and Maxwell, 1987), pp. 605–623; Ussher, *Company Law in Ireland* (Sweet and Maxwell, 1986), pp. 207–218; Courtney, *The Law of Private Companies* (Butterworths, 1994), pp. 301–304.

[4] See Chap. 8, paras 8–03–8–05.

are in a position to advise shareholders whether to recommend or reject an offer in the case of a public listed company. Consequently, their influence on the success or failure of an offer is considerable.

18–09 In *Re Smith & Fawcett Ltd.*,[5] the Court of Appeal held that directors are obliged to exercise their discretion bona fide in what they consider is the interests of the company and not for any collateral purpose. It would clearly be an improper motive if the directors were to organise the sale of assets if this was not in the shareholders best interests. Similarly, it would be improper for the directors to recommend a takeover offer made by an MBO team if this were not indeed in the shareholders' best interests.

18–10 Directors also owe a duty to the company to avoid self dealing. A director is not entitled to retain any unauthorised profit made in connection with the performance of his duties[6] or to divert corporate opportunities.[7] A director should avoid conflict of interest situations. In *Aberdeen Railway Co. v. Blaikie Bros.*[8] Lord Cranworth noted that:

> "[I]t is a rule of universal application, that no one, having [fiduciary] duties to discharge, shall be allowed to enter into engagements in which he has, or can have, a personal interest conflicting, or which possibly may conflict, with the interests of those whom he is bound to protect . . . So strictly is this principal adhered to, that no question is allowed to be raised as to the fairness or unfairness of a contract so entered into."[9]

This principle was held to apply by the Court even where the company obtained full value or profited from the transaction. Only full disclosure of the contract to the members and the ratification of the contract in general meeting will thus serve to meet the director's duty.[10] If the director fails to disclose his or her interest, the contract will be voidable at the instance of the company against any party who had notice of the breach.[11] However, it should be noted that the usual bars to rescission apply and the company may thus be denied rescission where restitution is impossible or where third party rights are affected. In addition to rescinding the contract, the company is entitled to recover any resulting benefit from the director.

---

5 [1942] Ch. 304.
6 *Regal (Hastings) Ltd v. Gulliver* [1967] 2 A.C. 134; *Industrial Development Consultants Ltd v. Cooley* [1972] 1 W.L.R. 443; *Cockburn v. Newbridge Sanitary Steam Laundry Co.* [1915] 1 I.R. 237.
7 *Cook v. Deeks* [1916] 1 A.C. 554.
8 (1854) 1 Macq. 461.
9 *ibid.*, at 471.
10 *Benson v. Heathorn* (1842) 1 Y&CCC 326.
11 *Transvaal Lands Co. v. New Belgium (Transvaal) Land and Development Co.* [1914] 2 Ch. 488.

18–11   The difficulty however, is that by adopting a suitable article in the company's constitution, a director may avoid the fiduciary principle as it applies to transactions in which he or she has an interest. Regulation 83 of Part I of Table A provides that:

> "A director who is in any way, whether directly or indirectly, interested in a contract or proposed contract with the company shall declare the nature of his interest at a meeting of the directors in accordance with section 194 of the Act."

Article 84 prohibits a director from voting "in respect of any contract or arrangement in which he is so interested, and if he shall so vote, his vote shall not be counted".[12] However this prohibition does not apply *inter alia* to "any contract or arrangement with any other company in which he is interested only as an officer of such other company or as a holder of shares or other securities in such other company." Regulation 85 provides that:

> "A director may hold any other office or place of profit under the company (other than the office of auditor) in conjunction with his office of director for such period and on such terms as to remuneration and otherwise as the directors may determine, and no director or intending director shall be disqualified by his office from contracting with the company either with regard to his tenure of any other such office or place of profit or as vendor, purchaser or otherwise, nor shall any such contract or any contract or arrangement entered into by or on behalf of the company in which any director is in any way interested, be liable to be avoided, nor shall any director so contracting or being so interested be liable to account to the company for any profit realised by any such contract or arrangement by reason of such director holding that office or of the fiduciary relation thereby established."

18–12   A director who is part of an MBO consortium which acquires the shares or the assets of the company will obviously have a financial interest in the contract, and must thus disclose it to the company. Failure to do so would lead to the reapplication of the *Aberdeen Railway Co.* principle and the invalidation of the contract.[13] In *Lee Panavision Ltd v. Lee Lighting Ltd.*[14] the Court of Appeal held that the desirability of applying uniform tests meant that the procedure for the disclosure of interests under section 317 of the Companies Act 1985 [equivalent to section 194 of the 1963 Act] should be imported into Regulation 85 of Table A of the Act. Accordingly, Regulation 85 was deemed to require a director to disclose the nature and extent of any material interest in a

---

[12]   Reg. 1 Pt. II of Table A provides that whereas regs 83 and 85 apply to private companies, reg. 84 does not.

[13]   *Movietex Ltd. v. Bulfield* [1988] B.C.L.C. 104.

[14]   [1992] B.C.L.C. 22 affirming [1991] B.C.L.C. 575.

contract with the company to the board of directors at the meeting at which the contract was first considered. Knowledge of the interest by pre-meeting informal disclosure was insufficient.

18–13 A further difficulty with using fiduciary duties to ensure that directors manage the conflict of interest inherent in an MBO is that traditionally directors are deemed to owe their fiduciary duties to the company itself and not to individual shareholders. Therefore, the company is the proper plaintiff in an action against a director for a breach, not a shareholder.[15] This may make enforcement of fiduciary duties difficult.[15a]

II. COMPANIES ACTS

18–14 The fiduciary duties imposed on directors in respect of conflict of interest situations are supplemented by certain provisions in the Companies Acts.[15b] These provisions prohibit certain transactions involving directors and allow other subject to certain onerous disclosure or approval requirements.

(1) Section 194 of the Companies Act 1963

18–15 Section 194(1) of the Companies Act 1963 ("the 1963 Act") provides that:

> "It shall be the duty of a director of a company who is in any way, whether directly or indirectly, interested in a contract or proposed contract with the company to declare the nature of his interest at a meeting of the directors of the company."

Section 47(1) of the Companies Act 1990 ("1990 Act") provides that any reference in section 194 to a contract is to be construed as including a reference to "any transaction or arrangement made or entered into" whether or not constituting a contract.

(a) Declaration and Notice of Interest

18–16 In the case of a proposed contract, the declaration must be made at the meeting of the directors at which the question of entering into the contract is first taken into consideration. If the director was not interested at that stage, the declaration should be made at the next meeting of the directors held after he or she becomes interested. If the

---

[15] *Foss v. Harbottle* (1843) 2 Hare 461, *Percival v. Wright* [1902] 2 Ch. 421.
[15a] See Chap. 13, paras 13.06–13.10 and Chap. 19, paras 19–49–19–52.
[15b] Gower, *op. cit.*, R. 3a at 623–640; Courtney, *op. cit.*, n.3a at 266–28.

director's interest only commences after the contract is made, the declaration must be made at the first meeting of directors held after the director becomes interested.[16]

18–17 Section 194(3)[17] of the 1963 Act provides that the declaration must notify the directors either:

(a) that the director is a member of a specified company or firm and is to be regarded as interested in any contract which may, after the date of the notice, be made with that company or firm or

(b) that the director is to be regarded as interested in any contract which may after the date of the notice be made with a specified person who is connected[18] with him.

The notice will only be effective, however, when it is given at a meeting of the directors or when the director takes reasonable steps to secure that it is brought up and read at the next meeting of the directors after it is given.[19]

18–18 A copy of every declaration and every notice must be entered in a special book kept for this purpose within three days after the making or giving thereof. This book must be available at the registered office for inspection by any director, secretary, auditor or member of the company. It must also be produced at every general meeting of the company. If requested in time, it must also be available at any meeting of directors.[20] Failure to make the book available is an offence rendering the company and every officer in default liable to a maximum fine of £500. Furthermore, if any inspection or production is refused, the court is empowered to order immediate inspection or production.[21]

---

[16] Companies Act 1963, s.194(2).

[17] As amended by section 47(3) of the Companies Act 1990.

[18] Within the meaning of section 26 of the Companies Act 1990. Section 26(1) provides that a person is connected with a director of a company if he is (a) that director's spouse, parent, brother, sister or child; (b) a person acting in his capacity as the trustee of any trust, the principal beneficiaries of which are the director, his spouse or any of his children or any body corporate which he controls; or (c) a partner of that director; unless that person is also a director of the company. Section 26(2) provides that a body corporate shall also be deemed to be connected with a director of a company if it is controlled by that director. Section 26(3) provides that a director shall be deemed to control a company for the purposes of the section if, but only if, he is, alone or together with any of the persons set out in section 26(1)(a)(b) or (c), interested in more than one-half of the equity share capital of the company or entitled to exercise or control the exercise of more than one-half of the voting power at any general meeting of that body.

[19] Companies Act 1963, s.194(4).

[20] *ibid.*, s.194(5)(a).

[21] *ibid.*, s.194(5)(b).

(b) Enforcement

Section 194(6) of the 1963 Act provides that any director who fails to comply with section 194 will be liable to a fine not exceeding £500. In addition, section 194(7) specifically states that:

> "nothing in this section shall be taken to prejudice the operation of any rule of law restricting directors of a company from having any interest in contracts with the company".

In *Guinness v. Saunders*,[22] a director had entered into a contract entitling him to a bonus in the event that the Guinness bid for Distillers was successful. The contract was not disclosed in accordance with section 317 of the Companies Act 1985 which is the equivalent of section 194 of the 1963 Act. Guinness' articles of associations, like Table A, provided that a director would not be liable to account to the company for the benefits arising from such a contract if they were disclosed. The Court of Appeal held that as the interest was not disclosed as required by the Articles, the transaction was voidable at the instance of the company and any benefits received by the director were recoverable by Guinness. It is important to note that Lord Goff opined that the breach of section 317 itself did not have any effect upon the contract. Gower referred to this as a regrettable conclusion and one which the legislature could not have intended.[22a] However, the House of Lords determined that in this case *restitutio in integrum* was not possible and it found that the contract was invalid on a different basis.

18–19 Where articles equivalent to Table A are incorporated by a company, failure by its directors to disclose interests will entitle the company in most cases to recover any benefits. The situation is not so clear, where the Table A articles are avoided by the company. Gower suggests that the contract would be voidable in any case under equitable principles because articles cannot contract out of a statutory duty.[23]

(2) Section 29 of the Companies Act 1990

18–20 Section 29 of the 1990 Act restricts *inter alia* the ability of a director to acquire non-cash assets from the company. Section 29(1) states that a resolution of shareholders at general meeting[24] is required in advance where a company proposes to enter into an arrangement:

---

[22] [1990] 2 A.C. 663. See also *Hely-Hutchinson v. Brayhead Ltd.* [1968] 1 Q.B. 549 (CA).
[22a] Gower, *op. cit.*, n.3a at p. 614.
[23] *op. cit.*, n.3a at pp. 562–564.
[24] If the director is a director of its holding company, a resolution in general meeting of the holding company is required.

"(a) whereby a director of the company or its holding company or a person connected with such a director[25] acquires or is to acquire one or more non-cash assets of the requisite value from the company; or

(b) whereby the company acquires or is to acquire one or more non-cash assets of the requisite value from such a director or a person so connected."

18–21   An MBO of the assets of the undertaking would obviously involve an arrangement under paragraph (a). A "non-cash asset" is defined as "any property or interest in property other than cash, and for this purpose "cash" includes foreign currency".[26] A non-cash asset is "of the requisite value" for the purposes of this section if at the time the arrangement is entered into "its value is not less than £1,000 but, subject to that, exceeds £50,000 or 10 per cent of the amount of the company's relevant assets".[27] Where accounts have been prepared and laid in accordance with section 148 of the 1963 Act, a company's "relevant assets" is the value of its net assets in respect of the last preceding financial year. If no accounts have been laid, the "relevant assets" will be the amount of its called-up share capital. Obviously, where an MBO is proposed, these limits would be breached.

18–22   Any reference to the "acquisition" of a non-cash asset includes a reference to the creation or extinction of an estate or interest in, or a right over, any property and also a reference to the discharge of any personal" liability other than a liability for a liquidated sum.[28]

(a) Effect of a Contravention of Section 29

18–23   In order to ensure compliance, section 29(3) of the 1990 Act provides that an arrangement entered into by the company in contravention of section 29 will be voidable at the instance of the company. In addition, any transaction entered into in pursuance of the prohibited arrangement will also be voidable.

18–24   There are three occasions set out in section 29(3) of the 1990 Act in which a breach will not have this effect. First, where restitution of any money or other asset, the subject of the prohibited arrangement, is no longer possible or where the company has been indemnified in pursuance of section 29(4)(b) by any other person for the loss or

---

[25] Within the meaning of section 26 of the Companies Act 1990.
[26] Companies Act 1990, s.29(9)(a).
[27] *ibid.*, s.29(2).
[28] *ibid.*, s.29(9)(b).

damage suffered by it.[29] Secondly, the agreement or transaction will not be avoided if this would affect the rights of any person who is not a party to the agreement where those rights have been acquired bona fide for value and without actual notice of the contravention.[30] The final circumstance is where the arrangement is affirmed by the company in general meeting within a reasonable period. If the prohibited arrangement involves the transfer of an asset to or by a director of its holding company or a person connected with such a director, the arrangement must be affirmed with the approval of the holding company given by a resolution in general meeting.[31] These are akin to the common law bars to rescission.

18–25 Section 29(4) provides that where an arrangement is entered into with a company by a director of the company or its holding company or a person connected with him, that director, the connected person and any other director who authorised the prohibited arrangement or any transaction entered into in pursuance of the arrangement will be liable:

(a) to account to the company for any gain which he has made directly or indirectly by the arrangement or transaction; and

(b) jointly and severally with any other person liable under this subsection to indemnify the company for any loss or damage resulting from the arrangement or transaction.

This liability exists whether or not the arrangement or transaction has been avoided in pursuance of section 29 (3) above. However, where an arrangement is entered into by a company and a person connected with a director of the company or its holding company, that director may avoid liability if he shows that he took all reasonable steps to secure the company's compliance with section 29. In any case, a connected person and any other directors who authorise the prohibited arrangement or any transaction in pursuance of the prohibited arrangement will not be liable if at the time the arrangement was entered into they were unaware of the relevant circumstances constituting the contravention.[32]

---

[29] *ibid.*, s.29(3)(a).
[30] *ibid.*, s.29(3)(b).
[31] *ibid.*, s.29(3)(c).
[32] *ibid.*, s.29(5).

(b) Exemptions

18–26   In certain specified circumstances shareholder approval will not be necessary for an acquisition of a non-cash asset. First, shareholder approval will not be necessary for any arrangement for the acquisition of a non-cash asset by a holding company from any of its wholly owned subsidiaries or from a holding company by any of its wholly owned subsidiaries or by one wholly owned subsidiary of a holding company from another wholly owned subsidiary of that same holding company.[33] Secondly, shareholder approval will not be necessary for any arrangement for the acquisition of a non-cash asset which is entered into by a company which is being wound up unless the winding up is a members' voluntary winding up.[34] Finally, shareholder approval is unnecessary in the case of an arrangement whereby a person acquires or is to acquire an asset from a company of which he is a member if the arrangement is made with that person in his character as such member.[35]

(3) Section 41 of the Companies Act 1990

18–27   Sections 41 and 42 of the 1990 Act require disclosure of certain transactions involving directors.[36] Section 41(1)(c) provides that the group accounts prepared by a holding company must disclose particulars of:

> "any other transaction or arrangement with the company or with a subsidiary of the company in which a person who at any time during the relevant period was a director of the company or its holding company had, directly or indirectly a material interest".

Section 41(2)(c) provides the accounts prepared by any company other than a holding company in respect of the relevant period must disclose particulars of:

> "any other transaction or arrangement with the company in which a person who at any time during the relevant period was a director of the company or of its holding company had, directly or indirectly a material interest."

18–28   Section 41(5) offers some clarification of the interpretation of section 41(1)(c) and section 41(2)(c). For the purposes of these two subsections:

---

[33] *ibid.,* s.29(7)(a).
[34] *ibid.,* s.29(7)(b)
[35] *ibid.,* s.29(8).
[36] *ibid.,* ss.41 to 43 apply to group accounts prepared in accordance with the European Communities (Companies: Group Accounts) Regulations, 1992 (para. 17 of the sched. to the Regulations).

"a transaction or arrangement between a company and a director of the company or of its holding company or a person connected with such a director shall (if it would not otherwise be so treated) be treated as a transaction, arrangement or agreement in which that director is interested".[37]

In addition, it provides that:

"an interest in such a transaction or arrangement is not material if in the opinion of the majority of the directors (other than that director) of the company which is preparing the accounts in question it is not material (but without prejudice to the question whether or not such an interest is material in any case where those directors have not considered the matter."[38]

18–29 The particulars which are required to be disclosed must be given by way of notes to the accounts.[39] Section 42 provides that the particulars which must be disclosed are particulars of the principal terms of the transaction, arrangement or agreement. In the case of an arrangement requiring disclosure under section 41(1)(c) or section 41(2)(c) this should include:

– a statement of the fact either that the transaction or arrangement was made or subsisted, as the case may be, during the financial year in respect of which those accounts are made up;

– the name of the person for whom it was made, and, where that person is or was connected with a director of the company or of its holding company, the name of that director;

– the name of the director with the material interest and the nature of that interest; and

– the value of the transaction or arrangement or, as the case may be, the value of the transaction or arrangement to which the arrangement relates.

18–30 Section 41(7) provides that section 41(1) and (2) do not apply in relation to the following transactions, arrangements or agreements:

"(a) a transaction, arrangement or agreement between one company and another in which a director of the first company or of its subsidiary or holding company is interested only by virtue of his being a director of the other;

(b) a contract of service between a company and one of its directors or a director of its holding company or between a director of a company and any of that company's subsidiaries;

---

[37] *ibid.*, s.41(5)(a).
[38] *ibid.*, s.41(5)(b).
[39] *ibid.*, s.41(3).

    (c) a transaction, arrangement or agreement which was not entered into during the relevant period for the accounts in question and which did not subsist at any time during that period; and

    (d) a transaction, arrangement or agreement which was made before the commencement of this section and which does not subsist thereafter."

(4) Other Statutory Disclosure Requirements

18–31   The directors of the offeree involved in the MBO may attempt to finance their takeover bid for the company: by obtaining a loan from the company or organising to have the company guarantee or provide security for a loan; by negotiating a severance payment from the company; or obtaining some other form of financial assistance from the company. Any such arrangements with the company are strictly regulated by statute.

(a) Payment for Loss of Office

18–32   As noted previously,[40] sections 186, 187 and 188 of the 1963 Act require the disclosure and approval of payments to directors for loss of office.[41] Section 186 applies where the payment is made by the company itself. Sections 187 requires disclosure and approval for payments made by any party to a director in connection with the transfer of the whole or part of the undertaking or property of a company. Section 188 requires that where payment is made to a director as "compensation for loss of office" or "in connection with his retirement from office", in connection with a general offer to acquire shares of his company, the director should ensure that the payment is disclosed in the offer document. Where the directors attempted to secure payments of this type from the company in order to fund the acquisition, they would therefore have to seek the shareholders' approval.

(b) Loans to Directors

18–33   Section 31(1) of the 1990 Act prohibits a company making a loan to a director or to a director of its holding company or to a person connected with such a director. Sections 31(1) also restrains the company giving a guarantee or security or entering a credit transaction as a creditor for such persons benefit.

---

[40] See Chap. 8, para. 8–29 and Chap. 11, para. 11–55.
[41] Section 189(3) provides that bona fide payments by way of damages for breach of contract or by way of pension in respect of part services are not included under sections 186, 187 or 188.

The restrictions do not apply, however, if the aggregate of all such transactions entered into by the company comes to less than 10 per cent of the company's net assets.[42] Neither do the restrictions apply to transactions entered into by the company in the ordinary course of its business on an arm's length basis.[43]

18–34 If a prohibited transaction is entered into, the effects are similar to a breach of section 29 discussed above. The transaction will be voidable at the option of the company unless (a) *restitution in integrum* is no longer possible or the company has been indemnified for the loss or (b) rescission would affect third party rights.[44] In addition, the director or connected person and any other directors who authorised the transaction may have to account to the company for any gain made by him and to indemnify the company for any loss it incurs.[45] Disclosure of such arrangements or agreements to enter into such arrangements are also required in the accounts pursuant to sections 41, 42 and 43 of the 1990 Act.[46]

(c) Financial Assistance for the Purchase of Own Shares

18–35 In addition to the above restrictions, any such assistance provided by the company itself may be viewed as breaching section 60 of the 1963 Act which prohibits the giving by a company "whether directly or indirectly, and whether by means of a loan guarantee, the provision of security or otherwise any financial assistance for the purpose of or in connection with a purchase or subscription made or to be made by any person of or for any shares in the company". This issue is addressed in chapters 11 and 14.[46a]

III. IRISH TAKEOVER RULES

18–36 Where the company being acquired is "a relevant company" for the purposes of the Irish Takeover Panel Act 1997,[47] the Irish Takeover Panel Act 1997, Takeover Rules, 1997 ("the Rules") will apply. Chapters 11 and 12 have set out the procedures to be followed and the relevant rules which apply where the shares of a company are acquired.[48]

---

[42] *ibid.*, s.32(1).
[43] *ibid.*, s.37.
[44] *ibid.*, s.38(1).
[45] *ibid.*, s.38(2).
[46] *ibid.*, s.41(1)(a), (b).
[46a] See Chap. 11, paras 11–42–11–46; Chap. 14, paras 14–12–14–17.
[47] See Chap. 3, para. 3–18.
[48] As noted in Chapter 3, the Takeover Rules do not apply to the acquisition of the business or the assets of a target company.

However, because of the nature of the transaction and the resulting conflict of interest, additional rules have been introduced to deal with MBOs.

(1) Independent Advice

18–37   Rule 3.1(a) requires the offeree board to obtain competent independent advice and to communicate the substance and source of such advice to shareholders together with their own considered views. However, any director with a conflict of interest is excluded from the formulation and communication of advice. A conflict of interest arises where, for example, there are a number of directors common to both offeror and offeree or where a person is a substantial shareholder in both companies.[49] In an MBO, a director will be regarded as having a conflict of interest if it is intended that he or she will have "a continuing role", whether in an executive or non-executive capacity, in either the offeror or offeree if the offer is successful.[50] The requirement for competent independent advice is particularly important in the case of MBOs and similar transactions. As the responsibility of the adviser is particularly significant, the board of the offeree or potential offeree should appoint an adviser as soon as possible after becoming aware that an offer may be made.[51]

18–38   The independence of the adviser must be beyond question in the case of MBOs. Rule 3.3 lists persons who are disqualified from giving independent advice under Rule 3 unless the Panel agrees otherwise. A person who controls or is controlled by or is under the same control as the financial or other adviser (including a stockbroker) to the offeror is not an appropriate person to give this independent advice to the offeree board.[52] A person who controls or is controlled by or is under the same control as the financial or other adviser (including a stockbroker) to the board of the offeree is not an appropriate person to give independent advice to the offeror. Furthermore, a person who has a significant interest[52a] in or financial connection which would create a conflict of interest with an offeror, offeree or any other party to the transaction is not an appropriate person to give advice to that board.

---

[49] Note 2 on R. 3.1.
[50] Note 3 on R. 25.1.
[51] Note 1 on R. 3.1.
[52] R. 3(3)(a).
[52a] Note 3 R. 3.3 provides that for this purpose, the panel will normally consider a shareholding of 20 per cent or more to be a significant interest.

(2) Equality of Information

18–39 Rule 20.2 requires that competing offerors are provided by the offeree with any requested information to the extent that the same information has been made available by the offeree to other offerors. In the case of an MBO, competing offerors should be provided with the same information, if specifically requested, as is generated by the offeree (including the management of the offeree acting in that capacity) which is passed to external providers or potential providers of finance to the offeror. The directors of the offeree involved in the MBO are obliged to co-operate with the offeree's independent directors and their advisers in the assembly of this information. The purpose of this rule is to ensure equality of information between competing offerors. This in turn guarantees that shareholders are free to make a fully informed decision between equally prepared offerors. Rule 20.3 requires the offeror, if so requested, to promptly furnish the independent directors of the offeree or its advisers with all the information that has been furnished by the offeror to external providers of finance for the buy-out. If this information has not been generated by the directors involved in the MBO acting in their capacity as management of the offeree, it would not seem to follow that this information would need to be disclosed to competing offerors pursuant to R.20.2.

(3) Documentation to the Offeree's Shareholders

18–40 Rule 25.1(d) provides that directors with conflicting interests should not be joined with the remaining directors in expressing their view of the offer in the board circular to shareholders. The participation of a director in an MBO would obviously lead to such a conflict of interest.[53] In addition, the nature of the conflict should be clearly explained in any document issued to shareholders. Depending on the circumstances, a director who has a conflict of interest may be required to make a responsibility statement clarifying that he or she does not accept responsibility for the views of the board on the offer.[54] It should also be remembered that directors participating in an MBO will be presumed to be acting in concert with each other and with the MBO vehicle during the offer period or at any time when they reasonably believe an offer to be imminent.[55]

---

[53] Note 3 on R. 25.1.
[54] Note 2 on R. 25.1.
[55] R. 3.3, pt. A.

IV. STOCK EXCHANGE LISTING RULES

18–41   As noted in Chapter 5 above, Chapter 11 of the Stock Exchange Listing Rules provides that where any transaction is proposed between a listed company (or any of its subsidiary undertakings) and a related party, a circular and the prior approval of the company in general meeting will generally be required.

(1) Definitions

18–42   A "transaction with a related party" is defined as:

> "(i) a transaction (other than a transaction of a revenue nature in the ordinary course of business) between a company, or any of its subsidiary undertakings, and a related party; or
>
> (ii) any arrangements pursuant to which a company, or any of its subsidiary undertakings, and a related party each invests in, or provides finance to, another undertaking or asset."[56]

18–43   The definition of "related party" is defined as:

> "(i) a substantial shareholder;
>
> (ii) any person who is (or was within the 12 months preceding the date of the transaction) a director or shadow director of the company or any other company which is (and, if he has ceased to be such, was while he was a director or shadow director of such other company) its subsidiary, undertaking or parent undertaking or a fellow subsidiary undertaking of its parent undertaking;
>
> . . .
>
> (iv) an associate of a related party within (i) or (ii) above."[57]

The parties included in paragraph (ii) and (iii) are obviously the relevant parties for the purposes of an MBO. An associate of a director would include:

 (i) that individual's spouse or child (together "the individual's family");

 (ii) the trustees (acting as such) of any trust of which the individual or any of the individual's family is a beneficiary or discretionary object[58]

(iii) any company in whose equity shares the individual or any member or members (taken together) of the individual's family or the individual and any such member or members (taken together) are directly or indirectly interested (or have a conditional or

---

[56] Listing Rules para. 11–1(a).
[57] Listing Rules para. 11–1(b). Para. 11–1(b)(iii) was deleted in January 1999.

contingent entitlement to become interested) so that they are (or would on the fulfilment of the condition or the occurrence of the contingency) be able:

- to exercise or control the exercise of 30 per cent or more of the votes able to be cast at general meetings on all, or substantially all, matters; or
- to appoint or remove directors holding a majority of voting rights at board meetings on all, or substantially all, matters.[59]

For the purposes of determining whether a company is an associate of a director under paragraph 11.1(d)(iii) above, it should be noted that where more than one of the directors of the listed company, its parent undertaking or any of its subsidiaries is interested in the equity shares of another company, then the interests of those directors and their associates will be aggregated when determining whether such a company is an associate of the director.[60] Consultation with the Exchange at an early stage is required prior to entering into a transaction which could be a transaction with a related party if clarification if needed as to the application of Chapter 11.[61]

(2) Usual Requirements

18–44 Where a company proposes to enter into a transaction with a related party, the company must make any appropriate announcement required by Chapter 10 depending on the classification of the transaction. The announcement must contain the details required to be included in a Class 2 transaction notification,[62] the name of the related party concerned and details of the nature and extent of the interest of the related party in the transaction.[63] The company must send its shareholders a circular containing the information required by paragraph 11.10. even further information.[64] This includes:

(a) the name and address of the company, the documents which are required to be on display, major interests in shares, material contracts, details of the consideration and significant changes in the company's trading or financial position since the last published accounts;

---

[58] Other than a trust which is either an occupational pension scheme or an employees' share scheme which does not, in either case, have the effect of conferring benefits on persons all or most of whom are related parties.

[59] Listing Rules para. 11–1(d).

[60] Listing Rules para. 11–2.

[61] Listing Rules para. 11–3.

[62] Listing Rules para. 10–31.

[63] Listing Rules para. 11–4(a).

[64] Listing Rules para. 11–4(b).

(b)   the directors' interests in shares, the directors' interests in unusual transactions and the directors' service contracts;

(c)   full particulars of the transaction, including the name of the related parties concerned and the nature and extent of their interests in the transaction;

(d)   in the case of an acquisition or disposal of an asset, an independent valuation;

(e)   a statement by the directors (other than any director who is, or an associate of whom is, a related party, or who is a director of a related party, in respect of the transaction) that the transaction is fair and reasonable so far as the shareholders of the company are concerned and that the directors have been so advised by an independent adviser acceptable to the Stock Exchange;

(f)   where applicable, a statement that the related party will abstain, and has taken all reasonable steps to ensure that its associates will abstain, from voting at the meeting;

(g)   if the transaction also falls within Class 1, the information required to be included in a Class 1 circular;

(h)   details of any other transactions entered into by the company (or any of its subsidiaries) with the same related party (and any of its associates) which have not been approved by shareholders, if required by paragraph 11.9; and

(i)   where a statement or report attributed to a person as an expert is included in any circular which does not comprise listing particulars, a statement that it is included, in the form and context in which it is concluded, with the consent of that person.

18–45   Shareholder approval must be obtained either prior to the transaction being entered into or, if it is expressed to be conditional upon such approval, prior to the completion of the transaction.[65] The related party must not vote on the resolution for this approval and must take all reasonable steps to ensure that its associates do not vote.[66] Although paragraphs 11.7 and 11.8 sets out certain circumstances in which the usual requirements will not apply,[67] none of the exceptions are likely to apply in an MBO.

---

[65]   Listing Rules para. 11–4(c).
[66]   Listing Rules para. 11–4(d). See also Appendix 1, para. 20 to Chap. 13 of the Listing Rules.
[67]   See Chap. 5, paras 5–46–5–47.

18–46   The variation or novation of an existing agreement between the company or any of its subsidiaries and a related party will be subject to the requirements set out above whether or not, at the time the original agreement was entered into, that party was a related party.[68]

(3) Aggregation

18–47   The Stock Exchange requires the aggregation of all transactions entered into by the company (or any of its subsidiary undertakings) with the same related party (and any of its associates) in any 12 month period which have neither been approved by the shareholders nor described in a circular complying with the requirements of paragraph 11.10.[69] If the aggregate transactions would be classified as a Class 2 or larger transaction, the Stock Exchange may require the company to comply with the usual requirements (of paragraph 11.4) in respect of the latest transaction. In such a case, the Stock Exchange may also require that the circular to shareholders provide all relevant details of each of the transactions being aggregated. The purpose of this is clear to prevent the related party building up an interest surreptitiously.

V. IRISH ASSOCIATION OF INVESTMENT MANAGERS GUIDELINES

18–48   In the event of an MBO, the Irish Association of Investment Managers recommends the appointment of a separate committee consisting wholly, or mainly of non-executive directors with direct access to independent advisers. It suggests that the independent advisers have access to all the information necessary to allow them to give a fully informed opinion on the merits of the offer. This committee should then issue a separate statement to shareholders giving both its views on the bid and the views of the advisers.[70]

---

[68] Listing Rules para. 11–6.
[69] Listing Rules para. 11–9.
[70] IAIM Statement of Best Practice on the Role and Responsibilities of Directors of Public Limited Companies (May 1992).

PART 6

RESISTING TAKEOVER BIDS

CHAPTER 19

REGULATING DEFENSIVE ACTIONS

Introduction

19–01 When a offeror makes an offer for a target company, the offeree's management have three options. They may remain neutral, they may endorse the offer, converting it to a friendly takeover, or they may oppose it, rendering it a hostile offer. It is unusual for directors to choose to remain neutral as they will generally have a definite view on the offer. If the directors decide to recommend the offer to their shareholders, the whole procedure will become easier for the offeror as it will have the directors' co-operation in executing the offer. Where the directors are opposed to the bid and the offerors pursue it despite this, the directors may attempt to frustrate the bid. A conflict of interest is inevitable in such circumstances. If the bid succeeds, the directors will lose their management posts. If the bid fails, they will retain their positions. This is true irrespective of the value offered to the offeree's shareholders. One must question thus, whether, in rejecting the bid, the directors are motivated by their own interests or those of their shareholders.

19–02 Part A of this Chapter considers the theories underlying the issue of management involvement in resisting a hostile takeover offer. In order to determine how these theories have been applied, Part B examines the general legal restrictions on the ability of management to frustrate or pre-empt a hostile takeover bid. Chapter 20 will then outline the various tactics which may be used to frustrate takeover offers and the legal principles which apply specifically to these tactics.

A. The Theory

19–03 A number of often conflicting theories have been advanced in respect of the issue of whether the executive directors should be entitled to take action to prevent a bid being made or action which would frustrate a bid once it had been made.[1] Some theories suggest

---

[1] See generally: Easterbrook & Fischel, "The Proper Role of a Target's Management in Responding to a Tender Offer" 94 Harv. Law Rev. 116 (1981); "Gilson Seeking

that directors should be prohibited from taking any form of defensive action and some suggest that directors should be authorised to take any form necessary. Yet a further thesis advocates authorising directors solely to seek further offers from third parties thereby promoting an auction. This is a special case for consideration as although it may not prevent the offeree being acquired, it may frustrate the intentions of the original offeror.

I. A PROHIBITION ON DEFENSIVE ACTIONS BY DIRECTORS

19–04 A number of theories have been advanced in support of the proposition that directors should not be allowed to engage in defensive actions which might lead to the frustration of a potential or an actual takeover offer. Many of these theories are based on the acceptance of takeovers as a positive element with the resulting implication that anything which prevents offers being made or completed is necessarily negative.

(1) Shareholders are Disadvantaged

19–05 In Chapter 2, the many positive effects of hostile takeovers were considered such as increased efficiency and the positive disciplinary effects on management.[1a] Such benefits would appear to suggest that hostile takeovers should be encouraged or at least not be frustrated by the offeree's management. The counter argument suggests that defensive actions lead to increased premiums for shareholders and should thus be permitted.

19–06 In a seminal article, Easterbrook and Fischel argue that while defensive actions may indeed lead to an increased premium for the offeree's shareholders, such actions decrease the likelihood of a takeover offer being made in the first place. They thus argue that shareholders are disadvantaged by defensive tactics and they recommend a rule of management passivity in the face of a hostile takeover bid.[1b] By

---

Competitive Bids Versus Pure Passivity in Tender Offer Defense" 35 Stan. Law Rev. 51 (1982); Gilson, "A Structural Approach to Corporations: The Case Against Defensive Tactics in Tender Offers" 33 Stan. Law Rev. 819 (1981); Gilson, "The Case Against Shark Repellent Amendments" 35 Stan.L.Rev. 775; Bebchuk, "The Case for Facilitating Competing Tender Offers: A Reply and Extension" 35 Stan.L.Rev. 23 (1982); Bebchuk, "The Case for Facilitating Competing Tender Offers" 95 Harv. Law Rev. 1029 (1982); Easterbrook & Fischel, "Auctions and Sunk Costs in Tender Offers" 35 Stanford Law Rev. 1; and "Coffee Regulating the Market for Corporate Control: A Critical Assessment of the Tender Offer's Role in Corporate Governance" 84 Col. Law Rev. 1145–1296.

[1a] See Chap. 2, paras 2–09–2–14 *et seq.*
[1b] Easterbrook & Fischel, "The Proper Role of a Target's Management in Responding to a Tender Offer" (1981) 94 Harv. Law Rev. 1161.

eliminating management resistance, they suggest that companies are more likely to make offers and the offers which are made are more likely to succeed. In this way, the effect of management passivity is to increase the number of takeovers in the marketplace. Easterbrook & Fischel argue that, by contrast, defensive actions are likely to affect the size of the premium which must be paid to secure control. For example, creating "golden parachutes" which are payments to displaced management makes the offeree more expensive. The increase in price is simply a transfer payment from the offeror's shareholders to the offeree's shareholders or in this case to management of the offeree. For example, in 1996, Wells Fargo completed a $12.3 billion hostile takeover of another Californian bank First Interstate. Approximately 75 per cent of the top 500 executives in First Interstate subsequently left their jobs, most with large lump sum payments as a result of golden parachute provisions. The bank's combined workforce was reduced by 23.5 per cent. Acquisitions of this type may be viewed, Easterbrook and Fischel argue, not as efficient wealth creation but as inefficient wealth transfer. Neither the offeror nor the offeree actually benefit from inflated prices, merely the offeree's shareholders or management and the offeror's financiers. If the offeree's shareholders or management are to obtain all the gains from the transaction, no one will have an incentive to make a takeover offer. In addition, Easterbrook and Fischel argue, defensive actions may give management an effective veto on any proposed takeover bid.

19–07   One criticism of Easterbrook and Fischel's zero premium policy is that it goes well beyond the minimal goal of preventing management from blocking the market's operation and actually seeks to dictate the terms of the bargain, thereby influencing the wealth distribution of the parties.[2] This constrains the bargaining which, under the Coasean analysis,[3] leads to the efficient allocation of assets. Other critics argue that although bargaining consumes resources and would be socially inefficient if it accomplished nothing, it is productive in the long run because it increases the magnitude of the gains to be partitioned.[4] Bargaining guarantees that no exchange occurs unless subjective values are recognised. It thus allows for "pareto efficiency" of exchanges. The

---

[2]   Coffee, "Regulating the Market for Corporate Control: A Critical Assessment of the Tender Offer's Role in Corporate Governance" 84 Colum. Law Rev. 1145 at 1165.

[3]   The Coase theorem suggests that if both parties to a transaction behave rationally, liability only determines the distribution of profits, and it does not affect the allocation of resources. This means that the efficient outcome will occur regardless of the choice of legal rule. Ronald Coase, "The Problem of Social Cost" (1960) 3 J.L.& Econ. 1.

[4]   Haddock, Macey & McChesney, "Property Rights in Assets and Resistance to Tender Offers" 73 Virg. Law Rev. 701 at 707.

term pareto efficiency was coined by an Italian sociologist Vilfredo Pareto. It refers to an allocation which is efficient in the sense that it is not possible to reallocate resources in such a way that at least one person is better off (in his own judgement) and no one else is worse off (in his own judgement).[5]

19–08 In addition, Haddock, Macey and McChesney argue that bargaining enhances the subjective and objective values of the items to be exchanged. They accept that if the market for corporate control[6] is the only cause of takeovers such that offerors create all the gains in takeovers, a no-resistance rule might be efficient. However, given that the cause of takeovers may vary substantially from one takeover to the next, they argue that compelling a no-resistance response is unjustified. It is also likely that the offeree may create gains too. If this were not the case, there would be no incentive for potential offerees to approach potential offerors. Another reason they put forward to encourage bargaining is that it makes takeovers less likely in cases where there are no gains, only transfers at stake. Because individuals who make valuable firm-specific investments value the firm's existing configuration more highly than do a majority of shareholders, their inability to bargain would discourage their firm-specific investments in the first place.

(2) Conflict of Interest

19–09 In a hostile takeover, the offeree's management clearly have a substantial interest in preserving their company's independence. By maintaining the status quo, the directors preserve their jobs, their salaries and their status. Yet, directors are required to act in the best interests of their shareholders and often shareholders' interests will be better served by recommending the bid. This causes an immediate conflict of interest between their own personal interests and those of the shareholders. Indeed, the less effective they have been as managers, the greater their incentive to frustrate a takeover. Because of the difficulty already alluded to of defining defensive actions, the fear exists that directors may disguise a policy of resistance to all takeovers as a policy of searching for a better offer than any made so far.

II. PERMITTING DEFENSIVE ACTIONS BY DIRECTORS

19–10 As will become clear in Part B, the generally accepted view appears to be that directors should be permitted to engage in defensive

---

[5] Pareto, *Trattato di Sociologia Gererale* (1916).
[6] Chap. 2, paras 2–11–2–14.

actions, albeit within certain imposed limitations. A wide range of theories have been advanced to support intervention by directors.

(1) Takeovers Should be Avoided

19–11 In Chapter 2, the exploitation theories of takeovers were explained.[6a] It was argued for example, that takeovers yield negative social effects such as employee displacement, asset stripping and monopolies. Overpayment theory also suggests that takeovers result in offerors overpaying for the offerees and increasing gearing unnecessarily. Acceptance of these theories would suggest favouring a policy of active defence on the part of directors with a view to minimising the detrimental effects of hostile takeovers.

(2) Expertise

19–12 Another argument which favours allowing management defend their companies against unwelcome takeovers is the premise that "management know best". This suggests that directors, as experts, are the best persons to assess the value of an offer and, as such, they are better placed than shareholders to determine whether an offer should be available to shareholders. Of course, such a theory assumes that directors will consider only the interests of the shareholders and not their own positions. It is also argued that this theory assumes that left to their own devices, shareholders will make the wrong decision.[7] This error, it is said, stems either from shareholders' irrational behaviour or from the fact that they are not equipped with the skills or the information to make the right decision. Alternatively, they may be too apathetic to make any decision at all. Individual shareholders, in general, do not demonstrate any great interest in participating in the running of their companies. They do not appear to believe that their individual votes are likely to affect the outcome of any decision making process.[8] They are thus, likely to remain rationally apathetic. Acquiring and analysing information about corporate matters tends to be costly and difficult. Motivating and organising fragmented groups of shareholders to vote in a particular manner is also costly for shareholders and generally unsuccessful. It is thus easier for management to do this at the company's expense through the use of the proxy machinery. For this reason Berle and Means noted that proxy

---

[6a] See Chap. 2, paras 2–15–2–17.
[7] Lipton, "Takeover Bids in the Target's Boardroom" 35 Bus. Law 101 at 113.
[8] One interesting point however made by Easterbrook and Fischel is that even though shareholders rarely use their voting powers, they obviously value them. Stock with voting rights is always more expensive ("Voting on Corporate Law" (1983) 26 J.L. & Econ. 395).

machinery in a company whose ownership is fragmented allows management to become a "self-perpetuating body".[9]

19–13   The argument that shareholders are unable to make a correct assessment of the value of shares would not appear to be consistent with financial theory. As noted in Chapter 2, shareholders are assumed to incorporate any new information about shares immediately into the share price so that the share price reflects the true value of the shares.[9a] In addition, Gilson emphasises that "management discretion to prevent a tender offer simply cannot be justified on paternalistic grounds".[10] Easterbrook and Fischel argue that "the most significant conceptual impediment to judicial and perhaps even legislative adoption of a rule requiring managerial passivity has been the notion that assessing the economic merits of tender offers, like judging the merits of any other prospect facing the corporation, is peculiarly within the ability of management".[11] In their note of dissent to the Jenkins Committee Report, Mr. Brown, Sir Erskine and Professor Gower stated:

> "It is also said that shareholder control is inefficient, since directors, as a class, know better what is good for business and for the shareholders than the shareholders themselves. In the normal case this is usually true. But if shareholder control is destroyed and nothing put in its place, we have to go still further and say that business efficiency is best ensured by allowing the directors to function free from any outside control, except that of the courts in the event of fraud or misfeasance, and by making themselves irremovable, without their own consent, however inefficient they may prove to be."[12]

(3) Safeguarding the Interests of Non-Investor Groups

19–14   Another argument in favour of defensive actions suggests that the directors of the offeree have a duty to consider the interests of non-investor groups such as employees, customers, creditors and the community. In consideration of these interests, directors may thus be compelled to defend against the bid. There are a number of problems with this thesis. First, there is no empirical evidence to suggest that these other non-investor parties suffer as a result of a takeover. Secondly, it is difficult to imagine how management of the offeree could know the

---

[9]   Berle and Means, *The Modern Corporation and Private Property*, originally published in 1932 (1991 ed., New Brunswick: Transaction Publishers), Book I, Chap. V, 82.

[9a]   See Chap. 2, para. 2–08.

[10]   Gilson, "A Structured Approach to Corporations: the Case Against Defensive Tactics in Tender Offers" 33 Stan. L. Rev. 819 at 862. See also Gilson, "Seeking Competitive Bids versus Pure Panivity in Tender Offer Defences", 33 Stan. L. Rev. 51; and Gilson, "The Case Against Stark Repellants" 35 Stan. L. Rev. 775.

[11]   *op. cit.*, n.1, 1194.

[12]   Company Law Committee, Cmnd. 1749, para. 8.

policies intended to be pursued by the new owners in advance. It would thus be impossible for them to determine the effect of these polices on third parties. A third argument which has been advanced is that the interests of non-investors should not be the concern of directors.[13] In *The Modern Corporation and Private Property*,[14] Berle and Means argued that in ceding control, shareholders lost any right to direct the firm or to claim that the corporation should be operated in their sole interest. In order to survive they said, 'the 'control' of the great corporations should develop into a purely neutral technocracy, balancing a variety of claims by various groups in the community and assigning to each a portion of the income stream on the basis of public policy rather than private cupidity".[15] Engel described the basis question of corporate social responsibility as being, "whether it is socially desirable for corporations organised for profit voluntarily to identify and pursue social ends where this pursuit conflicts with the presumptive shareholder desire to maximise profit".[16]

19–15 There is by no means a unanimous view that corporate social responsibility is desirable. One problem with the doctrine is that it would involve a relaxation of the objective of management to operate the business in the interests of shareholders. It has been suggested that a principle of divided loyalty ultimately would harm everyone by reducing the willingness of people to entrust their money to managers. Posner stated that, "in competitive markets, a sustained commitment to any goal other than profitability will lead to bankruptcy unless collusion is permitted".[17] Easterbrook and Fischel argued that the adoption of constraints additional to those required by law would be inefficient and counter-productive.[18] Another problem is that the doctrine would require the design of a mechanism to ensure that the components of "public interest" are properly weighted in the decision making process. Any social goal, Engel argued, would need a "broad social consensus".[19] Berle and Means themselves accepted that the larger interests of society can become paramount only "when a convincing system of community obligations is worked out".[20] The social goal would probably need a clear

---

[13] For a more detailed discussion see Clarke, "Corporate Responsibility In Light Of The Separation Of Ownership And Control" (1997) 19 *Dublin University Law Journal* 50. J.E. Parkinson, *Corporate Power & Responsibility* (Clarendon Press: Oxford, 1993) Chaps. 9 & 10, Wedderburn, "Companies and Employees: Common Law or Social Dimension?" (1993) 109 L.Q.R. 220 and Dodd "For Whom are Corporate Managers Trustees?" 45 *Harv. L. Rev.* 1145 (1932).
[14] *op. cit.* n.9.
[15] Book IV *op. cit.*, above, n.9, Chap. IV 312.
[16] Engel, "An Approach to Corporate Social Responsibility" (1979) 32:1 Stan.L.Rev.1.
[17] *Economic Analysis of Law* (2nd ed., 1977), 310.
[18] Easterbrook and Fischel, "The Corporate Contract" (1989) 89 Colum. Law Rev. 1416.
[19] Engel, above, n.16, 27.
[20] *op. cit.*, Book IV, above, n.9, Chap. IV, 313.

social signal to help companies determine which actions are in further-
ance of the goal. It should not thus be left to companies themselves to
make a decision which is after all a political rather than a corporate one.
Social policy is typically a matter for the democratically elected legislature
not individuals selected by private, non-representative, non-accountable
groups. Critics of corporate social responsibility have asked why, if there
is a generally accepted consensus, has this not already been reflected in
the dealings of the legislature.[21] In contrast, Parkinson believes that some
forms of socially responsible behaviour are capable of correcting forms of
market failure, and contrary to the efficiency argument will promote
rather than diminish allocative efficiency.[22] He suggests that the doctrine
also has a role to play in compensating for the limited capacity of
conventional external regulation.[23]

(4) Avoiding Diseconomies

19–16   Coffee warns that four principal diseconomies are risked by a
movement toward a substantially higher frequency of takeovers.[24] First, a
higher frequency of takeovers may enhance the likelihood of inefficient
transfers of control. This argument is based on the overpayment
hypothesis addressed in Chapter 2.[24a] The inefficient transfer could thus
be the result of empire building or error. In addition the "small market
effect" referred to in paragraph 2–19 leaves smaller publicly held companies vulnerable to larger inefficient companies. Clearly, if it becomes too
easy to acquire a company, there will be socially excessive investment in
search.[25] Secondly, Coffee argues that an increase in takeover activity
might cause a shift in managerial behaviour in the direction of risk
preference. In order to stave of the threat of a takeover, management in
vulnerable companies might accept high risk gambles. Examples of such
high risk strategies are the purchase of other companies or the divestment
of attractive assets. Thirdly, Coffee warns of excess deterrence. He refers
to this as a "demoralisation cost" which arises to the extent that employee
performance and loyalty deteriorate in an environment characterised by
a high rate of change in corporate control. These problems may also be
acerbated by assimilation difficulties. The final and possibly most
important dis-economy of increased frequency of control transactions is
the risk that the market for managerial services might be substantially

---

[21]   Engel, above, n.19 at 36.
[22]   Parkinson, *Corporate Power and Responsibility* (Clarendon Press, Oxford, 1993),
       pp. 309–317.
[23]   *ibid.*, pp. 317–330.
[24]   Coffee, "Regulating the Market for Corporate Control" 84 Col. L. Rev 1145.
[24a] See Chap. 2, paras 2–18–2–20.
[25]   *op. cit.*, n.24, 1047.

impaired. As executive tenure is made less secure by a higher frequency of takeovers, "the capacity of firms to secure executive services will be reduced in direct proportion to their need to resort to it."[25a]

III. AUCTIONS – A SPECIAL CASE

19–17   Auctions, unlike other responses, need not thwart the acquisition of the offeree or help managers appropriate any of the gains of the process for themselves. They are therefore more difficult to evaluate than are tactics designed to thwart all acquisitions. On one hand, it may seem that it is in the interests of the offeree's shareholders that management solicit higher offers and encourage an auction. Shareholders in such cases are likely to produce significantly higher premia. This provides an incentive to shareholders to invest in companies. On the other hand, as noted above, Easterbrook and Fischel argue that shareholders' interests are better served by a system which increases the probability that offers being made. They thus recommend that auctions should not be encouraged.[26]

19–18   Easterbrook and Fischel make their argument on the basis that as price rises, demand falls. They therefore contend that auctioneering should be subject to the same treatment as manager's other responses to tender offers, because it needlessly reduces the efficacy of the tender offer process. The company which identifies an attractive target by discovering mismanagement in another company incurs sunk costs. As soon as it makes an offer, other potential acquirers learn the offeree's identity and the accompanying documentation may disclose much of what the offeror has learned. Subsequent offerors do not incur the same level of investigative and evaluation costs and can thus afford to pay more. Easterbrook and Fischel also maintain that it is easy for management to conduct a defensive strategy under the guise of running an auction. For example, they might strike deals with favoured parties or selectively release information to them.

19–19   A number of arguments have been raised countering these views. Clearly, the first offeror always has a time advantage and an informational advantage which gives it a strategic advantage. In relative terms the sunk costs are often a small proportion of the entire purchase price. Also, advisers often operate a system of "no foal no fee" charges.[27] In addition, the unsuccessful offeror in a competitive auction

---

[25a] Coffee, *op. cit.*, above, n.24, at p. 1159.

[26] *op. cit.*, above, n.1 at pp. 1177–78.

[27] Bebchuk, "The Case for Facilitating Competing Tender Offers" 95 Harv. Law Rev. 1029 (1982) at 1037

may still gain from the process by tendering the shares it has already acquired to the successful offeror. Bebchuk suggests that one way in which offerors could be rewarded for searching is by raising the percentage of the offeree's stock which may be purchased without disclosure. This would suggest that the unsuccessful offeror will not really loose out from the whole process. However, Coffee has argued that some decline in offeror's price is inevitable.[28] First, there is a stigma associated with being a offeror which is viewed as not seriously attempting to seek control. Secondly, there is no assurance that sufficient shares will be tendered and bought to make a profit.

19–20   Coffee examines the effect of defensive tactic charters on both the probability of an offer being made and the size of the premium if the offer is made.[29] If defensive tactic charters decrease the first but increase the second, their net effect would be indeterminate as an a *priori* matter. Thus, it would be difficult to justify a *per se* objection to them. Whether they increase the premium more than they reduce the possibility of an offer is "an issue that depends on the elasticity of the demand for control". Easterbrook and Fischel maintain that the shareholders' supply curve is perfectly elastic with the result that all shares should be repurchasable at a price only nominally higher than the current market price.[30] In support of this position, they argue that if existing shareholders thought that the current market price was appreciably below that justified by the company prospects, they would buy shares at that price and the price would thus rise to a new equilibrium. Coffee disputes this and says there are many reasons shareholders do not buy. Economic theory, Coffee argues, has long recognised that rational individuals may have different buying and selling prices. They may lack sufficient wealth to buy the remaining shares or they may wish to hold a diversified portfolio. In addition, tax considerations or other legal restrictions may prevent further purchases.

19–21   Economists argue that as a general principle, allocating resources among competing claimants by price is desirable because it places resources with the most efficient users. Thus, even if competitive bidding reduces the overall number of offerors, the increase in efficiency from allocating the offeree's assets to their most efficient user must be balanced against the reduction of efficiency from fewer offers. While

[28] *ibid.* at 1176.
[29] *op. cit.*, n.24, Coffee notes that defensive tactics also have a third effect. They can increase the likelihood of equal treatment of all shareholders by in effect forcing the offeror to pay the same premium to all shareholders. This happens under Irish law anyway.
[30] "Corporate Control Transaction" 91 Yale L.J. 698 (1982) at 726–27.

this balance cannot be easily identified, the greater the importance of synergy as an explanation for the acquiring company's gains, the more important the efficiency gain through price competition relative to the efficiency loss due to a lower frequency of tender offers".[31] Easterbrook and Fischel, however, argue that the allocational benefits of auctions are small if not negative. Clearly, abandoning the rule of auctioneering to enhance further rewards for search can only be justified if the resulting increase in offer frequency can be so large that it will outweigh the loss of the rule's significant positive effect on premiums. Bebchuk maintains that the frequency effect is small and the premium effect large so that on balance auctions aid the offeree.[32] The error in this approach, Easterbrook and Fischel maintain is that it assumes that investors can identify potential targets in advance of bids. Only if they can do this could they identify themselves as target shareholders with an interest in high premia. An investor is just as likely to be a offeror as an offeree.[33] Thus, shareholders should be interested in improving the lot of shareholders as a whole rather than merely shareholders in the offeror.

B. Regulation of Defensive Actions

19–22 This part of the Chapter examines the general legal principles which currently curtail the ability of management to frustrate takeover offers. One problem which arises at the outset is the difficulty of defining defensive actions. For example, some actions may constitute unusual steps which are deliberately pursued with the clear intention of frustrating takeover offers. An example of such an action might be the creation of "poison pills" which are rights or warrants granted to security holders which only become exercisable upon the publication of a takeover offer for the company. Other actions may appear to constitute actions performed in the normal course of business which may simply have the effect of frustrating a takeover offer. An example of such an action might be the disclosure of favourable information about the offeree which leads to an increase in its share price.

---

[31] Gilson, "A Structural Approach to Corporations: The Case Against Defensive Tactics in Tender Offers" (1981) 33 Stan. Law Rev. 819, at 872.

[32] Bebchuk, "The Case for Facilitating Competing Tender Offers" (1982) 95 Harv. Law Rev. 1029 at 1038.

[33] Easterbrook & Fischel, "Auctions and Sunk Costs in Tender Offers" 35 Stanford Law Rev. 1 at 8.

I. SECTION 205 OF THE COMPANIES ACT 1963

19–23   Although Section 205 of the Companies Act 1963 ("the 1963 Act") does not refer specifically to directors' defensive measures it can be used to limit the ability of directors to adopt certain defensive measures.[33a] Section 205 (1) provides as follows:

> "Any member of a company who complains that the affairs of the company are being conducted or that the powers of the directors of the company are being exercised in a manner oppressive to him or any of the members (including himself), or in disregard of his or their interests as members, may apply to the court for an order under this section."

If defensive actions are deemed by the court to constitute oppressive behaviour or actions in disregard of a members interests, a remedy may be available under this section.

(1) Oppressive Behaviour

19–24   Section 205 will provide a remedy to shareholders where the directors are exercising their powers or conducting the affairs of the company in a manner which is regarded as oppressive to the complainant or in disregard to his interests.

19–25   The term "oppressive" was originally defined by Lord Simonds in *Scottish Co-operative Wholesale Society v. Meyer* according to a dictionary definition as something "burdensome, harsh and wrongful".[34] In *Re Jermyn Street Turkish Baths Ltd.*,[35] the Court of Appeal held that to establish oppression, the applicant must show that he is being constrained to submit to something which is unfair to him as a result of an act or omission by the majority shareholders. On the advice of the Jenkins Committee in the UK,[36] the term "oppressive" was subsequently removed and replaced by the term "unfairly prejudicial" in section 429 of the UK Companies Act 1985. The Jenkins Committee noted that the term "oppression" suggests a higher degree of culpability than was intended. It seemed to suggest that the law had to be broken or a shareholder's rights had to be infringed. The Committee suggested that to be effective, the section had to extend to cases in which the acts complained of falls short of actual illegality. The Committee equated the term "unfairly prejudicial" with Lord Cooper's understanding of "oppression" in *Elder v. Elder and Watson Ltd.*[37] as:

[33a] Courtney, *The Law of Private Companies*, (Butterworth, 1994), pp. 424–442; Ussher, *Company Law in Ireland* (Sweet and Maxwell, 1986), pp. 256–268; Forde, *Company Law* (Mercier Press, 1992), pp. 355–362.
[34] [1959] A.C. 324 at 342.
[35] [1971] 3 All E.R. 184.
[36] Company Law Committee, Cmnd.1749. paras. 2–03–2–05 and 2–12.
[37] [1952] S.C. 49 at 55.

"a visible departure from the standards of fair dealing, and a violation of the conditions of fair play on which every shareholder who entrusts his money to a company is entitled to rely".

19–26   Lord Simond's definition in the *Scottish Co-operative Wholesale Society* case, was accepted by Keane J. in the Irish High Court in *Re Greenore Trading Co. Ltd.*[38] In this case, a company which was found to have used its own money in the purchase of its own shares contrary to section 60 of the 1963 Act was deemed to have engaged in behaviour which was burdensome, harsh and wrongful. In making this decision, the Court also stressed the importance of "looking at the business realities of the situation" as opposed to adopting "a narrow legalistic view". In certain cases, the conduct complained of may be unlawful.[39] It should be noted however, that mere trivial illegalities are unlikely to constitute oppression. In *Re Clubman Shirts Ltd.*,[40] O'Hanlon J. stated:

> "I would not classify as oppressive conduct within the meaning of the Act, the omission to comply with the various provisions of the Act referable to the holding of general meetings and the furnishing of information and copy documents. These were examples of negligence, carelessness, irregularity in the conduct of the affairs of the company, but the evidence does not suggest that these defaults or any of them formed part of a deliberate scheme to deprive the petitioner of his rights or to cause him loss or damage."[41]

19–27   Relief under section 205 is also possible in cases where the management conducts the affairs of the company in a lawful but oppressive manner. Such conduct may be deemed oppressive even though it may be performed honestly and in good faith.[42] In *Re Clubman Shirts Ltd.*,[43] the behaviour of the directors in failing to consult a major shareholder when the company was in dire financial straits and threatened with receivership and liquidation was deemed oppressive. In *Irish Press plc v. Ingersoll Irish Publications Ltd.*[44] Barron J. determined that oppression exists "where a deliberate plan to damage the interests of a company is carried out by a shareholder in the manner by which it exercises its powers to conduct the affairs of the company". The facts of this case merit further study. In 1989, Irish Press Plc ("PLC") and Ingersoll Irish Publications Limited ("IPL") entered into an agreement to the effect that the three newspapers owned by PLC would be run by

---

[38]   Unreported, High Court, March 28, 1980 .

[39]   *Re Westwinds Holding Company Ltd.*, unreported, High Court, May 21, 1974.

[40]   [1983] I.L.R.M. 323.

[41]   *ibid.*, at 327. See also *Re Saul D Harrison & Sons plc* [1995] 1 B.C.L.C. 14.

[42]   *Re Irish Visiting Motorists Bureau Ltd.*, unreported, High Court, Kenny J., January 27, 1972.

[43]   [1983] I.L.R.M. 323.

[44]   Unreported, High Court, December 15, 1993.

one new company and the titles would be owned by another new company. The shareholding in each of these new companies was to be held equally between the two parties to the agreement. It was agreed that the editorial policy of the papers was to be controlled by PLC and the management of the newspapers was to be in the hands of IPL. Two main documents were executed, the subscription and shareholders agreement and the management agreement. In January 1990, various personnel of the Ingersoll Group arrived in Dublin to conduct the management of the newspapers in accordance with the management agreement. Subsequently however, as a result of financial difficulties experienced by the Ingersoll Group abroad, all but one of the personnel subsequently ceased working on the management of the papers and subsequently new persons were nominated. The High Court found that IPL's behaviour constituted oppression by (a) insisting on seeking to operate the terms of the management agreement when that agreement itself was no longer in existence and (b) running the affairs of the company in its interests. The High Court held that when the management activities agreed ceased, the agreement itself was being repudiated and insistence on its subsistence constituted oppression.

19–28 Whilst it is useful to examine the circumstances in which behaviour has been deemed to be oppressive for the purposes of section 205 in the past, it must also be noted that the term "oppressive" is wide and general and the circumstances in which it applies cannot therefore be exhaustively categorised. As Lord Wilberforce noted in the House of Lords in *Ebrahimi v. Westbourne Galleries Ltd*:[45]

> "Illustrations may be used, but general words should remain general and not be reduced to the sum of particular instances".

In that case, Lord Wilberforce considered the concept of "injustice and fairness" as a basis of a just and equitable winding up under section 210 of the UK Companies Act 1948 (the forerunner in the UK of section 459 of the Companies Act 1985). He stated:

> "The words [just and equitable] are a recognition of the fact that a limited company is more than a mere legal entity, with a personality in law of its own: that there is room in company law for recognition of the fact that behind it, or amongst it, there are individuals, with rights, expectations and obligations inter se which are not necessarily submerged in the company structure. That structure is defined by the Companies Act 1948 and by the articles of association by which the shareholders agree to be bound. In most companies and in most contexts, this definition is sufficient and exhaustive, equally so whether the company is large or small. The "just and equitable"

---

[45] [1973] A.C. 360 at 374–375.

provision does not . . . entitle one party to disregard the obligation he assumes by entering a company, nor the court to dispense him from it. It does, as equity always does, enable the court to subject the exercise of legal rights to equitable considerations; considerations, that is, of a personal character arising between one individual and another, which may make it unjust, or inequitable, to insist on legal rights or to entitle them in a particular way."[46]

19–29   This concept was developed further in *Re Saul D Harrison & Sons plc,*[47] where an appeal was heard by the Court of Appeal against an order striking out an application for an order under section 459 of the UK Companies Act 1985 as disclosing no cause of action. Hoffmann L.J. accepted that the test of unfairness is objective and then proceeded to examine the factors to be considered by a court in determining whether conduct is unfair. He stated that the starting point in any case under section 459 will be to ask whether the conduct of which the shareholder complains is in accordance with the articles of association or any other contractual arrangement governing the relationship between the share-holders.[48] Hoffmann L.J. then dealt with the narrow class of cases in which there are understandings between the parties which are not set out in the articles or other contractual arrangements but which may give rise to understandings whose breach may be actionable under section 459. Hoffmann L.J. relied on the above extract from *Westbourne Galleries* as a basis for deciding thus:

> "the personal relationship between a shareholder and those who control the company may entitle him to say that it would in certain circumstances be unfair for them to exercise a power conferred by the articles upon the board or the company in general meeting. I have in the past ventured to borrow from public law the term "legitimate expectation" to describe the correlative "right" in the shareholder to which such a relationship may give rise. It often arises out of a fundamental understanding between the shareholders which formed the basis of their association but was not put into contractual form, such as an assumption that each of the parties who has ventured his capital will also participate in the management of the company and receive the return on his investment in the form of salary rather than dividend."[49]

However, Hoffmann L.J. then referred to the following extract which followed directly from the previous extract from Lord Wilberforce's judgment in *Westbourne Galleries*:

> "It would be impossible, and wholly undesirable, to define the circum-stances in which these conditions may arise. Certainly the fact that the

---

[46]   *ibid.* at 379.
[47]   [1995] 1 B.C.L.C. 14.
[48]   However, his Lordship held that section 459 did not entitle an applicant to relief for trivial or technical breaches of the articles. Such breaches would constitute unlawful but not unfair conduct.
[49]   *ibid.* at 19.

company is a small one, or a private company, is not enough. There are very many of these where the association is a purely commercial one, of which it can safely be said that the basis of association is adequately and exhaustively laid down in the articles. The superimposition of equitable considerations requires something more which typically may include one, or probably more, of the following elements: (i) an association formed or continued on the basis of a personal relationship, involving mutual confidence—this element will often be found where a pre-existing partnership has been converted into a limited company; (ii) an agreement, or understanding, that all, or some (for there may be "sleeping" members), of the shareholders shall participate in the conduct of the business; (iii) restriction upon the transfer of the members' interest in the company—so that if confidence is lost, or one member is removed from management, he cannot take out his stake and go elsewhere.

It is these, and analogous, factors which may bring into play the just and equitable clause, and they do so directly, through the foce of the words themselves."[50]

Thus, Hoffmann L.J. held, in the absence of "something more", there is no basis for a legitimate expectation that the board and the company in general meeting will not exercise whatever powers they are given by the articles of association. In the case at hand, Hoffman L.J. determined that there was nothing more.

19–30　Care should be taken however that the legitimate and proper workings of business and capital investment should not be inhibited by unfounded threats of action under section 205. In *Re A Company*, commenting on a petition under section 459 of the UK Companies Act 1985, Hoffmann J. noted:

" . . . the very width of the jurisdiction means that unless carefully controlled it can become a means of oppression."[51]

In this case, Hoffman J. determined that a section 459 action was unwarranted. In this case and in the two subsequent cases,[51a] Hoffman J. emphasised that in an ordinary course of breakdown of confidence between the parties where the articles provide for a mechanism for determining a fair price. An appropriate solution is for the petitioner to be able to sell his shares at a fair price. In such cases, Hoffman J. stated, maintenance of a petition under section 459 would ordinarily be an abuse of the process. However, Hoffman J. accepted that oppression would have occurred if and when the member leaving the business sought to realise his investment and was prevented from doing so on reasonable terms. These cases were referred to by the Supreme Court in

---

[50] *op. cit.*, n.45 at 379.
[51] (No. 007623 of 1986) [1986] B.C.L.C. 362 at 367.
[51a] *In Re a Company* [1987] BCLC 94 and *In Re a Company* [1989] BCLC 365.

Horgan v. Murray[51b] in considering an application to strike out a petition under section 205 as a n abuse of process. The Supreme Court held that there was an issue to be tried as to whether there was oppression and as to the appropriate remedy for the court to provide.

19–31 Whilst it is clear that a reference to "unfairly prejudicial conduct" is different to "oppression", post 1985 English caselaw continues to be cited before the Irish Courts. The principles laid down by the House of Lords in Westbourne Galleries were adopted by Gannon J. *In Re Murph's Restaurant.*[51c] In addition, in the two recent interlocutory motions, *Feighery v. Feighery and Others,*[52] and *McGilligan v. O'Grady*[53] the *Westbourne Galleries* case was argued before the Irish courts. In the former of the two Irish cases, it was argued before the High Court that in determining relief the court must have regard to the contractual rights of a member of the company, his statutory rights and also (on the basis of the *Ebrahimi* decision) to wider equitable considerations arising from the rights, expectations and obligations of the members *inter se*. In particular, it was contended that equitable rights flow from the fact that the company was a quasi-partnership between the petitioner and the other family members, operating on the basis of mutual trust and confidence between them.

(2) Acting in Disregard of Members' "Interests"

19–32 Section 205 serves as a protection for shareholders' "interests" rather than merely their "rights". The latter term would be more limiting as shareholders' rights stem either from their contract with the company under section 25 of the 1963 Act or from the Companies Acts in general. The term "interests" however is interpreted more broadly to mean "benefits"[54] or "expectations".[55] The difference between the two interpretations becomes clear when one considers that although an opportunity to sell their shares for the maximum price available to an unmeritorious bidder may not be a right of a shareholder, clearly it would be of benefit to that shareholder.

19–33 The leading case on "acting in disregard to members' interests" is *Re Williams Group Tullamore Ltd.*[56] In this case, the company's share structure provided that the preference shareholders were entitled to non-

---

[51b] [1998] 1 I.L.R.M. 110.
[51c] [1979] I.L.R.M. 141.
[52] Unreported, High Court, February 25, 1998.
[53] [1999] I.L.R.M. 303.
[54] Ussher, *op. cit.*, n.33a, pp. 264–265.
[55] *Gower's Principles of Modern Company Law* (Sweet & Maxwell, 1997), at p. 742.
[56] [1985] I.R. 613.

cumulative dividend rights of 8 per cent and were also the only shareholders entitled to attend and vote at general meetings. The company
then decided to pay a large dividend to all the company's shareholders on
a *pro rata* basis. The effect of this scheme would be to provide preference
shareholders with a figure in excess of their fixed 8 per cent. A number of
ordinary shareholders claimed that this scheme disregarded their interests
as members. The Court determined that the share structure envisaged
that the ordinary shareholders would receive a higher return for the
higher risk they bore. As the proposed scheme would benefit only the
preference shareholders, it was held to be "contrary to the interests of the
ordinary shareholders" and oppressive to them.

(3) *Locus Standi*

19–34   The remedy is only available to a member of the company, and
would be no use for example to an unsuccessful offeror. The term
"members" is defined by section 31 of the 1963 Act as the subscribers of
the memorandum of the company who are automatically entered as
members in its register of members and all other persons who agree to
become members and whose names are entered in its register of
members.

(4) Remedies

19–35   Where misconduct or abuse of powers are found to have
occurred, the court has a wide discretion in the type of order it chooses
to make under section 205. Section 205(3) provides that:

> "If, on any application under subsection (1) or (2) the court is of opinion that
> the company's affairs are being conducted or the directors' powers are being
> exercised as aforesaid, the court may, with a view to bringing to an end the
> matters complained of, make such order as it thinks fit, whether directing or
> prohibiting any act or cancelling or varying any transaction or for regulating
> the conduct of the company's affairs in future, or for the purchase of the
> shares of any members of the company by other members of the company
> or by the company and in the case of a purchase by the company, for the
> reduction accordingly of the company's capital or otherwise."

The court has authority thus to direct or prohibit any act, cancel or vary
any transaction, regulate the conduct of the company's affairs or order
the purchase of the members shares and even have the company
wound up. It may take any of these actions in order "to [bring] to an
end the matter complained of". Where an order under section 205
would not end the matter complained of, the court will not grant relief
under section 205(3), but may instead make an order for the winding
up of the company. As Barron J. noted in the *Ingersoll* case:

> "Where there are equal shareholdings in a company and where the reality is that the shareholders have entered into a partnership the Court will where necessary apply the principles of the Law of Partnership."[57]

19–36   Section 213 of the 1963 Act allows a company to be wound up by order of the court in certain specified circumstances, two of which are of particular relevance in this context. Section 213(f) allows a company be wound up if:

> "the court if of opinion that it is just and equitable that the company should be wound up".

Section 213 (g) allows a company be wound up if:

> "the court is satisfied that the company's affairs are being conducted, or the powers of the directors are being exercised, in a manner oppressive to any member or in disregard of his interests as a member and that, despite the existence of an alternative remedy, winding up would be justified in the general circumstances of the case so, however, that the court may dismiss a petition to wind up under this paragraph if it is of opinion that proceedings under section 205 would, in all the circumstances, be more appropriate."

19–37   In *In Re Murph's Restaurants Limited*,[58] the High Court case considered a company in which three brothers were equal shareholders. Two of the brothers sought improperly to oust the third from the management of the company. The latter brought a petition to have the company wound up. At the hearing of the petition, the other two brothers argued than an order under section 205(3) would have been more appropriate. The petitioner objected to the application being dealt with under the provisions of section 205 on the grounds that his two brothers were seeking to buy him out at a gross undervalue. Gannon J. found as a fact that the petitioner was being oppressed and took the view that the appropriate order was to make an order for the winding up of the company and not an order within the provisions of section 205. He stated:

> "It is clear from the evidence that there is no form of Order of the nature indicated in Section 205(3) which could bring to an end the matters complained of by Brian in the proceedings or which could regulate the affairs of the company for the future. It appears to me that the circumstances in which by Order under Section 205 the Court may direct the purchase of the shares of a member by other members or by the company are circumstances in which the Court would do so "with a view to bringing to an end the matters complained of" by the person applying to the Court. It is my opinion that in this case with the fundamental relationship between Brian,

---

[57]   *op. cit.*, above, n.44 at 70.
[58]   [1979] I.L.R.M. 141.

Kevin and Murph sundered that proceedings under Section 205 would not in any circumstances be appropriate."[59]

19–38 In *Re Vehicle Buildings v. Insulations Limited*,[60] a petition to wind up a company was brought on behalf of a 50 per cent shareholder. This was opposed by the other shareholder who submitted that the petitioner had not established deadlock in the affairs of the company and that if she had, the cause was brought about by her own conduct. The petition was supported by three out of four creditors who appeared at the hearing. Murphy J. was satisfied that is was just and equitable that the company should be wound up even though the blame for the situation in which the parties found themselves had not been determined by the court. In *Feighery v. Feighery*,[60a] the petitioner sought an injunction to restrain the company from resolving to remove him as a director in accordance with section 182 of the Companies Act 1963. Laffoy J. rejected a submission that the application of the principles in *Re Murph's Restaurant* justified the granting of interlocutory relief restraining the director's removal in circumstances where a serious case had been established. She stated that she was not satisfied that she had jurisdiction to override the shareholder's statutory power under section 182. She noted that the relief granted in *Re Murph's Restaurant* was a winding-up order under section 213.

In *McGilligan v. O'Grady*[60b] an appeal was heard against the granting of an interlocutory injunction restraining the defendants from removing the plaintiff as director pursuant to section 182 pending the hearing of the section 205 action. Having determined that the plaintiff had established an arguable case that oppression existed, Keane J., in the Supreme Court stated:

> "It is undoubtedly the case that, if there is a relationship between shareholders in a company indicating a degree of mutual confidence and trust, the court may order the winding up of the company on the just and equitable ground where one or more of the shareholders and/or directors exercised their powers in a manner which is inconsistent with that relationship. Specifically, this may arise where the right of the shareholder to participate in the management of the company is infringed, as, for example, by the removal of a director."

Keane J. held that the fact that the shareholders are entitled to remove a director is not a material factor in determining whether the section is a ground for relief under section 205. Nor is it relevant, he noted, in

---

[59] *ibid.* at 152
[60] [1986] I.L.R.M. 239.
[60a] *op. cit.*, n.52.
[60b] [1999] 1 I.L.R.M. 303.

determining whether that conduct should lead to the winding up of a company on the just and equitable ground.

19–38A   In *Re Greenore Trading Company Limited*,[61] an order was made under Section 205. In this case, a private company had been established by three shareholders, one of whom agreed to buy out the third in a manner which Keane J. held to be irregular and oppressive of the petitioner. Keane J. stated:

> "It is obvious that the present circumstances would justify an Order being made for the winding up of the company under Section 213 (f) and (g). It is agreed, however, that such an Order, in the present circumstances, would not be in the interests of the members; and, accordingly, the remedy for the oppressive conduct must be the alternative remedy provided by Section 205. I think that the only effective method of bringing to an end the oppressive conduct of which the Petitioner complains is an Order for the purchase of his shares by (the other shareholder)."[62]

In fixing the price to be paid for these shares it was held that they should be purchased at a fair price and that that meant not only their value but also the Petitioner's proportion of undistributed profits. In so doing Keane J. expressed himself as in effect providing compensation for injury inflicted by the oppressor, and in so doing referred to the *Scottish Co-operative Wholesale Society* case where it was accepted that the correct principle in valuing the shares was to consider what would have been the value of the shares at the commencement of the proceedings had it not been for the effect of the oppressive conduct of which complaint was made.

19–39   These cases were followed by Barron J. in *Ingersoll* who concluded that:

> "where a deliberate plan to damage the interests of a company is carried out by a shareholder in the manner by which it exercises its power to conduct the affairs of the company, such behaviour is oppression. The behaviour is wrongful and the remedy is to remove the oppression and to compensate the party wronged. Even though it might be just and equitable to wind up the company, this will not be done if to do so the wronged party will be unfairly prejudiced. The remedy to the party wronged should, where possible, be to put it back into the position in which it was prior to the oppression."[63]

The remedy sought where the directors are behaving oppressively in the conduct of a takeover offer may be an injunction to prevent the

---

[61]   [1980] I.L.R.M. 94.
[62]   *ibid.* at 101.
[63]   *op. cit.*, n.44 at 79.

directors from frustrating the bid and to force the directors to allow the shareholders an opportunity to accept the bid. Alternatively, the court may be asked for an order to cancel an arrangement entered into by the directors contrary to their responsibilities.

(5) In the Context of Frustrating Actions

19-40 Where directors attempt to frustrate a takeover offer, they generally perform a single action such as issuing shares, altering the memorandum and articles of association etc. In *Re Westwinds Holdings Co.,*[64] Kenny J. indicated that a single instance of oppressive behaviour could give rise to an action under the terms of section 205. In the *Greenore Trading case*, Keane J. had avoided making such a ruling in the course of finding that the actions of a majority shareholder in buying out another shareholder with company money constituted oppressive behaviour. Keane J. held that the single action of buying the shares amounted to a multiplicity of unlawfulness because the relationship between the two parties had broken down, because the petitioner was not informed that company funds would be used and because the company was in a poor financial state.[65] The English courts, on the other hand, would appear to suggest that the phrase "the affairs of the company *are being*" or "the powers of the directors of the company *are being* exercised" implies that the oppression should still be happening.[66]

19-41 In *Re A Company,*[67] the court had to determine whether section 459 of the Companies Act 1985 could protect members who claimed to have suffered "unfair prejudice" in the course of competing offers made for a private company. In this case, two competing takeover offers were made for the shares of a private company. The petitioners alleged that the directors had breached their duty to the company by failing to recommend acceptance of the higher offer and by failing to state that they would exercise their discretion under the articles to enable the transfer of shares to the higher bidder. These breaches of duty, the petitioners claimed, amounted to unfair prejudice of members under section 459. The directors argued that section 459 protected the petitioners interests as members not as prospective vendors. Hoffmann J. disagreed and said that one of the interests of shareholders is to be able to sell his shares at the best price, and if he has been prevented from doing this, he has been prejudiced in his interests as a member. Hoffmann J. went on to state that fairness requires that the directors

---

[64] Unreported, High Court, May 21, 1974.
[65] See Ussher, *op. cit.*, above, n.33a, 260 & 261.
[66] *Re Westbourne Galleries Ltd.* [1970] 3 All E.R. 374.
[67] No. 008699 of 1985, [1986] B.C.L.C. 382.

give shareholders sufficient advice and information to allow them reach a proper decision and not give them misleading advice or exercise their fiduciary duties in a way which would prevent or inhibit shareholders from choosing a better price.

II. FIDUCIARY DUTIES

19–42 The extent to which the directors of the offeree can take action to thwart a bid is limited by the fiduciary duties they owe to the company. Fiduciary duties require directors to act bona fide in the interests of the company and to exercise their powers for the particular purpose for which they were conferred and not for some extraneous purpose. The difficulty with using the common law to restrict the directors' activities in this context is that it is difficult to establish that the directors have actually breached their duties. In *Clark v. Workman*,[68] Ross J. affirmed that the court had no jurisdiction to interfere in questions of internal management once the directors were acting bona fide and within their powers:

> "The Court has no right to say how much is to be distributed in dividends or how much is to be added to the reserve account; what contracts for material are to be accepted, what remuneration is to be paid to their employees and such like. All of these things must be dealt with by the directors and no Court can interfere so long as they are acting within their powers."[69]

(1) Acting in the Interests of the Company

19–43 In determining whether the directors have acted in good faith, the courts will consider whether they have acted in what they honestly believed to be the best interests of the company. In *Re Smith & Fawcett*, Lord Greene noted that directors must act:

> "bona fide in what they consider – not what a court may consider – is in the interest of the company".[70]

Similarly, the Australian High Court in *Harlowe's Nominees Ltd. v. Woodside (Lakes Entrance) Oil Co.* held:

> "that ultimate question must always be, whether in truth the [new] issue was made honestly in the interests of the company. Directors . . . may be concerned with a wide range of practical considerations, and their judgment, if exercised in good faith and not for irrelevant purposes, is not open to review in the courts."[71]

---

[68] [1920] 1 I.R. 107.
[69] *ibid.*, at 116.
[70] [1942] 1 All E.R. 542 at 543.
[71] (1969–70) 121 C.L.R. 483 at 493.

This business judgment doctrine recognises the legitimacy of the board as decision maker and its right to make the wrong decision.[72] These cases suggest that the directors subjective view of the interests of the company will be accepted by the courts without question.

19–44   Gower has suggested that the weakness of the "good faith" test has placed greater weight on the "proper purpose" test which has an objective basis. Even where the directors have acted in good faith in what they view to be the interests of the company, they may not exercise their powers for a purpose different from that for which the powers were conferred.[73] The difficulty here is that powers can be exercised for more than one motive – one motive which is in keeping with the objects of the company and the second which is an improper motive.[74] For example, a director may use his powers to issue shares both to raise necessary capital and to issue them to a friendly party to frustrate a potential takeover. In *Nash v. Lancegaye Safety Glass (Ireland) Ltd*[75] the criteria was said to be the "but for" test. *i.e.* would the allotment not have been made but for the improper purpose. In that case an allotment of shares to one shareholder was made to increase that shareholder's voting strength. While, the directors may also have had the object of benefiting the company, Dixon J. accepted that:

> "This was certainly not their sole objective and I cannot say that it, in fact, contributed to their decision. Even if it did, it was conceded in argument that would not suffice to validate the resolutions if the motives were partly improper."[76]

In *Hogg v. Cramphorn Ltd.*[77] an allotment was recognised by the Court of Appeal as having a two-fold object; to benefit the company and to frustrate a takeover offer. As the "primary purpose" of the allotment was however to frustrate the offer, the directors were held to have breached their fiduciary duties. In *Teck Corporation Ltd. v. Millar*,[78] Berger J. in the British Columbia Supreme Court stated:

> "the directors must act in good faith. Then there must be reasonable grounds for their belief. If they say that they believe there will be substantial

---

[72] See Grantham, "The Content of the Director's Duty of Loyalty", (1993) JBL 149.

[73] Gower, *op. cit.*, above, n.55, 605.

[74] Gilson argues that examining the development and content of traditional fiduciary analysis demonstrates that it is incapable of resolving the problem posed by defensive tactics. The court, he argues, has been unable to distinguish defensive tactics from neutral corporate action, particularly where duel effects are present (*op. cit.* above, n.31, at 821).

[75] (1958) 92 I.L.T.R. 11.

[76] *ibid.* at p. 26.

[77] [1966] 3 All E.R. 420.

[78] (1972) 33 D.L.R. 288.

damage to the company's interests, then there must be reasonable grounds for that belief. If there are not, that will justify a finding that the directors were actuated by an improper purpose".[79]

This case appears to suggest the existence of an objective element in this traditional business judgment doctrine.

19–45 In *Howard Smith Ltd. v. Ampol Petroleum Ltd.*[80] two companies, Ampol Petroleum Ltd and Bulkships Ltd, ("Ampol and Bulkships") which held 35 per cent of the issued shares in RW Miller (Holdings) Ltd ("Miller") decided to acquire the remaining shares. Howard Smith Ltd announced its intention to make a higher bid for the shares. Miller's directors indicated that they intended advising shareholders to reject the offer from Ampol and Bulkships as being too low. The directors then allotted sufficient shares to Howard Smith Ltd to give it control. The twin effects of this allotment were to provide Miller with much needed capital and to reduce the proportionate shareholdings of Ampol and Bulkships. Despite this, the Privy Council held that the allotment was made for an improper purpose. Lord Wilberforce stated that the power of directors to allot shares under the articles is a fiduciary duty and must be exercised for the power for which it was granted:

> "The extreme argument on one side is that, for validity, what is required is bona fide exercise of the power in the interests of the company; that once it is found that the directors were not motivated by self-interest i.e. by a desire to retain their control of the company or their positions on the board – the matter is concluded in their favour and that the court will not enquire into the validity of the reasons for making the issue . . . On the other side, the main argument is that the purpose for which the power is conferred is to enable capital to be raised for the company and that once it is found that the issue was not made for that purpose, invalidity follows."[81]

However, in their Lordships opinion neither position was absolutely correct.

> ". . . Where the self-interest of the directors is involved, they will not be permitted to assert that their action was bona fide thought to be, or was, in the interest of the company . . . But, it does not follow from this, as the appellants assert, that the absence of any element of self-interest is enough to make an issue valid. Self-interest is only one, though no doubt the commonest instance of improper motive; and before one can say that a fiduciary power has been exercised for the purpose for which it was conferred a wider investigation may have to be made . . . On the other hand, taking the respondent's contention it is, in their Lordships' opinion too narrow an approach to say that

---

[79] *ibid.*, at 315–316.
[80] [1974] A.C. 821.
[81] *ibid.* at 834.

the only valid purpose for which shares may be issued is to raise capital for the company . . . the law should not impose such a limitation on directors' powers. To define in advance, exact limits beyond which directors must not pass is, in their Lordships' view impossible".[82]

Consequently, the view advocated by their Lordships was as follows

"It is necessary to start with a consideration of the power whose exercise is in question, in this case a power to issue shares. Having ascertained, on a fair view, the nature of this power, and having defined as can best be done in the light of modern conditions the, or some limits within which it may be exercised, it is then necessary for the court if a particular exercise of it is challenged, to examine the substantial purpose for which it was exercised and to reach a conclusion whether that purpose was proper or not. In doing so, it will necessarily give credit to the bona fide opinion of the directors if such is found to exist and will respect their judgment as to matters of management; having done this, the ultimate conclusion has to be as to the side of a fairly broad line on which the case falls."[83]

As the purpose of issuing shares in this case was found to be solely the dilution of the majority voting power held by Ampol and Bulkships so as to enable the minority of shareholders to sell their shares more advantageously, the allotment was deemed to have been made for an improper purpose. Lord Wilberforce stated that "the right to dispose of shares at a given price is essentially an individual right to be exercised on individual decision and on which a majority in the absence of oppression or similar impropriety is entitled to prevail."[83a] However, the Court held that the use by a director of fiduciary powers solely for the purpose of shifting the power to decide to whom and at what price shares are to be sold cannot be related to any purpose for which the power was conferred.

19–46 In *Re a Company, ex p Glossop*,[84] Hoffmann L.J. emphasised that "actions of the boards of directors cannot simply be justified by invoking the incantation "a decision taken bona fide in the interests of the company"". He also provides a useful summary of the principal established by the *Howard Smith* case as follows:

"The decision of the Privy Council in *Howard Smith Ltd. v. Ampol Petroleum Ltd* . . . clearly establishes that a decision can be attacked in the courts and upset notwithstanding (a) that the directors were not influenced by a "corrupt" motive, by which I mean any motive of personal gain as by obtaining increased remuneration or retaining office, and (b) that directors honestly

---

[82] *ibid.* at 834–835.
[83] *ibid.* at 835.
[83a] *ibid.* at 837–838.
[84] [1988] B.C.L.C. 570.

believed that their decision was in the best interests of the company as they saw its interests. Lord Wilberforce's observations, delivering the advice of the Board, acquit the directors of corrupt motive; he asserts the primacy of the board's judgment; but he goes on to assert that there remains a test applicable to all exercises of power given for fiduciary purposes, that the power was not to be exercised for any 'bye-motives'."[85]

(2) Fettering Directors' Discretion

19–47　As part of their fiduciary duties, directors are obliged not to fetter their discretion, without the consent of the company. In *Clark v. Workman*[86] the chairperson of a company board promised a third party that he would use his best endeavours to obtain the board's approval to a proposed transfer of a controlling interest in the company to that party. The director used his own casting vote to effect the transfer. Ross J. stated:

> "By agreeing thus he had fettered himself by a promise to the [third party], and had disqualified himself from acting bona fide in the interests of the company ... ".[87]

In *John Crowther Group Ltd v. Carpets International plc*,[88] Crowther entered an agreement to made an offer to buy the shares of a wholly owned subsidiary[89] of the defendant. As the defendant was a publicly listed company, the transaction had to be made conditional on the approval of the defendant's shareholders. As part of the agreement, the defendant agreed to "use all reasonable endeavours to procure" the acceptances including recommending the proposal to its shareholders and proposing resolutions of acceptance to its shareholders irrespective of any other offers that might be made for the shares. The High Court held that the agreement to use reasonable endeavours was subject to the director's fiduciary duty to act in the interests of the company and to make full and honest disclosure to their shareholders before they vote on any resolution.

19–48　As Gower notes however, it is not always easy to distinguish an agreement in which the directors fetter their discretion from one in which they exercise it.[90] In *Thorby v. Goldberg*[91] Kitto J. in the High Court of Australia stated

---

[85]　*ibid.* at 577.
[86]　[1920] 1 I.R. 107.
[87]　*ibid.* at 118.
[88]　[1990] B.C.L.C. 460. See also *Rackham v. Peek Foods Ltd.* [1990] B.C.L.C. 895.
[89]　The City Code on Takeovers and Mergers did not thus apply.
[90]　Gower, *op. cit.* above, n.55, 787–788.
[91]　(1964) 112 C.L.R. 597.

> "There are many kinds of transaction in which the proper time for the exercise of the directors' discretion is the time of the negotiation of a contract and not the time at which the contract is to be performed . . . If at the former time, they are bona fide of opinion that it is in the best interests of the company that the transaction should be entered into and carried into effect, I can see no reason in law why they should not bind themselves to do whatever under the transaction is to be done by the board."[92]

This principle was accepted in *Fulham Football Club v. Cabra Estates*[93] where the Court of Appeal upheld a contract entered into by the directors for the redevelopment of the football ground in which the directors agreed to support any planning application made by the developers in the forthcoming seven years. The Court stated that whilst the *Crowther* decision might be right on its facts, it should not be regarded as laying down a general proposition that directors can never bind themselves as to the future exercise of their fiduciary powers.

(3) To Whom are Fiduciary Duties Owed

19–49   Traditionally, fiduciary duties are deemed to be owed to the company. But, as noted in Chapter 13,[94] in certain exceptional circumstances, fiduciary duties may also be said to be owed to the shareholders. It is clear that duties may be imposed or accepted by parties additional to those duties which are derived from their particular office or status. In *Feighery v. Feighery and Others*,[95] it was argued on an interlocutory motion before the Supreme Court that in addition to a remedy under section 205, in the special circumstances which prevailed in the instant case the applicant's fellow directors and shareholders owed him fiduciary duties. This claim was based on the case of *Coleman v. Myers*[95a] and the judgment of Murphy J in *Crindle Investments and Others v. Wymes*.[95b] Paramount amongst fiduciary duties owed as between directors and shareholders, it was urged in the *Feighery* case, is the obligation imposed upon each director to use his power for a proper purpose. Laffoy J. held that even if there was an arguable case that fiduciary duties were owed to the directors, she did not have jurisdiction to hear this case for other reasons set out in para. 19–38 above.

19–50   A duty may also be owed to shareholders where a takeover offer is made. In *Heron International Ltd. v. Lord Grade, Association*

---

[92]   *ibid.* at 605–606.
[93]   [1994] 1 B.C.L.C. 363.
[94]   Chap. 13, paras 13.06–13.10.
[95]   Unreported, High Court, February 25, 1998.
[95a] [1977] 2 N.Z.L.R. 225.
[95b] Unreported, High Court, March 27, 1997.

Communications Corp plc and others,[96] Bell Group Ltd. ("Bell") and Heron International Ltd. ("Heron"), made competing takeover offers for shares in Association Communications Corp plc ("ACC"), a public quoted company. Under ACC's articles, directors were debarred from voting in respect of any transaction in which they were interested. In addition, the consent of the directors was required for the transfer of the shares. ACC's directors, who controlled 53 per cent of the company's voting shares, agreed to sell their shares to Bell although their offer was the lower of the two at 66p. The Heron offer of 90p per share was conditional upon the acceptance of the offer by TVP, a company owning 51 per cent of the target's shares and controlled by one of the directors. The plaintiffs, suing as representatives of the offeree's shareholders, sought an interlocutory injunction to prevent the transfer of the ACC shares to Bell. One of the issues to be determined related to the allegation of breach of duty. Lawton L.J. in the Court of Appeal stated that:

> "Where directors have decided that it is in the interests of a company that the company should be taken over, and where there are two or more bidders, the only duty of the directors, who have powers such as those contained in Art 29, is to obtain the best price. The directors should not commit themselves to transfer their own voting shares to a bidder unless they are satisfied that he is offering the best price reasonably obtainable. Where the directors must only decide between rival bidders, the interests of the company must be the interests of the current shareholders. The future of the company will lie with the successful bidder. The directors owe no duty to the successful bidder or to the company after it has passed under the control of the successful bidder. The successful bidder can look after himself, and the shareholders who reject the bid and remain as shareholders do so with their eyes open, having rejected that price which the directors consider the best price reasonably obtainable. Thus, as a result of Art 29, the directors owed a duty to the general body of shareholders ... to obtain for the shareholders the opportunity to accept or reject the best bid reasonably obtainable."[97]

On the facts however, the Court found that the directors had not behaved unreasonably as the conditions on which the Heron bid was made could not be satisfied for reasons outside their control. They had no alternative thus but to recommend the Bell offer.

19–51 In *Re A Company*[98] Hoffmann J. in the High Court took a different view. In this case two competing offers were made for the shares of a private company. The offer made by of one of the offerors was for £1.40 (as opposed to a £3 offer from the other offeror) and was

---

[96] [1983] B.C.L.C. 244.
[97] *ibid.* at 265.
[98] (No. 007623 of 1984) [1986] B.C.L.C. 382.

also made conditional on the offeree's articles of association being altered. At a meeting of shareholders called to alter the articles, sufficient shareholder support was not obtained. The chairperson of the offeree notified shareholders that the directors would not accept the higher offer. He also indicated that the higher offer could not succeed as a sufficient number of irrevocable commitments not to accept the offer had been made and the highest offeror could not be registered as owner under pre-emptive provisions in the articles. An application was made by the petitioner under section 459 of the Companies Act, 1985 alleging that the directors had breached their duty to the company by failing to recommend acceptance of the higher offer and by failing to state that they would exercise their discretion under the articles to enable the shares be transferred to the highest bidder. The directors sought to have the petition struck out as showing no reasonable cause of action. Hoffmann J. stated:

> "I cannot accept the proposition that the board must inevitably be under a positive duty to recommend and take all steps within their power to facilitate whichever is the highest offer. In such a case as the present where the directors propose to exercise their undoubted rights as shareholders to accept the lower offer in respect of their own shares and, for understandable and fully disclosed reasons, hope, in their personal capacities, that a majority of other shareholders will accept it as well, it seems to me that it would be artificial to say that they were under a duty to accept the higher offer."[99]

Hoffmann J. referred to the *Heron* case but stated that the passage quoted above on the duties of a board must be read in context, namely that the board was authorised under the articles to choose the bidder to whom shares could be transferred and had chosen the lowest bidder. By exercising the power in the way that it did, the board in that case deprived shareholders of the opportunity of accepting the higher bid. In this case, on the other hand, Hoffmann J emphasised:

> "the mere omission of the board positively to recommend the higher offer has not deprived shareholders of the opportunity to accept it."

Thus, he stated:

> "the imposition of positive duties of this kind in each case of rival bids would be a considerable extension of the principle applied in the *Heron* case. Nor do I think that an omission to act in this way must necessarily be unfair."[100]

Gower has noted that Hoffmann J's view on this matter would appear to be more consistent with the City Code which distinguishes between

---

[99] *ibid.* at 389.
[100] *ibid.* at 390.

advice to the shareholders which is subject to fiduciary duties and the directors decision in respect of their own shareholdings.[101] Although there was no duty to recommend the higher bid, Hoffman J. maintained that directors are obliged to provide sufficient information to shareholders to allow them to make an informed decision and the shareholders must not be misled by being given misleading advise.[102] In the circumstances, the Court found that the chairperson's circular was misleading as it failed to inform shareholders that the directors had the power to authorise a transfer of shares to the highest bidder and that in recommending the lower offer, the directors may have allowed their personal interests to outweigh their fiduciary duties. For this reason therefore, the application to strike out the petition under section 459 of the UK Companies Act 1985 was dismissed.

19–52 In *Dawson International plc v. Coats Patons*,[103] the situation was slightly different as only one bid had been made. In this case, the board of Coats Paton plc ("Coats") entered into an agreement with Dawson International plc ("Dawson") to accept the latter's offer for their own holdings and to recommend it to their shareholders. Viyella plc ("Viyella") then approached Coat's advisors indicating its wish to make an offer which would be at least as good as Dawson's. Viyella was given a sufficient indication of Dawson's offer to allow it to make a higher offer which the Board of Coats accepted. They announced and recommended the Viyella offer. Dawson declined to become involved in the contested takeover but sued for costs incurred in relation to making the offer. Lord Cullen, a judge of the Outer House of the Court of Session in Scotland, the court of first instance, held that the contract was enforceable and did not amount to a breach of the directors' duties. Coats' first argument was that it was beyond its corporate power to enter into this type of contract, as it could have no interest in the identity of its shareholders. On this point Lord Cullen stated:

> "I do not accept as a general proposition that a company can have no interest in the change of identity of its shareholders on a takeover. It appears to me that there will be cases in which its agents, the directors will see the takeover of its shares by a particular bidder as beneficial to the company."[104]

---

[101] Gower, *op. cit*, above, n.55, 786.

[102] *Re A Company*, above, n.98, at 388, *per* Hoffmann J.: "Whether or not the board of a company faced with competing bids is under a positive duty to advise shareholders to accept the higher offer, I think that if the board chooses to give advice on the matter, fairness requires that such advice should be factually accurate and given with a view to enabling the shareholders (who *ex hypothesi*, are being advised to sell) to sell, if they so wish, at the best price."

[103] [1989] B.C.L.C. 233.

[104] *ibid.* at 242–243.

Coats' second argument was that such a contract was beyond the authority of its directors because the directors owed a fiduciary duty to its shareholders in a takeover situation and the alleged agreement conflicted with this duty. Lord Cullen rejected this argument on the grounds that a fiduciary duty is owed to the company not to the shareholders. The directors did therefore possess the power to enter into this type of contract. Lord Cullen stated that if the directors gave advice to the shareholders during a takeover bid, any liability which they might incur would arise from ordinary principles of law such as fraud or negligence rather than from a fiduciary duty to shareholders. Lord Cullen followed Hoffman J. in *Re a Company* but distinguished the *Heron* case on the ground that that case was authority only for the proposition that directors must use a power under article 29 of the articles of association to approve transfers in the interests of the company and not merely in accordance with their own interests. Lord Cullen stated that the case was not an authority for the proposition that directors may not on behalf of the company agree to recommend a bid and not to encourage or co-operate with an approach from another bidder without being in breach of their fiduciary duty to the current shareholders. However, if directors do undertake to advise shareholders, Lord Cullen stated that they must do so in good fiath and ensure that shareholders are not misled. Coat's final argument was that even if a contract existed, it was conditional on no higher offer being made. On this point, Lord Cullen stated that the issue could only be decided after all the evidence had been heard on appeal, Lord Prosser considering the proof in the Inner House of the Court of Session,[105] accepted an amended argument put forward by Coats that Dawson had failed to establish a legally binding contract. His Lordship held that it was not necessary to infer contractual relations between the parties as this was not their intention. He felt that the parties actions could be fully explained by their desire to act in accordance with the City Code. This decision suggests that in deciding whether to recommend a bid, the directors may consider interests beyond those of the current shareholders. As noted in para. 19–48 above, this approach was confirmed by the Court of Appeal.[106]

III. PERSONAL ACTIONS

19–53   As is clear from the previous section, there may be exceptional circumstances in which company directors may owe fiduciary duties to shareholders. In such cases, a shareholder should be free to take action to enforce his own fiduciary rights. In addition, shareholders may be

---

[105] [1991] B.C.C. 278.
[106] See Sellar, "Analysis – *Dawson International plc v. Coats Paton plc*", 16 Co. Law 207.

accorded personal rights under the company's memorandum or articles of association or under the Companies Acts which are clearly enforceable by individual shareholders.[107] These cases must however be distinguished from cases where shareholders take actions against the directors in respect of a diminution in the value of their shareholding which are arguably unrelated to their personal rights.

19–54 In *Foss v. Harbottle*,[108] the Court held that where the company has suffered a loss, the company itself is the proper plaintiff. However, in certain exceptional cases, a plaintiff may be entitled to bring a derivative action on behalf of the company for loss suffered by the company.[108a] These exceptions are necessary in cases where the perpetrators of the wrong are in effective control of the company and the wrong is unlikely to be remedied.[109] Where the directors are alleged to have committed an unratifiable wrong, a derivative action will lie in respect of it. Derivative actions have been allowed in respect of: *ultra vires* or illegal transactions;[110] cases of fraud on the minority;[111] transactions where the requirement of a "special majority" or procedure have been ignored;[112] situations where the justice of the case demands;[113] or as noted above, cases where the shareholders' own personal rights have been breached.

19–55 In *Prudential Assurance Co Ltd v. Newman Industries Ltd.* (No. 2),[114] a minority institutional shareholder in the defendant company brought a personal action against the defendant and two of its directors. It was proposed to shareholders that the defendant company would acquire the assets of a company TPG in which the defendant was a substantial shareholder. The two directors held management positions in both companies. The plaintiff argued that the purchase price was excessive and that the circular explaining the transaction to shareholders and seeking a resolution sanctioning the transaction was misleading. The Court of Appeal held that a shareholder could not recover damages merely because the company in which it is interested has suffered damage.

Referring to the rule in *Foss v. Harbottle*, it was said:

---

107   *Pender v. Lushington* (1877) 6 Ch. D 70.
108   (1843) 2 Hare 461.
108a Courtney, *op. cit.*, 33a, pp. 453–460; Ussher, *op. cit.*, 33a, pp. 340–354 and Gower, *op. cit.*, 55, pp. 665–678.
109   *Wallersteiner v. Moir* (No. 2) [1975] 1 Q.B. 373.
110   *Cockburn v. Newbridge Sanitary Steam Laundry Co. Ltd.* [1915] 1 I.R. 237.
111   *Cook v. Deeks* [1916] 1 A.C. 554.
112   *Edwards v. Halliwell* [1950] 2 All E.R. 1064.
113   *Moylan v. Irish Whiting Manufacturers Ltd.* unreported, High Court, Hamilton J., April 14, 1980.

"This is not merely a tiresome procedural obstacle placed in the path of a shareholder by a legalistic judiciary. The rule is a consequence of the fact that a corporation is a separate legal entity. Other consequences are limited liability and limited rights. The company is liable for its contracts and torts; the shareholder has no such liability. The company acquires causes of action for breaches of contract and for torts which damage the company. No cause of action vests in the shareholder. When the shareholder acquires a share he accepts the fact that the value of his investment follows the fortune of the company and that he can only exercise his influence over the fortunes of the company by the exercise of his voting rights in general meeting. The law confers on him the right to ensure that the company observes the limitations of its memorandum of association and the right to ensure that other shareholders observe the rule, imposed on them by the articles of association."[115]

In terms of the diminution in the value of his shares, the Court held:

"But what he cannot do is to recover damages merely because the company in which he is interested has suffered damage. He cannot recover a sum equal to the diminution in the market value of his shares . . . because such a "loss" is merely a reflection of the loss suffered by the company. The shareholder does not suffer any personal loss. His only "loss" is through the company, in the diminution in the value of the net assets of the company, in which he has . . . a shareholding."[116]

19–56   In *Heron International Ltd v. Lord Grade, Association Communications Corp plc and others*,[117] the Court of Appeal stated that although personal and derivative actions may arise from the same events, the remedy in the personal action relates only to the harm inflicted directly upon the individuals. Reference was made to *Prudential Assurance Co Ltd v. Newman Industries Ltd.* (No. 2) and to the rule in *Foss v. Harbottle*. However, the Court emphasised that where the loss is suffered directly and exclusively by the shareholders in that because of the breach of the directors duty to advise their shareholders in relation to the prospective bid "they are deprived of the opportunity of realising their shares to greater advantage", there is in no sense a loss to the company and the rule in *Foss v. Harbottle* does not thus apply. Lawton L.J. held that a shareholder has a right of action in such a case for "a direct loss caused to his own pocket as distinct from a loss caused to the coffers of a company in which he holds shares".[118]

---

[114] [1982] 1 All E.R. 354.
[115] *ibid*. at 367.
[116] *ibid*. at 366.
[117] *op. cit.*, n.96.
[118] *ibid*. at 263.

19–57   In *Stein v. Blake and Others*,[119] the Court of Appeal held that the loss sustained by a shareholder by a diminution in the value of his shares by reason of the misappropriation of the company's assets was a loss which could only be recovered by the company and not by the shareholder, who has suffered no loss distinct from that suffered by the company. Millett J. pointed out that the only loss suffered by the plaintiff consists of the diminution in the value of his shareholding by reason of the misappropriation of the assets of the companies in which those shares subsist. He noted that such loss would be fully remedied by the restitution of the value of the misappropriated assets to the company. Millett J made the following important distinction:

> "It is not alleged that the plaintiff has been induced or compelled to dispose of his shares in the companies at an undervalue by reason of the diminution in value of their assets; he still has them."[120]

Thus, Millett J. determined that if the shareholder was allowed to recover for the diminution in the value of his shares, and the company for the misappropriation of their assets, the plaintiff would have double recovery. His Lordship distinguished between cases such as *Heron* where the alleged loss was suffered directly by the shareholder by virtue of the shareholder being compelled or induced to dispose of his shares at an undervalue. Such a loss would be "distinct from, and independent of the loss suffered by the company". In such a case:

> "Even if the company recovers in respect of the wrong done to it, this will not benefit the shareholder who has disposed of his shares, but rather the purchaser who acquired them, who may or may not be the wrongdoer or an associate of his."[121]

His lordship summed up as follows:

> "The distinction is between (i) the loss sustained by a shareholder by a diminution in the value of his shares by reason of the misappropriation of the company's assets and (ii) loss caused directly to a shareholder who has been induced to part with the shares at an undervalue. The shareholder has a personal cause of action to recover in respect of the second type of loss, but not the first".[122]

19–58   In *O'Neill v. Ryan, Ryan Air Ltd, Aer Lingus plc, Kennedy, GPA Group Ltd. and Transport Analysis Inc.*,[123] the plaintiff claimed that the alleged anti-competitive conduct of the last four named defendants

---

[119]   [1998] 1 All E.R. 724.
[120]   *ibid.* at 727.
[121]   *ibid.* at 727.
[122]   *ibid.* at 729.
[123]   [1993] I.L.R.M. 557.

caused damage to RyanAir Ltd, the second named defendant and thereby to the plaintiff by reducing the value of his shareholding in Ryan Air Ltd. The plaintiff argued *inter alia* that his claim came within one of the exceptions to the rule in *Foss v. Harbottle*. The Supreme Court held that the nature of the plaintiff's claim was such that it fell totally outside the rule in *Foss v. Harbottle*, which rule is concerned with answering the question of who was the proper plaintiff to bring an action in respect of the damage suffered by a company:

> "The exceptions made to the rule, which allow minority shareholders to bring a derivative or representative action, are made in order to ensure that a majority in control of the company should not be able with impunity to act illegally or oppressively or in such a way as to commit a fraud on the minority. But where a derivative or representative action is permitted as an exception to the rule, the action is brought in respect of damage to the company. Instead of the company itself bringing the action in respect of such damage, the exceptions permit one or more minority shareholders to bring it. But the action is always brought in respect of damage to the company."[124]

Since the plaintiff's claim was not in respect of damage to the company but in respect of alleged damage to his shareholding in the company, it was held to be totally different from the type of claim with which the rule in *Foss v. Harbottle* is concerned.

19–59 The plaintiff submitted that a shareholder in a company has a personal action in respect of the reduction in value of his shareholding resulting from damage to the company against the party who caused such damage. The Supreme Court relied on the *Prudential Assurance Co.* case as demonstrating that a shareholder has no right to bring a personal action in respect of the value of his shareholding resulting from damage to the company against the party who caused such damage. In addition to the explanations given in the *Prudential Assurance Co.* case, Blayney J. noted:

> "What is also a relevant consideration . . . is the consequences which would flow from giving shareholders in a company a personal action against a party causing damage to the company. It would enable a multiplicity of actions to be brought and deprive the company itself of the ability to control them. So it would be both harmful to companies and very much against the public interest in opening the door to irresponsible litigation."[125]

IV. THE IRISH TAKEOVER RULES

19–60 General Principle 8 of the scheduled principles set out in the Irish Takeover Panel Act 1997 provides that the offeree's directors owe

---

[124] *ibid.* at 567.
[125] *ibid.* at 570.

their shareholders a duty to act in disregard of their personal interests when giving advice and furnishing information in relation to the offer. In exercising this duty, the directors are required to take into consideration the interests of shareholders as a whole.[126] Furthermore, General Principle 9 requires directors to exercise their rights of control in good faith. These Principles, which seek to ensure that all actions of the offeree's directors are properly motivated are particularly important in the case of a hostile takeover offers.

19–61   General Principle 6 specifically prohibits the offeree's board from taking frustrating action without the approval of shareholders in general meeting. It states:

> "It is the duty of the directors of an offeree when an offer is made or when they have reason to believe that the making of an offer is imminent to refrain from doing anything as respects the conduct of the affairs of the offeree which might "frustrate that offer or deprive shareholders of the opportunity of considering the merits of the offer, except upon the authority of those shareholders given in general meeting."

Rule 21 gives effect to this principle. This rule restricts the power of the board of the offeree to engage in frustrating action either during the course of a takeover offer or at earlier time at which the board of the offeree has reason to believe that an offer may be imminent. It is important to emphasize from the outset that Rule 21 does not prevent the offeree board from mounting a robust defence to a takeover. It does not, for example, prohibit the board from putting forward arguments citing facts and figures in an attempt to reject the offer. Its intention is rather to prevent directors denying shareholders an opportunity to assess the offer and make their own decisions. Rule 21 expressly prohibits specific activities during this time without the approval of the offeree's shareholders in a general meeting or the consent of the Panel. The prohibited actions are:

– allotting or issuing any authorised but unissued shares;

– issuing or granting an option in respect of unissued shares;

– creating or issuing convertibles;

– selling, disposing or acquiring assets of a material amount[127] or operations yielding profits of a material amount, or agreeing to do so;

---

[126] The equivalent principle in the City Code also obliges directors to consider the interests of employees and creditors. This would obviously equip directors with additional arguments to justify opposing a bid.

[127] According to note 3 on R. 21, a "Material Amount" is calculated by comparing (a) the value of the assets acquired/disposed with the assets of the target (b) where

- entering into contracts otherwise than in the ordinary course of business;

- taking "any action as respects the conduct of its affairs the effect of which would be, or be likely, to frustrate the making or implementation of an offer".

This last all-encompassing provision incorporates all activities which would or would be likely to frustrate a bid and gives the offeree's shareholders wide control.[128]

19–62   There is no definition contained within Rule 21 of a "frustrating action". The actions specifically referred to in Rule 21 and in the Notes, however, set out the Panel's views on a number of specific cases. Note 4 indicates that the declaration and payment of an interim dividend by the offeree, otherwise than in the normal course, during an offer period may, in certain circumstances, be contrary to Rule 21 in that it could effectively frustrate an offer. Note 7 suggests that the amendment of or entry into a service contract with a director or the creation or variation of the terms of employment of, a director which leads to an abnormal increase in emoluments or a significant improvement in terms of service may be regarded by the Panel as an action requiring shareholder approval. An increase or improvement which results from a bona fide promotion or new appointment would not be so included. Note 8 provides that the Panel may consent to proposals by the offeree to grant options over shares, the timing and level of which are in accordance with its normal practice under an established share option scheme. Finally, note 9 provides that Rule 21 may apply to proposals affecting the offeree's pension scheme arrangements, such as proposals involving the application of a pension fund surplus, a material increase in the financial commitment of the offeree in respect of its pension scheme or a change to the constitution of the pension scheme. In all the above cases, the Panel should be consulted by the directors in advance in order to advise the parties.

19–63   It would appear that the decision as to whether activities are deemed frustrating requiring shareholder approval depends both on their timing and on their nature. Actions taken during a period when

---

appropriate, the aggregate value of the consideration with the assets of the target and (c), where appropriate, net profits attributable to the assets acquired/disposed with the assets of the target. The Panel will normally consider relative values of 10 per cent or more as being of a material amount, although values lower than 10 per cent may be considered material if the asset is of particular significance.

[128] This final provision is unique to the Irish Takeover Rules in that it is not expressly set out in the London Panel City Code.

an offer is imminent or has been made are more suspect. For example, in a situation where Company A owns a shareholding in Company B, exercising the voting rights attached to those shares would not normally require shareholder approval. However, if Company A is the subject of a takeover offer from Company B or if an offer is imminent, shareholder approval may become necessary. If Company B were required pursuant to the Stock Exchange Listing Rules to seek the approval of its shareholders to the making of an offer, Company A could not vote against the resolution unless it had obtained the approval of its own shareholders for such an exercise of shares might frustrate the offer. In addition, actions outside the normal course of business are more likely to be caught by Rule 21. In order to avoid doubt, the Panel should be consulted in advance of any action which might conceivable fall within the scope of this rule.

19–64   An exception to Rule 21 is provided for where the offeree board is acting in pursuance of a contract entered into prior to the announcement of the offer or prior to the board's belief that an offer is imminent. In addition, it is noted that where Rule 21 would otherwise apply, the requirement for a shareholders' meeting will nonetheless normally be waived by the Panel if this is acceptable to the offeror or, in a competitive bid situation, to each offeror.[129]

19–65   The Rules apply from the time an offer is made or is imminent. In addition, Rule 21 provides that Rule 21 and the General Principles apply where an offer lapses under Rule 12(b)(I) as a result of the initiation of proceedings by the European Commission or the referral by it to a competent authority of a Member State under the European Merger Regulation. In such circumstances, the rule and General Principles will apply during the course of the European Commission or Competent Authority proceedings.

---

[129]   Note 1 to R. 21.

CHAPTER 20

POSSIBLE DEFENSIVE ACTIONS

20–01 In this Chapter, an examination is undertaken of the specific defensive tactics which directors may seek to adopt in an attempt to frustrate a hostile takeover offer.[1] These tactics involve either the directors adopting a pre-emptive role in order to deter potential bidders or adopting a reactive role in respect of specified offers which have been made or which are imminent. In the former case, the Irish Takeover Panel Act 1997 Takeover Rules, 1997 ("the Takeover Rules") will not apply. The directors will thus have greater freedom in their actions. They will not have to refer to shareholders for approval unless otherwise required to do so by the company's articles of association, by statute or, in the case of a listed company, by the Stock Exchange Listing Rules. Directors will also have more time to consider alternative strategies and to put a suitable framework into place to defend against unwanted offers.

A. Defensive Measures in Advance of an Offer

I. CREATING VOTING AGREEMENTS BETWEEN SHAREHOLDERS

20–02 Substantial shareholders may agree to vote two or more separate blocks of shares together and not to sell them separately. This would allow each shareholder control and voting power in excess of their individual shareholding. Such shareholders would be more likely to withstand the advances of hostile offerors who would be aware that there would be insufficient levels of acceptances to execute their offers. The existence of such a pact would thus be likely to deter a potential offeror from making an offer without the consent of the shareholders.

---

[1] See also Weinberg and Blank in *Takeovers & Mergers* (Sweet & Maxwell), Part IIIB, Chap. 7, paras 3–780 to 3–832 or Ussher, *Company Law in Ireland* (Sweet & Maxwell, 1986) 101–106.

20–03   Before creating such voting agreements, shareholders of listed public companies should be aware that, in the event of a takeover or other relevant transaction as defined in the Irish Takeover Panel Act 1997, they will be deemed "concert parties" for the purposes of the Takeover Rules. Section 1(3) of the Irish Takeover Panel Act, 1997 states that:

> "two or more persons shall be deemed to be acting in concert as respects a takeover or other relevant transaction if, pursuant to an agreement or undertaking (whether formal or informal) between them, they actively co-operate in the acquisition by any one or more of them of securities in the relevant company concerned or in the doing, or in the procuring of the doing, of any act that results in an increase in the proportion of such securities held by any one or more of them and "acting in concert" shall be construed accordingly."

Furthermore, note 1(d) on rule 2.1 of Part A of the Takeover Rules states that agreements between a company, or the directors of a company, and a shareholder which restrict the shareholder or the directors from either offering for, or accepting an offer for, the shares of the company or from increasing or reducing shareholdings, may be relevant for the purposes of the definition of concert party. Forming such a voting agreement with the company may thus have implications under Rule 9 of the Takeover Rules. If the agreement results in the two parties being deemed to be "acting in concert" and the combined shareholding of the companies is 30 per cent or more, any further acquisitions by either party may trigger a requirement to make a mandatory bid for the entire shareholding of the company.[2]

II. CROSS – SHAREHOLDINGS

20–04   Cross-shareholdings are formed where two or more companies acquire stakes in each other. Each of the companies would thus be assured of the existence of a friendly shareholder who would agree not to sell their shares without their consent.

In a consultative document in 1990, the UK Department of Trade and Industry acknowledged that while it is desirable that companies are entitled to hold stakes in other companies for genuine investment reasons, cross-shareholdings are being used as a barrier to takeovers.[3]

20–05   The disclosure requirements, described in Chapter 13,[3a] ensures that where a particular person owns a significant shareholding in the

---

[2]   See Chap. 11, paras 11–64–11–75.
[3]   January 1990, 13.
[3a] Chap. 13, paras 13–93–13–100.

company, this fact will be disclosed to the company and in certain circumstances published. It should thus be possible to determine where cross shareholdings exist. Where an offer is made or is imminent, the Takeover Rules subject "associates" of offerors or offerees to extremely onerous disclosure obligations. A substantial shareholder may be deemed to be "an associate" of an offeror or offeree for the purposes of the Takeover Rules if that person "whether or not acting in concert with the offeror or the offeree owns or controls, or together with one or more persons acting in concert with him or her owns or controls, 5 per cent or more of any class of relevant securities of the offeror or the offeree".[4] A person with a cross-shareholding in the offeree may thus be deemed to be as associate of the offeree under the Takeover Rules.

20–06 For listed companies, the only real restriction to cross share-holdings is set out in the Stock Exchange Listing Rules. Where an application for listing is made for a class of shares, paragraph 3.18 of the Listing Rules requires that "a sufficient number" of those shares must be in public hands no later than the time of admission. Paragraph 3.19 states that 25 per cent of the shares in respect of which the application has been made would represent "a sufficient number". In addition, paragraph 9.37 requires a listed company to notify the Stock Exchange if the percentage of shares in public hands falls below 25 per cent. Paragraph 3.20 provides that shares will not be regarded as being in public hands if they are held, directly or indirectly, by:

- a director or a person connected with a director of the applicant or any of its subsidiary undertakings;

- the trustees of any employees' share scheme or pension fund established for the benefit of any directors or employees of the applicant or any of its subsidiary undertakings;

- any person who by virtue of any agreement is entitled to nominate a director to the applicant's board of directors;

- any person who is interested in 5 per cent or more of the shares of the relevant class.

An exception may be made in the latter case if the Stock Exchange determines that, in all the circumstances, such a person may be included.

20–07 An obvious form of cross-shareholding in a company by a friendly company would be a holding by a subsidiary company of

---

[4] R. 2.2(i).

shares in its holding company. Section 32(1) of the Companies Act 1963 ("1963 Act") introduces a general prohibition on companies being members of their holding companies. However, section 32(2) states that the prohibition shall not apply where the subsidiary is concerned as personal representative or as trustee, unless the holding company or a subsidiary of the holding company is beneficially interested under the trust.[5] Section 32 has, to a large extent, been supplanted by Part XI and in particular section 224(1) of the Companies Act 1990 ("the 1990 Act") which allows subsidiaries acquire and hold shares in their holding companies once certain conditions set out in section 224(2) to safeguard shareholders are fulfilled.[6] These conditions are as follows:

"(a) the consideration for the acquisition of such shares should be provided for out of the profits of the subsidiary available for distribution;

(b) upon the acquisition of such shares and for so long as the shares are held by the subsidiary –

   (i) the profits of the subsidiary available for distribution shall for all purposes be restricted by a sum equal to the total cost of the shares acquired;

   (ii) the shares shall, for the purpose of the consolidated accounts prepared by the holding company in accordance with sections 150 to 152 of the Principal Act, be treated in the same manner as is required in respect of shares held as treasury shares under section 43A of the Act of 1983 (inserted by section 232(c) of this Act); and

   (iii) the subsidiary shall not exercise any voting rights in respect of the shares and any purported exercise of those rights shall be void."

The last of these conditions would render the holding by a subsidiary of shares in its holding company of limited use in a hostile bid. A contract for the acquisition by a subsidiary of shares in its holding company must not be entered into without being authorised in advance both by the subsidiary and its holding company.[7] The procedures required for the granting, variation, revocation and release of this authority is set out in sections 212 to 217 of the 1990 Act. Part XI of the 1990 Act substantially implements Directive 92/101/EEC which amends the Second Directive (Formation and Capital of Public Limited Companies), Directive 68/151/EEC.[7a] The European Communities (Public Limited Companies Subsidiaries) Regulations 1997 completes the implementation process by extending the definition of "subsidiary"

---

[5] A beneficial interest to the extent that the company is interested by way of security for the purposes of a transaction entered into by it in the ordinary course of business is not included in the prohibition.

[6] However, section 224(5) provides that section 224 will not apply to shares held by a subsidiary in its holding company in the circumstances permitted by section 32 of the Act.

[7] Companies Act 1990, s.224(3).

[7a] O.J. No. L347, November 28, 1992 and O.J. No. L.65, March 14, 1968, pp. 8–12.

for the purposes of Part XI of the 1990 Act. In addition, the Regulations apply additional requirements to directly controlled subsidiaries. Regulation 5(2) prohibits a public company subsidiary from subscribing for the shares of its parent public company which are not fully paid, or providing financial assistance in accordance with sections 60(i)–(ii) of the 1963 Act for the purchase of, or subscription for, shares in its parent public company.

III. ISSUING BLOCKS OF SHARES TO FRIENDLY HOLDERS

20–08   Where a company's shares are held by a friendly shareholder, it is difficult for a hostile bidder to acquire ultimate control. A company may thus decide to issue shares to a trade partner, a pension fund or trustee for the company's employees.

In order to do this, the directors must ensure that they are entitled to issue shares. The right to issue shares is normally vested in directors either by the articles of association or by a special resolution of the company.[8] Section 20 of the Companies (Amendment) Act 1983 ("the 1983 Act") seeks to ensure that director's powers in this respect are not abused. Section 20(1) prohibits directors from exercising any power of the company to allot relevant securities, unless they are authorised to do so by the company in general meeting or by the articles of association of the company. Where the bidder is a listed company, paragraph 14.4 of the Stock Exchange Listing Rules sets out specific details which must be included in the circular issued to shareholders in connection with this resolution. Section 20(2) of the 1983 Act provides that authority for the purposes of the section may be given for a particular exercise of that power or for the exercise of that power generally. Section 20(10)(a) provides that the section will not apply to "shares shown in the memorandum to have been taken by the subscribers thereto or shares allotted in pursuance of an employees' share scheme".[9] Shares issued by the directors to an employee share scheme or to the trustees of such a scheme are thus excluded from the ambit of the Act. Resolutions of the company must be passed bona fide in the interests of the company.[10]

---

8   Companies Act 1963, First Schedule, Table A, Part I, Arts 2, 4 & 5.
9   Section 2(1) of the Companies (Amendment) Act, 1983 defines an "employees' share scheme" as "any scheme for the time being in force, in accordance with which a company encourages or facilitates the holding of shares or debentures in the company or its holding company by or for the benefit of employees or former employees of the company or of any subsidiary of the company including any person who is or was a director holding a salaried employment or office in the company or any subsidiary of the company".
10   *Allen v. Gold Reefs of West Africa* [1900] 1 Ch. 656.

20–09   Where the directors propose to issue additional shares to a specific third party, pre-emption rights will have to be overcome. As noted in Chapter 5,[10a] a company is generally prohibited from allotting any equity securities to any person without firstly making an offer to its shareholders to allot them a portion of the securities in proportion to their existing holding. Private companies may however, exclude pre-emption rights by inserting an appropriate provision in their memorandum or articles of association. For public companies also, provision may be made by the articles of association or by a special resolution of the company empowering the directors to allot shares without consideration to their shareholders pre-emption rights. As noted in Chapter 5, these powers are however strictly limited.

20–10   As noted in the previous Chapter, director's powers must not be exercised for an improper purpose. Thus, while the directors possess the power to issue shares, this power must not be abused. In *Piercy v. S Mills & Co,*[11] it was held that a power to issue shares in a limited company given to directors for the purpose of enabling them to raise capital when required for the purpose of the company is a fiduciary power to be exercised by them bona fide for the general advantage of the company. The Court held further that when the company is in no need of further capital, directors are not entitled to use their power of issuing shares merely for the purpose of maintaining their control or the control of themselves and their friends over the affairs of the company or merely for the purposes of defeating the wishes of the existing majority of shareholders. This case has been followed in many subsequent cases including *Hogg v. Cramphorn Ltd*[12] and *Howard Smith Ltd v. Ampol Petroleum Ltd.*[13]

20–11   Also noted in the previous Chapter[13a] is the availability of section 205 of the 1963 Act to shareholders in such cases. In *Nash v. Lancegaye Safety Glass (Ireland) Ltd.,*[14] shares were issued by the directors to a friendly shareholder who used to be a director. The Court held that the resolution to issue shares to this recipient was invalid because it had been passed with the purpose of conferring a benefit on the recipient and to increase the voting strength of the family of this recipient, thereby ensuring that the family and their friends could

---

[10a] See Chap. 5, paras 5–58–5–60 and Chap. 8, paras 8–12–8–16.
[10b] See Chap. 19, paras 19–43–19–47.
[11] [1920] 1 Ch. 77; [1918–19] All E.R. Rep. 313.
[12] [1966] 3 All E.R. 420; [1967] Ch. 254.
[13] [1974] 1 All E.R. 1126.
[13a] Chap. 19, paras 19–23–19–39.
[14] (1958) 92 I.L.T.R. 11.

control a majority of the votes. The Court ordered that the allotment of shares should be set aside and the share register amended.

20–12   As noted in paras 20.05–20.06 above, there are implications under the Stock Exchange Listing Rules and the Takeover Rules for substantial shareholders. In addition, the party to whom the additional shares are issued must ensure that its aggregate shareholding does not exceed the stipulated thresholds thus triggering a requirement to make a mandatory offer pursuant to Rule 9 of the Takeover Rules. Where the shares acquired are not sufficient to trigger the application of Rule 9 of the Takeover Rules, the Irish Takeover Panel Act, 1997 Substantial Acquisition of Shares Rules may still be relevant. These latter Rules which regulate the speed at which a company can build up its stake in another company are dealt with in Chapter 13.[14a]

IV. OBTAINING PROXY VOTES

20–13   The existence of proxy machinery in a company whose owner-ship is fragmented has been identified as one of the central causes for management becoming a "self-perpetuating body".[15] It is argued that individual shareholders, in general, do not demonstrate any great interest in participating in the running of their companies because they do not believe that their individual votes are likely to affect the outcome of any decision making process. They are thus, likely to remain rationally apathetic. One obstacle to shareholder participation is the expense and difficulty of acquiring and analysing information about corporate matters. In addition, motivating and organising fragmented groups of shareholders to vote in a particular manner is also costly for individual shareholders and generally proves unsuccessful. It is much easier for management to do this at the company's expense through the use of the proxy machinery. One interesting point however made by Easterbrook and Fischel[16] is that even though shareholders rarely use their voting powers, they obviously value them because shares with voting rights are always more expensive.

20–14   The use of proxy votes to defeat a takeover is particularly common in continental European countries where bearer shares are commonplace. The bearer share depository may utilise the proxy votes to ensure that control does not pass. In Germany, for example, banks may use the proxy votes of bearer shares to support their own share-

---

[14a] Chap. 13, paras 13–111–13–137.
[15] Berle and Means, *The Modern Corporation and Private Property*, originally published in 1932 (1991 ed., New Brunswick: Transaction Publishers), Book I, Chap. V, 82.
[16] "Voting on Corporate Law" (1983) 26 J.L. & Econ. 395.

holders.[17] In Ireland and the UK, shareholders often give proxies to management allowing them to vote the shares to support their own stated policies.

20–15 Section 136(1) of the 1963 Act allows any member of the company entitled to attend and vote at company meetings to appoint another person (whether a member or not) as a proxy to attend and vote.[18] Section 136(2)(b) states that unless the articles provide otherwise, a member of a company shall not be entitled to appoint more than one proxy to attend company meetings on the same occasion. It may be possible, however, for a corporate shareholder to divide its shareholding between two or more subsidiaries in order to increase the number of proxies entitled to attend. Once appointed, a proxy is then entitled to the same rights as the member to speak at the meeting and to vote on a show of hands and on a poll. To ensure that shareholders are aware of these procedures, every notice calling a company meeting must contain a statement to the effect that proxies may be appointed by members entitled to attend and vote.[19] In general, if invitations to appoint as proxy a person or one of a number of persons specified are issued at the company's expense, they must be sent to all members entitled to attend and vote, not merely to some of the members. Failure to comply with this obligation will render any officer of the company who knowingly and wilfully authorises or permit the issue of an invitation to selected members liable to a fine not exceeding £500.[20]

20–16 Paragraph 9.26 of the Stock Exchange Listing Rules imposes, as a continuing obligation on listed companies a requirement to send a proxy form with the notice convening the meeting of holders of listed securities to each person entitled to vote at the meeting. Paragraphs 13–28 and 13–29 of the Listing Rules deal specifically with proxy forms. Proxy forms are required to provide for two-way voting on all resolutions intended to be proposed apart from procedural resolutions. The form must state that the shareholder is entitled to appoint a proxy of his or her own choice and provide a space for the insertion of the name of the proxy. In addition, the form should state that if it is returned without an indication as to how the proxy is to vote on any particular

---

[17] Boyle and Sykes, *Gore-Browne on Companies* (Jordans), para. 40.18.3.

[18] Section 136(2) states that unless the articles provide otherwise section 136(1) will not apply in the case of a company not having a share capital.

[19] s.136(3).

[20] s.136(5). However, section 136(6) provides than an officer will not be liable under subsection (5) by reason only of the issue to a member at his written request of a form of appointment naming the proxy or of a list of persons willing to act as proxy if this form list is available upon request to all other members entitled to attend and vote.

matter, the proxy will exercise his or her discretion as to whether, and if so how, he or she votes. Where the resolutions to be proposed include the re-election of retiring directors and if the number or retiring directors standing for re-election exceeds five, the proxy form may give shareholders the opportunity to vote for or against the re-election of the retiring directors as a whole but must also allow votes to be cast for or against the re-election of the retiring directors individually.

The use of proxies in relation to acceptances during a takeover which is subject to the Takeover Rules is stricly regulated by Rule 18 of those rules.

V. DIRECT USE OF THE VOTES OF SHARES BENEFICIALLY HELD BY OTHER PARTIES OR HELD IN TRUST FOR OTHER PARTIES

20–17 An extreme example of directors controlling the votes on shares which they do not own is the use by the directors of the votes on shares in the company which the company itself beneficially owns. Section 43 of the 1983 Act restricts the use of such shares.

20–18 Section 43(1) provides that section 43 applies:

"to a public limited company:

(a) where shares in the company are forfeited, or are surrendered to the company in lieu, in pursuance of the articles for failure to pay any sum payable in respect of those shares;

(b) where shares in the company are acquired by the company otherwise than by any of the methods mentioned in section 41(4)[21] and the company has a beneficial interest in those shares;

(c) where the nominee of the company acquires shares in the company from a third person without financial assistance being given directly or indirectly by the company and the company has a beneficial interest in those shares; or

(d) where any person acquires shares in the company with financial assistance given to him directly or indirectly, by the company for the purpose of or in connection with the acquisition and the company has a beneficial interest in those shares."

Section 43(3) provides that the shares or any interest of the company in them must be cancelled and the company's nominal share capital must

---

[21] In general circumstances, section 41(1) of the Companies (Amendment) Act 1983 prohibits limited companies with share capital from acquiring their own shares. However, section 41(4) provides that this prohibition does not apply to: (a) the redemption of redeemable preference shares (b) the acquisition of any shares in a capital reduction (c) the purchase of shares pursuant to an order of the court or (d) the forfeiture of partly paid shares for non-payment of calls or an acceptance of a surrender of shares liable to be so forfeited. This issue is examined in paragraphs 20–62–20–68 of this Chapter.

be reduced unless disposed of within the relevant period. In the case of shares forfeited or surrendered to the company in lieu of forfeiture or acquired as mentioned in subsection (1)(b) or (c), the relevant period is three years from their forfeiture, surrender or acquisition. In the case of shares acquired as mentioned in subsection (1)(d), the relevant period is one year from their acquisition.[22] Section 43(4) denies the directors the use of the votes by providing that:

> "The company and, in a case falling within subsection (1)(c) or (d), the company's nominee or, as the case may be, the other shareholder must not exercise any voting rights in respect of the shares and any purported exercise of those rights shall be void".

20–19 Despite the objective underlying these provisions, Ussher maintains that the former freedom possessed by companies other than public limited companies, to retain the beneficial ownership of their own shares is preserved and in the case of companies limited by shares possibly enlarged by not requiring such shares to be held through the medium of a nominee.[23]

Where directors are trustees for example of an employee pension fund, they may be in a position to exercise the votes attaching to the shares. The directors will of course be restrained by the fiduciary duties of trustees to act in the best interests of the beneficiaries.

VI. CREATING NON-VOTING CAPITAL AND CAPITAL WITH ENHANCED VOTING RIGHTS

20–20 Capital with enhanced voting rights may be issued to the controllers or friendly shareholders and additional share capital with little or no voting power may be made available to the general investors. Alternatively, the voting rights attached to existing shares may be altered so as to give controllers or friendly shareholders enhanced voting rights. Such actions may pre-empt a hostile offer by ensuring that the valuable voting shares are concentrated in the hands of friendly parties.

(1) Voting Rights

20–21 The voting rights of shareholders are generally equitably divided. Regulation 63 of Table A of the First Schedule to the 1963 Act states that:

> "subject to any rights or restrictions for the time being attached to any class or classes of shares, on a show of hands every member present in person and every proxy shall have one vote, so, however, that no individual shall

---

[22] s.43(14).
[23] Ussher, *op. cit.*, n.1, 103.

have more than one vote, and on a poll every member shall have one vote for each share of which he is the holder".

Although this is the norm, Table A is not obligatory and companies may introduce their own articles of association instead.[24]

(2) Issuing Shares with Enhanced or Reduced Voting Rights

20–22   As noted in paragraphs 8–07–8–11, the right to issue shares is normally vested in directors either by the articles of association or by a special resolution of the company. In *Bushell v. Faith*,[25] the House of Lords acknowledged the right of a company to "issue a share with such rights or restrictions as it may think fit".[26] In this case, a resolution was proposed in a general meeting to remove a shareholder-director from his office as director. Although the resolution was carried by a show of hands, the director sought to utilise a provision in the articles of association of the company which provided that "in the event of a resolution being proposed at any general meeting of the company for the removal from office of any director, any shares held by that director shall on a poll of such resolution carry the right to three votes per share". The House of Lords upheld the right of the company to issue shares with such weighted voting rights. Often the ordinary shares will be the only shares carrying voting rights and the preferential share-holders will not be entitled to receive notice of or attend and vote at general meetings. It has been suggested however that preferential shareholders should have the right to vote on any resolution involving a variation of their rights or a reduction of capital or a winding-up.[27] The considerations outlined in paragraphs 20–08–20–12 as applying generally to the issue of shares would apply here too.

(3) Alteration of Existing Voting Rights

20–23   Management may decide to alter the voting rights attached to shares in order to maintain control. Section 15(1) of the 1963 Act allows a company by special resolution to alter its articles, subject to the provisions of the Act and to the conditions contained in the memorandum. The power to alter the articles of association must be exercised bona fide for the benefit of the company as a whole[28] and must not be exceeded.[28a]

---

[24] Section 13(2) of the Companies Act 1963 provides that if articles are registered, in so far as they do not exclude or modify the regulations contained in Table A, those regulations will apply.

[25] [1970] A.C. 1099.

[26] *ibid.* at 1109.

[27] *Gore Browne on Companies, op. cit.*, above, n.17, para. 14–6.

[28] *Clark v. Workman* [1920] 1 I.R. 107.

[28a] See Chap. 8, para. 8–04.

As noted in the previous Chapter, shareholders who believe that this power has been exceeded may bring an action for a declaration or alternatively, they make initiate an action under section 205 of the 1963 Act.

20–24 An alteration of any of the rights attaching to a class of shares may be treated in a slightly different manner. Section 38(2) of the 1983 Act provides that where the rights are attached to a class of shares in the company otherwise than by the memorandum, and the articles of the company do not contain provision with respect to the variation of the rights, the rights may only be varied:

(a) upon the consent of the holders of three-quarters in nominal value of the issued shares of that class or

(b) the passing of a special resolution at a separate general meeting of the holders of that class approving the variation.

In giving their consent, the shareholders must attempt to decide and act for the benefit of the class as a whole.[29] Where:

(a) the class rights are attached to a class of shares in the company by the memorandum or otherwise;

(b) the memorandum or articles provide for the variation of those rights; and

(c) the variation of those rights is connected with the giving, variation, revocation or renewal of an authority for the purposes of section 20 or with a reduction of the company's share capital under section 72 of the Companies Act 1963.

In addition to meeting the conditions set out in section 38(2)(a) or (b), any requirement in the memorandum or articles in relation to the variation of rights of that class must also be met. In other cases, a variation procedure in the memorandum[30] or articles effectively removes the need for shareholder approval at separate class meetings.

20–25 Paragraph 9.10.(c) of the Stock Exchange Listing Rules requires a listed company as part of its continuing obligations, to notify the Company Announcements Office without delay of any change in the rights attaching to any class of listed securities or to any securities into which listed securities are convertible. Listed companies must circularise their shareholders in connection with proposed amendments to the memorandum and articles of association. Paragraph 13–9 requires

---

[29] *Re Holders Investment Trust Ltd.* [1971] 1 W.L.R. 583.

[30] In practice, Ussher points out a class variation clause is unlikely to be inserted in a memorandum, as the insertion of class rights in a memorandum usually indicates a desire to protect them from alterability or a desire to allow alterability subject only to a stringent variation clause, *op.cit.*, above n.1, 281, fn.17.

that the circulars must include an explanation of the effect of the proposed changes.

20–26 In *Re Schweppes Ltd.*,[31] an issue of new shares ranking *pari passu* with existing shares was held not to be a variation of the latter's rights. In *Greenhalagh v. Ardene Cinemas Ltd. and Another*,[32] a private company resolved to subdivide its existing 10 s ordinary shares, most of which were held by persons opposing the appellant, Mr. Greenhalagh, into 2s ordinary shares. Because each share carried one vote, additional votes were created which led to the passing of a resolution agreeing to increase its share capital by the issue of further ordinary shares. Prior to these resolutions, Mr. Greenhalagh, who owned 2s shares, had effective control of the company. Mr. Greenhalgh's voting control was thus diluted significantly. The Court held the effect of the resolution was not to alter the voting rights of the 2s shares as they still retained the right to one vote per share. Lord Greene M.R. stated that if an attempt had been made to reduce these shares voting rights by providing for example for one vote for every five votes, this would have amounted to an interference with class rights. Alternatively, if an attempt had been made without subdividing the 10s shares to give them five votes per share, the rights attaching to the 2s shares may well have been varied because one of the rights attaching to the 2s shares was that they should have voting powers pari passu with the other ordinary shares. However, neither of these things were done. Furthermore, counsel for the appellant conceded that if a number of new 2s shares had been issued each carrying one voting right, this would not have amounted to an interference of the rights of the original 2s shares:

> "In order, therefore, to make good the argument that what was done was an interference with the voting rights of the class of shares, it had to be argued that those shares had attached to them a right . . . to object to the other ordinary shares being split so as to increase their voting power."[33]

No such right was found in this case. It must be remembered of course that this case pre-dated section 205 of the 1963 Act and if the same circumstances arose to-day, an action under that section would be more likely. The articles of association of a company may provide that particular matters which would not otherwise be deemed to be variations of class rights will be treated as such. This would mean that these matters would be subject to the variation of class rights procedures established by section 38 of the 1983 Act.[33a]

---

[31] [1914] Ch. 322.
[32] [1946] 1 All E.R. 512.
[33] *ibid.* at 516.
[33a] Stedman & Jones, *Shareholders' Agreements*, (Longman Group UK Ltd., 1986) p. 18.

(4) Use of Non-Voting Shares

20–27   In a note of dissent to the Jenkins Committee Report, Mr. Brown, Sir Erskine and Professor Gower noted this disapproval of non-voting shares maintaining:

> "To-day, non-voting shares are the simplest and most straightforward method whereby directors can render themselves irremovable without their own consent, notwithstanding that they only own or control a fraction of the equity".

Non-voting shares are not currently prohibited. The Stock Exchange does however require that the shares must be designated as non-voting shares. Similarly, where there are equity shares with different voting rights, the designation of each class of shares, other than those with the most favourable voting rights, must include the words "restricted voting" or "limited voting".[34]

20–28   The UK Law Society has stated its view that unequal voting rights are undesirable for companies which offer their equity share capital to the public.[35] Only in exceptional circumstances does it suggest maintaining an equity share structure with unequal voting rights. An example of such a circumstance is the maintenance by the Government of "golden shares" in companies of strategic national significance. The Minister for Finance has in the past retained shares in newly privatised companies such as Greencore and Irish Life. Although such a share does not generally carry voting rights or dividend rights, the Minister's consent is required in advance of certain significant acts or resolutions by the company. Consent would be needed for example for the disposal of assets other than in the ordinary course of the business, the alteration of specified articles of association, the issue of share capital with unusual voting rights or the winding up of the company. The existence of golden shares aimed at frustrating takeover bids has been the subject of recent controversy. In July 1999, the European Commission initiated legal proceedings against France, the UK, Italy, Spain, Portugal and Belgium for golden share laws designed to fend off takeovers. It was argued, for example, that the special powers attached to the share held by the French state in Elf Acquitaine, France's leading oil producer, contravened EU rules on the free movement of capital and the right of establishment.[35a]

---

[34] paras 2 and 3 to Appendix 1 to Chap. 13.
[35] Law Society Memorandum, "Barriers to Takeovers in the European Community" April 1990 No. 220.
[35a] *Financial Times*, July 29, 1999.

VII. PUTTING ASSETS OUTSIDE THE CONTROL OF SHAREHOLDERS

20–29   Often, a company becomes a takeover target because of its attractive assets. For example, a company with a lot of cash might be particularly vulnerable to a takeover bid. One way in which such a company could avoid being targeted is to put the desired assets outside the control of shareholders. This may be done by disposing of the assets totally. The cash rich company might thus utilise its resources by making an acquisition. Alternatively, it might seek to restrict the use of its assets. Even where directors are empowered by the articles of association to dispose of their assets, the Stock Exchange continuing obligations in relation to major disposals will apply.[36] In addition, as noted in the previous Chapter[36a], the disposal may be the subject of an action under section 205 of the 1963 Act for oppression or a common law action for breach of a fiduciary obligation.

20–30   In the *Savoy Hotel Ltd* case,[37] the directors of a company suspected that a competitor was making plans to acquire the company with a view to closing down the Berkeley Hotel in London and selling the building. The directors devised a complicated transaction, the effect of which was to prohibit the controllers of the company using the building as anything but a hotel without the permission of the trustees of the staff superannuation fund. The UK Department of Trade and Industry investigated and concluded that although the directors were acting bona fide in what they believed to be the interests of the shareholders, they had exercised their power to sell the hotel for an improper purpose *i.e.* to deprive shareholders of such control over company assets as they were entitled under company regulation. However, the directors remedied this defect by obtaining the subsequent approval of their shareholders to the sale.

VIII. POISON PILLS

20–31   The generic term "poison pill" refers to various defensive measures adopted by boards of directors which can lead to substantial economic repercussions for the acquirer.[38] The effect of these measures may be either to frustrate the offer totally or to place the board in a stronger negotiating position.

---

[36] See Chap. 5.
[36a] See Chap. 19.
[37] [1981] 3 All E.R. 646.
[38] Dawson, Pence and Stone, "Poison Pill Defensive Measures" 42 The Bus. Law. 423; Clemens, "Poison Debt: The New Takeover Defence" 42 The Bus. Law. 747; and Helman & Junewicz, "A Fresh Look at Poison Pills" 42 The Bus Law. 771.

(1) Rights to Purchase Additional Shares

20-32 One of the commonest forms of poison pill may be implemented through the granting by the target of rights to acquire additional shares at a set price. Alternatively, the poison pills may be in the form of convertibles, *i.e.* debentures which are convertible into equity or which carry the right to subscribe for equity. These rights are deemed exercisable only upon the occurrence of certain specified triggering events such as the announcement of a takeover offer or the change of control. These devices will make the target less attractive as it will make it more difficult and more expensive for a potential offeror to obtain voting control.

(2) Management Contracts or Long-Term Service Agreements

20-33 Another form of poison pill which may be introduced is termed a "golden parachute" or a "golden handshake". Such an arrangement requires directors of the offeree to be paid specified lump sums in the event of the company being acquired or possibly in the event of the termination of their employment with the company as a result of the acquisition. These arrangements make the target less attractive and potentially more expensive for the successful bidder. It is difficult for a potential offeror to estimate in advance how may employees may decide to accept this opportunity to resign. The potential offeror is therefore unable to estimate with any degree of certainty the final cost of the takeover. These arrangements may also lead to difficulties in maintaining the company's productivity during and subsequent to the acquisition. Supporters of these arrangements suggest that they constitute an attempt by the offeree's directors to ameliorate the harsh effects of the takeover process. By reducing the premium which can be paid for the offeree, some of the profits from the offeree's shareholder are thus redirected to the offerer's labour force. Furthermore, it has been suggested that the existence of golden parachutes is more likely to deter potential offerors who are uncertain about their managerial capacity or who overestimate their ability to manage the offeree. Thus, it is argued, poison pills of this type actually improve the overall efficiency results of the takeover by reducing inefficiency.[39]

(a) Service Contracts

20-34 Section 182(1) of the 1963 Act provides that a company may remove a director before the expiration of his term of office by ordinary resolution. This power may be exercised "notwithstanding anything in its articles or in any agreement between it and him". In the case of a

---

[39] Ryan, "Corporate Directors and the Social Costs of Takeovers – Reflections on the Tin Parachute" 64 Tulane Law Rev. 3.

private company, it is expressly stated that this subsection will not authorise the removal of a director holding office for life. However, such a director may be removed by altering the articles which lead to his appointment for life.[40]

20–35 In order to provide for security of tenure, directors may enter into independent service contracts with their companies. Such contracts may appoint them as directors for a fixed period of time. The existence of such a contract would allow the director to sue for damages for breach of contract in the event of his dismissal. Section 28 of the 1990 Act prohibits the conclusion of service contracts with a duration longer than five years, without the approval of the shareholders at a general meeting. Such approval is necessary where the contract cannot be terminated by the company by notice or where it can only be terminated in certain specified circumstances. While management cannot thus legislate for their continued existence with the company, they can, at least, make their departures sweeter.

20–36 Section 182(7) of the 1963 Act provides that:

> "Nothing in this section shall be taken as depriving a person removed thereunder of compensation or damages payable to him in respect of the determination of his appointment as director or compensation or damages payable to him in respect of the determination of any appointment terminating with that as director or as derogating from any power to remove a director which may exist apart from this section."

(b) Payments for Loss of Office

20–37 Management contracts may be introduced to ensure that management who are deprived of their jobs as a result of a hostile takeover will at least be compensated for their loss. These contracts are regulated by the Companies Acts 1963–1990, corporate governance codes, the Stock Exchange listing Rules and the Takeover Rules.

Companies Acts
20–38 Section 186 of the 1963 Act sets out the requirements for any payments proposed by a company to its directors by way of compensation for loss of office, or as consideration for or in connection with their retirement from office. Particulars of the payments proposed including the amount thereof must be disclosed to the members of the company[41] and the proposal must be approved by the company in

---

[40] Ussher, *op. cit.*, above, n.1, 91.
[41] *Re Duomatic Ltd.* [1969] 1 All E.R. 161.

general meeting. Disclosure and shareholder approval in advance are also required under section 187(1) of the 1963 Act for the making of payments to any director as compensation for loss of office in connection with the transfer of the whole or any part of the undertaking or property of a company. The same rule applies if the payment is made "as consideration for or in connection with" a director's retirement from office in connection with the transfer of the whole or any part of the undertaking or property of a company. Failure to comply with the requirements of section 187(1) will render the payment illegal and section 187(2) provides that the amount received shall be deemed to have been received by the director in trust for the company.

20–39   Section 188(1) of the 1963 Act imposes a duty on a director to disclose to shareholders payments made to him in connection with certain specified transfers by way of compensation for loss of office or as consideration for or in connection with his retirement from office in connection with a full or partial takeover of the company. The relevant transfers are transfers:

> "to any persons of all or any of the shares in a company being a transfer resulting from –
> (a) an offer made to the general body of shareholders; or
> (b) an offer made by or on behalf of some other body corporate, with a view to the company becoming its subsidiary or a subsidiary of its holding company; or
> (c) an offer made by or on behalf of an individual with a view to his obtaining the right to exercise or control the exercise of not less than one-third of the voting power at any general meeting of the company; or
> (d) any other offer which is conditional on acceptance to a given extent."

Thus it is clear that payments in connection with both complete and partial takeovers are included. This section could also include a situation where the payment is made by the offeree itself. Particulars of the proposed payments (including the amount thereof) must be included in or sent with any notice of the offer made for their shares which is given to any shareholders. Failure to comply with this requirement will render the director liable under section 188(2) to a fine of £125. While, this may not act as a substantial incentive to compliance, the potential effect of section 188(3) ensures enforcement. It provides that unless there has been compliance with section 188(1) and unless the making of the proposed payment is, before the transfer of any shares in pursuance of the offer, approved by a special meeting of the holders of the shares to which the offer relates and of other holders of shares of the same class, any sum received by the director on account of the payment shall be deemed to have been received by him in trust for the shareholders who sold their shares as a result of the offer. In addition, the director must meet the expenses of distributing this amount among the shareholders.

20–40　While sections 186, 187 and 188 ensures that shareholders will be disclosed and voted on by shareholders, the possibility always exists that disguised payments might be made to shareholders. Section 189(1) provides that where proceedings have been issued to recover money held in trust by directors under sections 187 and 188, payments made "in pursuance of any arrangement entered into as part of the agreement for the transfer in question, or within one year before or 2 years after that agreement or the offer leading thereto"; where "the company or any person to whom the transfer was made was privy to that arrangement" will be deemed to be payments held in trust. Furthermore, section 189(2) provides that both payments to directors for their own shares in the company in excess of the price which other shareholders could obtain and any valuable consideration given to directors in connection with transfers mentioned in sections 187 or 188 will be deemed to be payments by way of compensation for loss of office or as consideration for or in connection with his retirement from office. Section 189(3) provides that payments to directors by way of compensation for loss of office or as consideration for or in connection with his retirement from office include

> "payments to him by way of compensation for loss of office as director of the company or for the loss, while director of the company, or on or in connection with his ceasing to be a director of the company, of any other office in connection with the management of the company's affairs or of any office as director or otherwise in connection with the management of the affairs of any subsidiary company".

20–41　What is specifically not included however, is "any bona fide payment by way of damages for breach of contract or by way of pension in respect of past services". The term "pension" in this context is said to include "any superannuation allowance, superannuation gratuity or similar payment". Finally, section 189(4) is a saving provision providing that nothing in sections 187 and 188 will be taken to prejudice the operation of any rule of law requiring disclosure to be made with respect to any such payment as are therein mentioned or with respect to any other like payments made or to be made to the directors of the company. Nor will anything in these sections prejudice the operation of any rule of law in relation to the accountability (if any) of any director for any such payment received by a director.

Corporate Governance Codes and Stock Exchange Listing Rules
20–42　In addition to statutory restrictions on payments to directors, a number of self regulatory codes apply. The Irish Association of

Investment Managers ("IAIM") Statement of Best Practice recommends that service contracts for directors of public limited companies should not run for a period of more than three years and states that there may be circumstances where a rolling contract should be limited to a period of not more than two years. The IAIM also recommends that all service contracts should be approved by the company's Remuneration Committee which should be comprised of non-executive directors.

20–43 In recent years, there has been a proliferation of voluntary codes in the UK and Ireland culminating in the Principles of Good Governance and Code of Best Practice known as the "Combined Code".[41a] This Combined Code incorporates the recommendations of the Cadbury Committee and Hampel Committee reports on corporate governance together with those of the Greenbury Committee report on executive pay.[41b] Section 1 of the Combined Code contains the corporate governance principles and code provisions applicable to listed companies.[42] Part B of section 1 deals with the issue of directors' remuneration. The establishment of remuneration committees consisting entirely of non-executive directors, with no personal financial interests other than as shareholders, is recommended. This committee should determine, within agreed terms of reference, the company's policy on directors remuneration and its cost. In addition, it should determine specific remuneration packages for each of the executive directors, including pension rights and any compensation payments.[43] Every year, the board of directors should report to the shareholders on remuneration and this report should form part of, or be annexed to, the company's annual report and accounts.[44] This is intended to be the main vehicle through which the company reports to shareholders on directors' remuneration. While the Combined Code provides that this report need not be a standard item of agenda for AGMs, the board are required to consider each year whether the circumstances are such that the AGM should be invited to approve the policy set out in the report.[45]

[41a] The combined code: Principles of Good Governance and Code of Best Practice: the Committee on Corporate Governance (1998).

[41b] The Report of the Committee on the Financial Aspects of Corporate Governance: the Code of Best Practice (Gee Publishing, 1992); Directors Remuneration – Report of a Study Group chaired by Sir Richard Greenbury) (Gee Publishing, 1995) and the Committee on Corporate Governance: Final Report (Hampel Committee Report) (Gee Publishing, 1998).

[42] Section 2 contains the principles and code provisions applicable to institutional shareholders with regard to their voting, dialogue with companies and evaluation of a company's governance arrangements.

[43] s.1 B.2.1.

[44] s.1.B.3.1.

[45] s.1 B.3.5.

Furthermore, the conclusions of the board of directors on this issue must be minuted. In preparing the remuneration report, the board of directors are required to follow the provisions in schedule B to the Code. This schedule requires that the report should include full details of all elements in the remuneration package of each individual director, by name. Information on share options and pension entitlements should also be given for each director.[46] If grants under executive share-options or other long term incentive schemes are awarded in a single large block rather than phased, the report must explain and justify this. This would be important in respect of poison pills which are comprised of convertibles. Where any service contracts provide for a notice period in excess of one year, this must be disclosed. Importantly, any provisions for predetermined compensation on termination which exceed one year's salary and benefits should also be disclosed.

20–44   The Combined Code is to be appended to, but not form part of the Listing Rules of the London Stock Exchange and the Irish Stock Exchange. Paragraph 12.43(a) of the Irish Stock Exchange Listing Rules requires companies incorporated in Ireland to include a narrative statement in its annual report and accounts as to how it has applied the principles set out in section 1 of the Combined Code, providing explanation which enables its shareholders to evaluate how the principles have been applied. In addition para. 14–23 provides that, a statement should be included as to whether or not it has complied throughout the accounting period with the code provisions set out in section 1 of the Combined Code. A company that has not complied with all of the code provisions or, in the case of provisions involving continuing requirements, has complied for only part of the accounting period, must specify with which provisions it has not complied or for what period has it not complied. Reasons for any non-compliance must be given. Paragraph 12.43A(c) states that the annual report and accounts must include a report to the shareholders on behalf of the board. This report must include a statement on the company's policy on executive directors' remuneration.[47] The report must also state:

> "the amount of each element in the remuneration package for the period under review for all of the directors in aggregate analysed into executive and non-executive sections including, but not restricted to, fees, basic salary, the estimated money value of benefits in kind, annual bonuses, deferred bonuses, compensation for loss of office and payments for breach of contract or other termination payments, both for the current period and the previous

---

[46] Schedule B provides that the amounts received by directors under these headings should be subject to audit.

[47] paras 12–43A(c)(i).

financial period, and any significant payments made to former directors during the period under review".[48]

Details of any directors' service contract must be included where there is a notice period in excess of one year or provisions for pre-determined compensation on termination which exceeds one year's salary and benefits in kind. The reasons for such a lengthy notice period must also be included.[49] On this issue, the unexpired term of a service contract of any director proposed for election or re-election at the forthcoming annual general meeting must also be disclosed.[50] Details of share options, long-term incentive plans, defined benefit schemes, contributions to money-purchase schemes and the company's policy on the granting of options or awards under employee share schemes and long term incentive schemes must also be included.[51] Interestingly, an explanation and justification of any element of remuneration, other than basic salary, which is pensionable must also be included.[52]

Takeover Rules

20–45 Even where changes are made to directors' service contracts at a time when an offer has not been made and is not imminent, disclosure may be necessary in the documentation published during a subsequent offer. Rule 25.4(a) provides that the first major circular from the offeree board advising shareholders of an offer must contain particulars of all service contracts with more than 12 months to run of any director or proposed director of the offeree or any of its subsidiary or associated companies. If any such contract has been entered into or amended within six months prior to the date of the circular, Rule 25.4(b) requires particulars be given of the earlier contracts as well as the new contracts. Any increase in remuneration would count as an amendment. This will allow shareholders to judge the significance of any changes. The particulars which must be disclosed are:

 (i) the name of the director under contract;

 (ii) the expiry date of the contract;

(iii) the amount of fixed remuneration payable under the contract;

(iv) the amount of any variable remuneration payable under the contract with details of the basis for calculating such remuneration; and

---

[48] para. 12–43A(c)(ii) as inserted by the Green Pages.
[49] para. 12–43A(c)(vi)
[50] para. 12–43A(c)(vii). Where such a director does not have a directors' service contract, a statement to this effect should be included.
[51] para. 12–43A(c)(iii), (iv), (viii), (ix), (x) and (xi).
[52] para. 12–43A(c)(v).

(v) arrangements for company payments in respect of a pension or similar scheme.

Tin Parachutes

20–46 Where similar payments are available to middle management, the packages are known as "tin parachutes". These payments are generally available to employees who leave during a fixed interval after the takeover. Since courts tolerate golden parachutes which are disclosed and sanctioned, tin parachutes are also likely to be accepted. However, one must consider the extent to which directors are legitimately entitled to take into account the economic well being of non-shareholder groups. Their main concern must be with the interests of their shareholders.[53]

IX. BLACK BOOK

20–47 A "black book" is the term used to describe an outline of the actions to be taken if a takeover bid occurs. Planning these actions in advance will serve to focus directors' minds on possible frustrating activities in advance of a takeover. The directors will then have time to consider their options and to obtain shareholder approval where necessary. In the event of an offer being made, they will then be able to react in a more timely and effective manner. The black book may also prove a useful deterrent to potential offerors. It may alert them to the fact that anything but a friendly bid is unlikely to succeed or at the least a hostile bid would be costly, time consuming and difficult.

B. Defensive Tactics Once a Bid Has Been Made or is Imminent

20–48 Once a takeover bid has been made, the directors of listed public companies are more limited in their options than directors of private or unlisted public companies. As noted in the previous Chapter[53a], in addition to statutory and common law restrictions, Rule 21 of the Takeover Rules provides that directors of listed companies require the approval of their shareholders in advance of engaging in any defensive activities. Most of the following tactics would be viewed as actions likely to frustrate the making or the implementation of a takeover offer contrary to Rule 21 and shareholder approval would thus be needed.

---

[53] See Chap. 19, para. 19–14.
[53a] See Chap. 19, paras 19–60–19–65.

I. REFUSING TO REGISTER TRANSFERS

20–49   A transfer of shares is not complete until the transferee is registered in the books as a member of the company.[54] In *Kinsella v. Alliance & Dublin Gas Co.,*[55] Barron J. held that:

> "Persons entitled to stock must be registered in the register of shareholders. Until they are, they are not entitled to vote."

Thus one method, of avoiding a takeover offer is to refuse to register the successful bidder.

In the case of listed companies, paragraph 3.15 of the Stock Exchange Listing Rules provides that to be listed, securities must be freely transferable. However, in exceptional circumstances as approved by the Stock Exchange, an applicant for listing may take power to disapprove the transfer of shares, "provided that the exercise of such power would not disturb the market in those shares". These requirements are reflected in the first Appendix to Chapter 13 of the Listing Rules which sets out the matters which must be provided for in the articles of association of a listed company.

20–50   Directors of private companies may be given an absolute discretion under the articles to register or refuse to register persons. Model Regulation 3 of Part II of Table A states that "the directors may, in their absolute discretion, and without assigning any reason therefore, decline to register any transfer of any share, whether or not it is a full paid share." As with other powers, the directors must take care not to abuse these powers.[56] In *Re Smith and Fawcett Ltd.,*[57] the articles gave such absolute discretion to the directors. Lord Greens M.R commented

> "In the present case the article is drafted in the widest possible terms, and I decline to write into that clear language any limitation other than a limitation which is implicit by law, that a fiduciary power of this kind must be exercised bona fide in the interests of the company. Subject to that qualification, an article in this form appears to me to give the directors what it says, namely, absolute and uncontrolled discretion."[58]

In *Village Cay Marine Ltd. v. Landac et al,*[59] the Privy Council held that the question for the court in such cases was to determine whether the directors of a private company believed in good faith that the refusal of registration was in the interests of the company. Although the articles

---

[54] *Tangney v. The Clarence Hotels Company Ltd.* [1933] I.R. 51.
[55] Unreported, High Court, Barron J., October 5, 1982 at page 12 of the transcript.
[56] As discussed in Chap. 19, paras 19–42–19–52.
[57] [1942] 1 Ch. 304.
[58] *ibid.* at 308.
[59] [1998] 2 B.C.L.C. 327.

of association of the company allowed the directors to decline registration without assigning any reason, reasons were given by the directors for their refusal. The Privy Council held that the reasons given by the directors at the time of their refusal were only part of the evidence and the court was entitled to take into account the other reasons given in evidence at the trial. As noted in para. 15–06 above, the directors are obliged to notify the transferee of their decision to refuse to register the transfer within two months. In *Re Inverdeck Ltd*,[60] Carnwath J. held that the directors have a duty to register the applicant's transfer within two months or, alternatively, to give notice to the applicant of their refusal to do so. In that case the directors lost their right to refuse to register the transfer because of their delay.

II. ISSUING AND ALLOTTING ADDITIONAL SHARES

20–51 In order to avoid being acquired by a particular offeror, the offeree may issue shares to other persons with a view to ensuring the offer is rejected or depriving the bidder of control. This tactic was discussed in paragraphs 20–08–20–12 above. Where a hostile offer has already been announced, the shares may be allotted to a "white knight". The term "white knight" refers to a company whose offer is favoured by the offeree in a competitive takeover situation. The offeree's directors may have encouraged such a company to make an offer in the first place and they will generally co-operate with the directors of this company in making and effecting an offer. In recent times, a practice has arisen of offering a favoured offeror an inducement fee pursuant to which a cash sum will become payable by the offeree if, typically, specified events occur which have the effect of preventing the offer from proceeding, or causing it to fail. The London Panel has expressed concern that bona fide offers may be frustrated by reason of these arrangements and has issued a number of safeguards which must be complied with where inducement fees are proposed. These include the requirement that any inducement fee be *de minimis* (which normally means more than 1 per cent of the offer value) and confirmation by the offeree board and its financial adviser that, *inter alia*, they believe the fee to be in the best interests of shareholders. All such arrangements must be fully disclosed and the relevant document must be put on display. This area is likely to be the subject of review by the Irish panel in the near future.[60a]

In certain circumstances issuing and allotting shares to a favoured offeror may amount to a breach of fiduciary duties. In *Howard Smith v. Ampol*,[61] the "substantial purpose" of allotting shares to a white knight

---

[60] [1998] 2 B.C.L.C. 242.
[60a] Circular 1990/10 (July 16, 1999).
[61] [1974] A.C. 821.

was to prevent the plaintiffs bid from succeeding. This was deemed to be an abuse of power. Pre-emption rights make this a difficult tactic to utilise effectively as pre-emption rights require shares to be offered to existing shareholders in proportion to their existing holdings.[62]

III. COMMUNICATION WITH SHAREHOLDERS

20–52   The directors of the offeree may seek to dissuade their shareholders from accepting the offer by arguing that the offer undervalues the company or is not otherwise in the shareholders best interests. Alternatively, the offeree's directors may criticise the offeror. This may be particularly effective in a securities exchange offer where the offeror is providing consideration in the form of its own shares. In such a case, the offeree's directors can argue that the offer undervalues the offeree's shares. Even where the consideration offered is in the form of cash, the directors can still criticise the philosophy, history and labour relations record of the offeror. In this case however, it becomes more difficult to criticise the actual bid itself, as the shareholders will be immediately aware of the real premium being offered on the current market price.

(1) The Views of the Offeree's Directors

20–53   If the directors of the offeree company reject the offer and provide cogent arguments to their shareholders for doing so, this may be sufficient in itself to frustrate the offer. Yet the communication of such views is mandated by the Takeover Rules. From the outset, shareholders in the offeree company will be aware of their directors views. General Principle 4 requires that shareholders to whom an offer is made should be given sufficient information and advice to enable them to reach a properly informed decision. For this purpose, the information must be accurate and adequate and must be furnished to them in a timely fashion. Rule 23(a) repeats this requirement. Once an offer is made, Rule 3.1(a) requires the offeree board to obtain competent independent advice and communicate both the substance and the source of this advice to shareholders. In addition, the offeree board must inform shareholders of its "considered views" of the bid. If the board considers it impossible to express a view on the merits of an offer or to give a firm recommendation for acceptance to shareholders, or if there is a divergence of views among members of the offeree board or between the offeree board and the independent adviser as to either the merits of the offer or the recommendation to be made, Rule 3.1(b) requires the offeree board to make this clear in its circular to shareholders. The

---

[62] See Chap. 5, paras 5–58–5–60 and Chap. 8, paras 8–12–8–16.

circular must also set out fully the arguments for acceptance and for rejection, emphasising the important factors. Rule 3.1(a) excludes any director with a conflict of interest from the formulation and communication of advice to shareholders. As noted in the previous Chapter[62a], where directors of an offeree are to be replaced following the acquisition, it may be said that there is a conflict of interest. Note 2 on rule 3.1 cites as an example of a conflict of interest significant cross-shareholdings between an offeror and offeree or the existence of common directors or substantial shareholders. These are examples of conflicts which would give a director an interest in seeing the takeover offer succeed rather than fail.

20–54 Rule 25 deals specifically with offeree board circulars. Rule 25.1(a) repeats the obligation imposed on the offeree board to circulate to its shareholders its views on the offer and any alternative offers together with the independent advice received. Rule 25.1(d) provides that any director with a conflict of interest should not be joined with the rest of the directors in expressing their opinion on the offer. In addition, the nature of the conflict should be clearly explained in any document sent to shareholders. The views of the board of the offeree on the offeror's plans for the company and its employees should be disclosed.[63] In addition, the first major circular sent to shareholders should include certain important details which are necessary to allow shareholders make an informed assessment. These include for example details of shareholdings and dealings in the offeror and offeree[64], the directors' service contracts,[65] arrangements in relation to dealings,[66] material contracts[67] and material changes of information.[68]

(2) Standards of Accuracy

20–55 Subject to the rules on confidential information and defamation, in ordinary circumstances a company is generally entitled to communicate freely with its shareholders. However, where an offer is imminent or has been made, the Takeover Rules regulate the type of information which may be disclosed and the manner of its disclosure. These effect of these Rules is to substantial curtail the ability of the offeree's directors to frustrate a bid by announcing favourable information about the offeree or by disclosing negative information about the

---

[62a] Chap. 19, para. 19–09.
[63] R. 25.2.
[64] R. 25.3.
[65] R. 25.4.
[66] R. 25.5.
[67] R. 25.6.
[68] R. 25.7.

offeror or the offer. The highest standard of care will be expected from the offeree. These rules were considered in detail in Chap. 12 above.

20–56 All documents, advertisements or statements issued by the offeree or on its behalf in connection with the offer must satisfy the same standards of accuracy, completeness and fair presentation as would be required of a prospectus. The sources of any material facts published must be clearly stated and quotations may not be used out of context.[69] In addition, documents issued to shareholders of the offeree and advertisements published in connection with the offer by either the offeror or offeree must contain a responsibility statement issued by the directors of the offeror or offeree as the case may be.[70] The directors must state that to the best of their knowledge and belief, having taken all reasonable care to ensure that such is the case, the information contained therein is in accordance with the facts and does not omit anything likely to affect the import of such information.[71] Not only is the offeree prohibited from issuing statements which are factually incorrect, but it is also prohibited from issuing statement which may mislead shareholders and the market or may create uncertainty.[72]

20–57 The contents of profit forecasts and asset valuations made by the offeree during the course of the offer are also regulated.[73] In addition, the offeree is prohibited from issuing statements which include estimates of the anticipated financial effects of a takeover unless they consult with the Panel in advance and unless they include in the statement:

(i) the basis of the belief (including sources of information and any assumptions made) supporting the estimate;

(ii) reports by financial advisers and auditors that the estimates have been made with due care and consideration;

(iii) an analysis and explanation of the constituent elements of the estimate;

(iv) a base figure for any comparisons drawn and

(v) a disclaimer.[74]

---

[69] R. 19.1.
[70] R. 19.2.
[71] Rule 19.2 will not apply to product advertisements or corporate image advertisements not bearing on an offer or potential offer, advertisements which are notices relating to court schemes or to advertisements which contain only information already published in a circular which included a directors' responsibility statement.
[72] R. 19.3.
[73] Rs. 28 & 29.
[74] R. 19.3(b).

Most advertisements in connection with the offer are prohibited unless they have been approved in advance by the Panel.[75] Furthermore, telephone campaigns and interviews are strictly regulated in order to ensure that new information is not released to selective shareholders and also to ensure that the information which is released is accurate and does not mislead shareholders.[76]

IV. PROMOTION OF AUCTIONS

20–58 Although the offeree's directors or their advisers are not prevented from seeking an alternative offeror and thus promoting an auction for the offeree, their dealings with this white knight are strictly regulated.

20–59 Rule 20.2 restricts the abilities of the offeree board to engage in favouritism in the form of passing salient information exclusively to the white knight. It provides that the offeree shall promptly provide any information, including particulars of shareholders if, and to the extent that the same or substantially the same information has previously been made available by the offeree to another offeror. There are two prerequisites to the operation of this rule. First, the rule only applies where the existence of the other offeror has been announced. Secondly, and more importantly, the information to be passed on is any information which has been "specifically requested by an offeror". The onus therefore is on the hostile offeror to be aware of the information it wishes to access in order to lodge a specific request for it. It is not entitled, by asking in general terms, to receive all the information supplied to a competing offeror. This still allows the offeree board a certain degree of latitude to pass on certain information to a favoured offeror in the safe knowledge that it is unlikely to be specifically requested by the hostile offeror.

20–60 Another potential defensive action is the giving of an irrevocable undertaking to a white knight in order to frustrate a hostile offer. General Principle 7 obliges directors to "give careful consideration" before entering into any commitment with the offeror (or any other person) which would restrict their freedom to advise the offeree's shareholders in the future. This Principle will affect a director's ability to enter into irrevocable commitment with one offeror to the detriment of another in a competitive bid situation. Rule 24.5 provides that unless the Panel consents otherwise, "the offer document shall contain a statement as to whether or not any agreement, arrangement or understanding

---

[75] R. 19.4.
[76] R. 19.5 & 19.6.

(including any compensation arrangement) having any connection with or dependence upon the offer exists between the offeror or any person acting in concert with it or any associate of it and any of the directors, recent directors, holders or recent holders of securities of the offeree and shall contain full particulars of any such agreement, arrangement or understanding." The effect of this rule would be to prevent the directors, or any of them, coming to a secret arrangement with a white knight.

V. GREENMAIL

20–61 This tactic involves the repurchase by an offeree of securities acquired by the offeror normally at a substantial profit.[76a] It is thus equated with bribing an offeror to go away. Regulations dealing with a company's ability to purchase its own shares would restrict an offeree's ability to defend a takeover offer in this way. It should be noted that the repurchase of shares can be problematic from a tax perspective. If the shares are bought back by the company by means of a standard stock transfer form, stamp duty is assessable in the normal way. If the shares are bought on foot of a contract or share purchase agreement and the shares certificates are merely handed over to the company, no share transfer form is necessary and thus no stamp duty is chargeable under section 59 of the Stamp Act, 1891.[76b] Capital Gains Tax ("CGT") is also relevant in this context. Where a company buys its own shares, there is no tax charge on the portion of the sale proceeds representing the return of the shareholder's capital (which is taken to be the original subscription price paid for the shares). Any sum received in excess of this will be treated as a distribution. The effect of this is that an individual shareholder will be subject to income tax on the distribution rather than being subject to CGT. Unfortunately, this distribution treatment will not be as beneficial as CGT treatment as the income tax rate is higher than the current rate of CGT applicable to gains of this nature which is 20 per cent. For a corporate shareholder, the benefits are, however, greater. A corporate shareholder will be receiving franked investment income which will not be subject to corporation tax. As a result, the corporate share-holder would probably prefer to secure a distribution as opposed on CGT treatment. There are two circumstances in which CGT treatment rather than income tax treatment will apply to the buy-back by a company of its shares. The first of these is where a company whose shares are listed in

---

[76a] See the *Stamp Duty Work Manual* and *Practices of the Revenue Commissioners*, (The Revenue Commissioners, 1998).

[76b] ss. 173–186 Taxes and Consolidation Act, 1997. See also Brennan & Moore, *Corporation Tax*, (The Institute of Taxation of Ireland, 1998).

the official list of a stock exchange or dealt in on an unlisted securities market, buys back its shares. The second case where CGT treatment applies is where certain conditions set out in the legislation apply. These are: the company is an unquoted trading company; the buy-back is for the benefit of the company's trade; the shareholder is resident and ordinarily resident in Ireland; the shares have been held for five years; after the transaction, the shareholders holds less than 30 per cent of the company; and there is substantial reduction in the vendor's interest after the transaction, *i.e.* the relevant shareholding has been reduced by 25 per cent.[76b]

(1) Companies (Amendment) Act 1983

(a) Prohibition

20–62   Section 41(1) of the 1983 Act prohibits a company from acquiring its own shares "whether by purchase, subscription or otherwise".[77] This prohibition safeguards the general principle of capital maintenance and also prevents a company increasing the demand for and thus the price of its own shares. This prohibition is however subject to a number of exemptions set out in section 41 of the Act.

(b) Exemptions

20–63   A company limited by shares is allowed pursuant to section 41(2) to acquire any of its own fully paid shares "otherwise than for valuable consideration". Thus where a company has been given the shares, or bequeathed the shares, it can accept them. It should be remembered that a "valuable consideration" need not necessarily be an adequate or a commensurate consideration. In *Currie v. Misa*,[78] Lush J. noted:

> "A valuable consideration, in the sense of the law, may consist in some right, interest, profit or benefit accruing to the one party or some forbearance, detriment, loss or responsibility, given, suffered or undertaken by the other."[79]

A number of other exemptions are permitted by section 41(1).[80] These include:

– the redemption of preference shares issued prior to May 5th, 1959 in pursuance of section 65 of the 1963 Act;

– the acquisition of any shares in a reduction of capital duly made;

---

[77] At common law, limited companies were also prohibited from purchasing their own shares. See *Trevor v. Whitworth* (1887) 12 App. Cas. 409.
[78] (1875) L.R. 10 Ex 153.
[79] *ibid.* at 162.
[80] As amended by section 232(a) of the Companies Act 1990.

- the purchase of any shares in pursuance of a court order under section 15 of the 1983 Act,[81] section 10 of the 1963 Act[82] or section 205 of the 1963 Act;[83]

- the forfeiture of any shares, or the acceptance of any shares surrendered in lieu, in pursuance of the articles for failure to pay any sum payable in respect of those shares; or

- the redemption or purchase of shares in pursuance of Part XI of the Companies Act 1990.

(c) Acquisition of Shares Under of Part XI of the Companies Act 1990

20–64 Part XI of the 1990 Act allows a company, subject to certain conditions, to issue redeemable shares of any class[84] and to convert normally irredeemable shares into redeemable ones.[85] As noted above, Part XI also allows subsidiary companies to acquire shares in their own holding companies, again subject to certain conditions.[86] In addition, section 211(1) of Part XI allows a company, if so authorised by its articles, to purchase its own fully paid shares including any redeemable shares.

20–65 Many of the same conditions which apply to the redemption of shares apply to the acquisition of a company's own shares.[86a] Shares may not be purchased at any time when the nominal value of the issued share capital which is not redeemable would be less than 10 per cent of the nominal value of the company's issued share capital.[87] The funds used to purchase the shares (up to the nominal value of the shares) and to pay for any premium on the shares must normally be profits available for distribution.[88] Alternatively, where the company proposes to cancel the shares, the purchase price (up to the nominal value of the shares) may be met out of the capital obtained for a fresh share issue made for this particular purpose.[89] In such a case the premium will still be met out of profits available for distribution.[90] A

---

[81] In connection with the re-registration of a public limited company as a private company.
[82] In connection with the alteration by a company of its objects clause.
[83] As a remedy for minority oppression.
[84] Companies Act 1990, s.207.
[85] *ibid.* s.210.
[86] *ibid.* s.224. See para. 20–07.
[86a] s.211(2) provides that ss. 207(2), 208 and 209 apply in this manner to the acquisition of a company's own shares.
[87] *ibid.* s.211(3).
[88] *ibid.* s.207(2)(d)(i).
[89] *ibid.* s.207(2)(d)(ii).
[90] *ibid.* s.207(2)(e).

premium may be met out of the proceeds of a fresh issue, to the extent that any balance in the share premium account which represents premium which arose on the issue of the particular shares which are being purchased and the balance in the share premium account must be reduced accordingly.[91]

20–66 A company is prohibited from making an off-market purchase of its own shares otherwise than in pursuance of a contract authorised by a special resolution of the company. An "off-market" purchase is defined as a purchase otherwise than on a recognised stock exchange or a purchase of shares which are not subject to a marketing arrangement[92] on that stock exchange.[93a] A "market purchase" by contrast is a purchase on a recognised stock exchange of shares which are subject to a marketing arrangement.[94] The votes attaching to the shares which are to be acquired by the company may be cast against the special resolution but may not be cast in favour of it.[95] The special resolution will only be effective if a copy of the proposed contract of purchase or a memorandum evidencing it is available for inspection by shareholders for 21 days prior to the shareholders meeting and at the meeting itself.[96]

20–67 A company is prohibited from making a market purchase of its own shares unless the purchase has first been authorised by the company in general meeting.[97] The authority granted for a market purchase in the case of a public limited company must specify the maximum number of shares authorised to be acquired and must determine the maximum and minimum prices which may be paid for the shares.[98] In addition, any authorisation granted in the case of a public limited company for a market or off-market purchase must specify the expiry date of the authorisation which date must not be more than 18 months from the date on which the authority was granted.[98a]

20–68 Where the purchase price is met out of profits available for distribution and the shares acquired are to be cancelled, an amount equal to the nominal value of the shares acquired must be credited to

---

[91] *ibid.* s.207(2)(f).
[92] Section 212(2) provides that a marketing arrangement includes both a listing and a dealing arrangement which does not involve the Stock Exchange's prior authorisation and does not have time limits.
[93] *ibid.* s.212(1)(a).
[94] *ibid.* s.212(1)(b).
[95] *ibid.* s.213(3).
[96] *ibid.* s.213(5).
[97] *ibid.* s.215(1).
[98] *ibid.* s.215(3).
[98a] *ibid.* s.216(1).

the capital redemption reserve fund.[99] The same rule applies if the purchase price is met partly or wholly out of the proceeds of a fresh share issue and the aggregate amount of those proceeds is less than the aggregate nominal value of the shares acquired. If the purchase price is met out of profits available for distribution, the company may hold the shares as treasury shares instead of cancelling them. However, the nominal value of treasury shares held by a company may not, at any one time, exceed 10 per cent of the nominal value of the company's issued share capital.[100] The company is not entitled to exercise any voting rights in respect of these shares or to claim a dividend.[101] Treasury shares may be cancelled or re-issued but the maximum and minimum prices at which treasury shares may be re-issued off-market will be determined in advance by the company in general meeting in accordance with the provisions of the Act.[102]

(2) Takeover Rules

20–69 Where the company purchases or redeems its own shares it must ensure that a mandatory general offer is not triggered by Rule 37. Rule 37.1(a) provides that if a person or a any person acting in concert acquires control of or consolidates control in a relevant company "wholly or partly" by reason of the redemption or purchase by that company of its own securities, unless the Panel allows otherwise, such person or persons must extend offers in accordance with the requirements of Rule 9.2, 9.3 and 9.4 to the holders of each class of equity share capital in the relevant company, whether or not such class confers voting rights, and also to the holders of each class of voting non-equity share capital of which such person or persons hold shares. The percentage figures to determine an acquisition of control or a consolidation of control are the same as are applied by Rule 9.

20–70 A holder of securities of a relevant company (not being a director of that company) who is not acting in concert with any one or more of the directors of that company will not be required to make the mandatory offer if, as a result of the purchase or redemption by the company of its own securities, the aggregate percentage of the voting rights in the company conferred by the securities held by them and any concert parties is increased to or beyond or by the relevant percentage level for the acquisition or consolidation of control.[103] This exemption

---

[99] *ibid.* s.208(b).
[100] *ibid.* s.209(2)(a).
[101] *ibid.* s.209(3).
[102] *ibid.* s.209(6)(a).
[103] R. 37.1(b).

will only apply if the Panel is satisfied that neither the holder of securities nor any concert party purchased voting securities of the company at a time when they had reason to believe that such a redemption or purchase would take place. Unless the Panel consents or the shareholders in general meeting consent, the offeree may not redeem or purchase any of its own shares during the course of an offer or at any earlier time at which the offeree board has reason to believe that an offer may be imminent.[104] The only exception to this is where the purchase or redemption is in pursuance of a contract entered into prior to the announcement of the offer. This means that if an offeree were to engage in greenmail, it would have to seek the approval of its shareholders.

20–71   In addition, as noted in Chapter 13 above, restrictions may be imposed on dealings in shares of the offeree company. For example, Rule 4.2(a) would prohibit the offeror selling any securities of the offerree except with the consent of the Panel and following an announcement that such sales may be made. Rule 4.2(c) would prohibit an offeror from dealing in securities of the offeree after deciding not to proceed with the offer until an announcement to this effect has been made.

(3) Stock Exchange Listing Rules

20–72   Chapter 15 of the Stock Exchange Listing Rules set out the rules which apply when a company wishes to purchase its own listed securities. These rules apply whether the purchase is to be a market purchase or an off market purchase within the meaning of section 212 of the 1990 Act.[105]

20–73   Paragraph 15–1 of the Listing Rules provides that purchases by a company of its own securities should not take place at a time when, under the provisions of the Model Code, a director of the company would be prohibited from dealing in its securities. The company would not be allowed to deal thus at a time when a director is in possession of unpublished price-sensitive information in relation to those securities. Arguably, if an offeree were to acquire its own shares from a company which had privately signalled its interest to the company, this could be deemed as acting on the basis of inside information. Whilst, the company would be dealing with another party, the potential offeror, who also possessed the information, it could distort the market price for the securities. If the offer is already publicly disclosed, this would be avoided.

---

[104]   R. 37.2(a).
[105]   Para. 15–12 of the Listing Rules provides that the rules will not apply, however, to transactions entered in the ordinary course of business by securities dealing businesses or on behalf of third parties by the company or any members of its group.

20–74   Where the company decides to submit a proposal to share-holders to authorise the purchase of its own equity shares, this decision must be notified to the CAO without delay. The notification must state whether the proposal relates to specific purchases or to a general authorisation. In the case of the former, the names of the persons from whom the purchases are to be made must be included. The outcome of the shareholders meeting must also be notified without delay.[106] Whilst the circular need not generally be submitted to the Stock Exchange for approval its contents are strictly regulated. Where general authority is sought, a statement of the directors' intentions regarding utilisation of that authority must be included. The method of acquiring the shares (if known), the number to be acquired and details regarding price should be included. In addition, if the authority relates to a specific purchase from a specific party or parties, the name of the party or parties together with all the material terms of the proposal should be included.[107]

20–75   In order to ensure equality of treatment of shareholders, the price offered by the company for its shares may be regulated. Purchases by a company of less than 15 per cent of any class of its equity shares pursuant to a general authority granted by shareholders may be made through the market only if the price to be paid is not more than 5 per cent above the average of the market values of those shares for the previous five business days. This will not apply however where a tender or partial offer is made to all holders of the class of securities on the same terms.[108] Purchases by a company of more than 15 per cent of any class of its equity shares pursuant to a general authority granted by shareholders must generally be made by way either of a tender or a partial offer to all shareholders.[109] This restrictions would severely curtail the ability of a company to use green mail.

20–76   Once the purchase takes place, the CAO must be notified as soon as possible and in any event not later than 8.30am on the business day following the calendar day on which dealing occurred. The CAO must be notified of the date of purchase, the number of equity shares purchased and the purchase price for each or the highest and lowest price paid.[110]

20–77   Where listed securities convertible into equity shares of the class proposed to be purchased are already in issue, a meeting of these security

---

[106]   para. 15.3.
[107]   para. 15.4. The information required by paragraph 14.1 must also be included.
[108]   para. 15.6.
[109]   para. 15.7.
[110]   para. 15.9.

holders must be convened to obtain their approval to the purchase. This will not, however, be necessary where the trust deed or terms of issue of the convertibles provide for the company purchasing its own shares.[111]

VI. MANAGEMENT BUY-OUTS AND LEVERAGE BUYOUTS

20–78   This is the ultimate defence because once the acquisition is completed it cannot be overcome by a bidder except through negotiations with management.[112] Because there is an immediate conflict of interest where directors of the offeree are also involved with the offeror, management buy-outs are highly regulated. This is dealt with in greater detail in Chapter 18.

VII. REVERSE BEAR HUG

20–79   This term refers to the situation where the offeree board responds to an offer by expressing a willingness to negotiate a friendly acquisition, but at a price far in excess of the proposal. This may be used as a delay tactic, *e.g.* in order to give them an opportunity to identify a white knight.

VIII. SANDBAG

20–80   In keeping with the militaristic terminology of the terms "hostile bids" and "defensive actions", many of the tactics mentioned to frustrate unwelcome bids are named after U.S. military strategies. A "sandbag" tactic is used by the offeree to delay the making of a takeover offer by the potential offeror. A delay might be necessary to find a white knight to make a competing bid or perhaps to increase the offeror's cost in the hope of rendering the acquisition uneconomical. Some critics have argued that statutory framework for regulating the conduct of takeovers in Ireland would present itself as just such an opportunity. The fear is that an offeree would use the judicial review procedure to delay the making of an offer. As noted in Chapter 3,[112] the drafting of the provisions of the Irish Takeover Panel Act 1997 seeks to minimise this possibility.

IX. SHOWSTOPPER

20–81   The term "showstopper" generally refers to legal action initiated by the offeree with a view to putting a permanent end to the offer.

---

[111]   para. 15.10.
[112]   See Chap. 3, paras 3–47–3–51.

Normally, this involves the offeree board arguing that the acquisition would be anti-competitive. For example, the offeree's directors may refer the offer to the Competition Authority under the Competition Act 1991 in an attempt to get the acquisition prohibited. The objective of a defence strategy based on competition policy is not to persuade shareholders of the undesirability of the offer but to frustrate the offer totally. A strict interpretation of the Rule 21 prohibition on directors taking any action as respect the conduct of its affairs the effect of which would be, or be likely, to frustrate the implementation of an offer would also rule out an appeal to the competition agencies.

X. SCORCHED EARTH

20–82   This involves the offeree convincing the offeror that the offeree's defence would be so vigorous, that it would substantially reduce its value to the offeror. This tactic was adopted very successfully by a U.S. publishing company which persuaded its important authors to advise a bidder that they would sever their ties with the target if the offer was successful.[113]

XI. PAC MAN

20–83   This defence tactic is named after the computer game. It involves the offeree launching a bid for the offeror. Such a tactic was used, for example, by French Oil group Elf following a hostile bid by rival Total Fina. One disadvantage with such a tactic is that instead of the original offeree's shareholders receiving a premium on the acquisition, the original offeror's shareholders receive the premium. Such a tactic may not thus receive the approval of the offerees shareholders.

---

[113]   Referred to in Gilson, "The Case Against Shark Repellant Amendments: Structural Limitations on the Enabling Concept", 35 Stan. Law Rev. 775.

APPENDIX 1

CITY CODE ON MERGERS AND TAKEOVERS

General Principles

1. All shareholders of the same class of an offeree company must be treated similarly by an offeror.

2. During the course of an offer, or when an offer is in contemplation, neither an offeror, nor the offeree company, nor any of their respective advisers may furnish information to some shareholders which is not made available to all shareholders. This principle does not apply to the furnishing of information in confidence by the offeree company to a bona fide potential offeror or vice versa.

3. An offeror should only announce an offer after the most careful and responsible consideration. Such an announcement should be made only when the offeror has every reason to believe that it can and will continue to be able to implement the offer. responsibility in this connection also rests on the financial adviser to the offeror.

4. Shareholders must be given sufficient information and advice to enable them to reach a properly informed decision and must have sufficient time to do so. No relevant information should be withheld from them.

5. Any document or advertisement addressed to shareholders containing information or advice from an offeror or the board or the offeree company or their respective advisers must as is the case with a prospectus, be prepared with the highest standards of care and accuracy.
   All parties to an offer must use every endeavour to prevent the creation of a false market in the securities of an offeror or the offeree company. Parties involved in offers must take care that statements are not made which may mislead shareholders or the market.

7. At no time after a bona fide offer has been communicated to the board of the offeree company, or after the board of the offeree company has reason to believe that a bona fide offer might be imminent, may any action be taken by the board of the offeree company in relation to the affairs of the company, without the approval of the shareholders in general meeting, which could effectively result in any bona fide offer being frustrated or in the shareholders being denied an opportunity to decide on its merits.

8. Rights of control must be exercised in good faith and the oppression of a minority is wholly unacceptable.

9. Directors of an offeror and the offeree company must always, in advising their shareholders, act only in their capacity as directors and not have regard to their personal or family shareholdings or to their personal relationships with the companies. It is the shareholders' interests taken as a whole, together with those of employees and creditors, which should be considered when the directors are giving advice to shareholders. Directors of the offeree company should give careful consideration before they enter into any commitment with an offeror (or anyone else) which would restrict their freedom to advise their shareholders in the future. Such commitments may give rise to conflicts of interest or result in a breach of the directors' fiduciary duties.

10. Where control of a company is acquired by a person, or persons acting in concert, a general offer to all other shareholders is normally required; a similar obligation may arise if control is consolidated. Where n acquisition is contemplated as a result of which a person may incur such an obligation, he must before making the acquisition, ensure that he can and will continue to be able to implement such an offer.

APPENDIX 2

AMENDED PROPOSAL FOR A 13TH EUROPEAN PARLIAMENT AND COUNCIL DIRECTIVE ON COMPANY LAW CONCERNING TAKEOVER BIDS[1]

(O.J. No. C 378/97, p. 10)
(Text with EEA relevance)
COM(97) 565 final – 95/0341(COD)
(Submitted by the Commission pursuant to Article 189a(2) of the EC Treaty on 11 November 1997)

INITIAL PROPOSAL AMENDED PROPOSAL

THE EUROPEAN PARLIAMENT AND
THE COUNCIL OF THE EUROPEAN UNION, Unchanged

Having regard to the Treaty establishing the
European Community, and in particular
Article 54 thereof,

Having regard to the proposal from the
Commission,

Having regard to the opinion of the Economic
and Social Committee[2],

Acting in accordance with the procedure referred
to in Article 189b of the Treaty[3],

Whereas it is necessary to coordinate certain
safeguards which Member States require of
companies and firms within the meaning of the
second paragraph of Article 58 of the EC Treaty
for the protection of members and others, in
order to make such safeguards equivalent
throughout the Community;

Whereas it is necessary to protect the interests of
shareholders of companies governed by the laws
of a Member State when these companies are
subject to a takeover bid or to a change of control
and their securities are admitted to trading on a
regulated market within the scope of this Directive;

Whereas only action at Community level can
ensure an adequate level of protection for
shareholders throughout the Union and provide
for minimum guidelines for the conduct of
takeover bids; whereas Member States acting
independently are not able to establish the same

---

[1] O.J. C 162, 6. 6. 1996, p. 5.
[2] O.J. C 295, 7. 10. 1996, p. 1.
[3] European Parliament opinion of 26 June 1997 (O.J. C 222, 21. 7. 1997, p. 20).

689

level of protection especially in the case of cross-border takeovers or purchases of control;

Whereas the adoption of a directive is the appropriate procedure for laying down a framework consisting of certain common principles and a limited number of general requirements which Member States will be required to implement through more detailed rules according to their national systems and their cultural contexts;

Whereas Member States should take the necessary steps in order to protect shareholders having minority holdings after the purchase of the control of their company; whereas such a protection can be ensured either by obliging the person who acquired the control of a company to make a bid to all shareholders for all or for a substantial part of their holdings or by providing for other means which attain the objective of at least an equivalent level of protection of minority shareholders;

Whereas each Member State should designate an authority or authorities to supervise all aspects of the bid and to ensure that parties to takeover bids comply with the rules made pursuant to this Directive; whereas the different authorities must cooperate with one another;	Whereas each Member State should designate an authority or authorities to supervise the entire course of the bid and to ensure that parties to takeover bids comply with the rules made pursuant to this Directive; whereas the different authorities must cooperate with one another;
Whereas it is desirable to encourage the voluntary control exercised by self-regulatory bodies in order to avoid recourse to administrative or judicial action;	Unchanged
Whereas to reduce the scope for insider dealing offerers should be required to announce their intention of launching a bid as soon as possible and to inform the supervisory authority and the offeree company's board of the bid before they are made public;	
Whereas the addressees of a takeover bid should be properly informed of the terms of the bid by means of an offer document;	Whereas the addressees of a takeover bid should be properly informed of the terms of the bid by means of an offer document; whereas appropriate information should also be given to the representatives of the company's employees or, failing that, to the employees directly;
Whereas it is necessary to set a time limit for takeover bids;	Unchanged
Whereas to be able to perform their functions satisfactorily, supervisory authorities must at all times be able to require the parties to the bid to provide information on it;	

Appendices

Whereas to avoid operations which frustrate the bid it is necessary to limit the powers of the board of directors of the offeree company to engage in operations of an exceptional nature;

Whereas the board of the offeree company should be required to make public a document setting out its opinion on the bid and the reasons on which it is based;

Whereas it is necessary that Member States provide for rules covering the cases when the bid may be withdrawn or declared void once the offer document has been made public, the right of the offerer to revise its bid, the possibility of competing bids for the securities of a company which are necessarily to the advantage of its shareholders and the disclosure of the result of the bid,

HAVE ADOPTED THIS DIRECTIVE:	**HAVE ADOPTED THIS DIRECTIVE:**
Article 1	*Article 1*
Scope	**Scope**
The coordination measures prescribed by this Directive shall apply to the laws, regulations and administrative provisions or other mechanisms or arrangements of the Member States relating to takeover bids for the securities of a company governed by the law of a Member State, where such securities are admitted, wholly or partially, to trading on a market in one or more Member States which is regulated and supervised by authorities recognized by public bodies, operates regularly and is accessible, directly or indirectly, to the public.	The coordination measures prescribed by this Directive shall apply to the laws, regulations and administrative provisions of the Member States, including mechanisms or arrangements established by organizations officially authorized to regulate the markets, relating to takeover bids for the securities of a company governed by the law of a Member State, where such securities are admitted, wholly or partially, to trading on a market in one or more Member States which is regulated and supervised by authorities recognized by public bodies, operates regularly and is accessible, directly or indirectly, to the public.
Article 2	*Article 2*
Definitions	**Definitions**
FOR THE PURPOSE OF THIS DIRECTIVE:	Unchanged

– "takeover bid" ("bid") shall mean an offer made to the holders of the securities of a company to acquire all or part of such securities by payment in cash and/or in exchange for other securities. A bid may be either mandatory, if so provided by Member States as a means to protect minority shareholders, or voluntary,

– "offeree company" shall mean a company whose securities are the subject of a bid,

691

– "offerer" shall mean any natural person or legal entity in public or private law making a bid,

– "offerer" shall mean any natural person or legal entity in public or private law making a bid in accordance with the legislation of the Member State deter mined as provided for in Article 4(2),

– "securities" shall mean transferable securities carrying voting rights in a company or conferring entitlement to obtain transferable securities carrying such rights,

– "securities" shall mean transferable securities carrying voting rights in a company,

– "parties to the bid" shall mean the offerer, the members of the offerer's administrative or management board, if the offerer is a company, the addressees of the bid and the members of the administrative or management board of the offeree company.

Unchanged

Article 3

Protection of minority shareholders

1. Where a natural person or legal entity who, as a result of acquisition, holds securities which added to any existing holdings give him a specified percentage of voting rights in a company referred to in Article 1, conferring on him the control of that company, Member States should ensure that rules or other mechanisms or arrangements are in force which either oblige this person to make a bid in accordance with Article 10 or offer other appropriate and at least equivalent means in order to protect the minority shareholders of that company.

Article 3

Protection of minority shareholders

1. Where a natural person or legal entity who as a result of immediate or future acquisition, holds securities which added to any existing holdings directly give him a specified percentage of voting rights in a company referred to in Article 1, conferring on him the control of that company, Member States should ensure that rules or other mechanisms or arrangements are in force which either oblige this person to make a bid in accordance with Article 10 or offer other appropriate and at least equivalent means in order to protect the minority shareholders of that company.

2. The percentage of voting rights which confers control for the purposes of paragraph 1 and the way of its calculation shall be determined by the law of the Member State where the supervisory authority is located.

2. The percentage of voting rights which confers control for the purposes of paragraph 1 and the way of its calculation shall be determined by the Member State where the supervisory authority is located in accordance with Article 4(2). That authority shall also be responsible for determining whether and to what extent the provisions of paragraph 1 apply to the temporary holding of securities or to the acquisition of a majority holding without there being any intention to exercise control over the company.

Article 4

Supervisory authority

1. Member States shall designate the authority or authorities, which will supervise all aspects of the bid. The authorities thus designated may

Article 4

Supervisory authority

1. Member States shall designate the authority or authorities, which will supervise the entire course of the bid. The

include associations or private bodies. Member States shall inform the Commission of the designations and shall specify all divisions of functions that may be made.

2. The authority competent for supervising the bid shall be that of the Member State in which the offeree company has its registered office if the securities of the company are admitted to trading on a regulated market in that Member State. Otherwise, the competent authority shall be that of the Member State on whose regulated market the securities of the company were first admitted to trading and are still traded.

3. Without prejudice to their duty of professional secrecy, the competent authorities of the Member States shall cooperate, in so far as is necessary for the performance of their duties and for this purpose shall supply each other with any information that may be necessary.

4. The supervisory authorities shall have all the powers necessary for the exercise of their functions, which shall include responsibility for ensuring that the parties to a bid comply with the rules made pursuant to this Directive. In addition Member States can provide that their supervisory authorities may, on the basis of a reasoned decision, grant derogations from the rules drawn up in accordance with this Directive provided that in granting such derogations the supervisory authorities shall respect the principles mentioned in Article 5.

5. This Directive does not affect the power which courts may have in a Member State to decline to hear legal proceedings and to decide whether or not such proceedings affect the outcome of the bid provided that an injured party enjoys adequate remedies, whether through an appeals

authorities thus designated may include associations or private bodies. Member States shall inform the Commission of these designations and shall specify all divisions of functions that may be made.

2. The authority competent for supervising the bid shall be that of the Member State in which the offeree company has its registered office if the securities of the company are admitted to trading on a regulated market in that Member State. Otherwise, the competent authority shall be that of the Member State on whose regulated market the securities of the company were first admitted to trading and are still traded and the law applicable shall be that of that Member State. If that condition is not met either, the competent authority shall be that of the Member State on whose regulated market the company's securities are principally traded during the period of acquisition of the securities conferring control of the company and the law applicable shall be that of that Member State.

3. Each Member State shall require any individuals who are or have been employed by the supervisory authorities to be bound by professional secrecy. Without prejudice to their obligation not to divulge information covered by professional secrecy, the supervisory authorities of the Member States shall cooperate, in so far as is necessary for the performance of their duties and for this purpose shall supply each other with any information that may be necessary.

4. The supervisory authorities shall have all the powers necessary for the exercise of their functions, which shall include responsibility for ensuring that the parties to a bid comply with the rules made pursuant to this Directive.

5. This Directive does not affect the power of Member States to designate the judicial or other authorities responsible for dealing with disputes and for deciding on irregularities committed during the bid procedure, provided that

procedure operated by the supervisory authority or through the right to take proceedings before the courts to claim compensation.

an injured party enjoys appropriate and adequate remedies to defend its interests and, where appropriate, obtain compensation for any loss suffered.

<table>
<tr><td>

Article 5
General principles

1. For the purposes of the implementation of this Directive, Member States shall ensure that the rules or other arrangements made pursuant to this Directive respect the following principles:

(a) all holders of securities of an offeree company who are in the same position are to be treated equally;

(b) the addressees of a bid are to have sufficient time and information to enable them to reach a properly informed decision on the bid;

(c) the board of an offeree company is to act in the interests of the company as a whole; including employment;

(d) false markets must not be created in the securities of the offeree company, of the offerer company, or of any other company concerned by the bid;

(e) offeree companies must not be hindered in the conduct of their affairs for longer than is reasonable by a bid for their securities.

2. In order to attain the objective set out in paragraph 1, Member States shall ensure that rules are in force which satisfy the minimum requirements set out in the following Articles.

</td><td>

Article 5
General principles

Unchanged

(a) all holders of securities of an offeree company who are in the same position are to be given equivalent treatment;

Unchanged

(c) the board of an offeree company is to act in all the interests of the company,

(d) false markets must not be created in the securities of the offeree company, of the offerer company, or of any other company concerned by the bid in such a way that the rise or fall in the prices of the securities becomes artificial and the normal functioning of the markets is disrupted:

Unchanged

</td></tr>
</table>

<table>
<tr><td>

Article 6
Information

1. Member States shall ensure that rules are in force requiring that the decision to make a bid is made public and that the supervisory authority and the board of the offeree company are informed of the bid before this decision is made public.

</td><td>

Article 6
Information

1. Member States shall ensure that rules are in force requiring that the decision to make a bid is made public and that the supervisory authority and the board of the offeree company are informed of the bid before this decision is made public. As soon as the bid has been made public, the board of the offeree company shall inform the representatives of its employees or, where there are no such representatives, the employees themselves.

</td></tr>
</table>

2. Member States shall ensure that rules are in force requiring the offerer to draw up and make public in good time an offer document containing the information necessary to enable the addressees of the bid to reach a properly informed decision on the bid. Before the offer document is made public, the offerer shall communicate it to the supervisory authority.

2. Member States shall ensure that rules are in force requiring the offerer to draw up and make public in good time an offer document containing the information necessary to enable the addressees of the bid to reach a properly informed decision on the bid. Before the offer document is made public, the offerer shall communicate it to the supervisory authority. When it is made public, the board of the offeree company shall communicate it to the representatives of its employees or, where there are no such representatives, to the employees themselves.

3. Those rules shall require that the document states at least:

Unchanged

– the terms of the bid,

– the identity of the offerer or, where the offerer is a company, the type, name and registered office of that company,

– the securities or class, or classes of securities for which the bid is made,

– the consideration offered for each security or class of securities and the basis of the valuation used in determining it with particulars of the way in which that consideration is to be given,

– the consideration offered for each security or class of securities and the basis of the valuation used in determining it with particulars of the way in which that consideration is to be given, and in particular the methods and terms of payment to shareholders resident in a Member State other than that of the offeree company's registered office or than that in which the securities are listed.

– the maximum and minimum percentages or quantities of securities which the offerer undertakes to acquire,

Unchanged

– details of any existing holdings of the offerer in the offeree company,

– all conditions to which the offers is subject,

– the offerer's intentions with regard to the future business and undertakings of the offeree company, its employees and its management,

– the offerer's intentions with regard to the future business and undertakings of the offeree company, its employees and its management, including any change in the conditions of employment,

– the period for acceptance of the bid, which may not be less than four weeks or more than 10 weeks from the date on which the document is made public,

– the period for acceptance of the bid, which may not be less than four weeks or more than 10 weeks from the date on which the document is made public, except where duly justified authorization has been given by the supervisory authority,

– where the consideration offered by the offerer includes securities, information about those securities.

Unchanged

– the conditions under which the offerer is to finance its bid.

4. Member States shall ensure that rules are in force requiring that the parties to a bid provide the supervisory authority at any time on request with all information in their possession concerning the bid which the supervisory authority considers necessary for the discharge of its functions.

4. Member States shall ensure that rules are in force requiring that the parties to a bid provide the supervisory authority at any time on request with all information in their possession concerning the bid which is necessary for the supervisory authority to discharge its functions.

Article 7
Disclosure

1. Member States shall ensure that rules are in force which require a bid to be made public in such a way as to avoid the creation of false markets in the securities of the offeree company or of the offerer.

Article 7
Disclosure

1. Member States shall ensure that rules are in force which require a bid to be made public in such a way as to avoid the creation of false markets in the securities of the offeree company, of the offerer or of any other company affected by the bid, particularly through the publication or dissemination of false, exaggerated, or tendentious information.

2. Member States shall ensure that rules are in force which provide for the disclosure of all information or documents required in such a manner as to ensure that they are both readily and promptly available to the addressees of the bid.

2. Member States shall ensure that rules are in force which provide for the disclosure of all information or documents required in such a manner as to ensure that they are both readily and promptly available to the addressees of he bid, including those resident in a Member State other than that of the offeree company's registered office or than that in which the securities are listed and to the representatives of the employees of the offeree company or, where there are no such representatives, to the employees themselves.

Article 8
Obligations of the board of the offeree company

Member States shall ensure that rules are in force requiring that:

(a) after receiving the information concerning the bid and until the result of the bid is made public, the board of the offeree company should abstain from any action which may result in the frustration of the offer, and notably from the issuing of shares which may result in a lasting impediment to the offerer to obtain control over the offeree company, unless it has the prior

Article 8
Obligations of the board of the offeree company

Member States shall ensure that rules are in force requiring that:

(a) fter receiving the information concerning the bid and until the result of the bid is made public, the board of the offeree company should abstain from any action which may result in the frustration of the offer, and notably from the issuing of shares which may result in a lasting impediment to the offerer to obtain

authorization of the general meeting of the shareholders given for this purpose,

control over the offeree company, unless it has the prior authorization of the general meeting of the shareholders given for this purpose, during the period of acceptance of the bid;

(b) the board of the offeree company shall draw up and make public a document setting out its opinion on the bid together with the reasons on which it is based.

Unchanged

Article 9
Rules applicable to the conduct of bids

Article 9
Rules applicable to the conduct of bids

In addition Member States shall ensure that rules are in force which govern the conduct of bids at least for the following matters:

Unchanged

(a) withdrawal or nullity of the bid,
(b) revision of bids,
(c) competing bids,
(d) disclosure of the result of bids.

Article 10
Mandatory bid

Article 10
Mandatory bid

1. Where a Member State provides for a mandatory bid as a means to protect the minority shareholders, this bid shall be launched to all shareholders for all or for a substantial part of their holdings at a price which meets the objective of protecting their interests.

1. Where a Member State provides for a mandatory bid as a means to protect the minority shareholders, this bid shall be launched to all shareholders for all or for a substantial part of their holdings at a price which ensures equal treatment for shareholders. The term "substantial part" should not be interpreted as meaning less than 70 % of the securities, except where duly justified authorization has been given by the supervisory authority.

2. If the mandatory bid comprises only a part of the securities of the offeree company and the shareholders offer to sell to the offerer more shares than the partial offer covers, shareholders should be treated equally by means of a pro rata treatment of their shareholdings.

Unchanged

Article 11
Transposition of the Directive

Article 11
Transposition of the Directive

1. Member States shall ensure that the laws, regulations and administrative provisions or other mechanisms or arrangements necessary for them to comply with this Directive are in force before 1 April 1998.

1. Member States shall ensure that the laws, regulations and administrative provisions or other mechanisms or arrangements necessary for them to comply with this Directive are in force before 1 January 1999.

697

2. Member States shall communicate to the   Unchanged
Commission the provisions or other
arrangements referred to in paragraph 1,
making express reference to this Directive.

Article 12
Addressees of the Directive

Article 12
Addresses of the Directive

This Directive is addressed to the Member States. Unchanged

Appendix 3

Amended Proposal for a European Parliament and Council Directive on Company Law Concerning Takeover Bids

THE EUROPEAN PARLIAMENT AND THE COUNCIL OF THE EUROPEAN UNION,

Having regard to the Treaty establishing the European Community, and in particular Article 44 thereof,
Having regard to the proposal from the Commission,
Having regard to the opinion of the Economic and Social Committee,
Acting in accordance with the procedure referred to in Article 251 of the Treaty,

(1) Whereas it is necessary to co-ordinate certain safeguards which Member States require of companies and firms within the meaning of the second paragraph of Article 48 of the EC Treaty for the protection of members and others, in order to make such safeguards equivalent throughout the Community;

(2) Whereas it is necessary to protect the interests of holders of securities of companies governed by the law of a Member State when these companies are subject to a takeover bid or to a change of control and their securities are admitted to trading on a regulated market within the scope of this Directive;

(3) Whereas only action at Community level can ensure an adequate level of protection for holders of securities throughout the Union and provide for minimum guidelines for the conduct of takeover bids; whereas Member States acting independently are not able to establish the same level of protection especially in the case of cross-border takeovers or purchases of control;

(4) Whereas the adoption of a directive is the appropriate procedure for laying down a framework consisting of certain common principles and a limited number of general requirements which Member States NMII be required to implement through more detailed rules according to their national systems and their cultural contexts;

(5) Whereas Member States should take the necessary steps in order to protect holders of securities having minority holdings after the purchase of the control of their company; whereas such a protection must be ensured by obliging the person who acquired the control of a company to make a bid to all holders of securities for all of their holdings; whereas it should be allowed, during a transitional period, to ensure this protection through other appropriate and at least equivalent means on the condition that these means are specific to the transfer of control and include specific financial compensations for the minority shareholders, whereas Member States may, in addition to the protection provided for by a mandatory bid or other equivalent means, provide for further instruments aiming at the protection of the interests of holders of securities;

(6) Whereas the obligation to make a bid to all holders of securities does not apply to those controlling holdings already in existence at the time of the Directive entering into force;

(7) Whereas Member States may establish further instruments for the protection of the interests of holders of securities, such as the obligation to make a partial bid where the offeror does not acquire control of the company, or the obligation to make a bid simultaneously with the·acquisition of the control of the company;

(7a) Whereas the obligation to launch a bid does not apply in the case of the acquisition of securities which do not carry voting rights in ordinary general meetings; whereas Member States may however extend this obligation to the acquisition of securities which only carry voting rights in specific circumstances or which do not carry voting rights;

(8) Whereas each Member State should designate an authority or authorities to supervise the aspects of the bid governed by this directive and to ensure that parties to takeover bids comply with the rules made pursuant to this Directive; whereas the different authorities must cooperate with one another;

(8a) Whereas, in order to be effective, takeover regulation must be flexible and capable of dealing with new circumstances as they arise, and must accordingly provide for the possibility of exceptions and derogations; whereas, however, in applying any rules or exceptions laid down or in granting any derogations supervisory authorities must respect certain general principles;

(9) Whereas supervision can be exercised by self-regulatory bodies;

(9a) Whereas, in accordance with general principles of Community law, and in particular the right to a fair hearing, decisions of a supervisory authority will in appropriate circumstances be susceptible to review by an independent court or tribunal; whereas, however, this Directive leaves it to Member States to determine whether rights are to be made available which may be asserted in administrative or judicial proceedings, whether in proceedings against a supervisory authority or proceedings between parties to a bid;

(9b) Whereas it is necessary to create a EU-wide clarity and transparency in respect of legal issues to be settled in event of take-over bids and to prevent pattern of EU corporate restructuring from being distorted by arbitrary differences in governance and management cultures;

(10) Whereas to reduce the scope for insider dealing offerors should be required to announce their decision of launching a bid as soon as possible and to inform the supervisory authority of the bid;

(11) Whereas the holders of securities should be properly informed of the terms of the bid by means of an offer document; whereas appropriate information should also be given to the representatives of the company's employees or, failing that, to the employees directly;

(12) Whereas it is necessary to regulate the period for the acceptance of the bid;

(13) Whereas to be able to perform their functions satisfactorily, supervisory authorities must at all times be able to require the parties to the bid to provide information on it and shall co-operate and supply information without delay to other authorities supervising capital markets in an efficient and effective manner;

(14) Whereas to avoid operations which frustrate the bid it is necessary to limit the powers of the board of directors of the offeree company to engage in operations of an exceptional nature without unduly hindering the offeree company to carry out its normal course of business;

(15) Whereas the board of the offeree company should be required to -make public a document setting out its opinion on the bid and the reasons on which it is based including its views on the effects of implementation on all the interests of the company and specifically employment;

(16) Whereas it is necessary that Member States provide for rules covering the cases when the bid lapses, the right of the offeror to revise his bid, the possibility of competing bids for the securities of a company which are to the advantage of its

holders of securities, the disclosure of the result of the bid and the irrevocability of the bid and conditions permitted,

(17) Whereas it is important to entrust the Contact Committee set up by Article 20 of Directive 791279/EEC with the task to assist Member States and the supervisory authorities in the implementation of this Directive, particularly in areas such as cross-border takeover bids and the mutual recognition of offer documents, and to advise the Commission, if necessary, on additions or amendments to this Directive,

HAVE ADOPTED THIS DIRECTIVE:

Article 1

Scope

1. The co-ordination measures prescribed by this Directive shall apply to the laws, regulations, administrative provisions, codes of practice or other arrangements of the Member States, including arrangements established by organisations officially authorised to regulate the markets ("rules"), relating to takeover bids for the securities of a company governed by the law of a Member State, where such securities are admitted to trading on a regulated market within the meaning of Article 1(13) of Directive 93/22/CEE in one or more Member States.

2. The measures prescribed by this Directive shall not apply to takeover bids for securities issued by companies the object of which is the collective investment of capital provided by the public, and which operate on the principle of risk spreading, and the units of which are, at the holders' request, repurchased or redeemed, directly or indirectly, out of the assets of those companies. Action taken by such companies to ensure that the stock exchange value of their units does not significantly vary from their net asset value shall be regarded as equivalent to such repurchase or redemption.

Article 2

Definitions

For the purposes of this Directive:

(a) "takeover bid" ("bid") shall mean a public offer (other than by the offeree company itself) made to the holders of the securities of a company to acquire all or part of such securities. A bid may be either mandatory or voluntary, and must follow or have as its objective the acquisition of control;

(b) offeree company "shall mean a company whose securities are the subject of a bid";

(c) offeror shall mean any natural person or legal entity in public or private law making a bid;

(d) "persons acting in concert" shall mean persons or legal entities who co-operate with the offeror or the offeree company on the basis of an agreement, either express or tacit, either oral or written, and aimed respectively at obtaining control of the offeree company or frustrating the successful outcome of the bid.

Persons controlled by another person within the meaning of Article 8 of Directive 88/627/EEC shall be deemed to be persons acting in concert with such persons and with each other;

(e) "securities" shall mean transferable securities carrying voting rights in a company:

(f) "parties to the bid" shall mean the offeror, the members of the offeror's administrative or management board, if the offeror is a company, the offeree company, holders of securities of the offeree company and the members of the administrative or management board of the offeree company, or persons acting in concert with such parties.

Article 3
General principles

1. For the purposes of the implementation of this Directive, Member States shall ensure that the rules or other arrangements made or introduced pursuant to this Directive respect the following principles:

   (a) all holders of securities of an offeree company of the same class are to be given equivalent treatment; in particular, if a person acquires control of a company, the other holders of securities are to be protected;

   (b) holders of securities of an offeree company are to have sufficient time and information to enable them to reach a properly informed decision on the bid;

   (c) the board of an offeree company is to act in the interests of the company as a whole, and must not deny the holders of securities the opportunity to decide on the merits of the offer;

   (d) false markets must not be created in the securities of the offeree company, of the offeror company, or of any other company concerned by the bid in such a way that the rise or fall in the prices of the securities becomes artificial and the normal functioning of the markets is distorted;

   (e) an offeror shall announce a bid only after ensuring that it can fulfil in full any cash consideration if so offered and after having taken all reasonable measures to secure the implementation of any other type of consideration;

   (f) offeree companies must not be hindered in the conduct of their affairs for longer than is reasonable by a bid for their securities.

2. In order to attain the objective set out in paragraph 1, Member States:

   (a) shall ensure that rules are in force which satisfy the minimum requirements set out in this Directive;

   (b) may have additional conditions and more stringent provisions than required by this Directive to regulate bids.

Article 4
Supervisory authority

1. Member States shall designate the authority or authorities, which will supervise the bid as far as it is governed by rules made or introduced pursuant to this Directive. The authorities thus designated must be either public authorities or associations or private bodies recognised by national law or by public authorities expressly empowered for that purpose by national law. Member States shall ensure that these authorities exercise their functions impartially and independently from all parties to the bid. Member States shall inform the Commission of these designations and shall specify all divisions of functions that may be made.

2.(a) The authority competent for supervising the bid shall be that of the Member State in which the offeree company has its registered office if the securities of that company are admitted to trading on a regulated market in that Member State.

(b) If the securities of the offeree company are not admitted to trading on a regulated market in the Member State in which the company has its registered office, the authority competent for supervising the bid shall be that of the Member State on whose regulated market the securities of the company are admitted to trading. If the securities of the company are admitted to trading on regulated markets in more than one Member State, the authority competent for supervising the bid shall be that of the Member State on whose regulated market the securities were first admitted.

(c) If the securities are first admitted to trading on regulated markets within more than one Member State as referred to under paragraph (b) sentence 2 simultaneously, the offeree company has to determine the competent authority for supervising the bid by notifying these regulated markets and their supervisory authorities on the first trading day.

Transitional clause

If the securities are admitted to trading on regulated markets in more than one Member State at the date mentioned in Article 11(1) and were admitted simultaneously, the supervisory authorities of these Member States shall agree on who is to be the competent authority for supervising the bid within four weeks after the date mentioned in Article 11(1). Otherwise the competent authority shall be determined by the offeree company on the first trading day following the expiry of the period of time mentioned in sentence 1.

(d) Member States shall ensure that rules are in force requiring the decisions referred to under paragraph (c) to be made public.

(e) In the cases referred to under (b) and (c) above, matters relating to the consideration offered in the case of a bid, and particularly the price, and matters relating to the procedure of the bid, in particular the information on the offeror's decision to make an offer, the contents of the offer document and the disclosure of the offer, shall be dealt with in accordance with the rules of the Member State of the competent authority. In matters relating to the information for employees of the offeree company and in matters relating to company law, in particular the percentage of voting rights which confers control and any derogation from the obligation to launch a bid, as well as the conditions under which the board of the offeree company may undertake any action which might result in the frustration of the offer, the applicable rules and the competent authority shall be those of the Member State in which the offeree company has its registered office.

(3) Member States shall ensure that all persons employed or formerly employed by the supervisory authorities shall be bound by professional secrecy. Information covered by professional secrecy may not be divulged to any person or authority except by virtue of provisions laid down by law.

(3a) The supervisory authorities of the Member States under this Directive and other authorities supervising capital markets, in particular in accordance with Directive 88/627/EEC, Directive 89/592/EEC and Directive 93/22/EEC, shall co-operate and supply each other with information, wherever necessary for the application of the rules drawn up in accordance with this Directive and in particular in cases covered by Article 4(2) (b), (c) and (e). Information thus exchanged shall be covered by the obligation of professional secrecy to which the persons employed or formerly employed by the supervisory authorities receiving the information are subject. The cooperation should include the ability to serve the legal documents necessary to enforce measures taken by the competent authorities in connection to the bids, as well as other such assistance as may be reasonably requested by the supervisory authorities concerned for the purposes-of investigating any actual or alleged breaches of the rules made or introduced to implement this Directive.

4. The supervisory authorities shall have all the powers necessary for the exercise of their functions which shall include the duty to ensure that the parties to a bid comply with the rules made pursuant to this Directive.

Provided that the general principles referred to in Article 3(l) are respected, Member States may provide in their rules made or introduced pursuant to this Directive that their supervisory authorities may in particular types of cases and, on the basis of a reasoned decision, in specific appropriate cases grant derogations from these rules .

5. This Directive does not affect the powers of the Member States to designate judicial or other authorities responsible for dealing with disputes and for deciding on irregularities committed in the bid procedure nor does it affect the power of Member States to regulate whether and under which circumstances parties to the bid are entitled to bring administrative or judicial proceedings. In particular this Directive does not affect the power which courts may have in a Member State to decline to hear legal proceedings and to decide whether or not such proceedings affect the outcome of the bid. This Directive shall not affect the powers of the Member States to determine the legal position concerning the liability of supervisory authorities or concerning litigation between the parties to a bid.

Article 5
Protection of minority shareholders; mandatory bid

1. Where a natural person or legal entity who, as a result of his own acquisition or the acquisition by persons acting in concert with him, holds securities of a company referred to in Article 1 which added to any existing holdings and the holdings of persons acting in concert with him directly or indirectly give him a specified percentage of voting rights in that company, conferring on him the control of that company, Member States shall ensure that rules are in force which oblige this person to make a bid as a means to protect the minority shareholders of that company. This bid shall be addressed to all holders of securities for all their holdings at an equitable price. When the consideration offered by the offeror does not consist of liquid securities admitted to trading on a regulated market in the sense of Article 1 (l), such consideration has to include a cash consideration at least as an alternative.

1 a. If in the case of a voluntary bid made in accordance with this Directive to all holders of securities for all their holdings control has been obtained, the obligation to launch a bid does no longer apply.

2. By derogation to paragraph 1, Member States which provide, at the time of adoption of this Directive, for other appropriate and at least equivalent means in order to protect the minority shareholders of that company, may continue to apply such means for one year following the date mentioned in Article 11(1), on the condition that these means.

(a) are specific to the transfer of control and

(b) include specific financial compensations for the minority shareholders.

2a. In addition to the protection provided under paragraphs 1 and 2, Member States may provide for further instruments aiming at the protection of the interests of holders of securities as far as these instruments do not hinder the normal course of the bid referred to in paragraph 1.

3. The percentage of voting rights which confers control for the purposes of paragraph 1 and 2 and the way of its calculation shall be determined by the rules of the Member State where the company has its registered office.

Article 5a

Amendment of Article 1(1) of Directive 88/627/EEC

Paragraph 1 of Article 1 of Directive 88/627/EEC is replaced by the following paragraph:

> "1. Member States shall make subject to this Directive natural persons and legal entities in public or private law who acquire or dispose of, directly or through intermediaries, holdings meeting the criteria laid down in Article 4(1) which involve changes in the holdings of voting rights in companies incorporated under their law the shares of which are admitted to trading on one or several regulated markets within the meaning of Article 1(13) of Directive 93/22/EEC."

Article 6

Information

1. Member States shall ensure that rules are in force requiring that the decision to make a bid is made public without delay and that the supervisory authority is informed of the bid. Member States may require that the supervisory authority is informed before this decision is made public. As soon as the bid has been made public, the board of the offeree company shall inform the representatives of its employees or, where there are no such representatives, the employees themselves.

2. Member States shall ensure that rules are in force requiring the offeror to draw up and make public in good time an offer document containing the information necessary to enable the holders of securities of the offeree company to reach a properly informed decision on the bid. Before the offer document is made public, the offeror shall communicate it to the supervisory authority. When it is made public, the board of the offeree company shall communicate it to the representatives of its employees or, where there are no such representatives, to the employees themselves.

Where the offer document is subject to the prior approval by the supervisory authority and once it has been approved, it shall be recognised, subject to any translation, in the other Member State or Member States on whose markets the securities of the offeree company are admitted to trading, without its being necessary to obtain the approval of the supervisory authorities of that or those Member States and without their being able to require additional information to be included in the offer document. The supervisory authorities may, however, require that the offer document include information specific to the market of the Member State or Member States on whose markets the securities of the offeree company are admitted to trading concerning the formalities to be complied with for accepting the bid and for receiving the consideration due at the close of the bid as well as the tax arrangements to which the consideration offered to the -holders of securities will be subject.

3. Those rules shall require that the offer document state at least:

(a) the terms of the bid;

(b) the identity 6f the offeror and where the offeror is a company, the type, name and registered office of that company;

(c) the securities or class, or classes of securities for which the bid is made;

(d) the consideration offered for each security or class of securities and, in the case of mandatory bids, the basis of the valuation used in determining it, with particulars of the way in which that consideration is to be given;

(e) the maximum and minimum percentages or quantities of securities which the offeror undertakes to acquire;

(f) details of any existing holdings of the offeror, and of persons acting in concert with him, in the offeree company;

(g) all conditions to which the offer is subject;

(h) the offeror's intentions with regard to the future business and undertakings of the offeree company, its employees and its management, including any material change in the conditions of employment;

(i) the period for acceptance of the bid;

(j) where the consideration offered by the offeror includes securities of any kind information about those securities;

(k) information on the financing for the bid;

(l) the identity of persons and entities acting in concert with the offeror or with the offeree company, in the case of companies together with their type, name and registered office, and their relationship with the offeror and where possible with the offeree company.

4. Member States shall ensure that rules are in force requiring that the parties to a bid provide the supervisory authorities of their Member State at any time on request with all information in their possession concerning the bid which is necessary for the supervisory authority to discharge its functions.

Article 6a

Period for Acceptance

1. Member States shall provide that the period for acceptance of the bid to be specified by the offeror in the offer document in accordance with Article 6(3)(i) may not be less than two weeks or more than ten weeks from the date of publication of the offer document. Member States may provide that the period of ten weeks may be prolonged on the condition that the offeror gives at least two weeks prior notice of its intention to close the bid.

2. Member States may provide for rules modifying the period mentioned in the preceding paragraph in specific appropriate cases. Member States may authorize the supervisory authority to grant a derogation from the period mentioned in the preceding paragraph in order to allow the offeree company to organise a general meeting to consider the bid.

Article 7
Disclosure

1. Member States shall ensure that rules are in force which require a bid to be made public in such a way as to ensure market transparency and integrity for the securities of the offeree company, of the offeror or of any other company affected by the bid, and which particularly avoid the publication or dissemination of false or misleading information.

2. Member States shall ensure that rules are in force which provide for the disclosure of all information or documents required in such a manner as to ensure that they are both readily and promptly available to the holders of securities at least in those Member States, where the securities of the offeree company are admitted to trading on a regulated market and to the representatives of the employees of the offeree company or, where there are no such representatives, to the employees themselves.

Article 8
Obligations of the board of the offeree company

1. Member States shall ensure that rules are in force requiring that:
   (a) at the latest after receiving the information referred to in Article 6(l), first sentence, concerning the bid and until the result of the bid is made public or the bid lapses, the board of the offeree company should abstain from completing any action other than seeking alternative bids which may result in the frustration of the offer, and notably from the issuing of shares which may result in a lasting impediment to the offeror to obtain control over the offeree company, unless it has the prior authorization of the general meeting of the shareholders given for this purpose, during the period of acceptance of the bid;
   (b) the board of the offeree company shall draw up and make public a document setting out its opinion on the bid, together with the reasons on which it is based, including its views on the effects of implementation on all the interests of the company, including employment.

2. Member States may allow the board of the offeree company to increase the share capital during the period for acceptance of the bid on the condition that prior authorization has been received from the general meeting of shareholders not earlier than 18 months before the beginning of the period of acceptance of the bid, with full recognition of the right of pre-emption of all shareholders as provided for in Article 29(1) of Directive 77/91 /EEC.

Article 9
Rules applicable to the conduct of bids

In addition Member States shall ensure that rules are in force which govern the conduct of bids at least for the following matters:
   (a) lapse of the bid;
   (b) revision of bids;
   (c) competing bids;
   (d) disclosure of the result of bids;
   (e) irrevocability of the bid and conditions permitted.

Article 10
Mandatory bid

Article redundant: see Article 5.

Article 10a
Contact Committee

1. The Contact Committee set up by Article 20 of Directive 79/279/EEC shall also have as its functions:
  (a) to facilitate, without prejudice to the provisions of Articles 226 and 227 of the Treaty, the harmonized application of this Directive through regular meetings dealing in particular with practical problems arising in connection with its application;
  (b) to advise the Commission, if necessary, on additions or amendments to this Directive.

2. It shall not be the function of the Contact Committee to appraise the merits of decisions taken by the supervisory authorities in individual cases.

Article 10b
Sanctions

Each Member State shall determine the sanctions to be applied for infringement of the measures taken pursuant to this Directive. The sanctions shall be sufficient to promote compliance with those measures.

Article 10c

Three years after the date referred to in Article 11(1), the Council and the Parliament, acting on a proposal from the Commission, shall examine and if need be revise Article 4(2) in the light of the experience acquired in applying this Article.

Article 11
Transposition of the Directive

Member States shall ensure that the laws, regulations and administrative provisions or other mechanisms or arrangements necessary for them to comply with this Directive are in force before 2 . . . [4 years after the entry into force of this Directive].

2. Member States shall communicate to the Commission the provisions or other arrangements referred to in paragraph 1, making express reference to this Directive.

Article 12
Addressees of the Directive

This Directive is addressed to the Member States.

DECLARATIONS TO BE INCLUDED IN THE COUNCIL MINUTES

(1) Re Article 4(4) second subparagraph

"*The Commission and the Council* agree that national law may provide that when a natural person or a legal entity makes a voluntary public offer to acquire the securities of a given company conferring the control, this offer may be limited to the acquisition f at least 60% of the voting rights on condition that the offer has been approved by the majority of all shareholders with voting rights, excluding from the calculation securities that are held by the offeror and persons acting in concert with the offeror, and by any shareholder, who alone or in concert holds more than 10 % of the voting rights. The abovementioned approval is independent from the decision by each individual shareholder whether or not to accept the offer."

(2) Re Article 4(4) second subparagraph

"*The Commission* declares that the words "on the basis of a reasoned decision" do not impose on the supervisory authorities the obligation of issuing a written decision when granting derogations of minor importance."

(3) Re Article 5(l) last sentence

"*The Commission and the Council* state that, in accordance with tne framework character of this Directive, Member States may provide more stringent requirements, in particular that the consideration offered by the offeror has to include a cash consideration."

(4) Re Articles 10a and 4(2)(e)

"*The Commission and the Council* agree that it should be a priority for the Contact Committee provided for in Article 10a to develop guidelines to facilitate agreement on the respective roles of supervisory authorities in Article 4(2)(e) cases."

(5) Re Article 4(3a)

Unilateral statement by the Irish delegation

"in reference to the obligation to serve legal documents at the beginning of the third sentence of Article 4(3a), *the Irish delegation* confirms that its interpretation of this provision is that compliance will be on the basis of what is reasonably possible for supervisory authorities to deliver in this area of co-operation."

(6) Re Article 4(5)

Unilateral statement by the United Kingdom delegation

"*The United Kingdom* delegation wishes to make clear that it regards the wording in Article 4(5) as a fundamental pre-requisite of its support for the Directive as a whole."

INDEX

Goodwill
due diligence exercise, 15–41
valuation of, 1–16
"Green pages", 5–05
Greenmail *see under* **Defensive actions**
**Guinness Ireland Group
Limited/United Beverages
Holdings Limited merger,**
6–100—6–103

Health and safety at work, due
diligence exercise, 15–66—15–68
Herfindahl Hirschman Index (HHI),
6–87, 6–95, 6–102
Holding company
cross-shareholdings, 20–07
listing, 1–03
public listed companies, 1–03
shareholding, 1–03
Horizontal mergers
anti-competitive agreements, 6–04
merger category certificate, 6–95—
6–98
Horizontal takeover
cost reducing synergies, 2–10
definition, 1–04
Hostile takeovers
defensive actions *see* **Defensive
actions**
meaning, 1–08
private information theory, 2–27
valuation of target, 1–13

ICC Bank plc
see also **Banks**
Central Bank, and, 7–41
ICC Bank Act 1992, 7–40—7–41
privatisation, 7–40
Income tax, shareholders, and, 8–01
Industrial banks, 7–03
see also **Banks**
Insider dealing
common law, 13–06—13–10
IAIM Code of Best Practice, 13–48—
13–54
company responsibilities, 13–50
investors and analysts,
responsibilities of, 13–51
"materially affected", 13–49
objectives, 13–48
stockbrokers, 13–53
"unpublished price-sensitive
information", 13–49

**Insider Dealing Directive and
Companies Act 1990**
agents, exemptions for, 13–31
co-operation between relevant
authorities, 13–44—13–45
dealing in securities, 13–19—
13–21
exemptions, 13–29—13–32
generally, 13–03, 13–11
good faith, transactions entered
into in, 13–30
inside information, 13–12—13–15
confidentiality of, 13–15
definition, 13–12
materiality of, 13–13
nature of information, 13–14
penalties, 13–33—13–37
compensation, 13–33—13–35
fines, 13–36
imprisonment, 13–36
transaction void and
unenforceable, 13–37
person connected with the
company, 13–17—13–18
position of companies, 13–27—
13–28
primary insiders, 13–16
prohibitions, 13–16—13–26
role of the Stock Exchange,
13–38—13–43
secondary insiders, 13–23
shares acquired under will or
profit sharing scheme, 13–29
territorial scope, 13–46—13–47
tippees, 13–23
Model Code
clearance to deal, 13–62—13–64
close period, definition, 13–60
company, restrictions on dealing,
13–68
compliance with, 13–56
dealing
definition, 13–58
restrictions, 13–59—13–61,
13–68
directors
compliance, 13–56
responsibilities, 13–65
employees
compliance, 13–56
responsibilities, 13–65
enforcement, 13–66—13–67
prohibition periods, 13–63

**London Panel on Takeovers and
Mergers** *(cont.)*
procedure, 3–07—3–09
Rules Governing Substantial
Acquisitions of Shares, 3–04,
3–05
sanctions, 3–08
self-regulatory basis, 3–10, 4–02,
4–18, 4–27
London Stock Exchange
see also **Stock exchanges**
Admissions Directive, 5–14
Alternative Investment Market
(AIM) *see* **Alternative
Investment Market**
"Big Bang", 10–13
generally, 5–11A—5–12
Interim Reports Directive, 5–14
Listing Particulars Directive,
5–14
Listing Rules, 5–05
Official List, 5–13—5–15
SEAQ, 5–13
SEATS PLUS, 5–13, 5–17
SETS, 5–13
"Yellow Book", 5–05

Machinery, due diligence exercise,
15–29—15–31
Management buy-in, 18–01n
Management buy-outs
attractions of, 18–03
common law fiduciary duties,
18–08—18–13
Companies Acts, 18–14—18–30
declaration and notice of interest,
18–15—18–19
defensive actions, as, 20–78
directors, disclosure of certain
transactions involving, 18–27—
18–30
generally, 18–01—18–02, 18–06—
18–07
IAIM Guidelines, 18–48
Irish takeover rules
documentation to offeree's
shareholders, 18–40
equality of information, 18–39
generally, 18–36
independent advice, 18–37—
18–38
mezzanine debt, 18–04
regulation, 18–06 *et seq*

restriction on acquisition of non-
cash assets from company,
18–20—18–26
exemptions, 18–26
sale agreement, warranties in, 16–34
statutory disclosures
certain transactions involving
directors, 18–27—18–30
financial assistance for purchase
of own shares, 18–35
generally, 18–31
loans to directors, 18–33—18–34
payment for loss of office, 18–32
Stock Exchange Listing Rules
aggregation, 18–47
definitions
related party, 18–43
transaction with a related
party, 18–42
generally, 18–41
usual requirements, 18–44—
18–46
vehicle for, 18–04—18–05
Mandatory offer
Irish Takeover Panel, rules of,
3–33—3–34, 11–64—11–75
procuring issue of shares to offeror,
11–84—11–85
Rule 9 mandatory offer
consideration, 11–71—11–72
exemptions, 11–75
generally, 3–34, 11–26, 11–48,
11–64, 11–84—11–85
merger approval, 11–68—11–70
minimum acceptance condition,
11–67
offeree's directors, 11–73
requirement for general offer to
all shareholders, 11–65
resources, 11–66
voluntary offers, 11–74
Market for corporate control *see*
**Rationale for mergers and
acquisitions**
Market hypothesis, 2–23—2–26
Markowitz efficient portfolios, 2–05
see also **Portfolio theory**
Merchant banks, 7–03
see also **Banks**
Mergers
causes of *see* **Rationale for mergers
and acquisitions**
definitions, 1–03

Transfer of undertakings *(cont.)*
transfer, what constitutes
contracting out of services,
9–18—9–22
generally, 9–09
licenses and franchises, 9–15—
9–17
part of undertaking, 9–10—
9–14
what is being transferred, 9–23—
9–24
what is not transferred, 9–25
Transparency Directive
draft 13th Directive, amendment by,
4–39
generally, 4–13
information to be published, 4–39,
13–97
TRAX, 5–25
Trustee savings banks
see also **Banks**
amalgamations, 7–35
merger of ACC Bank plc and TSB,
7–37
re-organisation, 7–36
Trustee Savings Bank Act 1989,
7–34—7–39

Valuation of target
capital asset pricing model, 1–22
discounted cash flow, 1–18—1–19
dividend valuation, 1–17
earnings value, 1–20—1–21
generally, 1–13—1–14, 1–23
hostile takeover, 1–13
insider dealing restrictions, and, 1–13
net asset value, 1–15—1–16
goodwill, 1–16
pre-emption rights, and, 1–14
private companies, 1–14
public companies, 1–14
shareholders agreements, and, 1–14
Vertical mergers, merger category
certificate, 6–99
Vertical takeover
cost reducing synergies, 2–10
definition, 1–04

Wall Street Rule, 2–13
Warranties *see under* **Sale agreement**
Waste, due diligence exercise, 15–64—
15–65
Welfare, exploitation theories, 2–15—
2–16
Winners curse theory, 2–20
see also **Overpayment theory**